WORLD WAR II PACIFIC

BATTLES AND CAMPAIGNS FROM GUADALCANAL TO OKINAWA 1942-1945

DANIEL WRINN

CONTENTS

In the first six months of a war with the United States, I will run wild and win victory upon victory. But then, if the war continues after that, I make no such guarantees.

— Admiral Isoroku Yamamoto

PREFACE

The first months of World War II were a disaster for the United States. The Japanese caught the Pacific Fleet flat-footed in Pearl Harbor at anchor. Their attack dealt a massive blow to American naval power.

The Imperial Japanese forces took full advantage of the initiative. They made a lightning assault to take the Philippines, Thailand, Guam, Singapore, the Dutch East Indies, New Britain, Rabaul, and Hong Kong. They moved deeper into China and took Burma and New Guinea. It was an unstoppable victory after victory, and the Japanese Empire seemed invincible.

OPERATION WATCHTOWER

THE 1942 INVASION AND BATTLE FOR GUADALCANAL

INTRODUCTION

In early summer 1942, intelligence reported that a Japanese airfield was being constructed in the Solomon Islands near Lunga Point on Guadalcanal. This triggered a demand for immediate offensive action in the South Pacific.

Admiral Ernest King was the Chief of Naval Operations in the Pacific. He was the leading advocate in Washington for starting an offensive. His views were shared by Admiral Chester Nimitz, the commander-in-chief of the Pacific Fleet. Admiral Nimitz had already proposed sending the 1st Marine Raider Battalion to destroy a Japanese seaplane base on Tulagi. An island twenty miles north of Guadalcanal, across the Sealark Channel.

The Battle of the Coral Sea had interrupted a Japanese amphibious assault on Port Moresby, at the time the Allied base of supply in eastern New Guinea. The completion of the Guadalcanal airfield would signal the beginning of the renewed enemy advance to the south. This increased the threat to the lifeline of American aid to Australia and New Zealand. On July 23, 1942, the Joint Chiefs in Washington agreed to seize the line of communications in the South Pacific. The Japanese advance had to be stopped at any cost.

The Joint Chiefs created Operation Watchtower and the plan to invade and seize the islands of Guadalcanal and Tulagi.

The Solomon Islands are nestled in the backwaters of the South Pacific. Spanish fortune hunters discovered these islands in the sixteenth century. No European powers saw any value in these islands until Germany expanded its colonial empire two hundred years later. In 1884, Germany decreed a protectorate over the Bismarck Archipelago, in northern New Guinea, and the northern Solomons. Great Britain jumped into action and established a protectorate over the southern Solomon Islands and annexed the remainder of New Guinea. By 1905, the British crown passed administrative control over its territories in the region to Australia and the domain of Papua. Its capital was at Port Moresby.

After World War I, Germany's holdings in the region fell under the administrative control of the League of Nations. The seat of the colonial government was at Rabaul on New Britain. The Solomons are 10° below the equator. Hot, humid, and plagued by torrential rains.

By late January 1942, Japanese forces had seized Rabaul and fortified it. The site was an excellent harbor and had several airfield positions. The Japanese carrier and aircraft losses at the Battle of Midway had caused the Imperial Japanese Headquarters to cancel their plan of invading Midway, Fiji, New Caledonia, and Samoa. But the plans to construct a significant seaplane base at Tulagi went forward. The new location offered one of the best anchorages in the South Pacific. Strategically located over five hundred miles from the New Hebrides and just short of eight hundred miles from New Caledonia, and only one thousand miles from Fiji. It was the perfect location.

The Tulagi outpost on Guadalcanal was evidence of a sizable Japanese force in the region. Starting with the 17th Army, headquartered at Rabaul, and enemy 8th Fleet, the 11th Air Fleet and the 1st, 7th, 8th, and 14th Naval Base Forces, were also on New Britain. In early August 1942, Japanese intelligence units picked up transmissions between Noumea and Melbourne. Enemy analysts decided that Admiral Ghormley had ordered an offensive force to assault the Solomon Islands or at New Guinea. The warnings were passed to the Imperial Japanese Headquarters in Truk but were ignored.

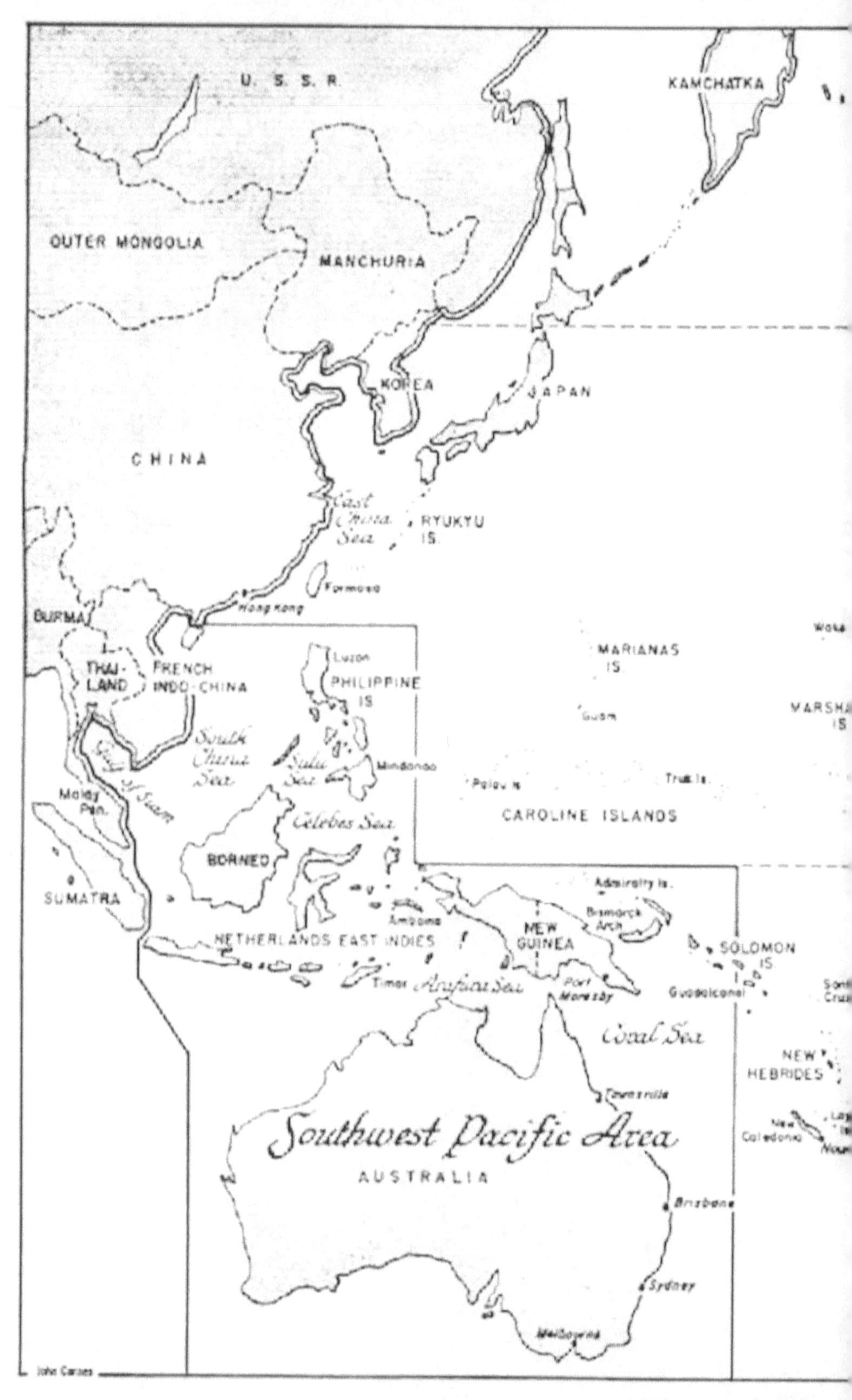

U. S. S. R.
KAMCHATKA
OUTER MONGOLIA
MANCHURIA
KOREA
JAPAN
CHINA
East China Sea
RYUKYU IS.
Formosa
Hong Kong
BURMA
Luzon
MARIANAS IS.
Wake
THAI-LAND
FRENCH INDO-CHINA
PHILIPPINE IS
Guam
MARSHA IS
South China Sea
Sulu Sea
Mindanao
Palau Is.
Truk Is.
Malay Pen.
Celebes Sea
CAROLINE ISLANDS
BORNEO
Admiralty Is.
SUMATRA
Amboina
Bismarck Arch.
NEW GUINEA
SOLOMON IS
NETHERLANDS EAST INDIES
Santa Cruz
Timor
Arafura Sea
Port Moresby
Guadalcanal
Coral Sea
NEW HEBRIDES
Townsville
New Caledonia
Noumea
Southwest Pacific Area
AUSTRALIA
Brisbane
Sydney
Melbourne
John Carnes

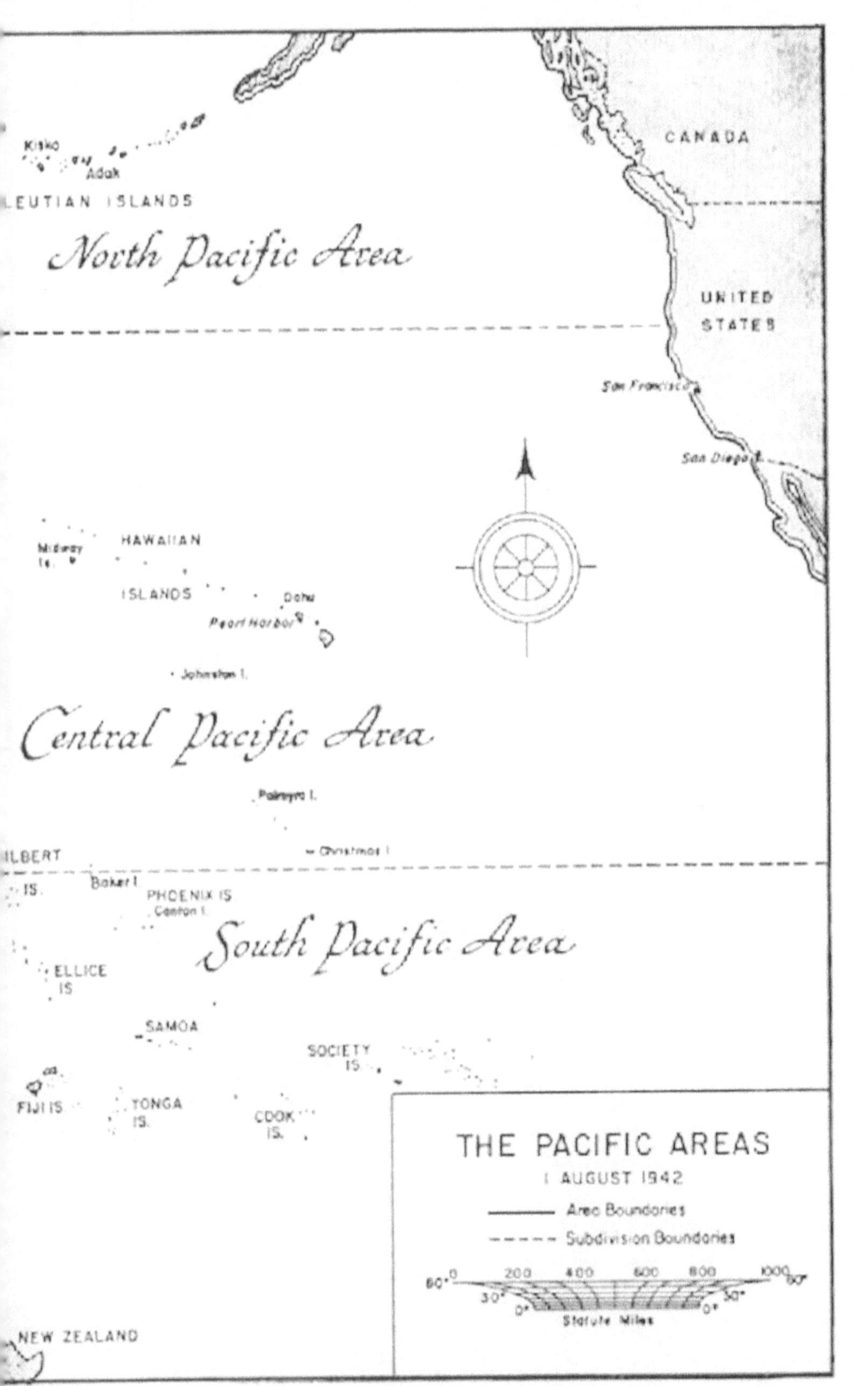

Kiska
Adak
ALEUTIAN ISLANDS
North Pacific Area
CANADA
UNITED STATES
San Francisco
San Diego
Midway Is.
HAWAIIAN
ISLANDS
Oahu
Pearl Harbor
Johnston I.
Central Pacific Area
Palmyra I.
Christmas I.
GILBERT
IS.
Baker I.
PHOENIX IS
Canton I.
South Pacific Area
ELLICE
IS
SAMOA
SOCIETY
IS.
FIJI IS
TONGA
IS.
COOK
IS.
NEW ZEALAND
THE PACIFIC AREAS
1 AUGUST 1942
Area Boundaries
Subdivision Boundaries
0   200   400   600   800   1000
Statute Miles

AUGUST 1, 1942

The invasion force was on its way to targets in Guadalcanal, Tulagi, and the tiny islands of Tanambogo and Gavutu close to Tulagi's shore. The landing force would be composed of Marines. The covering and transport forces were supplied by the US Navy with the reinforcement of Australian warships. The 1st Marine Division was slated to make the landings. Five US Army divisions were located in the Southwest Pacific. Three in Australia, the 37th and 5th Infantry were in Fiji and an Americal Division on New Caledonia.

None of these divisions were trained for amphibious warfare, and all were vital parts of defensive garrisons in the Pacific. The 1st Marine Division began arriving in New Zealand in mid-June after the 5th Marines had reached Wellington. The rest of the unit's reinforced divisions were still preparing to embark. The 1st Raider Battalion was on New Caledonia, 1st Marines were at San Francisco, and the 3rd Defense Battalion was at Pearl Harbor. The 2nd Marine Division, who would eventually replace the 1st Division, 7th Marines, was stationed in British Samoa, while the rest loaded out from San Diego. The landing force infantry regiments all had battalions of artillery attached from the 11th Marines.

The news that this division would be the landing force for Operation Watchtower came as a shock to Major General Alexander Vandegrift. He had expected that the 1st Division would have at least six months of training in the South Pacific before seeing any kind of action. Combat loading took precedence over any administrative loading of supplies. Equipment, weapons, ammunition, and rations were positioned to come off the ship with the assault troops. The combat troops replaced the civilian longshoremen. They unloaded and reloaded the cargo and passenger vessels often during rainstorms, which hampered the task, but the job got done.

All division forces got their share of labor on the docks as the various shipping groups arrived. Time was running out. General Vandegrift convinced Admiral Ghormley and the Joint Chiefs that he would not meet the proposed D-Day of August 1, and only possibly meet the extended landing date of August 7.

An amphibious operation is a complicated affair when the forces involved are assembled on brief notice from all over the Pacific. The pressure placed on Vandegrift was intense. The US Navy ships were the key to success, and they were scarce. The previous battles of the Coral Sea and Midway had damaged the Imperial Japanese fleet's offensive capabilities and crippled its carrier forces. But their enemy naval aircraft could fight as well ashore as afloat, and enemy warships were still numerous and lethal.

American losses at Pearl Harbor, Coral Sea, and Midway were considerable. The Navy knew their ships were in short supply. The day was coming when America's shipyards and factories would fill the seas with warships of all types, but they had not arrived in 1942. The name of the game for the US Navy was calculated risk. And now the risk seemed too great. The Operation Watchtower landing force might need to be a casualty. The US Navy never ceased to risk its ships in the waters of the Solomon Islands. This meant the naval lifeline to the troops ashore was stretched thin.

The tactical command of the invasion forces approaching Guadalcanal in early August was vested in Vice Admiral Frank Fletcher as the expeditionary force commander (Task Force 61). His forces consisted of the amphibious shipping carrying the 1st Marine Division, under Admiral Richmond Turner. Admiral Leigh Noyes contributed the land-based air forces that were commanded by Admiral John McCain. Fletcher's support forces comprised three fleet carriers, the *Wasp*, the *Saratoga*, the *Enterprise*, and the battleship *North Carolina*, six cruisers, sixteen destroyers, and three oilers. Admiral Turner's covering force included five cruisers and nine destroyers.

Onboard the transports approaching the Solomons, the Marines were expecting a tough fight. They knew little about any targets, even less about their opponents. The available maps were based on outdated hydrographic charts and information provided by former island residents. The maps based on aerial photographs were of poor quality and often mismapped.

On July 17, a couple division staff officers, Lieutenant Colonel Merrill Twining and Major William McKean, joined the crew of a B-17 flying from Port Moresby on a reconnaissance mission over Guadalcanal. They reported that they saw no extensive defenses along the beaches of Guadalcanal's north shore.

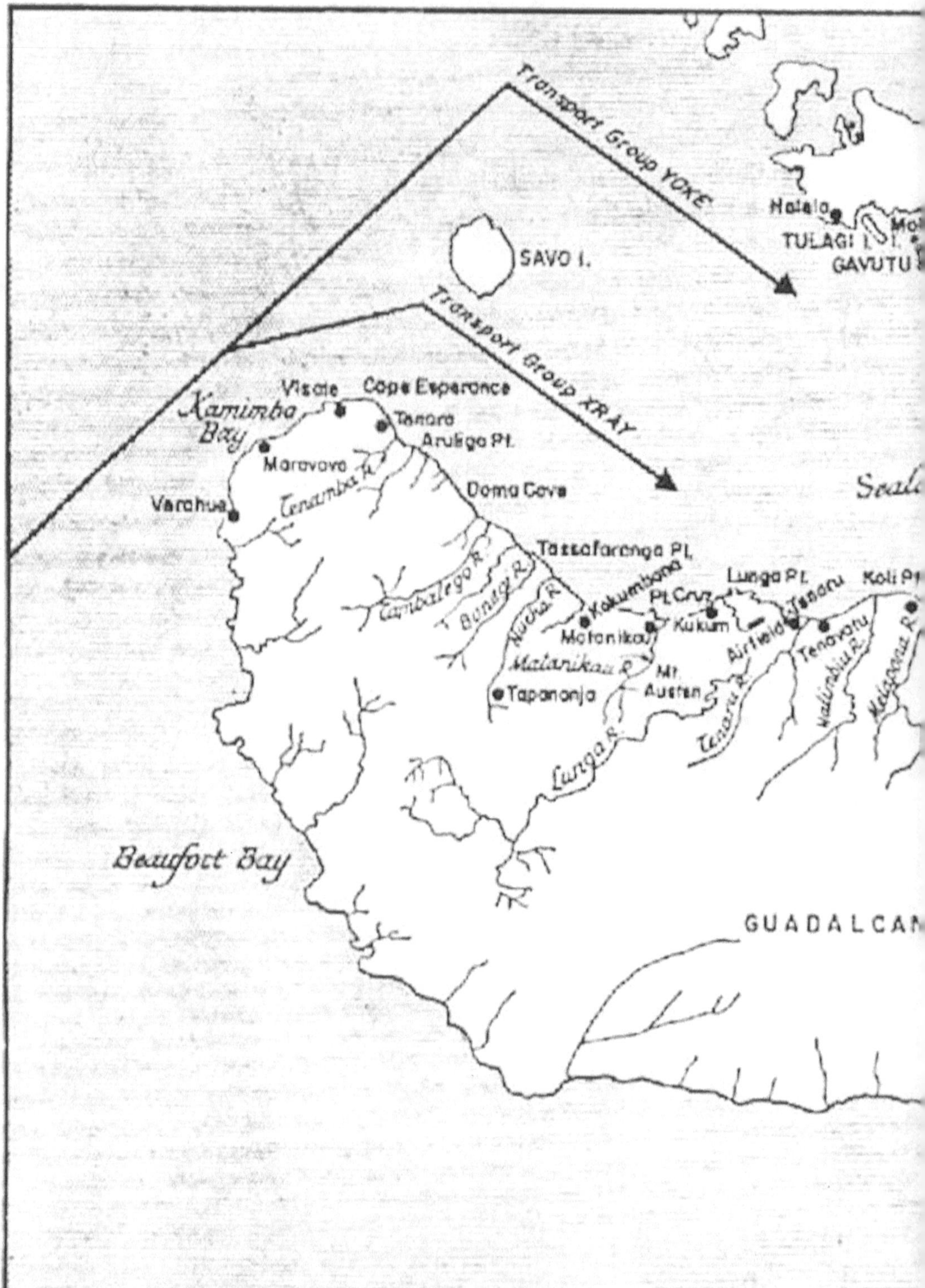

Transport Group YOKE
Transport Group XRAY
SAVO I.
Halalo
TULAGI I.
GAVUTU
Visale
Cape Esperance
Kamimba Bay
Tanaro
Aruligo Pt.
Maravovo
Doma Cove
Tenambu R.
Varahue
Scale
Tassafaronga Pt.
Tambalego R.
Bunag R.
Nueha R.
Kokumbona
Pt. Cruz
Lunga Pt.
Tananu
Koli Pt.
Matanikau
Kukum
Airfield
Matanikau R.
Mt. Austen
Tenaru R.
Tenavatu
Koliumbiu R.
Matanga R.
Tapananja
Lunga R.
Beaufort Bay
GUADALCAN
John Carnes

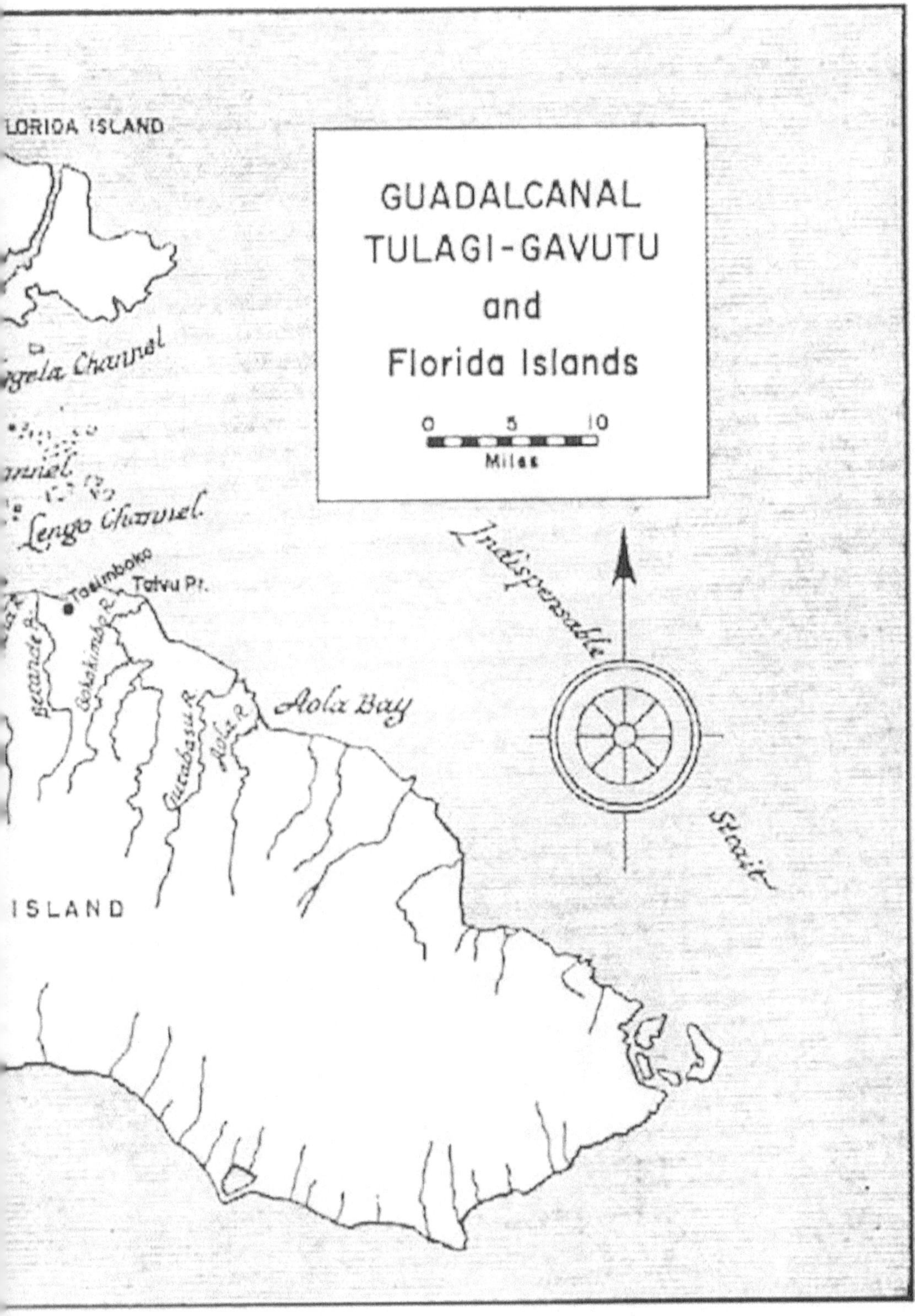

FLORIDA ISLAND
GUADALCANAL
TULAGI-GAVUTU
and
Florida Islands
0   5   10
Miles
Sealark Channel
Lengo Channel
Taivu Pt.
Tasimboko
Aola Bay
ISLAND
Indispensable
Strait

GUADALCANAL AND FLORIDA ISLANDS

The G-2 Intelligence officer, Lieutenant Colonel Frank Goettge, determined that approximately 8,400 Japanese occupied Guadalcanal and Tulagi. Admiral Turner's staff concluded that the Japanese were around 7,000 men. In comparison, Admiral Ghormley's Intelligence officer put the enemy strength at just over 3,000 men. He was the closest to the actual total of Japanese troops of 3,457 men. Over 2,500 of these men stationed on Guadalcanal were Korean laborers working on the airfield.

The Marine Corps had overwhelming superiority over the Japanese. The Marine Division had 19,514 officers and enlisted. This included the Naval Medical and Seabee engineer units. The infantry regiments numbered exactly 3,168 and had a headquarters company, weapons company, and three battalions. Each infantry battalion (933 Marines) was organized into a headquarters company, a weapons company, and three rifle companies. The artillery regiment had 2,581 officers and men. They were organized into 105mm howitzer and three 75mm howitzer battalions. A special weapons battalion of antiaircraft and antitank guns, a parachute battalion, and a light tank battalion contributed to additional combat power. An engineer regiment (2,450 Marines) with battalions of pioneers, engineers, and Seabees provided a hefty combat and service element. The total was completed by division headquarters, battalion headquarters, military police companies, and the division's service troops. The 1st Raider Battalion and the 3rd Defense Battalion had been added to Vandegrift's command to provide more infantry and a much-needed coastal defense for supplying antiaircraft guns and crews.

The 1st Division's heaviest ordinance had been left behind in New Zealand. Limited ship space and time meant that the division's big guns, 155mm howitzer Battalion, and all of the Motor Transport Battalion's 2 1/2 ton trucks were not loaded. Colonel del Valle commanded the 11th Marines. He was distressed at the loss of his heavy howitzers. And equally concerned that the essential sound and flash ranging equipment necessary for effective counter-battery fire was left behind. There was not enough room for extra clothing, bedding rolls, and other supplies essential to support and reinforce the division for sixty days of combat. An additional ten days' supply of ammunition also remained in New Zealand.

In the opinion of several 1st Division historians and veterans from the landing, the men approaching the transports "thought they'd have a tough time getting ashore." They were confident young men and sure that they would not be defeated, but most men were entering combat for the first time. While there were combat veteran officers and NCOs within the division, most men were going to their first battle. The 1st Marines commanding officer Colonel Clifton Cate estimated that over 90% of his men had enlisted directly after Pearl Harbor.

The fabled fame of the 1st Marine Division from the later World War II, Korean War, Vietnam War, and the Persian Gulf War—the most highly decorated division in the US Armed Forces—had not yet established its reputation. The convoy of ships, with its protective screen of carriers, reached Koro in the Fiji Islands on July 26. The practice landings did little more than exercise the transports landing craft since reefs prevented an actual beach landing.

The rendezvous at Koro gave the senior commanders a chance to have a face-to-face meeting. Turner, McCain, Fletcher, and

Vandegrift got together with Ghormley, and Chief of Staff, Admiral Daniel Callahan. They learned that the 7th Marines on Samoa were to be prepared to embark on four days' notice to reinforce Operation Watchtower. Admiral Fletcher added some bad news to this. Because of the threat of land-based air assaults, he could not "keep the carriers in the area for more than forty-eight hours after the landing." Vandegrift protested he needed at least four days to get the division's gear ashore. Fletcher grudgingly kept his carriers at risk for another day.

On the 28th, the ships sailed from the Fiji Islands. They proceeded as if they were heading toward Australia. At noon on August 5, the convoy and its escorts turn north for the Solomon Islands. They were undetected by the Japanese. The assault force reached their target during the night of August 7 and split into two landing groups. The first was Transport Division X-Ray. They had fifteen transports headed for the north shore of Guadalcanal, east of Lunga Point. Transport Division Yoke followed with eight transports headed for Tulagi, Gavutu, Tanambogo in nearby Florida Island, which loomed over the other smaller islands.

Vandegrift's plans for the landing would put two of his infantry regiments—the 1st Marines and the 5th Marines—ashore on both sides of the Lunga River. They would be ready to seize the airfield and attack inland. The 11th Marines, the 3rd Defense Battalion, and most of the division's supporting units, would land near Lunga and be prepared to take advantage of the beachhead. Twenty miles across the Sealark Channel, the division's assistant commander, Brigadier General William Rupertus, would lead the assault forces to take Tulagi, Gavutu, and Tanambogo. The 1st Raider Battalion, 2nd Battalion, 5th Marines (2/5 Marines), and the 1st Parachute Battalion would patrol the nearby shores of Florida Island. The rest of Colonel John Arthur's regiment would await orders in reserve.

They slipped through the channels on both sides of the rugged Savo Island. Heavy clouds and dense rain blinded the task force until the moon came out and silhouetted the islands. Onboard his command ship, General Vandegrift wrote to his wife: "*Tomorrow morning at dawn, we land on our first major offensive of the war. Our plans have been made and God grant us our judgment has been sound. Whatever happens, I want you to know I did my best. Let us hope that will be good enough.*"

At 0641, on August 7, Turner signaled his ships to land the landing force. Just twenty-eight minutes before, *Quincy* started shelling the Guadalcanal beaches. When the sun came up that Friday at 0650, Marine assault troops touched down at 0909 on Red Beach, on Guadalcanal's north shore. To the men's surprise—and relief—no Japanese resisted the landing. The assault troops moved off the beach and into the surrounding jungle. They waded through the steep banked Ilu River and headed toward the enemy airfield. The 1st Marines that followed could cross the Ilu on a bridge the engineers had thrown up with an amphibian tractor bracing its middle. The silence was eerie. The absence of opposition worried the rifleman. The Japanese troops, mostly Korean laborers, fled to the west, terrified by a week's worth of B-17 bombardments, naval gunfire, and the imposing sight of the ships offshore. The situation was not the same across the Sealark. The Marines on Guadalcanal heard echoes of a firefight across the channel.

The Japanese on Tulagi would refuse to give up without a vicious, no surrender battle to the death. After the Marines landed, they moved inland toward the ridge that ran lengthwise through the island. The Marine battalions encountered pockets of resistance in the undergrowth of the island's thick vegetation. They maneuvered to outflank and overrun the opposition. The Marine advance was steady but riddled with casualties. By nightfall, they had reached the former British residency overlooking the Tulagi harbor and dug in for the night. They were across from the hill that overlooked the Japanese position—a ravine on the island's southern tip. The 2/5 Marines cleaned out its sector of enemy insurgents. By the end of their first day, the 2nd Battalion had fifty-six men killed and wounded. The 1st Raider Battalion's casualties was ninety-nine Marines.

During the night, the Japanese swarmed from hillside caves in four separate ambushes, trying to penetrate the raider's lines. They were unsuccessful, and most died in their suicidal efforts. At dawn, the 2nd Marines landed and reinforced the attackers. By the afternoon of August 8, the mop-up was completed and the battle for Tulagi ended. The fight for tiny Tanambogo and Gavutu, both little more than small hills rising out of the sea connected by a one hundred yard causeway, had fighting just as intense as that on Tulagi.

The combat area was much smaller than the opportunities for fire support from offshore ships. Carrier planes were limited once the Marines landed on the beachhead. Naval gunfire began from the light cruiser *San Juan*. F4F Wildcats flying from the *Wasp* attacked enemy positions on the island. The 1st Parachute Battalion landed 395 men in three waves on Gavutu. The Japanese, with secured cave positions, opened fire on the second and third waves, pinning down the 1st Marines on the beach. Major Williams took a bullet in the lungs and was evacuated. Thirty-two Marines were killed under withering enemy fire. This time the 2nd Marines' reinforcements were really needed. The 1st Battalion's Company B landed on Gavutu and attempted to take Tanambogo. The attackers were driven to the ground and had to pull back to Gavutu.

After a rough night of fighting with the defenders of both islands, the 3rd Battalion, 2nd Marines, reinforced the men already ashore and mopped up each island. The Marines' butcher's bill on the three islands was almost 150. The wounded numbered just under 200. The surviving Japanese fled to Florida Island, which had been scouted out by the 2nd Marines on D-Day and found to be clear of enemy soldiers. The Marine landings and concentration of shipping in Guadalcanal waters acted as a magnet to the Japanese at Rabaul. Admiral Ghormley's headquarters was heard on D-Day, "desperately calling for the dispatch of surface forces to the scene" and to designate transports and carriers as targets for massive bombing. The messages were sent uncoded and emphasized the imminent danger of the threatened garrison. The Japanese response was quick and would be characteristic in the upcoming months of air and land battles to come.

On August 7, an Australian coastwatcher warned of a Japanese airstrike that was composed of light, heavy, and fighter-bombers fast approaching toward the island. Fletcher's pilots, whose carriers were positioned one hundred miles south of Guadalcanal, intercepted the approaching planes, twenty-five miles out, before they could attack Marine positions. This setback did not discourage the Japanese. Other aircraft and ships were en route to the inviting target.

On August 8, the Marines consolidated their positions ashore, taking the airfield on Guadalcanal and establishing a beachhead. Supplies were unloaded as fast as the landing craft could make the turnaround from ship to shore. Still, the men allocated on shore to handle the influx of rations, ammunition, tents, and aviation gas were woefully inadequate. The beach became a dumpsite. Just as the supplies were landed, they needed to be moved to other positions near Kukum Village and Lunga Point within the planned perimeter. Luckily, the lack of Japanese ground opposition allowed Vandegrift to shift the supply beaches west to a new beachhead.

Japanese bombers penetrated the American fighter screen on August 8. They dropped bombs from twenty thousand feet or higher to escape the antiaircraft fire. The enemy planes were inaccurate while they concentrated on the ships in the channel damaging several and sinking the destroyer *Jarvis*. In the fight to turn back the attacking planes, the carrier fighter squadrons lost twenty-one Wildcats.

The Japanese targeted the Allied ships. The Japanese commanders at Rabaul underestimated the strength of General Vandegrift's forces. They thought the Marine landings were made up of a reconnaissance force of 2,000 men on Guadalcanal. By the evening of August 8, Vandegrift had 10,900 troops ashore on Guadalcanal and another 6,075 on Tulagi. Three infantry regiments landed with supporting 75mm howitzer battalions—the 2nd and 3rd Battalions. 11th Marines on Guadalcanal and the 3rd Battalion, 10th Marines on Tulagi. The 5th Battalion, 11th Marines' 105mm howitzers supported the assault.

Later that night, a cruiser force of the Imperial Japanese Navy reacted to the American invasion with an intense response. Admiral Turner had positioned three cruiser destroyer groups to block the Tulagi approaches. During the Battle of Savo Island, the Japanese showed their superiority of night assaults and fighting at this stage of the war. They smashed two of Turner's covering forces without any loss. Four heavy cruisers sunk—three American, one Australian —and another lost her bow. As the sun came up on what would soon be called "Ironbottom Sound," the Marines watched with grim faces as Higgins boats swarmed out to rescue survivors. American casualties were 1,300 sailors dead and another 700 wounded. Japanese casualties were less than 200 men.

The cruiser *Chokai* was the only Japanese ship to suffer damage in the encounter. The American cruisers *Vincennes*, *Astoria*, and *Quincy*, were sunk as well as the Australian HMAS *Canberra*. She was critically damaged and sunk by American torpedoes. Both the cruiser *Chicago* and the destroyer *Talbot* were damaged. Luckily for the Marines on shore, the Japanese force—five heavy cruisers, two light cruisers, and a destroyer—departed before dawn.

When the Japanese attack force leader, Vice-Admiral Gunichi Mikawa, returned to Rabaul, he had expected to receive the praise of his superiors. He got that, but he also found himself the subject of criticism. Admiral Yamamoto, the Japanese fleet commander, chided his subordinates for failing to attack the transports. Mikawa replied he didn't know Fletcher's aircraft carriers were that far off Guadalcanal.

This disaster prompted the American admirals to re-examine naval support for shore operations. Fletcher was concerned for the safety of his aircraft carriers. He'd already lost a quarter of his fighter aircraft. The expeditionary force commander had lost a carrier at Midway and Coral Sea. He felt he couldn't risk losing a third, even if it meant abandoning the men on the island. Before the Japanese cruiser attack, he got Ghormley's permission to withdraw.

The admiral told General Vandegrift that Fletcher's impending withdrawal would have to pull out the amphibious force's ships. The Savo Island battle was essential in reinforcing the decision to flee before Japanese enemy aircraft would strike. The next day the transports steamed away to Noumea. The unloading of ship supplies were interrupted while the ships fled. The forces ashore had seventeen days worth of rations—after counting Japanese food—and only four days' supply of ammunition for all weapons. The naval ships fled with most of the supplies and with the majority of the 2nd Division Marines still on board. The Marines were left at the island of Espiritu Santo in the New Hebrides. Colonel Arthur and the Infantry Marines were distraught that they could not reinforce their comrades until they finally reached Guadalcanal on October 29.

General Vandegrift ordered the remaining rations reduced to two a day for the Marines on the beachheads. Most of the Marines were smokers and now smoked Japanese brand cigarettes. The fast-burning tobacco scorched their lips because of the separate paper filters that came with the cigarettes.

The withdrawing naval ships also took with them precious, valuable engineering tools as well as some of the empty sandbags. The Marines used discarded Japanese shovels to fill remaining sandbags. They strengthened their defensive positions along the beaches between the Tenaru River and the ridges west of Kukum.

A Japanese counter landing was a distinct threat. Inland of the beaches, Marines in foxholes had defensive gun positions, and they lined the west bank of the Tenaru. They maintained higher ground over the hills that faced west toward the Matanikau River and Point Cruz. South of the airfield were densely jungled ridges and ravines. The beachhead perimeter was guarded by outposts manned by combat support troops. Frontline positions included the engineers and amphibious tractor battalions. In fact, any Marine with a rifle—virtually every Marine—stood a night defensive duty. No place within the perimeter could be counted safe from enemy infiltration.

As Turner's transport sailed away, the Japanese began a pattern of harassing air attacks on the beachhead. Sometimes the raids came during the day. But the 3rd Battalion's 90mm antiaircraft guns forced the bombers to fly too high for effective bombing. The erratic pattern of bombs meant no safe place near the airfield, the preferred target, and no place could claim it was bomb free. Japanese air attacks became the new norm and severely harassed Allied positions, dropping bombs and flares indiscriminately.

The nightly visitors' aircraft engines soon became well-known sounds. They were called "Washing Machine Charlie" and later "Louis the Louse" when they signaled Japanese bombardment. When "Charlie" was used, it meant a twin-engine night bomber. "Louis" was a cruiser floatplane that signaled to the bombardment ships. But the harassed Marines use these names interchangeably.

Even though most of the division's heavy engineering equipment had disappeared with the naval transports, the resourceful Marines soon completed the airfield's runway with captured Japanese gear. On August 12, Admiral McCain's aide piloted in a PBY-5 Catalina. A flying boat landed on what was now officially Henderson Field, named for a Marine pilot, Major Loftin Henderson lost at Midway. The Navy decided that fighters could use the airfield and flew off with several loads of wounded Marines. The first of 2,879 to be evacuated. Henderson Field was the centerpiece of General Vandegrift's strategy. He would hold it at all costs.

The tiny airstrip was only two thousand feet long and lacked a taxiway and adequate drainage. Torrential downpours riddled the runway with potholes. It was rendered unusable but was essential for the success of the landing force. With the airstrip operational, supplies could be flown in and wounded flown out. At least in the Marines' minds, the lifeline of Navy ships was no longer available for the remaining Marines. General Vandegrift's Marines were dug in on Henderson Field on the west and east.

The Imperial Japanese headquarters in Rabaul planned what they considered the most effective response to the Marine offensive. Their faulty intelligence estimated that the Americans had two thousand men. Several Japanese officers believed that a smaller force would quickly overwhelm the Marines' invasion. On August

12, CINCPAC determined that a sizable Japanese force was massing at Truk to steam to the Solomons and attempt to remove the Americans. The heavy carriers *Zuikaku* and *Shokaku* and the light carrier *Ryujo* were dispatched. After the stinging losses at Savo Island, the only significant American naval force increase in the Solomons was the new battleship, the *South Dakota*.

The Japanese Imperial headquarters in Tokyo had ordered General Hyakutake's 17th Army to attack the Marine perimeter. For his assault force, he chose the 35th Infantry Brigade, commanded by Major General Kawaguchi. Kawaguchi's primary force was in Palaus. General Hyakutake chose the 28th—a crack infantry regiment commanded by Colonel Ichiki—to land first. Alerted for their mission while still on Guam, the Ichiki detachment assault echelon, one battalion of nine hundred men, was transported to the Solomon Islands on the only shipping available, six destroyers. The troops only carried small amounts of supplies and ordinance. A follow-on force of twelve hundred troops was to join the assault battalion on Guadalcanal.

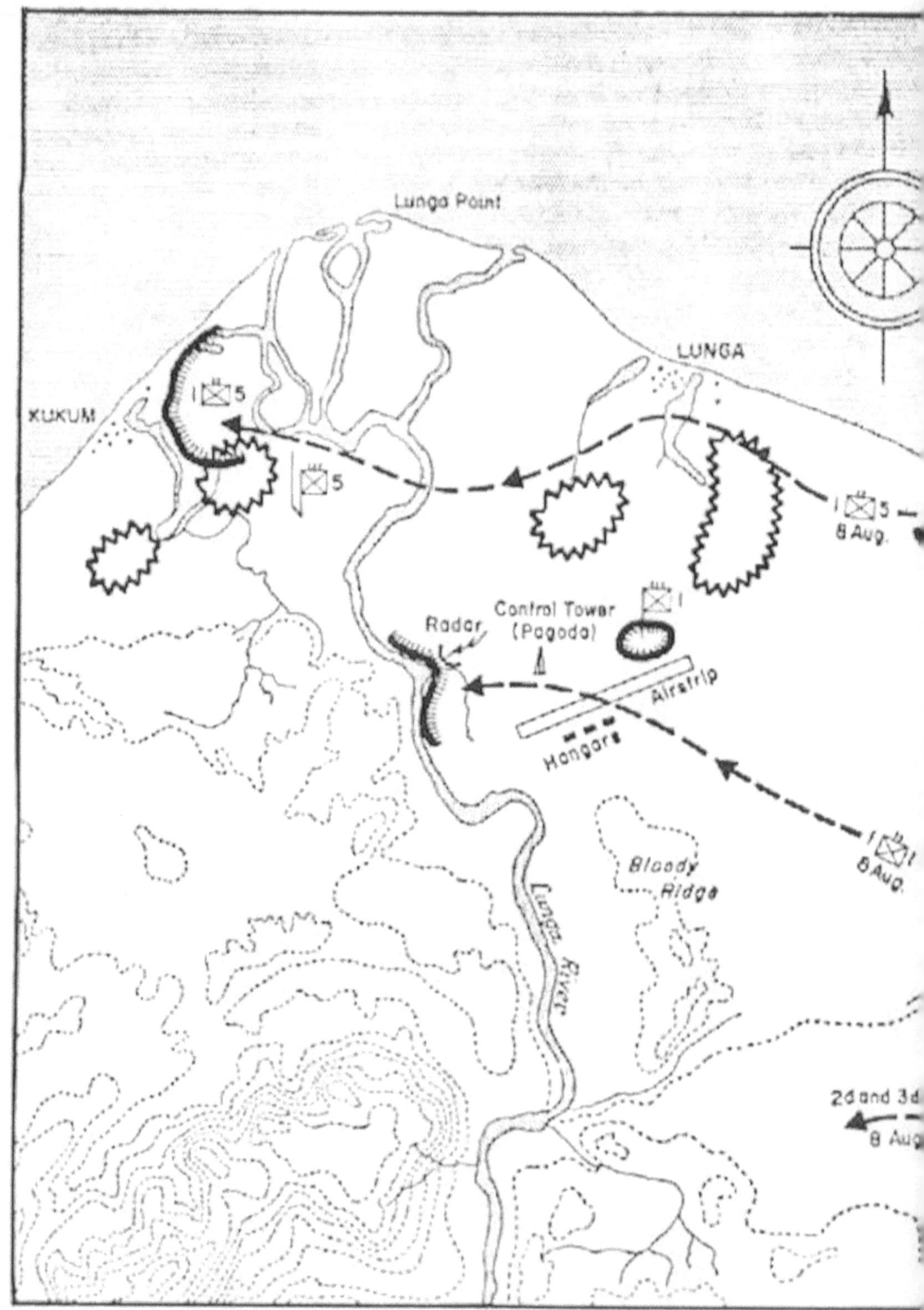

Lunga Point
LUNGA
KUKUM
Radar
Control Tower
(Pagoda)
Airstrip
Hangars
Lunga River
Bloody
Ridge
1 X 5
5
1 X 5
8 Aug.
1 X 1
1 X 1
8 Aug.
2d and 3d
8 Aug.

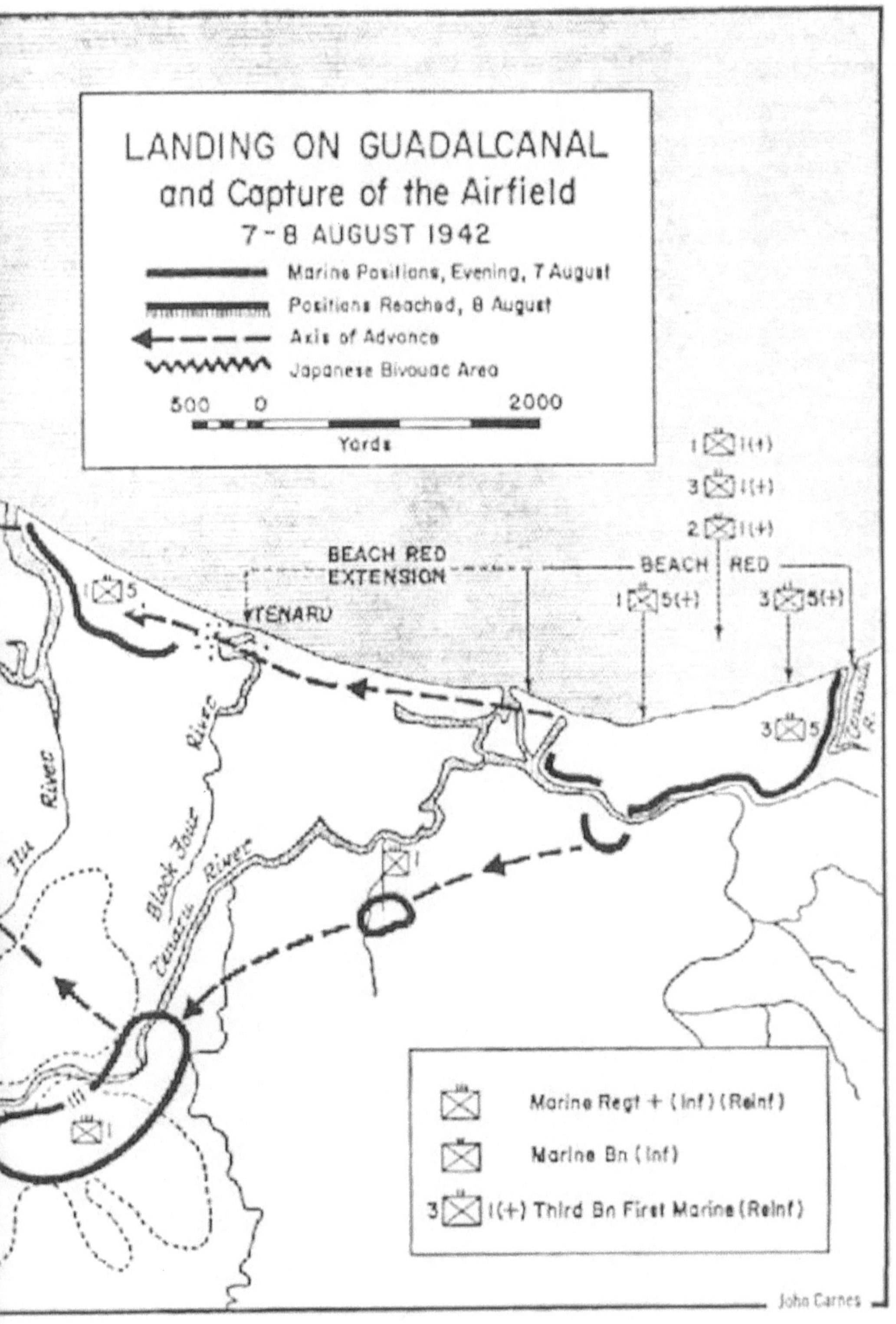

LANDING ON GUADALCANAL
and Capture of the Airfield
7 - 8 AUGUST 1942
Marine Positions, Evening, 7 August
Positions Reached, 8 August
Axis of Advance
Japanese Bivouac Area
500   0   2000
Yards
BEACH RED EXTENSION
BEACH RED
YTENARU
1 5
1 5(+)
3 5(+)
3 5
1 I(+)
3 I(+)
2 I(+)
Tiu River
Black Jour River
Tenaru River
Ilu River
Marine Regt + (Inf) (Reinf)
Marine Bn (Inf)
3 I(+) Third Bn First Marine (Reinf)
John Carnes

BATTLE OF THE EASTERN SOLOMONS

While the Marine landing force headed to Guadalcanal, the Japanese were already on the island, providing an unpleasant reminder that they were full of fight. A Japanese captured naval officer told Marine officers that the Japanese group was ready to surrender near the village of Kokumbona, seven miles west of Matanikau. This was the area that Colonel Goettge believed held most of the enemy troops who had fled the airfield. On August 12, a reconnaissance patrol of twenty-five men led by Goettge himself left the perimeter by landing craft. Their patrol landed near their objective. They were ambushed—and nearly wiped out.

Three Marines survived by swimming back to the lines. The rest of the other patrol Marines and their bodies were never found. After losing Goettge and his men, the perimeter became more vigilant. On August 14, a coastwatcher named Martin Clemens calmly exited the jungle and into the Marine perimeter. He'd observed the Japanese landing from the southern hills of the airfield and brought his bodyguard of native policeman with him. Jacob Vouza was a local and a retired sergeant major of the British Solomon Islands Constabulary. He volunteered his men to search out the Japanese east of the perimeter where they might have landed.

The news of Japanese sightings to the east and west of the perimeter were balanced out by news that more Marines had already landed. These Marines were aviators. On August 20, two squadrons of Marine aircraft groups were launched from the escort carrier *Long Island,* some two hundred miles southeast of Guadalcanal. Captain John Smith led nineteen Grumman F4F Wildcats of the Marine Fighting Squadron onto the narrow runway in Henderson Airfield. Captain Smith's fighters were followed by Major Richard Mangrum's Marine Scout-Bombing Squadron with twelve Douglas SBD Dauntless dive bombers.

They wasted no time. The Marine pilots were soon an action against the Japanese naval aircraft. Captain Smith shot down his first enemy Zero fighter on August 21. Three days later, the Wildcats intercepted a strong Japanese aerial attack and shot down sixteen enemy planes. In this fight, Captain Marion Carl, a Midway veteran, shot down three planes. The coastwatchers alerted the Cactus Air Force to an impending air attack. Thirteen of sixteen enemy bombers were engaged and destroyed. Three of the destroyed enemy dive bombers damaged three enemy destroyers attempting to reach Guadalcanal.

On August 22, five Bell P-400 Air Cobras of the Army's 67th Fighter Squadron landed at Henderson Airfield, followed later in the week by nine more Air Cobras. These Army planes had serious climb rate and altitude deficiencies. They would see the most action in ground combat support roles.

On August 24, the American attacking aircraft now included Navy scout bombers from the *Saratoga*'s Scouting Squadron. They turned back a Japanese reinforcement convoy of destroyers and warships.

This frenzied action became known as the Battle of the Eastern Solomons. Japanese destroyers had already delivered the vanguard of the Ichiki force at Taivu Point. A Marine patrol ambushed a substantial Japanese force at Taivu on August 19. The dead Japanese were quickly identified as Army troops. In the debris of their defeat, Marines found fresh uniforms and large amounts of communication equipment. This signaled a new phase of fighting.

The Japanese encountered up to this point had all been naval troops.

Marines dug in along the Ilu River, often mislabeled as the Tenaru on Marine maps, and were ready for Colonel Ichiki. The Japanese commander's orders were to "quickly recapture and maintain the airfield at Guadalcanal," in his own directive, his troops were to fight "to the last breath of the last man." And that is what they did.

Colonel Ichiki decided to not wait for the rest of his regiment. Sure of the fact he only faced two thousand Marines, Ichiki marched out from Taivu to the Marine lines. Before he attacked, a bloody figure stumbled out of the jungle with a warning that the Japanese were coming.

Sergeant Major Vouza had been captured by the Japanese. They found a small American flag hidden in his loincloth. The Japanese tortured him to get more information on the details of the Marine Invasion Force. He was tied to a tree, bayoneted twice through the chest, and beaten with rifle butts. Sergeant Major Vouza showed true grit as he chewed through his bindings to escape.

He was taken to Colonel Edwin Pollock, whose 2nd Battalion, 1st Marines held the Ilu River mouth defenses. He warned that over five hundred Japanese soldiers were close behind him. The sergeant was rushed to an aid station and then the division hospital. He miraculously survived his ordeal and was awarded the Silver Star for his heroic actions. Sergeant. Major Vouza was also made an honorary sergeant major of the US Marines.

On August 21 at 0130, Japanese troops stormed the Marines' lines in the screaming frenzy display of "spiritual strength," to destroy their weak American enemy. As the Japanese charged across the sandbar, astride the river Ilu's mouth. The US Marines cut them down. After a mortar assault, the Japanese tried again to storm past the sandbar. A section of 37mm guns pounded the enemy force with lethal effect. The 1st Battalion, 1st Marines, moved upstream at daybreak. And waded across the sluggish fifty-foot wide stream and moved to flank the Japanese. Wildcats strafed the beleaguered enemy force. Five light tanks blasted the retreating Japanese. By 1700—as the sun was setting—the battle ended.

Colonel Ichiki, disgraced by defeat, burned his regimental colors and shot himself in the face. Eight hundred Japanese soldiers joined him in his ritual suicidal death. The few survivors fled eastward toward Taivu Point. Japanese Admiral Tanaka, whose reinforcement troops of destroyers and transports were responsible for the Japanese troop build-up on Guadalcanal, remarked about this foolish unsupported attack: "*This tragedy should have taught us the hopelessness of bamboo spear tactics.*"

Colonel Ichiki's overconfidence was a common trait, and weakness, among Japanese Army commanders. After the 1st Marines' fight with the Ichiki detachment, General Vandegrift was inspired to write, and recalled: "These youngsters are the darndest people when they get started."

The Marines on Guadalcanal, both veteran and newly enlisted, were becoming fast accomplished jungle fighters. No longer were they "trigger-happy" as many had been in the first days ashore, shooting at shadows and imagined enemy. They were now waiting for targets, patrolling with enthusiasm, and more sure of themselves. The miscalled battle of the Tenaru had cost the regiment thirty-four killed in action and seventy-five wounded. Most of the division's Marines were now bloodied. What the men on Tenaru, Gavutu, Tulagi, and those of the Ilu had proved was that the 1st Marine Division could and would hold fast to what it had done.

While the 1st Division's Marines and sailors got a breather as the Japanese regrouped for another attack, the action in the air over the Solomon's intensified. Every day, Japanese aircraft arrived before noon to bomb the perimeter. Marine fighter pilots fought the twin-engine Betty bombers as easy targets. Japanese Zero fighters were another story. While the Wildcats were a much sturdier aircraft, the Japanese Zeros advanced speed and better maneuverability gave them an advantage in a dogfight. The American planes, when warned by the coastwatchers of Japanese attacks, had time to climb above the oncoming enemy and attacked by making firing runs during high-speed dives. These tactics made the airspace over the Solomon Islands dangerous for the Japanese. On August 29, the carrier *Ryujo* launched aircraft for a strike against the airstrip.

Captain Smith's Wildcats shot down sixteen with a loss of four. Japanese air assaults continue to strike at Henderson Airfield without letting up. Two days after the *Ryujo* raid, Japanese bombers inflicted massive damage to the airfield. They set aviation fuel ablaze in incinerated parked aircraft. The Marine retaliation was to shoot down another thirteen enemy planes.

On August 30, two more MAG-23 squadrons flew into Henderson Airfield. These reinforcements were more than welcome. The frequent damage caused by combat attrition with scant facilities to repair and no access to parts kept the number of aircraft available a diminishing resource.

General Vandegrift needed infantry reinforcements as much as he needed additional aircraft. He brought the now combined Parachute and Raider Battalions, under the command of the 2/5 Marines, over to Guadalcanal from Tulagi.

The division commander ordered a significant increase in reconnaissance patrols to search and destroy Japanese soldiers. On August 27, the 1st Battalion, 5th Marines made a landing near Kokumbona and marched back to the beachhead with no results. While the Japanese dug in out beyond the Matanikau, they waited and watched for a better opportunity to attack.

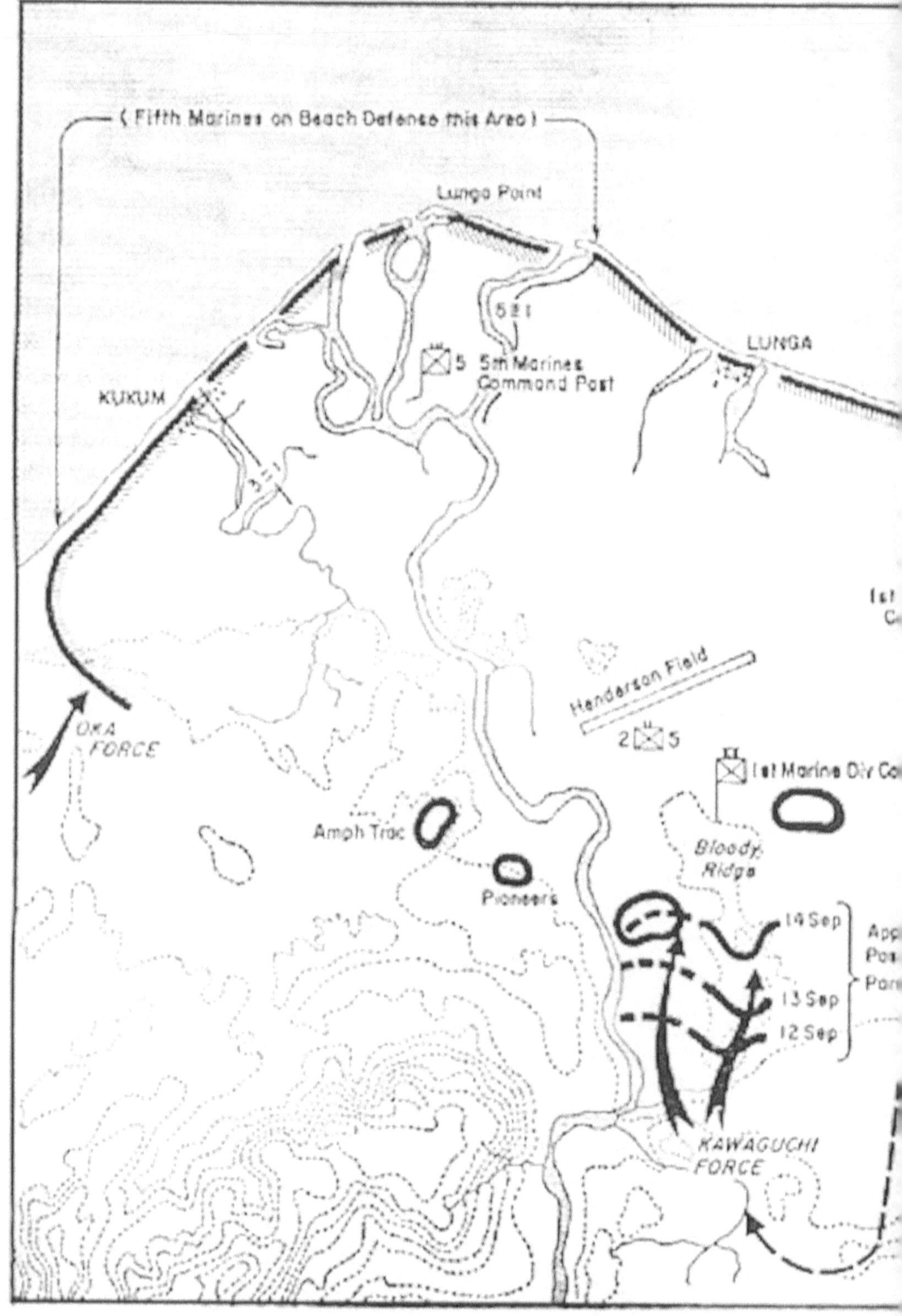
(Fifth Marines on Beach Defense this Area)
Lunga Point
5 5 1
5 5m Marines Command Post
LUNGA
KUKUM
1st Co
ORA FORCE
Henderson Field
2 5
1st Marine Div Co
Amph Trac
Bloody Ridge
Pioneers
14 Sep
App Par Par
13 Sep
12 Sep
KAWAGUCHI FORCE

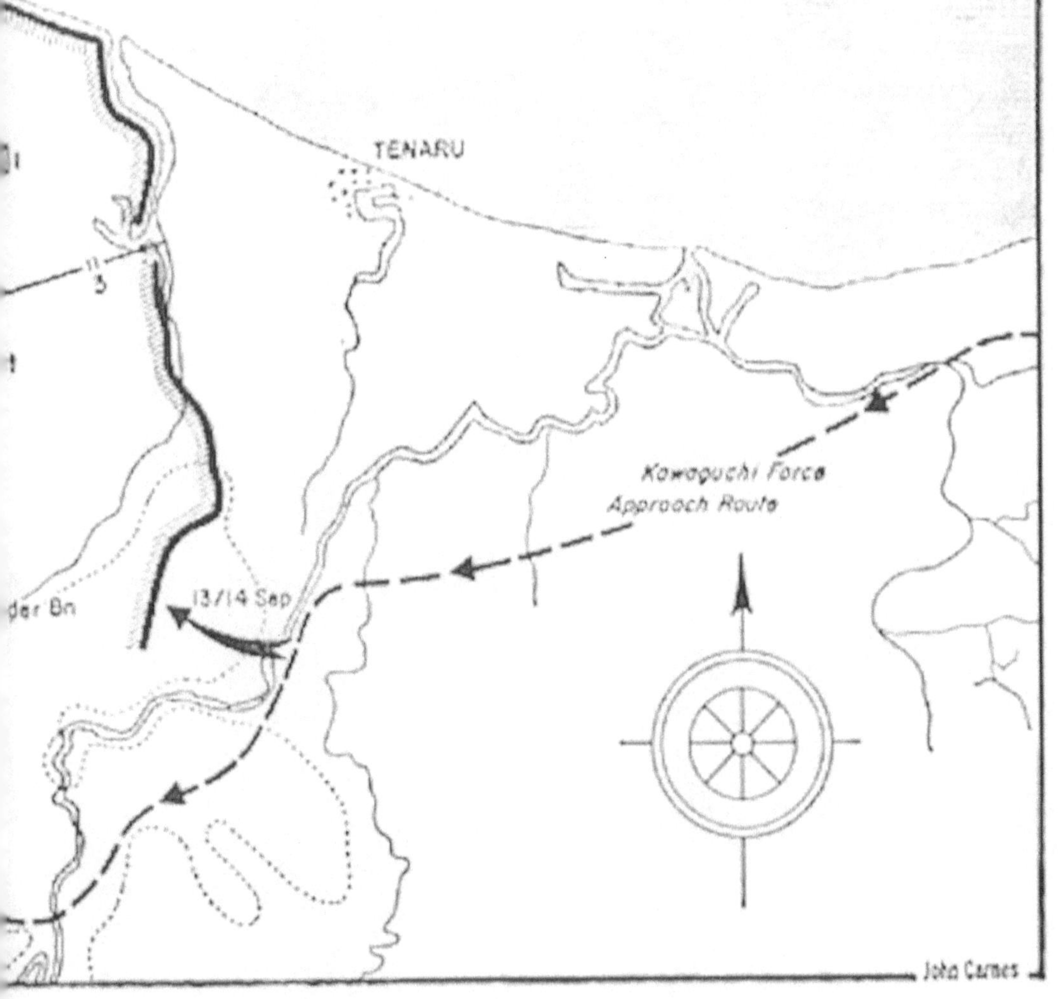

EDSON'S (BLOODY) RIDGE
12-14 SEPTEMBER 1942
Marine Positions 13 September
Axis of Japanese Attack
500   0   1000   2000
Yards
TENARU
Kawaguchi Force
Approach Route
der Bn
13/14 Sep
John Carnes

COLENEL EDSON'S BLOODY RIDGE

Admiral McCain visited Guadalcanal at the end of August. He arrived in time to greet the aerial reinforcements he had ordered, just in time for a taste of the Japanese nightly bombings. He got first-hand experience of another unwanted feature of the Cactus Air Force nights: being bombarded by Japanese cruisers and destroyers. General Vandegrift noted that Admiral McCain had gotten a dose of the "normal ration of shells." The admiral had seen enough and signaled his superiors; it was time to increase support for the Guadalcanal Operations.

He noted that it was "imperative and that the situation admits no delay whatsoever." He sent another message to admirals Nimitz and King: "Cactus can be a sinkhole for enemy air power and must be consolidated, expanded, and exploited to the enemy's mortal hurt."

On September 3, the commanding general of the 1st Marine Aircraft Wing, General Roy Geiger, and his assistant wing commander, Colonel Woods, moved forward into Guadalcanal and took charge of the air operations. These veteran Marine aviators signaled an instant lift to the morale of the pilots and ground crews. It reinforced the belief that they were on the leading edge of air combat, they were now setting the pace for the rest of Marine Corps aviation. General Vandegrift could turn over the day-to-day management of the aerial defenses of Cactus to the able and experienced General Geiger. There was no shortage of targets for the mixed air force of Marine, Navy, and Army flyers. Daily attacks by the Japanese, coupled with steady reinforcement attempts by enemy destroyers and transports, meant that every type of plane would lift off of the Henderson runway and was airborne as often as possible. The Seabees had begun work on a second airstrip, Fighter One, which would relieve most of the pressure of the primary airfield.

By now, most of General Kawaguchi's troops had reached Guadalcanal. Those who hadn't, missed landfall forever because of the American air assaults. Kawaguchi gambled with a surprise attack on the heart of the Marines' position. He planned a thrust from the jungle directly to the airfield. To reach his jump-off position, Kawaguchi would have to move through rugged terrain unobserved, carving his way through the dense vegetation and out of sight of the Marine patrols. This strenuous approach route would lead them into a prominent ridge topped by Kunai Grass that wove snakelike through the jungle to within a mile of the Henderson runway. Unknown to Japanese intelligence, Vandegrift Moved his HQ to a sheltered spot toward the inland base of the ridge, a better-protected site from enemy bombing and shell fire.

The success of the Japanese general's plan depended on the Marines keeping that inland perimeter thinly manned. They concentrated their forces on the west and east flanks. This would not happen. All available intelligence, including captured enemy maps, pointed to the likelihood of an attack on the airfield. Vandegrift moved his combined Parachute/Raider Battalion to the most apparent enemy approach throughout the ridge.

Colonel Edson's men scouted Savo Island after moving into Guadalcanal and destroyed a Japanese supply base at Tasimboko. Another shorter raid took up positions on the forward slopes of the ridge at the edge of the encroaching jungle on September 10. Their commander said that he was convinced they were in the path of the next Japanese attack. The earlier patrols had spotted a sizable Japanese assault force approaching. Colonel Edson patrolled extensively as his men dug in on the ridge. In the flanking jungle, Marines contacted enemy patrols who confirmed that Japanese troops were out front. Kawaguchi had two thousand of his men with him; enough, he thought, to punch through into the airfield.

Japanese bombers had dropped five-hundred-pound bombs along the ridge on the 11th, and enemy ships began showering the area after nightfall on the 12th, once the threat of American air attacks subsided. The first Japanese thrust came at 2100 against Edson's left flank. They boiled out of the jungle, the enemy soldiers attacked fearlessly into the face of machine gun and rifle fire. They closed into bayonet range. The Marines pushed them back. Then they came on again—a coordinated attack against the right flank—and penetrated the Marines' positions. They were forced back again. A third attack ended the night's action, it was a close fight, but by 0230, Colonel Edson told Vandegrift his men could hold. And they did.

On the morning of September 13, Colonel Edson called his company commanders together and told them: "They were just testing, just testing. They will be back."

All defenses were ordered merged, and positions improved. He pulled his lines toward the airfield along the center spine of the ridge. The 2/5 Marines, were back up on Tulagi. They were moved into position to reinforce him again.

The following night's assaults were as fierce as any Marine had yet to see. The Japanese fought hand-to-hand everywhere. They were in the Marines' foxholes and gun pits, and streaming past positions to attack from the rear. Sergeant Major Banta shot one in the command post. Colonel Edson appeared wherever the fighting was the toughest, encouraging his men to their utmost efforts. The hand-to-hand battles spilled out into the jungle on both flanks of the ridge. Engineer positions were attacked. The 5th Marine reserves were ordered into the fight. Artillery from the 5/11 Marines fired

105mm howitzers at called out targets. The range became as short as fifteen hundred yards from tube to impact.

The Japanese could stand no more. They pulled back at dawn. On the slopes of the ridge in the surrounding jungle, they left over seven hundred bodies, with another five hundred men wounded. The remnants of the Kawaguchi force staggered back toward their lines to the west. A grueling, hellish eight-day march that killed most of the enemy.

The cost to Edson's force for its epic defense was also heavy. He lost fifty-nine men, ten missing in action, and nearly two hundred wounded. Coupled with the casualties and losses of Tulagi, Gavutu, and Tanambogo, this signaled the end of the 1st Parachute Battalion as an effective fighting force. Less than ninety men of the parachutists' original strength could walk off the ridge soon to be known as Bloody Ridge or Edson's Ridge. Due to his inspirational and heroic actions, Colonel Edson was awarded the Medal of Honor.

Over the next two days, the Japanese attempted to support Kawaguchi's attack on the ridge against the flanks of the Marine perimeter. In the east, enemy troops tried to penetrate the lines of the 3rd Battalion, 1st Marines. Artillery fire caught them out in the open on the grass plane, causing over two hundred dead. To the west, the 3rd Battalion, 5th Marines continued to hold ridge positions that covered the coastal road and heroically fought off a determined Japanese attack force that skirmished its front lines.

7TH MARINES REINFORCE THE BATTALION

The victory at Colonel Edson's Bloody Ridge boosted the Allied home front morale. It reinforced the idea, for the men ashore on Guadalcanal, that they could take out anything the enemy could send up against them. At higher levels of military command, the leaders were unsure if the ground Marines and their motley air force could hold out against the Japanese forces.

Captured Japanese dispatches uncovered the myth of the two thousand man sized defending force. The Imperial Japanese sent a sizable naval force and two divisions of Japanese troops to engage and conquer the Americans on Guadalcanal. The Cactus Air Force, boosted by Navy carrier squadrons, made the planned reinforcement a high-risk venture. This was a risk the Japanese were prepared to take.

On September 18, the long-awaited 7th Marines, reinforced the 1st Battalion, 11th Marines, and other division troops. When the men from Samoa landed, they were greeted with open arms by the Marines already on the island. The 7th had been the 1st regiment of the 1st Division to go overseas. Its men, many thought then, were likely the first Marines to see combat. The division had sent some of the best Marines to Samoa, but now they had returned. A salty combat veteran of the 5th Marines said to a friend in the 7th that he was tired of waiting "to see our first team get into the game." A separate supply convoy reached the island at the same time as the 7th's arrival, bringing with it the first resupply of ammunition and aviation fuel since D-Day.

The naval force covering for the supply and reinforcement convoys was attacked by Japanese submarines. The battleship *North Carolina* was damaged and the carrier *Wasp* was torpedoed and sunk. The destroyer *O'Brien* was hit so severely, she broke up and sank on her way to drydock. The Navy accomplished the mission. The 7th Marines were landed, but with a terrible loss of life. One of the few optimistic outcomes of the devastating Japanese torpedo attack was the remainder of the *Wasp's* aircraft joined the cactus Air Force. Similar to what the planes of the *Enterprise* and *Saratoga* had done with their carriers. This left the *Hornet* as the only whole fleet carrier in the South Pacific.

As the ships that brought in the 7th Marines withdrew, they took with them the survivors of the 1st Parachute Battalion with sick bays full of badly wounded men. General Vandegrift now had control over five artillery battalions, one under strength raider battalion, and ten battalions of infantry. The 3/2 Marines, arrived from Tulagi. The defensive perimeter was reorganized into ten sectors. He gave the engineer, pioneer, and amphibian tractor battalions sectors along the beach. The other sectors were manned by the infantry battalions, which included the jungle's inland perimeter. Each infantry regiment was assigned to battalions, one to be kept in reserve and one battalion online.

General Vandegrift had a select group of infantrymen training to be scouts and snipers under Colonel "Wild Bill" Whaling. An experienced jungle fighter, marksman, and hunter, he was appointed to run a school to sharpen the divisions' fighting skills. As the men finished their training under Colonel Whaling and went back to their outfits, others took their place and were available to scout and spearhead operations.

Now that General Vandegrift had over nineteen thousand men onshore. He planned to take a forward position on the east bank of the Matanikau River. He probed the Japanese reaction with a strong force of Marines. General Vandegrift chose the fresh 1st Battalion, 7th Marines, commanded by Lieutenant Colonel Lewis "Chesty" Puller, to move inland along the slopes of Mount Austin and to patrol north toward the coast and the Japanese held area.

Puller's battalion ran into Japanese troops bivouacked on the slopes of Mount Austin on the 24th and, in a sharp firefight, lost seven men and twenty-five wounded. Vandegrift had sent the 2/5 Marines, to reinforce Puller and help carry wounded men out of the jungle. Puller advanced with reinforcements moving along the east bank of the Matanikau River. He reached the coast on September 26 as planned. He encountered intense fire from ridges west of the river. He attempted to cross with the 2/5 Marines but was beaten back.

The 1st Raider Battalion was ordered to attack on the 27th and establish a patrol base west of the Matanikau River before they were sent inland to outflank the Japanese. The battalion, now commanded by Edson's former XO, Lieutenant Colonel Samuel Griffith, ran into a hornet's nest of Japanese who had crossed the Matanikau River during the night. A garbled message led Colonel Edson to believe that Griffith's men were advancing according to the plan. He landed companies of the 1/7 Marines behind the Matanikau River and struck the Japanese from the rear. Another assault was launched across the river.

This landing was made without incident, and the 7th Marines moved inland only to be cut off and ambushed by the Japanese. A rescue force was ordered to assist. They moved with difficulty through Japanese fire and landing craft. The Marines evacuated after a tough fight under covering fire from a destroyer and machine guns of an overhead SBD. The 7th Marines returned to the perimeter, landing near Kukum. The Raider, and 5th Marines Battalions pulled back from the Matanikau. The Japanese strongly contested any westward advance, and it cost the Marines sixty men killed and over one hundred wounded.

The Japanese soldiers who the Marines had encountered were men from the 4th Regiment of the 2nd (*Sendai*) Division. Prisoners confirmed that the division was landing on the island. This included the enemy's reinforcement of 105mm howitzers, guns capable of shelling the airfield from positions as far out as Kokumbona. This was direct evidence of a new and more potent enemy attack.

September drew to a close, and several of the senior officers, picked in the order of when they joined the division, were sent back to the states. They would provide training and organization at a new level of combat expertise with the several new Marine Corps units now forming. The air wing was not ready to return its experienced pilots to the rear. The vital combat knowledge they possessed was needed in the training pipeline. But they, the survivors, would soon rotate back to the rear, some for a much needed R&R before returning to combat and others to lead new squadrons into the fight.

JAPANESE OFFENSIVE ON MARUYAMA TRAIL

On September 30, a B-17 carrying Admiral Nimitz made an emergency landing on Henderson Airfield. The admiral made the most of the opportunity. He took a tour of the front lines, saw Edson's Bloody Ridge, and spoke to several Marines. He reaffirmed to General Vandegrift that the overriding mission was to hold the airfield. He awarded Navy Crosses to several Marines, including General Vandegrift, and promised all the support he could give. He left the next day visibly encouraged by what he had seen.

The next Marine assault involved a punishing return to Matanikau. Whaling commanded five infantry battalions along with his men in the 3/2 Marines. He surged inland, clearing the way for the 7th Marines. Their objective was to drive through and hook toward the coast, destroying the Japanese along the Matanikau. Colonel Hudson's 2nd and 3rd Battalions were set to attack across the river's mouth. The rest of the division's artillery was positioned to fire in the support role.

Whaling's force moved into the jungle upstream of the Matanikau. They encountered Japanese troops that harassed his forward elements, but not in enough strength to stop the advance.

He bypassed the enemy and dug in for the night. Behind him was the 7th Marines, prepared to move through the lines, cross the river, and attack north toward the Japanese. The 5th Marines Assault Battalion moved toward the Matanikau. They ran into the Japanese in strength less than four hundred yards from the river.

They had run into a strong advance element of the Japanese 4th Regiment, which had crossed the Matanikau to set up a base from which they could fire artillery into the Marine perimeter. The fighting was intense. Even though the 2nd Battalion encountered little opposition and broke through to the riverbank, they turned north. They hit the inland flank of the enemy troops. General Vandegrift sent a company of raiders forward to reinforce the 5th and maintain a holding position toward the beach.

On October 8, rain poured all day long, stopping virtually all forward progress. It did not stop the hand-to-hand fighting around the pockets of Japanese. When the enemy troops retreated, they attempted to escape the encircling Marines. They smashed into the raiders' position near their escape route. Wild hand-to-hand combat ensued, and only a few Japanese broke through to reach across the river. The rest died fighting.

The next day, Whaling's force, flanked by the 2nd and the 1/7 Marines, crossed the Matanikau. They turned and continued to follow ridgelines to the sea. Puller's battalion discovered several Japanese in a ravine to his front, fired his mortars, and called in artillery. His men used rifles and machine guns to pick off enemy troops trying to escape. When his ammunition ran short, Puller pushed inland toward the beach to link up with Whaling's force, which had encountered no opposition. The Marines then recrossed the Matanikau River, joined Colonel Edson's troops, and marched back to the perimeter. They left a strong combat outpost at the Matanikau now clear of Japanese. Vandegrift, informed by intelligent sources that a major Japanese attack was coming from the west, consolidated his positions.

He left no sizable Marine force more than a day's march from the perimeter. The Marine advance on October 8 had thwarted the Japanese plans for an early attack and cost the enemy over seven hundred dead. The Marines paid a hefty price as well, 65 killed and 130 wounded.

Disease was killing men in numbers equal to the battle casualties. Crippling stomach cramps known as gastroenteritis and other tropical fungus infections like "jungle rot," infamous for uncomfortable rashes on men's armpits, elbows, feet, and crotches—a product of seldom being dry. If it didn't rain, sweat provided moisture. Along with this came hundreds of malaria cases. Atabrine tablets were some relief. Besides turning the skin yellow, they were not effective enough to stop the spread of the mosquito-borne infection. Malaria attacks were becoming so severe that nothing short of complete prostration, becoming a litter case, could earn a rest in the hospital. These diseases affected the men who had been on the island the longest, especially those who experienced the early days with short rations. General Vandegrift suggested that when his men got relieved, they should not be sent to another tropical island hospital. But to a place where a genuine change of atmosphere and climate existed. He asked for Wellington or Auckland in New Zealand to be considered.

Under present circumstances, there was no relief for the men starting their third month on Guadalcanal. The Japanese did not abandon their plan to seize back Guadalcanal and gave painful evidence of their intentions in mid-October. General Hyakutake landed on Guadalcanal to oversee the Imperial Japanese offensive. The elements of General Maruyama's *Sendai* Division was already a factor in the fighting near the Matanikau River. More enemy troops were coming. The Japanese were taking advantage that the Cactus Air Force flyers had no night attack capability. They planned to ensure that no planes at all would rise from Guadalcanal to meet them.

On October 11, US Navy surface ships assisted in stopping the "Tokyo Express." The nickname given to Admiral Tanaka's almost nightly reinforcement for his covering force of five cruisers and destroyers. Admiral Scott, who commanded Renell Island, got word enemy ships were approaching Guadalcanal.

Admiral Scott's mission was to protect an approaching reinforcement convoy. He steamed at flank speed eager to engage the enemy. He encountered more ships than expected, three heavy cruisers and two destroyers, as well as six destroyers escorting two seaplane carrier transports. Scott maneuvered between Cape Esperance and Savo Island—Guadalcanal's western tip. He engaged the bombardment group head-on.

Alerted from the scout plane on his flagship, *San Francisco*, the spotting's later confirmed by radar on the *Helena*. The Americans could open fire first because the Japanese had no radar and did not know of their presence. When the Japanese enemy destroyer sank immediately, two cruisers were severely damaged. Another remaining cruiser and destroyer turned away from the hellish inferno of American fire. Admiral Scott's own force was punished by enemy fire, which damaged two cruisers and two destroyers, one of which, the *Duncan*, sank the next day. The Cactus Air Force flyers spotted two reinforcement destroyer escorts retreating and sank them both. Named The Battle of Cape Esperance, it would be counted as an American naval victory—one sorely needed.

A welcome reinforcement convoy arrived on the island on October 13 when the 164th Infantry Regiment of the newly formed Americal Division arrived. These soldiers were members of a National Guard outfit from North Dakota. They were equipped with Garand M1 rifles—a weapon most overseas Marines had only heard of. The rate of fire of the semi-automatic Garand outperformed the single shot, bolt action Springfield's that the Marines carried, and the bolt action rifles carried by the Japanese. Most 1st Division Marines believed their Springfield's were more accurate and a better weapon. This did not stop some light-fingered Marines from acquiring these new weapons when the occasion presented itself. Such an opportunity arose when the soldiers were landing, and supplies were being moved to the dumps.

Flights of Japanese bombers appeared over Henderson Field, unscathed by the defending fighters, and started dropping bombs. The soldiers headed for cover, and the alert Marines inured to the bombing, used this interval to "liberate" interesting crates and cartons. The news that the Army had arrived spread across the island like wildfire. There was hope. It meant the Marines may eventually be relieved.

If the bombing wasn't enough grief, the Japanese opened on the airfield with their 150mm howitzers. The men of the 164th, commanded by Colonel Robert Hall, got a rude welcome to Guadalcanal. On that night, October 13, they shared a terrifying experience with the Marines that no one would ever forget.

The Imperial Japanese were determined to knock out Henderson Field to protect their soldiers landing in strength west of Koli Point. The enemy commander sent the battleships *Kongo* and *Haruna* into Ironbottom Sound to bombard the Marine positions. The Japanese flare planes signaled the bombardment, seventy-five minutes of sheer hell, 14-inch shells exploding with such a devastating effect that even cruiser fire was barely noticed.

No place was safe. No one was safe. No dugout could withstand the fury of 14-inch shells. One seasoned veteran used to being cool under enemy fire said nothing was worse in war than being helpless on the receiving end of naval gunfire. "Huge trees being cut apart and flying about like toothpicks," he said.

The airfield and surrounding area were reduced to a fiery shambles when dawn broke. The naval shelling, and artillery fire and bombing left the Cactus Air Force commander, General Geiger, with only a handful of aircraft still operational. Henderson Airfield was now thickly cratered with shells and bombs, and a death toll of forty-one. The Cactus Air Force flyers had to attack because the morning revealed a shore and sea full of inviting targets.

Japanese transports and landing craft had broken through. The enemy was now everywhere near Tassafaronga. The escorting cruisers and destroyers had proven to be a formidable screen of antiaircraft. Every American plane that could fly was in the fight. General Geiger's aid, Major Jack Cram, took off, in the generals PBY, rigged with two torpedoes. He put one into the side of an enemy transport as it unloaded. A new squadron of F4Fs took part in the day's action. He landed, refueled, and took off again to join in the fight. After an hour, when he landed again, he had four enemy bomber kills. Bauer, had over twenty Japanese aircraft kills and in later air battles, was killed in action. He was posthumously awarded the Medal of Honor along with four other Marine pilots in the early days of the Cactus Air Force.

General Hyakutake believed the Japanese had now landed enough troops to destroy the Marines occupied beachhead and seize the airfield. He approved General Maruyama's objective to move most of the *Sendai* Division out of sight through the jungle without engaging the Marines. They were to strike south near Edson's Ridge. With seven thousand men, each carrying a mortar or artillery shell, they trekked along the Maruyama Trail. General Maruyama had approved the trail's name to show his deep confidence. He intended to support this attack with infantry guns and heavy mortars—70mm pack howitzers. The men had to push, lug, and drag the supporting guns over miles of broken ground, two major streams, the Matanikau and the Lunga, and through heavy underbrush, for their commander's path to glory.

General Vandegrift knew the Japanese were going to attack. Patrols and reconnaissance flights had shown the push would come from the west, where the enemy reinforcements had landed. The American commander changed his disposition. There were now Japanese troops east of the perimeter, but not in any considerable strength. The 164th Infantry Regiment, reinforced by the Marine Special

Weapons Unit, was put into the fight to hold the sixty-six-hundred-yard eastern flank.

They curved inland to meet up with the 7th Marines near Edson's Ridge. The 7th Marines held twenty-five-hundred-yards of the ridge to the Lunga. From the Lunga, the 1st Marines had a thirty-five-hundred-yard sector of jungle which ran west to the point of the line curving back again toward the beach in the 5th Marines' sector. Since the attack was expected from the west, the 3rd Battalion's Marines kept a strong outpost position forward of the 1st Marines' lines along the east bank of the Matanikau.

In the lull before the attack—if Japanese destroyer cruiser bombardments, artillery harassment, and bomber attacks could be called a lull—General Vandegrift was visited by the commandant of the Marine Corps, Lieutenant General Thomas Holcomb. The commandant flew in on October 21 to see for himself how the Marines were faring. It proved to be an occasion for both senior Marines to meet the new commander of the South Pacific, Admiral "Bull" Halsey. Admiral Nimitz had announced Halsey's appointment on October 18. The news was welcome in the Marine and Navy ranks throughout the Pacific.

Halsey's well-deserved reputation for aggressiveness promised renewed attention to the situation on Guadalcanal. On the 22nd, Holcomb and Vandegrift flew to Noumea to meet with Halsey. They gave a round of briefings about the Allied situation. After Vandegrift described his position, he argued against the diversion of reinforcements intended for the Cactus Air Force to any other South Pacific venue. He argued that he needed all of the Americal Division and another two Marine Division regiments to beef up his forces. He also said that more than half of his veterans were worn out by over three months of fighting the ravages of jungle incurred diseases. Admiral Halsey told the Marine Corps general: "You go back there, Vandegrift. I promise to get you everything I have."

When General Vandegrift returned to Guadalcanal, Admiral Holcomb moved on to Pearl Harbor to meet with Admiral Nimitz. He brought with him Halsey's recommendation that, landing force commanders, once established onshore, would have equal command status with Navy amphibious force commanders. At Pearl Harbor, Admiral Nimitz approved Halsey's recommendations as well as in Washington. This meant that the command status of all future Pacific amphibious operations was determined by the events of Guadalcanal.

Another piece of news Vandegrift received from Holcomb, was that if Pres. Roosevelt did not reappoint him, (which was likely because of his age), he would recommend that Vandegrift be appointed as the next Commandant of the Marine Corps. This news did not divert Vandegrift's attention when he flew back to Guadalcanal. The Japanese were in the middle of their offensive. An enemy patrol accompanied by two tanks on the twentieth tried to find a way through the line held by the 3/1 Marines. A sharp-shooting 37mm gun crew knocked out a lead tank, and the enemy's force fell back. In the meantime shelling the Marines' positions with artillery.

On sunset the next day, the Japanese tried again, this time with more artillery fire and more tanks in the fray. But again, a 37mm gun knocked out the lead tank and discouraged the attack. On October 22, the enemy paused, waiting for General Maruyama's force to get inland. The 23rd was planned as the day of the main Japanese assault. They dropped a heavy rain of artillery and mortar fire on Marine positions near the Matanikau River mouth. At dusk, nine 18 ton medium tanks clanked out of the trees onto the river sandbar. Eight of them were peppered by the 37mm. One tank made it across the river, a Marine blasted its track off with a grenade, and a 75mm half-track was destroyed in the ocean surf. The remaining enemy infantry was annihilated by Marine artillery fire. Hundreds of Japanese casualties and three more tanks were destroyed. A later inland thrust further upstream was beaten back. The coastal attack did nothing to General Maruyama's island offensive. This caused Vandegrift to move one battalion, the 2nd Battalion, 7th Marines, into the four-thousand-yard gap between the Matanikau perimeter and position. This move proved helpful since one of General Maruyama's attacks was headed directly to this area.

Although patrols had encountered no Japanese south or east of the jungle perimeter up to the 24th, these attempts had alerted everyone. General Maruyama was satisfied his men had struggled to gain the appropriate assault positions after delaying the attack for thirty-three days. He began his assault on October 24, but the Marines were waiting. An observer spotted an enemy officer surveying Edson's Ridge on the 24th. Scout snipers reported smoke from rice fires rising from the valley two miles south of "Chesty" Puller's positions. Six battalions of the Japanese *Sendai* Division were poised to attack. Near midnight, the first elements of the enemy hit and bypassed a platoon-sized outpost forward of Puller's barbed wire entanglements. Puller's men waited, straining to see through the dark night in the driving rain. When the Japanese charged out of the jungle attacking Puller's area near the ridge in the flat ground to the east, the Marines reacted with everything they had. They called in artillery, fired mortars, and relied heavily on crossing fields of machine gun fire to cut down enemy infantrymen. Japanese mortars, artillery, and other supporting armaments were thrown back along the Maruyama Trail. They had proved too much of a burden for the infantrymen to carry.

This drove a wedge into the Marine lines. But everything straightened out with repeated counterattacks. Puller realized his battalion was being hit by a strong Japanese force capable of repeated attacks. He requested reinforcements. The Army's 3rd Battalion, 164th Infantry, was ordered to move forward. Men slipped and slid in the rain as they trudged a mile south along Edson's Ridge. Puller met Colonel Robert Hall at the head of the column, and they walked down the length of the Marine lines peeling off Army squads one at a time to feed into the lines. The enemy attacked again throughout the night. Marines and soldiers fought back together.

By 0330, the Army battalion was completely assimilated into the 1/7 Marines' lines, and the enemy attacks were getting weaker. The Americans returned fire. They used flanking fire from machine guns and the 37mm guns remaining in the positions held by the 2nd Battalion and 164th Infantry on Puller's left. Near dawn, General

Maruyama pulled his men back to regroup and prepare to attack again.

At daylight, Puller and Hall reordered the lines. They put the 2nd Battalion and the 164th into their own positions on Puller's left flank. The driving rains had turned Henderson Field into a quagmire. This grounded the Cactus Air Force flyers. Japanese planes used this "free ride" to bomb Marine positions. Enemy artillery fire continued along with a pair of Japanese destroyers adding in on the bombardment until they got too close to shore. The 3rd defense Battalion's 5-inch guns repelled them. As the sun rose, the runways dried and afternoon enemy attacks were now met by the Cactus Air Force fighters—who downed twenty-two Japanese planes with only a loss of three.

As night came on again, General Maruyama tried more of the same with the same result. The Marine/Army lines held, and the Japanese were cut down in droves by rifle, mortar, machine gun, 37mm, and artillery fire from the west. The Japanese mounted three attacks on positions held by the 2/7 Marines. The enemy broke through the positions held by Company F. Still, a counter-attack led by the battalion's XO drove off the Japanese again at daylight. The American positions were secured, and the enemy had retreated. They would not return. The Imperial Japanese offensive using the *Sendai* Division was defeated.

Over thirty-five hundred Imperial Japanese troops died during these attacks. General Maruyama's boast that he would "exterminate the enemy Americans around the airfield in one blow" had proven empty. The remainder of his force now limped back over the Maruyama Trail, with mostly wounded men. The soldiers and Marines, together, lost just under three hundred men killed and wounded.

The existing records are sketchy and incomplete. One result of the battle was a warm welcome to the 164th Infantry from the 1st Marine Division. Vandegrift commended Hall's battalion and said: "The division was proud to have serving with it another unit which had stood the test of battle."

Through the heroics of two nights of constant brutal fighting, several Marines were singled out for recognition. Two outstanding Marines were Sergeant John Basilone of the 1/7 Marines, and Sergeant Mitchell Paige of the 2nd Battalion. Both of these Marines were machine gun section leads recognized as having performed above and beyond the call of duty in the inspiring words of their Medal of Honor citations.

FIGHTING WITHDRAWAL ALONG THE BEACH

While the Marines and soldiers battled the Japanese ashore, A patrol plane sighted a sizeable Japanese fleet near the Santa Cruz Islands, east of the Solomons. The enemy force was formidable for battleships and for carriers with twenty-eight destroyers and eight cruisers. Admiral Halsey was poised for a victorious attack after the capture of Henderson Field. He signaled Admiral Kincaid, with the *Hornet* and *Enterprise* carrier groups, and ordered them to attack.

On October 26, American planes located the Japanese carriers. The Japanese *Zuiho*'s flight deck was damaged by the scout bombers, canceling their flight operations. But three other carriers launched strikes. A dogfight raged overhead as each side's planes strove to reach the other's carriers. The *Hornet* was hit repeatedly by torpedoes and bombs. Two Japanese pilots crashed their planes into the deck. The damage to the ship was so massive, the *Hornet* was abandoned and sunk. The *Enterprise*, the battleship *South Dakota*, the light cruiser *San Juan*, and the destroyer *Smith* were also hit. The destroyer *Porter* was sunk. On the Japanese side—no ships were sunk. Three carriers and two destroyers were damaged. One hundred Japanese planes were lost. Seventy-five US planes went down. This was considered a standoff. The Imperial Japanese Navy could have continued their attacks but were discouraged by the defeat of their ground forces and withdrew to attack another day.

The enemy naval force departure marked a period in which sizable reinforcements reached the island. The 2nd Marines' headquarters found transport space to come up from Espiritu Santo on October 29. Colonel Arthur moved his regiment from Tulagi to Guadalcanal, changing out the 1st and 2nd Battalions for the well bloodied 3rd Division, which took up the Tulagi duties. The 2nd Marines' battalions at Tulagi had performed the task of scouting and securing all the small islands of the Florida group. They were frustrated, only being able to watch the battles taking place across the Sealark Channel. These Marines could now take part in the big show.

US planes flew into the Cactus fields from the island of New Caledonia. Squadrons of MAG-11 fighters moved forward from New Caledonia to Espiritu Santo to be closer to the battle. The flight echelons could now operate forward to Guadalcanal with relative ease. Two batteries of 155mm guns landed on November 2, providing Vandegrift with his first artillery units capable of matching the enemy's long-range 150mm guns. The 8th Marines had arrived from American Samoa. The full-strength regiment, reinforced by the 75mm howitzers of the 1st Battalion, 10th Marines, added another four thousand men to the defending forces. These fresh troops reflected a renewed emphasis at all levels of command, ensuring that Guadalcanal would hold no matter the cost. The reinforcement/replacement pipeline was being filled. The rest of the 2nd Marine Division, and the Army's 25th Infantry Division arrived. More planes of every type from American as well as Allied sources were slated to reinforce and replace the battle-weary Cactus Air Force veterans.

The increased pace of reinforcement was provided by Pres. Roosevelt. Cutting through the demands for American forces worldwide, he told each of the Joint Chiefs, on October 24, that Guadalcanal must be reinforced immediately. The operational pace on Guadalcanal did not slacken after the Japanese offensive was pushed back. General Vandegrift wanted to clear the area immediately west of the Matanikau of all troops, forestalling another buildup of attacking forces. Admiral Tanaka's Tokyo express was still operating despite punishing attacks by the Cactus aircraft and American motor torpedo boats now based at Tulagi.

On November 1-5, Marines backed up by the newly arrived 2nd Marines, attacked across bridges engineers had laid over the Matanikau River the previous night. Inland, Colonel Whaling led his scout snipers in a screening movement with the main driving attack to protect the flank. The opposition was fierce in the shore area where they drove forward toward Point Cruz, but Whaling's group encountered little resistance. At nightfall, when the Marines dug in, the only sizable enemy force was in the Point Cruz area. In the days of bitter fighting, Corporal Anthony Casamento, a badly wounded machine gun squad leader in Edson's 1st Battalion, distinguished himself so well that he was recommended for a Navy Cross. Many years later, in August 1980, Pres. Jimmy Carter approved the award for the Medal of Honor in its stead.

The attack continued with the reserve 3rd Battalion moving into the fight and all 3/5 Marine units moving to surround enemy defenders. On November 3, the Japanese pocket just west of the base at Point Cruz was eliminated. Well over three hundred enemy soldiers had been killed. The Marines encountered light resistance and slowly advanced across the rugged terrain one thousand yards beyond the 5th Marines' action.

The offensive objectives seemed well in hand, and the advance halted. Intelligence was reported that a substantial enemy reinforcement attempt was underway. General Vandegrift pulled most of his men back to safeguard the perimeter of the airfield. This time he left a regiment to outpost the ground that had been gained. Colonel Arthur's 2nd Marines reinforced the Army's 164th Infantry.

Vandegrift emphasized the need to be cautious because the Japanese were again discovered in strength, east of the perimeter. On November 3, Lieutenant Colonel Hanneken's 2/7 Marines on a reconnaissance in force toward Koli Point, could see the Japanese ships clustered, eight miles from the perimeter. His men encountered strong Japanese resistance from fresh troops, and he pulled back. A regiment of the enemy's 38th Division landed as Hyakutake used the Japanese Navy to attack the perimeter from both flanks.

Hanneken's battalion executed a fighting withdrawal along the beach. They took fire from the jungle inland. A rescue force was soon put together comprised of two tank companies, the 1/7 Marines, and the 2nd and 3rd Battalions of the 164th Infantry. The Japanese troops, members of the 38th Division Regiment and remnants of Kawaguchi's brigade, fought to hold ground as the US Marines and Army drove forward along the coast. Marines and soldiers attempted to outflank the enemy in the jungle. This battle lasted for days, supported by Cactus Air, naval gunfire, and the newly landed 155mm guns.

The Japanese commander received new orders as he struggled to hold back the Americans. He was to move inland and break off the action in March to rejoin the main Japanese forces west of the perimeter—a tall order to fill. This two-pronged attack had been abandoned. The Japanese managed the 1st part. Japanese soldiers found a gap in the 164th line and broke through along a meandering jungle stream. They left 450 dead throughout a seven-day battle. The Army and the Marines had lost forty dead in one hundred and twenty-five wounded. The enemy soldiers who broke out from the encircling Americans escaped into worse circumstances.

Admiral Turner had employed one of his several plans for alternate landings and beachheads. All of which General Vandegrift opposed. At Aola Bay, forty miles east of the main perimeter, the Navy put an airfield construction and defense force ashore on November 4. While the Japanese were still battling Marines near Tetere, Vandegrift persuaded Turner to detach part of his landing force, the 2nd Raider Battalion, to sweep west and destroy any enemy forces it encountered.

Colonel Carlson's Raider Battalion had already seen action before reaching Guadalcanal. An additional two companies had reinforced the Midway Island offenders when the Japanese attacked in June. The remainder of the battalion landed on the Macon

Islands and destroyed the garrison. For his part in the fighting, Sergeant Clyde Thomason was awarded a Medal of Honor, the first Marine enlisted to receive his country's highest award in World War II.

Marching from Aola Bay, The 2nd Raider Battalion encountered the Japanese attempting to retreat to the west. On November 12, the raiders beat off attacks by two enemy companies. They pursued the Japanese, fighting a series of small actions over the next five days before making contact with the main Japanese force. For two weeks, the raiders came down from the jungle ridges into the perimeter, harassing the retreating enemy. They killed over five hundred Japanese soldiers. Their losses were only sixteen dead and eighteen wounded. This mission at Aola Bay provided the 2nd Raider Battalion a starting point for its month-long jungle campaign but proved to be a bust. The site chosen for an airfield was unacceptable—too wet and unstable. The entire force moved to Koli Point in early December, where another airfield was constructed.

The build-up on Guadalcanal continued. On November 11, guarded by a destroyer/cruiser covering force, a convoy was attacked by enemy bombers. Three transports were hit, but the men still landed. These men were badly needed. Vandegrift's veterans on Guadalcanal were ready to be replaced.

Malaria cases were averaging over one thousand a week besides related diseases. Enemy soldiers who had been on the island for any length of time were in no better shape. Rations and medical supplies were scarce. The entire thrust of the Japanese reinforcement effort continued to get troops and combat equipment ashore. In Tokyo, the idea prevailed that despite all evidence to the contrary, one overwhelming coordinated assault would crush the American resistance. The enemy drive to take Port Moresby, New Guinea, was put on hold to put all of their effort into driving the Americans off Guadalcanal.

On November 12, Japanese naval forces converged on Guadalcanal to cover the landing of the main body of the 38th Division.

Admiral Callahan's cruisers and destroyers moved in to confront the enemy. Coastwatcher and scout plane sightings and radio intercepts identified two carriers, two battleships, four cruisers, and a host of destroyers heading toward Guadalcanal. The battleships were led by *Hiei* and *Kirishima* with the light cruiser *Nagura,* and fifteen destroyers spearheaded the bombardment and attack.

Just after midnight, Callahan's cruisers picked up the Japanese on radar and continue to close. The battle was fought at such a short-range that each side fired at their own ships. Callahan's flagship, *San Francisco,* was hit fifteen times. Callahan was killed; his ship limped away. The cruiser *Atlanta* was also hit and set ablaze. Admiral Scott, who was on board, was killed. Despite the hammering by the Japanese fire, the Americans held and continued fighting. The battleship *Hiei* was hit by over eighty shells. Badly damaged, it retired, and with it the rest of the attack force. Four destroyers were damaged, and three others were sunk. The Americans accomplished their purpose. They'd forced the Japanese to turn back. But the cost was high. Two antiaircraft cruisers, the *Juneau* and the *Atlanta,* were sunk. For destroyers, the *Laffey,* the *Monssen,* the *Cushing,* and the *Barton* also went to the bottom. The *San Francisco,* the heavy cruiser *Portland,* and the destroyers *Sterret* and *Aaron Ward* were also damaged. Only one destroyer of the thirteen American ships engaged, the *Fletcher,* was unscathed when survivors retired to the New Hebrides.

At dawn came the Cactus bombers and fighters. They attacked the crippled *Hiei* and pounded it ruthlessly. The Japanese were forced to scuttle her on the 14th. Admiral Halsey ordered his only surviving carrier, the *Enterprise,* out of Guadalcanal to get it out of reach of Japanese aircraft. He sent in his battleships the *South Dakota, Washington,* and escorting destroyers north to meet the Japanese. Some of the *Enterprise's* planes flew into Henderson Field to help even the odds.

On November 14, Cactus and *Enterprise* flyers found a Japanese destroyer/cruiser force that had pounded the island the night before. They damaged four cruisers and a destroyer. They quickly refueled and rearmed and went on the hunt for the approaching

Japanese troop convoy. They hit several transports and sank one. Army B-17s from Espiritu Santo scored one hit and several near hits, bombing from over 17,000 feet. In a persistent pattern of attack, return, refuel, rearm, and resume, Guadalcanal planes hit nine transports—sinking seven. Many of the five thousand troops on the damaged ships were rescued by Tanaka's destroyers.

The Japanese fired furiously and laid smokescreens to protect the transports. General Tanaka later recalled: "Bomb's wobbling down from highflying B-17s, of carrier bombers roared toward targets as though to plunge full in the water, releasing bombs and pulling out barely in time; each miss sending up towering columns of mist and spray; every hit raising clouds of smoke and fire."

Despite the intensive attack, Tanaka continued on to Guadalcanal with four transports and four destroyers. Imperial Japanese intelligence learned of the oncoming American battleship force and rushed to warn Tanaka. Japanese admirals sent their own cruiser/battleship force to intercept. The Americans led by Admiral Lee on the *Washington*, reached the Sealark Channel by 2100 on the 14th. A Japanese cruiser was picked up north of Savo Island an hour later, and battleship fire repelled her. The Japanese now understood the opponents they expected would not be the cruisers. This clash, fought in the glare of gunfire and Japanese searchlights, was the most significant fight at sea for Guadalcanal. When the battle was over, the American battleships' 16-inch guns had more than matched the Japanese. Both *South Dakota* and *Washington* were damaged so severely they were forced to withdraw.

One Japanese and three American destroyers were sunk. When the Japanese attack force retired, Admiral Tanaka ran his four transports onto the beach. He knew they would be targets at daylight. Most men on board managed to get ashore before the expected pummeling by American warships, planes, and artillery. The Japanese had landed ten thousand troops of the 38th Division. But they were in no shape to ever again attempt a massive reinforcement. The horrific losses caused by the frequent naval clashes, which seemed to favor the Japanese, did not represent a standoff. Every American ship damaged or lost would be replaced. Every

Japanese ship was precious to their steadily diminishing fleet. The air fighting losses on both sides were overwhelming. The Japanese would never recover from the loss of its experienced carrier pilots. In the Battle of the Philippine Sea between Japanese and American carriers, it would be called the "Mariana's Turkey Shoot" because of the ineptitude of the Japanese trainee pilots.

The enemy troops fortunate enough to reach land were not ready to assault the American positions. The 30th Division and the remnants of the various Japanese units attempting to penetrate the Marine lines needed to be trained in built into a coherent attack force before General Hyakutake could have any reasonable attempt at taking Henderson Field. General Vandegrift now had enough men and fresh units to replace his veteran troops along the front lines. He swapped the 1st Marine Division with the Army's 25th Infantry. Admiral Turner told Vandegrift to leave all of his heavy equipment on the island, and when he pulled out "in hopes of getting your units re-equipped when you come out."

He told Vandegrift that the Army would now command the final phases, since it would provide most combat forces once the 1st Division Marines departed. Major General Alexander Patch, commander of the Americal Division, would relieve Vandegrift as senior American officer ashore. His air support would continue to be Marine dominated with General Geiger, now on Espiritu Santo with 1st Wing headquarters fighter squadrons, to maintain the offensive. The Guadalcanal air command would be a mixture of Marine, Navy, Army, and Allied squadrons.

The sick list of the 1st Marine Division in November was over three thousand men with malaria. The men of the 1st Division still manned the frontline foxholes and rear areas, if any place within Guadalcanal's perimeter could properly be called a rear area. The men were exhausted. They had done their part of the fighting and they all knew it. On November 29, General Vandegrift was handed a message from the Joint Chiefs of Staff. The crux of it read: "1st

Marine Division is to be relieved without delay. And will proceed to Australia for rehabilitation and employment."

The word spread that the 1st Division was leaving and where it was going. Australia was not yet the special place it would become in the division's future, but anywhere was better than Guadalcanal.

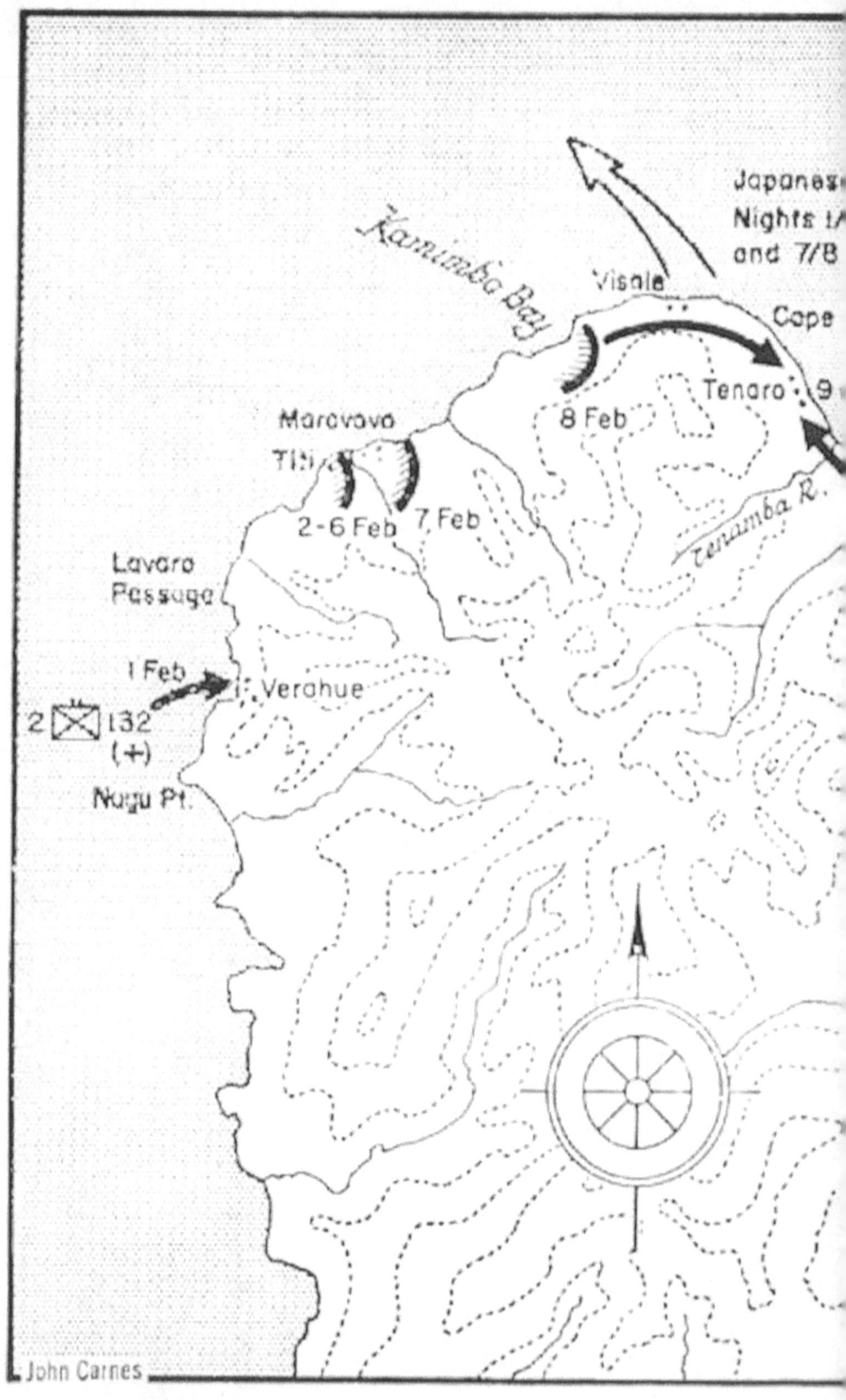

Kamimba Bay
Japanese
Nights 1/
and 7/8
Visale
Cape
Tenaro
9
8 Feb
Marovovo
Tenamba R.
Ti:
2-6 Feb
7 Feb
Lavoro
Passage
1 Feb
Verahue
2 132
(+)
Nugu Pt.
John Carnes

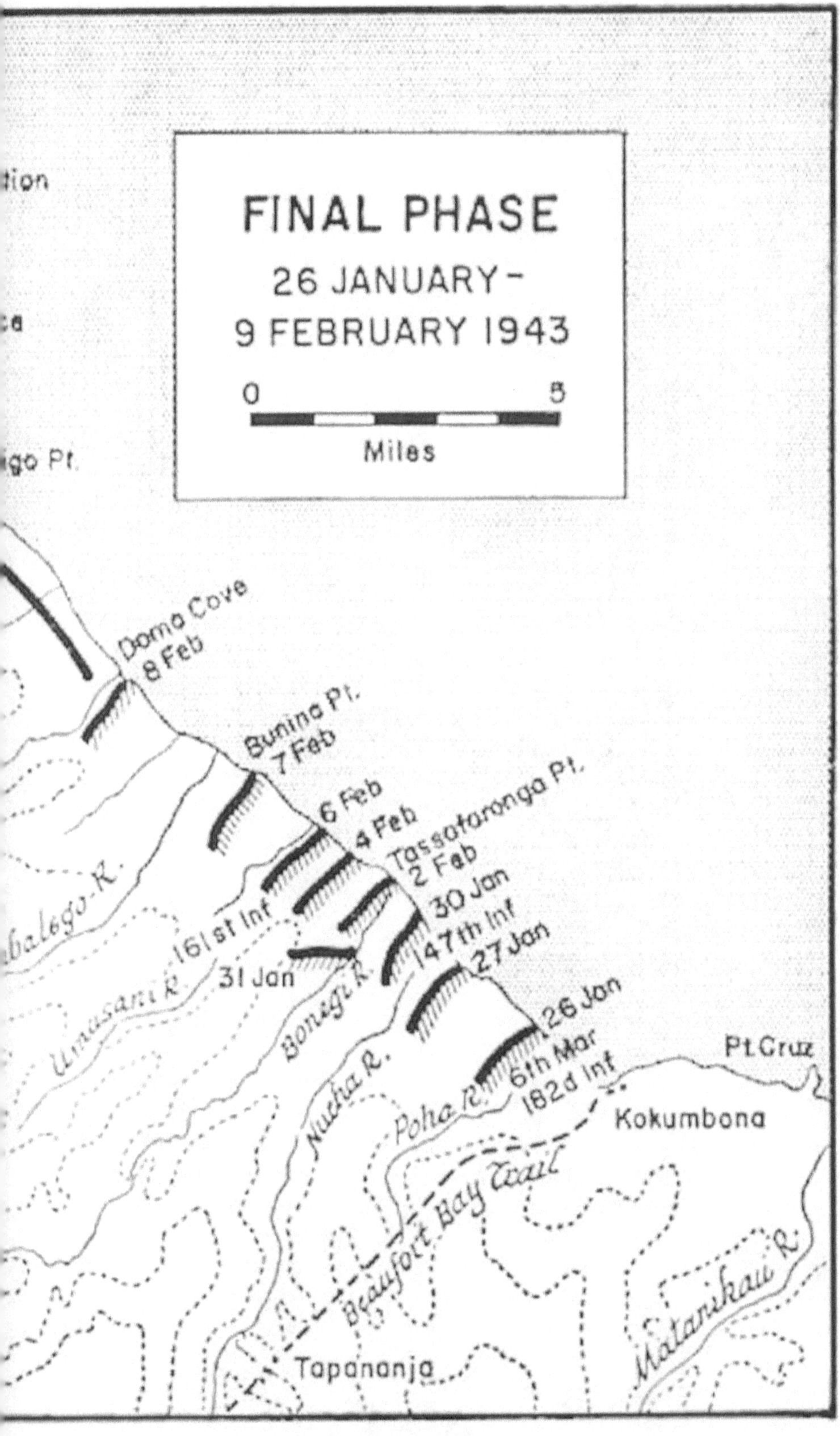

FINAL PHASE
26 JANUARY -
9 FEBRUARY 1943
0
5
Miles
Doma Cove
8 Feb
Bunina Pt.
7 Feb
6 Feb
4 Feb
Tassafaronga Pt.
2 Feb
30 Jan
161st Inf
147th Inf
31 Jan
27 Jan
26 Jan
6th Mar
182d Inf
Pt. Cruz
Kokumbona
Umasani R.
Bonegi R.
Nueha R.
Poha R.
balego R.
Beaufort Bay Trail
Matanikau R.
Tapananja
tion
go Pt.

DEFEAT OF JAPANESE FORCES ON GUADALCANAL

On December 7, one year after the Japanese assault on Pearl Harbor, General Vandegrift sent a message to all under his command thanking them for their steadfastness and courage. He reminded them of their unbelievable achievements they'd made on Guadalcanal, now a synonym for disaster and death in the Japanese language. On December 9, he handed over his command to General Patch and flew out to Australia.

Elements of the 5th Marines boarded ship. The 1st, 11th, and 7th Marines soon followed together with the rest of the division's supporting units. The men that left with him were tired, thin, hollow-eyed, and demoralized.

This group of young men had grown considerably older in only four months. They left behind 681 dead Marines in the island cemetery. The final regiment of the 132nd Infantry of the Americal Division landed on December 8 as the 5th Marines prepared to leave. The 2nd Marine Division's regiments were already on the island. The 6th Marines were on their way to rejoin. Many of the men of the 2nd Marines, who landed on D-Day August 7, should have also left. They took little comfort in the thought that they, by all rights, should be the first of the 2nd Division to leave Guadalcanal whenever the day came.

A steady stream of replacements and ground reinforcements came to General Patch in December. He was still not ready to undertake a full-scale offensive until the 25th Division, and the rest of the 2nd Marine Division arrived. He kept all reconnaissance patrols and frontline units active—especially toward the western flank. The island commanders' air defense capabilities multiplied. The Cactus Air Force was organized into a fighter command and a strike and bomber command. They now operated from the newly redesignated Marine Corps airbase. Henderson Airfield had a new airstrip, Fighter Two. Fighter Two replaced Fighter One, which had suffered severe drainage problems.

General Lewis Woods took over as senior aviator when General Geiger returned to Espiritu Santo. Geiger was relieved on December 26 by General Francis Mulcahy, the commanding General of the 2nd Marine Aircraft Wing. New bomber and fighter squadrons were added regularly. The Army added a bomber squadron of B-26s. The Royal New Zealand Air Force flew in a reconnaissance squadron of Lockheed Hudsons. The US Navy sent a squadron of PBY Catalina patrol planes, with night-flying capability.

This aerial buildup forced the Imperial Japanese to curb air attacks and make their daylight naval reinforcement attempts an event of the past. The nighttime visits of the Tokyo Express destroyers now only brought supplies encased in metal drums rolled over the ship sides, hoping to float into shore. The men on shore desperately needed everything that could be sent, even by this method. But most of the drums never reached the beaches.

No matter how desperate the enemy situation was becoming, the Imperial Japanese were prepared to fight. General Hyakutake continued to plan the seizure of the airfield. He ordered the commander of the *Eighth Area Army* to continue the offensive. General Imamura had fifty thousand men to add and reinforce to the embattled Japanese troops on Guadalcanal.

Before the enemy units could be used, the Americans were prepared to move out from the perimeter on their own offensive. They knew that the Mt. Austin area was a continuing threat to their inland flank. General Patch committed the American's 132nd Infantry to clearing the mountain's wooded slopes on December 17. The Army was successful in isolating the major Japanese force in the area by early January. The 1/2 Marines took uphill positions to the southeast of the 132nd to increase flank protection. By now, the 25th Infantry Division had arrived. So had the 6th Marines and the rest of the 2nd Division's headquarters and support troops. General De Carre took charge of all Marine ground forces on the island. The 2nd Division's commander General John Marston remained in New Zealand because he was senior to General Patch.

General Patch was in command of three divisions and designated as the XIV Corps Commanding General on January 2. His Corps headquarters numbered less than twenty officers and men, almost all taken from Americal staff. General Sebree, who had already led both Army and Marine units in attacks on the Japanese, took command of the Americal Division. On January 10, General Patch gave the signal to start the most vigorous American offensive in the Guadalcanal campaign. The mission of the troops was to attack and destroy remaining Japanese forces on Guadalcanal.

The objective of the Marine Corps attack was a line fifteen hundred yards west of the jump-off positions. These lines ran inland from Point Cruz to the vicinity of Hill 66—three thousand yards from the beach. To reach Hill 66, the 25th Infantry Division attacked with the 27th and 35th Infantry driving west and southwest across a scrambled series of ridges. The going was rough against a dug-in enemy. Elements of two regiments of the 38th Division gave way reluctantly and slowly. By the 13th, American soldiers aided by 1/2 Division Marines had won through two positions on the southern flank of the 2nd Marine Division.

On January 12, the Marines began their advance with the 8th Marines along the shore and 2nd Division Marines inland. At the base of Point Cruz in the 3/8 Marine sector, regimental weapons company half-tracks ran over half a dozen enemy machine gun nests. This attack was held up by an extensive emplacement unit. The weapons company commander, Captain Henry Crow, took charge of the squad of Marine infantrymen taking cover from enemy fire with the classic line: "You'll never get a Purple Heart hiding in a foxhole. Follow me!"

The men followed and destroyed the emplacement.

The going was difficult along the front of the advancing assault companies. The remnants of the Japanese *Sendai* Division were dug in on a series of cross compartments. Their fire took Marines in the flank advances. The progress was slow despite massive artillery support and naval gunfire from offshore destroyers. In over two days of heavy fighting, flamethrowers were used for the first time, and tanks were brought into play. The 2nd Division Marines were relieved, and the 6th Marines moved into the attack along the coast while the 8th Marines advanced inland. Naval gunfire spotted by officers onshore improved the accuracy. The Marines and Army reached their initial core objective on the 15th. In the attack zone, over six hundred Japanese had been killed.

The battle-weary 2nd Marines had seen their last infantry action on Guadalcanal. A new unit now came into being. It was a composite Marine/Army division, or CAM division, formed from units of the 2nd Marine Divisions and the Americal Division. The directing staff was from the 2nd Division since the entire Americal Division was responsible for the main perimeter.

Two of their regiments, 147th, and 182nd Infantry, moved up to attack in line with the 6th Marines still strung out along the coast. The 8th Marines were pinched out of the front lines by a narrowing attack corridor as inland mountains and hills pressed closer to the coastal trail. The 25th Division advance across this rugged terrain was tasked with outflanking the enemy in the vicinity of Kokumbona, while the CAM Division continued to drive west. On the 23rd, as the CAM troops approached Kokumbona, the infantry of the 1st Battalion surged north from the hills and overran the village and Japanese base. They offered a steady but slight resistance to the American advance and withdrew west toward Cape Esperance.

The Imperial Japanese would not attempt to retake Guadalcanal. These were the orders sent in the Emperor's name. Senior staff officers were dispatched to make sure they were followed. The Imperial Japanese Navy would make its final runs of the Tokyo Express, only this time in reverse, to evacuate the garrison to fight later battles to hold the Solomons. Enemy ships were massing to the northwest. General Patch took steps to guard against overextending his forces. Especially faced with what appeared to be another enemy attempt at reinforcement. He pulled back the 25th Division to bolster the primary perimeter defenses and ordered the CAM Division to continue its attack. Marines and soldiers moved out on January 26, gaining over one thousand yards on the first day and two thousand the next. The Japanese contested every attack—but not in strength.

By January 30, the sole frontline unit in the American advance was the 147th Infantry; the 6th Marines held positions to its rear.

The Japanese destroyer transports made their first run to the island on the night of February 2, evacuating twenty-three hundred men from positions near Cape Esperance. On the night of February 5, they returned and evacuated most *Sendai* survivors, and General Hyakutake and his 7th Army staff.

On February 8, the final evacuation was carried out, and a three thousand man rearguard action was embarked. The Japanese withdrew over eleven thousand men in those three nights and evacuated over thirteen thousand soldiers from Guadalcanal. The Americans would meet many of these soldiers again in later battles, but not the six hundred evacuees who died—too sick and worn out to survive the rescue.

On February 9, American soldiers advancing west and east met at Tenaro village on Cape Esperance. The only Marine ground unit still in action was the 3/10 Marines, supporting the advance. General Patch reported the complete and total defeat of Japanese forces on Guadalcanal. No organized Japanese units remained.

On January 31, the 2nd Marines boarded ships to leave Guadalcanal. As with the 1st Marine Division, some of these men were so beaten down by malaria that they had to be carried on board. Observers were struck again as these young men had considerably aged in the last few months, "with their skin cracked, and furrowed, and wrinkled." On February 9, the rest of the 8th Marines boarded the transports. The 6th Marines, with only six weeks on the island, left on the 19th. All troops headed for Wellington, New Zealand. They left behind, on the island as a legacy of the 2nd Marine Division, 263 men dead.

The total cost of the Guadalcanal campaign to the American ground combat forces was 1,598 officers and men killed. 1,152 of them were Marines.

The wounded totaled 4,709. Of these 2,799 were Marines. Marine aviation casualties were 147 killed and 127 wounded.

The Japanese lost nearly 25,000 on Guadalcanal. About half killed in action—the rest died from wounds, starvation, and illness.

At sea, each side lost a similar number of fighting ships. The Japanese lost two battleships, three carriers, twelve cruisers, and twenty-five destroyers—all were irreplaceable. While the Allied ship losses were substantial and costly: they were not fatal. All lost ships were ultimately replaced. Over six hundred Japanese planes were shot down. Worse than the loss of aircraft was the death of over two thousand experienced pilots and aircrew. The Allied plane losses were only half that of the enemy's number, and the pilot and aircrew losses were substantially lower.

President Roosevelt, awarded General Vandegrift the Medal of Honor for outstanding and heroic accomplishment for his leadership of the American forces on Guadalcanal from August 7 to

December 9, 1942. He also awarded a presidential unit citation to the 1st Marine Division for "outstanding gallantry, reflecting courage and determination of an inspiring order."

Included in the division citation and award, besides the organic units of the 1st Division with the 2nd and 8th Marines and attached units of the 2nd Marine Division, all of the Americal Division, the 1st Parachute Battalion, 1st and 2nd Raider Battalions, elements of the 3rd, 5th and, 14th Defense Battalions, the 1st Aviation Engineer Battalion, the 6th Naval Construction Battalion, and two motor torpedo boat squadrons. The vital Cactus Air Force was included. Represented by seven Marine headquarters and service squadrons, sixteen Marine flying squadrons, sixteen Naval flying squadrons, and five Army flying squadrons.

The Guadalcanal victory was a crucial turning point in the Pacific War. The Japanese offensive was ended. The Imperial Japanese pilots, seamen, and infantry had been in close combat with the Americans and their allies. There were still years of fierce fighting ahead, but now there was no question of the eventual outcome.

OPERATION GALVANIC

1943 BATTLE FOR TARAWA

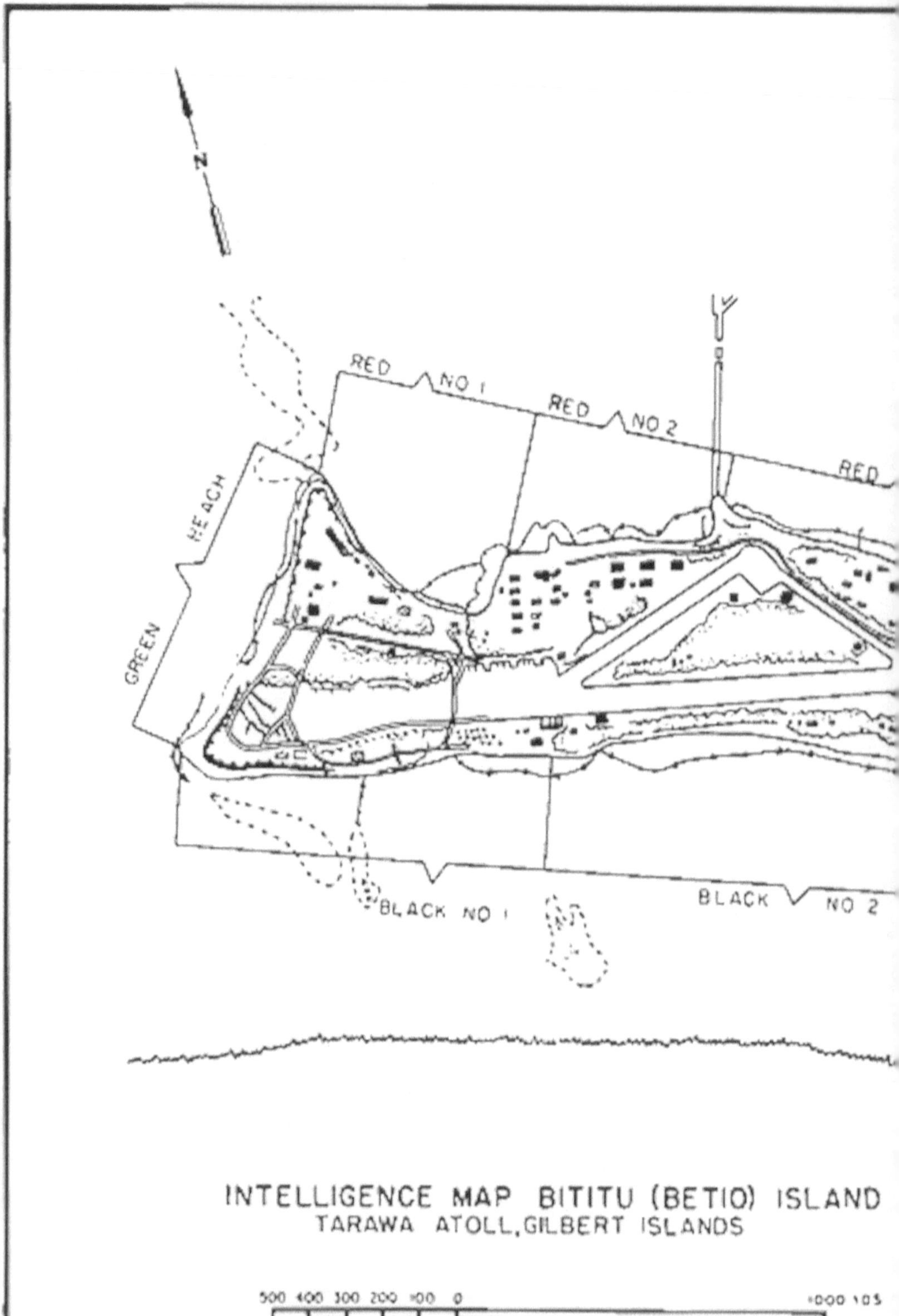

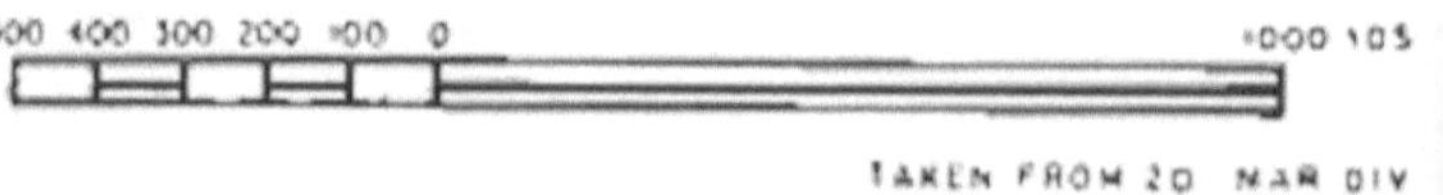
N
RED NO 1
RED NO 2
RED
GREEN BEACH
BLACK NO 1
BLACK NO 2
INTELLIGENCE MAP BITITU (BETIO) ISLAND
TARAWA ATOLL, GILBERT ISLANDS
500 400 300 200 100 0
1000 YDS
TAKEN FROM 2D MAR DIV
SPECIAL ACTION REPORT

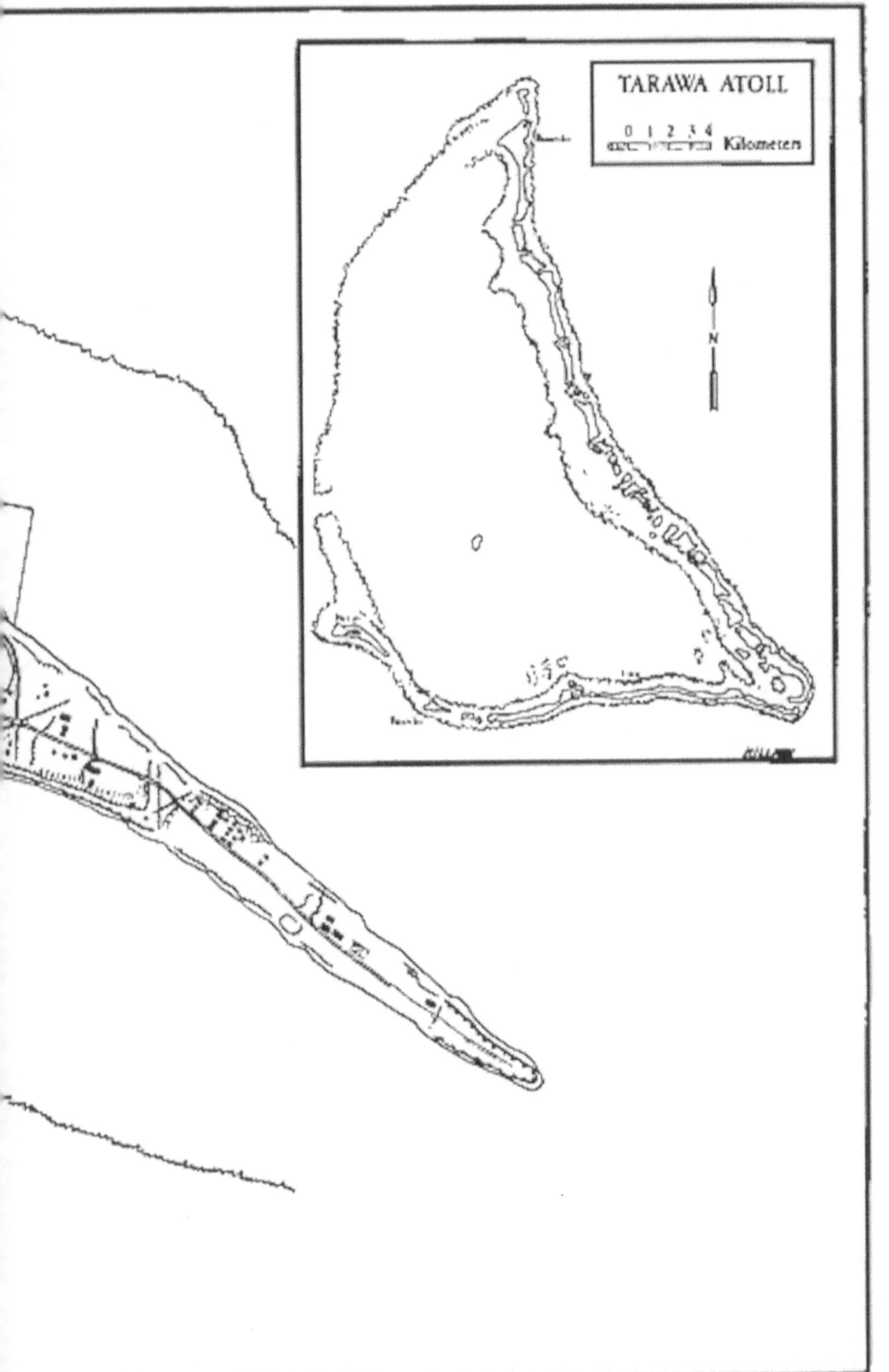

TARAWA ATOLL
0 1 2 3 4 Kilometers
N

INTRODUCTION

In August 1943, Admiral Spruance, the Central Pacific Naval Force Commander, met in secret with General Julian Smith and other 2nd Marine Division staff officers. Admiral Spruance told the Marines to prepare for an amphibious assault in the Gilbert Islands by November. The Marines were well aware of the Gilbert Islands. Under Colonel Evans Carlson, the 2nd Marine Raider Battalion had attacked Makin only a year before. Intelligence reported that the Japanese had fortified Betio Island in the Tarawa Atoll. Imperial Japanese Marines guarded an airstrip that Admiral Spruance designated the prime target for the 2nd Marines.

Colonel Shoup was General Smith's operation officer. He studied Betio's primitive chart and saw the tiny island was surrounded by a barrier reef. Colonel Shoup asked if any of the Navy's shallow draft experimental plastic boats would be provided. He was disappointed to hear that only the usual wooden landing craft would be available for this assault. The operation on Tarawa had become a tactical watershed. This would be the first large-scale test of American amphibious forces against a strongly fortified beachhead. The Marine assault on Tarawa Atoll's islet, Betio, was one of World War II Pacific Theater's bloodiest. After the assault, *Time* magazine published its post-battle analysis: *Over three thousand United States Marines, mostly now dead or wounded, gave the nation a new name to stand behind those of Concord Bridge, the Bon Homme Richard, Little Big Horn, the Alamo, and Belleau Wood. This new name is Tarawa.*

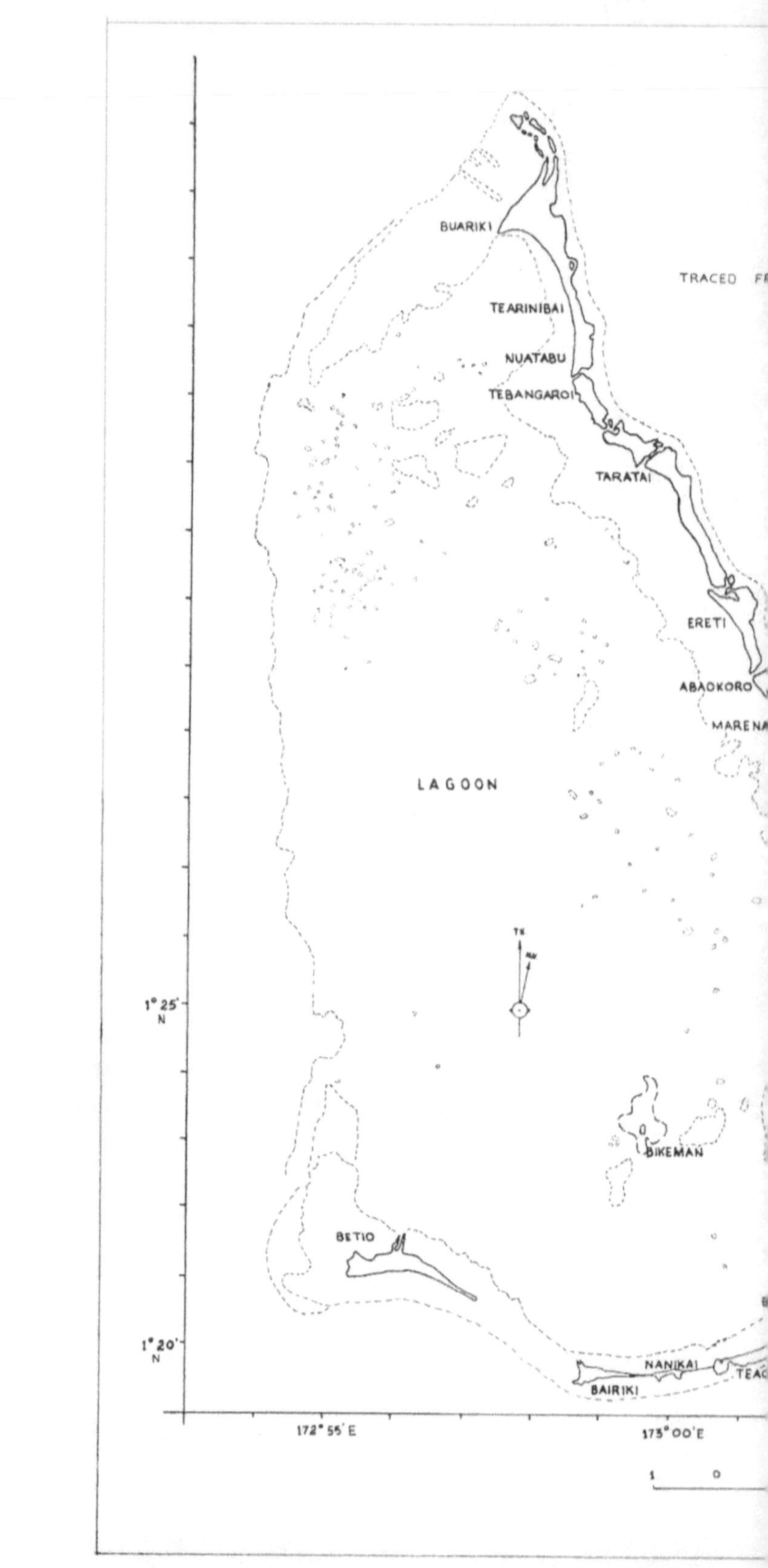

TRACED FR
BUARIKI
TEARINIBAI
NUATABU
TEBANGAROI
TARATAI
ERETI
ABAOKORO
MARENA
LAGOON
TN
MN
BIKEMAN
BETIO
NANIKAI
TEAO
BAIRIKI
1° 25' N
1° 20' N
172° 55' E
173° 00' E
1   0

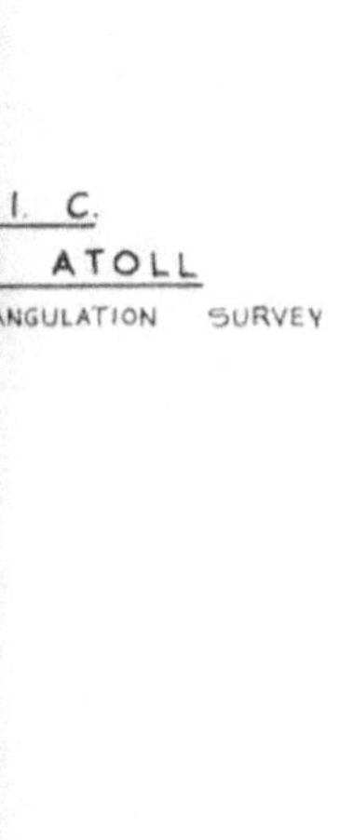
I. C.
ATOLL
ANGULATION   SURVEY

PACIFIC
OCEAN
KAINABA
NABEINA
TABITEUEA
ABATAO
BUOTA
BONRIKI
TEMAIKU
BIKENIBEU
EITA
TABORIO
173°05'E
173°10'E
3   4   5
LANDS & SURVEYS,   BETIO
February 1974.

THE YOGAKI PLAN

The Gilbert Islands comprise sixteen scattered atolls along the equator in the Central Pacific. Tarawa Atoll is over 2,000 miles southwest of Pearl Harbor and 540 miles southeast of the Marshall Islands. Betio is the principal islet in the Tarawa Atoll.

Three days after Pearl Harbor, the Japanese seized Makin and Tarawa from the British. After a raid in August 1942, the Japanese realized their vulnerability in the Gilbert Island chain. After the attack, the *6th Yokosuka Special Naval Landing Force* was dispatched to the islands, led by Admiral Saichiro, a well-known engineer. He directed the construction of advanced and sophisticated defensive positions on the Tarawa Atoll. Admiral Saichiro's vision was to make Tarawa so formidable that any American amphibious assault would stall at the water's edge, and allow the Japanese time to annihilate the landing force.

The Japanese strategy was outlined in the *Yogaki* Plan. Its principal point was to defend Eastern Micronesia from an Allied invasion. Admiral Nimitz took the Japanese threat of counterattack with bombers, submarines, and their main battle fleet, seriously. Admiral Nimitz told Spruance, "Get the hell in and the hell out." The overall theme of this island assault was to seize the Gilbert Island targets with lightning speed.

Codename "Operation Galvanic" was assigned by the Joint Chiefs of Staff to capture Tarawa and Makin in the Gilbert Islands. The 2nd Marine Division was given the invasion of Tarawa while the Army's 165th Regimental Combat Team would assault Makin. All three of the landing force commanders assigned to Operation Galvanic had the last name Smith. The senior general was Holland "Howling Mad" Smith, who commanded the V Amphibious Corps. General Julian Smith commanded the 2nd Marines. And General Ralph Smith was in charge of the 27th Infantry Division.

Admiral Kelly Turner, a veteran of the bloody Guadalcanal Campaign, was assigned command of all amphibious assault forces for Operation Galvanic. Admiral Turner was accompanied by General Holland Smith and was given Task Force 52 for the assault on Makin.

Admiral Harry Hill was assigned command of Task Force 53 for the assault on Tarawa. General Julian Smith and Admiral Harry Hill discussed the plans on board the battleship *Maryland*. These two officers couldn't be more different. Admiral Hill was impetuous and outspoken, while General Smith was reflective and reserved. They worked together well and outlined a plan for the assault on the Gilbert Islands. Admiral Spruance set the D-Day for November 20, 1943.

Colonel Shoup came up with an outline for tackling Betio's barrier reefs. The Marines used LVT-1s (Landing Vehicle Tracked or "Alligators"), an amphibian tractor, during Guadalcanal. The Alligators were unarmored logistical vehicles. They were not assault craft, but true amphibians—capable of being launched at sea and moving through moderate surf to reach the shore. Colonel Shoup discussed the potential idea of using the LVT assault craft with the 2nd Amphibian Tractor Battalion commander, Major Henry Drews. The major liked the idea but warned Shoup that many tractors were in poor condition after the Guadalcanal Campaign. Major Drews could provide only seventy-five Alligators—nowhere near enough to transport all the assault waves. Worse, the thin hulled tractors were vulnerable to enemy fire and would need armor plating. Colonel Shoup ordered Major Drews to modify the tractors with whatever armor plating he could scrounge together.

General Julian Smith knew that the armored LVT-2s, known as "Water Buffalo", were stockpiled in San Diego. He submitted an urgent request for one hundred newer models to be dispatched immediately. General Holland Smith endorsed the request while Admiral Turner disagreed. The argument was intense. Admiral Turner did not dispute the need for Marines to have a reef crossing capability. He objected to the fact these newly ordered vehicles would need to be transported to Tarawa. They'd require LSTs (Tank Landing Ships). The LSTs slow speed (8 knots max) would require an additional convoy, independent escorts, and increased risk of losing the initiative and strategic surprise. General Smith reduced the debate to the essentials: "No LVTs, No operation."

Admiral Turner eventually agreed, but it would not be a complete victory for the 2nd Marines. Fifty of the new one hundred LVT-2s would support the Army's landing at Makin against a lighter opposition. The Marine vehicles scheduled to arrive would not be there in time for any workup training or rehearsal landings. The first time the Marine Infantry would lay eyes on the LVT-2s would be in the predawn hours of Tarawa's D-Day—if at all.

TASK FORCE 53

Replacement troops poured into New Zealand. General Smith requested the reassignment of Colonel Edson to be his division chief of staff. The fiery Colonel Edson was now a Marine Corps legend for his heroic exploits on Guadalcanal. He worked tirelessly to forge the new recruits and veterans into an effective amphibious assault team. The intelligence reports from Betio were startling. The island was void of any natural fortifications to conceal enemy fire. And too narrow, inhibiting any maneuvering room, which favored the Japanese. Betio was 800 yards at its widest point and less than three miles long. It also contained no natural elevation higher than ten feet above sea level. Colonel Edson observed that every place on the island could be covered by machine gun and direct rifle fire.

These elaborate defenses were prepared by Admiral Saichiro. He used minefields, long strings of barbed wire to protect beach approaches, and concrete and steel pillboxes and bunkers. The Japanese built a barrier of coral and logs around much of the islands. They use tank traps to protect fortified command bunkers and firing positions inland of the beach. Of the island's five hundred pillboxes, most were covered by steel plates, logs, and sand.

The Japanese defenders on the island had 8-inch turret-mounted naval rifles, "Singapore guns." They also had many anti-aircraft, anti-boat, heavy caliber coastal defense and field artillery guns, and howitzers. They had an abundant amount of 50mm mortars, dual-purpose 13mm heavy machine guns, and light tanks with 37mm guns. During August, the Japanese high command replaced Saichiro with Admiral Shibasaki, an officer with a reputation for being more of a fighter than an engineer.

Intelligence estimated the total strength of the enemy garrison on Betio was 4,800 men. Twenty-six hundred of them were Imperial Japanese Marines, first-rate naval troops, nicknamed "Tojo's best." Colonel Edson's 1st Raider Battalion had taken nearly 100 casualties wrestling Tulagi from these elite Japanese naval troops in the previous August. Admiral Shibasaki boasted that a million Americans couldn't take Tarawa in a hundred years. His optimism was understandable at the time, because Tarawa was the most heavily defended island ever invaded by Allied forces in the Pacific.

Task Force 53 desperately needed detailed tide information. Colonel Shoup was confident that the LVTs could negotiate the reef during any tide. Still, the rest of the tanks, artillery, assault troops, and reserve forces would need to come ashore in Higgins boats (LCVPs). The water depth over the reef was four feet, it was enough to float a loaded Higgins boat. If less than four feet, the troops would need to wade several hundred yards ashore against an array of deadly Japanese weapons.

A New Zealand reserve officer, with fifteen years' experience sailing Tarawa's waters, predicted: "there won't even be 3 feet of water on that reef when the assault begins."

Colonel Shoup took his warning seriously and made sure that all troops knew in advance that there would be a 50-50 chance of having to wade ashore. Besides the island's physical constraints and daunting Japanese defenses, Shoup proposed a landing plan that included a preliminary bombardment and advance seizure of neighboring Bairiki Islands, to be used as an artillery firebase and a decoy landing. General Smith took this proposal to Pearl Harbor and recommended it to the significant officers involved in Operation Galvanic: Admirals Spruance, Turner and Nimitz, and General Holland Smith.

The restrictions imposed by CinCPac were sobering. Admiral Nimitz declared that the requirement for strategic surprise would limit any bombardment of Betio to only three hours on the morning of D-Day. He also ruled out Bairiki's advance seizure and any decoy landings to defend against the Japanese fleet. To make things worse, General Holland Smith announced that the 6th Marines would be withheld and used as a reserve force. The 2nd Marine Division's tactical options had been stripped away. Ordered into a frontal assault against the teeth of Japanese defenses on Betio with only a three-hour bombardment. Without the 6th Marines attacking the island fortress, that would mean only a 2:1 troop superiority—well below the doctrinal minimum.

Colonel Shoup returned to New Zealand and prepared a modified operations order and selected the landing beaches. The southwestern tip of Tarawa near the lagoon entrance looked like the profile of a crested bird lying on its back. The Japanese concentrated their defenses on the southern and western coasts (the bird's head and back). Northern beaches had calmer lagoon waters and only one deadly exception. Defenses in this sector were incomplete, but being improved daily. A thousand-yard pier that jutted north over the fringing reef into deeper lagoon waters (the bird's legs, sticking upward) was an attractive logistics target. He selected the northern coast for landing beaches—but there was no safe avenue of approach.

The northern shore of Betio from the departure line within the lagoon was designated for the three landing beaches, each 600 yards in length. Moving from west to east, Red Beach One, made up the bird's beak and neck from the northwestern tip of Betio to a point just east, Red Beach Two made up the bird's breast from the juncture to the pier, and Red Beach Three from the pier eastward. Green Beach on the western shore, along with other beaches, would be designated as contingencies.

General Smith planned to land with two regiments abreast and one in reserve. Losing the 6th Marines forced him to make a significant change. Colonel Shoup's modified plan now assigned the 2nd Marines, reinforced by 2/8 (2nd Battalion, 8th Marines) as the main assault force. The rest of the 8th Marines would make up the divisional reserve. An advanced seizure of the pier by First Lieutenant Hawkin's Scout-Sniper Platoon would precede the main assault.

General Smith scheduled a large-scale amphibious exercise in Hawkes Bay on November 1. He planned for New Zealand trucks to haul the men back to Wellington at the end for a large dance. The entire 2nd Marine Division boarded the sixteen amphibious ships for the routine exercise. It was all a ruse. The ships weighed anchor and headed north to begin Operation Galvanic.

Task Force 53 assembled in New Hebrides on November 7. Admiral Hill arrived onboard the *Maryland*. Now that the Marines were keenly aware and operations were underway, they were more interested in the fourteen new Sherman tanks on board the *Ashland*. The 2nd Marine Division had never operated with medium tanks before. The rehearsal landings did little to prepare the Marines for the assault on Betio. Fleet carriers and air wings were assaulting other targets in the Solomons. Sherman tanks had nowhere to offload: the new LVT-2s were still somewhere to the north, underway for Tarawa. And naval gunships were bombarding Erradaka Island, away from the troops landing at Mele Bay.

One positive aspect of the amphibious assault rehearsal was that the Marines could practice embarking on rubber rafts. In the prewar Fleet Marine Force, the first battalion in each regiment was designated the Rubber Boat Battalion. This common site of a mini-flotilla inspired catcalls from other Marines. The main contentious issue during the post-rehearsal critique was the naval gunfire plan. The target island would receive the greatest concentration of naval gunfire in the war to date. Admiral Turner was optimistic about the outcome; he made his plans clear that they did not intend to just neutralize or destroy the island—but obliterate it. General Smith reminded the senior naval officers that the Marines crossed the beach with bayonets. Their only armor would be khaki shirts.

While on New Hebrides, Colonel Marshall, the commander of

Combat Team Two became too ill to continue. General Smith promoted Colonel Shoup to relieve Colonel Marshall. Shoup knew the 2nd Marines, and he knew the plan. The architect was now the executor.

Once underway, Admiral Hill ordered the various commanders of Task Force 53 to brief troops on the destination and mission. Tarawa was a surprise to most of the men. Many had believed they were heading for Wake Island. On the day before D-Day, General Smith sent a message to the 2nd Division officers and men. In his message, he reassured his men that the Navy would stay and provide support throughout the campaign—unlike in the Guadalcanal Campaign. The troops attentively listened to these words coming over the loudspeakers: "We are embarked on a great offensive to destroy the enemy in the Central Pacific. The Navy will screen our operation and support our attack tomorrow with the greatest concentration of naval gunfire and aerial bombardment in the history of war. The Navy will remain with us until our objective has been secured. Garrison troops are already en route to relieve us as soon as we have completed our work. Good luck and God bless you all."

As the sun set on Task Force 53 on the evening of D -1, it seemed strategic surprise had been attained. More good news came with the report that small convoys of LSTs transporting the LVT-2s arrived safely from Samoa and had joined the formation. All the pieces were coming together.

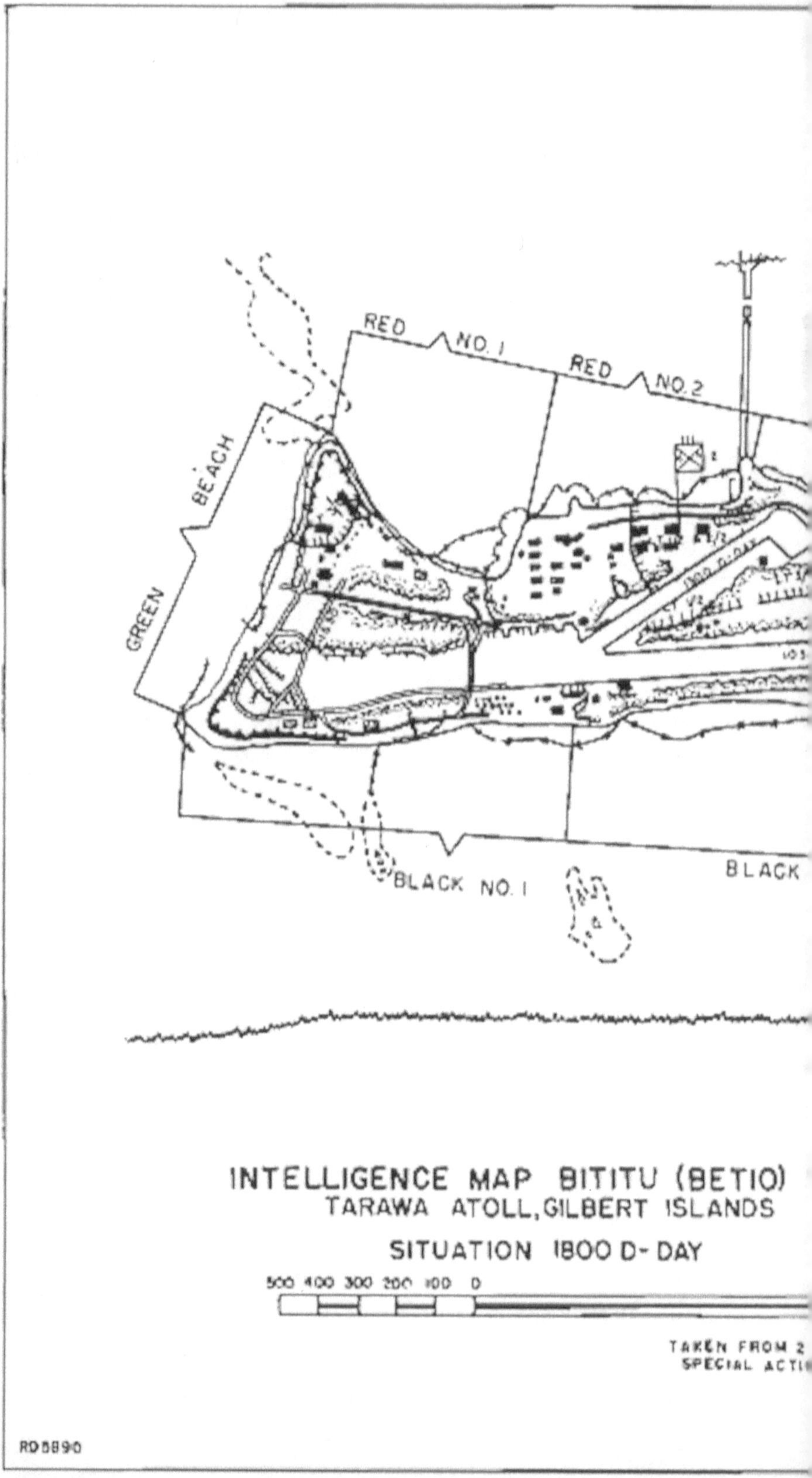

RED NO. 1
RED NO. 2
GREEN BEACH
BLACK NO. 1
BLACK
INTELLIGENCE MAP BITITU (BETIO)
TARAWA ATOLL, GILBERT ISLANDS
SITUATION 1800 D-DAY
500 400 300 200 100 0
TAKEN FROM 2
SPECIAL ACTI
RD5890

.... ADVANCES DURING DAY
POSITIONS AT SUNSET
NO. 3
N
NOTE: LINES ARE GENERAL INDICATION ONLY.
GAPS WERE COVERED BY SMALL GROUPS
AND BY FIRE. SECONDARY LINES WERE
ESTABLISHED WHERE POSSIBLE BEHIND
FRONT LINES.

D-DAY AT BETIO

Shortly after midnight on D-Day, the crowded transports of Task
Force 53 arrived off Tarawa. The sailors cheered as the public

address system played the Marine Hymn to the 2/2 Marines scrambling over the sides and down the cargo nets at 0320.

This was when things started to go wrong.

Admiral Hill, the amphibious task force commander, realized the transports were in the wrong anchorage. He directed the fire support ships to immediately shift to the correct site. While the landing craft bobbed away along in the wake of the ships, several Marines were halfway down the cargo nets when the ships unexpectedly weighed anchor. Choppy seas made matching the exact LVTs with their assigned assault teams dangerous in the darkness.

Few tactical plans survived the opening rounds of execution in this amphibious operation. The D-Day plan was for the H-Hour assault wave to start at 0830. A fast carrier strike would initiate the action with a thirty-minute bombing raid at 0545. After that, the fire support ships would bombard the island from a close range for the next two hours. The planes would then return for a final strafing run, five minutes before H-Hour, and then shift to inland targets while the Marine Corps stormed ashore.

None of this went according to plan.

The Japanese were alerted by the predawn activities offshore and initiated the battle. Their garrison opened fire on Task Force 53 with big naval guns at 0505. The *Maryland's* and *Colorado's* main batteries returned fire at once, and several 16-inch shells found their mark. A huge fireball signaled the destruction of an enemy ammunition bunker at one of the Japanese's gun positions. After other fire support ships joined in, Admiral Hill ordered a cease-fire thirty-five minutes later. He'd expected the air attack to begin. A long silence and no air assault.

The carrier air group changed plans. They postponed the strike by thirty minutes. Their modifications were never relayed to Admiral Hill. Hill's problems were aggravated by the communication loss on his flagship after the ship's main battery's initial crushing salvo. The Japanese coastal defense guns were damaged, but still dangerous. This mistake gave the Japanese almost thirty minutes to adjust and recover. Admiral Hill was frustrated at every turn and ordered his ships to resume firing at 0605. At 0610, carrier fast attack planes appeared. They bombed and strafed the island for the next few minutes. Throughout this confusion, the sun rose into a macabre background of thick, black smoke.

The destroyers, cruisers, and battleships of Task Force 53 bombarded Betio for the next few hours. The shock and awe of the shelling was a vivid experience for the Marines. A combat photographer, Staff Sergeant Hatch, recalled: "We really didn't see how we could do anything but just go in there and bury the Japanese. This wasn't even going to be a fight. Surely no mortal man could live through this destroying power. Any Japs on the island would have to be dead by now."

Staff Sergeant Hatch was proved wrong by a geyser of water fifty yards to the starboard side of his ship. The Japanese resumed fire and targeted the vulnerable troop transports underway for the second time that morning.

General Smith and Admiral Hill onboard *Maryland* struggled to get information throughout the long day. Their best source of information was from a Kingfisher observation aircraft, launched by the battleships. Admiral Hill asked the pilot if the reef was covered with water and received a negative answer. The first wave of LVTs, with over seven hundred embarked Marines, left the assembly area and headed toward the departure line.

The embarked Marines in the LVTs had a difficult, long morning. Cross deck transfers were dangerous in choppy seas while 8-inch shells exploded around them. They began a long run to the beach— ten miles away. The LVTs started on time but fell behind schedule quickly. The LVT-1s of the first wave failed to maintain the 4-knot speed of advance due to a strong westerly current. This, combined with the weight of the improvised armor plating, reduced the buoyancy. A psychological factor was also at work. Colonel Edson had criticized the LVT crews for landing five minutes early during the rehearsal. He had made it clear that early arrival was inexcusable and preferred a late arrival. The three struggling columns of LVTs would not make the beach by the intended hour of 0830. This caused H-Hour to be postponed twice to 0900. All hands did not receive this information.

Two destroyers, *Dashiell* and *Ringgold,* entered the lagoon, following the minesweepers to provide close fire support. Once in the lagoon, the minesweeper *Pursuit* became the primary control ship and directly took a position on the departure line. The *Pursuit* turned her searchlights seaward and provided the LVTs with a beacon of light through the thick smoke and dust. At 0825, as the first wave of LVTs crossed the line, they were still 6,000 yards away from the target beaches.

Minutes after, carrier aircraft roared over Betio, right on time for the original H-Hour but unaware of the new times. Admiral Turner specifically provided all of the players in Operation Galvanic with this warning: "Times to strafe the beaches regarding H-Hour approximate. The distance of the boat from the beach will be a governing factor."

Admiral Hill called them off. The assault planes remained on station with depleted ammunition and fuel levels.

The LVTs chugged shoreward in three long waves. They were separated by 300-yard intervals. Wave One contained forty-two LVT-1s, followed by Wave Two with twenty-four LVT-2s, and Wave Three with twenty-one LVT-2s. Behind these tracked vehicles were Waves Four and Five of Higgins boats. Each of the assault battalion commanders were in Wave Four. Astern, the *Ashland* ballasted down and launched fourteen LCMs (or Landing Craft Mechanized), all carrying a medium Sherman tank. Four other LCMs trailed, transporting light tanks with 37mm guns.

Just before 0800, Colonel Shoup and elements of his tactical command post debarked and headed to the line of departure. A bulky sergeant stood close to Shoup and shielded the radio from the salt spray. Of all the communication failures and blackouts on D-Day, Shoup's radio remained functional longer. It served him better than radios of any other commander—Japanese or American—on the island.

At 0854, Admiral Hill ordered a cease-fire, even though the assault waves were still 4,000 yards out from shore. Colonel Edson and General Smith objected. Still, Admiral Hill considered the enormous pillars of smoke unsafe for overhead fire support. After the bombing ceased, the LVTs made their final approach into the teeth of long-range machine-gun fire and artillery airbursts. The artillery could have been fatal to troops crowded into the open-topped LVTs, but the Japanese had loaded the projectiles with high explosives instead of steel shell fragments, which only doused the Marines with "hot sand." This was the last tactical mistake the Japanese made on D-Day.

The aborted airstrike returned at 0855 for five minutes of ineffective strafing along the beaches. The pilots followed their wristwatches instead of the progress of the lead LVTs. Two naval landing boats started toward the end of the long pier at the reef's edge. 1stLt. Hawkins and his Scout Sniper Battalion with a squad of combat engineers charged out. They made quick work of Japanese gun placements along the pier with their flamethrowers and explosives.

The LVTs of Wave One struck the beach and crawled over the reef. These parts of Colonel Shoup's plan were executed flawlessly. The bombardment, as extraordinary as it had been, failed to soften the Japanese defenses. Little of the ships' fire had been directed against the landing beaches.

Admiral Shibasaki vowed to defeat the amphibious assault units at the water's edge. The well-protected Japanese shook off the sand and manned their guns. The curbing of all naval gunfire for the first thirty minutes of the assault was a fateful mistake for Admiral Hill. This gave the Japanese time to shift their forces from the southern and western beaches to reinforce the northern positions. The Japanese defenders were stunned and groggy from the naval pounding and sight of the LVTs crossing the barrier reef. However, Admiral Shibasaki's killing zone was still intact. The Japanese met the amphibious assault waves with a steady volume of combined arms fire.

The first wave of LVTs approaching the final 200 yards of beaches Red One and Red Two were the most challenging. Well aimed fire from anti-boat, 40mm, and heavy and light machine guns hammered the Marines. The assault team fired back with their .50-caliber machine guns mounted on each of the LVT-1s, firing over

10,000 rounds. The exposed gunners were easy targets, and dozens were cut down. The LVT battalion commander, Drews—who worked with Shoup to make this assault possible—took over a machine gun from a fallen crewman and was killed instantly by a bullet through his eye. One of Major Drew's company commanders mentioned later he saw a Japanese officer standing defiantly on the seawall, waving his pistol, "just daring us to come ashore."

The LVTs pushed through. The touchdown times staggered at intervals of ten minutes on each beach. The first LVT to land was a vehicle nicknamed "My Deloris," driven by PFC Moore. My Deloris was the right guide vehicle on Red Beach One and hit the beach squarely on "the bird's beak." PFC Moore tried to drive his LVT over the 5-foot seawall, but the vehicle stalled in a vertical position while Japanese machine guns riddled troops inside. PFC Moore reached for his rifle and found it shot in half. He later recalled what happened next on the LVT: "The sergeant stood up and yelled, 'everybody out!' but as soon as the words left his mouth, machine-gun bullets ripped the top of his head off."

PFC Moore and a handful of others escaped the LVT and destroyed two machine-gun positions a few yards away. All would either be killed or injured during the assault . Few of the LVTs could negotiate the 5-foot seawall. While the LVTs stalled on the beach, they were vulnerable to howitzer and mortar fire, as well as hand grenades thrown into the troop compartments by Japanese troops on the other side of the barrier.

One crew chief of the vehicle, Corporal Spillane, a baseball prospect with the St. Louis Cardinals before the war, caught two Japanese grenades barehanded in midair and tossed them back over the wall. He caught a third grenade that exploded in his hand and fatally wounded him.

MAELSTROM ON BETIO

Waves Two and Three of the LVT-2s were protected by a 3/8 inch boilerplate hastily installed in Samoa. These waves suffered even more intense fire. The large-caliber anti-boat Japanese guns destroyed several of the LVT-2s. Machine gunner PFC Baird, aboard one of the embattled LVTs, recounted what he saw: "After we were 100 yards in, the enemy fire was awful damn intense and only getting worse. They were knocking us out left and right. A tractor would get hit, stop, and burst into flames. Men jumped out like torches."

PFC Baird's LVT was hit by a shell and killed many of the troops. He recalled: "I grabbed my carbine and an ammunition box. I stepped over a couple fellas lying there dead and put my hand on the side to roll over into the water. I didn't want to put my head up. The bullets poured over us like a sheet of rain."

The LVTs executed the assault according to General Smith's expectations. Eight out of the eighty-seven vehicles in the first three waves were lost in the assault. Fifteen others were so damaged and riddled with holes that they sank when reaching deep water while seeking to shuttle more troops to shore. Within ten minutes, the

LVTs landed over 1,500 Marines on Betio's north shore. While a brilliant start to the operation, the problem was sustaining the momentum of the assault. The neap tide predictions were accurate. No landing craft could cross that reef on D-Day.

Colonel Shoup hoped that enough LVTs would survive to permit a wholesale transfer operation with the boats along the edge of the reef. It would not work. The LVTs suffered more casualties. Several vehicles, afloat for only five hours, ran out of gas. Others needed to be used immediately for the evacuation of wounded Marines. The already flawed communications deteriorated even more as the radio sets suffered water damage from enemy fire. The surviving LVTs continued on. But after 1015, most troops had waded ashore from the reef, crossing distances of 1,000 yards, under well-aimed fire. The Marines of the 3/2 were walloped on Red Beach One. Company K suffered casualties from the stronghold on the left. Company I crossed the seawall but paid a high price— losing their company commander before he could even debark from his LVT. Both units lost more than half of their men within the first two hours.

Major Michael Ryan's Company L was forced to wade ashore when their boats grounded on the reef, taking over 35% casualties. Major Ryan spotted one lone trooper through the fire and smoke scrambling over a parapet on the beach to the right, marking a new landing point. When Company L finally reached the shore, Major Ryan looked back over his shoulder, and all he could see were heads with rifles held over them. He ordered his men to make as small of a target as possible. Ryan assembled the various stragglers in a sheltered area along Green Beach.

In the fourth wave, Major Schoettel remained in his boat with the remnants of his Marines. He was convinced that his landing team had been destroyed beyond relief. He had no contact with Major Ryan. Schoettel received fragmented reports that seventeen of his thirty-seven officers were combat ineffective casualties.

In the center, the 2/2 Marines were thumped hard coming ashore. The Japanese strong point in the re-entrant between the two beaches created turmoil among the Marines scrambling over the sides of their stalled and beached LVTs. Five out of six of Company E's officers were killed. Company F took 50% casualties getting ashore and negotiating the seawall to seize a foothold. Company G barely clung to a crowded stretch of beach along the seawall in the middle. Two infantry platoons and two machine gun platoons were driven away from their beach. They were forced to land on Red Beach One, joining "Major Ryan's orphans."

When Lieutenant Colonel Amey's boat ran against the reef, he hailed a passing LVTs for a transfer. After that, Lieutenant Colonel Amey's LVT became hung up on a barbed wire obstacle several hundred yards off Red Beach Two. Amey drew his pistol and shouted for his men to follow him into the water. As he got closer to the beach, Colonel Amey turned to encourage his men: "Come on! These bastards can't beat us."

A machine gun fire burst hit him in the throat—killing him instantly. His XO, Major Rice, and another LVT landed far to the west behind Major Ryan. Lieutenant Colonel Walter Jordan was the senior officer present with the 2/2. He was one of the several observers from the 4th Marine Division, and only one of a handful of survivors from Amey's LVT.

Lieutenant Colonel Jordan did what any Marine would do under the circumstances: he took command. Jordan tried to rebuild the pieces of the landing team into a cohesive fighting force.

The only amphibious assault unit that got ashore without significant casualties was the 2/8 on Red Beach Three, east of the pier. This good fortune was attributed to the continued direct fire support the 2/8 received, throughout its run to the beach, from the two destroyers in the lagoon. The fire support from the two ships provided a preliminary fire from such a short-range. It kept the Japanese defenders on the island's eastern edge buttoned up. As a result, the 2/8 only suffered less than 25% casualties in the first three LVT waves. Company E made a significant penetration by crossing the barricade and the taxiway. Still, five of its six officers were shot down in the first ten minutes ashore. The 2/8 was fighting against one of the most sophisticated defensive positions on the islands. These fortifications to their left flank would keep the Marines boxed in for the next forty-eight hours.

Major "Jim" Crowe was the commander of the 2/8 Marines. A former enlisted man, gunner, distinguished rifleman, and star football player, he was a tower of strength through the battle. He carried a combat shotgun cradled in his arm. With his trademark red mustache, he exuded professionalism and confidence that were sorely needed on Betio that day. Major Crowe ordered the coxswain of his Higgins boat to "put the god damn boat in." The Higgins boat hit the reef at high speed, sending Marines sprawling. Crowe quickly recovered and ordered his men over the sides and then led them through hundreds of yards of shallow water. They reached the shore intact only four minutes behind the last wave of LVTs.

Crowe was accompanied by a combat photographer who recalled the major clenching a cigar in his teeth and standing upright, growling at his men: "Look, these sons of bitches can't hit me. Why do you think they can hit you? Get your asses moving. Go!"

Red Beach Three was in capable hands.

By 0945 on Betio, Major Crowe was well-established, with a penetration to the airfield. A distinct gap existed between the 2/8 and the survivors of 2/2 in small clusters along Red Beach Two under Colonel Jordan's command. It was a dangerous gap because of the Japanese fortifications between Beaches One and Two. Only a few members of 3/2 on the left flank and a growing collection of Marines under Major Ryan were on Green Beach.

Major Schoettel was floating beyond the reef. Colonel Shoup was likewise in a Higgins boat, but starting his move toward the beach. Other Marines waded ashore under increasing enemy fire. The tanks were forced to unload from the LCMs at the reef's edge, searching for recon teams to lead them ashore.

Communications were a nightmare. The TBX radios of Crowe, Shoup, and Schoettel were still operational. But there was either dead silence or complete havoc on the command nets. No one on the flagship knew of Major Ryan's successful debark on the western end, or of Colonel Amey's death and Colonel Jordan's assumption of command. An early report from an unknown source flashed over the command nets: "Have landed. Unusually heavy opposition. Casualties 70%. Can't hold."

Colonel Shoup ordered the 1/2 regimental reserve to land on Red Beach Two and work west. This would take time because the men were still awaiting orders at the line of departure, but all were waiting embarked in boats. Colonel Shoup assembled enough LVTs to transport companies A and B. The 3rd Infantry Company and the Weapons Company had yet to wade ashore through this chaotic assault. Most of the LVTs were destroyed en route by anti-boat guns. Japanese gunners now had the range down pat. Five vehicles were driven away by the intense fire and landed west at Major Ryan's position, giving him another 113 troops to add to Green Beach.

The rest of companies A and B stormed ashore and penetrated several hundred feet, expanding the perimeter. Other troops sought refuge along the pier and tried to commandeer a passing LVT. Many of the regimental reserve 1/2 troops did not complete the landing until the following morning. It was typical for an LVT driver and his gunners to be shot down by enemy machine gun fire. The surviving crewmen would get the stranded vehicle started again, but only in reverse. The vehicle would back wildly through the entire impact zone before breaking down again, causing several men to not reach the shore until sunset.

Naval commanders received their first clear signal that things were going wrong on the beach when a derelict LVT chugged astern with no one at the controls. They dispatched a boat to retrieve the vehicle and discovered three dead Marines aboard the LVT. Their bodies were brought on board and buried with full honors at sea. These were the first of hundreds of men consigned to the deep because of the maelstrom on Betio.

After the communications were restored on the *Maryland,* General Smith tried to make sense of the conflicting and intermittent messages coming in through the ship's command net. At 1036 General Smith reported to the V Amphibious Corps: "Successful landing on beaches Red Two and Three. Toehold on Red One. And committing one LT from division reserved. Still encountering strong resistance."

Colonel Shoup was trying to navigate getting ashore. When his Higgins boat was stopped at the reef, he transferred into a passing LVT. He joined Colonel Evans Carlson, a legend for his exploits on Guadalcanal and Makin. He took command of the 1/10 Artillery detachment. Their LVT made three attempts to land—each time the enemy fire was too intense. On the third attempt, the vehicle was hit and disabled. Shoup took a painful shell fragment wound in his leg but led his men out of the LVT and into the fight. He stood in waist-deep water surrounded by thousands of dead fish and floating bodies. Shoup manned his radio and tried desperately to get organized combat units ashore to sway the fight's balance.

Colonel Shoup had hoped that the Sherman tanks could break the gridlock. This was the combat debut of the Marine Corps' medium tanks but was discouraging on D-Day. The 2nd Marine Division did not understand how to employ tanks against fortified positions. When four Shermans reached Red Beach Three, later in the morning, Major Crowe waved them forward with orders to knock out all enemy positions. The tank crews, who were buttoned up under fire, were practically blind in their tanks. With no accompanying infantry, they were destroyed one by one. Some were knocked out by the Japanese 75mm guns, while others were damaged by friendly fire from American dive bombers.

Six other Shermans that tried to land on Red Beach One were preceded by a dismounted guide to warn off underwater shell craters. These guides were shot down every few minutes by Japanese marksmen. Each time, another volunteer would step forward to continue the movement. Combat engineers had blown a hole in the seawall for the tanks to pass through, but the way was blocked with wounded and dead Marines. Rather than run over their fellow Marines, the tank commander reversed his column and went around toward a second opening blasted in the seawall.

While the Shermans operated in murky, chaotic waters, four tanks foundered in shell holes on the detour. Inland on the beach, one of the surviving Sherman's engaged a Japanese light tank. The medium American tank demolished its small opponent, but not before the doomed Japanese tank released one final 37mm round— a phenomenal shot—right down the barrel of the Sherman.

RED BEACH TWO

By the end of the day, only two of the fourteen Sherman tanks were still operational. Maintenance crews worked desperately to retrieve a third tank, *Cecilia,* on Green Beach for Major Ryan. Japanese gunners sank all four of the LCMs transporting the light tanks into the battle before the boats even reached the reef. The tank battalion commander, Colonel Swenceski, was assumed killed in action while wading ashore. He was severely wounded but survived by crawling on top of a pile of dead bodies to keep from drowning until he was discovered the next day.

Colonel Shoup sent a message to the flagship at 1045 on D-Day voicing his frustration: "Our tanks no good. Stiff resistance, need half-tracks."

The regimental weapons company's half-tracks with their 75mm guns fared no better getting ashore than any other combat units that morning. One half-track was sunk in its LCM transport by long-range artillery fire before reaching the reef. A second half-track ran the entire gauntlet but got stuck in the loose sand at the water's edge and was destroyed. The situation was now critical.

Individual courage and initiative inspired the scattered remnants throughout the chaos along the exposed beachhead. Staff Sergeant Bordelon was a combat engineer attached to the 2/2. After a Japanese shell disabled his LVT and killed most of the troops en route to the beach, Bordelon rallied the survivors and led them ashore on Red Beach Two. He stopped only long enough to prepare explosive charges. He knocked out two Japanese positions that had been firing on the assault waves. After attacking a third emplacement, he was hit by machine-gun fire but refused medical help and continued fighting. Staff Sergeant Bordelon bolted back into the water and rescued a wounded Marine calling for help. As more intense fire opened up from another enemy position, Bordelon prepared one final demolition package and charged the Japanese gun position in a frontal assault. This is where his luck ran out. He was shot and killed. He later became the first of four men in the 2nd Marine Division to be awarded the Medal of Honor.

In another instance, Sergeant Roy Johnson single-handedly

attacked a Japanese tank. He scrambled to the turret and dropped a grenade inside while sitting on the hatch, waiting for the detonation. Sergeant Johnson survived this but was later killed in the fighting on Betio. In the seventy-six hour battle, he was one of the 217 Marine sergeants to be wounded or killed.

A captain on Red Beach Three, who was shot through both arms and legs, sent a message to Major Crowe apologizing for letting him down.

Major Ryan later recalled a wounded Sergeant, who he'd never seen before, limping up to him and asking where he was needed most.

PFC Moore, who was earlier disarmed and wounded, trying to drive "My Dolores" over the seawall, carried ammo to the machine gun crews for the rest of the day until he was evacuated to one of the transports.

Other brave Marines retrieved a pair of 37mm antitank guns from a sunken landing craft. They manhandled them across several hundred yards under terrifying enemy fire. They dragged them across the beach to the seawall. While two Japanese tanks approached the beachheads, the Marines lifted the 900-pound anti-tank guns on top of the seawall. They calmly loaded, aimed, and fired. Knocking out one of the Japanese tanks at close range and chasing off the other.

Robert Sherrod was an experienced war correspondent for *Time* magazine. The landing on D-Day at Betio was the most frightening experience of his life. Sherrod accompanied Marines from the fourth wave of 2/2 and tried to wade ashore on Red Beach Two. In his own words: "No sooner did we hit the water than the Japanese machine guns really opened up on us. It was so painfully slow, we waded in such deep water. We had 700 yards to walk slowly into direct machine-gun fire, looming into larger targets as we rose onto the higher ground. I was so scared, more than I'd ever been before. Those who weren't hit would always remember how the machine-gun bullets hissed into the water, inches to the right, inches to the left."

Colonel Shoup moved toward the beach parallel to the pier. He ordered Major Ruud's 3/8 Marines to land on Red Beach Three—east of the pier. There were now no organized LVT units to transport the reserve battalion to the fight. Major Ruud was ordered to approach as near as he could to the landing boats and then wade the remaining distance into shore. Ruud received his orders from Shoup at 1104. While the two officers were never more than a mile apart from each other for the next six hours, they could not communicate.

Major Ruud divided his landing team into seven waves. Once the boats approached, the reef confusion began. The Japanese zeroed their anti-boat guns on the landing craft with fearsome accuracy. They scored several direct hits as the bow ramp dropped. A distinct *clang* from an impacting shell would signal a split second before the explosion. Staff Sergeant Hatch watching from the beach later recalled: "It happened at least a dozen times. The boat was blown completely out of the water and smashed bodies all over the place. I watched a Jap shell hit a landing craft directly that brought many Marines ashore. The explosion was horrific, and parts of the boat flew in all directions."

Navy coxswains watching the slaughter directly ahead stopped their boats seaward of the reef and ordered troops to debark. Many Marines loaded with extra ammunition or radios instantly sank into the deep water—many drowned. The reward for the troops whose coxswains made it into the reef was less sanguine. They waded through 600 yards of withering crossfire. Heavier, by far, than what the first assault waves experienced at H-Hour. The first wave slaughter of companies L and K was terrible. Over 70% fell while attempting to reach the beach.

Colonel Shoup and his party frantically waved to groups of Marines to seek the pier's protection. While many did, several NCOs and officers had been hit, making the stragglers disorganized. The pier was a questionable shelter; it received sniper fire, and intermittent machine-gun fire from both sides. Colonel Shoup was struck in nine places. A bullet came close to penetrating his bull-like neck. His runner crouching behind him was shot between the eyes by a Japanese sniper.

The commander of the 3/8 Weapons Company, Captain Carl Hoffman, fared no better getting ashore than the infantry companies ahead. His landing craft took a direct hit from a Japanese mortar, and he lost six or eight men right there. Captain Hoffman's Marines veered toward the peer and then waded toward shore. Ruud was unable to contact Shoup. And instead radioed his regimental commander, Colonel Elmer Hall: "Third wave landed on Red Beach Three. Practically wiped out. Fourth wave landed but only a few Marines ashore."

Colonel Hall was in a small boat near the line of departure, unable to respond. General Hermle, Assistant Division Commander, intervened with this message: "Stay where you are or retreat out of gun range."

This only added to the confusion. Major Ruud did not reach the pier until late afternoon. At 1730 he was able to lead what was left of his men ashore.

Many Marines did not straggle in until the following day. Colonel Shoup dispatched what was left of the 3/8 to support Major Crowe's besieged 2/8. Other Marines were used to plug the gap between the 2/8 and the combined troops of the 2/2 and the 1/2.

When Colonel Shoup finally reached Betio and established his command post. He was fifty yards in from the pier along the blindside of a Japanese occupied bunker. Shoup posted guards to keep the enemy from launching any attacks. Still, the site's approaches were exposed, just like any other place on the flat island. Over twenty messengers were shot while bearing dispatches to and from Colonel Shoup.

Combat photographer Sherrod crawled to look out at the exposed water on both sides of the pier. He counted over fifty disabled LVTs, boats, and tanks.

Colonel Shoup admitted to him, "We need more men. We're in a tight spot." The situation did not look good.

Shoup's first order of business after reaching dry ground was to seek updated reports from his landing team commanders. Tactical communications were worse now than they had been during the morning assault. Colonel Shoup still had no contact with any troops on Red Beach One, nor could he raise General Smith on *Maryland*. A messenger arrived with a report from 2/2: "All communications out except runners. We need help. Situation bad. CO killed. No word from E Company."

Colonel Shoup found Colonel Jordan and ordered him to take command of the 2/2. Shoup reinforced him with elements of the 1/2 and 3/8. He gave Jordan an hour to organize and rearm the assorted attachments. Shoup then ordered him to proceed inland to attack the airstrip and expand the beachhead. Colonel Shoup then ordered Colonel Carlson to hitch a ride to the *Maryland* and inform General Smith of the situation personally. He told Carlson to tell the general, "We're going to stick it out and fight."

Carlson departed immediately. But because of the hazards and confusion between the line of departure and the beach, he did not reach the flagship with his message until 1800.

FOG OF WAR

Colonel Shoup focused his attention on the critical matters of resupply. Beyond the pier were over a hundred small craft that circled aimlessly. They carried assorted supplies from cargo and transport ships. They unloaded as quickly as they could in compliance with Admiral Nimitz's orders of "Get the hell in and then get the hell out."

The unorganized unloading hindered the fight ashore. Shoup was not sure of which boat held what supplies. He sent word that only the most critical supplies were to be sent to the pier: LVT fuel, ammunition, water, blood plasma, and more radios. The naval gunfire support since the landing was terrific, but it was time for the Marines to bring their own artillery to the beachhead. The original plan of landing the 1/10 Marines at Red Beach One was no longer practical.

Shoup conferred with Lieutenant Colonel Presley Rixey and agreed to land on Red Beach Two's left flank with the 75mm howitzers. These expeditionary guns would be broken down and manhandled ashore. Lieutenant Colonel Rixey had seen close up what happened when the 3/8 tried to wade ashore from the reef. He went after the last few LVTs. There were only enough operational vehicles for two sections of Batteries A and B. In the confusion, three Battery C sections followed the LVTs toward the shore in their open boats. Luck smiled on the artillerymen. The LVTs landed with intact guns in the late afternoon. When the trailing boats were hung up on the reef, Marines dragged the heavy components through the bullet swept waters to the pier and made it ashore by twilight. There was now close-in fire support available at dawn.

General Julian Smith knew little of what was happening. He continued trying to piece together the tactical situation onshore. Smith received reports from staff officers afloat and in float planes. He decided the situation in the early afternoon was in desperate straits.

Although he had elements of five infantry battalions ashore, their toehold was unstable. General Smith decided the gap between Red Beach One and Red Beach Two had not been closed. And that the left flank on Red Beach Three was not secure. Smith assumed that Shoup was still alive and in command, but he could not afford to gamble. Over the next few hours, the commanding general did his best to influence all-action ashore from the flagship. Smith's first step was to send a radio message to General Holland Smith. He requested the use of the 6th Marines to division control because the situation was in doubt. He also ordered his last remaining landing team, 1/8 Marines, to the line of departure. General Julian Smith reorganized another emergency division composed of engineers, artillery, and service troop units.

General Julian Smith ordered General Hermle to proceed to the end of the pier and assess the situation and report back. Hermle took his small staff and promptly debarked from the *Monrovia* headed toward the smoking island—but the trip took four hours. During this time, General Julian Smith received a message from Major Schoettel, still afloat seaward at the reef: "Command post located on back of Red Beach One. Situation as before. Lost all contact with assault elements."

General Smith replied: "Land at any cost. Regain control of your battalion and continue to attack."

Major Schoettel reached the beach at sunset. It was well into the next day before he could work west and consolidate the scattered Marines. General Smith received authorization to take control of the 6th Marines at 1525. Smith now had four battalions of landing teams available at his disposal. The question was how to feed them into the fight without getting them annihilated like Major Ruud's experience trying to land the 3/8.

Again, General Smith's communications failed him. At 1740 he received a message from Hermle that he had reached the pier and was under fire. Ten minutes later, Smith ordered Hermle to take command of all forces onshore. Hermle never received these orders. General Smith did not know his message failed to get through, and Hermle remained at the pier sending runners to Colonel Shoup, who told him to "Get the hell out from underneath that pier." They tried with little success to unscrew the two-way movement of casualties and supplies to shore.

Throughout the long day, Colonel Hall and his staff languished in their Higgins boats next to the 1/8 waiting at the line of departure. They were wet, cramped, hungry, and tired with many seasick Marines. Later in the afternoon, General Smith ordered Hall to land all of his remaining units on the beach on the northeast tip of the island and work west toward Colonel Shoup's ragged lines. This was extremely risky. General Smith's primary concern was that the Japanese would counterattack from the eastern tail of the island against his left flank. Once he had the 6th Marines, General Smith later admitted he would've sacrificed a battalion landing team if it meant saving the landing force from being overrun by a Japanese counterattack during the night.

Luckily, Hall never received this message from General Smith. Later that afternoon, a float plane reported to Smith that a unit crossed the departure line and headed for the left flank of Red Beach Two. General Smith assumed it was Hall going to the wrong beach. But this was the beginning of Rixey's artillerymen moving ashore. The 8th Marines spent the night in their boats waiting for orders. General Smith did not discover this until early the next morning.

On Betio, Major Ryan reported to Colonel Shoup that several

hundred Marines and two tanks had penetrated over 500 yards beyond Red Beach One on the island's western end. This was now the most successful progress of the day and welcome news to Shoup, because he'd feared the worst. He'd assumed Schoettel's companies and all other strays who'd veered in that direction were wiped out. This was more news that Shoup could not convey to Smith.

Major Ryan's troops were effective on the western end. They learned how to best operate the medium tanks and carved out a substantial beachhead. They overran several Japanese pillboxes and turrets. Aside from the tanks, Ryan's men had only infantry weapons. They had no demolitions or flamethrowers. Major Ryan new from his earlier experiences fighting in the Solomons that positions reduced by only grenades could come alive again. He decided by late afternoon to pull back his thin lines and consolidate. In his words: "I was convinced that without any flamethrowers or explosives to clean them out, we needed to pull back . . . to a perimeter that could be defended against a counterattack by Japanese troops still hidden in the bunkers."

The fundamental choice by Marines on Betio was whether to stay put on the beach or try and crawl over the seawall to fight inland. Much of the day, the fire came across the coconut logs so intensely that a man could lift his hand and get it shot off. Late on D-Day, many Marines were too demoralized to advance. Major Ravoth Tompkins brought messages from General Hermle to Colonel Shoup. Tompkins arrived on Red Beach Two at the foot of the pier at dusk on D-Day. He was appalled at the sight of so many Marine stragglers. Tompkins wondered why the Japanese didn't just use mortars on the first night. He later reported that Marines lying on the beach were so thick you couldn't walk through them.

The conditions on Red Beach One were congested as well, but there was a difference. Major Crowe was everywhere, "as cool as icebox lettuce." There weren't any stragglers. Crowe fed small groups of Marines into the lines, reinforcing his precarious hold on the left flank. Captain Hoffman of the 3/8 Marines welcomed the integration of Crowe's 2/8 Marines. Hoffman needed help as darkness fell. He recalled: "There we were, toes in the water, casualties everywhere, dead and wounded all around us. But finally, a few Marines started to inch forward, a yard here, a yard there."

It was enough, Hoffman could see well enough to call in naval gunfire support. His men dug in for the night. To the west of Major Crowe's lines, and inland from Colonel Shoup's command post, was Company B of the 1/2. They had settled in for the expected counterattack. Scattered in the bloody landing at midday, Company B had men from 12 to 14 different units, including sailors, who swam ashore from sinking boats. These men were all well-armed and no longer stragglers.

Of the 5,000 Marines that stormed the beaches of Betio on D-Day, 1,500 of them were missing, dead, or wounded by nightfall. The survivors held only a quarter of a square mile of coral and sand. Colonel Shoup later described the location of his beachhead lines the night of D-Day as "a stock market graph." The Marines went to ground in the best fighting positions they could secure, whether in inland shell holes or along the splintered seawall. Despite the defensive positions and scrambled units, the fire discipline of the Marines was superb. The troops shared a grim confidence. They'd already faced the worst in getting ashore. They were ready for any *banzai* charges in the dark.

General Smith on the *Maryland* was concerned. He recalled: "This was the crisis of the battle. Three-fourths of the island was in enemy hands. A concerted Japanese counterattack would've driven us into the sea."

Smith reported up his chain of command to Admirals Spruance, Turner, and Nimitz that the issue still remained in doubt. Admiral Spruance's staff began drafting plans for an emergency evacuation of the landing force.

Throughout the night of D-Day, the main struggle was Shoup and Hermle's attempt to try and advise General Smith of the best place to land the reserves the following morning. General Smith was astonished to learn at 0200, that Colonel Hall was not ashore but still at the line of departure awaiting orders. Smith again ordered combat team eight to land on the eastern tip of the island at 0900 on D +1.

General Hermle finally caught a boat back to one of the destroyers. He relayed Shoup's request to land reinforcements on Red Beach Two. General Smith modified Colonel Hall's orders. Smith ordered Hermle back to the flagship, irked at his assistant for not getting ashore and taking command. In the end, General Hermle had done Smith a useful service by relaying the advice from Colonel Shoup. As much as the 8th Marines would bleed in the next morning's assault, a landing on the island's eastern end would have been a disaster. Reconnaissance after the battle discovered those beaches to be the most intensely mined on the entire island.

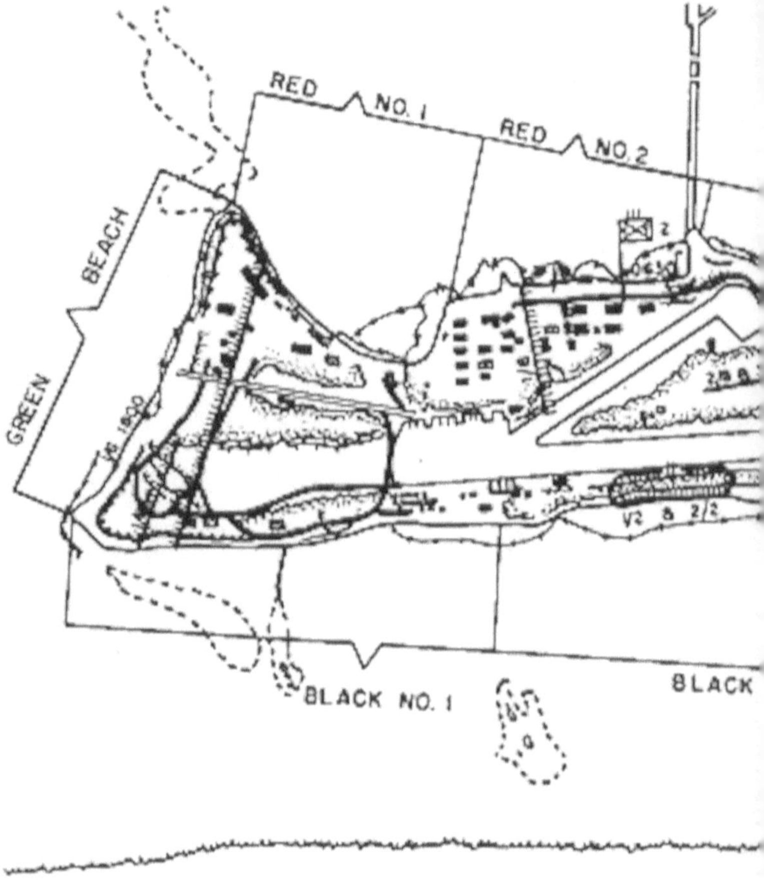

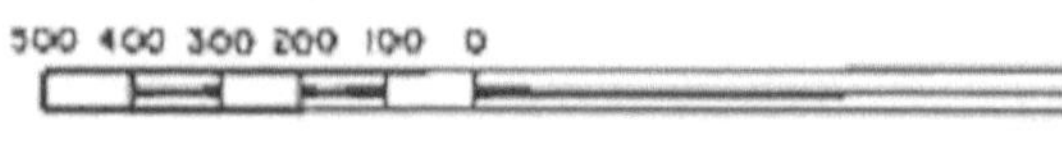

RED NO. 1
RED NO. 2
GREEN BEACH
BLACK NO. 1
BLACK
V2 & 2/2

INTELLIGENCE MAP BITITU (BETIO)
TARAWA ATOLL, GILBERT ISLANDS
SITUATION 1800 D+1

500 400 300 200 100 0

TAKEN FROM 2
SPECIAL ACTI

RD 5890

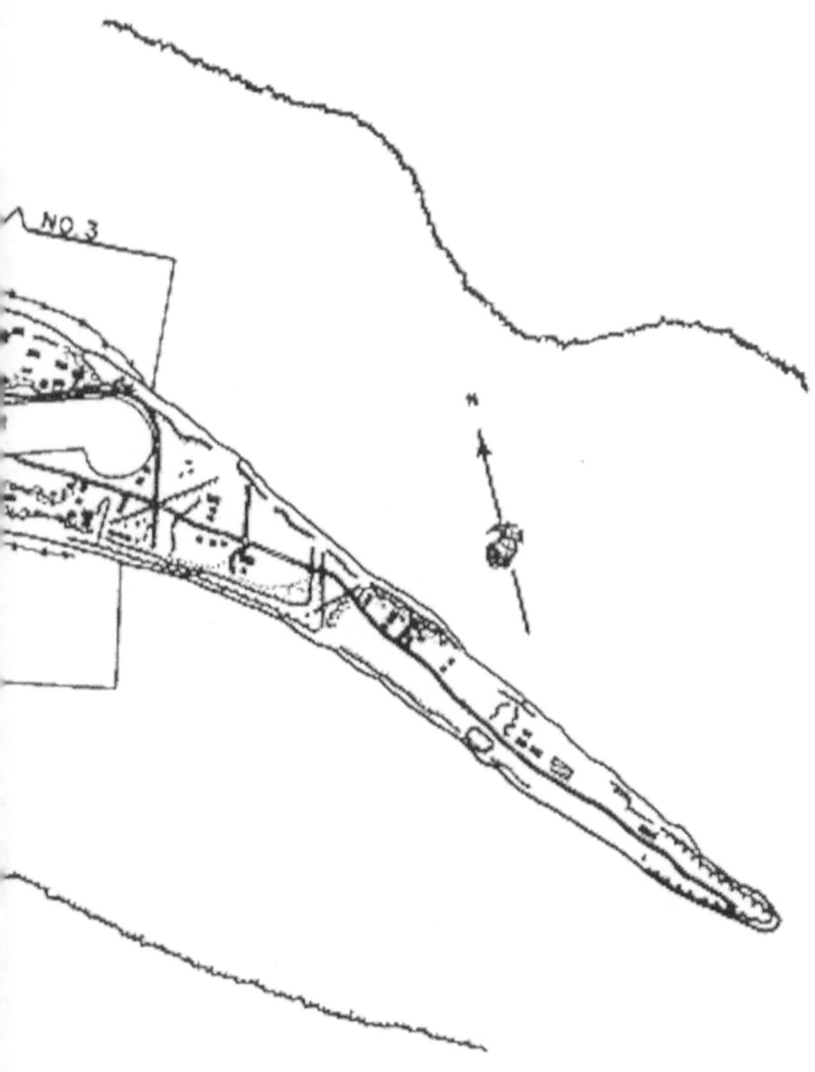

INITIAL LANDING
POSITIONS AT SUNSET
NO. 3
N
NOTE: LINES ARE GENERAL INDICATION ONLY.
GAPS WERE COVERED BY SMALL GROUPS
AND BY FIRE. SECONDARY LINES WERE
ESTABLISHED WHERE POSSIBLE BEHIND
FRONT LINES.

D +1 AT BETIO

The tactical situation on Betio was perilous for most of the second day. During the morning, the Marines paid in blood for every attempt to land reserves or advance the ragged beachheads. Tarawa's beaches were gruesome and filled with the dead and dying. Colonel Shoup surveyed the beach at first light and was horrified. In his own words: "It was a dreadful sight, bodies drifted slowly in the water just off the beach. The stench of dead bodies covered the island like a cloud."

The smell wafted out a bad omen to the line of departure for the 1/8 Marines getting ready to start their run into the beach. With an imperfect knowledge of the scattered forces and his faulty communications, Colonel Shoup ordered each landing team commander to attack. Colonel Jordan would take the south coast. Rudd and Crowe were to reduce the Japanese strongholds to their left and front. Major Ryan was to take all of Green Beach.

Colonel Shoup's predawn request to General Smith relayed a specific landing of the 1/8 on Red Beach Two close to the pier. Unfortunately, this critical component of Shoup's request did not survive the communications route to Smith. The commanding general ordered Major Lawrence C. Hays Jr. and Colonel Hall to land on Red Beach Two at 0615. Hays and Hall were oblivious of the situation ashore and assumed that the 1/8 would make a covered landing.

The Marines of the 1/8 had spent eighteen hours in the embarked Higgins boats, making endless circles through the night. The troops cheered when the boats finally made their turn toward the beach.

Things went wrong quickly. The tides failed to provide enough water for the boats to cross the reef. Hays' men debarked over the obstacle and started the 500-yard trek to shore. Dangerously far to the right flank and within the zone of Japanese guns firing from the strong re-entrant point. They were in the worst place they could be. Japanese gunners began an unrelenting fire. Japanese snipers raked the Marines from the disabled LVTs they had infiltrated during the night. Multiple machine guns opened up on the waiting troops from every beached interisland schooner at the reef's edge. Hays' men fell at every turn.

The Marines tried to stop the slaughter. Colonel Shoup called for naval gunfire support. Two 75mm howitzers protected by a sand berm, erected from a Seabee bulldozer, fired at the blockhouses at the Red Beach One/Two border using delayed fuses in high explosive shells. A squadron of F4F Wildcats attacked the Japanese defenders with machine guns and bombs. While these measures helped, the Japanese had caught the Marines in a withering crossfire.

Correspondent Sherrod watched this bloodbath in horror. In an hour, Sherrod counted at least two hundred bodies that did not move on the dry flats. He recalled: "One boat blows up, then another. The survivors start to swim for shore, but machine-gun bullets dot the water all around them. Far worse today than yesterday."

First Lieutenant Dean Ladd jumped into the water from his boat and was shot in the stomach. He recalled the troops' strict orders to not stop for the wounded and expected to die on the spot. One of his riflemen, PFC Sullivan, ignored the orders and saved his lieutenant's life. Ladd's rifle platoon suffered twenty-four casualties during the ship to shore assault.

First Lieutenant Frank Plant, the air liaison officer, was with Major Hays in the command Higgins boat. After the call, the craft slammed into the reef, Major Hays shouted for the men to debark. As he jumped in the water, the troops that followed him were cut down by the murderous fire. Lieutenant Plant helped to pull the wounded back into the boat. He later wrote that the water all around him was colored purple with blood. As he hurriedly caught up with Hays, he was terrified at the sudden appearance of what he thought were Japanese fighters roaring toward him. But they were the Navy Wildcats screaming in to attack the Japanese. The pilots were excited but inconsistent. While one bomb hit the Japanese defenders, others missed by over 200 yards and contributed to the dying Marines' chaos. An angry Colonel Shoup came on the radio: "Stop strafing. Bombs hitting our own troops."

It was only sheer courage of the survivors that got them ashore under such a hellish crossfire. Major Hays reported to Shoup at 0800 with only half of his landing team. He had taken over three hundred casualties while other men were missing and scattered along the beach and pier. His unit had lost all of its heavy weapons, demolitions, and flamethrowers. Colonel Shoup directed Hays to attack west. Both men knew that small arms and courage would not overtake the Japanese in their fortified positions.

The combined forces of Majors Rudd in Crowe on Red Beach Three were full of fight and had sufficient weapons. Their left flank was flush against three large Japanese bunkers, each mutually supporting each other and unassailable. The stubby pier slightly to the east of the main pier turned into a bloody no-man's-land as the two sides fought for possession. Learning from the mistakes of D-Day, Major Crowe ensured his one surviving Sherman was always accompanied by infantry.

Rudd and Crowe benefited from the intense air support and naval gunfire on their left flank. Crowe was later to write that he was unimpressed with the aviators' effectiveness and accuracy, and that the aircraft never did that much good. But he was enthusiastic about the naval guns: "I had the three destroyers supporting me: the Ringgold, the Daschle, and the Anderson. Anything I asked for, I got. I authorized a direct fire from one of the destroyers in the lagoon at a command bunker only 50 yards ahead of us during the fight. They slammed the fire in there, and you could see arms and legs and everything just go up like that."

Colonel Jordan managed to get some of his troops across the fire-swept airstrip inland from Red Beach Two all the way to the southern coast—making a significant penetration. Their toehold was precarious, and his Marines suffered heavy casualties. He recalled that he could not see the Japanese. Still, the fire came from every direction when Jordan lost contact with his lead elements. Colonel Shoup ordered him across the island to reestablish command. Jordan did so at a significant hazard to himself. By the time his reinforcements arrived, Jordan had only fifty men, who could be accounted for, from his landing team's 2/2 rifle companies. The colonel organized and supplied these men to the best of his abilities. Then, at Shoup's orders, he merged them with the reinforcements and stepped back into his original role as an observer.

SCOUT SNIPER PLATOON

The heroics of the 2nd Marines Scout Sniper Platoon had been spectacular from the start, when they led the assault on the pier, just before H-Hour. 1stLt. Hawkins was an example of having a cool disregard for danger in every tactical situation.

While he displayed superhuman bravery, it would not protect him in the turmoil. A Japanese shell had wounded him on D-Day, and he shook off any attempts to treat his injuries. At dawn on D +1, he led his men in a series of attacks on Japanese strong points. Hawkins crawled up to a pillbox, fired his weapon point-blank through the gun ports, and threw grenades inside to finish the job. He was shot in the chest but continued to attack and took out three more pillboxes personally. Just after that, a Japanese shell tore him apart.

The division mourned his death, and he was awarded the Medal of Honor posthumously. Colonel Shoup recalled: "It's not often that you can credit a first lieutenant with winning a battle, but Lieutenant Hawkins came as near to it as any man possibly could have."

It was now up to Major Ryan and his makeshift battalion on the western side of Betio to make the most considerable contribution to winning the battle. Ryan's fortunes were enhanced by three developments during the night.

1. The Japanese did not counterattack his thin lines.
2. Seabees repaired his medium tank, *Cecilia*.
3. The arrival of a naval gunfire spotter, Lieutenant Thomas Green, with a fully functional radio.

Ryan organized a coordinated attack against the Japanese pillboxes, gun emplacements, and rifle pits concentrated on the island's southwestern corner. Slowed by communication failures, Ryan could talk to the fire support ships but not Shoup. It took hours for his runners to negotiate the fire gauntlet and return with answers from Shoup's CP.

Ryan's first message to Shoup revealed his attack plans but was delayed because Shoup called in an airstrike. After two more runners, the airstrike was canceled, and Ryan called in a naval gunfire strike on the southwest targets. Two of the destroyers in the lagoon responded accurately and promptly. Major Ryan launched a coordinated tank/infantry assault at 1120. In less than an hour, his makeshift force had seized all of Green Beach and was ready to move eastward toward the airfield and attack.

The communications were still awful. Major Ryan twice reported that the southern end of Green Beach was intensely mined. That message reached no higher headquarters. General Smith on the *Maryland* did not receive any direct word of Major Ryan's successes. Smith was delighted when he learned he could land reinforcements on the covered beach and keep the unit integrity intact.

General Smith conferred with Colonel Holmes, commander of the 6th Marines, as to the best way of getting the fresh combat teams into the fight. Due to the heavy casualties taken by Hays' battalion on Red Beach Two, Smith reassessed his landing on an unknown eastern end of the island. Major Ryan's good news quickly solved this problem. Smith ordered Holmes to land one of his battalions by rubber raft on Green Beach and have the second landing team boated in and prepared to wade ashore in support.

General Smith received reports that the Japanese troops were retreating from the eastern end of Betio by wading across to the next islet: Bairiki. The Marines did not want to fight the same deadly enemy twice. Holmes ordered the 2/6 to land on Bairiki and "seal the back door." The 1/6 was ordered to land on Green Beach by rubber boat. The 3/6 was held in reserve and prepared to land at any assigned spot, probably Green Beach. Smith ordered the light tanks of Company B to land on Green Beach, supporting the 6th Marines.

These tactical plans took much longer to execute than envisioned. The 1/6 was waiting and ready to debark when their ship *Feland* was ordered underway because of a submarine threat. It would be hours before the *Feland* could return close enough to Betio and launch the rubber boats and the Higgins tow craft. These light tanks were now among the few critical items not loaded into the transports because they were in the very bottom of the cargo holds. During the first thirty-five hours of the landing, poor loading practices had further scrambled all supplies and equipment into intervening decks. It would take hours to clear the tanks and get them loaded on board.

Frustrated by the long delays, Shoup sent a message at 1345, asking for flamethrowers. He desperately wanted the 1/6 ashore to begin their attack. Colonel Shoup, and his small staff were continually frustrated by logistical support problems. His team organized men to strip the dead of first-aid pouches, canteens, and ammunition. He also organized a shore party to create a false beachhead at the end of the pier.

The primary control officer onboard the minesweeper, *Pursuit*, Captain McGovern, eventually brought order by taking strict control of all unloading supplies. He used the surviving LVTs to keep the shuttle of casualties moving seaward and bring all critical items from the pier head to the beach.

This task was completed by men who hadn't slept in days and worked under constant enemy fire.

TIDE OF BATTLE

The handling of casualties was the most pressing logistical problem on D +1. The 2nd Marine Division was served heroically by its Navy corpsmen and doctors. Over ninety of these medical specialists were casualties in the onshore fighting.

Lieutenant Herman Brukhardt established an emergency room in a captured Japanese bunker. Some of the former occupants came to life, firing their rifles more than once. But, in over thirty-six hours and under brutal conditions, Lieutenant Brukhardt treated 126 wounded men, only losing four.

The casualties were at first evacuated to the far off troopships. Because a long journey was so dangerous and wasteful of the few available LVTs or Higgins boats, the Marines began to deliver casualties to the destroyer *Ringgold* in the lagoon. Even though her sickbay had been destroyed by a 5-inch Japanese shell on D-Day, the destroyer still actively fired in support missions and accepted dozens of casualties.

Admiral Hill dispatched the troopship, *Doyen*, into the lagoon early on D +1 to be used as a primary critical receiving ship. Lieutenant Commander Oliver led a surgical team of five men with recent combat experience from the Aleutian Islands. In three days,

Oliver's team treated over 550 wounded Marines. In his own words: "We'd run out of sodium pentathol and had to use ether. If a bomb would've hit us, Doyen would have blown off the face of the planet."

The Navy chaplains were also hard at work wherever the Marines were fighting onshore. They had heartbreaking work: administering last rites to the dying, consoling the wounded, and praying for the souls of the dead before the bulldozer came to cover the bodies from the unforgiving tropical sun.

The tide of battle now shifted toward the Americans by the middle of the afternoon on D +1. While the fighting was still intense, and Japanese fire deadly, the surviving Marines were now moving. No longer gridlocked in dangerous toeholds, Colonel Rixey's howitzers made a new definition of close-in fire support. Supplies of fresh water and ammunition were improved. Morale was rising. The troops knew the 6th Marines would come in soon. Colonel Rixey later wrote: "I thought up until 1300 today it was touch and go, after that I knew we would win."

Despair spread among the Japanese defenders. While they had shot down Marines at every turn they could—another would appear in his place: rifle blazing, well supported by naval and artillery guns. The great Japanese *Yogaki Plan* was a failure. Only a few enemy aircraft would attack the island every night. American transports were never seriously threatened, and the Japanese fleet never joined the battle. Japanese troops began to commit suicide rather than risk being captured.

Colonel Shoup noticed the shift in momentum. Despite his frustration over the miscommunications and delays, he was in good spirits. He sent a situation report to General Smith at 1600—with a famous last line: "Casualties: many. Percentage dead: unknown. Combat efficiency: We are winning."

At 1655, the 2/6 landed on Bairiki against light opposition. During the night, the 2/10 landed on the same island and began firing its howitzers. Rixey's fire direction center on Betio helped this process. The forward artillery observer, attached to Major Crowe's 2/8 on Red Beach One, adjusted the fire of the Bairiki guns he'd practiced on in New Zealand. General Smith finally had artillery in place on Bairiki.

Meanwhile, the 1/6 were finally on the move. After a day of many false starts, the Marines prepared for their assault mission, which General Smith had changed from the east end to Green Beach. When the *Feland* returned to within a reasonable range, the 1/6 Marines disembarked. They used the tactics developed with the Navy during the rehearsal on Efate. The men loaded onboard the Higgins boat's, which towed their rubber raft to the beach. The Marines embarked on board the rafts with up to ten troops per craft and began the 1,000-yard paddle toward Green Beach.

Major "Willie K." Jones, commander of the 1/6 Marines, later remarked that he did *not* feel like the "admiral of the condom fleet," as he helped paddle his raft shoreward. He noted that his battalion was spread out over the ocean from horizon to horizon. Major Jones was alarmed at the frequent appearance of anti-boat mines moored to the coral heads beneath the surface, endangering his 150 rubber rafts.

His rafts passed over the mines without incident. Jones also had two LVTs accompanying his ship to shore movement, each preloaded with rations, ammo, water, medical supplies, and spare radio equipment. While guided in by the rafts, one of the LVTs made it ashore, but the second drifted into a mine that blew the heavy vehicle ten feet in the air, killed most of the crew, and destroyed all of the supplies. It was a severe but not critical loss. The landing force suffered no other casualties coming ashore, thanks to Major Ryan's men. Jones' battalion was the first to land intact on Betio.

It was well after dark by the time Major Jones assumed his defensive positions behind Major Ryan's lines. The light tanks of Company B continued their attempt to come ashore on Green Beach. Because of the high surf and the distance between the reef, the beach hindered the landing effort. While a platoon of six tanks eventually reached the beach, the rest of the company moved its boats toward the pier and worked all night to get ashore onto Red

Beach Two. The 3/6 Marines remained afloat in Higgins boats beyond the reef for an uncomfortable night.

That evening Colonel Shoup turned to war correspondent Robert Sherrod and said: "We're winning, but the bastards have a lot of bullets left. I think we should clean it all up tomorrow."

After dark, General Smith sent Colonel Edson ashore to command all Betio and Bairiki forces. Colonel Shoup had done a magnificent job, but it was now time for the senior colonel to take command. Edson had two artillery battalions and eight reinforced infantry battalions deployed on the two islands. The 3/6 Marines were scheduled to land early on D +2. Virtually all combat and support elements of the 2nd Marine Division would now be deployed.

Edson found Shoup's command post at 2030. He greeted the barrel-chested warrior still on his feet, haggard and grimy but full of fight. Colonel Edson took command and allowed Colonel Shoup to concentrate on his own reinforced combat team, and they began making plans for the next morning.

Years later, General Julian Smith looked back on the pivotal day of November 21, 1943, and wrote: "We were losing until we won. Many things went wrong, and the Japanese inflicted severe casualties on us, but from this point on, the issue was no longer in doubt at Tarawa."

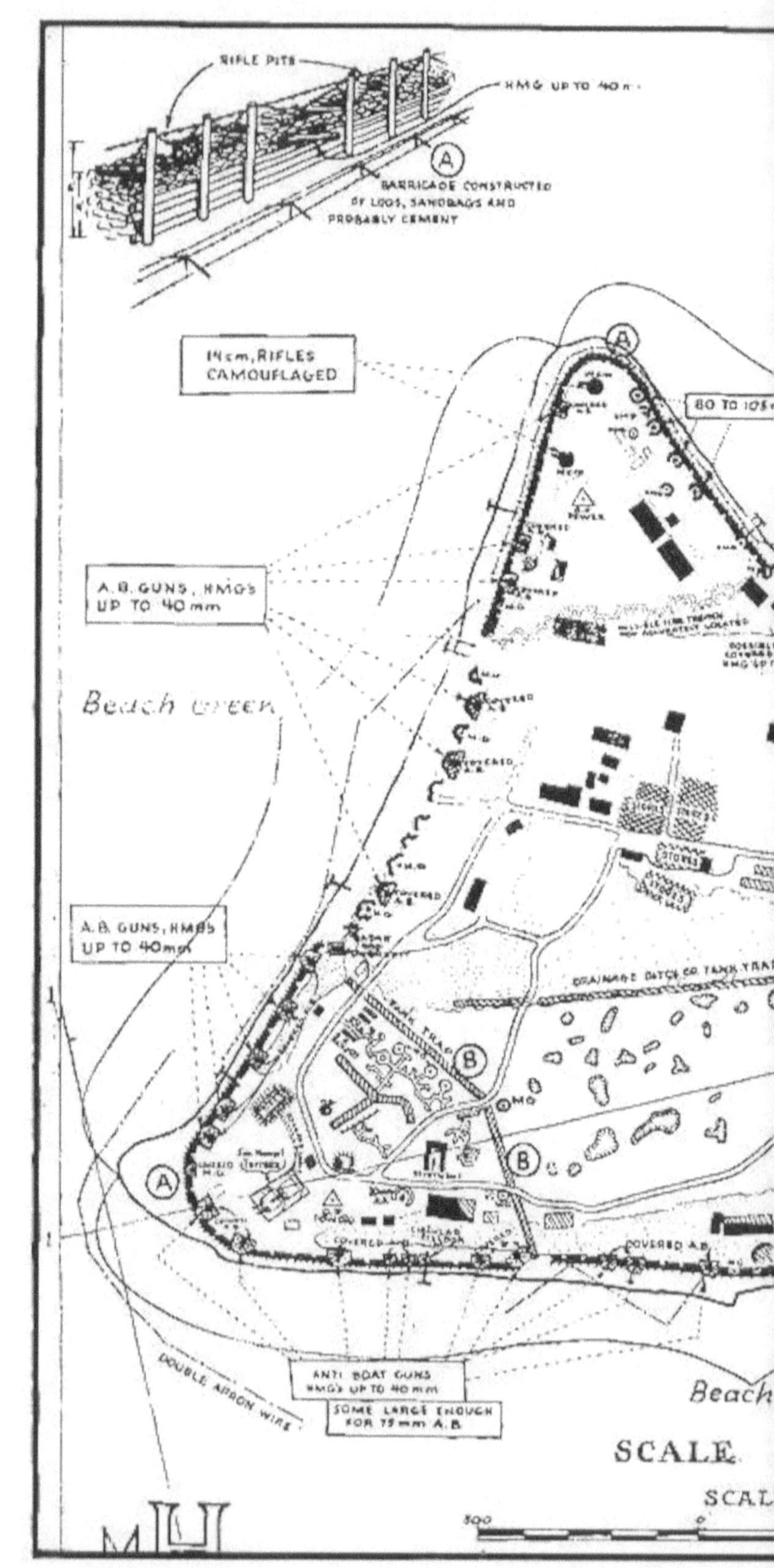

RIFLE PITS
HMG UP TO 40 m
A
BARRICADE CONSTRUCTED OF LOGS, SANDBAGS AND PROBABLY CEMENT
14 cm. RIFLES CAMOUFLAGED
A.B. GUNS, HMG's UP TO 40 mm
A.B. GUNS, HMG's UP TO 40 mm
80 TO 105
Beach Green
DRAINAGE DITCH OR TANK TRAP
TANK TRAP
DOUBLE APRON WIRE
ANTI BOAT GUNS HMG's UP TO 40 mm
SOME LARGE ENOUGH FOR 75 mm A.B.
COVERED A.B.
Beach
SCALE
SCAL
500

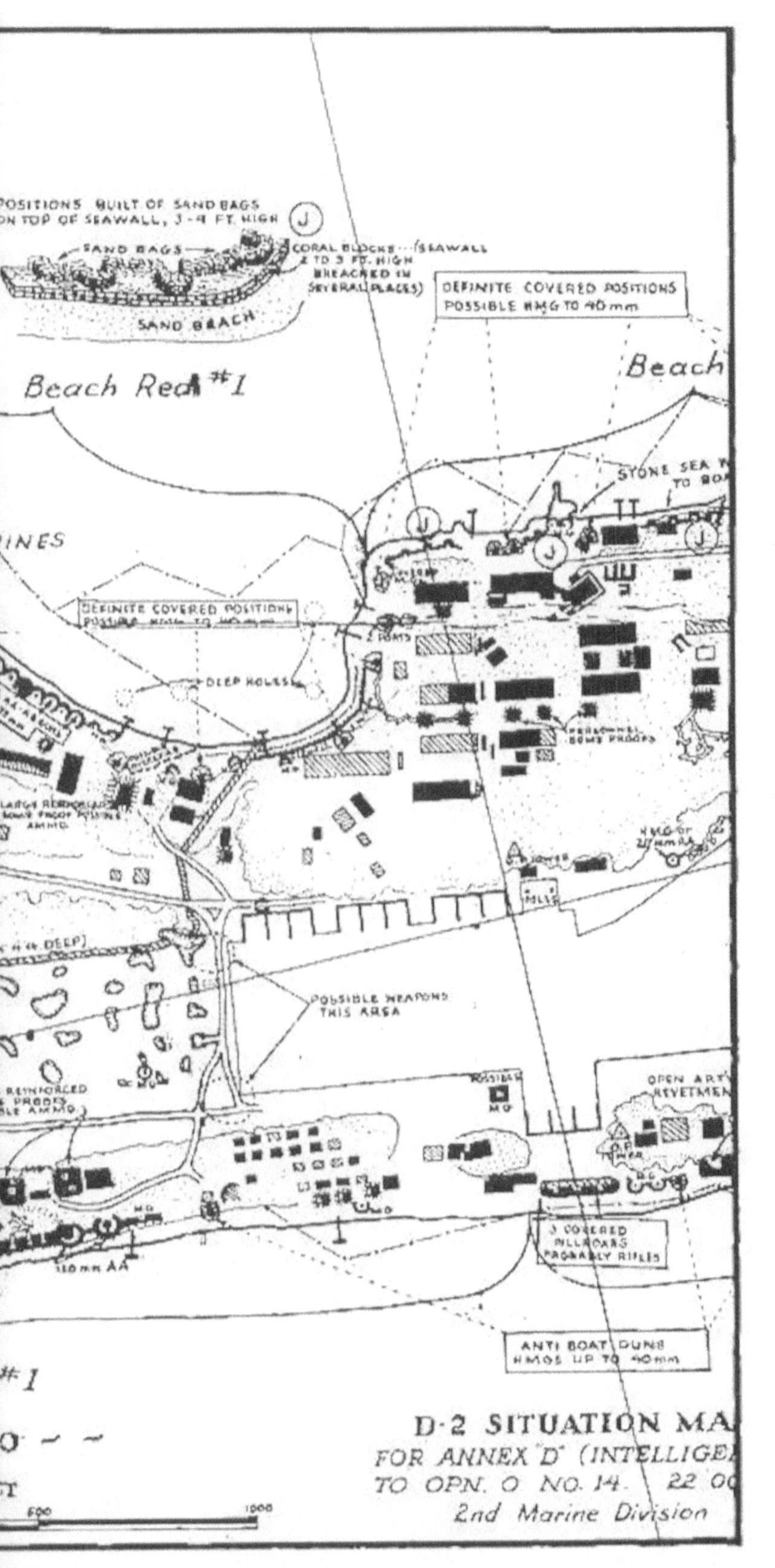

POSITIONS BUILT OF SAND BAGS
ON TOP OF SEAWALL, 3-4 FT. HIGH
SAND BAGS
CORAL BLOCKS (SEAWALL
2 TO 3 FT. HIGH
BREACHED IN
SEVERAL PLACES)
SAND BEACH
DEFINITE COVERED POSITIONS
POSSIBLE HMG TO 40mm
Beach Red #1
Beach
STONE SEA WALL
TO BOAT
J
J
J
RINES
DEFINITE COVERED POSITIONS
POSSIBLE HMG TO 40mm
2 HMGS
DEEP HOLES
PERSONNEL
BOMB PROOFS
AA REVETMENTS
HMG OR
2/18mm AA
LARGE REINFORCED
BOMB PROOF POSITION
AMMO.
TOWER
MLLS
POSSIBLE WEAPONS
THIS AREA
H (4' DEEP)
POSSIBLE
MG
OPEN ART
REVETMENT
REINFORCED
E PROOF
LE AMMO.
O.P.
AREA
MG
MG
3 COVERED
PILLBOXES
PROBABLY RIFLES
110 mm AA
ANTI BOAT GUNS
HMGS UP TO 40 mm
#1
D-2 SITUATION MAP
FOR ANNEX "D" (INTELLIGENCE)
TO OPN. O NO. 14.   22 0
2nd Marine Division
500   1000

D +2 AT BETIO

War correspondent Keith Wheeler from *the Chicago Daily News* sent this dispatch from Tarawa on D +2: "It looks like the Marines are winning on this blood-soaked, bomb-hammered, stinking little island."

Colonel Edson's plan of attack on D +2 was to have the 1/6 Marines attack eastward along south beach and link up with the 1/2 and 2/2. He issued his attack orders at 0400 and attached the 1/8 to the 2nd Division Marines. They were to attack at daylight to the west along north beach and eliminate all Japanese resistance pockets between Red Beach One and Two. After that, the 1/8 would continue the attack east.

Edson arranged for air support and naval gunfire to strike the eastern end of the island at twenty-minute intervals throughout the morning. The 3/6 Marines were still embarked at the line of departure and would await Colonel Shoup's call on Green Beach.

The key to the success of this plan was an eastward attack by fresh troops from Major Jones' landing team. Colonel Edson could not raise the 1/6 on any radio net and sent his assistant division operations officer, Major Tompkins, to deliver the attack order in person to Jones. Major Tompkins' odyssey from the command post to Green Beach took over three hours. He was almost shot, several times, by Japanese snipers and nervous American sentries. The radio net started to work again just before Tompkins reached the 1/6 Marines. Major Jones later wrote he never told Tompkins he already had the attack order when the exhausted messenger arrived.

Major Hays promptly launched his attack at 0700 on Red Beach Two. He attacked westward on a three company front. His engineers used Bangalore torpedoes and satchel charges to neutralize many inland Japanese positions. But the strongpoints along the re-entrant were a deadly and veritable hornet's nest. Light Marine tanks made courageous frontal attacks against the Japanese fortifications. The tanks fired their 37mm guns point-blank at the Japanese fortifications, but were inadequate for the task. One tank was destroyed because of enemy fire, and the other two withdrew. Major Hays called for a section of 75mm half-tracks. One half-track was lost instantly, but the others used their more massive guns to considerable advantage.

The left flank and center companies curved around behind the main Japanese strongpoints, cutting the enemy off from the rest of the island. Along the beach, the progress was measured in yards. A small Japanese party tried a sortie from the strong points against the Marine lines. Now the Marines were finally given actual targets in the open—they cut the Japanese down in short order.

Major Jones made his final preparations for the assault to the east on Green Beach, with the 1/6 Marines. He had access to several light tanks available from the platoon that came ashore the prior evening. Major Jones preferred the medium tanks' effectiveness and borrowed two medium battle-scarred Sherman's from Ryan for the assault. Major Jones ordered the tanks to range no further than fifty yards ahead of his lead company. He personally kept in radio contact with the tank commander. Jones assigned a platoon of .30-caliber water-cooled machine guns to each rifle company and attached combat engineers with flamethrowers and demolition squads. Due to the nature of the terrain and the necessity for giving Major Hays' battalion a wide berth, Jones constrained his attack to a zone of only one-hundred yards wide. In his words:

"This was one of the most unusual tactics I'd ever heard of. As I moved to the east on one side of the airfield, Larry Hays moved to the west of me, exactly opposite."

Major Jones' plan was well executed. He had the advantage of a fresh tactical unit in place with integrated supporting arms. The 1/6 Marine landing team made rapid progress along the south coast, killing over two hundred Japanese defenders. American casualties were light at this point, and he reached the thin lines held by the 2/2 and the 1/2 in less than three hours.

Colonel Shoup called Major Jones to his command post at 1100 to brief him on the afternoon plan of action. Major Jones' XO, Major Francis Beamer, was to take and replace the lead rifle company. Enemy resistance had stiffened, and the company commander had just been shot and killed by a sniper. The oppressive heat was taking its toll on the Marines. While Beamer made superhuman efforts to get more salt tablets and water for his men, several of his troops had fallen out and become victims of heatstroke. First Sergeant Lewis Michelony later wrote: "Tarawa's sands were as white as snow and as hot as red white ashes from a heated furnace."

On Green Beach, only 800 yards behind the 1/6 Marines, the landing team of the 3/6 Marines streamed to shore. While the landing took several hours to execute, it was uncontested. Not until 1100 did Jones' lead elements link up with the 2nd Marines before the 3/6 were fully established onshore.

The 8th Marines attack order was the same as the previous day: attack Japanese strong points to the east. These obstacles were just as difficult on D +2. Three of the Japanese fortifications were especially formidable:

1. A steel pillbox near the contested pier
2. A large bombproof shelter further inland
3. A coconut log emplacement with multiple machine guns

All three obstacles had been designed by the master engineer, Admiral Saichiro. These strongpoints, mutually supported by fire and observation, had effectively contained the combined Marine forces of the 3/8 and the 2/8 since the assault on D-Day.

Major Crowe reorganized his tired forces into another assault. The former marksmanship instructor got cans of lubricating oil out and made his troops field strip and clean their M1s before the attack. Crowe placed his Battalion XO, Major William Chamberlin, in the center of the three attacking. Chamberlin was a former college economics professor and was no less dynamic than his red mustached commander. Still nursing a painful wound in his shoulder received at D-Day, Chamberlin was a major player in the repetitive assaults against the three Japanese strong points. First Sergeant Michelony later wrote about Chamberlin: "He was a wild man, a guy anybody would be willing to follow."

Chamberlin took his mortar crew and scored a direct hit on top of the coconut log emplacement at 0930. He penetrated the bunker and detonated the ammunition stocks. It was a stroke of great fortune for the Marines. At the same time, the medium tank *Colorado* penetrated the steel pillbox with its 75mm guns. Now, two of the three emplacements were overrun.

The massive bombproof shelter was still lethal. Flanking attacks were getting shot to pieces before they could gather any momentum. The solution was to get to the top of the sand-covered mound and drop thermite grenades or explosives down the air vents to force the Japanese outside. This formidable task went to Major Chamberlin, Lieutenant Alexander Bonnyman, and a squad of combat engineers.

Machine gunners and riflemen opened up a sheet of fire against the strongpoint's firing ports. Bonnyman led a small band and raced across the sands up the steep slope. The Japanese knew they were in mortal danger. Dozens of them poured out of the rear entrance, attacking the Marines on top. A Marine stepped forward and emptied his flamethrower into the onrushing Japanese—then charged them with an M1 carbine. The Marine was shot dead and his body rolled down the slope. But other Marines were inspired to overcome the Japanese counterattack.

The remaining combat engineers rushed to place explosives

against the rear entrances. Hundreds of demoralized Japanese broke out in panic and fled eastward; the Marines shot them to pieces. The tank crew fired one "dream shot" canister round. It killed at least twenty Japanese.

Lieutenant Bonnyman's bravery resulted in a posthumous Medal of Honor. The third to be awarded to the Marines on Betio. His single-handed sacrifice almost ended the stalemate on Red Beach Three. There's no coincidence that two of these highest awards were received by combat engineers. The bravery and courage under fire represented hundreds of other engineers on only a slightly less spectacular basis. Almost an entire third of the combat engineers who landed in support of the 2/8 ended up as casualties. According to Second Lieutenant Beryl W. Rentel, the surviving combat engineers used: "Eight cases of TNT, eight cases of gelatin dynamite, and two 54-pound blocks of TNT to destroy Japanese fortifications. The engineers used an entire case of dynamite and both large blocks of TNT to destroy the large bombproof shelter alone."

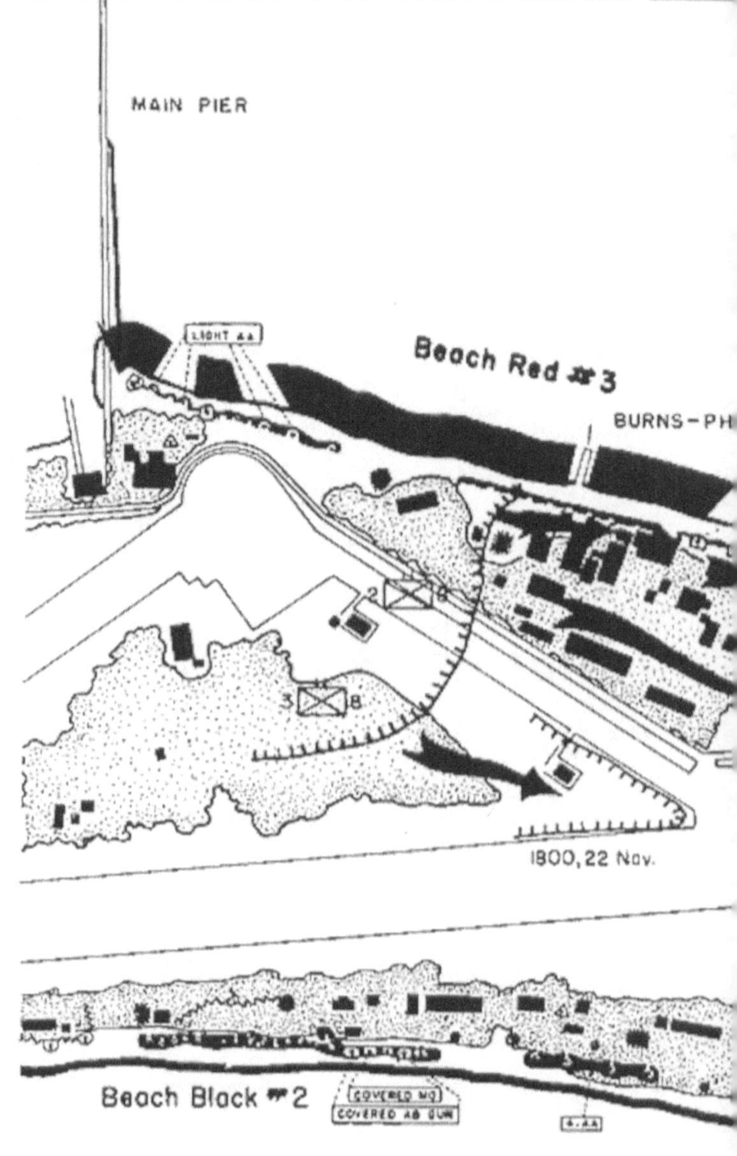

MAIN PIER
Beach Red № 3
LIGHT AA
BURNS-PH
2
3 8
1800, 22 Nov.
Beach Black № 2
COVERED MG
COVERED AA GUN
AA AA
BETIO
TARAWA ATOLL, GILBERT ISLANDS
ATTACK OF THE 2d BN., 8th MARINES
NOV 22, 1943
100   0   100   200   300   400 Yds.
TAKEN FROM 2d BN 8th MARINES
SPECIAL ACTION REPORT.
RD 5890

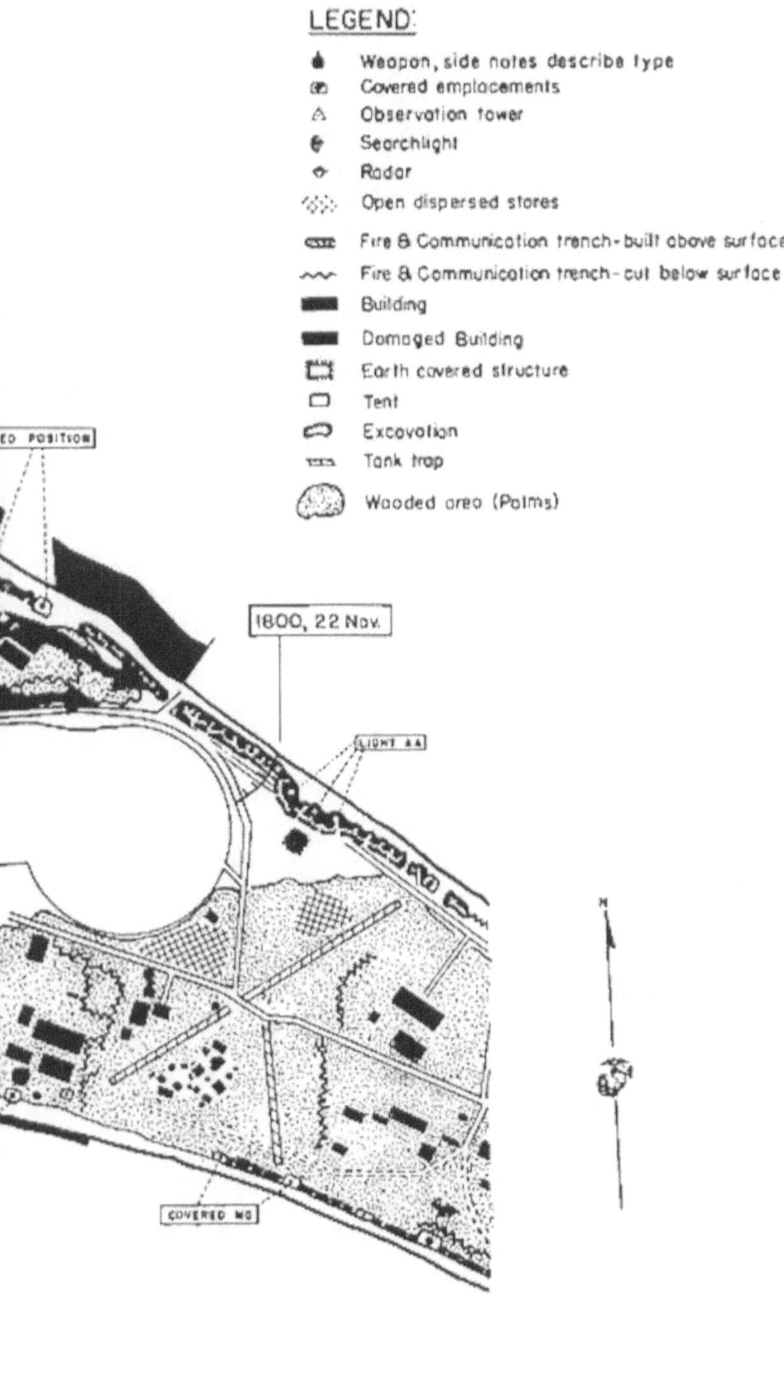

LEGEND:
Weapon, side notes describe type
Covered emplacements
Observation tower
Searchlight
Radar
Open dispersed stores
Fire & Communication trench-built above surface
Fire & Communication trench-cut below surface
Building
Damaged Building
Earth covered structure
Tent
Excavation
Tank trap
Wooded area (Palms)
RED POSITION
1800, 22 Nov.
LIGHT AA
COVERED MG
N

STRONG RESISTANCE

During the chaotic, murderous fighting in the 8th Marines' zone, Admiral Shibasaki was killed in his blockhouse. The unyielding Japanese commander's failure to provide any backup communications to the above-ground wires, which were destroyed during the preliminary D-Day bombardment, kept him from influencing the battle. The Imperial Japanese archives showed that Shibasaki transmitted one last message to Tokyo early in the morning on D +2: "Our weapons have been destroyed. From now on, everyone is attempting the final charge. May Japan exist for 10,000 years."

General Julian Smith arrived on Green Beach just before noon. Smith conferred with Major Ryan and observed the deployment of the 3/6 Marines inland. General Smith realized he was far removed from the main action toward the center of the island. He returned to his landing craft and ordered the coxswain to make for the pier. It was here that the commanding general received his rude welcome to Betio.

Major Hays' 1/8 Marines were besieging the Japanese strongpoints at the re-entrant. But the Japanese defenders still had control over the approaches to Red Beaches One and Two. The defenders' well-aimed machine gun fire disabled Smith's boat and killed his coxswain. The other occupants of his group leaped over the gunwale and into the water. Major Tompkins, the right man in the right place, waded through Japanese fire for a half-mile to find the general another LVT. This LVT drew fire and wounded the coxswain, further alarming the remaining occupants. General Smith did not reach Colonel Edson and Shoup's combined command post until 1400.

In the meantime, Colonel Edson had assembled his commanders and issued orders to continue the attack to the east that afternoon. The 1/6 Marines would continue along the narrowing south coast, supported by the howitzers and all available tanks from the 1/10. Colonel Hall would lead two battalions of the 8th Marines and continue advancing along the north coast. Air support and naval gunfire would blast the areas for two hours in advance.

Colonel Hall spoke up about his exhausted and decimated Marine landing teams. They'd been in direct contact and ashore since D-Day morning. He told Edson the two landing teams had enough strength for only one more assault, and then they must get relieved.

Colonel Edson promised to exchange the exhausted 2/8 Marines with the fresh 2/6 Marines on Bairiki at the first opportunity after this assault.

The 1/6 Marines started their attack at 1330. They ran into heavy opposition. They took deadly fire from heavy Japanese weapons mounted in turret type emplacements near the south beach. While this took ninety minutes to overcome, the light tanks were brave but ineffective. It took sustained 75mm fire, from two Sherman medium tanks, to neutralize the Japanese emplacements. Resistance was fierce throughout the zone, and the 1/6 Marines' casualties mounted. They'd taken eight-hundred-yards of enemy territory quickly in the morning, but by the long afternoon had attained half that distance.

The 8th Marines, after having destroyed their three bunker nemesis, made excellent progress at first, but then ran out of steam after they passed the eastern end of the airfield. Colonel Shoup was right in his estimation that the Japanese defenders, while leaderless, still had plenty of bullets and fight left.

Major Crowe reorganized his leading elements into defensive positions for the night. He placed one company north of the airfield. The end of the airstrip was covered by fire, but unmanned.

On nearby Bairiki Island, the 2/10 Marines fired artillery missions to support Major Crowe. Company B of the 2nd Medical Battalion established a field hospital, handling the overflow of casualties. The 2/6 Marines, eager to get into the fight, waited in vain for boats to move them onto Green Beach. Landing craft were mostly unavailable. They were crammed with miscellaneous supplies as the transports and cargo ships continued a general unloading—regardless of the troops' needs ashore. Navy Seabees on Betio were already repairing the airstrip with bulldozers, under enemy fire. Occasionally, Marines would call in for help from the Seabees to seal up a bothersome bunker. A bulldozer would arrive and do the job nicely.

Shore party Marines and Navy beachmasters on the pier kept the supplies coming in and the wounded going out. Colonel Edson requested a working party at 1552 to clear bodies from around the pier that hindered shore party operations. Later that afternoon the first Jeep got ashore. A wild ride along the pier with every remaining Japanese sniper trying to shoot the driver. War correspondent Sherrod commented: "If a sign of certain victory was needed, this is it. The jeeps have arrived."

One of Colonel Hall's Navajo Indian code-talkers had been mistaken for a Japanese and was shot. This was because of the strain of the prolonged battle. A derelict, blackened LVT drifted onshore filled with dead Marines. At the bottom of the pile was one Marine who was still alive. Still breathing, after two-and-a-half days of an unrelenting hell. He looked up and gasped, "Water. Pour some water on my face, will you?"

Shoup, Edson, and Smith were near exhaustion. While the third day on Betio had been a day of spectacular gains, progress was excruciatingly slow. And the end was not in sight. General Smith sent this report to General Hermle, who had taken his place on the

Maryland: "Situation not favorable for rapid cleanup on Betio. Heavy casualties among officers make leadership difficult. Still strong resistance. Many emplacements intact on eastern end of the island. Japanese strong points westward of our front lines within our position have not been reduced. Progress costly and slow. Complete occupation will take at least five days more. Air and naval bombardment a great help but does not take out emplacements."

General Smith took command of operations at 1930. He had seven thousand Marines onshore fighting against one thousand Japanese defenders. Aerial photographs showed many defensive positions were still intact on Betio's eastern tail. Smith believed he would need the entire 6th Marines to complete the job. At 2100 the 6th Marines landed. Smith called a meeting to assign orders for D +3.

The 3/6 Marines would pass through the lines of Major Jones' 1/6 Marines to have a fresh Battalion lead the eastward assault. The 2/6 Marines would land on Green Beach and move east to support the 3/6. All available tanks would be assigned to the 3/6. Colonel Shoup's 2nd Marines, with the 1/8 still attached, would continue to assault the Japanese re-entrant strongpoints. The remaining 8th Marines would be shuttled to Bairiki. The 4/10 would land its heavy 105mm guns on Green Beach to increase the howitzer battalions' firepower that was already in action.

Imperial Japanese soldiers began vicious counterattacks during the nights of D +2 and D +3. Major Jones believed his exposed forces would be the target for any *Banzai* attacks and took his precautions. He gathered his artillery forward observers and naval fire control spotters. Jones arranged for field artillery support starting from seventy-five yards from his front lines to 500 yards out, where naval gunfire would take over. Major Jones put Company A to the left of the airstrip and Company B on the right along the south shore; while he worried about the 150-yard gap across the runway to Company C, he realized there was no solution. Jones used a tank to bring up stockpiles of small arms ammunition, grenades, and water to be kept fifty yards behind the lines.

At 1930, the first Japanese counterattack began. Fifty Japanese soldiers snuck past Major Jones' outposts through thick vegetation and penetrated the border between the two companies south of the airstrip. Major Jones' reserve force was composed of his headquarters' cooks, bakers, and admin people. They contained the penetration and killed many Japanese in the two hours of close-in fighting. Direct and intense fire from the howitzers of the 1/10 and 2/10 stopped the Japanese from reinforcing their penetration. By 2130, the lines were stabilized, and Jones placed a company one hundred yards to the rear of his lines. All he had left was a composite force of forty Marines.

At 2300, the Japanese attacked Jones' lines again. They made a loud disturbance across from Company A's lines. Clinking canteens against their helmets, taunting Marines and screaming *Banzai*, while a second force attacked Company B in a silent rush. The Marines repelled this attack but used their machine guns, revealing their positions. Major Jones requested a full company from the 3/6 to reinforce the 2nd Marines to the rear of the fighting.

The third attack came at 0300. The Japanese moved multiple 7.7mm machine guns into nearby wrecked trucks and opened fire on Marine weapons positions. Major Jones called for star shell illumination from the destroyers in the lagoon. A Marine sergeant crawled forward against this oncoming fire to lob grenades into the improvised machine-gun nests. This did the job and silenced the battlefield once again.

Three hundred Japanese launched a frenzied attack at 0400 against the same two Marine companies. The Marines repulsed them with every available weapon. Japanese soldiers were caught in a murderous crossfire from the 10th Marine howitzers. Two destroyers in the lagoon, *Sigsbee* and *Schroeder*, opened up on the Japanese flanks. Waves of screaming attackers took vicious casualties but kept coming. Groups of men locked together in bloodied hand-to-hand combat. PFC Jack Stambaugh of Company B killed three Japanese soldiers with his bayonet before an officer beheaded him with a samurai sword. Another Marine jumped in and knocked out the Japanese officer with his rifle butt. The acting commander of Company B, First Lieutenant Norman Thomas, reached Major Jones on the field phone and said: "We're killing them as fast as they come at us, but we can't hold out much longer. We need reinforcements."

Major Jones replied: "We haven't got them. You've got to hold."

The Marines lost 42 dead and 114 wounded in the wild fighting —but they held. In less than an hour, it was all over. The supporting arms never stopped shooting down the Japanese, either attacking or retreating. Both destroyers emptied their magazines of 5-inch shells. The 1/10 Marines fired over 1,400 rounds that night. As dawn broke, Marines counted over 200 dead Japanese within fifty yards of their lines. An additional 130 bodies laid beyond that range, badly mangled by naval and artillery gunfire. Other bodies laid scattered throughout the Marine lines. Major Jones had to blink back his tears of pride and grief as he walked his lines. One of his Marines grabbed his arm and said: "They told us we had to hold, and by God, we did."

COMPLETING THE TASK

Japanese counterattacks during the nights of November 22 and 23 broke the back of their defense. If they'd remained in their bunkers until the bitter end, the enemy could have taken a higher toll of Marine lives. Rather than facing an inevitable defeat, over 600 Japanese soldiers chose to die by taking an offensive night action.

After the bloody counterattacks during the night, the 2nd Marine Division still had over five more hours of tough fighting on Betio before the island could be conquered. Later in the morning General Smith sent this report to Admiral Hill on the *Maryland*: "Enemy counterattack was defeated decisively. Last night destroyed bulk of hostile resistance. Expect complete annihilation of all enemy on Betio this date. Recommend you and staff come ashore to get information on type of hostile resistance which will be encountered in future operations."

After a preliminary bombardment, the fresh troops of the 3/6 Marines weaved through Major Jones' lines and began their attack to the east. The Marine assault tactics were now well refined. The 3/6 Marines made rapid progress, led by tanks and combat engineers with flamethrowers and high explosives. Only one well-armed bunker, along the north shore, provided any substantial opposition.

The 3/6 Marines took advantage of the heavy brush along the south shore and bypassed the obstacle. They left one rifle company to encircle and eventually overrun it. Momentum was with the Marines. The remaining Japanese troops seemed dispirited. By 1300, the 3/6 reached the eastern tip of Betio and inflicted over five hundred Japanese casualties at the loss of only thirty-four Marines.

Lieutenant Colonel MacLeod sent a report that summarized the Japanese defenders' collapse in the eastern zone that followed their counterattacks: "At no time was there any determined defensive. We used flamethrowers and could've used more. Medium tanks were excellent. Light tanks did not fire one shot."

The hardest fighting of the fourth day was on the border of Red Beach One and Two. Colonel Shoup directed the combined forces of the 1/8 and 3/2 against the re-entrant strongpoint. The Japanese in these positions were the most disciplined and deadliest on the island. In these bunkers, Japanese anti-boat gunners had thoroughly disrupted over four different battalions' landings and almost killed General Smith the day before. The seaward approaches to the strongpoints were littered with bloated bodies and destroyed LVTs.

Major Hays finally received his flamethrowers and began the attack with the 1/8 from the east, making steady—painstaking progress. Major Schoettel was eager to atone for what may have been perceived as a lackluster performance on D-Day. Schoettel attacked and pressed the assault with troops from the 3/2 from the west and south. Completing the circle, Colonel Shoup ordered a platoon of infantry and two 75mm half-tracks out to the reef, keeping the enemy pinned down from the lagoon.

The exhausted Japanese defenders either fought to the end or committed *hara-kiri*. The 1/8 Marines had been attacking this forti-fied strongpoint ever since the bloodied landing on the morning of D +1. In only forty-eight hours, the 1/8 Marines fired over 55,000 rounds of .30-caliber rifle ammo. The real damage was done by the engineers' special weapons, and by direct fire from the 75mm half-tracks. After the Marines captured the largest concrete pillbox posi-tion near the beach, they could approach the remaining bunkers more safely. It was all over by 1300.

When the fighting was still underway, a Navy fighter plane landed on Betio's airstrip and weaved around the Seabee trucks. Marines rushed over to the aircraft to shake the pilot's hand.

At 1245, Admiral Hill and his staff came ashore. The senior naval officers were impressed by the great strength of the Japanese bunker system. They realized the need to reorganize bombardment strategies. Hill praised the Marines for making such a landing and called Betio a "little Gibraltar."

When Colonel Shoup reported to General Smith that the ultimate objectives had been seized, Smith shared the excellent news with Admiral Hill. Between them, they had worked together to achieve this victory. They drafted a message to Admiral Turner and General Holland Smith announcing the end of organized resistance on Betio.

Working parties were organized to identify the dead. Many of the bodies were so severely shattered or burned that it was difficult to distinguish between friend and foe. The stench and decay of death was overwhelming. War correspondent Robert Sherrod wrote: "Betio would be more habitable if the Marines could leave for a few days, and the million buzzards swirling overhead could finish their work."

Chaplains accompanied burial teams equipped with bulldozers. Administrative staff worked diligently to prepare accurate casualty lists. Even more casualties were expected in mop-up operations over the surrounding islands including Apamama, also known as Abemama Atoll. A distressing report was issued that over one-hundred Marines were missing. The changing tides swept many bodies of the assault troops out to sea. One of the first pilots ashore reported seeing dozens of floating corpses miles away over the horizon.

The Japanese defenders were nearly annihilated in the battle. The Marines, supported by carrier aviation, naval gunfire, and Army Air Force units, killed 98% of the 4,836 enemy troops on Betio during the assault. Only seventeen Japanese soldiers were taken prisoner. The only Japanese officer captured in the fighting was Kiyoshi Ota. A thirty-year-old ensign in the *7th Sasebo Special Landing Force*, from Nagasaki. Ensign Ota recounted that the Japanese garrison had expected landings along the southwest sectors instead of the northern beaches. He also believed the reef would have protected the Japanese defenders during the low tide.

Before General Julian Smith announced the Marines' victory at Betio, General Ralph Smith, his Army counterpart, reported: "Makin Taken." In three days of hard fighting over on Butaritari Island, the Army had wiped out the Japanese garrison at the cost of 204 American casualties.

Many exhausted and grimy Marines on Betio had been awake since the night before the landing. Captain Carl Hoffman later wrote in his memoirs: "There was no way to rest. There was virtually no way to eat. Most of it was close, hand-to-hand fighting, and survival for three and a half days. One of my men mixed me a canteen full of hot water, coffee, chocolate, sugar, he gave it to me and told me he thought I needed something. It was the best meal I'd ever had."

Marines were surrounded by the devastation on Betio after the fighting. Chaplain Willard walked along Red Beach One, now finally clear of enemy pillboxes, and scratched out a note to his wife: *"I'm on Tarawa in the midst of the worst destruction I've ever seen. Walking along the shore, I counted seventy-six dead Marines staring up at me, half in and half out of the water. An LVT is jammed against the seawall barricade. Three waterlogged Marines lay dead beneath it. Four others are scattered nearby, and there is one hanging on a 2-foot high strand of barbed wire who doesn't even touch the coral flat at all. What I see in this god-awful place I am certain is one of the greatest works of ruin wrought by any man."*

Japanese forces in the Gilbert Islands took a bloody toll from the Marine invasion force. Japanese submarines arrived in the area during D +2. The *I-175* sunk the carrier *Liscome Bay* with a torpedo as the sun rose on November 24 off of Makin. A horrific explosion —the flash was seen at Tarawa, over 90 miles away—the ship sank quickly, taking 644 souls with her to the bottom.

The Marines conducted a flag-raising ceremony later that same morning. There were few surviving palm trees to select as a flagpole. A field musician played the bugle calls, and Marines all over the island stood and saluted. Each reckoning the cost.

More good news came from the V Amphibious Corps Reconnaissance Company. They had landed on Apamama by rubber rafts from the submarine *Nautilus*. On the night of November 21, while the small Japanese garrison kept the scouts at bay, the *Nautilus* surfaced and fired its deck guns, killing many Japanese defenders— the rest committed *hara-kiri*. After the island was deemed secure, the 3/6 Marines took control of Apamama until other defense forces could arrive.

On November 24, amphibious transports entered the lagoon and loaded Marine combat teams 2 and 8. Many Marines believed going back to a ship, after the carnage of Betio, was like going to heaven. Navy personnel were generous and kind. The Marines were treated to a full-scale turkey dinner served by Navy officers. Many Marines still suffered from post-combat trauma.

The 2nd and 8th Marines were on their way to Hawaii, while the 3/6 Marines were on their way to Apamama. The 2/6 Marines were beginning their long trek through the other islands of the

Tarawa atoll. Under Jones, the 1/6 Marines were the last infantry unit on Betio. Their work was tedious and heartbreaking. They buried the dead, flushed out the last of the diehard snipers, and hosted visiting dignitaries.

General Holland Smith, the V Amphibious Corps commander, flew to Betio on November 24. He spent an emotional afternoon viewing the death and destruction with General Julian Smith. General Holland Smith was shaken by what he'd seen and the Marines' sacrifices on the island. He concluded: "The sight of our dead Marines floating in the waters of the lagoon and lying along the blood-caked beaches is one I will never forget. Over the pitted, blasted island hung a miasma of coral dust and death, nauseating and horrifying."

The generals came upon one site that moved all of them to tears. A dead Marine leaned against a seawall, his arm upright from his body weight. Just beyond his upraised hand on top of the seawall was a blue-and-white flag. A beach marker to direct succeeding waves where to land. General Holland Smith cleared his throat and said, "How can men like that ever be defeated?"

Company D of the 2nd Tank battalion was the designated scout company for Tarawa's 2nd Marine Division. Elements of these scouts had landed on the Buota and Eita Islands while the fighting raged on Betio. The scouts discovered a sizable Japanese force. On November 23, the 3/10 Marines landed on Eita. The battalion's howitzers were initially intended to increase support fire on Betio. When the island finally fell, the artillery turned their guns to support the 2/6 clearing out the rest of the islets in the Tarawa Atoll.

At 0500 on November 24, the 2/6 Marine landing team under Colonel Murray boarded boats from Betio and landed on Buota. Murray moved his Marines at a fierce pace, wading across the sand-spits that joined the succeeding islands. Murray learned from friendly natives that a Japanese infantry force of 175 waited ahead on the larger island of Buariki. The lead elements of the 2/6 caught up with the enemy on November 26. After a sharp fire exchange in thick vegetation, Murray pulled his troops back. He positioned his forces for an all-out assault in the morning.

The November 27, Battle of Buariki was the last engagement in the Gilberts. It was no less deadly than the preceding encounter with the *Special Naval Landing Forces*. Colonel Murray assaulted the Japanese defensive positions at dawn. He received supporting fire from Battery G before the lines became too intermingled in the melee.

The fighting was not unlike Guadalcanal: hand-to-hand brawling in the tangled underbrush. The Japanese did not have the elaborate defenses found on Betio. But the Imperial Naval soldiers took advantage of as much cover and concealment as they could. They made every shot count and fought to the death. All 175 of them were killed. Colonel Murray's victory came at a high cost. 32 Marines killed and 60 more wounded. The next day, the Marines crossed to the last islet and found no more Japanese defenders. General Julian Smith announced on November 28 that the remaining enemy forces on Tarawa had been wiped out.

Admiral Nimitz had arrived on Betio just before General Julian Smith's announcement. Nimitz noted that the primary Japanese defenses were still intact. He had his staff diagnose the exact construction methods the Japanese used. In less than a month, an identical set of pillboxes and bunkers were built on naval bombardment islands in the Hawaiian island chain.

Admiral Nimitz presented a few of the many to come combat awards to the 2nd Division Marines. The Presidential Unit Citation was awarded to the entire division. Colonel Shoup received the Medal of Honor. Major Crowe and his XO, Major Chamberlin, received the Navy Cross, as well as Colonel Amey, Major Ryan, and Corporal Spillane--the LVT crew chief and St. Louis Cardinals prospect, who caught the Japanese hand grenades in midair on D-Day before his luck ran out.

While some senior officers were jealous of Colonel Shoup's Medal of Honor, General Julian Smith knew whose strong shoulders carried the critical first thirty-six hours of the assault. Shoup recorded in his combat notebook: "With God and the Navy in support of the 2nd Marine Division, there was never any doubt that we would take Betio. For several hours, however, there was a considerable haggling over the exact price we would pay for it."

SIGNIFICANCE OF TARAWA

The high cost of the battle for Tarawa was twofold: the Marine casualties in the assault, followed by the nation's despair and shock after hearing the battle reports. At first, the gains seemed small. The "stinking little island" of Betio was eight thousand miles away from Tokyo. But the practical lessons learned in the complexity of amphibious assault outweighed the initial public outrage.

Casualty figures for the 2nd Marine Division and Operation Galvanic were 3,407. There were 1,027 dead Marines and sailors. An additional 88 Marines were missing and presumed dead, and 2,292 Marines and sailors wounded. Guadalcanal's campaign cost a similar number of Marine casualties—but spread over six months.

Tarawa losses happened in 76 hours. The killed to wounded ratio at Tarawa was excessive and reflected the savagery of the fighting. Overall, the casualties among the Marines engaged in the fight was around 19%. A steep but *acceptable* price. Many battalions suffered much higher losses. The 2nd Amphibian Tractor Battalion lost half of their men. This battalion also lost 35 of the 125 LVTs on Betio.

Headlines of "The Bloody Beaches of Tarawa" alarmed the American public. This was partially the Marines' own doing. Many combat correspondents were invited along for Operation Galvanic. They had shared the worst of what Betio had to offer in the first thirty-six hours. They only reported what they had observed. Marine Sergeant James Lucas, whose account of the fighting received front-page coverage in both *The New York Times* and *The Washington Post* on December 4, 1943, read: "Grim Tarawa Defense a Surprise, Eyewitness of Battle Reveals; Marines Went in Chuckling, To Find Swift Death Instead of Easy Conquest."

Remarks made by senior Marines involved in Operation Galvanic to the media did little to help soothe public concerns. General Holland Smith likened the assault on D-Day to Pickett's charge at Gettysburg. Colonel Edson said the assault force "paid the stiffest price in human life per square yard" at Tarawa than any other engagement in the Marine Corps' history. War correspondent Robert Sherrod wrote of seeing one-hundred Marines gunned down in the water in five minutes on D +1. It did not help when the Marine Corps headquarters waited an additional ten days after the battle to release the casualty list.

The atmospheres at Pearl Harbor and Washington were tense during this period. General Douglas MacArthur was still bitter that the 2nd Marine Division had been taken from his Southwest Pacific Command. He wrote to the Secretary of War and complained that "these frontal attacks by the Navy, like Tarawa, were unnecessary and a tragic massacre of American lives."

American mothers wrote letters by the hundreds, one accusing Admiral Nimitz of "murdering her son."

Frank Knox, the secretary of the Navy, called a press conference in which he blamed a "sudden shift in the wind" for exposing the reef and preventing reinforcements from landing. Congress began a special investigation. Fortunately, the Marines had General Vandegrift in Washington as the newly appointed 18th Commandant. Vandegrift, a highly decorated and widely respected veteran of Guadalcanal, reassured Congress and pointed out that "Tarawa was an assault from beginning to end."

The casualty reports were less extraordinary than the American public expected. In an editorial by *The New York Times* on December

27, 1943, the paper complemented the Marines for overcoming Tarawa's sophisticated defenses and zealous garrisons. The editorial warned that any future assaults, in the Marshall Islands, could be even deadlier: "We must steel ourselves now to pay that price."

After the war, the controversy continued when General Holland Smith publicly claimed that Tarawa was a mistake. Admiral Nimitz replied by saying that Tarawa's capture knocked down the front door to the Japanese defenses in the Central Pacific.

Nimitz launched the Marshalls Campaign only ten weeks after the seizure of Tarawa. The photo-reconnaissance and attack aircraft from the captured airfields at Apamama and Betio proved vital.

The battle for Tarawa's capture would become the textbook on amphibious assault to guide and influence all subsequent landings in the Central Pacific. Nimitz believed that the prompt and selfless analysis immediately following Tarawa were of great value. He wrote: "From analytical reports of the commanders and from their critical evaluations of what went wrong, of what needed improvement, and of what techniques and equipment proved out in combat, came a tremendous outpouring of lessons learned."

Many senior officers later agreed that the conversion of the logistical LVTs to assault craft made the difference between victory and defeat on Betio. A further consensus was that the LVT-1s and LVT-2s used in the operation were only marginal against the heavily defensive fire. The LVT-1s (Alligators) needed heavier armament, more powerful engines, auxiliary bilge pumps, self-sealing gas tanks, and wooden plugs the size of 13mm bullets. More importantly, there needed to be more LVTs, at least 300 per division. Colonel Shoup wanted to keep the use of LVTs as reef-crossing assault vehicles a secret, but there were too many reporters on the scene.

Naval gunfire got mixed reviews. Marines were enthusiastic about the destroyers' responses in the lagoon but critical about the preliminary bombardment's extent and accuracy—especially when it was ended so prematurely on D-Day. Major Ryan later wrote that the significant shortcomings in Operation Galvanic were: "Overestimating the damage that could be inflicted on a heavily defended position by an intense but limited naval bombardment, and by not sending in its assault forces soon enough after the shelling."

Major Schoettel later wrote that of the pounding his battalion received from emplacements within the seawall, he'd have recommended a direct fire against the beach by 40mm guns from close-in destroyers. The hasty saturation fires, considered adequate by planners because of strategic surprise, proved virtually useless. Any amphibious assaults against fortified atolls would need sustained, aimed, and deliberate fire.

No one could question the bravery of the aviators who supported the assault on Betio. But many questioned whether they were trained and armed adequately for such a difficult target. The need for closer integration of all supporting arms was clear.

Communications throughout the assault on Betio were terrible. Only the resourcefulness of a few radio operators and the bravery of individual runners kept the assault coherent. The Marines needed waterproof radios. The Navy needed a dedicated amphibious command ship, not on board a major combatant whose massive guns knocked out the radio nets with each salvo. These command ships, the AGC's, would appear later during the Marshalls Campaign.

Other amphibious revisions to the doctrine were immediately enacted. The priority of unloading supplies would become the tactical commander's call onshore, not the amphibious task force commander. Betio showed the critical need for underwater swimmers to stealthily assess and report the surf, beach, and reef conditions to the task force before the landing. This concept was first envisioned by amphibious warfare prophet Major Earl "Pete" Ellis in the 1920s, and quickly came to fruition. Admiral Turner created a fledgling UDT (Underwater Demolition Team) for the Marshall Islands assault.

The Marines also learned that the new medium tanks would become valuable assets with proper combined arms training. Future tank training would now emphasize integrated tank, engineer, infantry, and artillery operations. Tank and infantry communications would need immediate improvement. Most casualties among tank commanders on Betio resulted from individuals needing to dismount their vehicles to speak with the infantry in the open.

Backpack flamethrowers won universal approval from the Marines on Betio. Each commander recommended increases in range, quantity, and mobility for these assault weapons. Suggestions were that larger versions should be mounted on LVTs and tanks, predicting the appearance of "Zippo Tanks" in later Pacific campaigns.

General Julian Smith summed up the lessons he learned at Tarawa with this comment: "We made fewer mistakes than the Japs did."

Military historian Philip A. Crowl wrote in his assessment of the battle for Tarawa: "The capture of Tarawa despite all defects in execution, conclusively demonstrated that the American amphibious doctrine was valid, that even the strongest island fortress could be seized."

Future landings in the Marshall Islands would use this doctrine to achieve objectives against similar targets with fewer casualties and in less time. The benefits of Operation Galvanic quickly outweighed the steep initial costs. In time, Tarawa became a symbol of sacrifice and courage for Marine raiders and Japanese defenders alike.

Ten years after the battle, General Julian Smith saluted the heroism of the Japanese who chose to die almost to the last man. He then turned to his beloved 2nd Marine Division shipmates in Task Force 53 at Betio: "For the officers and men, Marines and sailors, who crossed that reef, either as assault troops, or carrying supplies, or evacuating wounded, I can only say that I shall forever think of them with the feeling of the greatest respect and reverence."

TARAWA TODAY

Decades after World War II, Tarawa remains mostly unchanged. Visiting Betio Island, you can still see wrecked LVTs and American tanks along the beaches as well as ruined Japanese pillboxes and gun emplacements. The imposing concrete bunkers created by Admiral Shibasaki still stand, as impervious to time as they were to the naval guns of Task Force 53. At the turn of the century, island natives found a buried LVT containing skeletons of its Marine crew inside —one Marine still wearing his dog tags.

In 1968, General David Shoup was recalled from retirement to active duty for nine days to dedicate a large monument on Betio. He commemorated the twenty-fifth anniversary of the famous fight and later told *The National Observer*: "My first reaction was that Betio Island had shrunk a great deal. It seems smaller now in peace than in war."

While Shoup toured the ruined fortifications, he recalled the desperate, savage fighting. He pondered why the two nations spent so much for so little. In seventy-six hours of fighting, nearly 6,000 Americans and Japanese died on the tiny island.

In the late 1980s, the American Memorial had fallen into disrepair. It was in danger of being dismantled for a cold storage plant to be used by Japanese fishermen. The 2nd Marine Division Association and Long Beach journalist, Tom Hennessey, began a lengthy campaign to raise enough funds to get a new, more stable monument. They brought a 9-ton block of Georgia granite with the inscription "To our fellow Marines, who gave their all." They dedicated this Memorial on November 20, 1988.

Betio is now part of the Republic of Kiribati. Tourist facilities have been developed to accommodate the large number of veterans who return every year. In author James Ullman's opinion, the small island still resembles what it probably looked like on D-Day almost 78 years ago. Ullman visited Tarawa several years ago and wrote a fitting eulogy: "A familiar irony that old battlefields are often the quietest and gentlest of places. It has been true of Gettysburg, Cannae, Austerlitz, Verdun—and is true of Tarawa."

OPERATION BACKHANDER

1944 BATTLE FOR CAPE GLOUCESTER

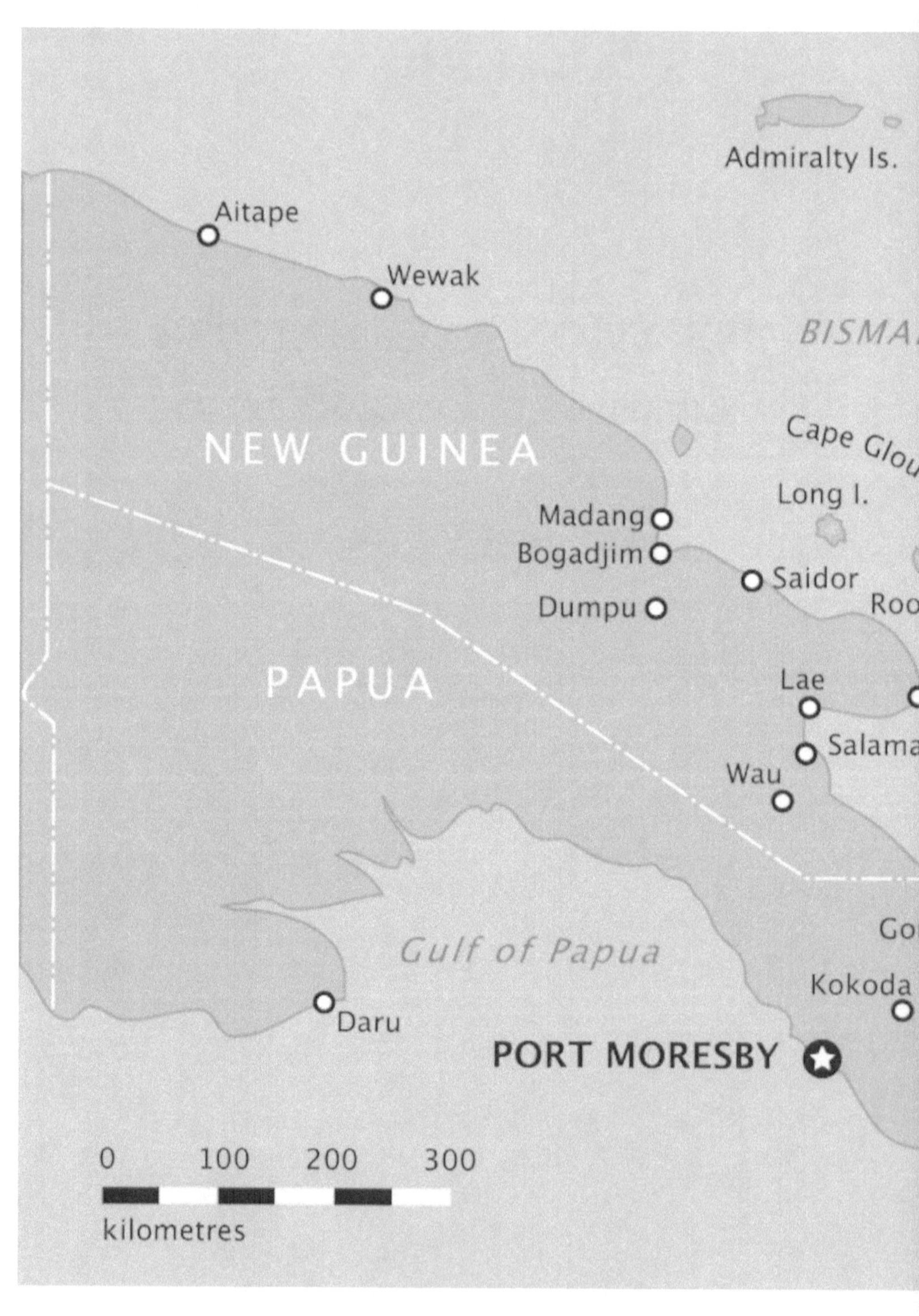

Admiralty Is.
BISMA
Aitape
Wewak
Cape Glou
Long I.
NEW GUINEA
Madang
Bogadjim
Saidor
Dumpu
Roo
PAPUA
Lae
Salama
Wau
Gulf of Papua
Gor
Kokoda
Daru
PORT MORESBY
0   100   200   300
kilometres

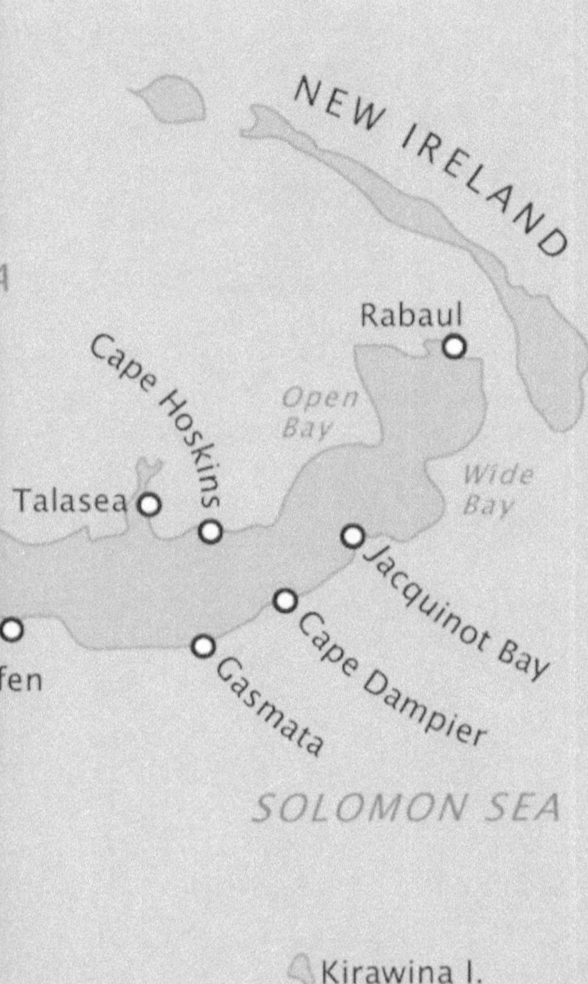

NEW IRELAND
Rabaul
Open Bay
Wide Bay
Cape Hoskins
Talasea
Jacquinot Bay
Cape Dampier
Gasmata
fen
SOLOMON SEA
Green I.
Buka I.
BOUGAINVILLE
Torokina
Shortland Is.
Treasury Is.
Kirawina I.
Goodenough I.
Woodlark I.
Fergusson I.
Normanby I.
Milne Bay
AL SEA
N

INTRODUCTION

Early on the morning of December 26, 1943, Marines stood ready off the coast of Japanese-dominated New Britain. The outline of the mile-high Mount Talawe was just visible in the twilight. American and Australian cruisers shattered the early morning calm with ammunition flying from their destroyers' guns. The 1st Marine Division, was commanded by Major General William H. Rupertus, arriving from the recently finished Guadalcanal Campaign. The men steeled their nerves, waiting for daylight and the signal to assault the Yellow Beaches near Cape Gloucester.

Fire support ships blazed away for ninety minutes. They attempted to neutralize entire areas rather than destroy pinpointed targets because the dense jungle concealed most of the individual Japanese fortifications and ammunition dumps.

At dawn on D-Day, Army airmen joined the bombardment. B-24 Liberator bombers flew at such an altitude that the Marines could barely see them. They dropped five-hundred-pound bombs on the beaches, scoring a hit on one of the enemy fuel dumps at the Cape Gloucester airfield—releasing a fiery geyser that leapt hundreds of feet into the air. A squadron of B-25 medium bombers and A-20 light bombers followed them, attacking from a lower altitude, hammering the Japanese antiaircraft batteries.

US B-25 Mitchell Bombers

Then the attention shifted to the assault beaches. Landing craft carrying two battalions of the 7th Marines started toward the shore. An LCI (Landing Craft, Infantry), with multiple rocket launchers, took positions on the flank of the first wave bound for each beach. They unleashed a hellish barrage, keeping the Japanese troops pinned down after the destroyers and cruisers shifted their fire to avoid putting the assault troops in danger.

At 0745, Higgins boats brought the first wave toward Yellow Beach 1. They grounded onto a narrow strip of volcanic sand that measured just under five hundred yards from one end to the other, bringing the 3rd Battalion Marines' lead elements. Two minutes later, the 1st Battalion landed on Yellow Beach 2. Separated by a thousand yards of jungle and a seven-hundred-yard shoreline. Neither battalion encountered any organized resistance. The

Marines used a smokescreen that drifted across the beaches. This hampered the later waves of landing craft and blinded Japanese observers on Target Hill overlooking the beachhead. No enemy manned the log-and-earth bunkers that might have raked the assault force with deadly fire.

The Yellow Beaches on the north coast of the peninsula pointed west toward Cape Gloucester. Codenamed Operation Backhander, this access point was the primary objective: two airfields at the cape's northwestern tip. By capturing the airfields, the 1st Marine Division would allow Allied airmen to step up attacks on the Japanese fortress at Rabaul, three hundred miles away at the north-eastern edge of New Britain—the opposite end of the long, cres-cent-shaped island. The capture of these Yellow Beaches was vital for the New Britain Campaign, but two additional landings also took place. The first occurred on December 15, landing at Cape Merkus on Arawe Bay along the south coast. The second at Green Beach on the northwest coast, also on December 26.

The Cape Merkus landing was across the channel from the islet of Arawe. Its purposes were to disrupt motorized barges and other Japanese small-craft moving men and supplies along the southern coast of New Britain and to divert attention from Cape Gloucester. The Marine amphibian tractor crews used the slower and more vulnerable LVT-1 Alligators and the new armored LVT-2 Water Buffaloes to carry soldiers from the 112th Cavalry to make landings on Orange Beach at the western edge of Cape Merkus.

The destroyer *Conyngham* provided fire support enhanced by rocket equipped DUKW's (a 2.5-ton, six-wheel, amphibious truck known as duck) and a submarine chaser designated as the control craft. A last-minute bombing silenced the beach defenses and enabled the LVT Water Buffaloes to crush enemy machine guns that survived the opening bombardment.

Two diversionary landings by soldiers paddling ashore in rubber boats were less successful. Savage enemy fire forced one group to turn back just short of its objective on Orange Beach, but the other gained a foothold on Pilelo Island and killed the small group of Japanese defenders. Enemy airmen reported the assault force approaching Cape Merkus. Japanese bombers and fighters from Rabaul attacked within two hours of the landing. The Japanese executed sporadic airstrikes throughout December with diminishing ferocity. They ultimately shifted their troops to meet the threat in the south.

Then there was the secondary landing on December 26. Battalion Landing Team 21 was a 1,500 man assault force, from the 2/1 Marines, commanded by Lieutenant Colonel James Masters. They started toward Green Beach supported by American destroyers *Smith* and *Reid* with their 5-inch naval gunfire. LCMs (Landing Craft, Medium) carried amphibian trucks, driven by soldiers, fitted with rocket launchers. They fired from the landing craft as the assault force attacked the beach. The first wave landed at 0750, with two others closely following ashore. The Marines carved out a beachhead 1,200 yards wide and 500 yards inland, encountering no opposition. Their mission was to sever the coastal trail that passed west of Mount Talawe and prevent Japanese from reinforcements reaching the Cape Gloucester airfields.

Following the coastal trail proved more difficult than expected. The local villagers tilled and cleared garden plots, leaving them for the jungle to reclaim. This left a maze of trails—some fresh, some faint—but most led nowhere. The Japanese did not take advantage of the confusion caused by the path tangling until early morning on December 30. They attacked the Green Beach force and took advantage of the heavy rain that muffled sounds and reduced visibility. When the Japanese began their assault, the Marines called down mortar fire within 20 yards of their defensive positions. A battery of the 11th Marines was reorganized as an infantry unit because the cannoneers couldn't find suitable targets for their 75mm howitzers.

Gunnery Sergeant Guiseppe Guilano materialized at critical moments and fired a light machine gun from his hip. His bravery and cool disdain for danger earned him a Navy Cross. While some Japanese troops penetrated the position, a counterattack led by Company G drove them off. This brutal fighting cost the Marines six dead and seventeen wounded. Ninety Japanese soldiers perished, and five surrendered.

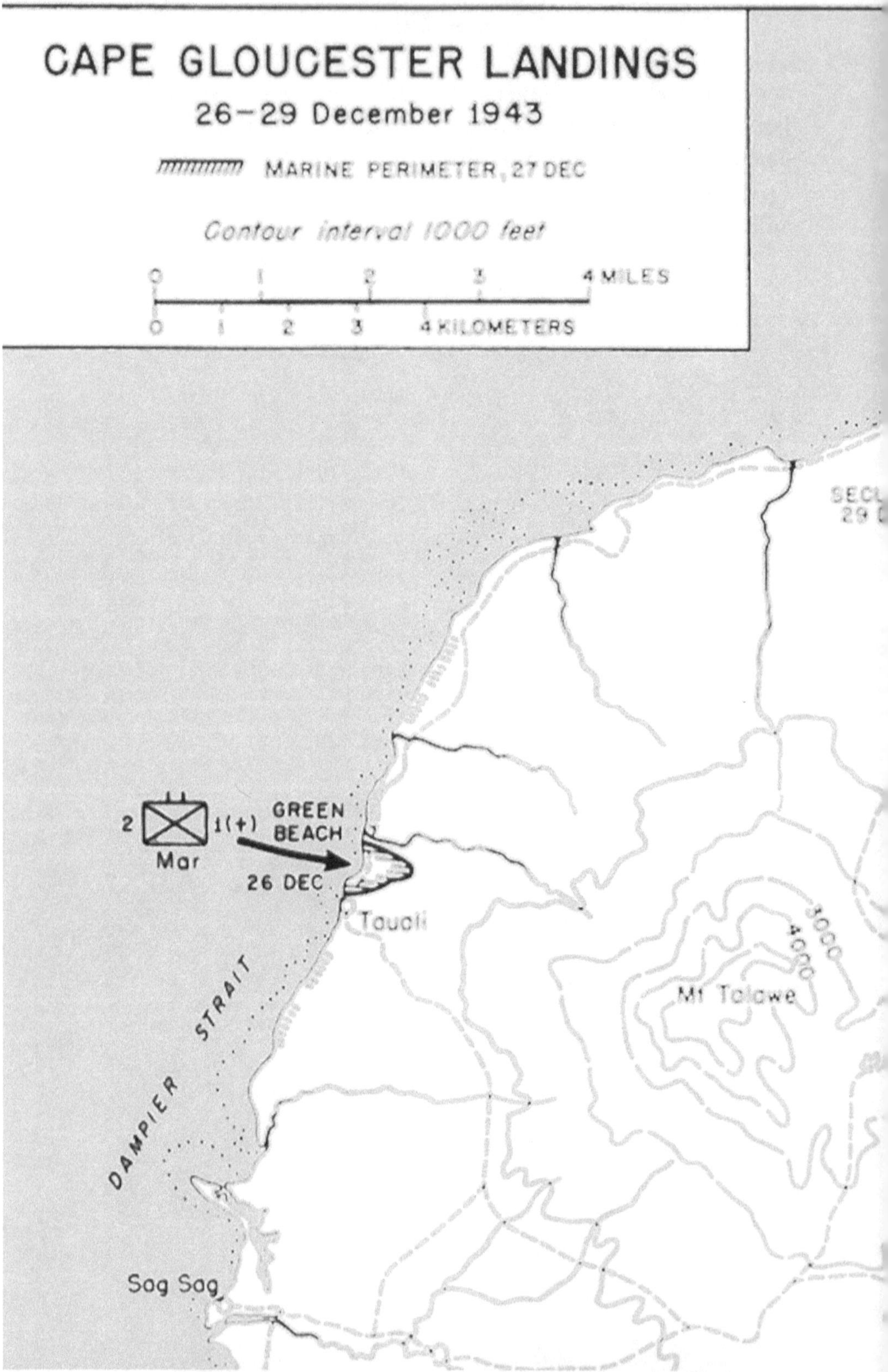

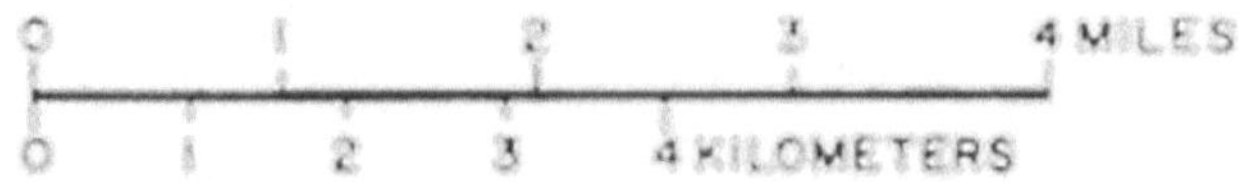

CAPE GLOUCESTER LANDINGS
26–29 December 1943
MARINE PERIMETER, 27 DEC
Contour interval 1000 feet
0   1   2   3   4 MILES
0   1   2   3   4 KILOMETERS
SECU
29 D
2   1(+)   GREEN BEACH
Mar
26 DEC
Tauali
DAMPIER STRAIT
Mt Talawe
3000
4000
Sag Sag

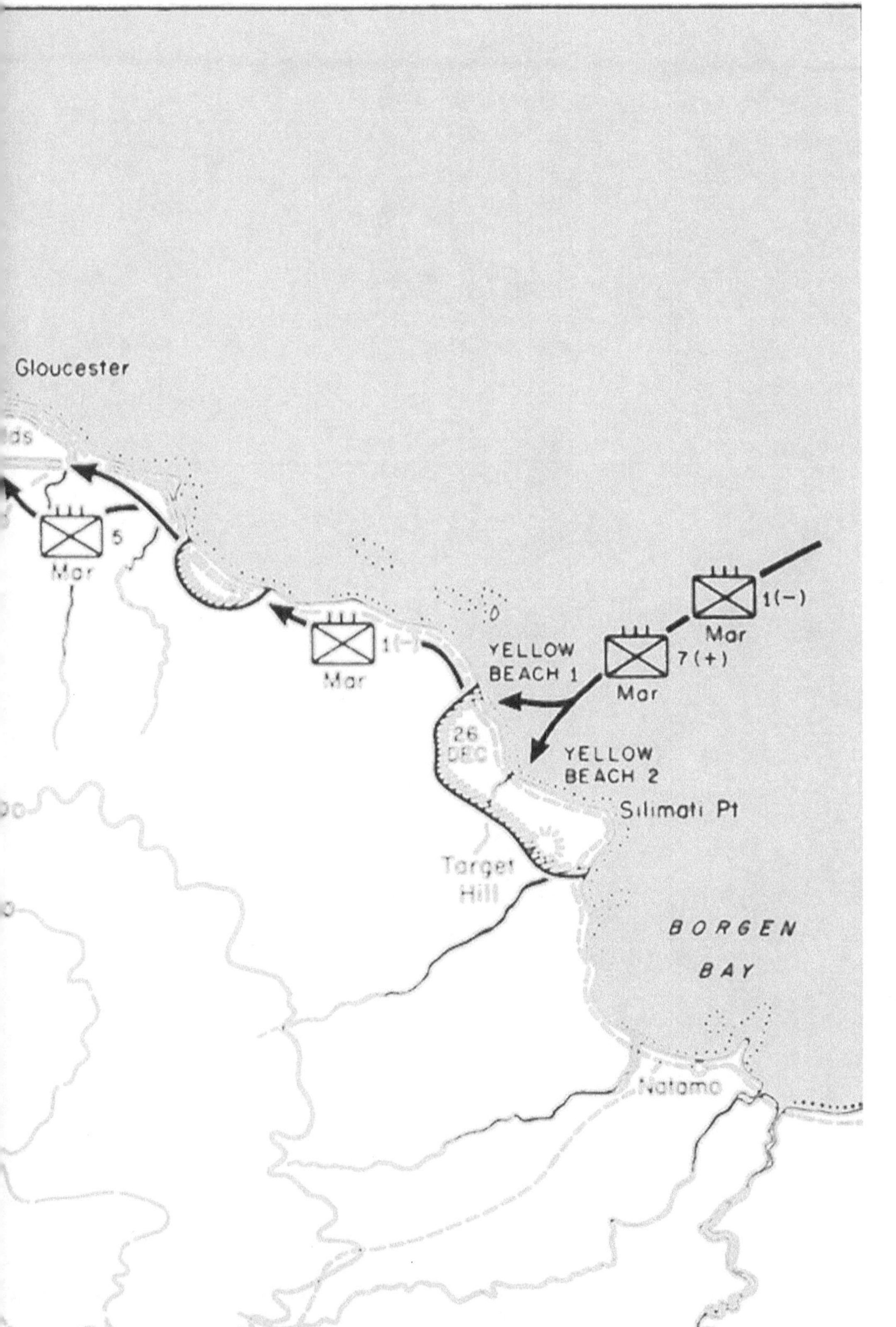

Gloucester
ds
5
Mar
1 (-)
Mar
YELLOW
BEACH 1
7 (+)
Mar
1 (-)
Mar
26
DEC
YELLOW
BEACH 2
Silimati Pt
Target
Hill
BORGEN
BAY
Natamo

ESTABLISHING THE BEACHHEAD

The Japanese had a mixture of combat and service troops in western New Britain. They used motorized barges to shuttle cargo and troops along the coast from Rabaul to Cape Gloucester. They utilized their fleet of trawlers and schooners enhanced by destroyers from the Japanese Navy for any more extended movements.

Japanese troops that defended western New Britain were known as the *Matsuda Force*. General Iwao Matsuda was a military transportation specialist and a commander of an infantry regiment in Manchuria. When he arrived in February 1943 on New Britain, he took control of the battle-tested *141st Infantry* from the Philippines conquest and additional antiaircraft and artillery units. Matsuda established his headquarters near Kalingi, the coastal trail northwest of Mount Talawe, five miles from the airfields at Cape Gloucester. He ultimately changed his location to reflect his tactical challenges.

The Allies increased their threat to New Britain as 1943 wore on. Japanese headquarters at Rabaul assigned General Matsuda's force to the *17th Division* under Lieutenant General Sakai, recently arriving from Shanghai. Sakai's division was attacked en route and lost two of their four transports to submarine torpedoes and mines. An Allied air attack nearly wiped out the third convoy. This deprived the Japanese defenders of three thousand replacement and service troops. Lieutenant General Sakai deployed the remainder of his forces to western New Britain under Matsuda's tactical command.

The mid-December Cape Merkus landings caused General Matsuda to shift his troops to combat the threat. This redeployment did not account for the lack of resistance at the Yellow Beaches. Matsuda was familiar with the terrain of western New Britain. He did not believe the Americans would storm the small strips of sand that extended a few yards inland, backing up to a swamp. Matsuda did not know the American maps labeled the beaches as a "swamp forest." Even though the aerial photography taken after the initial preliminary airstrikes revealed no shadow within the bomb craters —there was evidence of a water level high enough to fill these depressions to the brim. Matsuda knew the airfields were the obvious prize and did not believe that the Marines would plunge into the muck and risk becoming bogged down short of achieving their objective.

Matsuda forfeited the immediate advantage of opposing the Marine assault force at the water's edge. Enemy troops were suffering the long-term indirect effects of eroding Japanese fortunes, beginning at Guadalcanal and New Guinea. The Allies dominated the skies over New Britain, blunted any air attacks on the beach at Cape Merkus beachhead, and bombed at will throughout the island. While the airstrikes did minor damage, except for Rabaul, they demoralized the Japanese troops suffering from medicine and supply shortages because of the submarine and air attacks. An ineffective network of primitive trails hugged the coastline and increased General Matsuda's dependence on barges. The capture of Cape Merkus made his barges, convoys, and coastal shipping vulnerable to aircraft, and later to gunboats and torpedo craft.

The two battalions that landed on the Yellow Beaches crossed the sands and plunged through a wall of undergrowth into a swamp forest. A Marine could slog through knee-deep mud, step into a hole, and then end up damp to his neck. A Japanese counterattack while the Marines lurched through the swamp forest could have inflicted severe casualties. General Matsuda lacked the roads and vehicles to shift his troops in time to take advantage of the terrain. The Japanese defenders were immobile on the ground and tried to retaliate by air. A flight of enemy aircraft sent from Rabaul was intercepted by Army P-38s. Two Japanese bombers evaded the Army fighter planes and sank the destroyer *Brownson* with a direct hit, followed by an immense explosion. She took 108 crewmen with her; the rest were rescued by destroyers *Daly* and *Lamson*.

When the first Japanese bombers came into view, a squadron of Army B-25s flew over LSTs (Landing Ships, Tank) attacking targets at Borgen Bay, south of the Yellow Beaches. Gunners on board the LSTs opened fire at the enemy aircraft but mistook friend for foe and shot down two American bombers and damaged two others. The Allied planes, shaken by the experience, dropped their bombs too soon on the 11th Marines' artillery positions at the left flank of Yellow Beach 1—killing one Marine and wounding fifteen others. A Marine battalion commander from the artillery regiment later wrote: "It was like trying to dig a hole with my nose as the bombs exploded. Trying to get down into the ground just a little bit more."

By the afternoon of D-Day, the 1st Marine Division had established a beachhead. The 7th Marines' assault battalions had pushed ahead and captured Target Hill on the left flank before pausing to await reinforcements. Two more battalions arrived during the day: Landing Team 31 came ashore at 0815 on Yellow Beach 1. They weaved through the 3/7 Marines and veered to the northwest, leading the way toward the airfields at 0845. The 2/7 Marines landed and waded through the swamp forest between the 1st and 3rd Battalions, expanding the beachhead. The next infantry unit was the 1/1 Marines, reaching Yellow Beach 1 at 1300 to join the 3rd Battalion advancing on the airfields. The 11th Marines, despite the accidental bombing, set up their artillery with the help of amphibian tractors. Some of the amphibious tractors brought the 75mm howitzers from the LSTs directly to the battery firing positions. Other tractors were used to break a trail through the undergrowth to pull the more massive 105mm weapons.

Army trucks loaded with supplies came ashore from the LSTs. Logistical plans called for these vehicles to move forward as mobile supply dumps, but the swamp forest proved impossible for the wheeled vehicles. Drivers abandoned their trucks to avoid being left behind when the ships moved out from the threat of Japanese bombers. The Marines built roads and corduroyed them with logs or shifted the cargo onto the amphibian tractors. Even with this enormous effort, the convoy still got underway with over 100 tons of supplies left on board.

While the cargo and reinforcements crossed the beach, the Marines advanced inland and encountered the first real Japanese resistance. On December 26 at 1015, the 3/1 Marines pushed ahead, forced into a column of companies by a swamp on the left flank that narrowed the frontage.

The Japanese opened fire from camouflaged bunkers, killing the commander of Company K and his executive officer. These sturdy Japanese bunkers proved impervious to the bazooka rockets, which failed to detonate in the soft earth covering the structures. And the 37mm guns could not penetrate the logs protecting the Japanese defenders.

An LVT-1 Alligator that had delivered supplies for Company K attempted to crush one bunker—but got wedged between two trees. Japanese snipers killed the tractor's two machine gunners before the driver could break it free. When the tractor lunged ahead, it caved in one bunker, silencing enemy fire and enabling Marines to isolate the three others and destroy them—killing twenty-five Japanese. A platoon of M4 Sherman tanks joined in to lead the advance beyond this first strongpoint.

Japanese troops of the *1st Debarkation Unit* provided the initial opposition, but Matsuda had alerted his nearby infantry units to converge onto the beachhead. A Japanese battalion moved into position late in the afternoon on D-Day. They were opposite the 2/7 Marines who clung to a crescent-shaped position with both flanks protected by marshlands.

After sunset, only muzzle flashes pierced the darkness as the firing intensity increased. The Japanese were preparing to counterattack. Amphibian tractors could not make supply runs until it was light enough to avoid the fallen tree trunks and roots when navigating through the swamp forest. Before dawn, Lieutenant Colonel "Chesty" Puller, the XO of the 7th Marines, organized the men of the service company and regimental headquarters into carrying parties. He loaded them with ammunition and waded with them through the dangerous swamp. Only one misstep and a Marine carrying bandoliers of rifle ammo or containers of mortar shells could slip, stumble, and drown.

When the regimental commander reinforced the Marines with Battery D, of the 1st Special Weapons Battalion, Colonel Puller had the men leave the 37mm guns behind and carry the ammunition instead. A guide from headquarters met the column that Puller had pressed into service. He led the Marines forward through a blinding downpour, driven sideways by a monsoon gale. Obscured landmarks forced the heavily laden Marines to blindly wade onward. Each man clung to the belt of the man in front. Not until 0805, over twelve hours after the column started its march, did the Marines reach their goal, put down their loads, and take up their rifles to fight.

The 2/7 Marines had been fighting for their lives since the first storm struck. A curtain of rain prevented mortar crews from seeing their aiming stakes. The battalion commander described these men firing as just "guessing by God's will." Mud got into most of the small arms ammo and jammed machine guns and rifles. Marines abandoned their water-filled foxholes while the defenders hung on fighting.

At dawn, Japanese soldiers moved toward the right flank of the 2/7 Marines, attempting to outflank them. They were possibly forced into that direction by the Marines' defensive fire. When Battery D arrived and moved into the threatened area, they forced the Japanese to break off their action and regroup.

DEFENSE OF HELL'S POINT

The overall plan for the 1st Division Marines' maneuver called for Combat Team C to take and hold a beachhead at Target Hill. Combat Team B would advance on the airfields. Due to the enemy build-up to prepare for the attack, General Rupertus requested the release of the division reserve, Combat Team A, to reinforce the

Marines. The Army agreed and sent the 1st, 2nd, and 3rd Battalions in support.

The division commander landed them on Blue Beach, three miles right of the Yellow Beaches. By using Blue Beach, this placed the 5th Marines closer to Cape Gloucester and the airfields. Not every element of Combat Team A received these orders. Several units touched down on the Yellow Beaches instead and moved on foot to their planned destination.

While General Rupertus laid out plans to commit the reserve troops, Combat Team B advanced toward the airfields. Marines initially encountered light resistance but were warned of a maze of trenches and bunkers stretching inland from a promontory—earning the name Hell's Point. Japanese troops built these defenses to protect the beaches where General Matsuda had expected the Allies to land. The 3/1 Marines attacked the Hell's Point position on the flank instead of a head-on frontal assault. Overrunning this complex set of defenses proved a lethal task.

Rupertus delayed the attack to give the division reserve, the 5th Marines, time to come ashore. On December 28, after the 2/11 Marines and Army A-20s bombarded the dug-in enemy, the assault troops suffered another delay. They waited several hours for a platoon of M4 Sherman medium tanks to increase the attack's intensity. At 1100, the 3/1 Marines moved ahead. Company I and the medium Sherman's led the way. At the same time, Company A waded through jungle and swamp intending to seize the ridge's inland point extending from Hell's Point. Despite the obstacles in their path, Company A surged from the jungle at 1145, crossing the tall grass field until repulsed by intense enemy fire. By late afternoon, Company A broke off the attack. Attackers and defenders were short of ammunition and exhausted. The 2/11 Marines covered Company A's withdrawal behind an onslaught of fire. By nightfall, the Japanese had abandoned their positions.

The attached Shermans with Company I collided head-on with the primary defenses fifteen minutes after Company A assaulted inland of the ridge. The Japanese had modified their defenses since the December 26 landings. They hacked fire lanes in the undergrowth, cut new gun ports and bunkers, and moved men and weapons to oppose the Allied attack along the coastal trail parallel to the shore instead of over the beach. The Marines advanced in drenching rain and encountered jungle-covered enemy positions protected by mines and barbed wire.

Medium Sherman tanks, protected by riflemen, crushed the bunkers and weapons inside. Company I drifted to the left flank during the fight, and Company K, reinforced with a platoon of Sherman tanks, closed the gap between the coastal track and Hell's Point. This unit used the same tactics as Company I. A rifle squad followed each of the Shermans after the tanks cracked the twelve bunkers and fired inside. The riflemen killed anyone attempting to fight or flee. Nine Marines were killed and thirty-six were wounded in this assault while over two hundred and sixty Japanese died fighting.

After the Marines shattered the Hell's Point defenses, two battalions of the 5th Marines joined in the airfield's advance. The 1st and 2nd Battalions moved out in a column. In front of the Marines was a swamp only a few inches deep. The downpour increased the depth to over five feet making it hard for the shorter Marines. The 5th Marines lost time wading through the swamp. This delayed the attack while the leading elements chose a piece of open and dry ground to establish a perimeter while the remaining Marines caught up.

The 1/1 Marines encountered only scattered resistance—mostly sniper fire—as they weaved along the coast beyond Hell's Point. Advancing with half-tracks carrying 75mm guns, artillery, medium Sherman's, and even rocket-firing DUKWs, the 1st Marines held a line extended inland from the coast. The 3/1 Marines and the 2/5 Marines advanced on the flanks and formed a semicircle around the airfield.

Colonel Sumiya of the *53rd Infantry Regiment* was the Japanese officer in charge of defending the airfields. On December 29, he fell back to gain time. Sumiya gathered the surviving troops for Razorback Hill's defense, a ridge running diagonally across the southwestern approaches to the airfield. The 5th Marines attacked on December 30, supported by artillery and tanks. Sumiya's troops had built sturdy bunkers, but the chest-high grass covering Razorback Hill did not stop the Allied assault like the jungle at Hell's Point.

The Imperial Japanese fought bravely to hold their position, even stalling the Marines' advance. But the Japanese had neither the firepower nor the numbers to overcome. During the Japanese assault, one platoon of Company F beat back three *banzai* attacks.

Medium Shermans allowed the Marines to smash the remaining bunkers in their path and kill the enemy troops within. By nightfall on December 30, the Marine landing force overran the airfield defenses. At noon the next day, General Rupertus hoisted the American flag next to the wreckage of a Japanese bomber at Airfield No. 2—the larger of the airstrips.

The 1st Marine Division seized the objective for the Battle of Cape Gloucester. But the airstrips proved only marginal value to the Allies. Airfield No. 1 was overgrown with sharp, tall kunai grass. Craters from American bombs pockmarked the surface of Airfield No. 2. After its capture, Japanese hit-and-run planes added more bomb craters, despite antiaircraft fire from the 12th Defense Battalion. Army aviation engineers worked desperately around the clock to get Airfield No. 2 back in operation. This task took until the end of January 1944. Army aircraft based here defended against air assaults for as long as Rabaul remained an active Japanese airbase.

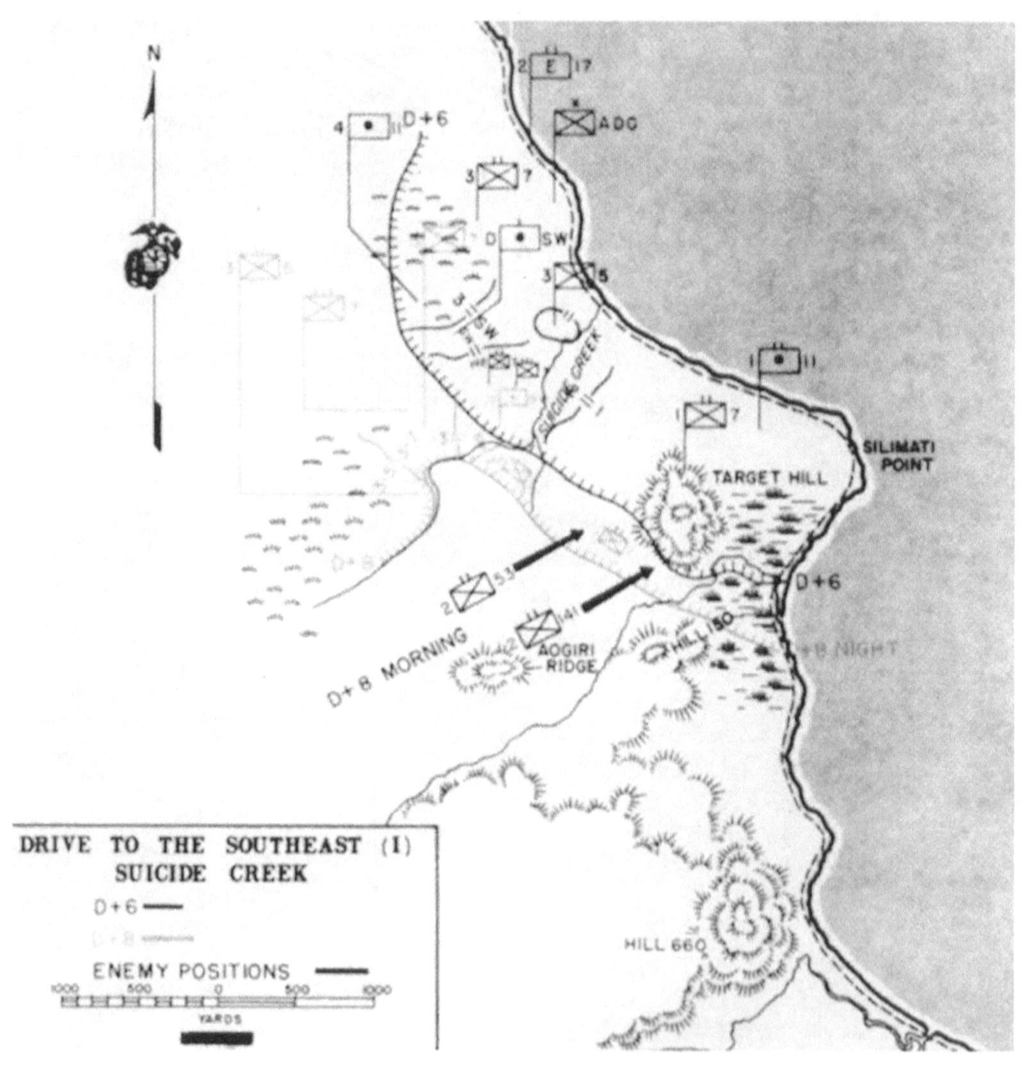

N
2 E 17
4 D+6
ADC
3 7
D SW
3 5
SUICIDE CREEK
1 11
SW
1 7
TARGET HILL
SILIMATI POINT
2 53
D+6
D+8 MORNING
141
HILL 150
D+8 NIGHT
AOGIRI RIDGE
HILL 660
DRIVE TO THE SOUTHEAST (I)
SUICIDE CREEK
D+6
D+8
ENEMY POSITIONS
1000 500 0 500 1000
YARDS

CROSSING SUICIDE CREEK

While Major General Rupertus directed the airfields' capture, Brigadier General Lemuel Shepherd had come ashore on December 26 and took command of the beachhead. Shepherd had coordinated the logistics activity and assumed responsibility to expand the perimeter southwest and secure Borgen Bay's shores. He used a shore party of engineers, transportation, and service troops to handle the logistics. The 3/5 Marines arrived on December 30 to help the 7th Marines enlarge the beachhead.

General Shepherd had limited knowledge of the Japanese deployments to the south and west of the Yellow Beaches. Thick vegetation concealed swamps, streams, ridgelines, trenches, and bunkers. The progress made toward the airfields showed a Japanese weakness in that area and a potential strength in Borgen Bay and the Yellow Beaches vicinity. To resolve the uncertainty of the enemy's intentions and numbers, General Shepherd issued orders to probe enemy defenses on January 1, 1944.

Colonel Katayama commanded the *141st Infantry* and prepared a counterattack. Katayama intended to hurl three reinforced battalions against the Allies at Target Hill. Japanese headquarters believed 2,500 Marines were now ashore on New Britain, 10% of the total. Colonel Katayama thought his force was strong enough to do this job.

Katayama waited and gathered his strength, giving Shepherd time to make the first move. Midmorning on January 2, the 1/7 Marines stood ready near Target Hill. The 2nd Battalion waited along a stream known as Suicide Creek. The 3/5 Marines advanced into the jungle to cover the 3/7 Marines on one flank. As the units pivoted, they would cross Suicide Creek to squeeze out of the 2/7th Marines and provide Shepherd with a reserve.

The change in direction through thick vegetation proved exceptionally difficult. In the words of one Marine: "You'd step from your line, take ten paces, and turn around to guide your buddy, and nobody was there. I can tell you it was a very small war and a very lonely business."

The Japanese troops were dug in south of Suicide Creek. From there, they resisted every attempt by the Marines to cross the stream that day. This created a stalemate until Seabees from Company C built a corduroy road. They punched through the swamp forest behind the Yellow Beaches for the tanks to move forward and smash through enemy defenses.

While Marines waited at Suicide Creek on Sherman tanks, Katayama attacked Target Hill. He took advantage of the darkness. His infantry cut steps into the lower slopes so troops could climb more efficiently. The Japanese followed their preconceived plan, to the letter, of advancing up the steps and slipping past the Company A, 7th Marines' thinly held lines. At midnight enemy troops stormed the strongest of the company's defenses. Japanese mortars fired to soften the defenses and screen the approach. Still, they could not conceal the sound of the soldiers working their way up the hill, and the Marines were ready. While Japanese supporting fire proved to be inaccurate, one round did score a direct hit on a machine gun position killing the gunner and wounding two others. The injured Marines kept on firing their weapon until someone else could take over. This lone gun fired over five thousand rounds and helped stop the Japanese thrust, ending at dawn. The Japanese could not crack the 1/7 Marines' lines or loosen their grip on Target Hill.

A dead Japanese officer on Target Hill had documents that cast a new light on enemy defenses south of Suicide Creek. On a crudely drawn map, Aogiri Ridge was discovered. This enemy strongpoint was unknown to General Shepherd's intelligence section. Observers on Target Hill searched for the Aogiri Ridge trail network, but the jungle canopy frustrated their efforts.

Marine patrols on Target Hill found dozens of enemy bodies. They captured documents that, when translated, listed forty-seven killed Japanese and fifty-five wounded. Using field glasses to scan the jungle south of Suicide Creek, the 17th Marines finished the road to allow the Sherman tanks to test the stream's defenses.

On the afternoon of January 3, three Sherman tanks reached the creek. They realized the bank dropped off too sharply for them to negotiate. The engineers called in a bulldozer; they lowered its blade to gouge out the lip of the embankment. The Japanese realized the danger if the tanks could cross the creek and opened fire on the bulldozer, wounding the driver. A Marine climbed into the exposed driver seat until he was also wounded. Another Marine jumped forward, but instead of climbing onto the machine, he walked alongside and used its bulk for cover. He manipulated the controls with an ax handle and a shovel. By dark, he'd finished the job of converting the impossible bank into a ramp the Shermans could cross.

At dawn on January 4, the first Sherman went down the ramp and across the stream. As the tank emerged on the other side, Marines cut down two Japanese soldiers trying to detonate mines against the tank's sides. Other Shermans followed, accompanied by infantry, and smashed open the bunkers barring the way. The 3/7 Marines surged across the creek and joined the other battalions on the far right of the line that crossed the jungle, concealing Japanese defenses at Aogiri Ridge.

Now across Suicide Creek, the Marines advanced on Aogiri

Ridge, another name for Hill 150. The Marine advance rapidly took the hill, but the Japanese resistance in the vicinity did not stop. Enemy fire wounded the commanding officer of the 3/5 Marines and killed his executive officer. On the morning of January 8, Lieutenant Colonel Lewis W. Walt, the executive officer of the 5th Marines, took command of the 3rd Battalion. Walt continued the attack from the previous day. His Marines encountered savage fire, and through the thick jungle they moved up a steep slope. The battalion formed a perimeter and dug in as night approached. Sudden skirmishes and random Japanese fire punctuated the darkness. The determined resistance and nature of the terrain convinced Colonel Walt that he had a fight on his hands for Aogiri Ridge.

Drenching rain, mud, and rampaging streams blunted the shock action and firepower of the tanks. The heaviest weapon the Marines could bring forward was a 37mm gun. The 11th Marines hammered the crest of Aogiri Ridge while the 7th Marines probed the flanks. The 3/5 Marines advanced in the center, seizing a narrow segment of the slope. By nightfall, Colonel Walt reported that his men had "reached the limit of their physical endurance and morale was low. It was now a question of whether they could hold their hard-earned gains."

The Marine crew of the 37mm gun opened fire to support the afternoon's last attack. After only two rounds, four of the nine men handling the weapon were wounded. Colonel Walt called for volunteers. When no one responded, he crawled to the gun and pushed the weapon up the incline. After firing two more rounds and cutting a swath to the undergrowth, his third-round destroyed an enemy machine gun. From there, other Marines took over, and the new volunteers cut down the enemy. The new 37mm improvised gun crew continued to fire canister rounds every few yards until they manhandled the weapon to the crest. From there, the Marines dug in 10 yards away from bunkers the Japanese had built on the crest of the reverse slope.

At 0130 on January 10, the Japanese charged through a curtain of rain, firing and shouting as they attacked. The Marines clinging to the ridge repelled this attack and the three others that followed, costing the Marines nearly all of their ammunition. Marine reinforcements scaled the muddy slope with clips and belts of ammo for the machine guns and rifles. Still, there was hardly any time to distribute the ammunition before the Japanese launched their fifth attack of the morning. Marine artillery decimated the enemy as the forward observers' vision was obstructed by rain and jungle; fire was adjusted by sounds more than sight. They moved the 105mm concentration to within fifty yards of the Marine infantrymen.

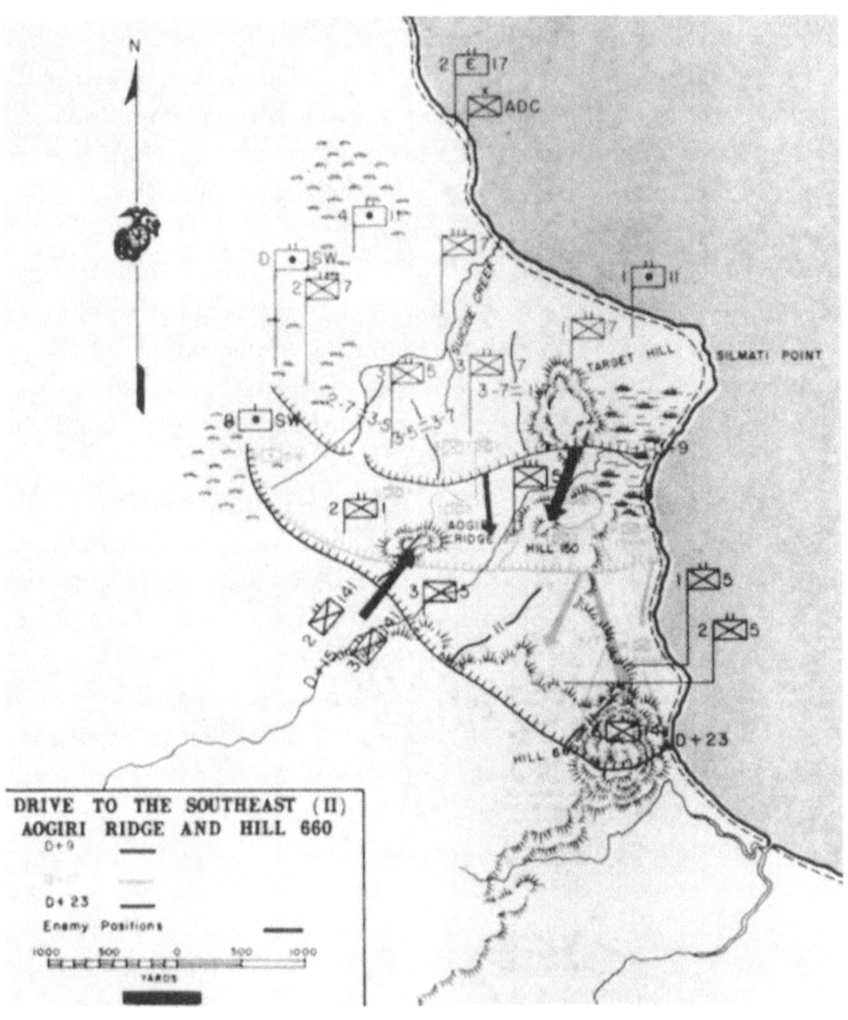

A Japanese officer emerged from the darkness and ran toward Colonel Walt's foxhole before fragments of a shell bursting in the trees cut him down. This was the climax of the enemy counterattack at Aogiri Ridge. The Japanese tide receded as daylight grew brighter. When the Marines moved forward at 0800, they did not find one living Japanese at Aogiri Ridge—now renamed Walt's Ridge in honor of their commander, who received the Navy Cross for his heroic leadership.

Only one Japanese stronghold in the vicinity of Walt's Ridge still survived. A supply dump along the trail linking the ridge to Hill 150. On January 11, the 1/7 Marines accompanied by two half-tracks and a platoon of light tanks eliminated the enemy resistance in four hours of fighting. It had been fifteen days of combat since the landings on December 26. It cost the division 182 killed and 640 wounded.

The next objective was Hill 660. It was to the left of General Shepherd's zone of action and inland of the coastal track. The 3/7 Marines got orders to seize the hill. Captain Joseph W. Buckley, commander of the 7th Marines Weapons Company, created a task force to bypass Hill 660 and block the coastal trail beyond the objective.

Buckley used two platoons of infantry, a platoon of 37mm guns, two half-tracks, and two light tanks. He assigned a platoon of pioneers from the 17th Marines with the bulldozer to trail the task force. They pushed through the mud and set up a roadblock to block the line of retreat from Hill 660. The Japanese attacked with long-range, plunging fire against Captain Buckley's task force as it advanced one mile along the trail. Because of the flat trajectory, the 37mm and 75mm guns could not destroy the enemy's automatic weapons. But the Marines succeeded in forcing enemy gunners to keep their heads down. As they advanced, Buckley's task force unreeled telephone wire to keep in contact with headquarters. Once the roadblock was in place and camouflaged, Buckley requested a truck bring in hot meals for his men. When the truck got bogged down—he sent the bulldozer to pull it free.

Buckley called in an aerial bombardment and artillery fire at

0930 on January 13. His tanks could not negotiate the ravines on the hillside. The climb became so steep that the riflemen had to sling their arms and seize handholds along the vines to pull themselves up. This is when the Japanese suddenly opened fire from trenches at the crest and pinned down the Marines climbing toward them. The Marines responded with mortar fire to silence the enemy lacking an overhead cover. Captain Buckley's riflemen followed closely behind the mortar barrage and scattered the defenders. Many trying to escape along the coastal trail were shot down by the task force waiting for them.

Because of the torrential rain, the Japanese did not counterattack until January 16. Two companies of Katayama's troops charged up the southwestern slope and were slaughtered by small arms and mortar fire. Of the enemy lucky enough to survive and try to break through the roadblock, forty-eight perished.

After the capture of Hill 660, the nature of the campaign changed. The Allies had captured their objective and eliminated any possibility of a Japanese counterattack against the airfield. Now the Marines would repel the Japanese, who harassed the secondary beachhead at Cape Merkus. Marines would also secure the jungle-covered mountainous interior of Cape Gloucester—south of the airfields between the Yellow and Green beaches.

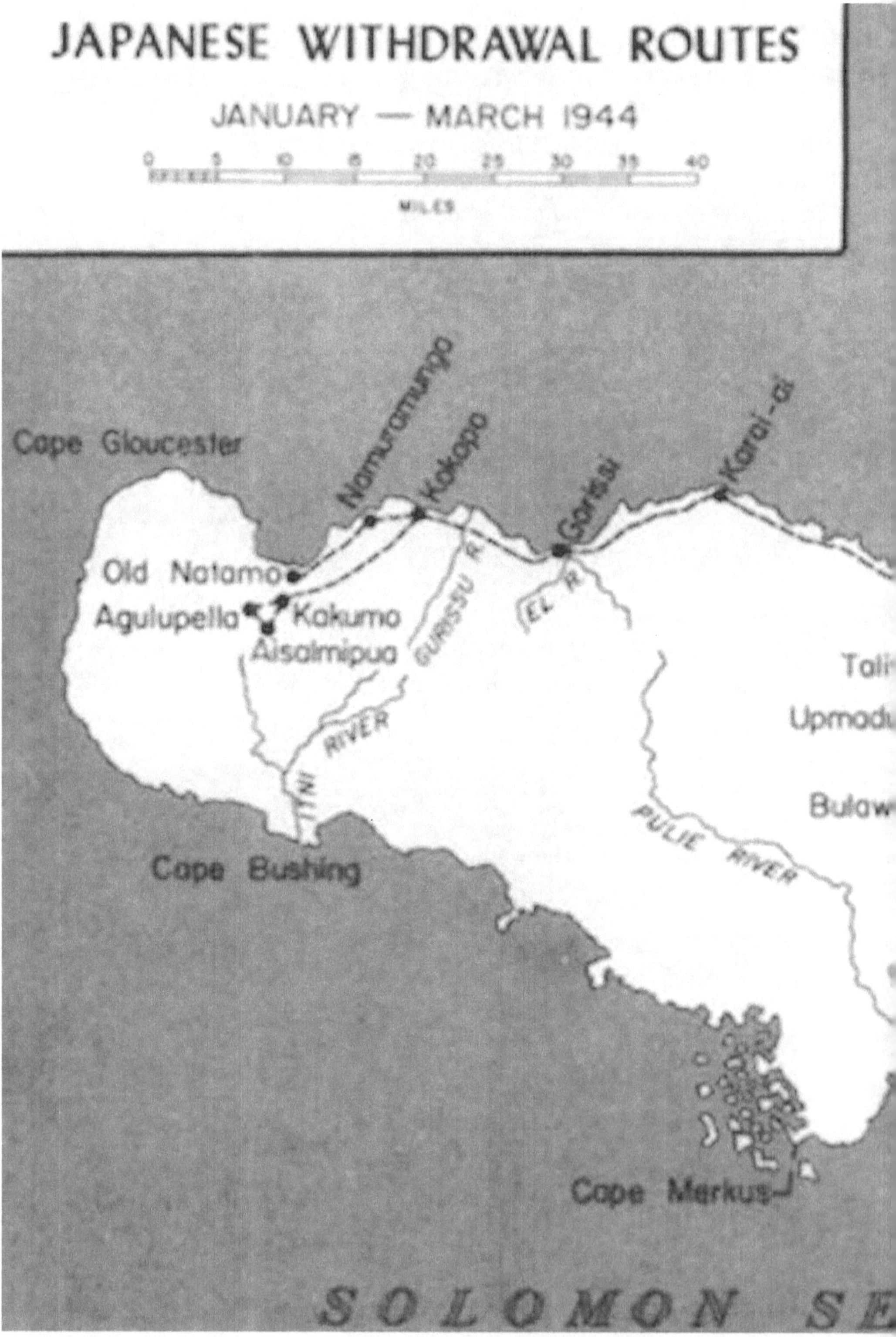

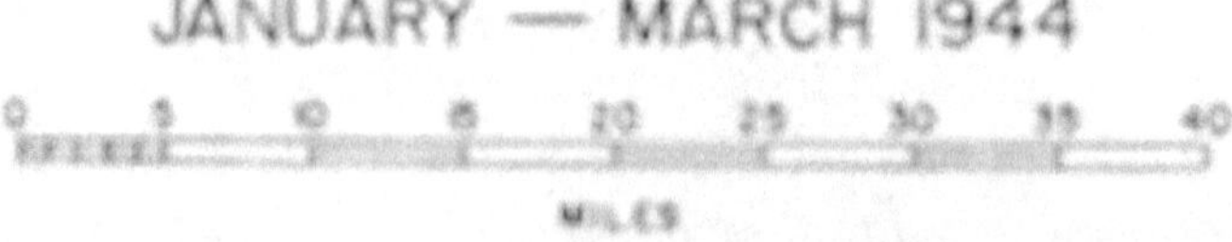

JAPANESE WITHDRAWAL ROUTES
JANUARY — MARCH 1944
0 5 10 15 20 25 30 35 40
MILES
Cape Gloucester
Namuramunga
Kokopo
Gorissi
Karai-ai
Old Natamo
Agulupella
Kakumo
Aisalmipua
GURISSU R.
EL R.
Tali
Upmadu
Bulaw
TINI RIVER
PULIE RIVER
Cape Bushing
Cape Merkus
SOLOMON SE

BISMARCK
SEA
Volupai
Talasea
Garu
Kilu
Lingo Linga
Kandoka
Numundo
San Remo
KAPULUK RIVER
KULU RIVER
VIA RIVER
ugitni

MOPPING UP IN THE WEST

The fighting at Cape Merkus on the south coast of western New Britain paled compared to Cape Gloucester's savage struggle. Japanese in the south were content to take advantage of the dense jungle and contain the 112th Cavalry on Cape Merkus. The Japanese commander, Major Komori, believed that the Allied landing force's plan was to capture an abandoned airfield at Cape Merkus. Komori built Japanese defenses to protect the airfield. He created a series of concealed bunkers with integrated fields of fire to hold the lightly armed cavalrymen in check while his troops directed harassing fire toward the beach.

The 112th Cavalry unit lacked heavy weapons. They called for 1st Marine Division tanks left behind on Finschhafen, New Guinea, because the other tanks were already turning up the mud at Cape Gloucester. Eighteen M5A1 light tanks from Company B of the 1st Marine Tank Battalion answered the call. They arrived at Cape Merkus and moved into position on January 15. The tanks attacked the next day after a squadron of Army B-24s dropped one-thousand-pound bombs on enemy jungle-covered defenses. The Marines followed up with artillery and mortars, joining in on the bombardment after two platoons of tanks and two infantry companies charged ahead.

Some tanks bogged down in the rain-soaked soil, and tank retrievers were needed to pull them free. Despite the nearly impenetrable thickets and deep mud, the tank infantry teams destroyed most of the Japanese bunkers. After eliminating the source of the harassing fire, the Allied troops pulled back. They destroyed a tank immobilized by a thrown track so the enemy could not create a pillbox. Another tank trapped in a crater was nearly destroyed—but Army engineers were able to free it and bring it back to service.

The January 16 attack broke the back of remaining Japanese resistance. Major Komori ordered a retreat to the vicinity of the airstrip, but the 112th Cavalry launched an attack that caught and shot them to pieces. By the time the Japanese dug in to defend the airfield—which the Americans had no intention of seizing—Komori's men lost 116 dead and 117 wounded with another 94 too sick to fight. Through starvation and sickness, the Japanese hung on until February 24, when Major Komori received orders to join the *Matsuda Force* in a general retreat.

On the other side of the island, after the victories at Hill 660 and Walt's Ridge, the 5th Marines focused on seizing control of the Borgen Bay shore's to the east of Yellow Beach 2. The 1/5 Marines followed the coastal trail until January 20, when the column smashed into a Japanese stronghold at Natamo Point. Documents captured earlier in the fighting described one enemy platoon supported by automatic weapons as dug in. Allied airstrikes and artillery could not suppress the enemy fire. The seized documents proved to be out of date when at least one company armed with 20mm, 37mm, and 75mm weapons stalled the Allied advance.

Marine reinforcements called in Sherman tanks that arrived in LSTs on January 23. That afternoon, supported by rocket firing DUKWs and artillery, the Marines overran Natamo Point. The battalion commander dispatched patrols along the west bank of the Natamo River. They outflanked strong enemy positions on the east bank near the stream's mouth. While the Marines executed this maneuver, the Japanese abandoned their defenses and retreated to the east.

The success at Borgen Bay and Cape Gloucester enabled the 5th Marines to probe the trails leading inward toward the village of Magairapua, where Katayama once had his headquarters. The 5th Marines led the way to trap enemy troops still bottled up on western New Britain.

Company L of the 1st Marines pursued the retreating Japanese from Cape Gloucester toward Mount Talawe. Marines crossed the mountain's eastern slope and weaved their way through a cluster of lesser outcroppings, through Mount Langila and into the saddle between Mounts Tangi and Talawe. They discovered four unoccupied bunkers situated to defend the track they'd followed, with another trail running east to west. Company L found the main route on the coast to the village of Agulupella from Sag Sag and ultimately onto Natamo Point on the northern coast.

Taking full advantage of this discovery, the 1st Marine patrol advanced south along the trail. At the same time, a composite company from the 7th Marines landed at Sag Sag on the West Coast and moved along an east-west track. Australian reserve officer, William Weidman, a former Episcopal missionary at Sag Sag, served as guide and contact for the natives. When enemy resistance stopped the 1st Marine patrol short of the trail junction near Mount Talawe, Company K of the 1st Marines attacked.

For three hours, the Marines of Company K tried to break through a line of bunkers concealed by jungle growth. The Marines took fifteen casualties and withdrew beyond the reach of the Japanese mortars. The Japanese broke from cover and pursued a brave but foolish move that exposed the enemy troops to a deadly fire. This vigorous pursuit along the coast and the inland trails failed to trap the Japanese. The Marines captured General Matsuda's abandoned headquarters in the shadow of Mount Talawe. Inside they found documents buried instead of burned—possibly because the smoke would bring down artillery fire or airstrikes. The Japanese general and his troops escaped.

. . .

General Shepherd believed that Matsuda was headed to the vicinity of Mount Talawe to the south. He organized a battalion of six rifle companies—nearly four thousand men—entrusted to Chesty Puller. This patrol would advance from Agulupella on the east-west track down to Government Trail. Then all the way to Gilnit, a village on the Itni River, inland of Cape Bushing on the southern New Britain coast. Before Colonel Puller could advance, the intelligence section discovered that the enemy was retreating to the northeast toward Rabaul. General Shepherd detached the newly arrived 1/5 Marines. He reduced Colonel Puller's force from almost 4,000 to 350 Marines for the jungle march to Gilnit.

During this trek, Puller's Marines depended on supplies dropped from Allied planes. Puller was also assigned 150 native bearers to carry rations and supplies. Air Force B-17s dropped tons of cargo. The patrol was only possible because of the supplies dropped from the sky. But this did little to ease the Marine discomfort of plodding through the mud.

Despite the air assistance, the march to Gilnit taxed Marine ingenuity and hardened them for future action. Colonel Puller, who had led many patrols during the American intervention in Nicaragua, seemed in good spirits during this action. Division supply clerks, aware of Pullers' disdain for any creature comforts, were startled when they read his requisitions for hundreds of insect repellent bottles. Puller later wrote: "We were always soaked and everything we owned was likewise, and that lotion made the best damn stuff to start a fire with that you ever saw."

Colonel Puller's Marines slogged toward Gilnit on the Itni River, killing seventy-five Japanese, capturing one straggler, and weapons and equipment odds and ends. One abandoned enemy pack contained an American flag, probably captured by a *141st Infantry* soldier during Japan's Philippine conquest. When the patrol reached Gilnit, they met no opposition. Puller's Marines made contact with an rmy patrol from Cape Merkus and then headed toward the northern coast on February 16.

. . .

On February 12, to the west, Company B of the 1st Marines boarded landing craft to cross the Dampier Strait to occupy Rooke Island, fifteen miles off the coast of New Britain. Division intelligence believed that the enemy garrison had departed. They were correct. The enemy withdrawal began on December 6, three weeks before the Cape Gloucester landings.

Colonel Sato and half of his *51st Reconnaissance Regiment* of 500 men sailed to Cape Bushing, where Sato led his command up the river and joined the main body of the *Matsuda Force* east of Mount Talawe. Instead of committing Sato's troops to the defense of Hill 660, Matsuda directed him to delay and harass the 1st and 5th Marines who converged on the inland trail net. Colonel Sato succeeded in stalling the Marine patrols. He bought time for Matsuda's forces to retreat to the northern coasts with the *51st Reconnaissance Regiment* serving as the rearguard.

Once the Marines realized what Matsuda was up to, cutting their line of retreat became the highest priority. They withdrew the 1/5 Marines from the Puller patrol on the eve of the march toward Gilnit. On February 3, General Shepherd realized the Japanese did not have the strength to mount a counterattack on the airfields and devoted all his resources to destroy retreating enemy troops. Shepherd chose the 5th Marines, now restored to three-battalion strength, to pursue the fleeing Japanese troops. While light aircraft scouted the coastal track, landing craft stood fast and waited to debark the regiment to cut off and destroy General Matsuda's force. Bad weather stalled the 5th Marines. Clouds concealed the enemy from aerial observation while the boiling surf ruled out landings on several beaches. With over 5,000 Marines and Army troops, the Allies rotated their battalions and sent out fresh troops each day. They also used ten LCMs (Landing Craft, Mechanical) to leapfrog the retreating Japanese.

Marines were not called upon to make marches for more than two days in a row, with few exceptions. After a one day hike, they either remained at camp for three days or made the next jump by

LCM. The 5th Marines expected a battle for the Japanese supply point at Iboki Point, but enemy troops dwindled. Instead of encountering resistance by a resolute and clever rearguard, the 5th Marines only found stragglers, most wounded or too sick to fight. Marines kept up pressure on retreating Japanese troops. On February 24, they took Iboki Point without loss or even one man wounded.

During this action, American amphibious forces seized Eniwetok and Kwajalein Atolls in the Marshall Islands. The Central Pacific offensive now gathered momentum. Allied carrier strikes proved Truk was too vulnerable to continue serving as a significant enemy naval base. Now conscious of the threat to their inner perimeter developing to the north, the Japanese pulled back the fleet units from Truk and aircraft from Rabaul. On February 19, two days after the Allies invaded Eniwetok, enemy fighters at Rabaul took off to challenge an American air raid. When the Japanese bombers returned the next day, not a single operational Japanese fighter remained at the airfields.

The defense of Rabaul now depended on ground forces. Lieutenant General Sakai, commander of the *17th Division*, received orders to not dig in near Cape Hoskins and instead move to Rabaul. Sakai assumed the supplies he'd positioned along the trail would enable at least the most spirited of Matsuda's troops to stay ahead of the Marines and reach the fortress.

What was left of the self-propelled barges could carry the remaining troops and heavy equipment needed to defend Rabaul. This retreat would be an ordeal for the Japanese. The 5th Marines had already showed how swiftly they could move by taking advantage of Allied controlled skies and coastal waters. A full two-week march separated the nearest of Matsuda soldiers from their destination. While attrition was heavy, those who could contribute the least to Rabaul's defenses fell by the wayside.

VOLUPAI - TALASEA
OPERATIONS
6 - 11 MARCH 1944
5th MARINES ROUTE OF ADVANCE
APPROXIMATE FORM LINES SHOWN
MILES
Volupai
Liapo
Big
Mt Wor
Kum
Mt Bagum
Bagum
Cape Bastion

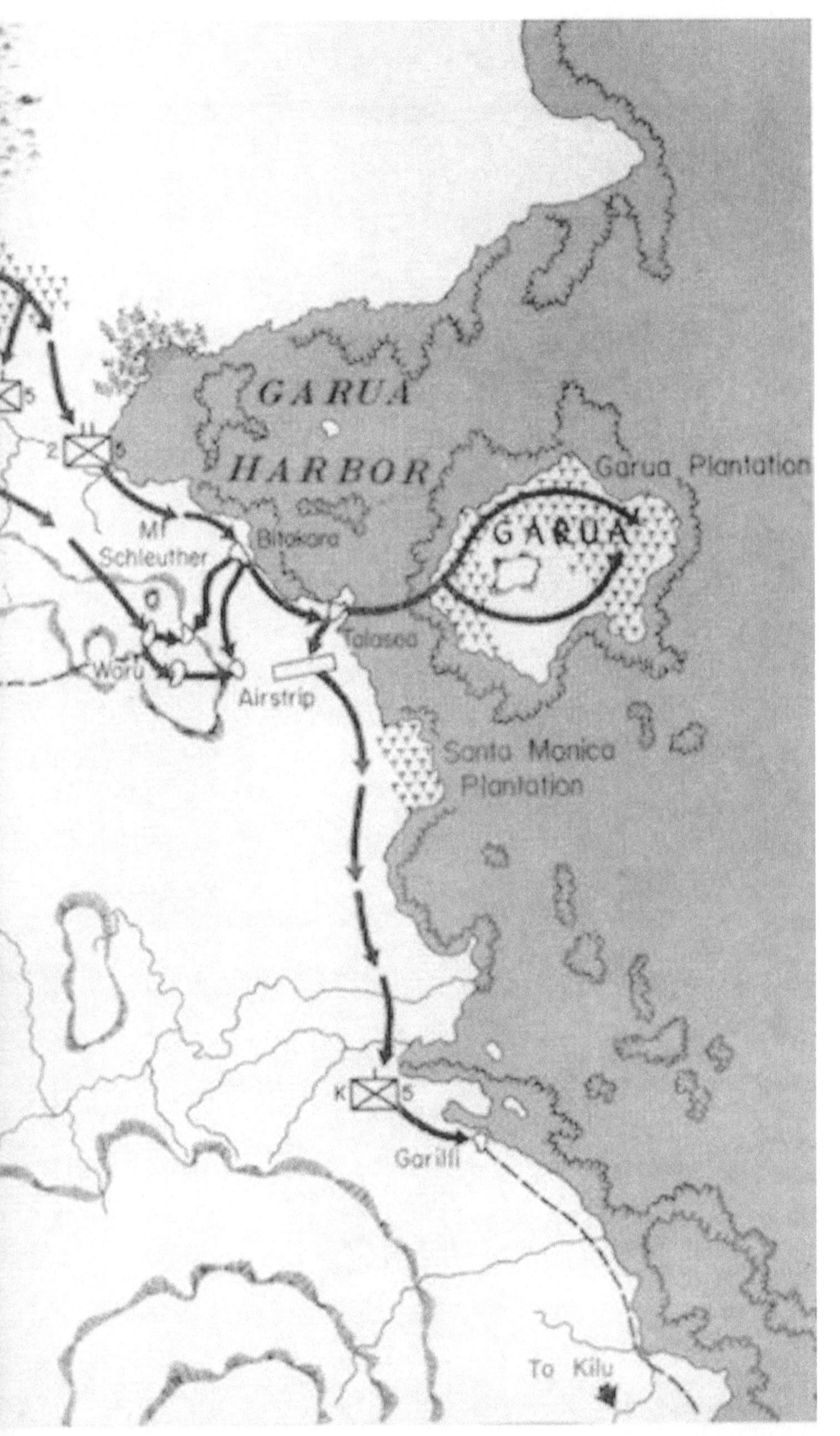

GARUA HARBOR
GARUA
Garua Plantation
Bitokara
Mt Schleuther
Waru
Talasea
Airstrip
Santa Monica Plantation
K 5
Garilli
To Kilu
2
5

LANDINGS AT VOLUPAI

March 6 was D-Day for the 5th Marines to land on the west coast of the Willaumez Peninsula—halfway between the base and the tip. Division intelligence believed that the Japanese strength between Talasea, site of the crude airstrip, and Cape Hoskins, across Kimbe Bay were equal to the 5th Marines. Still, most of the enemy troops were defending Cape Hoskins. If the intelligence estimates were correct, Sakai prepared the last defense of Cape Hoskins before ordered to retreat to Rabaul.

A torpedo boat landed a recon team at Bagum. Their orders were to discover the intent of Japanese preparations near Volupai, nine miles from Red Beach, chosen for the assault. They learned Red Beach was lightly defended from native sources who'd worked at a plantation operated in the area before the war. The natives confirmed the Marine estimates of an enemy force of 600 men, two-thirds of them near Talasea, armed with artillery and mortars.

The Royal Australian Air Force, based out of Kiriwina Island to the south, bombed the Volupai region for three days. A force of 5th Marines, designated as Landing Team A, loaded into a small flotilla of landing craft set out from Iboki Point with an escort of torpedo boats.

On March 6, at 0835, the first amphibian tractors carrying assault troops clawed their way onto Red Beach. Sherman tanks in Army LCMs opened fire with machine guns. They waited to direct their 75mm weapons against any enemy gunner opposing the Allied landing force. Aside from difficult-to-pinpoint small arms fire, enemy opposition consisted mainly of mortar barrages, screened by the terrain. As Japanese mortar shells burst among the approaching landing craft, Captain Theodore A. Petras, flying a Piper L-4 Grasshopper, dove low over mortar positions and dropped hand grenades from the cockpit. Natives warned the Allied assault forces of a machine gun nest dominating the beach from the slopes on Little Mount Worri. The 1/5 Marines leading the way found it abandoned and encountered no serious opposition as they dug into protect the beachhead.

Four Sherman's supported the 5th Marines as they pushed farther inland, pressing their attack. One of the medium tanks got bogged down on Red Beach's soft sand, but the other three continued in a line. The lead tank lost momentum on a muddy rise, and two Japanese soldiers carrying landmines surged from cover to attack. Company E rifleman cut one down, but the other detonated his mine against the tank, killing himself and a Marine trying to stop him. The explosion jammed the tank's turret and stunned the crewmen inside, shaken but not wounded. The damaged Sherman moved aside to allow the other two tanks to pass, returning to the trail only to hit another mine.

After losing two tanks, one temporarily immobilized, and the other permanently out of action, the 5th Marines continued their advance. During the fighting at a Volupai coconut plantation, a dead Japanese soldier's body had a map showing the enemy positions around Talasea. By early afternoon, regimental intelligence distributed the information, which proved valuable for future operations.

Company E of the 5th Marines followed the trail to the plantation. At the same time, Company G kept pace, crossing the western shoulder of Little Mount Worri. Five P-39s from Airfield No. 2 at

Cape Gloucester supported the attack. The pilots could not pinpoint the troops below and instead bombed Cape Hoskins, where there was no danger of hitting any Marines. Even without the aerial attack, the 2/5 Marines overran the plantation by nightfall and dug in for the night. Marines counted thirty-five Japanese killed.

Throughout the fighting, Combat Team A took eighty-four casualties. The artillery batteries suffered a more significant number of casualties than rifle companies.

The 2/11 Marines set up their 75mm howitzers on the open beach—exposed to fire from the 90mm mortars, which Captain Petras showered with hand grenades. Some of the Navy Corpsmen on Red Beach, who helped the wounded artillerymen, ended up as casualties themselves. Thirty-four of the Marines killed and wounded on March 6 were members of the artillery unit. The gunners succeeded in registering their fires that afternoon and harassing the enemy through the night.

While the Marines prepared to renew their attack on the next day, the Japanese opposed them in order to keep a line of retreat open for the *Matsuda Force*. By doing so, the Japanese fell back from their prepared positions on the fringes of the Volupai plantation. This included the mortar pits that had caused such havoc with the 2/11 Marines. They dug in on the northern slopes of Mount Schleuther, overlooking the trail leading from the plantation to Bitokara village on the coast. Company F was sent uphill to disrupt the Japanese plan, while Company E remained on the trail to build up a base of fire.

On the right flank, Company F, the weapons platoon, surged from the undergrowth. They surprised Japanese machine gunners setting up their weapon, killing them, and turning the gun against the enemy troops. Company F's advance caught the Japanese in mid deployment and drove them back, killing over forty of their men. The 5th Marines established a night perimeter that extended from Mount Schleuther to the trail and embraced a portion of both.

The March 7 action was a departure from the plan. Originally, the 3/5 Marines would assume responsibility for the beachhead.

Landing craft that had carried assault troops would depart from Red Beach on D-Day, and pick up the 3rd Battalion at Iboki Point, bringing them to Volupai. If the reinforcements were to arrive in time for an attack on the morning of March 7, this would require a dangerous nighttime Volupai approach through uncharted waters studded with sharp coral that could tear open the hull of the landing craft.

General Shepherd decided the risks of such a move outweighed the advantages and canceled it at the last moment. No boats started the return voyage to Red Beach until after daylight on March 7, delaying Marine reinforcements until late afternoon. This left the 1st Battalion with only enough time to send Company C a short distance inland on the trail to the village of Liappo. When the trail petered out among trees and vines, Marines hacked their way forward until they ran out of daylight short of their objective.

The 1/5 Marines resumed the advance on March 8. Companies A and B moved through parallel paths leading east of Little Mount Worri.

Company A Marines peered through dense undergrowth and saw a figure in a Japanese uniform and opened fire. This man was a native wearing clothing discarded by the enemy and serving as a guide for Company B. The shots triggered an exchange of fire that killed two Marines, wounded the guide, and several others. Afterward, the advance resumed, but through formidable terrain—muddy ravines choked with brush and vines—which slowed the Marines as darkness fell with the battalion still on the trail.

The 2nd Battalion probed deeper into the enemy defenses. Patrols pushed ahead on the morning of March 8. They found Japanese troops dug in at the Bitokara Mission. The enemy fell back before the Marines could charge their position. Marines occupied Bitokara and advanced as far as Talasea taking over the abandoned airstrip. Other Marine patrols climbed the steep slopes of Mount Schleuther and collided with the enemy troops. Fire from a 90mm mortar, 75mm gun, and small arms killed eighteen Marines. Rather than press the attack in the darkness, Marines withdrew from the mountain and dug in at the Bitokara Mission. Mortars and artillery hammered the defenses through the night, leaving one company to defend the Talasea airstrip.

On the morning of March 9, Company G of the 2nd Marine Battalion advanced up Mount Schleuther while companies B and C cleared villages around the base. Company G expected to meet strong opposition during its part of the coordinated attack. But the Japanese had withdrawn from the mountaintop and left behind one artillery piece, two stragglers, and three dead. Enemy troops had festooned the abandoned 75mm gun with vines serving as tripwires for a booby-trap. When Marines hacked at the vines to examine the weapon more closely, they released the firing pins and detonated a round in the chamber. Since the Japanese gun crew had plugged the bore before they fled, the explosion ruptured the breach block and wounded several Marines.

After yielding the dominant terrain, the Japanese chose not to defend any of the villages clustered at the mountain's base. This opened up a route for the 5th Marines across the Willaumez Peninsula to support further operations against General Matsuda's line of retreat. Since the March 6 offensive, the Allied force had killed an estimated 150 Japanese at the cost of seventeen dead and 114 wounded, most casualties taking place on the first day. The last phase of the fighting that began on Red Beach consisted of securing Garua Island, abandoned by the Japanese.

Results of the action at the base of the Willaumez Peninsula were mixed. The grassy Talasea airstrip lacked enough length to accommodate fighter planes. Still, the division's liaison planes made widespread use of it, landing on either side of a Japanese aircraft's carcass until the wreckage could be hauled away. The trail net was a web of muddy paths that required long hours of hard work by Company F of the 17th Marines. Army engineers used a 10-ton wrecker to recover three Sherman tanks that had become mired during the fighting. By March 10, the trails could support a further advance. Two days later, the 3/5 Marines provided a guard of honor. The same American flag flown over Airfield No. 2 on Cape Gloucester was raised over Bitokara.

FINAL COMBAT AND RELIEF

The Allied flotilla of Navy LCTs and Army LCMs supporting the Volupai landings continued to inflict damage on Japanese coastal traffic. On March 9, landing crafts carrying supplies around the tip of the peninsula spotted four enemy barges. They were beached and carelessly camouflaged. An LCT opened fire from its 20mm cannon and destroyed one of the Japanese barges. After that, two Army LCMs used their 37mm guns and opened fire on another barge beached on the shore.

The Japanese tried to make the best use of their shrinking number of barges, but the bulk of General Matsuda's troops moved overland. A hundred Japanese were dug in at Garilli, but by the time Company K of the 3/5 Marines attacked on March 11, the Japanese had withdrawn to a new trail three miles away. Marines fought a series of actions lasting four days. The Japanese retreated a few hundred yards, dragging their 75mm gun that anchored each of the blocking positions. On March 16, Company K received 81mm mortars from an arriving LCM. The enemy turned their cannon seaward to deal with the threat but could not hit the landing craft. After the Marine mortars landed, they were quickly put into action. Japanese troops again withdrew, but this time they faded away since the bulk of General Matsuda's force had escaped eastward.

The 5th Marines dispatched patrols southbound to the base of the Willaumez Peninsula, only capturing an occasional straggler, confirming the departure of General Matsuda's primary force. The 1st Marine Division established training sites, a comfortable head-quarters, and a hospital that used Japanese medicine stocks. Marines could swim in a rest area off the Garua beaches and hot springs ashore. The Navy then built a base on the Willaumez Peninsula for torpedo boats to harass surviving Japanese barges. On March 27, only the second day after the base was operating, Allied aircraft mistook two boats for enemy craft. They attacked—killing five and wounding eighteen sailors with friendly fire.

At the new training center on Garua, classes were taught to produce amphibious scouts for future operations. Headquarters decided that a reconnaissance of Cape Hoskins would be a suitable graduation exercise since aerial observers had seen no sign of enemy there. On April 13, sixteen trainees, two native guides, and a rifle platoon from the 2/5 Marines embarked on a pair of LCMs to Cape Hoskins. Two instructors stood by in one landing craft as the platoon established a trail block. Future scouts advanced toward the airfield at Cape Hoskins. The patrol encountered small arms and mortar fire en route to their objective. But the Marines had learned their lessons well, and they broke off the action and escaped with no casualties.

The Japanese had retreated. Major Komori's troops blazed the trail for Sato's command from Augitni to the northern coast. They encountered a dispiriting number of hungry stragglers as they marched toward Kandoka, a supply depot ten miles west of the Willaumez Peninsula. Komori's troops came under fire from an American landing craft as they crossed the Kuhu River. The rain-swollen river was a serious obstacle and became a detour that lasted two days until reaching a point where the stream narrowed.

On March 17, Komori's provisions ran out, forcing his troops to survive on birds, fish, and taro root, supplemented by coconuts from a nearby plantation. After losing a dozen men and additional time crossing the river, Komori's troops struggled into Kandoka. Only to discover that the food and other supplies had already been carried off to Rabaul. Major Komori pressed on through this crushing disappointment. His men continued to live off the land as best they could. Another five Japanese troops drowned in the fast-moving Kuhu River, and a native hired guide defected. Major Komori came down with a severe bout of malaria, and although physically weakened, he forced himself to continue.

Japanese survivors strived onward toward Cape Hoskins and ultimately into Rabaul. On Easter Sunday, 1944, a handful of half-starved enemy troops wandered onto the San Remo Plantation, where Marines had bivouacked after pursuing Japanese troops eastward from the Willaumez Peninsula. The Marine unit was preparing to pass in review for the regimental commander when a sentry saw them and opened fire. The ensuing firefight killed three Japanese. One of the dead was Major Komori. In his pack was a rusty revolver and a diary that described the suffering of his command.

Colonel Sato took the rest of the rearguard intended for the *Matsuda Force* and set out from Augitni on March 7. One day after Major Komori had sent word on the nineteenth that the 5th Marines' patrols had fanned out from the Willaumez Peninsula, where the reinforced regiment had landed two weeks earlier. When Sato reached Linga Linga he came across an abandoned Marine patrol bivouac. Sato's force had shrunk to less than 250 men, half the number he had starting out.

The following day, he was shocked when Allied landing craft appeared as his men prepared to cross the Kapaluk River. Sato set up a perimeter to repel the expected attack. The boats carried elements of the 2/1 Marines and landed a patrol from Company F on a beach beyond Kandoka. Another platoon was dispatched westward along the coastal track. Colonel Sato was only aware of the landing's general location and groped eastward toward the village. On March 26, they collided. The Japanese surprised the Marines crossing a small stream and pinned them down for three hours until Company F reinforcements forced the Japanese to break off, take to the jungle, and bypass Kandoka.

Colonel Sato's column disappeared into the jungle. One of the division's light airplanes scouting landing sites for the battalion sited the end of the column near Linga Linga. The Piper L-4 Grasshopper pilot sketched where the Japanese were and dropped the map to one of the troop-laden landing craft. The pilot then led the way to an undefended beach where the Marines waded ashore and set out to pursue Sato and his troops. On March 30, an eight-man Marine patrol spotted a pair of Japanese with their rifles slung. These enemy troops were members of a seventy-three man patrol—too many to handle.

After the enemy column moved off, the eight-man patrol hurried back to Kandoka and reported. Outfitted with more machine guns, mortars, and men. This reinforced rifle platoon returned to the trail. The Japanese encountered another Marine patrol, which took up a position on high ground commanding the trail. When the reinforced rifle platoon heard gunfire, they hurried to aid the other Marines. The resulting slaughter killed fifty-five Japanese troops, including Colonel Sato, who died, sword in hand, charging Marines. The Marines did not suffer one casualty during this encounter.

On April 9, the 3/1 Marines continued to search for enemy stragglers. The bulk of Matsuda's force, and whatever supplies it could transport, had retreated to Cape Hoskins.

Army troops were taking over for the Marines. It had now been four months since the landing at Cape Gloucester. The time had come for the amphibious forces to move on to an operation that would make better use of their specialized equipment and training. The last Marine action took place on April 22, when an ambush, sprung by the 2/5 Marines, killed twenty Japanese and caused the campaign's last Marine fatality. By seizing western New Britain as part of Rabaul's isolation, the division suffered 1,083 wounded and 310 killed in action—one-fourth of the Japanese casualties.

The capture of the Cape Gloucester airfields in early February 1944 tied down the 1st Marine Division for an extended period. This alarmed the recently appointed Commandant of the Marine Corps, General Vandegrift. Referring to an extended engagement in New Britain, he wrote: "Six months there, and [the 1st Marine Division] will no longer be a well-trained amphibious division."

Vandegrift urged US Fleet Admiral Earnest King to help him pry the division from General Douglas MacArthur's grasp so he could again engage in amphibious operations. Admiral Nimitz, the commander-in-chief of Pacific Ocean Areas, requested the 1st Marine Division for the Palau Islands' impending invasion. The capture would protect MacArthur's flank on his advance to the Philippines.

Admiral Nimitz made the Army's 140th Infantry Division available to MacArthur. He swapped a division capable of taking over the New Britain Campaign for one that could spearhead the amphibious offensive against Japan. MacArthur briefly kept control of one Marine division, Company A, 1st Tank Battalion. The unit's medium tanks landed on April 22 at Hollandia on the northern coast of New Guinea. A swamp behind the beachhead stopped the Shermans from assisting the inland advance.

The commanding general of the Army's 140th Infantry Division was Major General Isaac R. Brush. He arrived on April 10 and arranged for the relief. His advance echelon landed on the 23rd, with the rest of the division following five days after. The 1st Marine Division departed on April 6 and May 4. They left behind the 12th Defense Battalion, who continued to provide antiaircraft defense for the Cape Gloucester airfields until replaced by an Army unit later in May.

The 1st Marine Division had plunged into an unforgiving jungle and overwhelmed a resolute enemy. They captured the Cape Gloucester airfields and drove the Japanese from western New Britain in just over four months. Several factors helped the Marines defeat the Japanese. The Allied control of the air and sea provided mobility. It disrupted the coastal barge traffic, which the enemy depended on for the movement of large quantities of medicine and supplies desperately needed for the retreat to Rabaul. Landing craft armed with rockets, aided by tanks and rocket-equipped amphibian trucks fired from landing craft, helped support the landings. But the size of the island and the lack of fixed coastal defenses reduced the efficiency of naval gunfire.

Marines defied the swamp and undergrowth by using superior engineering skills and bringing forward tanks that crushed enemy emplacements—adding to formidable American firepower. Through photo analysis, an art that improved rapidly, the Americans misinterpreted the nature of the swamp forest. However, Marine intelligence made excellent use of captured Japanese documents throughout the campaign. But it was the courage and endurance of the average Marine who made victory possible on Cape Gloucester. A Marine braved discomfort, disease, and violent death during his time in this hellish green Inferno.

1944 BATTLE FOR SAIPAN

BREACHING THE MARIANAS

Dawn on June 15, 1944 would be a brutal day. Navy fire support ships off Saipan Island increased the previous day's firing. At 0542, Admiral Richmond Kelly Turner ordered, "Land the landing force." At 0700, the LSTs (Landing Ship, Tank) moved to a thousand yards behind the line of departure.

Troops waiting in the LSTs debarked into LVTs (Landing Vehicle, Tracked). Navy and Marine personnel took their positions with radio gear. They displayed flags to indicate which beach approaches they controlled.

Admiral Turner delayed H-hour for 10 minutes until 0840 to give the boat waves extra time to get into position. After the first wave headed full speed at the beaches, the Japanese were ready. They waited, poised to make the Marine assault units pay a heavy price in blood.

The first assault wave contained LVT [A]s (armored amphibian tractors) with their swiftly firing 75mm guns. Escorted by light gunboats firing 4.5-inch rockets and 40mm guns. The LVTs could negotiate their way through the reef. But the gunboats could not and had to turn around until they could uncover a passage through the reef.

Farther north at 0600, a diversionary landing was organized off Tanapag harbor by the 2nd, 24th, and 29th Marines. The Japanese were not deceived and didn't rush any reinforcements to the area. But the ruse tied up one complete enemy regiment.

When the LVTs reached the reef, the battle exploded. Water fountained from mortar and artillery shells exploding in every direction. Rifles, machine guns, and small arms fire joined the crescendo as the LVTs ground ashore.

Mayhem spread through the beaches, mainly in the 2nd Marine Division area. A northern current caused the 6th and 8th Marine assault battalions to land five hundred yards too far north. This created a gap between the 2nd and 4th Marine Divisions. Colonel Hogaboom, operations officer of the Expeditionary Troops wrote: "The opposition consisted primarily of artillery and mortar fire from weapons placed in well-deployed positions. Previously registered to cover the beach areas, and fire from small arms, automatic weapons, and anti-boat guns sited to cover the approaches for the nearest landing beaches."

The result was five of the 2nd Marine Division assault unit commanders wounded. Afetan Point, in the middle, was raked by deadly enfilade fire to the left and right. This allowed two battalions of the 23rd and 25th Marines to cross the gap. The original plan was for the assault troops to ride their LVTs to the first objective, the O-1 line. But the surge of enemy fire and natural obstacles prevented this.

A few units in the center of the 4th Division made it through, but fierce enemy resistance pinned them down on the left and right flanks. This prevented the two divisions from making direct contact.

In the 3rd Battalion, 24th Marine Regiment, a young lieutenant recalled his extraordinary experience on the beach when he came ashore: "All around us was chaos and bitter combat. Marine and Jap bodies laid in mangled and grotesque positions. Blasted and burnt-out pillboxes. Burning wrecks of LVTs knocked out by high-velocity Jap fire. The acrid smell of high explosives. Shattered trees. And the churned-up sand littered with discarded equipment."

After his company moved inland a short distance, he experienced the terrifying pre-registered Japanese artillery fire: "Wham! A shell landed right on top of us. I was too surprised to think, but instinctively, we all hit the deck and spread out. Then shells poured down on us: behind, ahead, on both sides, and right in our midst. They rocketed down like a freight train, thundering, and exploding into a deafening roar.

"I realized the first shell bursts we heard were ranging shots. Now the Japs had zeroed in on us, and we were pinned down in a full-fledged barrage. Their fire hit us with pinpoint accuracy, and it wasn't hard to see why: Fifteen hundred feet above us were Jap observation posts honeycombing the crest of Mt. Tapotchau."

That night the lieutenant and his runner shared a foxhole and split watches. Death came close again: "The hours of my watch passed slowly. I leaned over to shake my runner awake. 'It's time for your watch,' I whispered. 'Watch out for that place over there, might be Japs in it. Stay awake.' After that, I rolled over and was asleep in an instant.

"As if it was right away, someone shook me and insisted I wake up. I jerked and bolted upright—your reflexes act faster in combat, and you never entirely go to sleep. I glanced at my watch, and it was almost dawn. I turned to my runner, lying against me asleep. 'Let's go,' I said. 'Pass the word to squad leaders to get set.' But he didn't move. I shook him. Again, he didn't move. He was dead. With all the barbarity that war demands, I rolled him over, took his canteen, and poured the precious water into my own. Then I left him lying there. Dead."

The assault regiments took casualties from constant shelling zeroed in by spotters on high ground. Reinforcing and supply units piled up from the confusion on the landing beaches. Snipers lurked everywhere. The support waves experienced the same deadly enemy fire on their way to the beach. Many LVTs took direct hits, others were flipped over on their sides by waves or enemy fire—spilling equipment and personnel onto the reef. Casualties in both divisions mounted. Evacuating them to the ships was dangerous and difficult. The medical aid station set up ashore was also under enemy fire.

Marine artillery landed in the late afternoon on D-Day to support the infantry. They received deadly-accurate counter-battery fire from the Japanese. General Harry Schmidt, in command of the 4th Division, came ashore at 1930 and later wrote, "The command post during that time did not function very well. It was the hottest spot I was in during the war."

Major James (Jim) Donovan, executive officer of the 1/6 Marines, survived a mortar bombardment with uncanny timing and precision: "We entered a little village called Charan-Kanoa. We had stopped to get some water and were washing up and resting when mortar shells fell on us. We saw a tall smokestack hiding a Japanese forward observer. He was directing fire and looking right down on us. It didn't occur to anyone that someone could be up in that smokestack after all that naval gunfire and everything else fired into the area. But he was sure up there all right. He killed a lot of Marines from G Company that day.

"He caught us without foxholes. We had a false sense of security. We thought we could relax. Wrong. We had to dig holes in a hurry. It's hard to dig a hole when you're lying on your stomach digging with your chin, knees, toes, and elbows. While it's possible to dig a hole that way, we lost more Marines than we should have before someone located that Jap observer. I don't know how tall that smokestack was, but at least two or three stories high. From up there, he saw the entire picture, and he really gave it to us."

At night on D-Day, the Japanese continued to probe Marine positions. Fire from bypassed enemy soldiers and enemy attacks screened by a curtain of civilians. The 6th Marines dealt with the main counterattack on the far-left flank. Over two-thousand Japanese moved south from Garapan. And by 2200, they attacked. Led by tanks, they charged, but were met by a wall of fire from 37mm antitank guns, .30-caliber machine guns, and M-1 rifles. It was too much, and they pulled back.

The Japanese retreated, leaving seven hundred men dead and an abandoned tank. The body of the bugler who blew the charge slumped over the open hatch. A bullet had gone straight up his bugle and blew his brains out.

Illumination shells, fired from Navy ships, were vital for the Marine defense that night and on many other nights. Japanese records revealed, "as soon as the night attack units go forward, the enemy points out targets by using large star shells which turned night into day. Thus making the maneuvering of units extremely difficult."

Weary Marines tried to get some sleep along the irregular line of foxholes. Two things were clear: they had forced themselves onto a perilous beachhead through the teeth of fierce enemy fire, and a ferocious battle lay ahead.

While the Marines focused on survival and the immediate ground in front of them, Senior Command regarded the landing's initial success as a culmination of months of planning, organization, and training for a strategic strike on the crucial Japanese stronghold. The opportunity for this sprang from earlier victories in the Central Pacific. The Marine conquest of Tarawa in November 1943, followed by the joint Marine-Army capture of Eniwetok and Kwajalein in the Marshall Islands in February 1944, had broken the ring of Japanese defenses, and set the stage for future operations.

These earlier victories allowed the American operational timetable for the Central Pacific to move up by three months. After discussions on various alternatives (an attack on the Japanese base at Truk). The Joint Chiefs decided on their next objective: the Mariana Islands. There were three principal targets: Saipan, Tinian, and Guam. A bold decision because Saipan was over 1,300 miles from the Marshall Islands and 3,200 miles from Hawaii, but only 1,250 miles from Japan. These islands were linchpins in the defensive line, which the Japanese felt they had to hold after the previous losses in the Southwest and Central Pacific.

Saipan also represented a whole new kind of problem for an American assault. Instead of a small flat coral inlay on an atoll, it was a large island target of seventy-two miles. The terrain varied from swamps to flat cane fields to steep cliffs. The Japanese considered it *their* territory, although it was legally only a mandate provided by the Versailles Treaty's terms after World War I. The Japanese removed all outsiders and started military construction in 1934.

Attacking a formidable objective like Saipan demanded complex planning and a much greater force than previously needed in the Central Pacific. Admiral Raymond A. Spruance was in overall command of the force ordered to invade the Marianas. Admiral

Turner was in command of the Amphibious Task Force. Corps Commander, General Holland Smith was tasked with directing the landing forces on Saipan and then on to the neighboring island of Tinian.

The operational plan for the invasion of Saipan was code-named, Forager. It called for an assault on the western side of the island, with the 2nd Marine Division on the left and the 4th Marine Division on the right. The Army's 27th Infantry Division, led by Major General Ralph C. Smith, was held in reserve, ready to be fed into the battle if needed. While both Marine divisions had previously fought as a complete unit, the 27th had experienced only two minor landings (on Makin and Eniwetok islets).

These three divisions trained intensively in Hawaii. General Schmidt's 4th Marine Division trained on Maui. General Watson's 2nd Marine Division on Hawaii Island (Big Island). And Army General Ralph Smith's 27th Infantry Division on Oahu.

These were busy and hard-working months. Replacements arrived to fill gaps left by the recent battle casualties. These men needed to be well-versed in all the complexities of fieldwork. Most of the replacements were boys fresh from boot camp, ignorant of everything except for the barest essentials. Their weeks consisted of long marches, live fire, field combat problems, obstacle courses, judo, street-fighting, calisthenics, and several lectures on errors made during the recent Namur battle. An added emphasis was placed on how to attack fortified positions. They worked with demolition charges of TNT, dynamite, and plastic explosive. They learned to use flamethrowers until they could operate them forward and backward.

In May 1944, the final maneuvers for the practice landings were ready for all three divisions. The operational plan looked efficiently organized on paper. According to a young lieutenant on Maui it looked different: "To us, it was the same old stuff we'd been doing for a year. Filing up from compartments below decks to your assigned boat station. Going over the side. Hurrying down the net to beat the stopwatch and into the heaving LVCP (Landing Craft Vehicle Personnel). Endless hours of circling—wet, hungry, and bored. The K rations tasted like sawdust. The weather only got rougher, and some of the men got so seasick. All of us were soaking wet and so cold.

"When we finally headed back toward the transport and scrambled up over the cargo net, there was a sigh of relief. The next day was the same thing all over again. Only this time, we went ashore. Getting your only pair of socks and shoes wet, wading through the surf, and rushing onto the beach before all the sand mingled inside your shoes. Confusing and conflicting orders flowed down through the chain of command: move on, halt, go here, go there."

The attack force gathered at Pearl Harbor. Over eight hundred ships set out in the armada. Some for direct troop fire support, some for transport, and some (Fast Carrier Task Force) made advance airstrikes and then were tasked with dealing with any attacks the landing would provoke from the Japanese Navy.

General Holland Smith's V Amphibious Corps totaled over 71,000 Marines and Army troops. They sailed on May 25, headed for Saipan. The troops got their final briefings at sea. Maps of the island, based on recent aerial and submarine photographs, estimated 15,000 enemy troops (turned out to be over 30,000) along with their detailed attack plans for two Marine divisions.

Planes launched from American fast carriers on June 11. They softened up enemy targets and attacked Japanese land-based air. Two days later, the main enemy fleet headed to the Marianas for a decisive battle. Then on June 14, the old battleships of the US Navy, ready to dish up some payback from the Pearl Harbor disaster, moved in close to Saipan and hammered Japanese defenders with their heavy guns. UDTs (Underwater Demolition Teams) made treacherous swims close to the assault beaches. They checked channels, reefs, and reconnoitered beach defenses. Everything was ready for the landings.

The bloody business of D-Day was only the beginning—a long grueling fight had yet to come.

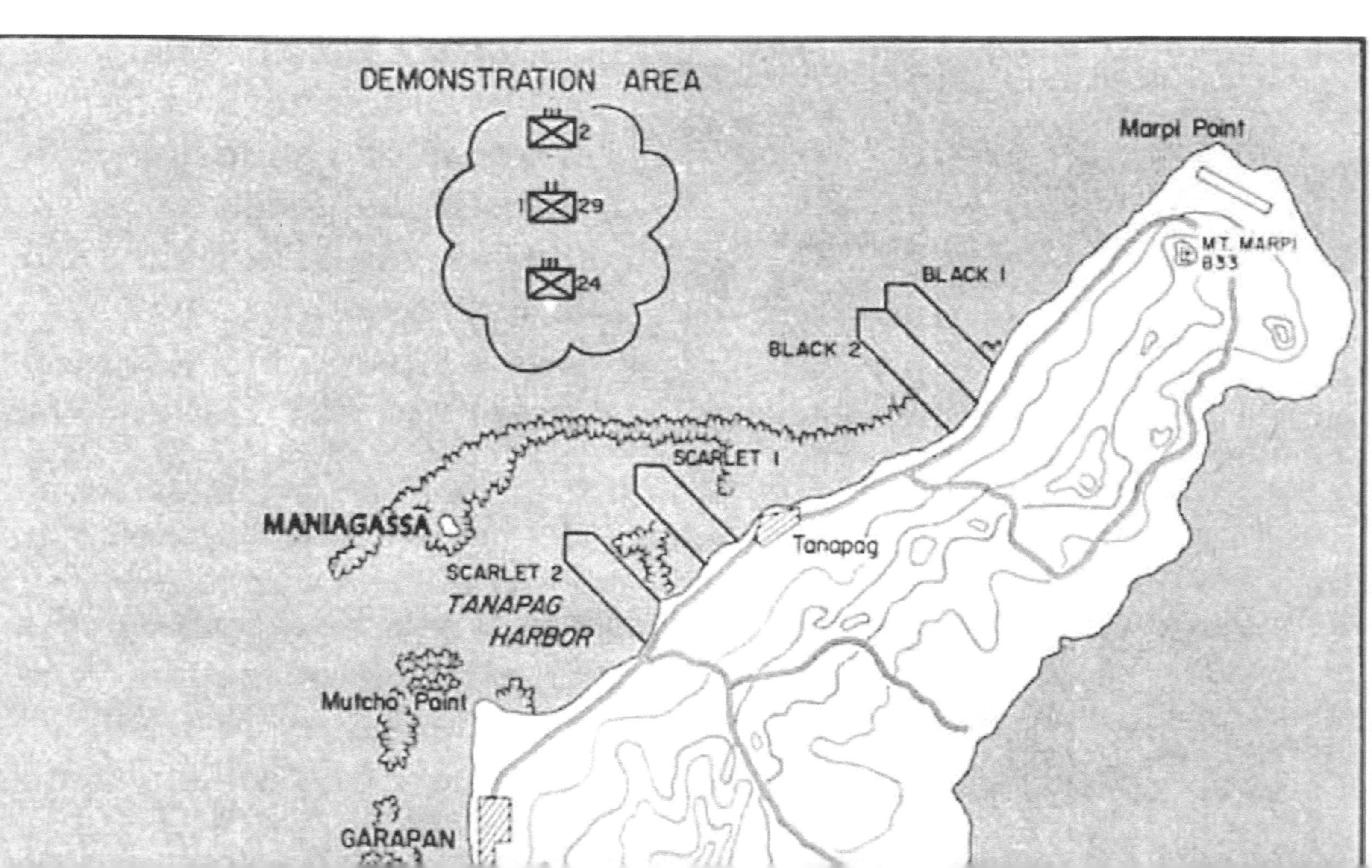

DEMONSTRATION AREA
2
1 29
24
Marpi Point
MT. MARPI
853
BLACK 1
BLACK 2
SCARLET 1
MANIAGASSA
SCARLET 2
TANAPAG
HARBOR
Tanapag
Mutcho Point
GARAPAN

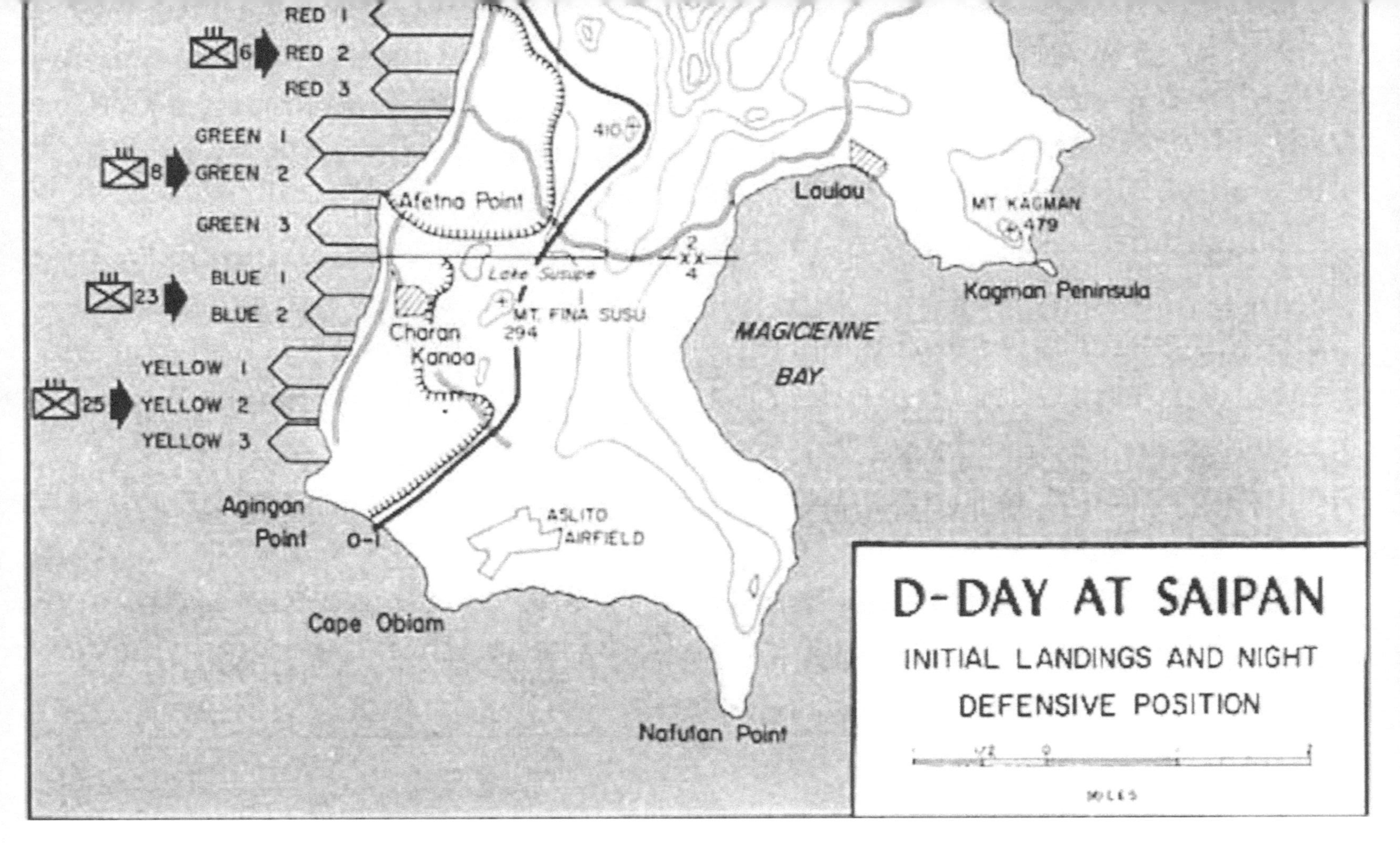

RED 1
RED 2
RED 3
6
GREEN 1
GREEN 2
GREEN 3
8
BLUE 1
BLUE 2
23
YELLOW 1
YELLOW 2
YELLOW 3
25
Afetna Point
410
Lake Susupe
MT. FINA SUSU
294
Charan Kanoa
Agingan Point
O-1
ASLITO AIRFIELD
Cape Obiam
Nafutan Point
Loulou
MT KAGMAN
479
Kagman Peninsula
MAGICIENNE BAY
2 XX 4
D-DAY AT SAIPAN
INITIAL LANDINGS AND NIGHT
DEFENSIVE POSITION
MILES
1/2 0 1

ASSAULT ON SAIPAN

June 16-17, 1944

For two days, the Marines assaulted along an irregular front. The 2nd Marines moved north toward Garapan. The 8th east into the swamps near Lake Susupe. And the 6th pushed northeast into Mount Tipo Pali.

It was close combat. No exceptions for battalion commanders. Colonel Chambers, commanding the 3/25 Marines of the 4th Division, described his experiences: "We got to a giant bomb crater. The soil had been all turned up, and around it was three Marines protected by the dirt. I called over to one of these Marines and asked what was going on. He said an antiaircraft gun was right in front of them. I crawled to within two feet of the top of that dirt and raised on my hands to see for myself.

"In less than thirty yards, I was looking into the muzzle of an 88mm antitank gun. The Japs had swung the damn thing around and pointed it right up the hill. I was looking clear down its muzzle. I dropped as hard as I could, and then the damn gun went off. The shell tore through the far side of the bomb crater and came through the dirt near where I was. It took the head off the Marine right next to me. The shell landed and detonated another thirty feet beyond me. Later that same day, we had another close call.

"We advanced and uncovered some Jap supply caches. One was an ammo dump. At 1500, the Japs blew the dump where I was standing and caused many concussion casualties—including myself. I still don't remember a thing about it. Marines told me that when the blast went off, I got thrown right up in the air and turned a complete flip and then landed on my face."

On the night of the 16th, the Japanese launched a major attack against the 6th Marines. This time with forty-four tanks. This battle was a madhouse of noise tracers and flashing lights. As tanks were hit and set on fire, they silhouetted other tanks that came out of flickering shadows to the front. Marines fired in with grenade launchers, 2.36-inch rocket launchers, 75mm self-propelled guns, artillery, and tanks. When it was over and dawn broke, the shattered hulks of twenty-seven Japanese tanks lay there smoking.

In the Susupe swamp, Marines drove inland to the east toward the objective of Aslito Airfield. In danger of overextending his lines. General Holland Smith pulled the 165th Infantry out of reserve and sent them ashore to reinforce the 4th Marine division. On the same day, General Ralph Smith came ashore to command the additional Army 27th Infantry Division units as they landed.

With the 24th Marines on its left flank and the 165th Infantry on its right, the 25th Marines advanced to the north edge of Aslito Airfield late on June 17. Patrols found the airstrip abandoned, but the 165th (tasked to capture it) waited until the next day.

On the same day, June 17, Admiral Spruance made a critical command decision. The formidable main Japanese fleet approached Saipan. He ordered his carriers to meet the enemy ships. That night, he withdrew his supply ships and transports from their offshore positions to a safe distance from the Japanese threat.

June 18, D +3

When the rifleman woke the following day, they looked out in amazement at an empty ocean. Waves of anxious questions must have raced through their minds. Where the hell are our ships? What about our food and ammunition? Will we have the star shell illumination and naval gunfire support? The rifleman in front-line combat had no way of knowing that 33,000 tons of cargo had already been unloaded before the ships withdrew.

That same morning, the 4th Marine Division's attack objective was the seizure of the O-3 line. This meant splitting the Japanese forces in two by reaching the east coast of Saipan. But first, the 23rd Marines had to seize a part of the O-2 line in its zone. This would be the division's line of departure. This meant that the entire division, with its three infantry regiments, the 23rd, 24th, and 25th Marines, jumped off at 1040.

Both the 24th and 25th Marines were able to reach O-3 before dark.

Intense Japanese mortar and machine-gun fire stalled the 23rd

Marines. The bombardment came from the east of Lake Susupe on the boundary line separating the two Marine divisions. This made it uncertain which division was responsible for destroying these enemy positions. It was impossible to fire artillery on them for fear of friendly fire. As a result, the 23rd Marines suffered heavy casualties. At days end, a gap still existed between the 2nd and 4th Marine Divisions.

In combat, the bizarre can become routine. One of the 23rd Marines' 75mm half-tracks fired into a Japanese cave. A dense cloud of noxious fumes poured out. A gas alarm sounded. This was serious trouble because the riflemen had long jettisoned the burdensome gas masks. Relief flooded through the men as they established the fumes weren't poisonous and came from picric acid the Japanese stored in the cave.

In the 2nd Division's zone to the north, the 8th Marines fought bitterly to control Hill 240. A heavily defended coconut grove required saturation fire from the artillery of the 10th Marines before the riflemen could smash their way in and destroy the enemy. By the night of June 18, the two Marine divisions had suffered over five thousand casualties.

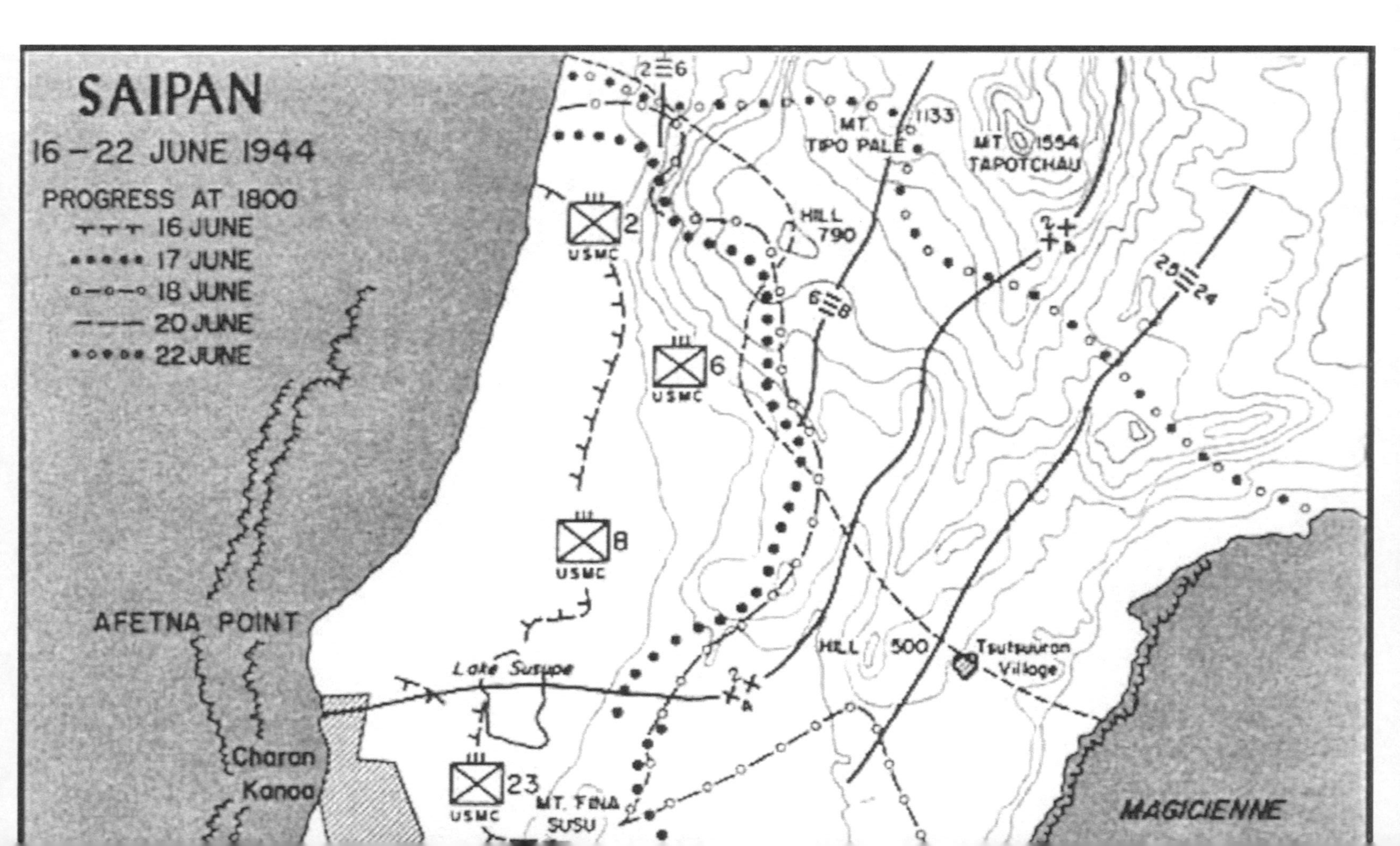

SAIPAN
16 – 22 JUNE 1944
PROGRESS AT 1800
16 JUNE
17 JUNE
18 JUNE
20 JUNE
22 JUNE
2 USMC
MT. TIPO PALE
1133
MT. 1554 TAPOTCHAU
HILL 790
6 USMC
8 USMC
AFETNA POINT
Lake Susupe
HILL 500
Tsutsuuran Village
Charan Kanoa
23 USMC
MT. FINA SUSU
MAGICIENNE

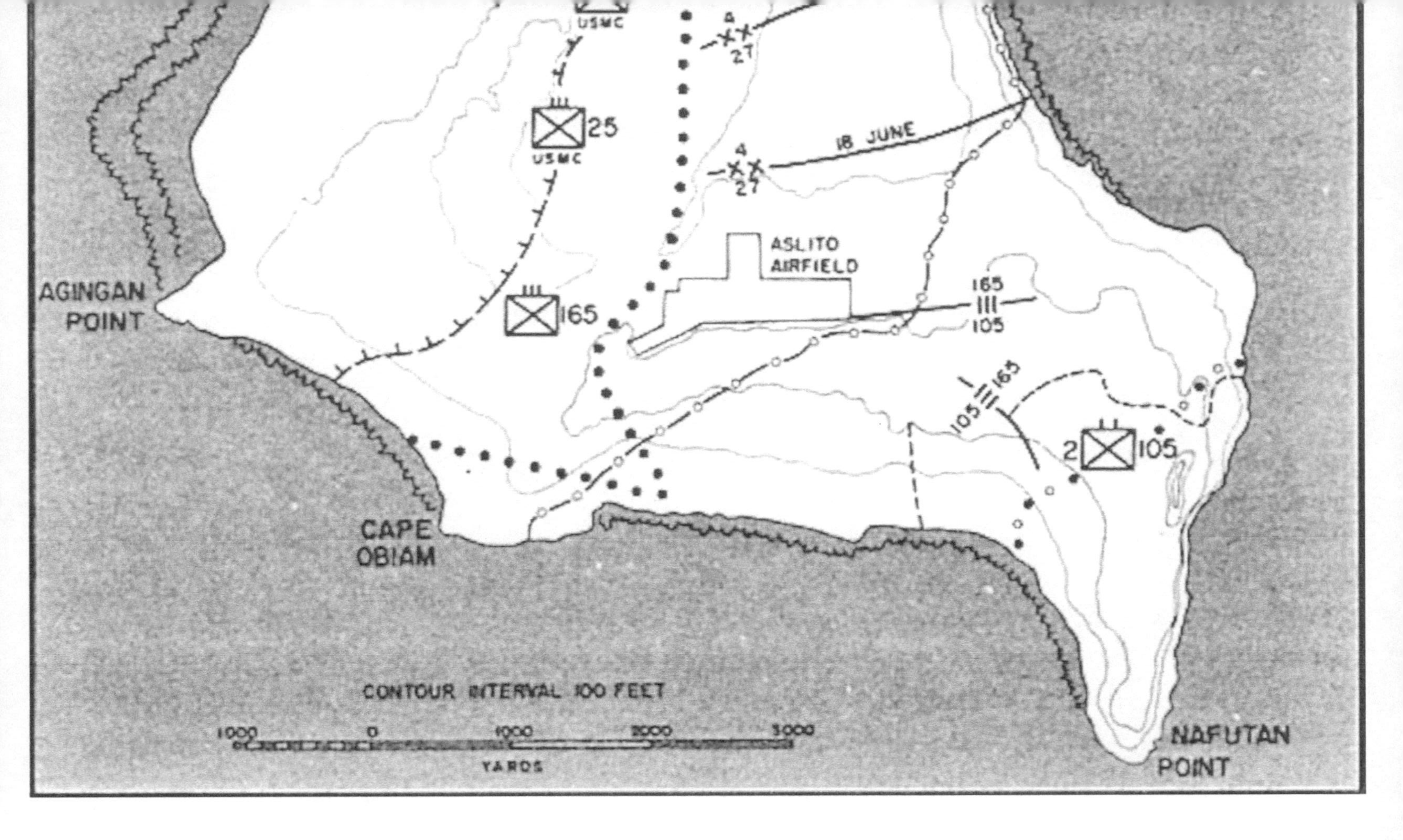

AGINGAN POINT
USMC
25
USMC
165
4
27
4
27
18 JUNE
ASLITO AIRFIELD
165
105
105
165
2
105
CAPE OBIAM
NAFUTAN POINT
CONTOUR INTERVAL 100 FEET
1000
0
1000
2000
3000
YARDS

GREAT MARIANA'S TURKEY SHOOT

June 19-22, 1944

The most significant event of the entire Saipan campaign took place at sea. The two carrier task forces clashed in a colossal air battle. And when it was over, the Japanese suffered a devastating loss of three-hundred and thirty planes out of the four hundred and thirty they'd launched. US Navy flyers called it "The Great Mariana's Turkey Shoot" because of the extreme loss inflicted on the Japanese.

With the help of American submarines and additional carrier plane attacks the next day, the Japanese attempt to relieve Saipan was smashed by a decisive US naval victory. The doom of the enemy garrison was now assured. The American supply ships returned offshore to unload their remaining cargo.

During this time, the 105th Infantry moved slowly along the south coast. They joined the 165th Infantry, sealing off Japanese survivors at Nafutan Point. Once the Japanese were trapped, the 105th were assigned to destroy them. The rest of the 27th Division, including the 165th Infantry, were ordered north as a reserve.

June 19–22 marked a shift in direction for American troops. By pivoting the 2nd Marines onto the far-left flank along the western shore, other Marine regiments swung around from their drive, which had reached the east coast at Magicienne Bay.

On June 20, the 4th Division confronted a key objective. A young lieutenant later recalled: "We had a perfect chance to watch a battalion of the 25th attack. They were in action less than a quarter mile from us. The whole landscape was spread out before us. They assaulted Hill 500, the dominant terrain feature of the entire area. It was obvious they were running into a solid wall of Jap fire. Using artillery timed fire, smoke, and tanks—they stormed to the top and took it. The use of those supporting arms was an overwhelming spectacle. From our vantage point, we watched the timed fire raging in cave entrances and down the face of the hill as if it were going down a stepladder. On lower levels, flamethrower tanks sprouted their napalm Jets upward into other caves. It was quite a show."

In the 2nd Division's area, the 8th Marines wheeled to attack north into the foothills of Mount Tapotchau. Both Marine divisions now faced serious problems. Their northern drive was stalled by

Lieutenant General Yoshitsugu Saitō's main line of defense, running east to west across the island. The terrain into where the attack had to go was a nightmare of caves, hills, valleys, ravines, and cliffs—fortified and defended to the death by Japanese troops.

On June 21, the frontline troops got a reprieve. They rested at their positions, caught up on deeply needed sleep, got some water, and even had a hot meal. They got their first 10-in-1 rations in addition to their K rations.

Intensive preparations were made for a coordinated attack by both Marine divisions the following day. Eighteen artillery battalions were massed for supporting fire. Combat efficiency was rated as satisfactory, despite the sobering total of over six thousand casualties.

On June 22, the Marines attacked all along the line. The 6th Marines overran parts of Mount Tipo Pali, while the 8th Marines worked their way into the maze of gullies and ridges forming Mount Tapotchau's foothills.

On the right flank, the 24th Marines were forced into the messy business of blasting caves along Magicienne Bay. In one of the mortar platoons, a weird encounter took place as described by Lieutenant Joe Cushing: "I bent over one of my mortars and checking the lay of it when I felt a tap on my shoulder, and a guy asked me, 'Hey Mac, are you Marine?' I turned around, and a Jap officer stood less than a foot away from me. I dropped to the ground speechless, and one of my men riddled that Jap from head to toe."

On the left of the 4th Division's area, the 25th Marines advanced 2,400 yards. The forward lines reached an area where the Kagman Peninsula jetted off to the east. This resulted in a substantially increased frontage that the two Marine divisions couldn't cover. To deal with this General Holland Smith ordered his reserve, the Army's 27th Infantry Division to the center of the line and left one battalion of the 105th Infantry in the rear to continue its attempt to eliminate Japanese pockets on the bypassed Nafutan Point.

June 22 marked the arrival of the 19th Fighter Squadron from the US Army Air Forces. P-47 Thunderbolts, launched from Navy escort carriers, landed at Aslito Airfield. The P-47s were fitted with launching racks for rockets by ground crews after they landed. Later that day, eight planes took off in the first support mission of the Saipan campaign. There were only two Marine observation squadrons, VMO-2 and VMO-4, involved in the battle for Saipan. They provided invaluable artillery spotting for the two Marine divisions.

While these developments took place, down in the rock-bottom basic life of infantry platoons, days of relentless combat pressure were embodied by the impact of the regular duties in high-stress levels on the platoon commanders: "I'd made a final inspection of the platoon position and then sacked in—exhausted. When it was my turn to stand watch, it took every reserve of willpower and strength to get up and go on duty. For hours, I alternated between fighting off sleepiness and sweating out the noises and movements that encircled us. I spotted a dark shape, darker than the other shadows. It was the size of a man's head. I watched for a long time, nerves on edge, finger on my M-1 carbine trigger. It moved. I fired a shot. Nothing happened. It would've been suicide to go over and investigate. In the darkness and jungle my men would have shot me in a second. So, when it came time for my relief, I pointed out the suspicious object to the next man and told him to watch closely. Then I collapsed into a dead-tired sleep.

"At dawn, first thing I did was look over where I'd shot the night before. Lying on top of a rock was a gas mask from one of my men. The owner had been sleeping right beside it—a miracle he hadn't been hit."

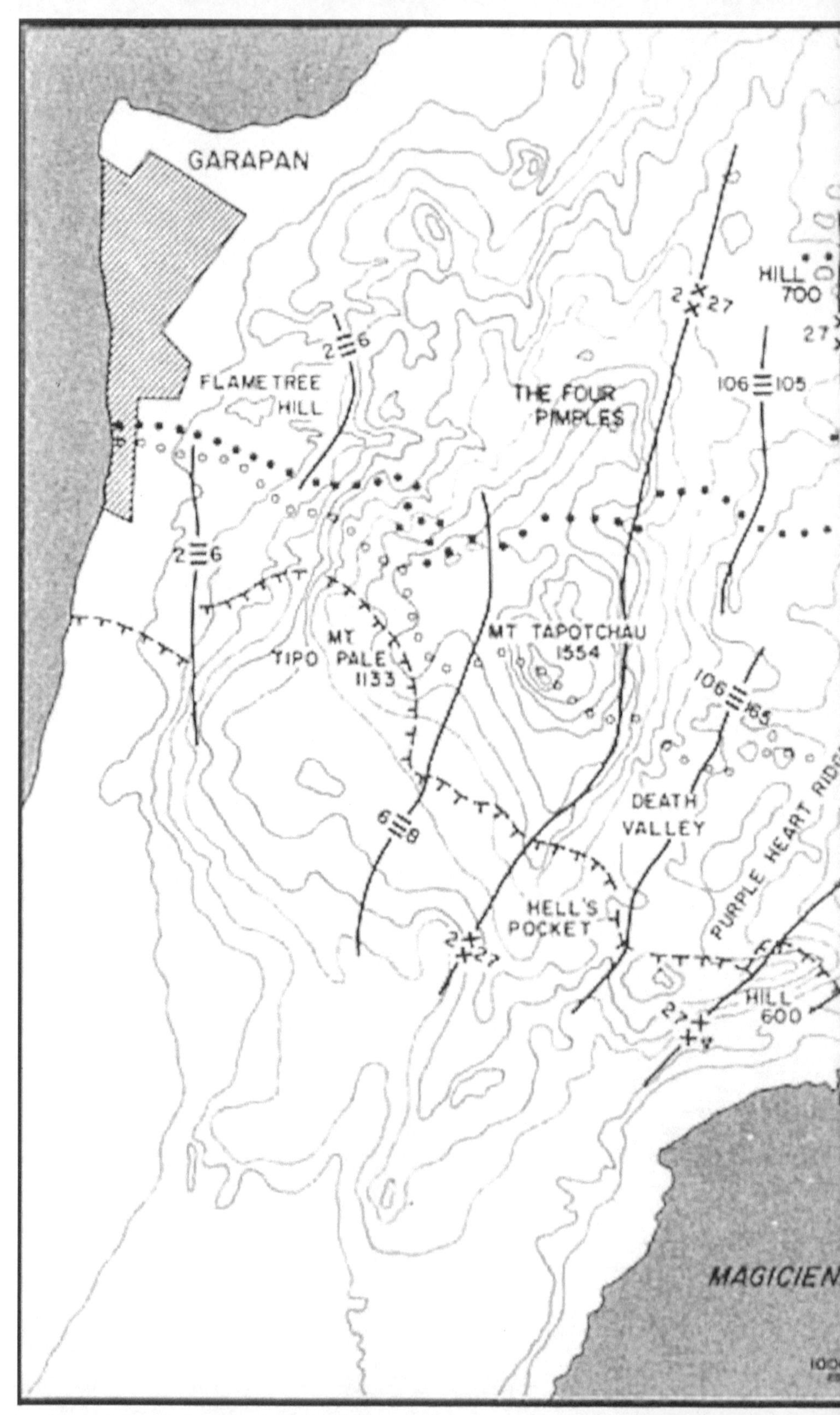

GARAPAN
HILL 700
2 X 27
27
106 ≡ 105
2 ≡ 6
FLAME TREE HILL
THE FOUR PIMPLES
2 ≡ 6
MT TIPO PALE 1133
MT TAPOTCHAU 1554
106 ≡ 105
DEATH VALLEY
PURPLE HEART RIDGE
6 ≡ 8
HELL'S POCKET
2 X 27
HILL 600
2 X 27
MAGICIEN
1000

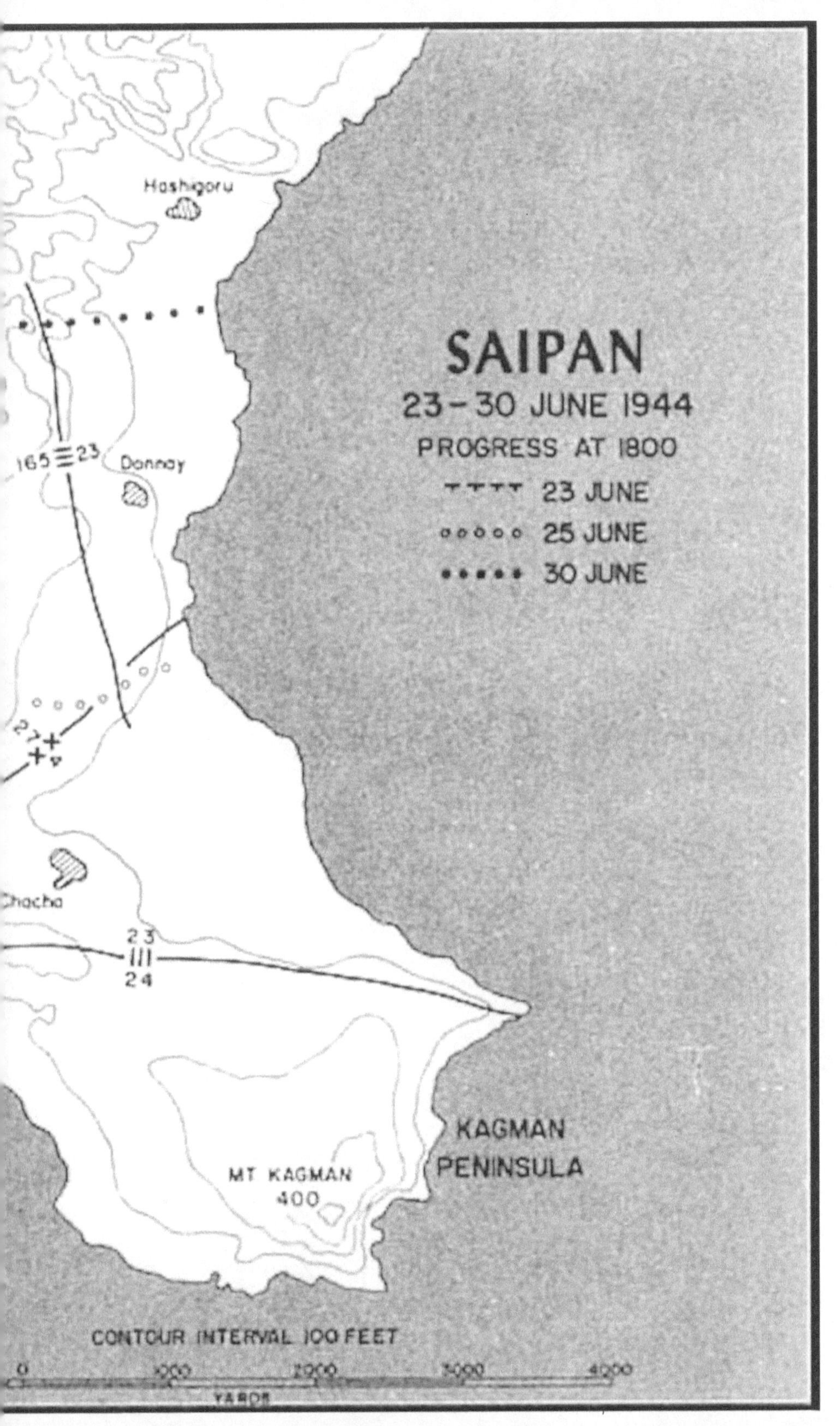

Hoshigoru
165 ≡ 23   Donnay
27 +
Chacha
2 3
|||
2 4
SAIPAN
23 – 30 JUNE 1944
PROGRESS AT 1800
ⴕⴕⴕⴕ   23 JUNE
ooooo   25 JUNE
•••••   30 JUNE
KAGMAN
PENINSULA
MT KAGMAN
400
CONTOUR INTERVAL 100 FEET
0   1000   2000   3000   4000
YARDS

MARINES STORM GARAPAN

July 1-4, 1944

General Holland Smith turned his attention to the operational plans for driving through the northern third of Saipan. He intended to bring the campaign to a successful, even if bloody, finish. His next objective ran eastward across the island to Tanapag and then up Garapan on the west coast. The 2nd Marine Division would be held in reserve near Flores Point.

This left the 4th Marine Division and the 27th Infantry Division ready to attack General Saitō's troops and defenses. The *easiest* assignment during this period fell on the shoulders of the 4th Marine Division on the east coast. They advanced over three thousand yards against light opposition, veering left and ending on July 4 with their left flank less than two-thousand yards north of Tanapag.

What seemed like light opposition to General Schmidt in his divisional command post looked quite different to a tired lieutenant who described a typical rifle platoon on the morning of July 1: "I took the rest of my men, and we cautiously combed the area. It was a terrible place. Rocks and creepers were so interwoven that they formed an impenetrable barrier. Visibility was limited to only a few feet. After my sergeant was wounded, the atmosphere of the place became even more tense.

"We found some rock crevices that the Japs might be hiding in. I tried calling to them in our Japanese combat phrases to come out and surrender. This proved fruitless. The Japs knew exactly where we were. I had no idea where they were. I tried to maneuver a flamethrower man into a position where he could give the crevice a blast without becoming a target. But because of the ground's composition, this proved impossible.

"It was then we heard a shot off to our left. We headed over to investigate and then all hell broke loose. An automatic Jap weapon opened to our left. We all hit the deck. No one was hit (for a change). But we couldn't locate the weapon. I called to the man over on the left flank. No answer. What happened?

"More enemy fire spattered our small group of Marines. The source was right on top of us. I told two of my men to throw grenades at the area they thought the fire was coming from—twenty feet away. Under that cover, we worked a rifleman forward a couple yards to get a bead on that Jap, but he couldn't spot him, and the enemy fire grew heavier.

"Here we were—isolated from the rest of the company with only six of us left—our flank man had disappeared. We took heavy fire from an uncertain number of Japs we couldn't locate right in our middle. Some men were getting jittery, so I tried to be as calm and cool as I could, although I didn't feel that way on the inside. I moved back to the other end of the hilltop and reported to our company commander on the phone. If I could get his okay, I would then [contact another one of our platoons] for reinforcements, and we could move back into this area and clear out the Jap pocket.

"Our relentless advance against the Jap defenses would often result in face-to-face encounters. After three days, I saw another remarkable act of bravery: Three of our tanks came down the road. They turned to the south, which took them off the high ground and into a cave with literally hundreds of Japs, swarming all over our tanks. We watched and heard the lieutenant who commanded them screaming for help on the radio—and I don't blame him. They formed a triangle and covered each other as best as they could."

The commanding officer closest to the crisis was Lieutenant Colonel Hollis "Musty" Mustain, in charge of the 1/25 Marines. He recalled the incident later: "My executive officer was a regular major named Fenton Mee. We were together and when the radio operators told us what was happening. I turned to Mee and said, 'Get some people in and get those damn tanks out.' Major Mee turned to his battalion CP (all staff people) and said, 'Let's get going.' Then he turned and took off. I can still see his face like it was yesterday—he must've figured he was going to get killed. But they got there, and the Japs pulled out. This saved our tanks. It was one of the bravest things I ever saw anyone do."

By July 4, only six officers remained out of twenty-eight, and three-hundred enlisted men out of the six hundred and ninety remained in those companies. Including the headquarters company, only 468 men remained in the battalion's original strength of over

1,050. One rifle company had to be disbanded. Another battalion repeated this macabre toll with twenty-two officers killed out of twenty-nine and four hundred and ninety enlisted men killed or wounded in action.

The 27th Infantry Division advanced in the center of the line of attack. They had a far easier time than in the grinding experience they had previously come through. Their advance also veered left and against "negligible resistance" with the enemy in full flight.

The 2nd Marines stormed into Garapan and seized Flametree Hill. The regiment found the town in shambles.

The town had been leveled by Marine artillery and naval gunfire. Twisted metal rooftops covered the area, shielding Japanese snipers. Several deftly hidden pillboxes were spread among the ruins. Engineers, covered by riflemen, slid behind obstacles, and set up explosives while flamethrowers seared the front. With the help of tanks and 75mm self-propelled guns, the 2nd Marines eliminated the scattered resistance before nightfall.

On the beaches, suppressing fire from the LVT(A)s of the 2nd Armored Amphibian Battalion destroyed Japanese weapons near the water. The 2nd Marines moved past the town into Flores Point, halfway to Tanapag. Their uniforms were filthy. Stiff with sweat and dirt from two weeks of fierce fighting. Marines gleefully dipped their heads into the cool ocean water.

The other two divisions had veered their attack to the left and already reached the northwest coast. The 2nd Marine Division went into reserve as planned on July 4. General Holland Smith anticipated the end in sight for Saipan. He wanted to rest the 2nd Division and use them for the next assault on neighboring Tinian Island.

The Japanese withdrew to a defensive line north of Garapan. The American attack not only shattered their manpower, artillery, and tanks, but the enemy was desperate for food. Many starving Japanese troops turned to eating field grass and tree bark.

TENNO HAIKA! BANZAI

July 5-8, 1944

The Japanese retreat left many of their men behind in caves to fight to the death. This tactic posed to American troops the life-threatening question of whether the civilians hidden inside should be saved.

First Lieutenant Fred Stott of the 1/24 Marines wrote of his experiences: "It was the twenty first day of the battle, and we trudged along a winding trail to relieve the 23rd Marines for an attack scheduled at 1300. A typical artillery barrage followed by *morale-lifting* rockets was unleashed against cave-dwelling Japs. But neither was effective. The Japs used civilian men, women, and children as decoys. The cost was heavy. Jap soldiers dressed as civilian prisoners succeeded in killing a dozen men from A Company."

This kind of treacherous warfare continued. The next day 1st Lieutenant Stott described how he dealt with the Japanese deception: "A few Japs played possum by smearing the blood of other dead Japs on themselves and lying still as the Marines walked up. I gave my Marines instructions to 'stick it if it didn't stink.' Marines had the grim duty of bayoneting all the bodies.

"We also picked up civilian prisoners, including women and children. Marines took some serious risks. They went into caves, not knowing whether there were soldiers hiding inside, in order to rescue civilians. The minute they got civilians out, they fed them with part of their rations and offered the men cigarettes."

After the 2nd Division was put into reserve, it was clear to General Holland Smith that a banzai attack would come. He warned all units to be alert and paid a personal visit on July 6 to General Griner, now in command of the 27th Infantry Division. He stressed the likelihood of an attack coming down the coastline onto the flat ground of Tanapag Plain.

General Holland Smith hade been furious with General Ralph Smith, and after discussing the matter with AdmiralTurner, he relieved Ralph Smith of command of the 27th Infantry Division on June 24 and sent him to Hawaii. By the Morning of the 25th he was temporarily replaced by Major General Jaraman, who was then replaced by Major General Griner on the June 28th. This conflict created a grudge between the Marines and the Army "that lasted well after the war."

While General Holland Smith had the authority to do this, many said it was a rash decision and that he hadn't considered the challenging terrain the 27th Division faced on Saipan. A report on an interview with General Holland Smith paraphrased him explaining that his decision was for the best because, under Ralph Smith, men were being wasted and more were dying than necessary, and they hadn't even accomplished their objective while the two Marine divisions had moved forward.

While General Holland Smith was preparing his men for a banzai attack, General Saitō and his Japanese troops were cornered in his sixth and last command post. It was a miserable cave north of Tanapag in the Paradise Valley. This valley was pounded by naval gunfire and artillery. Saitō only had fragments of his troops left. He was sick, hungry, and wounded. Saitō gave orders for one final and fanatical banzai charge while he committed *hara-kiri* in his cave.

On July 6 at 1000, he faced east and shouted: "Tenno Haika! Banzai" (Long live the Empire for ten-thousand ages). He drew his blood first with his sword and then his assistant shot him and Admiral Chūichi Nagumo in the back of the head with a pistol. But not before he ordered the commencement of the final attack at 0300 on July 7 and said [translated], "Whether we attack or whether we stay where we are, there is only death."

Another all-out enemy charge was nothing new to the Marines and soldiers on Saipan. One rifleman recounted his experiences: "Whenever we cornered the Japs, and there was no way out, we faced that damn banzai attack. The 23rd Marines had fought off a few of these on our Saipan adventures. I dreaded these attacks but also welcomed them. While they created a great deal of fear, when it was finally over, that sector was Jap-free.

"For hours, we heard them preparing for a banzai attack. It was their end, and they knew it. They wouldn't surrender. It was against their training and heritage. All that was left was one last charge of pouring all their troops into one concentrated place—trying to kill as many of us as they could."

The rifleman's account continued with dramatic descriptions of the stressful waiting he endured while listening to enemy shouts and screams going on for hours. The noise increased as Marine mortars and artillery hammered toward the shouting—adding to the deafening din. Marines waited in foxholes with clips of ammo placed close so they could reload fast. They fixed bayonets to their rifles—ensured knives were loose in their scabbards. They waited in jittery anticipation of the imminent attacks.

Listening to the screams, their senses were alert and finely tuned. But there was a silence. A silence that signaled the enemy's advance. Then: "What sounded like a thousand people screaming all at once. A horde of madmen broke out of the darkness. Screams of 'banzai' choked the air—Japanese officers led these 'devils from hell' with their swords drawn and swishing in circles over their heads. Japanese soldiers followed their officers, firing their weapons and screaming 'banzai' as they charged.

"Our weapons opened up. Mortars and machine guns fired like gangbusters. They didn't fire in bursts of three or five, but belt after belt of ammo went through the gun. The gunner swiveled the barrel to the left and right. Jap bodies mounted up in front of us, but they still charged, running over their comrades' fallen bodies. Mortar tubes and machine gun barrels got so hot from the rapid-fire —they could no longer be used.

"While each attack had taken its toll, they still came in droves. To this day, I can even now visualize the enemy only a few feet away —bayonets aimed at us as we emptied clip after clip into them. Their momentum carried them into our foxholes, right on top of us. Then, after pushing the dead Jap body off me, I'd reload and do it all over again.

"Deafening screams, bullets whizzing around us, the reek of death and smell of Japanese gunpowder permeated the air. I was full of fear and hate and the desire to kill. I believed the Japanese were a savage animal, a devil, a beast, not human. The only thought I had was to kill, kill, kill—until finally, it ended."

That was the mayhem General Holland Smith predicted as the final spastic effort of the Japanese. And it came in the early morning hours of July 7. The pivotal moment in the Battle for Saipan. The Japanese tactical objective was to smash through Garapan and Tanapag, reaching down to Charan-Kanoa. It was a fearful charge of fire and flesh, primitive and savage. Some of the Japanese troops were only armed with rocks or with a knife mounted on a pole.

This banzai charge also hit the 105th Infantry dug in for the night on the main line of resistance. With the regimental headquarters directly behind them, the 105th left a five-hundred-yard gap between them which they planned to cover by fire. The Japanese found this gap, poured through, and headed pell-mell for the regimental headquarters. The men of the frontline battalions fought bravely but failed to stop the banzai onslaught.

Behind the 105th were three artillery battalions of the 10th Marines. The gunners couldn't set their fuses fast enough, even when cut down to five-tenths of a second, to stop the Japanese enemy on top of them. They lowered their muzzles of their 105mm howitzers and spewed ricochet fire by bouncing shells off the ground. Many of their other guns couldn't fire at all because the Army troops ahead of them mixed in with the Japanese attackers.

Marines in the artillery battalions fired every type of small weapon they could. One of their battalions was almost wiped out when the battalion commander was killed. The cane fields to the front swarmed with enemy troops. Guns were overrun, and Marine artillerymen, after removing their guns' firing locks, fell back and joined the fight as infantry.

As the firestorm broke on the 105th, men of the nearby 165th Infantry were ordered "to stand where they were and shoot Japs" without moving forward. By 1600 that afternoon, after coming to the aid of the shattered 105th, the 165th was still three hundred yards short of making contact.

Savage hand-to-hand fighting took the momentum out of the Japanese surge. They were finally stopped by the 105th, less than eight hundred yards south of Tanapag. By 1800, the lost ground had been regained.

A shocking day of casualties. The 105th Infantry's two battalions took 917 casualties while killing 2,291 Japanese. One Marine artillery battalion had 127 casualties but had accounted for 322 of the enemy. The final count of the Japanese dead reached a staggering total of 4,321, some due to shell fire, but the vast majority were killed in the banzai charge.

During the bloodshed, there were countless acts of bravery. Recognized and later awarded the Army Medal of Honor for leadership and "resistance to the death" were Army Colonel William O'Brien, commanding a battalion of the 105th, and one of his squad leaders, Sergeant Tom Baker.

While most attention was centered on the bloody coastal battle, the 23rd Marines attacked a strong Japanese force well protected by caves in an inland cliff. The key to eliminating them was truck-mounted rocket launchers, lowered over the cliff by chains attached to tanks. Once lowered to the base, their fire, supplemented by offshore rocket gunboats, snuffed out the remaining enemy resistance.

The next day on July 8, saw the beginning of the end. The Japanese spent the last of their manpower on banzai charges. It was now time for the final American mop-up. LVTs rescued men of the 105th Infantry who'd waded out from the shore to the reef to escape the Japanese. General Holland Smith placed most of the 27th Infantry Division back into reserve. He then put the 2nd Marine Division back in the line of attack with the 105th Infantry attached. Together with the 4th Marine Division, they swept north toward the end of the island.

Along the coast was a bizarre spectacle that presented a macabre end to the campaign: Japanese troops in the area had destroyed themselves with suicidal rushes from the high cliffs to the rocky beach below. Japanese troops were observed, along with hundreds of civilians, wading out to sea and drowning themselves. Some troops committed hara-kiri with knives or destroyed themselves with grenades. Some officers even used their swords to decapitate their troops.

UNBELIEVABLE SELF DESTRUCTION

July 9, 1944

It was to be the final day of a brutal campaign. The 4th Marines reached Marpi Point on the northern end of the island, while the 6th and 8th Marines came down from the hills to occupy the last western beaches.

Colonel Chambers watched as this grim scene played out: "We moved along the cliffs and caves, uncovering civilians along the way. Japanese soldiers refused to surrender and would not allow civilians to surrender. I watched as women, some carrying children, stumbled out of the caves toward our lines. They were shot down by Japanese troops in the back. I watched more women carrying children come out to the cliffs that dropped to the ocean.

"These were steep cliffs. Some women came down and threw their children into the ocean and jumped after them to commit suicide. I watched one group of about nine civilian men, women, and children get into a little huddle and blow themselves up. It was the saddest and most terrible thing I've ever seen, and yet I presume quite consistent with the Japanese code of Bushido."

Another lieutenant from the same division witnessed other

unbelievable forms of self-destruction: "The interpreters were summoned, and they begged using an amplifier for civilians to come forward and surrender. No movement at first. Then people came closer into a compact mass. It seemed to be predominantly civilians, but several uniforms could be seen circling about in the throng—using the civilians for protection.

"As they huddled closer, I heard a weird singing chant. Then a Rising Sun flag unfurled. Movement grew more agitated. Men leaped into the sea. The chanting gave way to startled cries and then that popping sound of detonating grenades. It was a handful of soldiers determined to prevent the surrender or escape of the civilians by tossing grenades into the throng of men, women, and children. Then the Japs dived into the sea, from which escape was impossible. Exploding grenades shattered the mob into pieces of wounded and dying. It was the first time I actually saw water that ran red with human blood."

This kind of fanaticism characterized the Japanese. Not surprising that over 23,800 of the enemy were known dead—with uncounted thousands of others charred by flamethrowers and sealed forever in caves. Only 736 prisoners of war were taken, and of these 430 were Koreans. American casualties numbered exactly 16,612.

On July 9 at 1615, Saipan was declared secured (although mopping up continued for long after). The 4th Marine division was later awarded the Presidential Unit Citation for their outstanding combat performance on Saipan and later assault on the neighboring island of Tinian.

LEGACY OF SAIPAN

The fighting on Saipan not only caused many American casualties but foreshadowed the bloody fighting that lay ahead in the western and central Pacific. General Holland Smith called it, "the decisive battle for the Pacific offensive and opening the way to the home islands."

Japanese General Saitō wrote: "The fate of the Empire would be decided in this one action." Another Japanese admiral had agreed, "Our war was lost with the loss of Saipan." This was a truly strategic strike for victory in the Pacific War.

The proof of these vital decisions was demonstrated four months later when one-hundred B-29 bombers took off from Saipan bound for Tokyo. There were other significant results. The US had secured an advanced naval base to deliver punishing strikes close to enemy shores. Emperor Hirohito was forced to consider a diplomatic settlement of war. General Tojo, the premier, and his entire cabinet fell from power on July 18—nine days after losing Saipan.

The lessons learned in this grisly campaign would be applied to future amphibious operations. Flaws would be analyzed and corrected. The clear need to improve aviation support for ground troops led to better results in the Philippine Islands and Okinawa and Iwo Jima. Artillery spotting missions flown by the Marine Observation Squadron (VMO-2 and -4) set a pattern for the use of light planes in the future.

Naval gunfire support was also closely reviewed. General Saitō wrote, "If there were no naval gunfire, we could have fought it out with the enemy in a decisive battle." But over 8,500 tons of ammunition were fired by US Navy ships. The trajectory of the flat naval guns proved somewhat limiting, as the shells didn't have the penetrating and plunging effect needed against Japanese strongholds.

Lessons learned from the supply confusion that marred the early days on the beaches had improved little since the days of the Guadalcanal landing. The logistic problems arose because: once a beach was in friendly hands, ships unloaded as quickly as possible and sailors in the landing craft hurried to get into the beaches and back out again. Supplies were spread all over the beach, partly because of the enemy's artillery and mortar harassing fire on the beaches but also because of the Marine Corps' hard-driving rapid attack.

Estimates of resupply requirements were way too small. For example, a shortage of radio batteries was never corrected. There was insufficient time to sort and separate equipment and supplies adequately. This caused mix-ups with Marine uniforms getting into Army dumps, an Army supply showing up at Marine dumps.

After the beach chaos at Saipan, the Navy decided to organize a permanent shore party for the future. It would be responsible for the movement of all supplies from the beach to the dumps and then the later issue to the divisions.

The tactical lessons learned were also new to the Pacific war. Instead of assaulting a small atoll, the fighting had been one of movement on a sizable landmass, further complicated by a maze of caves and Japanese defensive systems. The enemy had defended caves before, but never on such a huge scale. On Saipan, these caves were both man-made and natural. Often, the vegetation gave them excellent camouflage. Some caves had steel doors which could be opened for an artillery piece or machine gun to fire and then withdraw before return fire could destroy them. Flame-throwing tanks proved useful in reaching these caves, but the range was limited on Saipan. This was improved for future operations.

The challenging experiences on Saipan led to a variety of changes that saved American lives in future Pacific campaigns. Losing the island was a strategic strike from which the Japanese would never recover—while the United States pressed forward to ultimate victory.

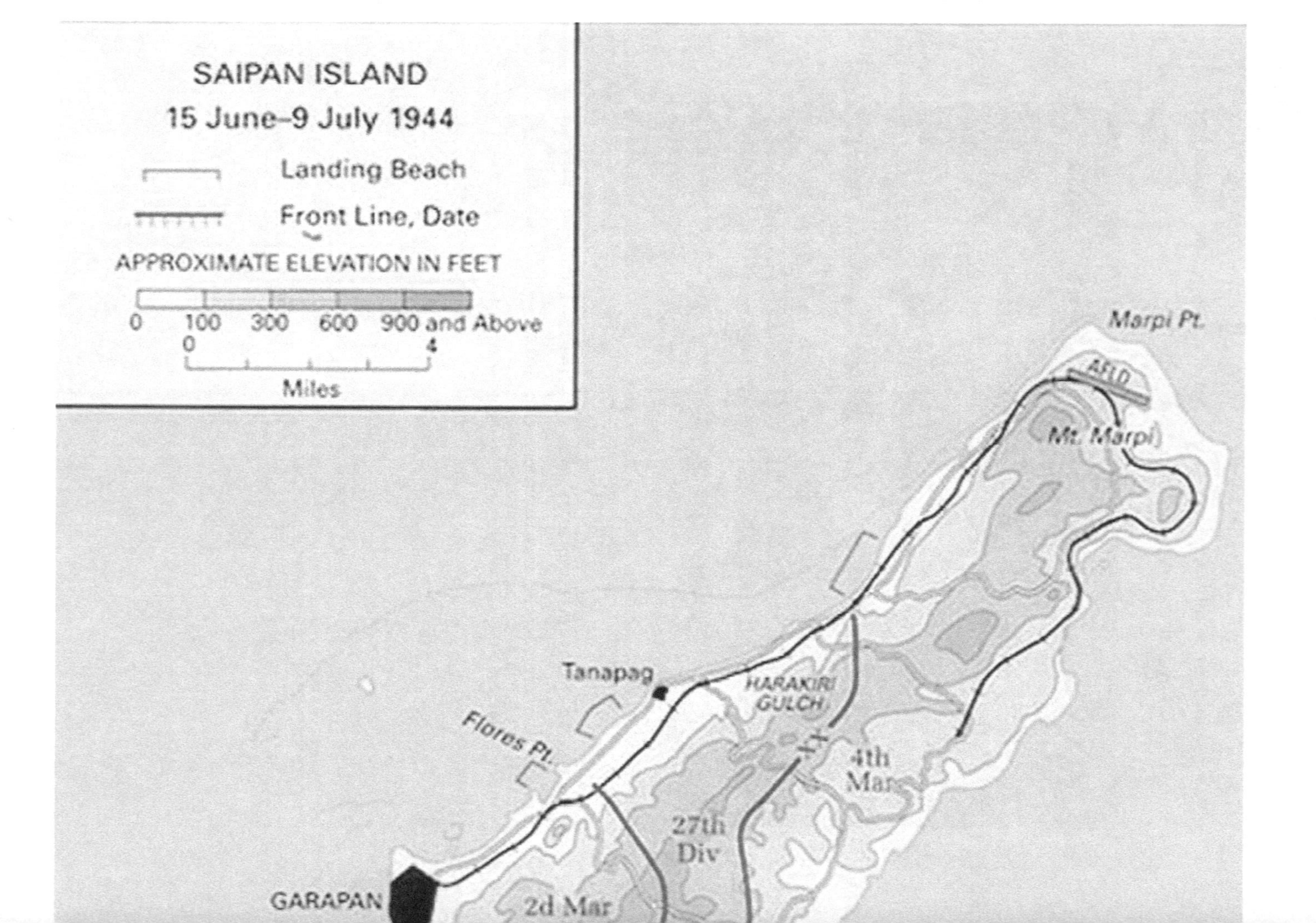

SAIPAN ISLAND
15 June–9 July 1944
Landing Beach
Front Line, Date
APPROXIMATE ELEVATION IN FEET
0 100 300 600 900 and Above
0 4
Miles
Marpi Pt.
AFLD
Mt. Marpi
Tanapag
HARAKIRI GULCH
Flores Pt.
XX
4th Mar
27th Div
GARAPAN
2d Mar

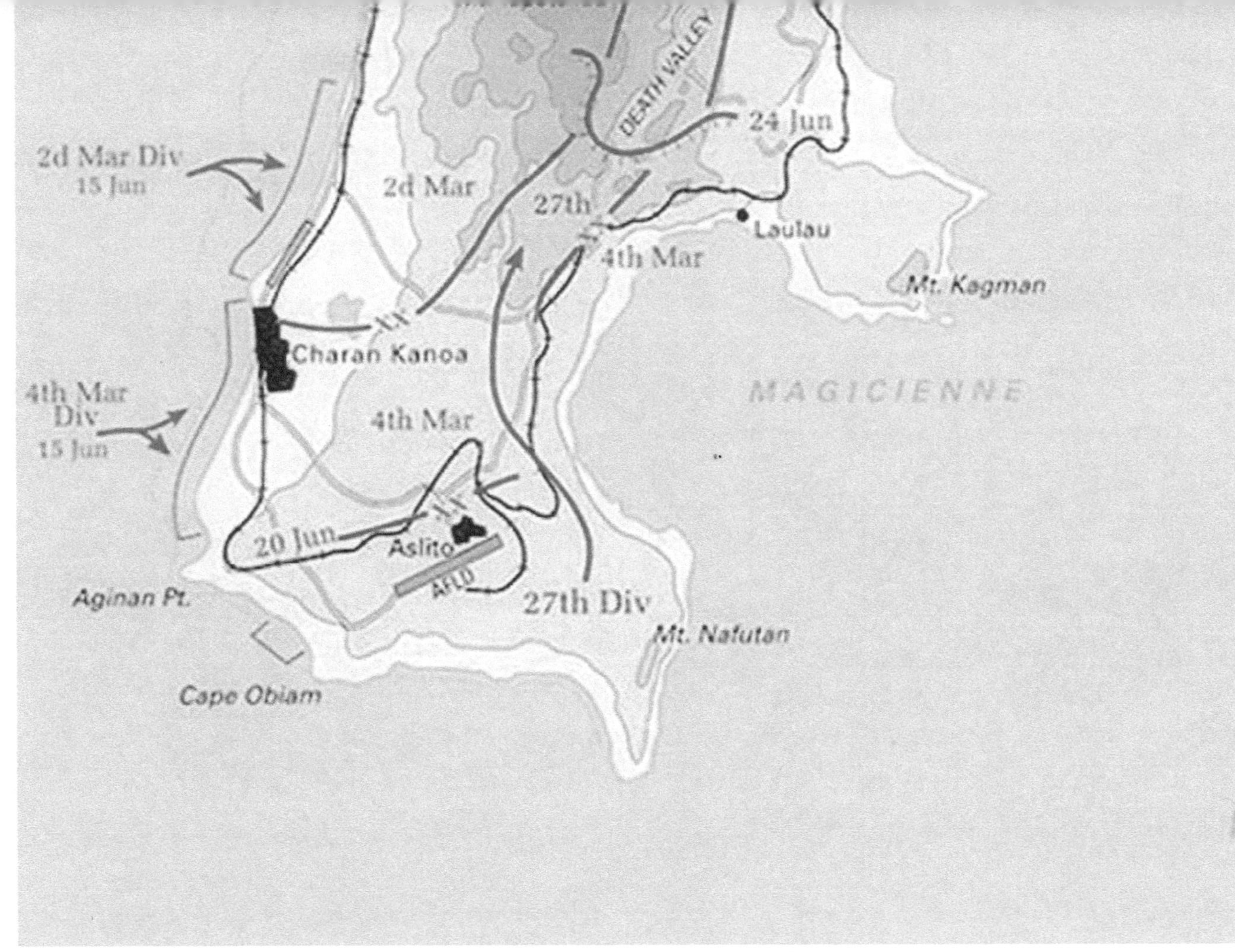

2d Mar Div
15 Jun
2d Mar
27th
4th Mar
DEATH VALLEY
24 Jun
Laulau
Mt. Kagman
Charan Kanoa
MAGICIENNE
4th Mar
Div
15 Jun
4th Mar
20 Jun
Aslito
AFLD
27th Div
Aginan Pt.
Mt. Nafutan
Cape Obiam

INVASION OF TINIAN

SCOUTING TINIAN'S BEACHES

Once the outcome of Saipan's battle was clear, the V Amphibious Corps Commanders turned their attention to the next objective: the island of Tinian. Three miles off Saipan's southwest coast and garrisoned with over nine-thousand Japanese troops. Many of the enemy combatants were veterans of the Manchurian Campaign, pummeled for over seven weeks by US Navy air and sea armadas.

The 2nd and 4th Marine Divisions, fresh from fighting on Saipan, were selected to assault Tinian. The vital question of where they would land was still undecided. There was firm support among assault planners to land on two narrow sand strips—codenamed White Beach 1 and White Beach 2—on Tinian's northwest coast. White Beach 1 was sixty yards wide, while White Beach 2 was one hundred and sixty.

Admiral Richmond Kelly Turner, overall commander of the Marianas' Expeditionary Force, was skeptical and suggested an alternative site codenamed Yellow Beach.

On July 3, 1944, Captain James Jones was put on alert for future reconnaissance of these potential landing sites. On July 9, the day Saipan was officially declared secured, Captain Jones got his orders from General Holland Smith. His men were to scout out Tinian's beaches and fortifications to determine the capacity to handle a landing force and keep it supplied.

Navy UDT (underwater demolition teams) would locate underwater obstacles and do the hydrographic work. Captain Jones chose Company A under the command of Captain Merwin Silverthorn and First Lieutenant Leo Shinn to command Company B. They rehearsed the operation off the beaches of Saipan's Magicienne Bay. On the evening of July 10, Navy and Marine units boarded the destroyer transports *Stringham* and *Gilmer* for the quick trip into the channel that separated the two islands.

At 2030 on July 10, the teams debarked in zodiac rubber boats and paddled to within five hundred yards of the beach, then swam the rest of the way in. Luckily, it was a black night, and although the moon rose at 2230, it was largely hidden by the clouds.

Yellow Beach was assigned to Silverthorn's Company A. He led eight UDT swimmers and twenty Marines ashore. They found a beach near Tinian Town flanked on each side by formidable cliffs. Several floating mines and underwater boulders barred the approach. On the beach, double-apron barbed wire had been strung.

Captain Silverthorn worked his way thirty yards inland in search of exit routes for the vehicles. Talkative Japanese workers were busy building pillboxes and entrenching blasting charges. Silverthorn spotted three Japanese sentries on the cliff overlooking the beach. Searchlights passed back and forth, scanning the beach approach, but Silverthorn and his men safely made it back to the *Stringham*. Yellow Beach as a landing site would not work.

In the northwest, the White Beaches reconnaissance was assigned to Company B. Strong currents push the rubber boats off course. The team heading for White Beach 1 was swept over a thousand yards north off course and never got ashore. The team headed for White Beach 2 wound up on White Beach 1 and reconnoitered the area. The *Gilmer* eventually picked up both parties. The following night, ten swimmers from Company A went to White Beach 2 and were successful.

Reports from the White Beaches were encouraging. The LVTs

(amphibian tractors) and other vehicles could negotiate the reefs and get ashore. Troops could also clamber over the low cliffs flanking the beaches with little difficulty. Marines disembarking from the boats on the reef could wade ashore through a shallow surf. The Navy's UDT teams confirmed the Marine intelligence and reported: "no man-made underwater obstructions or mines were found."

After the reconnaissance team returned from White Beach 2, Admiral Turner withdrew his objection, and the command decision was made to use the northwestern beaches. The assault was set for July 24 at 0730.

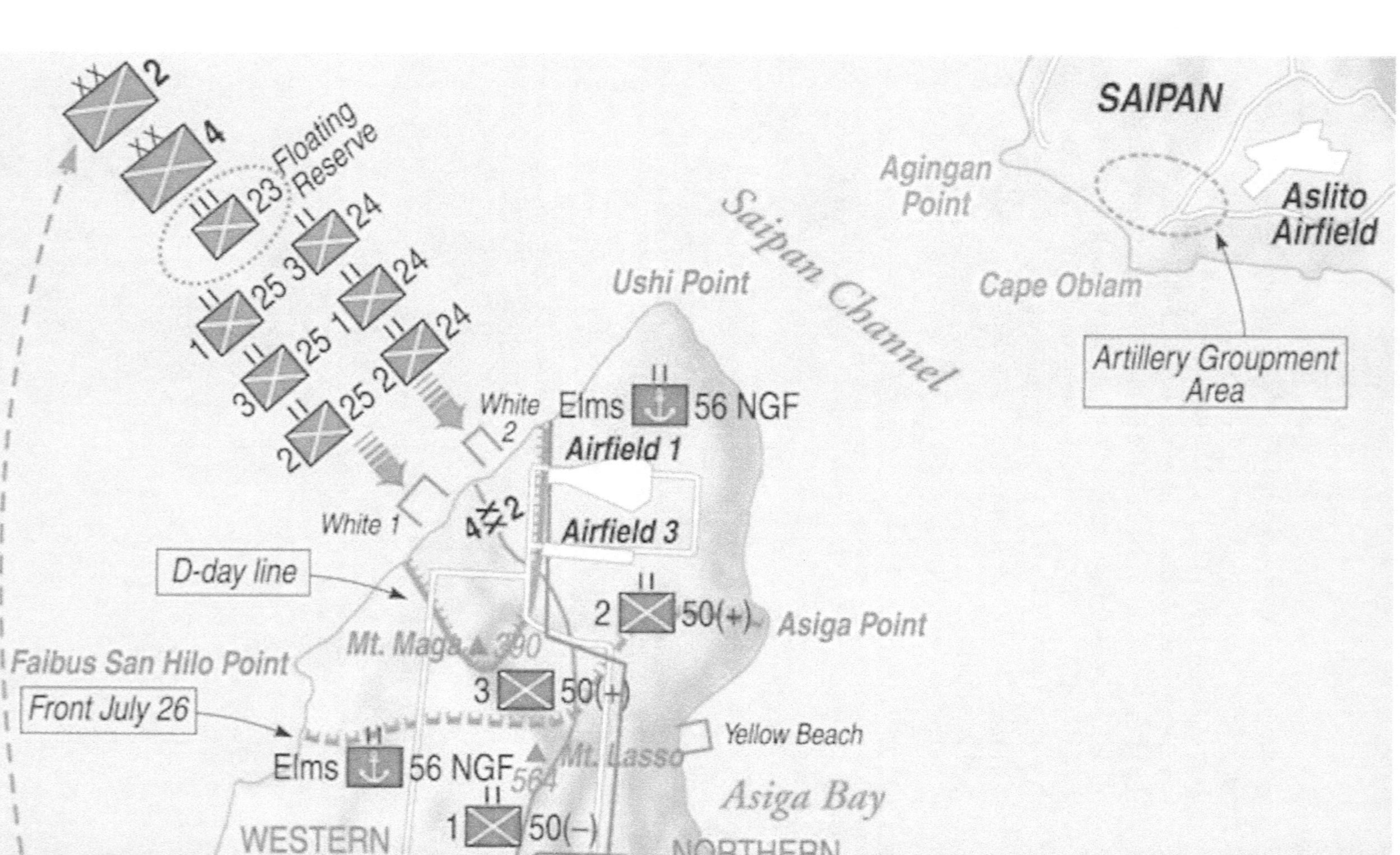

SAIPAN
Aslito Airfield
Artillery Groupment Area
Agingan Point
Cape Obiam
Saipan Channel
Ushi Point
White
2
Elms
56 NGF
Airfield 1
Airfield 3
D-day line
2
50(+)
Asiga Point
Floating Reserve
4
2
23
1 25 3
3 25 2
2
24
24
White 1
Mt. Maga 390
Faibus San Hilo Point
Front July 26
3
50(+)
Elms
56 NGF 564
Mt. Lasso
Yellow Beach
Asiga Bay
WESTERN
NORTHERN
1
50(-)
PACIFIC

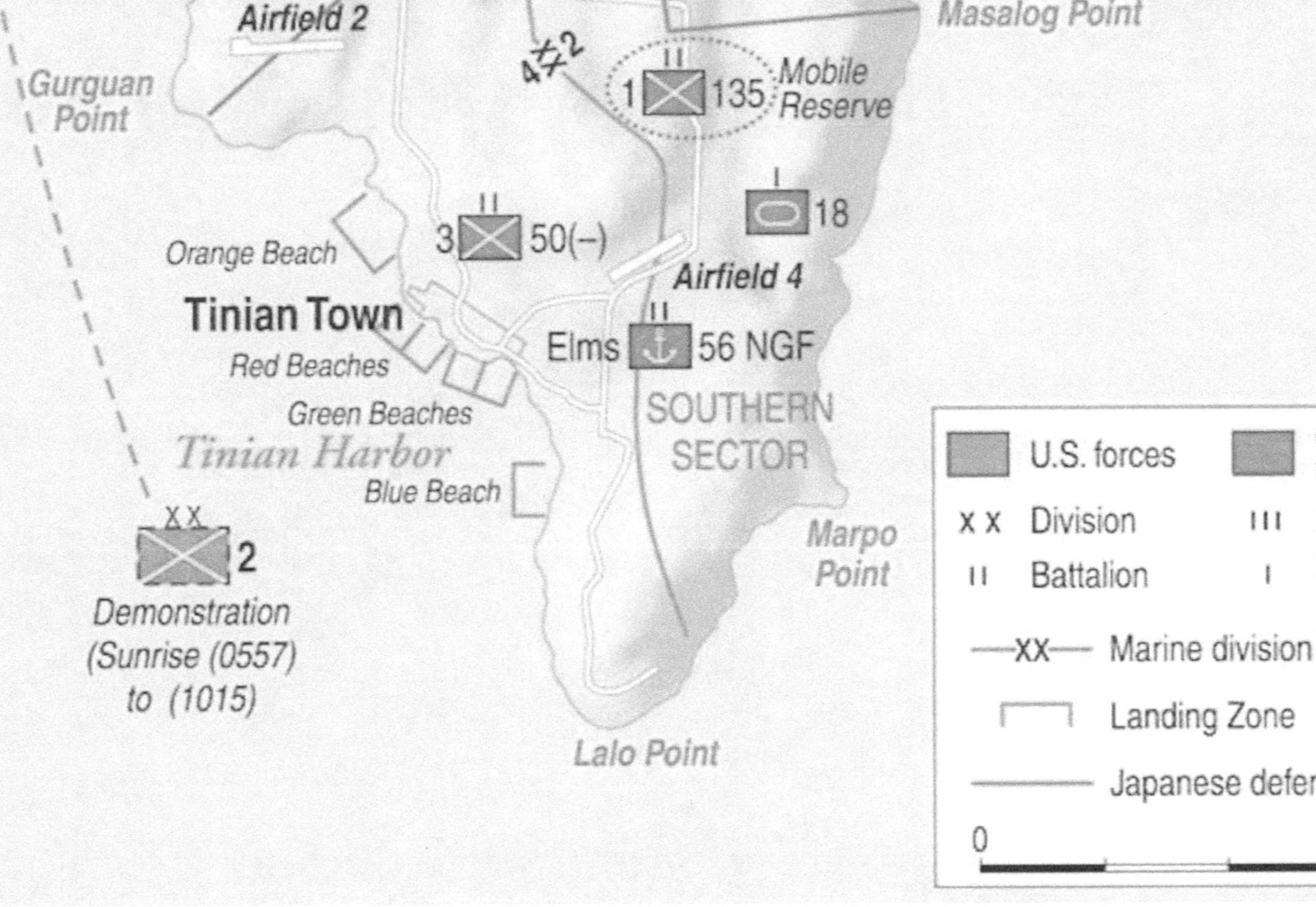

Airfield 2
Masalog Point
Gurguan Point
4/2
1 135 Mobile Reserve
Orange Beach
3 50(–)
18
Airfield 4
Tinian Town
Red Beaches
Elms 56 NGF
SOUTHERN SECTOR
Green Beaches
Tinian Harbor
Blue Beach
Marpo Point
X X 2
Demonstration
(Sunrise (0557) to (1015)
Lalo Point
U.S. forces
Japanese forces
X X Division
III Regiment
II Battalion
I Company
XX Marine division boundary
Landing Zone
Japanese defense sectors
0 3 miles

PLANNING THE ASSAULT

The 2nd and 4th Marine Divisions on Saipan were tasked with seizing Tinian. The Army's 27th Infantry Division would remain on Saipan in reserve. All three had been pummeled during the Saipan campaign. Together they'd suffered more than 14,000 casualties, with over 3,200 killed in action.

This would be the fourth assault in eighteen months for the 2nd Marine Division. The division left Guadalcanal in February 1943, suffering over one thousand casualties. Another 12,000 men had diagnosed malaria cases. Eight months later, on November 20, 1943 —the 2nd Marine Division had gone through one of the most intense seventy-two hours of combat in the history of island warfare at Tarawa. They endured 3,368 casualties, with just under a thousand dead.

Two and a half months before Tarawa, the division was still malaria-ridden, with troops hospitalized at a rate of over forty men a day. Ranks were filled with emaciated Marines, skin yellowed by the daily doses of the Atabrine pills. The Saipan operation took another heavy toll on these Marines seven months later: 1,304 killed and 5,027 wounded.

The 4th Marine Division had a busy but less demanding year.

They went directly into combat after their formation at Camp Pendleton. They landed on January 31, 1944, in the Marshall Islands. They suffered 787 casualties in the capture of Roi-Namur. They endured 6,025 casualties on Saipan, with more than 1,000 Marines killed. The Tinian landing would be the third assault in six months. It would also be the first under a new divisional commander—Major General Clifton Cates: a decorated World War I veteran who would later become the 19th Commandant of the Marine Corps in 1948.

"Troop morale in the Tinian operation was generally high," wrote Marine historian Carl Hoffman. "This fact takes on significance only when it's recalled the Marines had just survived a bitter month-long struggle with only a two-week lapse, and they were again ordered to assault enemy-held shores. Their spirit was more of a philosophical shrug accompanied by a 'here we go again' attitude rather than a resentment at being called upon again so soon."

The pre-invasion bombardment also helped the morale of the troops. For Jig -1 and Jig Day (Jig was the codename for D-Day on Tinian) Rear Admiral Harry Hill would command the Northern Landing Forces. He divided the island into five support sectors and assigned specific ships to each. He intended to deceive the Japanese about the true intentions of the Marine landing.

Tinian Town got the heaviest pounding the day before the landing: 2,785 rounds of 5- to 16-inch shells from battleships *Tennessee*, *Colorado*, *California*, and the cruiser *Cleveland* along with seven destroyers. *Colorado* had the best day with sixty rounds of 16-inch shells smashing the two six-inch coastal defense guns the Japanese had placed on the west near San Hilo Point—guns that could have covered the white beaches.

Due to lack of suitable targets and deception, White Beach area firing was insignificant. Naval gunfire and artillery barrages were stopped to allow massive airstrikes on railroad junctions, villages, pillboxes, cane fields, gun emplacements, and the beaches at Tinian Town. Over 350 Army and Navy planes took part in dropping over 200 rockets, 500 bombs, and thirty-four napalm bombs.

That night thirty-seven LSTs (Landing Ship, Tank) at anchor off Saipan reloaded with 4th Marine Division troops. Three days of rations, medical supplies, ammunition, water, vehicles, and other equipment were preloaded on July 15. The troops traveled light: a pair of socks, insect repellent, a spoon, emergency supplies in their pockets, and no pack on their back.

Historian Philip Crowl wrote, "I rode the ships with two transport divisions that would carry two regiments of the 2nd Marine Division on a diversionary feint against Tinian Town and would later disembark them across the Northwestern beaches." (A similar ruse was made by the 2nd Division Marines a year later off the southeast beach of Okinawa.)

The 4th Marine Division was selected as the assault division for Tinian. The beaches were not wide enough to accommodate battalions landing abreast, much less divisions. The assault troops landed in columns—companies, platoons, and even squads.

The 2nd Division would soon follow after taking part in a feint off the beaches of Tinian Town. They hoped to tie down the main Japanese forces while the 4th Division surprised the lightly defended northern beaches.

To give the 4th Marine Division more punch after the landing, the 2nd Marine Division was stripped of some of its artillery, tank, and firepower units. They would be at the lowest strength on Tinian of any Marine division involved in an amphibious operation in all of World War II.

Even after cannibalizing from the 2nd Marine Division, the 4th would still be "skinny," wrote Lieutenant Colonel "Jumping Joe" Chambers, who commanded the 3rd Battalion 25th Regiment (3/25) Marines and later earned a Medal of Honor on Iwo Jima. The division's infantry battalion only received one replacement after the fighting on Saipan. At full strength, they averaged 880 men—at Tinian, the average strength was down by more than 35% to just over 550 men.

Due to combat fatigue, heavy losses during previous weeks and months, and under-strength units: The Marines on Tinian played a cautious game. Admiral Turner said he'd give them two weeks to seize the island. General Harry Schmidt, now in command of V

Amphibious Corps, promised to get it done sooner. The island was secured after nine days. A Marine Historian wrote, "the operation could have been finished sooner if they used more aggressive tactics." But time was no great factor—the relatively slow pace of the operation probably contributed to keeping casualties at a minimum and helped reduce troop fatigue. Tinian may have been easy on the eyes, but the heat and humidity were brutal, the cane fields were hard going, and it was monsoon season.

JIG DAY LANDING

At 0330, July 24, troop ships moved out of Saipan's Charan Kanoa harbor. They carried the 2nd and 8th Infantry Regiments of the 2nd Marine Division. This deception mission would be far bloodier than the White Beach landings and far more costly than command expected. They had a powerful escort—the battleship *Colorado*, light cruiser *Cleveland*, and destroyers *Monssen*, *Wadleigh*, *Norman Scott* and *Ramey*.

The convoy moved into Sunharon Harbor across from Tinian Town just before dawn. At 0601, the attack transport *Calvert* lowered its landing craft, and by 0630, all twenty-two of its boats were in the water. Marines climbed down cargo nets, and within thirty minutes: US planes strafed and bombed the runs, paying particular attention to Tinian Town. Rockets and shells from battleships, light and heavy cruisers, destroyers, and over thirty gunboats saturated the beaches. Massed artillery battalions in southern Saipan thundered in with 155mm rounds.

After thirty minutes, the LVCPs (Landing Craft Vehicle Personnel, or Higgins boats) from the *Calvert* made a run toward the beach, taking on heavy artillery and mortar fire from shore. Rear Admiral Hill, trying to avoid casualties, ordered the boats to withdraw and reform. A second run followed and took on heavy fire from Japanese resistance on shore. Several of the boats were sprayed with shell fragments but continued until less than four hundred yards off the beach before turning back.

While the small boats engaged in this maneuver, the battleship *Colorado* came under fire at a range of just over 3,000 yards from two Japanese 6-inch guns near Tinian Town. These guns had gone undetected during the pre-invasion reconnaissance. Within fifteen minutes, Japanese gunners scored twenty-two direct hits on the *Colorado* and six on the destroyer *Norman Scott*. The casualties among the Marine detachments and crews were costly: 227 wounded and 69 killed. The *Colorado* limped back to Saipan. That Japanese battery survived for four entire days until finally destroyed by the battleship *Tennessee*.

The losses taken by these two ships alone exceeded those suffered by the larger Marine landing forces on the northwestern beaches. But this deception served its purpose. One battalion of the Japanese *50th Infantry Regiment* and elements of the *56th Naval Guard Force* froze in place around Tinian Town. This deception also convinced the Japanese commander Colonel Kiyochi Ogata that he had thwarted an invasion. His message to Tokyo described his forces repelled over one-hundred landing barges.

These "barges" reloaded back onto the *Calvert* at 1000. The convoy steamed north to the White Beaches, where the Marine 4th Division troops had landed after a mishap. A UDT party using floats and carrying explosives swam to White Beach 2 before dawn to blast away boulders and destroy beach mines. But a squall caused this mission to fail. Now the floats were scattered and explosives lost. The Marines would pay a heavy price for this aborted mission a few hours later.

To offset the UDT mission's failure, airstrikes were ordered at 0630. Observers claimed that five of the fourteen known beach mines had been destroyed. One battery of 155mm "Long Tom" guns on Saipan fired smoke shells at the Japanese command post on Mount Lasso. They also laid smoke in the woods, the bluffs, and beaches to hinder Japanese observation.

* * *

The 24th Marines were tasked with assaulting White Beach 1 while White Beach 2 went to the 25th Marines. Almost at once, two battalions of the 25th Marines loaded into sixteen LVTs and landed in columns of companies on White Beach 2. The 2nd Battalion was on the right and the 3rd Battalion on the left.

Units of the 24th Marines loaded into twenty-five LVTs and crossed the line of departure 3,500 yards offshore at 0715. Ahead of them were LCIs (landing craft, infantry) and a company of the 2nd Armored Amphibian Battalion. They raked the beaches with barrage rockets and automatic cannon fire. In the twenty-five-minute run to the beach, the trip-laden LVTs took scattered small arms and machine-gun fire.

At White Beach 1, a small Japanese beach detachment holed up in caves and crevices put up a fierce resistance with small arms fire. Company E gunners quickly destroyed them.

In less than an hour, the entire 1st and 2nd Battalions of the 24th Marines were ashore on White Beach 1 and prepared to move inland. The 2nd Battalion faced erratic small arms, mortar, and artillery fire during the first few hundred yards of its advance. After that, the battalion had an easy walk for the rest of the day, gaining their O-1 line objective by 1600. They also occupied the western edge of Airfield 3 and cut the main road that linked Airfield 1 with the eastern coast and southern Tinian. Still receiving sporadic small-arms fire, the battalion dug in for the night.

On the left flank, heavy fire stalled the 1st Battalion. Enemy shooters hid in patches of vegetation and cave positions. Flamethrower tanks were set up against these positions, but the Japanese kept up a stiff resistance. As a result, the 1st Battalion did not reach their objective—400 yards short of their objective by the afternoon. This left a gap between the two perimeters. The regimental 3rd Battalion waiting in reserve was called up.

The 25th Regiment ran into problems. The beach in the surrounding area had been seeded with mines that the UDT teams and offshore gunners failed to destroy. It took five hours to clear them out. Three LVTs and a jeep were destroyed in the process. Several booby traps were left for the Marines to deal with: Cases of beer and watches wired to explode in the hands of careless souvenir hunters.

Inland, troops from Ogata's *50th Infantry Regiment* put up a vigorous defense with mortars, anti-boat and anti-tank guns, and other automatic weapons placed in fortified ravines, pillboxes, caves and field entrenchments. A pair of 47mm guns kept Marines on the defensive. After they finally bypassed the difficult positions, they left fifty dead Japanese in the gun pits.

Colonel Chambers, the 3/25 Marines commander, later wrote of the confusion on the beach, "the confusion you always get when you land, and trying to reorganize under fire." One of his company commanders was killed fifteen minutes after landing. It took a while to get a replacement on scene and up to speed. Then there was still the problem of mines and artillery fire from the Japanese command post on Mount Lasso, less than two miles away.

By late afternoon Colonel Chambers' battalion had reached its objective of 1,500 yards inland to the center of the line and had tied the 24th onto its left flank. Other battalions of the 25th came up short of their O-1 line. This created a crescent-shaped beachhead that was 3,500 yards wide at the shoreline and bulged inland 1,500 yards at sunset.

But the day's greatest confusion came from the 23rd Marines. The regiment had been waiting on LSTs in division reserve during the landing. At 0740, troops were ordered to board LVTs parked cheek to jowl in the tank decks. Their engines were running and spewing carbon monoxide. After thirty minutes, the cooped-up troops developed headaches, got nauseous, and started vomiting.

Colonel Louis Jones ordered the men to unload and return topside until a launch order was finally received at 1030. The regiment debarked and eventually got ashore at 1400 despite an incredible series of communication breakdowns, where Colonel Jones at crucial times, was out of touch with his battalions and divisions.

Besides disrupted radio communications, Colonel Jones was stuck in an LVT with a bad engine. He waited seven hours to get ashore with his staff, leading to a division complaint about his regiment's tardiness. Command noted that "fortunately no serious harm was done by the delay."

But at the end of the operation, Colonel Jones left the division. He was promoted to brigadier general and assigned a position as assistant division commander of the 1st Marine Division leading up to the Okinawa landings.

A similar problem happened involving the 2nd Marine Division. After the feint at Tinian Town, the division sailed north and waited offshore of the White Beaches throughout the day. At 1530, the landing force commander, General Harry Schmidt, ordered a battalion from the 8th Marines to land on White Beach, backing up the 24th Marines. General Schmidt wanted a battalion ashore by 1600.

Because of the poor communications and transport confusion, the deadline was missed. It wasn't until 2100 when the unit entered into its log, "Dug in in assigned position."

But while all the details weren't perfect, the overall operation had gone well in the morning and afternoon. By the standards of

Saipan and Tarawa, casualties were light—225 wounded and 15 dead. The Japanese body count was over 435 men.

Despite narrow beaches, undiscovered mines, and drizzling rain, over 15,500 troops were still put ashore. Along with massive quantities of equipment and material, including four artillery battalions, twenty-four half-tracks with 75mm guns. Forty-eight medium and fifteen flamethrower tanks, which found the Tinian terrain agreeable for tank operations.

Tanks got into action early that morning and led the 24th in tank-infantry attacks. They'd also come to the aid of the 23rd Marines as the regiment moved inland to take over the division's right flank. Despite some units failing to reach their first objectives, the beachhead was large and extended inland nearly a mile and embraced defensible territory.

Not bad for a day's work.

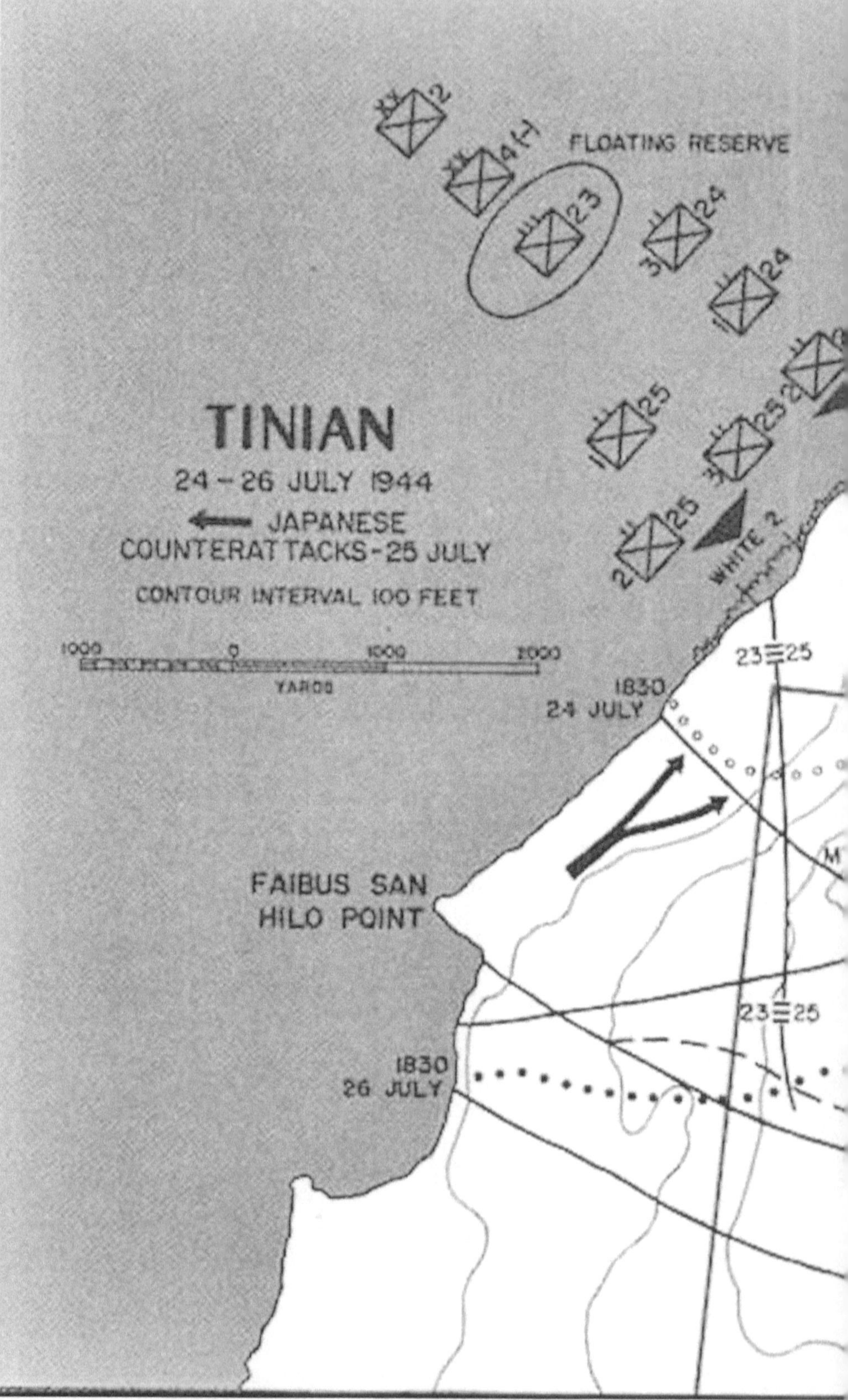

2
4(-)
FLOATING RESERVE
23
24
3
24
TINIAN
24-26 JULY 1944
JAPANESE
COUNTERATTACKS-25 JULY
CONTOUR INTERVAL 100 FEET
1000
0
1000
2000
YARDS
25
25
3
25
WHITE 2
2
23 25
1830
24 JULY
M
FAIBUS SAN
HILO POINT
23 25
1830
26 JULY

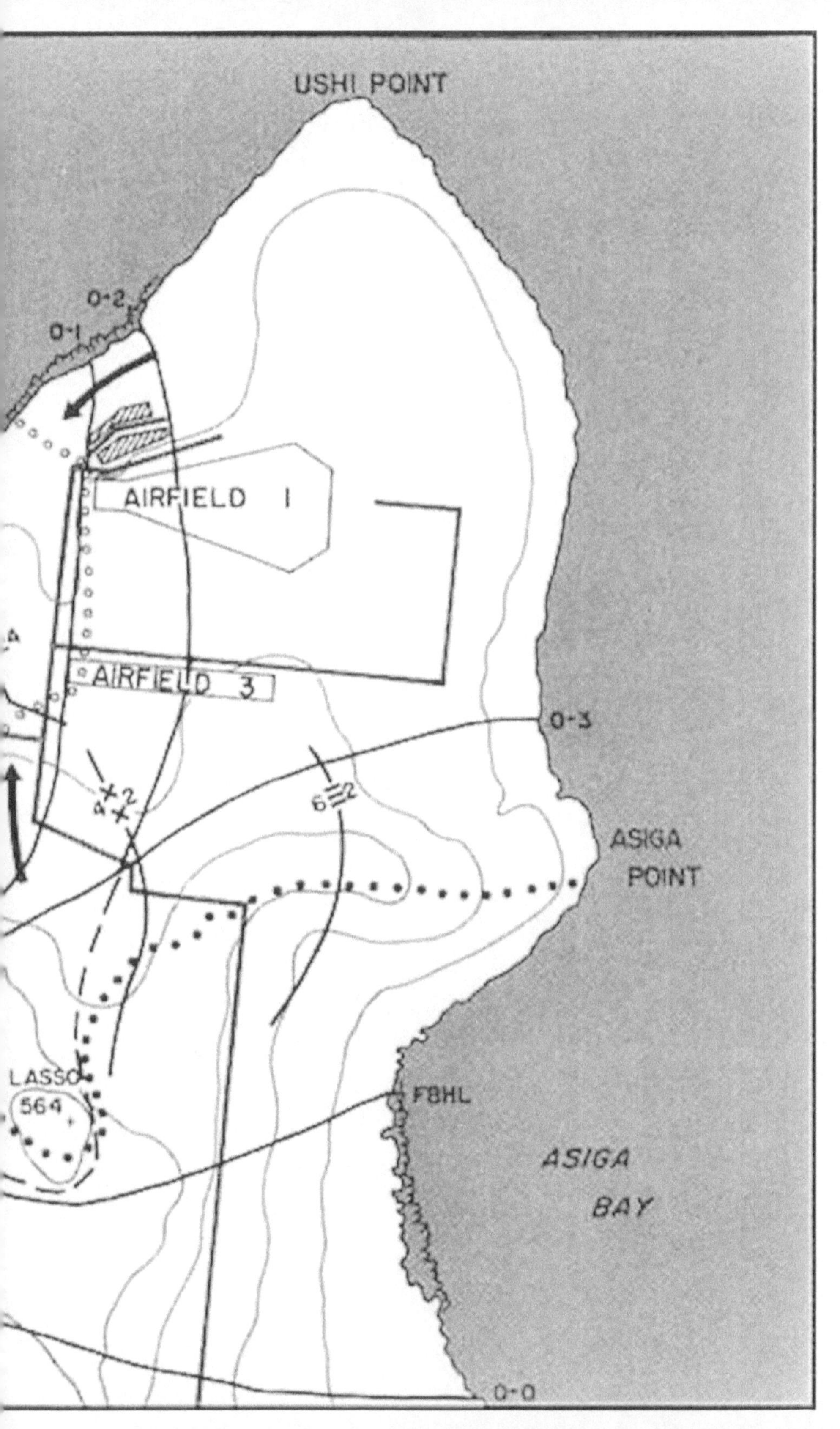

USHI POINT
O-2
O-1
AIRFIELD 1
AIRFIELD 3
O-3
ASIGA POINT
LASSO
564
F8HL
ASIGA BAY
O-0

JAPANESE COUNTERATTACK

At 1630, General Clifton B. Cates, in command of the 4th Marine Division, ordered his forces to button up for the night. Command expected a nighttime counterattack. Barbed wire, preloaded on amphibian vehicles, was strung along the front.

Stockpiled ammunition could be seen in every weapons position. Machine guns were emplaced to allow interlocking fields of fire. Target areas were assigned to mortar crews. Artillery batteries in the rear were pre-registered to hit enemy approach routes and fire illumination shells to light up the battlefield. Anti-tank 37mm guns with canister ammunition (antipersonnel shells firing large pellets for close infighting) were positioned upfront. This would ensure severe casualties and do the greatest damage to the enemy.

The Marines dug in and waited for whatever the night would bring. The 24th Marines were backed up by the 1/8 Marines, occupying the northern half of the crescent defense. The 25th with a battalion of the 23rd occupied the southern half of the crescent. The rest of the 23rd were in reserve, along with artillery battalions from the 10th and 14th Marines, waiting in the rear on high alert.

The Japanese prepared for their counterattack. Because of their shattered communication lines, it would not be a coordinated operation. Units would need to act independently. Colonel Ogata issued a general order on June 28: "destroy the enemy on beaches with one blow. Especially where time prevents quick movement of forces within the island."

The Japanese had 850 naval troops at the Ushi Point airfields on the Marines' northern flank. Opposite the center of the Marine lines, near Mount Lasso, were another two battalions of the *50th Infantry Regiment* and a tank company of 1,500 Japanese troops in total. On the west coast facing the Marines' right flank were another 250 men from an infantry company of the *50th Regiment*—along with an anti-tank squad and an anti-tank detachment.

The Japanese *Mobile Counterattack Force*—a 750-man battalion of the *135th Infantry Regiment*, equipped with new rifles and demolition charges, waited six miles from the White Beaches. Japanese movement toward the northwestern beaches within the Marine lines was treacherous. All daylight movement was closely monitored by air surveillance and vulnerable to American firepower.

But the battalion set out under its commander, Captain Izumi, and was hit frequently by unobserved artillery and naval gunfire. Izumi advanced and made his objective through skillful use of terrain for concealment. At 2230 he probed the center of the Marine lines where the 2/24 Marines were tied in with the 3rd Battalion.

According to a Marine Combat correspondent: "While most of the Japanese crept along forward of the lines, a two-man reconnaissance detail climbed up on a battered building forward of the 24th Marines and audaciously jotted notes or drew sketches of the front lines. When Marines recognized this impudent gesture, they rewarded them with a thundering concentration of artillery fire."

Another Marine wrote of his vivid memory that night: "A big gully ran from southeast to northwest into the western edge of our area. Anyone in their right mind would have figured that if there were going to be any counterattacks—they'd come from that gully.

"Throughout the night, Marines reported they heard a lot of

Japanese chatter from down in the gully. Then they hit us at about midnight in K Company's area. They hauled a couple of 75mm howitzers by hand with them, and when they got up to where they could fire at us—they hit us hard. I believe K Company did a damn good job, but about two-hundred Japs pushed through us [1,500 yards] to the beach area.

"Once the Japs hit the rear areas, all the artillery and machine guns started shooting like hell. Fire came in from the rear and grazed right up over our heads. During this, the enemy that hit Company L was putting up one hell of a fight about seventy-five yards from where I was—and there wasn't a damn thing I could do about it.

"Over in Company K's area is where the attack really developed. That was where Lieutenant McGuire and his 37mm guns on the left flank were firing canister. I watched two Marines manning a machine gun layout a cone of dead Jap bodies in front of them. A dead Jap officer laid right in there with them."

A Combat Marine correspondent later described this action: "Marines held their fire until the Japanese were less than a thousand yards away—then they opened up. The Japanese charged. Screaming '*banzai*' and firing machine guns and throwing grenades. It was near impossible for the Marines to hold on and continue firing. The next morning, we counted the Jap bodies piled in front of us. Over 250 dead Japanese soldiers.

"Just before sunrise, two tank companies showed up. They wanted to get right at the Japs and were sent off to an area held by Companies L and K. The major returned in less than fifteen minutes and said, 'you don't need tanks. You need undertakers. I've never seen so many dead Japs.'"

Another large party of Japanese troops was *stacked up* by the 75mm howitzer gunners of the 14th Marines supported by the 50-caliber machine guns of batteries E and F. These machine guns literally tore the Japanese to pieces. Over 600 Japanese were killed in their suicidal attack on the Marine center.

On the left flank, the 1/24 Marines came under attack at 0200 from 550 *Special Naval Landing Force* troops out of the barracks at the Ushi Point airfields. Company A was hit so hard it was at one point reduced to only 30 men with weapons. Company A was forced to draw reinforcements from corpsmen, engineers, communicators, and members of the shore party.

Illumination flares soared over the battlefield. This allowed Marines to use 37mm canister shells, mortars, and machine-gun fire to good effect. The fight continued until dawn, when medium tanks from the 4th Tank Battalion lumbered up to break up the last attacking Japanese troops. By this point, many Japanese had used their grenades to commit suicide.

As the sun rose, 470 Japanese bodies were counted in the defensive crescent, mostly in front of Company A's position.

The last enemy attack that night hit the right flank of the Marines at 0330. A handful of Japanese tanks rattled up from Tinian Town's direction to attack the 23rd Marines' position. They were met with fierce fire from anti-tank guns, Marine artillery, small arms, and bazookas.

Lieutenant Jim Lucas was a professional reporter who enlisted in the Marine Corps after the attack on Pearl Harbor and was commissioned in the field. He later wrote: "Three lead tanks broke through the wall of fire. One glowed a blood-red and turned crazily on its tracks before careening into a ditch. A second, mortally wounded, turned its machine guns on its tormentors, firing into the ditches in one last desperate effort to fight its way free. After another hundred yards, it stopped dead in its tracks.

"The third tank tried frantically to turn around and retreat, but our boys closed in and literally blasted it apart. Bazookas knocked out a fourth tank, killing the driver. The rest of the crew piled out of the turret screaming. The fifth tank was now surrounded and tried to flee. Our bazookas made quick work of it. Another hit set it on fire, and its crew was cremated.

"The sixth tank was chased off by a Marine driving a Jeep. But destroying these tanks did not end the fight on the right flank. Infantry from the Japanese *50th Regiment* continued to attack the 2/23 Marines. While they were repulsed and killed in large numbers, mainly through effective use of anti-tank 37mm guns with canister shot. In the last hopeless moments of the assault, some wounded Japanese destroyed themselves by detonating a magnetic tank mine, producing a horrific blast."

From a Japanese standpoint, that night's work was a disaster. Over 1,200 bodies were left on the battlefield: several hundred more carted away during the night. With fewer than one hundred Marines wounded or killed, losing these Japanese troops broke the back of the already poor defenses of Tinian. Now that their communications were shattered by sustained fire from Saipan and increasing fire from Tinian, survivors were capable of only the weakest, most dazed sort of resistance. During the next seven days, small groups of Japanese took advantage of the darkness to launch night attacks, but mostly, they only withdrew in no particular order until there was nowhere left for them to withdraw.

Most agreed that the battle for Tinian was over. But 4th Division intelligence officer Colonel Gooderham McCormick, a Marine reserve officer, later to become the mayor of Philadelphia, did not agree: "we believed after the counterattack the enemy was capable of a still harder fight. And from day-to-day during our advance expected an even more bitter fight that never materialized."

Hard work still lay ahead. A demanding task was the exhausting but straightforward job of humping through the cane fields and humidity with frequent monsoon downpours. Fearful of not only sniper fire, booby traps and mines but also fires that could sweep through the cane fields and incinerate anyone caught in its path.

PEOPLE SHOOTING GROUSE

Colonel "Bucky" Buchanan was an assistant naval gunfire officer for the 4th Division at Tinian. He wrote of his experiences: "We fought the same way at Tinian that we did on Saipan. It was a handholding, linear operation, like a bunch of bush beaters, people shooting grouse or something. The idea was to flush out every Jap consistently as we go down rather than driving down the main road with a fork and cutting this and that off in what I called creative tactics. This was the easiest and safest thing to do. Who can criticize it? We were successful. And again, what little resistance was left was pushed into the edge of the island—and quickly destroyed."

The grouse shooting metaphor was simple, but even the 4th Division commander, General Cates thought the campaign had a sporting aspect. "The fighting was different from most any that we'd experienced because it was good terrain. A good, clean operation the men really enjoyed."

Before the bush beating could begin in a proper order, three things needed to happen. First, the 2nd Division needed to be put ashore. This was completed on the morning of July 26.

Next, Japanese pockets of resistance and stragglers on the

island's northern sector had to be crushed. That job was completed on the 26th as the 2nd Marine Division swept across Ushi Point airfields and reached the east coast before turning south.

The 4th Division seized Mount Maga in the center of the island, also on the 26th. This forced Colonel Ogata and his staff to abandon their command post on Mount Lasso, which fell to the Marines without a struggle. Two days later, Navy Seabees had the Ushi Point airfields in operation for Army P-47 Thunderbolt Fighters.

The third objective was to drive south a skirmish line of infantry and tanks stretching across the 29 square mile island. This was also accomplished on the 26th. The 4th Division lined up in the western half of the island. The 23rd Marines were on the coast, with the 24th in the center and the 25th on the left flank. The 2nd Division lined up with the 2nd Marines on the east coast with the 6th Marines in the center now all tied into the 25th. The 8th Marines stayed in the north to mop up any further resistance.

This was achieved with only minor casualties. On July 26, Jig Day +2, the 2nd Division reported two dead and 14 wounded. These were the heaviest losses since the first day and night of fighting had been sustained by the 14th Marines, the 4th Division's artillery regiment, following the Japanese counterattack. An enemy shell smashed into the 1st Battalion's fire direction center, killing the battalion commander, intelligence officer, ops officer, and seven other staff members. Fourteen Marines in the battalion headquarters were also wounded. Nearly all the casualties sustained by the regiment during the Tinian campaign happened on that one day —July 25.

The morning of July 27, Jig Day +3, started the bush beating drive to the south. General Schmidt's plan for the first two days of the drive alternated between the two divisions' main thrust. The official history of the operation likens it to "a man elbowing his way through the crowd swinging on one arm then the other."

The 2nd Division got the heavier work on July 27. Artillery firing from southern Saipan had softened up suspected enemy positions early in the morning. At 0730, the 2nd Division began its advance. They advanced swiftly and were harassed by sporadic arms fire. By 1345 they'd reached their objective. They gained over 4,000 yards in less than six hours.

The 4th Division moved out late in the morning against "negligible opposition" and reached their objective by noon before calling it a day. A Japanese prisoner of war complained to his captors, "you couldn't drop a stick without bringing down artillery."

On the morning of July 28, the 4th Marines got the "swinging elbow" job. It was now apparent the remaining Japanese defenders were fleeing to the hills and caves along the southern coast. The opposition to the Marine advance was virtually nil. The 4th Marines moved more than two miles in less than four hours, with troops riding in half-tracks and tanks.

Starting again early in the afternoon in a *blitz* fashion, they overran the airfield at Gurguan Point before quitting for the day at 1730 after gaining just over 7000 yards—a little over 4 miles. The 2nd Division got light-duty and moved ahead a few hundred yards, reaching their objective in two hours, and digging in to wait for the next morning.

General Cates later wrote how he spurred on his 4th Division troops: "'Look men,' I said. 'The Hawaiian island of Maui is waiting for us. See the ships out there? The quicker you get this over with, the quicker we'll be back there.' They almost ran to the other end of that island."

On the 29th, General Schmidt dropped the elbowing tactic and ordered both divisions to move as far and as fast as sensible. Opposition had been so light that preparatory fires were canceled to save the dwindling artillery supply shells left on Saipan and to prevent any "waste of naval gunfire on areas largely deserted by the enemy."

While the 2nd Marines in the eastern terrain ran into pockets of resistance at Masalog Point, the 6th Marines encountered a twenty-man Japanese patrol attempting to penetrate the regiment's lines after dark. The 25th took heavy sniper fire as they moved through cane fields and engaged in a heavy firefight with Japanese troops fighting from dug-in positions later in the day. The Marines suffered casualties and one of their tanks was disabled in the fight. But the resistance was eventually overcome. The 24th Marines operating near the west coast ran into Japanese positions, including a series of mutually supporting bunkers. The 4th Tank Battalion reported that the area had to be overrun twice by tanks before the resistance ended.

By nightfall, more than half of Tinian was in Marine hands. The 4th Division Marines could see Tinian Town from their foxholes. While great for morale, the night was spoiled by weather and heavy enemy activity. A soaking rain poured through the night. Enemy mortars and artillery fired relentlessly, drawing counter-battery fire from Marine gunners. Mortars and small arms fire silenced probes in front of the 3/25 Marines—forty Japanese bodies were found in the area at dawn.

On July 30 (Jig Day +6), Tinian Town became the principal objective of the 4th Division. At 0730, all of the division's artillery battalions laid down preparatory fire in front of Marine lines. After ten minutes, the firing stopped, and the troops moved out. At once, two destroyers and a cruiser lying in Sunharon Harbor of Tinian Town started an hour-long bombardment to support the Marines. The 1/24 Marines advanced 600 yards before coming under heavy fire from the caves along the coast north of town.

With the help of tanks and armored amphibians operating offshore, this problem was solved. Flame-throwing tanks worked over the caves, allowing engineers to seal them with demolition charges. A 75mm gun hidden in one cave was found and destroyed.

The regiment entered the ruins of Tinian Town at 1430. Except for a lone Japanese soldier—eliminated on the spot—the town was deserted. After searching through the rubble for snipers and documents, Marines advanced to their O-7 line objective south of town. The greatest danger was from mines and booby traps planted in beach areas and roads.

As the 24th continued south, the 25th Marines seized Airfield 4 on the outskirts of Tinian Town. A Japanese prisoner revealed that the unfinished airfield was rushed to completion in order to accommodate relief planes promised by Tokyo. Only one plane was parked on the crushed coral airstrip—a lone Zero fighter. Flying suits, goggles, and other equipment were found in the supply room.

En route to the airfield, the 25th took light small arms fire and while crossing the airstrip, was mortared from positions in the south. This was the 25th's last action in the Tinian campaign. They went into reserve and were relieved by units of the 23rd and the 1/8 Marines.

The 2nd Division operating east of the 4th ran into intermittent opposition from machine gun positions and a 70mm howitzer. The 3/2 Marines of the 2nd Division had the roughest time. After they silenced the howitzer, they attacked across an open field and chased a Japanese force into a large cave. With the help of a flame-throwing tank, ninety-three Japanese were killed, and four machine guns destroyed.

Afterward, the battalion came under mortar fire. The unit commander, Colonel Walter Layer wrote: "It was beyond my memory as to the number of casualties the 3rd suffered at that time. I remember rendering first aid to wounded Marines and seeing seven wounded or killed by enemy mortar fire. Half-tracks and tanks took the enemy under fire, destroying enemy mortars."

There were more minor delays, but the division reached the objective on time and dug-in by 1830. Nearly eighty percent of the island was now in American hands.

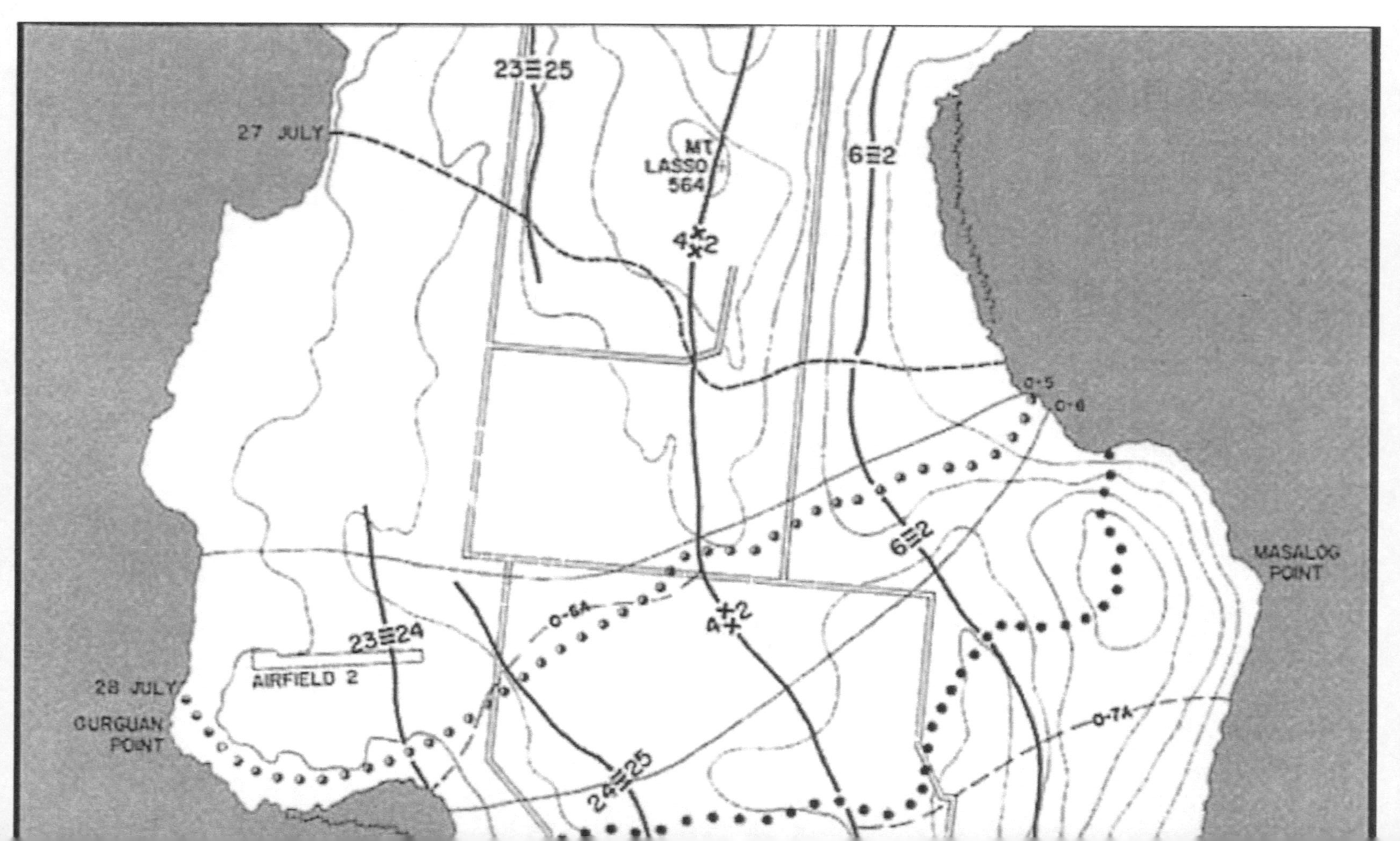

27 JULY
23≡25
MT LASSO 564
6≡2
4x2
0-5
0-6
6≡2
MASALOG POINT
0-6A
4x2
23≡24
AIRFIELD 2
28 JULY
GURGUAN POINT
24≡25
0-7A

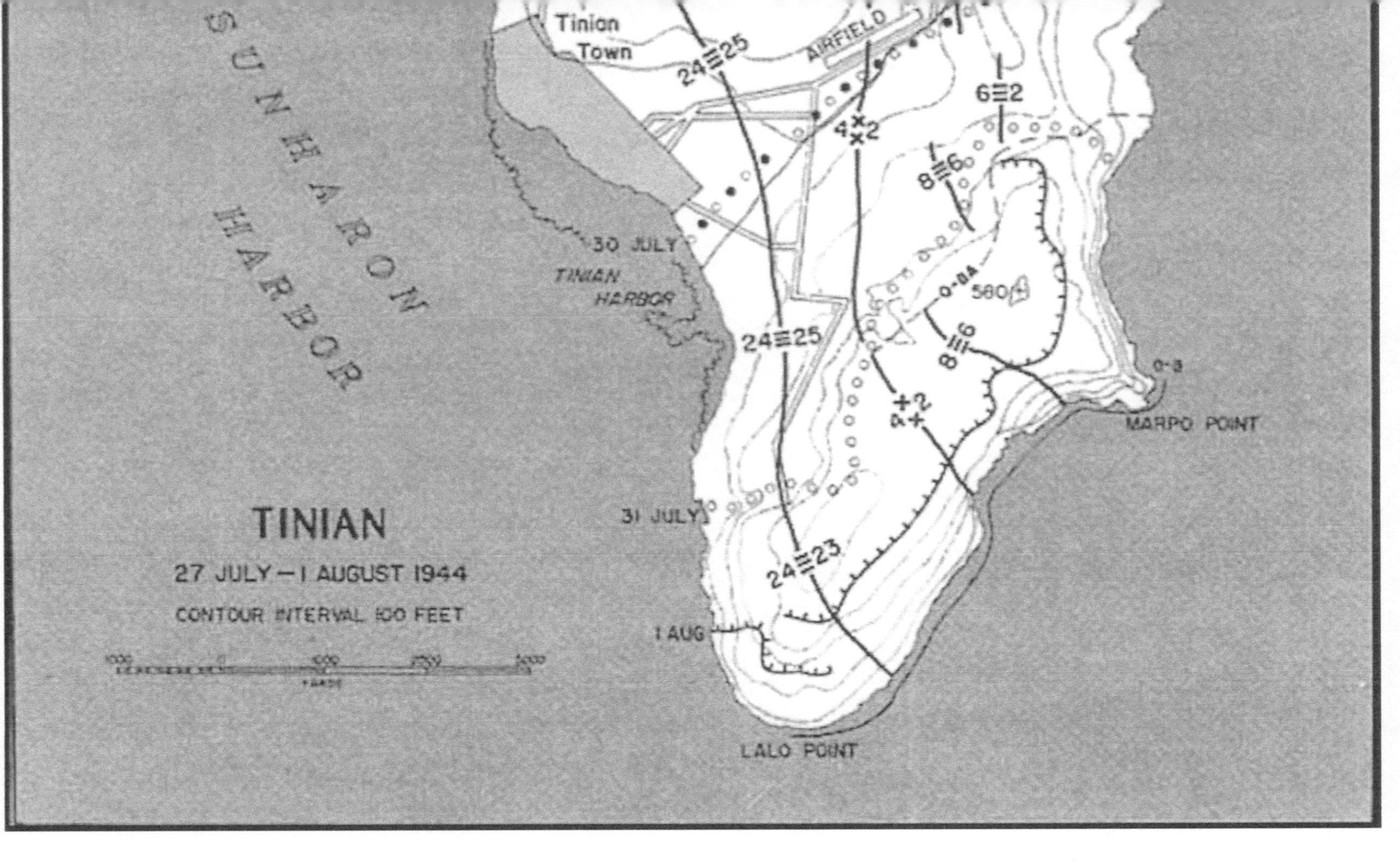

SUNHARON HARBOR
Tinian Town
Tinian
AIRFIELD
24≡25
6≡2
4×2
8≡6
30 JULY
TINIAN HARBOR
0-8A
580(A)
8≡6
24≡25
0-8
+2
4×
MARPO POINT
31 JULY
24≡23
1 AUG
LALO POINT
TINIAN
27 JULY — 1 AUGUST 1944
CONTOUR INTERVAL 100 FEET

END OF RESISTANCE

The Japanese were now confined to a small area of southeastern Tinian. Marines had advanced so quickly that only four miles of the island remained safe firing for ships not supporting battalions.

General Schmidt saw the end in sight in the late afternoon of July 30. He ordered the divisions to drive all the way to the southeast coastline and seize all territory remaining in enemy hands and destroy any Japanese troops.

This was not an insignificant assignment and caused the heaviest fighting since the Jig-Day counterattack. A Japanese officer captured on July 29 estimated that 500 troops of the *56th Naval Guard Force* and 2,000 troops of the *50th Infantry Regiment* were in battle-ready condition in the island's southeastern area. US intelligence estimated on July 29, based on daily reports from the divisions, that 2,800 Japanese troops had already been killed or taken prisoner up to that point. If this was true, then nearly two-thirds of the 9,000 Japanese defenders would still be alive and ready to defend the island.

The main Japanese force occupied rugged terrain that was difficult to reach and traverse—well suited for their defensive purposes. Outside of Tinian Town, the gentle landscape ended with the ground rising to plateaus of over 5,000 feet long and 2,000 yards wide—with altitudes over 500 feet. There were many caves. The plateaus were rocky and covered with thick brush. All along the east coast, cliff walls rose and seemed impossible to scale. Cliffs and jungle growth obstructed the approaches. The road in the center of the plateau led to its top and was reportedly mined. This plateau would be the last hold out for the remaining Japanese.

Next came the most intense bombardment any Japanese force had yet experienced in World War II. Marine artillery regiments on southern Saipan fired throughout the night of July 30 into the wooded cliff lines. Battleships *California* and *Tennessee* along with the heavy cruiser *Louisville* and light cruisers *Birmingham* and *Montpelier* began two sustained bombardments at 0600.

Firing for over an hour, they stopped to allow a forty-minute strike by 126 P-47 Thunderbolt Fighters, Mitchell Bombers, and Grumman Avenger Bombers from the carrier *Kitkun Bay*. These planes dropped seventy tons of explosives before the offshore gunfire resumed for another thirty minutes.

The battleships and cruisers fired over 600 tons of shells at their targets. The 10th and 14th Marines' artillerymen and gunners fired over 7,000 rounds during the night. According to a Japanese prisoner, the effect was "unbearable."

The following day, the 2nd Marines' task was to clear out the western coastal area with one battalion assigned for the plateau's seizure. The 2nd Marines intended to seal off the east coast at the base of the plateau. The 6th, 8th, and 23rd Marines would assault the cliff areas and advance to the top of the plateau.

The 24th Marines jumped off at 0830 and advanced into the coastal plains. They immediately encountered brush and undergrowth so dense that tank operations would be hampered. Armored amphibians lying offshore fired against enemy beach positions and covered the regiment's right flank as they made their way down the coast. A platoon-sized Japanese beach unit launched a foolish counterattack on the 1/24 Marines at 0950. The Japanese were destroyed. Flame throwing tanks burned off brush and undergrowth, which concealed the Japanese riflemens' positions.

The 3rd Battalion on the regiment's left flank assaulted the base of the plateau. They encountered minimal opposition until 1610 when they took machine gun and rifle fire from cliff positions. Tanks were called up but got caught in a minefield and were delayed for several hours while engineers cleared dozens of mines.

The 1/23 Marines encountered a similar problem. As the regiment approached the plateau, they ran into intense small arms fire from two positions. A small village at the base of the cliff and from the cliff face itself. They took fire from a "large caliber weapon." Marines pressed forward without tank support, running a few yards, then diving, and getting up to advance again. Marine tanks finally came in search of this elusive and well-concealed weapon. One tank took six hits from the Japanese gun. A second tank was hit, but in the process, a concrete camouflage bunker hiding a 47mm anti-tank gun and twenty enemy troops was destroyed.

The 2/23 Marines came under fire from machine gunners and riflemen. One of their supporting tanks was disabled by a mine. Its crew was taken to safety by another tank, but the disabled tank was taken over by the Japanese and used as an armored machine gun nest. Other tanks were dispatched to take it out. The 23rd Regiment also lost two 37mm guns and a 1-ton truck belonging to the regiment's half-track platoon. The guns and the vehicle got too far ahead and came under heavy fire before being abandoned. The platoon later retrieved one of the guns and removed the breech block from the other. The 50-caliber machine gun from its truck mounting was brought back.

By late afternoon, the 1/23 Marines got a foothold on top of the plateau. The 3rd Battalion soon followed. On their left flank, the 3/8 Marines shrugged off small arms fire to reach the cliff's base where they were delayed for the night. The 1st Battalion had better luck. Company A made it to the top of the plateau at 1630 and was soon followed by the entire battalion and Companies E and G from the 2/8 Marines.

Captain Carl Hoffman commander of Company G of the 2/8 Marines later wrote a definitive history of the Saipan and Tinian campaigns. In an interview, he described his own experiences on top of the plateau on the night of July 31: "By the time we got up there, there was enough daylight to get ourselves properly barbed wired in, get our fields of fire established, and site our interlocking bands of machine gun fire. All things necessary for preparing a good defense.

"By dusk the enemy started a series of probing attacks. Some Japs made it into our positions. It was such a black night that the Japs moving around in our positions made our troops edgy and they challenged everyone in sight. We didn't have any unfortunate incidents of Marines firing on Marines because we were all well-seasoned by this point.

"While the night wore on, the intensity of enemy attacks started to build and finally they launched a full-on banzai attack against our battalion. The strange thing the Japs did here was that they executed one wave attack after another against a 37mm firing canister ammunition. That gun just stacked up dead Japanese. As soon as one gunner dropped another took his place. [Eight out of the ten Marines manning that gun were killed or wounded.] We were shoulder high with dead Japs in front of that weapon. By the next morning, we had defeated the enemy. Around us were a lot of dead ones—hundreds of them. From then on, we were able to finish the rest of the campaign without any difficulty. People often said that the Tinian campaign was the easiest campaign—in the Pacific."

Marines in that 37mm position on the escarpment might

disagree with that assessment and think Tinian was the busiest campaign in the Pacific War.

Captain Hoffman had another vivid experience before leaving the island. He was obsessed with trumpets and carried his horn with him throughout the Pacific War: "On Tinian, I didn't take any chances sending my horn ashore in a battalion ambulance or a machine gun cart. I had it flown to me. One night my troops were in a small perimeter with barbed wire all around us on top of a cliff. My Marines were shouting requests: 'Pretty Baby' and 'Oh You Beautiful Doll' among others. While I was playing these tunes, all of a sudden, I heard the scream of *banzai*. One Jap soldier charged right toward me through the barbed wire. Marines had their weapons ready, and he must've been hit from fourteen different directions at once. He didn't even get to throw his grenade. He must not have liked my music. Not a supporter of my trumpet playing. But I continued with my little concert after we accounted for him."

In the early morning of August 1, a final banzai attack happened. A 150-man Japanese force attacked the 1/20 Marines on Hoffman's left flank. After twenty minutes, the attack's thrust was spent and at dawn, the Japanese withdrew. One-hundred mangled Japanese bodies laid in an area seventy yards in front of Company E from the 2/28 Marines. That night the 8th Marines took seventy-five casualties.

The next day the two divisions got back to work. The 2nd Division moved across the plateau toward the eastern cliffs. The 4th Division advanced toward the cliffs to the south and west. When they reached the edge of the escarpment and overlooked the ocean, their job was primarily done. At 1900, General Schmidt declared the island secured. This meant the organized resistance had ended. But not the killing. Hundreds of Japanese troops remained holed up in caves on the southern cliffs rising from the ocean.

On August 2, a Japanese force of 200 men charged and attacked the 3/6 Marines. After over two hours of combat, 119 Japanese were destroyed. This kind of contact continued for months. By the end of the year, the 8th Marines left on Tinian for mop-up operations had suffered sixty-seven casualties, with twenty-two Marines killed. Japanese losses were over 500 killed.

Beginning on August 1, there were large-scale surrenders by civilians fleeing the caves where they took refuge. Marine intelligence estimated that nearly 10,000 civilians were hiding in the southeast sector.

Marine General James Underhill took command of the island as military governor on August 10. He was responsible for the care and feeding of civilians. He wrote of his experiences: "Five hundred came through immediately, the next day eight hundred then one thousand, and then two thousand and so on. Numbers increased until we counted over 8,000. Another 3,000 hid in the caves and dribbled in over a period of months. It was 30 percent adult males, 20 percent adult females, and the rest were children. They were in terrible shape—hungry, sick, wounded. They had few possessions beyond the clothes on their backs.

"We estimate 4,000 civilians were killed in the bombardment of Tinian and the fighting on the island. On Saipan, Marines were helpless to prevent mass suicides among the civilian population. While we were more successful on Tinian, unfortunate incidents did occur. Civilians, for example, died under Marine fire after wandering into the lines at night."

Reports of suicides and ritual murders were common. This was taken from a report on August 3: "Several freak accidents occurred during the day. Japanese children were thrown by their parents over a cliff into the ocean. Japanese military grouped civilians in numbers of twenty and attached explosive charges to them, blowing them to bits. Both military and civilians lined up on the cliffs and hurled themselves into the ocean. Japanese soldiers pushed civilians over the cliff."

Some efforts to prevent these types of incidents were successful. Marines used amplifiers on land and offshore, promising good treatment to civilians and soldiers who would peacefully surrender. Many civilians, clad in colorful Japanese silk, responded to Marine promises, but it was plain from the expression on their faces that they expected the worst.

AFTERMATH OF TINIAN

By August 14, the entire 4th Division had embarked to base camp on Maui. On Tinian, they suffered over 1,100 casualties, with 210 killed. Their next assignment would be Iwo Jima.

The 2nd Division remained in the Mariana Islands. They set up base camp on Saipan. The 8th Marines remained on Tinian for mopping up until October 25, until the 2nd and 3rd Battalions were moved to Saipan. This left an unhappy 1st Battalion behind until getting relieved at the end of the year.

The overall cost for the 2nd Division on Tinian was 760 casualties, including 105 killed. This number did not include the casualties suffered after the island was "secured" on August 1.

The Japanese military losses based on the bodies counted and buried were over 5,000. Thousands more were assumed sealed up in underground fortifications and caves. The number of prisoners taken was 437.

The Army Air Corps now had the B-29 bases they needed for bombing Japan. With the capture of the Marianas, they were located only 1,200 nautical miles from the home islands of Japan. An ideal distance for B-29 bombers and their range of nearly 3,000 miles. Tinian became the home for two wings of the Twentieth Air

Force. After the conquest of Tinian, B-29s hammered the Japanese mainland in less than three months. Over the next year, B-29s flew nearly 30,000 missions out of the Marianas. They dropped over 150,000 tons of explosives which killed (by Japanese estimates) 250,000 people and left over nine million homeless with 2,200,000 homes demolished.

Tinian's place in history was cemented by the flight of the *Enola Gay* dropping a nuclear bomb on Hiroshima on August 6th, 1945. A few days later, another nuclear bomb was dropped on Nagasaki. The following day, the Empire of Japan surrendered.

When news of the official surrender reached the division on Saipan, one Marine recalled that he looked at Tinian's clean and rocky coast of the coral boulders where they'd gone ashore. He thought of the forbidding coast of Japan—the coast that could have awaited them in the fall. He said, "Tinian was a pretty good investment, I guess."

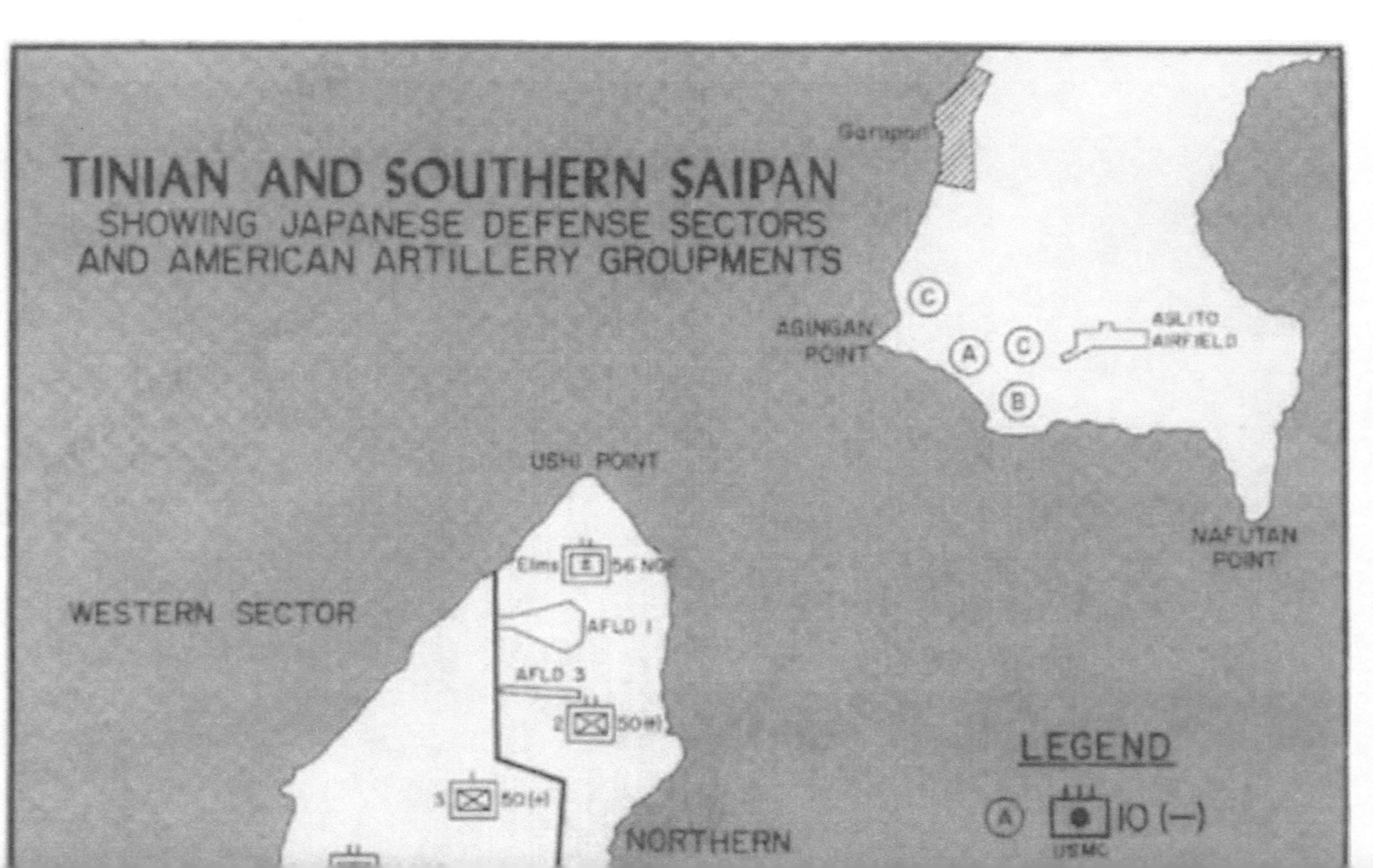

TINIAN AND SOUTHERN SAIPAN
SHOWING JAPANESE DEFENSE SECTORS
AND AMERICAN ARTILLERY GROUPMENTS
Garapan
ASLITO AIRFIELD
AGINGAN POINT
NAFUTAN POINT
USHI POINT
Elms 56 NGF
AFLD 1
AFLD 3
2 50(+)
3 50(+)
WESTERN SECTOR
NORTHERN
LEGEND
A IO (—)
USMC

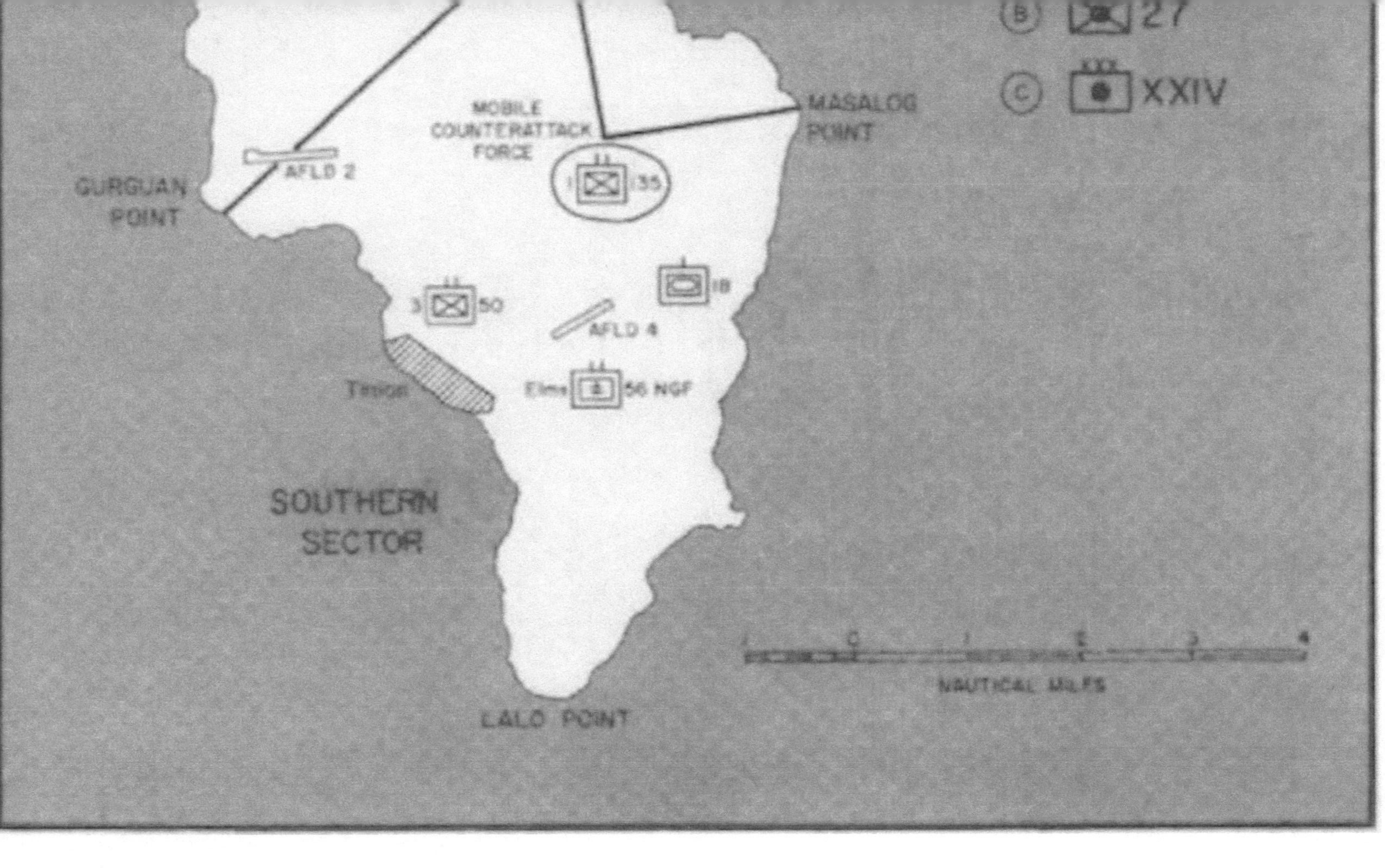

B 27
C XXIV
GURGUAN POINT
AFLD 2
MOBILE COUNTERATTACK FORCE
1 35
MASALOG POINT
3 50
1B
AFLD 4
Elms 56 NGF
Tmgo
SOUTHERN SECTOR
LALO POINT
NAUTICAL MILES

JAPANESE DEFENSE FORCE

The Japanese fortified Tinian and other islands in the Mariana's chain in direct violation of the League of Nation's Mandate. By 1944 the Tinian garrison numbered over 9,000 Navy and Army personnel and brought the island's total population to over 25,000.

The principal fighting force was the *50th Infantry Regiment*, a detachment from the *29th Division* on Guam. Stationed in Manchuria from 1941 until transferred to Tinian in March 1944. The troops were battle-hardened veterans of several Manchurian campaigns. Colonel Keishi Ogata commanded the regiment consisting of three 875-man infantry battalions, a 75mm mountain artillery battalion with twelve guns, communication, medical, and engineer companies. This also included a company of twelve light tanks, headquarters support personnel, and an anti-tank platoon. Ogata also had a battalion of the *135th Infantry Regiment* with a troop strength of 900 men. In total, more than 5,000 Japanese Army troops were assigned to the island's defense.

The Navy unit was the *56th Naval Guard Force*. A 1,400-man coastal defense unit supplemented by four construction battalions with a combined strength of 2,000 men. Other naval units totaling

1,000 men included a detachment of the *5th Base Force* and ground elements of seven aviation squadrons.

The Japanese Navy personnel totaled over 4,200 men and were under the immediate command of Captain Oichi Oya. Both Ogata and Oya were outranked by Vice Admiral Kakuji Kakuda, in command of the *1st Air Fleet* headquartered on Tinian. But as the invasion got closer, Kakuda had no air fleet to command. Of the estimated 111 planes based on Tinian's airfields, US airstrikes had destroyed seventy on the ground in early June. By July 24, at the time of the Tinian landing, none of Kakuda's planes were operational.

Kakuda was by Japanese physical standards a hulking figure. He was over six feet tall and weighed more than 200 pounds. He had an unquenchable thirst for liquor and lacked the fortitude to face the odds arrayed against him at Tinian. He was known as a drunk and an extremely unpleasant one, from many accounts.

Nine days before the invasion on July 15, Kakuda and his headquarters group attempted to escape in rubber boats to Aguijan Island and rendezvous with a Japanese submarine. They failed. They tried for five nights in a row with the same results before abandoning the effort on July 21. Kakuda fled with his staff officers to a cave on Tinian's east coast to await their fate.

A Japanese prisoner who later described Kakuda's escape attempt assumed he had committed suicide after the American landing—but that was never verified. Toward the end of the battle for Tinian, one of Kakuda's orderlies led an American patrol to his cave. This patrol was fired on, and two Marines were wounded. Another passing group of Marine pioneers sealed the cave with demolition charges, but it is still unknown whether Kakuda was inside.

Admiral Kakuda had no part in directing any Japanese resistance on Tinian. Colonel Ogata took command of defending the island. He assumed command of both Navy and Army forces. Japanese diaries, later found, showed the friction between the two men. In the *50th Regiment's* artillery battalion, a Japanese soldier wrote: "March 9: The Navy stays in dark buildings and has liberty every night with liquor to drink and fights. On the other hand, we stay in the rain and never get out on any pass—what a difference in discipline.

"June 12: Our anti-aircraft guns manned by the Navy spread black smoke where the enemy planes are not. Not one hit out of over a thousand shots. Our Naval Air Group has taken to its heels.

"June 15: The Naval aviators are thieves. When they ran off to the mountains, they stole Army provisions."

The island's geography dictated Tinian's defenses. It was encircled by coral cliffs that rose from the coastline as part of a limestone plateau that underlined the island. The cliffs were from five to ninety-five feet. Breaks in the cliff were rare and where they did happen were narrow. This left truly little beach space for any invasion force. All along the coastline of Tinian, only four beaches were worthy of the name.

Sunharon Harbor in front of Tinian Town was the most suitable target for an amphibious assault. It had several wide sandy strips. The harbor was mediocre but provided a fair-weather anchorage for ships to load and unload cargo at the two Tinian Town piers.

Colonel Ogata assumed this beach would be the first choice for the Americans. Of the over one-hundred guns in fixed positions on the island—6-inch British naval rifles and 7.7mm heavy machine guns—a third were assigned to the defense of Tinian Town, its beaches, and the airfield at Gurguan Point two miles northwest. Within a two-mile radius of the town were 1,400 men of the *56th Naval Guard Force* and the *135th Infantry Regiment* designated as the mobile counterattack force. Their area of responsibility extended out to Lalo Point on the southernmost part of the island and east to Masalog Point. This made up the "southern sector" of Ogata's defense plan.

The remainder of the island was divided into northeastern and northwestern sectors. The northeast sector had the Ushi Point airfields and a potential landing beach 125 yards wide south of Asiga Point on the island's east coast. Between 500 and 900 Navy personnel were stationed close to the Ushi Airfields. A battalion from the *50th Infantry Regiment* and an engineer group were stationed inland of Asagi Point. In the northwestern sector, there were two narrow strips of beach less than a thousand yards apart. One of them was sixty yards wide and the other twice as long. They were popular with Japanese civilians because the water was swimmable, and the sand was white. Known as the White Beaches—and to the Japanese's great surprise—as the American invasion route.

This sector was defended modestly by a single infantry company and one anti-tank squad, 450 yards northeast of the White Beaches. The gun crews were situated in placements containing a 47mm anti-tank gun, a 37mm anti-tank gun, and two 7.7mm machine guns.

Colonel Ogata established his command post in a cave on Mount Lasso in the center of the northern region, a little over two miles from the beaches on either side of the island. On June 25, he issued orders that said: "the enemy in Saipan can be expected to be planning a landing on Tinian. The area of that landing is estimated to be either Asiga Harbor [on the northeast coast] or Tinian Harbor." Three days later he followed up with a defense forces battle plan which outlined his two contingencies.

(1) In the event the enemy lands at Asiga Bay.

(2) In the event the enemy lands at Tinian Harbor (Sunharon Harbor).

Colonel Ogata issued a plan for the "Guidance of Battle" on July 7. He ordered his men to be prepared for the landings at Asiga Bay and Tinian Town and for a counterattack if the Americans invaded across the White Beaches.

According to his battle plan, in each of the three sectors, commanders were to destroy the enemy at the beach but also be prepared to shift two-thirds of their forces elsewhere. His reserve force was to maintain fortified positions and counterattack points while maintaining anti-aircraft observation and fire in the area. The mobile counterattack force had to rapidly advance to the landings depending on the attack and situation. In the event of a successful landing, his forces would "counterattack to the water and destroy the enemy on beaches with one blow, especially where time prevents quick movement of forces within the island."

If things went badly, they would fall back onto prepared positions in the southern part of the islands and defend each position to the death.

Many of these orders were contradictory and others were impossible to execute. But despite the odds against them—without air or sea support and confronted by three heavily armed divisions only three miles away on Saipan—the Japanese fighting spirit had not been broken by over forty days of heavy bombardment.

In the *50th Infantry Regiment*, a Japanese soldier wrote in his diary on June 30: "We spent over twenty days under unceasing enemy bombardment and air raids but have suffered only minor losses. Everyone from the commanding officer to the lowest private is full of fighting spirit. How exalted are the gallant figures of the Force Commander, the Battalion Commander, and their subordinates who have endured this violent artillery and air bombardment."

RECAPTURE OF GUAM

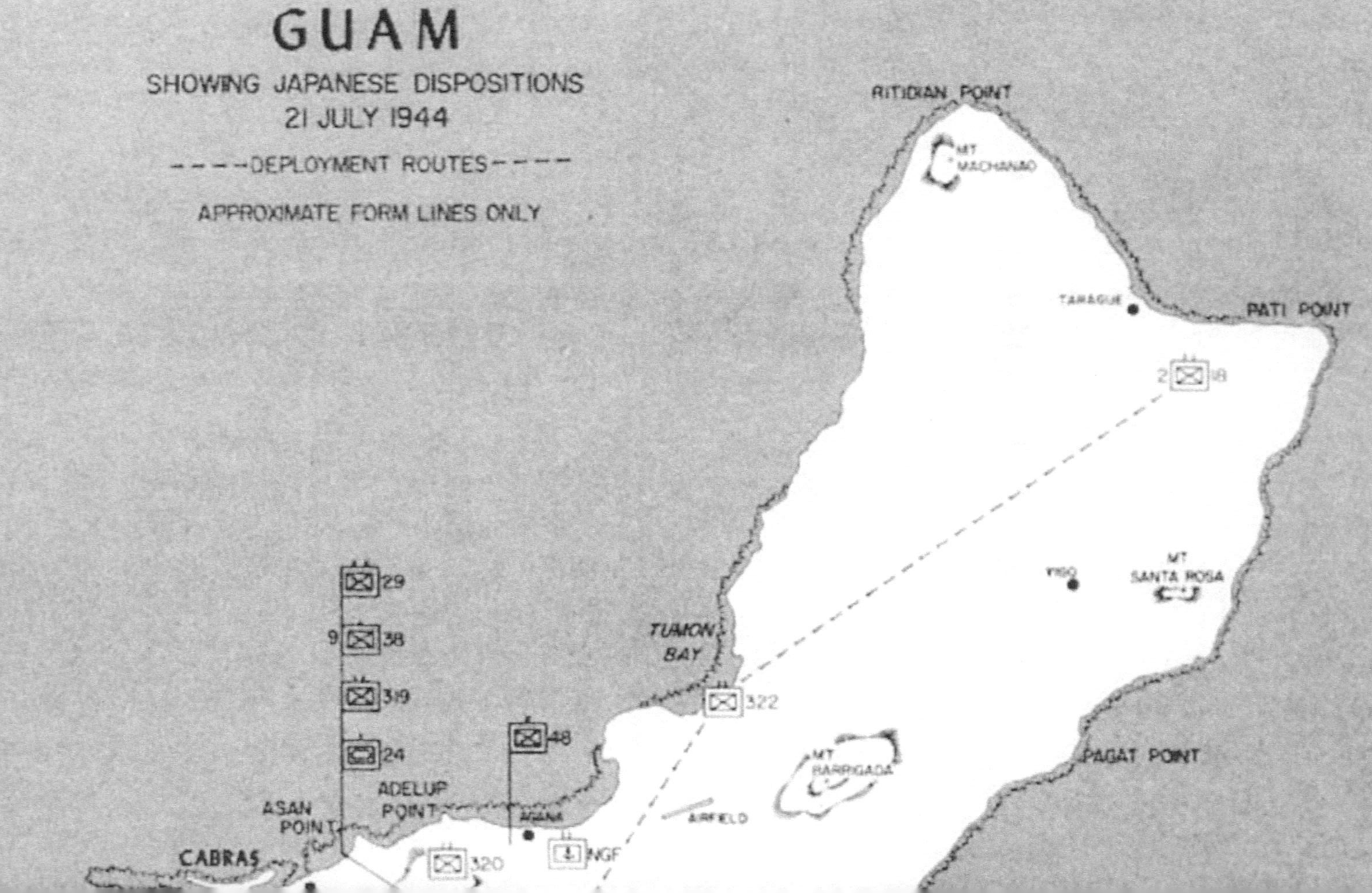

GUAM
SHOWING JAPANESE DISPOSITIONS
21 JULY 1944
DEPLOYMENT ROUTES
APPROXIMATE FORM LINES ONLY
RITIDIAN POINT
MT MACHANAO
TARAGUE
PATI POINT
YIGO
MT SANTA ROSA
PAGAT POINT
TUMON BAY
MT BARRIGADA
AIRFIELD
ASAN POINT
ADELUP POINT
AGANA
CABRAS
NGF
2 8
29
9 38
319
24
48
322
320

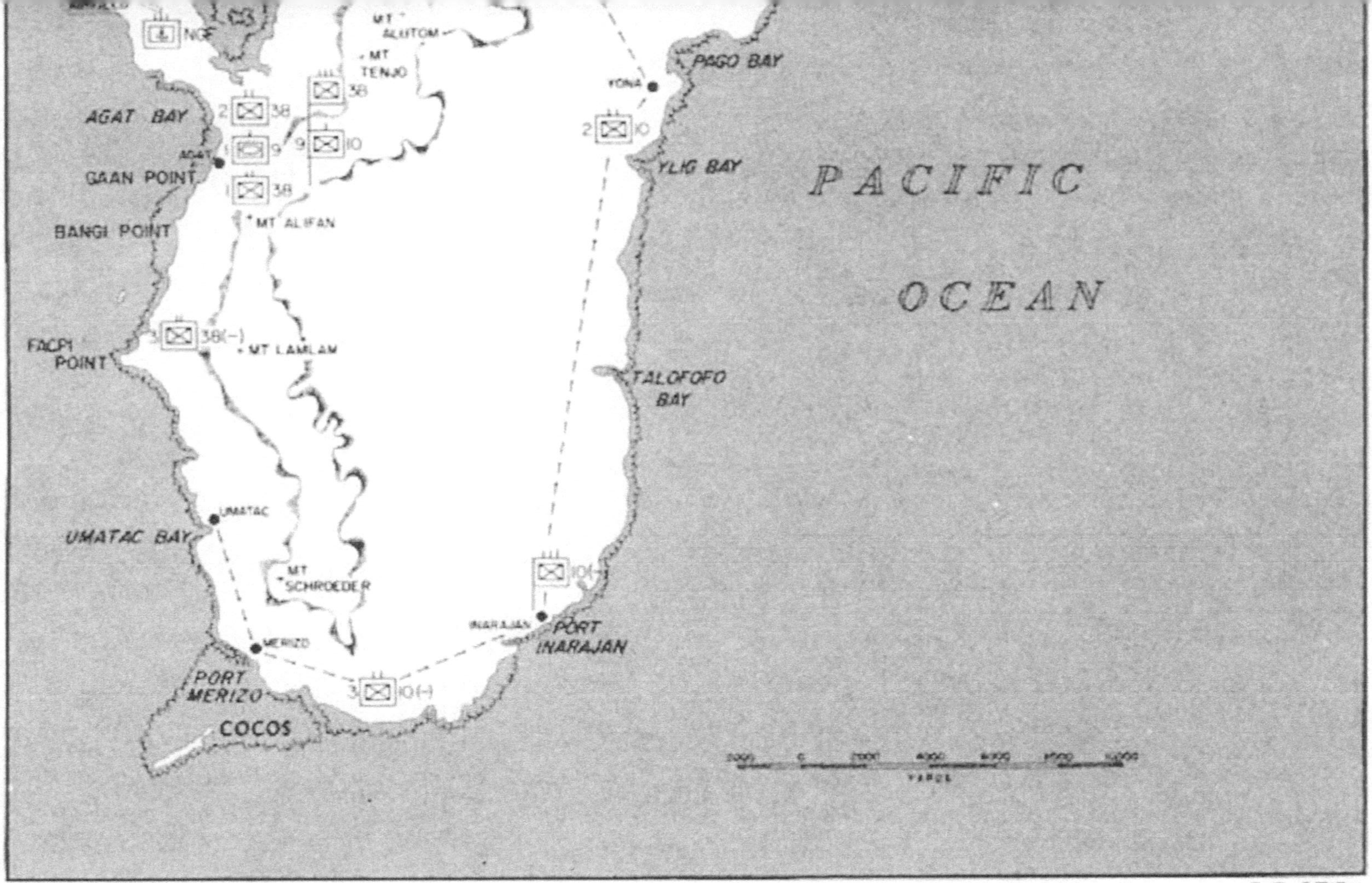

PACIFIC
OCEAN
AGAT BAY
GAAN POINT
BANGI POINT
FACPI POINT
UMATAC BAY
PORT MERIZO
COCOS
MT ALUTOM
MT TENJO
MT ALIFAN
MT LAMLAM
MT SCHROEDER
UMATAC
MERIZO
PAGO BAY
YONA
YLIG BAY
TALOFOFO BAY
INARAJAN
PORT INARAJAN
NGF
AGAT
YARDS
R F STIBIL

BACK TO GUAM

After a two-hour bombardment from six battleships, nine cruisers, and a handful of destroyers hammering the wrinkled black hills, cliffs, rice patties, and caves facing the attacking fleet on the west side of the island—liberation day began at 0530 on July 21, 1944.

Flames fountained from 14-inch guns belching thunder and fire. Setting off a spectacular blossom of flame on the inland hillsides and fields. The glow from the star shells illuminated the shore, the ships, and the troops lining the rails of the LSTs (Landing Ships, Tank), bringing the soldiers and Marines back to Guam.

The daylight shelling was enhanced by the bombing and strafing of carrier fighters, torpedo planes, and bombers for the pre-landing softening up. Task Force 58 had blasted Guam's airfield since June 11, while other bombardments had started as early as May 6.

Marine assault troops laden with fighting gear, and bayonets bulging from their packs, enjoyed their traditional Marine pre-landing breakfast of steak and eggs. The loudspeakers echoed: "Now hear this. . . Now hear this." Unit commanders on board the LSTs visited with their Marines and double-checked their gear. They straightened packs, gave encouraging pats on the shoulder, and squared away the lines of Marines going below to the well decks before boarding the LVTs (Landing Vehicles, Tracked).

Troops on board the attack transports went over the rail and down cargo nets. Weighed down with forty-plus pound packs and weapons—they held on for their lives. They clambered into their LCVPs (Landing Craft, Vehicle, Personnel) or Higgin's boats. If all went as planned, these troops would transfer from the landing craft to the LVTs at the reef's edge.

Aircraft roared overhead. Navy guns thundered a deafening background noise. The voice of Major General Roy Geiger, commander of III Amphibious Corps, boomed: "You've been honored. The nation watches you go to battle to liberate this former American bastion from the enemy. The honor bestowed on you is a signal one. May the glorious traditions of the Marine Corps esprit de corps spur you to victory. You have been honored."

On board the crowded and muggy well decks of the LSTs, troops climbed on board the LVTs. They waited in a hell of claustrophobia until the LSTs' bow doors dropped. The loaded LVTs rattled out over the ramps into the swell of the sea. Amphibian tractors circled near the lines of departure while a flight of attack craft from the *Wasp* drowned the amtrac engines' whine, whirling up clouds of fire and dust obscuring the landing beaches. Fifty-three torpedo planes, sixty-five bombers, and eighty-five fighters executed a bombing sweep and grass-cutting strafing along the northern landing beaches of Agana, heading south toward Bangi Point.

Task Force 53 commander, Admiral Richard Conolly, said: "I aim to get the troops ashore standing up." Conolly earned the nickname "Close-in Conolly" from his insistence on having naval gunfire support ships fire very close in to the beaches.

Private First Class James Helt was a radio man in the bow of an LVT moving toward shore. He later wrote about how he wondered if anything could still be alive on Guam.

Colonel Hideyuki Takeda, a staff officer in the defending *29th Division*, wrote the island could only be defended if the Americans did not land. In his diary, he also noted that the only respite from the barrage was a "stiff drink."

The bold and brave Navy UDT (Underwater Demolition Teams) cleared all the beach obstacles for the assault. Navy Chief James Chittum noted these pathfinders were often close enough to draw small arms fire. They exploded 650 wire obstacle cages filled with cemented coral on Asan. On Agat, they detonated a 200-foot hole for unloading in the coral reef. Navy UDT teams also removed half of a small freighter blocking the channel from the assault. Scouts and swimmers left a sign for this first assault wave at Asan: "Welcome Marines—USO This way."

At 0730, a flare was fired overhead the waiting flotilla. Admiral Conolly ordered: "Land the Landing Force." The first wave of the 3rd Marine Division broke the circle of waiting LVTs and formed a line to cross the 2,000 yards of water to the beach between Asan and Adelup. By 0830, the first elements of the 3rd Marine Division were on Guam. Less than five minutes later, the lead assault troops of the 1st Provisional Marine Brigade crossed the shell-cratered strand at Agat, six miles south of the beachhead at Asan-Adelup.

OPERATION FORAGER PLANNING

In late 1943, the Joint Chiefs of Staff decided to advance the direction of the Pacific War. In command of the Southwest Pacific, General MacArthur was ordered to head north through New Guinea to regain the Philippines. Admiral Nimitz, commander-in-chief of the US Pacific Fleet, proposed to move through the Central Pacific to secure a hold in the Marianas.

The strategic bombing of Japan would originate from captured airfields on Guam, Saipan, and Tinian. The new strategic weapon for the attacks would be the B-29 bomber with a range of 3,000 miles and the ability to carry over 10,000 pounds of bombs. The codename for this Marianas operation was "Forager." The drive in the Central Pacific started with the landings on Tarawa in November 1943. Followed by landings on Roi-Namur, Eniwetok, and Kwajalein.

Admiral Nimitz finalized his plans for Guam in 1944. He selected his command structure for the Marianas campaign. Admiral Spruance, coming off a tremendous victory at Midway, was designated Commander of the Fifth Fleet and all the Central Pacific Task Forces. Spruance would command all units involved in Operation Forager.

Admiral Turner, who had commanded naval forces at Guadalcanal's landings, was to head Task Force 51. Admiral Turner would also command the northern attack force for the invasion of Saipan and Tinian. Admiral Connolly who'd commanded the invasion forces at Roi-Namur in the Marshalls, would lead the southern attack force—Task Force 53 assigned to Guam.

General Holland Smith, the expeditionary troop commander for the Marianas, would be responsible for the northern troops and landing forces on Saipan and Tinian. Marine General Roy Geiger, an aviator who had conducted the Bougainville operation, would command the southern troops and the III Amphibious Corps landing forces on Guam.

Guam's invasion was originally set for June 18, the 3rd Marine Division, the 1st Provisional Marine Brigade, and the Army's 77th Infantry Division would lead the assault, but the 3rd and 1st Marine Division were held in floating reserve until the course of operations on Saipan became clear. The 77th stood by on Oahu, ready to be called in if needed.

Admiral Spruance kept the floating reserves southeast of Saipan, out of the path of any Japanese naval attack. A powerful Japanese fleet was eager to clash with the American invasion force and descended on the Mariana Islands. The opposing carrier groups fought it out nearby in the battle of the Philippine Sea, one of the most critical battles of the Pacific War. The Japanese Imperial Navy lost over 300 planes out of the 430 launched in the fight. On June 19, the clash would be forever known as "the Great Marianas Turkey Shoot." It was a catastrophe for the Japanese and ended once and for all any enemy air or naval threat to the Mariana Islands invasion.

The brutal fighting on Saipan eventually shifted in favor of the American Marines and soldiers battling the Japanese. The US Navy was now ready to direct their attention to Guam, currently slated to receive the most thorough pre-landing bombardment yet seen in the Pacific War.

After weeks at sea, the 3rd Division and 1st Brigade were given a break and a chance to lose their sea legs. The Task Force 53 convoy moved back to Eniwetok atoll, where a twenty-mile-wide lagoon became the forward naval base.

Marines welcomed the break and walked on the island's dry land—there was even warm beer to all those onshore. The Marine veterans of New Georgia, Eniwetok, and Bougainville had a chance to look over the soldiers from the Army's 77th Infantry Division arriving from Oahu. The recapture of Guam named W-Day was now set for July 21.

The 3rd Marine Division, under General Allen H. Turnage, had received their baptism of fire on Bougainville in November 1943 and spent the remaining months on Guadalcanal training and absorbing casualty replacements. The 1st Provisional Marine Brigade, organized on Guadalcanal, was also a veteran outfit. One of its infantry regiments, the 4th Marines, was formed from a disbanded raider battalion who'd fought in the Solomons. The III Amphibious Corps was prepared to land over 53,000 Marines, soldiers, and sailors.

General Takashina, commanding the Japanese *29th Infantry Division,* waited for the attack and was sure it would come, but he didn't know from where. The *29th* served in Manchuria until it was sent to the Marianas in February 1944. Its *18th Regiment* fell victim to an American submarine, the *Trout,* and lost 2,237 of its 3,000 men when the transport was sunk. They reorganized on Saipan, and the *18th Infantry Regiment* took two infantry battalions to Guam together with two tank companies.

Another regiment from the *29th,* garrisoned on Tinian, the *38th Infantry,* arrived on Guam in March. Other major Japanese defending units were the *10th Independent Mixed Regiment* and the *48th Independent Mixed Brigade* formed on Guam in March. With supporting troops, the Japanese defending forces numbered 11,000 men. Add to these 5,000 naval troops of the *54th Keibitai Guard Force* and 2,000 naval airmen reorganized as infantry to defend the Orote peninsula.

General Takashina was in overall tactical command of the 18,000 Army and Navy defenders. His immediate superior was General Obata, commanding the *31st Army* also on Guam, but not intentionally. Obata was trapped on Guam by the American landing on Saipan after making an inspection trip to the Palau Islands. He left the defense of Guam to Takashina.

It was no secret to the Japanese that the Americans planned to assault Guam. The invasion of Saipan and month-long bombardment by ships and planes left only the questions of when and where. With fifteen miles of potential landing beaches along the west coast, the Japanese couldn't be very wrong no matter where they decided to defend.

Tokyo Rose said they expected the Americans. On board ship, American troops heard her pleasant, beguiling voice on the radio while she made threats of dire things waiting to happen to the invasion troops. But she was never taken seriously by any of her American "fans."

General Kiyoshi Shigematsu, attempting to bolster the morale of his *48th Independent Mixed Brigade,* told his men: "the enemy is overconfident because of his successful landing on Saipan. They are now planning a reckless attack on Guam. We have an excellent opportunity to annihilate them on the beaches."

Hideki Tojo, Prime Minister of Japan, also had feisty words for his commanders: "The fate of Japan depends on the result of your operation, inspire the spirit of your officers and men to the very end. Continue to destroy the enemy gallantly and persistently—alleviate the anxiety of the emperor."

Fifty years later, a former Japanese lieutenant wrote of the incredible American invasion fleet offshore had "paved the sea" and recalled what he thought on July 21: "this is the day I will die."

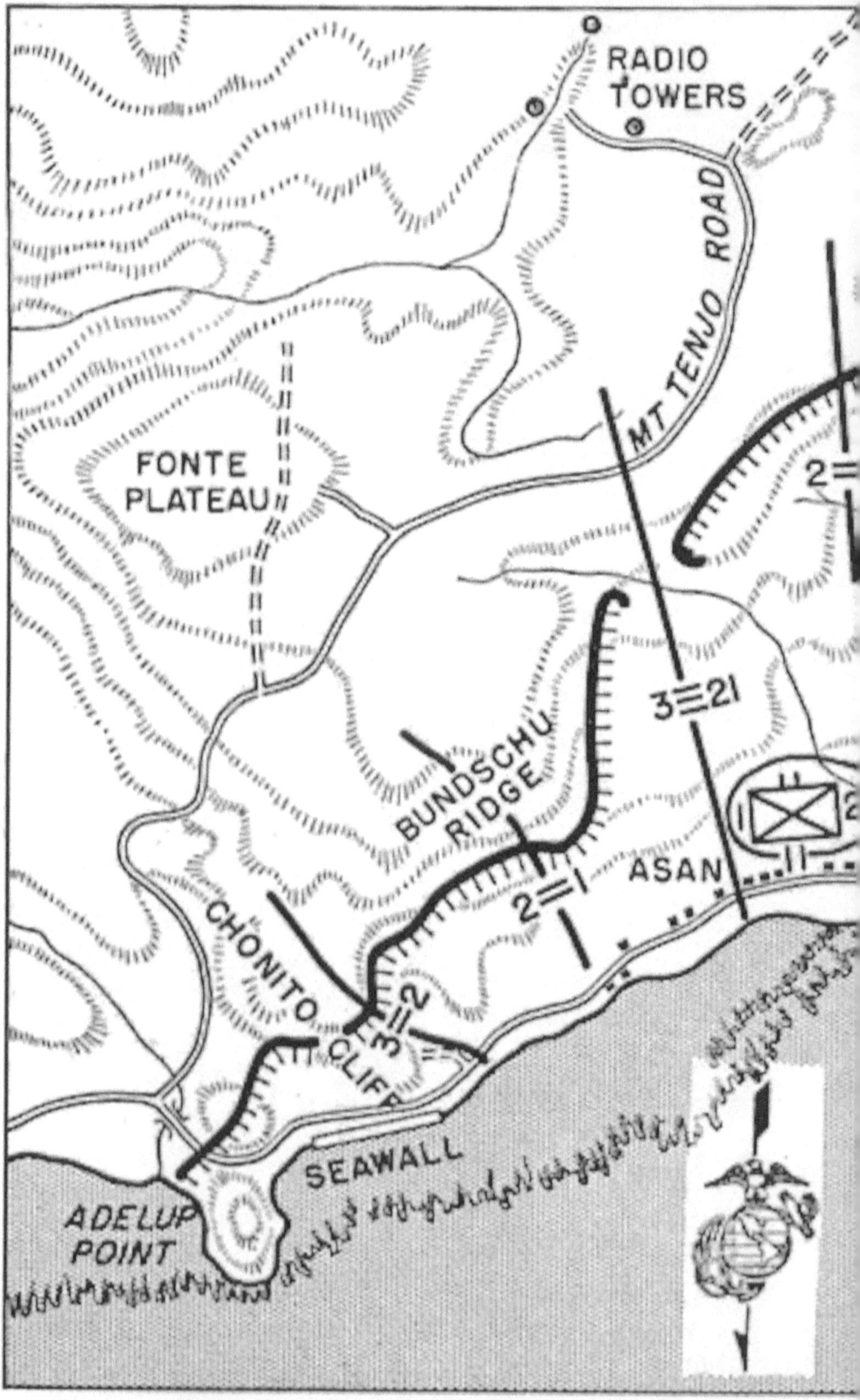

RADIO TOWERS
MT TENJO ROAD
FONTE PLATEAU
2≡
3≡21
BUNDSCHU RIDGE
2≡1
ASAN
CHONITO CLIFF
3≡2
SEAWALL
ADELUP POINT

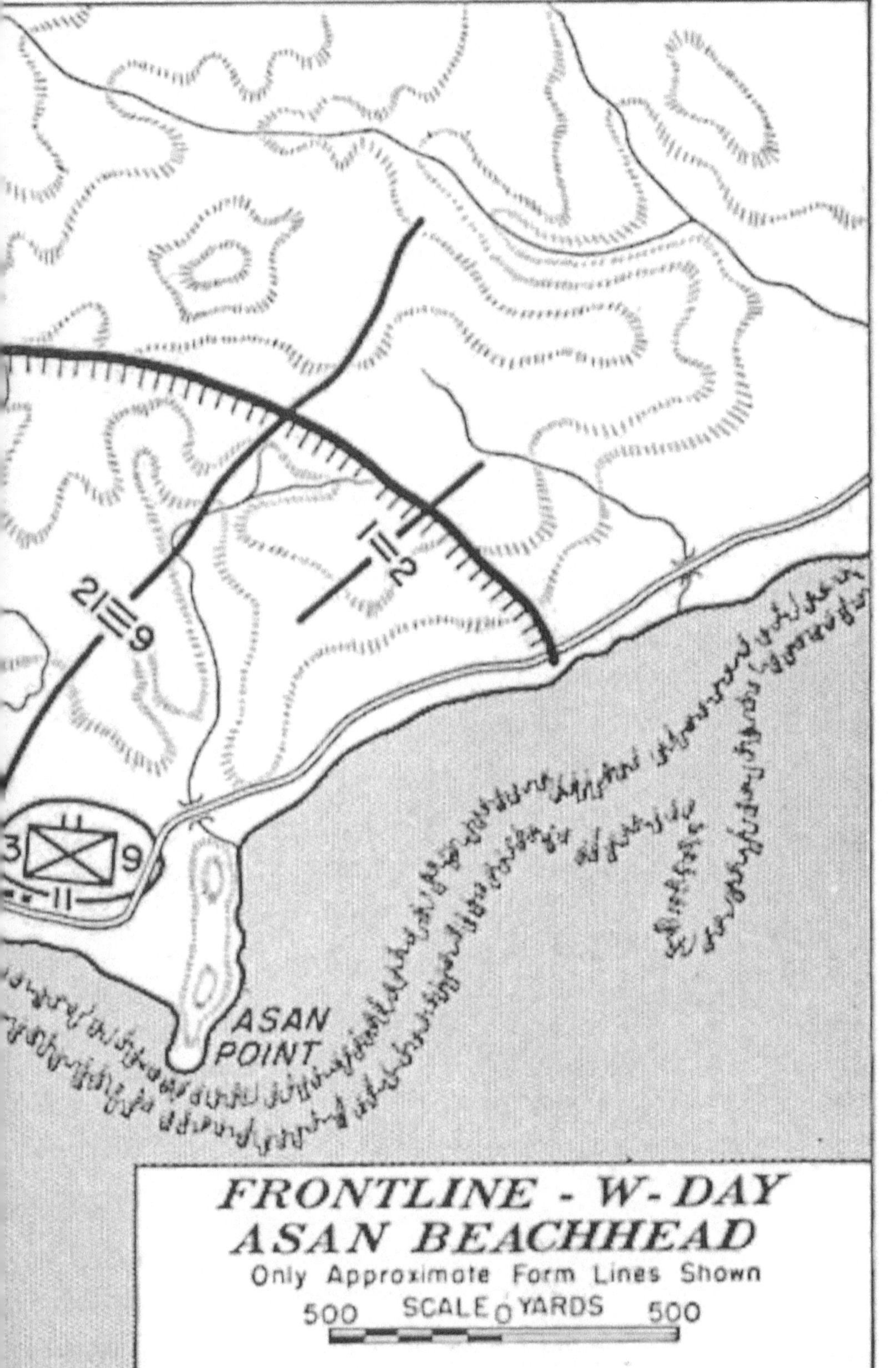

2 ║ 9
II 2
3 ⊠ 9
II
ASAN POINT
FRONTLINE - W- DAY
ASAN BEACHHEAD
Only Approximate Form Lines Shown
500   SCALE 0 YARDS   500

W-DAY IN THE NORTH

The 3rd Marine Division troops landed practically into the lap of General Takashina's U-shaped command post. The CP cave was carved out of sandstone cliff that overlooked the Asan-Adelup beachhead. Its looming heights dominated the beaches where the 3rd and 21st Marines were headed in for their assault.

W-Day on July 21, 1944, started as a beautiful day. But it soon turned hazy as the violent clouds of dust, smoke, and fire fountained into the sky. At 0805 an observer shouted into his microphone: "First wave on the beach." At 0833, the same man confirmed the battle was on and announced: "Troops ashore on all beaches."

The 3rd Marines struck out on the far left of the 2,500-yard beachhead toward Bundschu Ridge. Also known as Chonito Cliff, it had high, difficult ground that needed to be taken before the final beachhead line or the first goal of the landing could be achieved. The 21st Marines went straight up the middle. They advanced inland, securing the line of cliffs and defending them until the division caught up and could expand the beachhead outward. The 9th Marines landed on the right flank near Asan Point and moved inland over patties and across lower and easier to traverse hills, but all part of the same formidable enemy held ridgeline.

The 3/9 Marines took intense fire from the front and right flank near Asan Point and called in tanks for help. One company got to the ridge ahead of the others and threw the enemy off balance, making the regiments advance easier. The 9th Marines smashed through their initial objectives quickly and had to slacken their advance as to not thin out the division's lines.

The 21st Marines, in a stroke of luck later called unbelievable, found two unguarded defiles on both sides of the regiment's action zone. The 21st climbed straight to the clifftops and formed a bridge covering both defiles. This allowed the 2nd and 3rd Battalions to form a bridge covering both defiles while the 1st Battalion swept the area underneath the cliffs.

The 12th Marines were swiftly landed on the beach with their burdensome guns and equipment. The 3rd Battalion was registered and firing by noon. By 1620, every battery was in position and ready to support the offensive. According to Captain Austin Gattis of the 12th Marines: "We must attribute the success of our regiment setting up so quickly to training—because we'd done it over and over. It was an efficiency learned and practiced and it always gave the 12th a leg up."

On the left flank, the 3rd Marines got the worst of the enemy resistance. They took intense artillery and mortar fire coming in on the beaches, as well as advancing through the toughest terrain. Japanese machine gun fire laced with interlocking bands made the approaches to the steep cliffs deadly. The enemy defenders knew how to use their weapons well. Japanese troops would roll grenades down the escarpment onto the Marines. Snipers found protection and refuge in the countless folds and ridges of irregular terrain. The ridge tops were arrayed like breastworks of some nightmarish medieval castle. As if ten Japanese soldiers on top could hold off a hundred Marines below.

Japanese Lieutenant Kenichi Itoh wrote in his diary that even with a terrible bombardment he felt secure his countrymen could hold and possibly even win. He later wrote about that eventful day in July 1944, after the war. Lieutenant Itoh thought it was all a bad dream, and "absurd" to think that his forces could ever have withstood that onslaught.

On W-Day the 3/3 Marines were on the extreme left flank of the line facing Adelup Point. Marines seized territory in their zone with support from tanks and half-track-mounted 75mm guns. A little nose projecting from Chonito Ridge held up the regimental advance. Company A, under the command of Captain Geary Bundschu was able to secure a foothold within 100 yards of the promontory crest, but failed to hold their position in the face of intense machine gun fire. Captain Bundschu called for corpsmen and stretchers. He also requested permission to disengage, but his request was refused, and he was ordered to hold what he had.

The attack was ordered to continue in the afternoon under cover of a massive 81mm mortar barrage. No 2nd Battalion companies could gain any ground beyond what they already held. The Japanese *320th Independent Infantry Battalion* fought fiercely and held fast.

Two hours later, Company A was ordered to make another attack, according to a Marine Combat correspondent: "When the attack at 1700 went off, there was no change. The Marines made little progress. Company A attacked again and again and again.

They reached the top but failed to hold. After Captain Bundschu was killed, his company slid back to their former positions."

Throughout the days of brutal fighting, Marines attempted to envelop the Japanese in a pincer movement using companies A and C. On regimental orders, the assault started at 1100—but got nowhere at first. Company A got to the top but was thrown off. Company E advanced slowly. But after several probes into the Japanese resistance, Marines found the enemy was weakening.

By 1900, Company E Marines reached the top above Company A's position. The Japanese had finally pulled back. A further Marine advance confirmed the enemy's withdrawal.

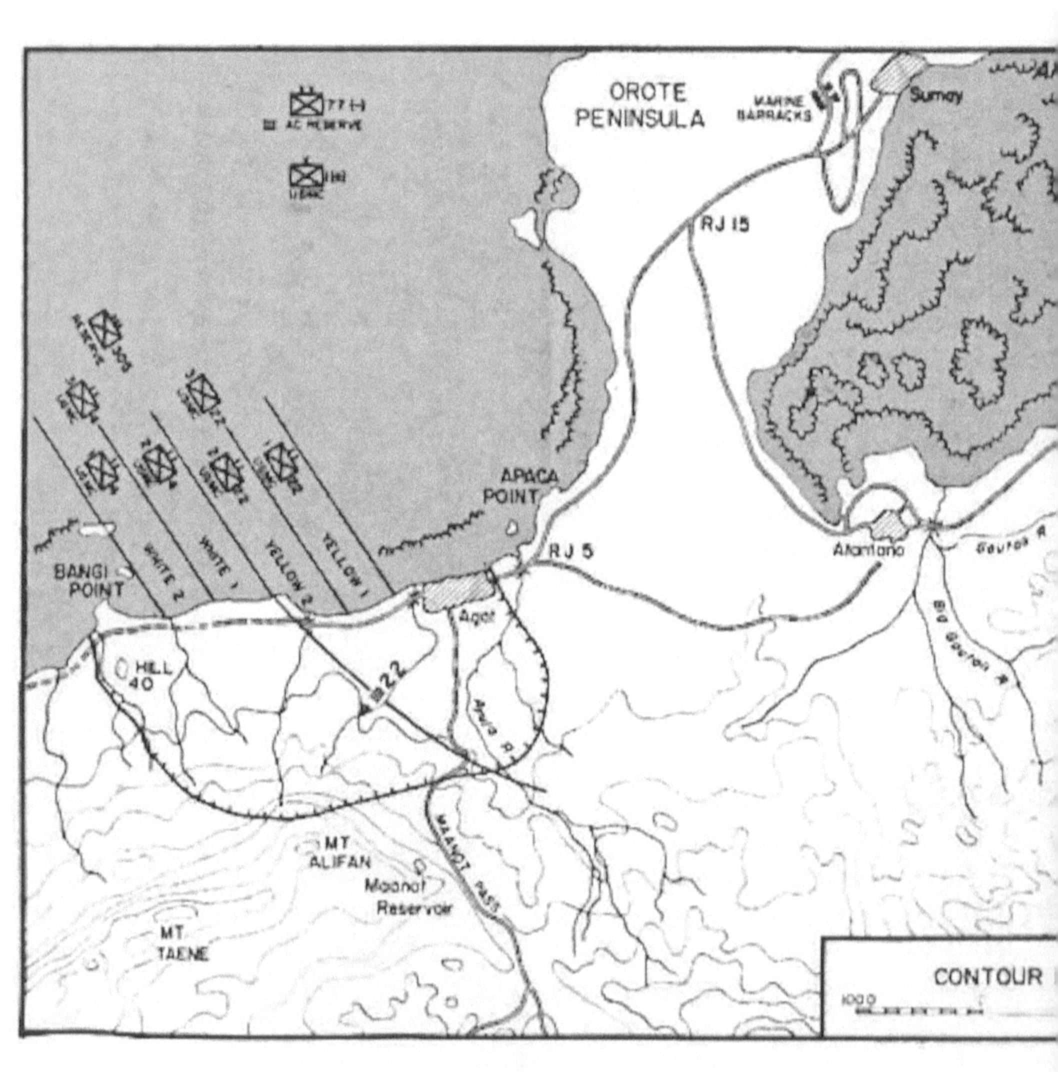
OROTE
PENINSULA
MARINE
BARRACKS
Sumay
RJ 15
77 (-)
III AC RESERVE
III AC
APACA
POINT
RJ 5
Atantano
Agat
Apra R.
Big Gautan R.
Gautan R.
BANGI
POINT
WHITE 2
WHITE 1
YELLOW 2
YELLOW 1
HILL
40
22
MAANOT PASS
MT
ALIFAN
Maanot
Reservoir
MT
TAENE
CONTOUR
1000

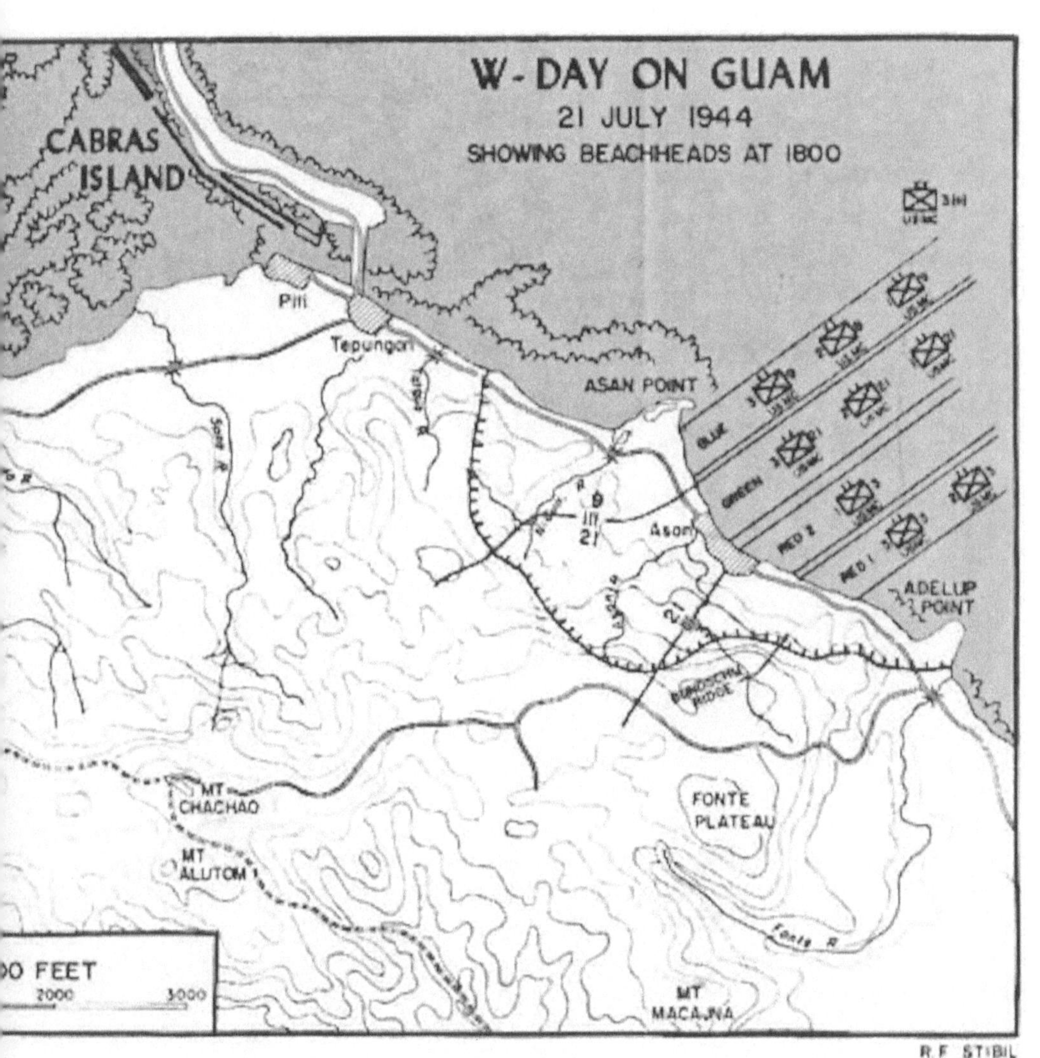

W-DAY ON GUAM
21 JULY 1944
SHOWING BEACHHEADS AT 1800
CABRAS ISLAND
Piti
Tepungan
ASAN POINT
Asan
BLUE
GREEN
RED 2
RED 1
ADELUP POINT
BUNDSCHU RIDGE
MT CHACHAO
MT ALUTOM
FONTE PLATEAU
MT MACAJNA
Fonte R
00 FEET
2000
3000
R. F. STIBIL

W-DAY IN THE SOUTH

In the south, near Agat, in spite of a favorable terrain for the attack, the 1st Brigade, led by General Lemuel C. Shepherd, encountered intense enemy resistance at the beachhead. Much more than the 3rd Division found on the northern beaches. Japanese machine gun and small arms fire, along with two 75mm guns from a concrete blockhouse with a four-foot-thick roof, greeted the invading Marines as the LVTs churned ashore.

The blockhouse had been well camouflaged and not spotted before the landing as a bombing target. As a result, Japanese guns knocked out twenty-four amtracs carrying elements of the 22nd Marines. The W-Day assault forces' first hours on the southern beaches posed a major problem.

The Agat assault was given the same thunderous naval gunfire support, which disrupted and shook the ground before the landings on the northern beaches. When the 1st Brigade assault wave was less than a thousand yards from the beach, hundreds of 4.5-inch rockets from LCI(G)s (Landing Craft Infantry, Gunboat) slammed into the strand.

While the LCVPs, LVTs, and the DUKWs (amphibious trucks) were still offshore, there was virtually no enemy fire from the beach.

Artillery observation planes reported no observed enemy fire. The defenders would respond in their own time. Because so many amtracs were lost as the assault waves neared the beaches, later in the day there would not be enough LVTs available for transferring men and supplies from boats to amtracs at Agat reef. The shortage of amphibious tractors would plague the brigade for days.

The precision of the Japanese guns caused severe damage to the cargo and assault craft on the beach. This became a real concern for General Shepherd. Most of the soldiers and some of the Marines who came in after the first assault waves waded ashore with full packs in waist high water. They faced the danger of both underwater shell holes and enemy fire. By the time the bulk of the 77th Division waded in, these twin threats were not as great because the Marines onshore were spread out and could keep the Japanese occupied.

The Japanese defenders prepared their defenses well—thick-walled bunkers and smaller pillboxes. On Gaan Point there were 75mm guns in the middle of the landing beaches. Crossfire from Gaan, coordinated with the machine guns on nearby Yona island, raked the beaches allocated to the 4th Marines. The 4th was tasked with establishing a beachhead and protecting the southernmost flank.

After vicious fighting, the 4th Marines advanced onto low ground and cleared Bangi Point where bunker walls could withstand a battleship round. The 4th Marines set up a roadblock on Harmon Road leading down from the mountains to Agat. Previous operations had taught the Marines that the Japanese would be back in strength at night.

After the Marines landed, they found an under-manned but excellent Japanese trench system on the beaches. While the pre-landing bombardment had driven many defenders back into their holes, they poured heavy machine gun fire and mortar fire down on the invaders. The preinvasion planning called for the Marine amtracs to drive a thousand yards inland before disembarking Marines. This tactic failed because of a heavily mined beachhead and anti-tank ditches along with other obstacles.

But the Marines attacked with such overwhelming force that they broke through. And by 1030, the assault forces were over one-thousand yards inland. Now, the 4th Marines Reserve Battalion had finally landed after taking heavy fire from emplaced enemy forces. Marines worked on clearing bypassed bunkers using the now landed tanks. By 1320, the blockhouse on Gaan Point was eliminated by advancing to the rear and blasting the surprised enemy gunners before they could offer any resistance. By this time, General Shepherd was on the beach and had opened his command post.

The 22nd Marines were battered by a hail of small arms and mortar fire when they hit their assigned beach. They suffered heavy losses in equipment and men during the first few minutes. According to Private First Class William Dunlap, the battalion's beloved chaplain who had been entrusted with everyone's gambling money to "hold for safekeeping," had been killed. Marines never for a minute considered he was just as mortal as they were.

The 1/22 Marines left their section of the landing zone and advanced to the shattered town of a gap where the battalion drove north and eventually sealed off a heavily defended road to Orote Peninsula, soon to be the scene of a major battle.

The 2/22 Marines was in the center of the beachhead and hurried the 1,000 yards inland from the beach. The battalion could have taken one of its W-Day goals of securing the local heights of Mount Alifan—if American bombs and not fallen short and stalled their attack.

The 1st Battalion moved into the ruins of Agat and secured it by 1020. While there was still minor small arms resistance in the rubble, by 1130 the battalion was also out on Harmon Road leading to the northern shoulder of Mount Alifan. As the Marines advanced, Japanese shells hit the battalion aid station, wounding and killing several members of the medical team and destroying supplies. It wasn't until later that afternoon that the 1st Battalion finally received another doctor.

On the right flank of the landing waves, the 1/4 Marines ran head-on into Hill 40 near Bangi Point—which had been thoroughly hammered by the Navy. The unexpected fierce defense on Hill 40 demonstrated that the Japanese recognized its importance, commanding the beaches where troops and supplies came ashore. It took tanks and the support of the 3rd Battalion to secure that position.

The 2/22 Marines, before dark on W-Day, could see the 4th Marines from across a deep gully. The 4th held a twisted, thin line extending over 1,500 yards from the beach to Harmon Road, while the 22nd Marines held the rest of the beach at 5,000 yards long and 1,500 yards deep. General Shepherd summed it up to General Geiger on nightfall of W-Day: "casualties at about 350. Critical shortages of fuel and ammunition of all types. Enemy unknown. Think we can handle it. Will continue as planned tomorrow."

Support troops helped to ensure that Marines could stay on shore once they landed. The support troops struggled since daylight, trying to manage the flow of vital supplies to the beaches. As darkness on W-Day approached, a black unit, the 4th Ammunition Company, guarded the brigade's ammunition depot ashore. During a sleepless night, these black American Marines killed fourteen enemy saboteurs sneaking into the ammo dump.

Poor communications delayed the order to land the Army's 305th Regimental Combat team for several hours. They were slated for a morning landing but there were no amtracs available, and the soldiers had to wade in from the reef. Some soldiers slipped underwater into shell holes and had to swim for their lives in high tide. When the rest of the 305th arrived on the beach, they were all soaked, and some were seasick.

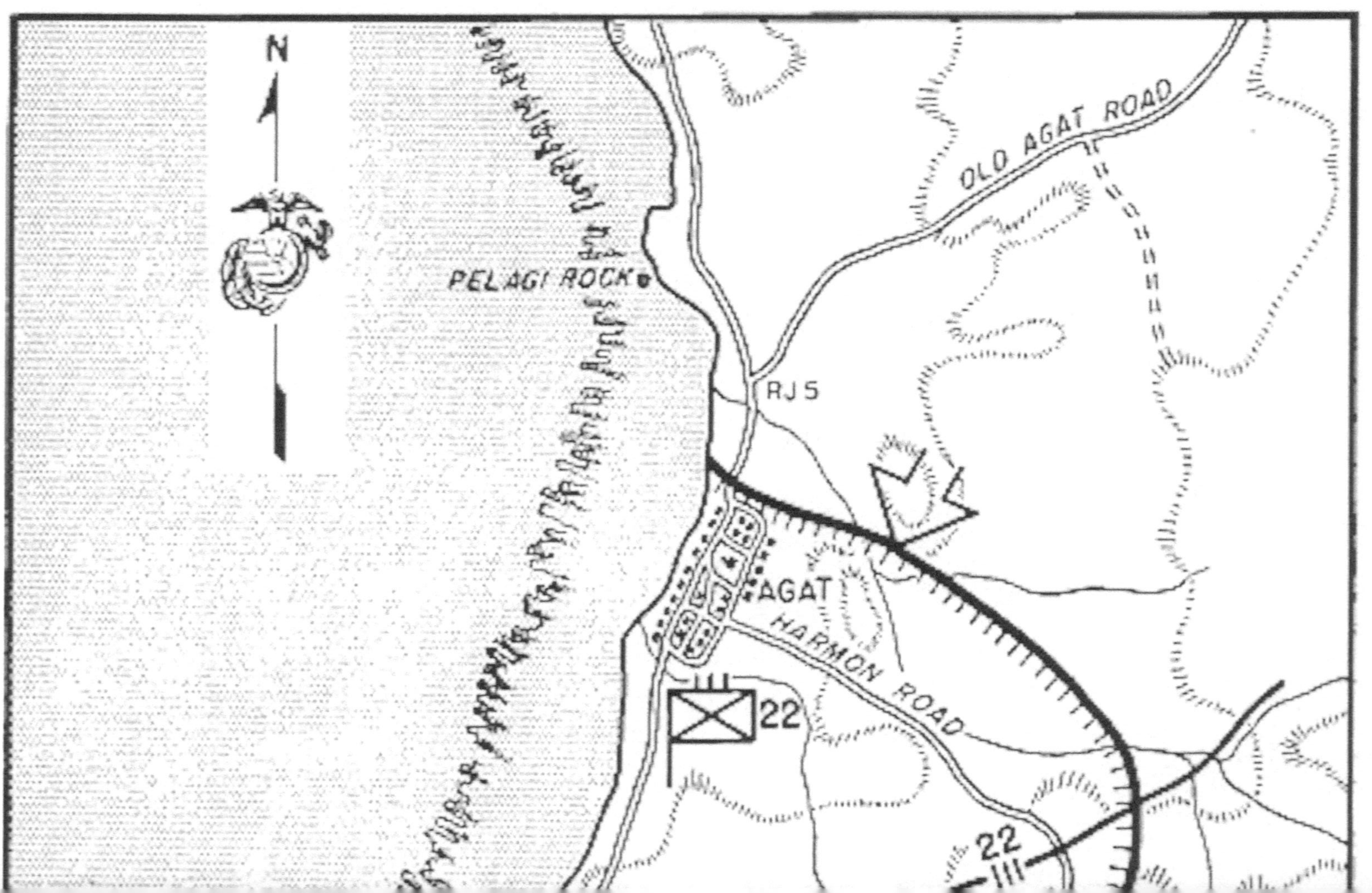

N
PELAGI ROCK
OLD AGAT ROAD
RJ 5
AGAT
HARMON ROAD
22
22

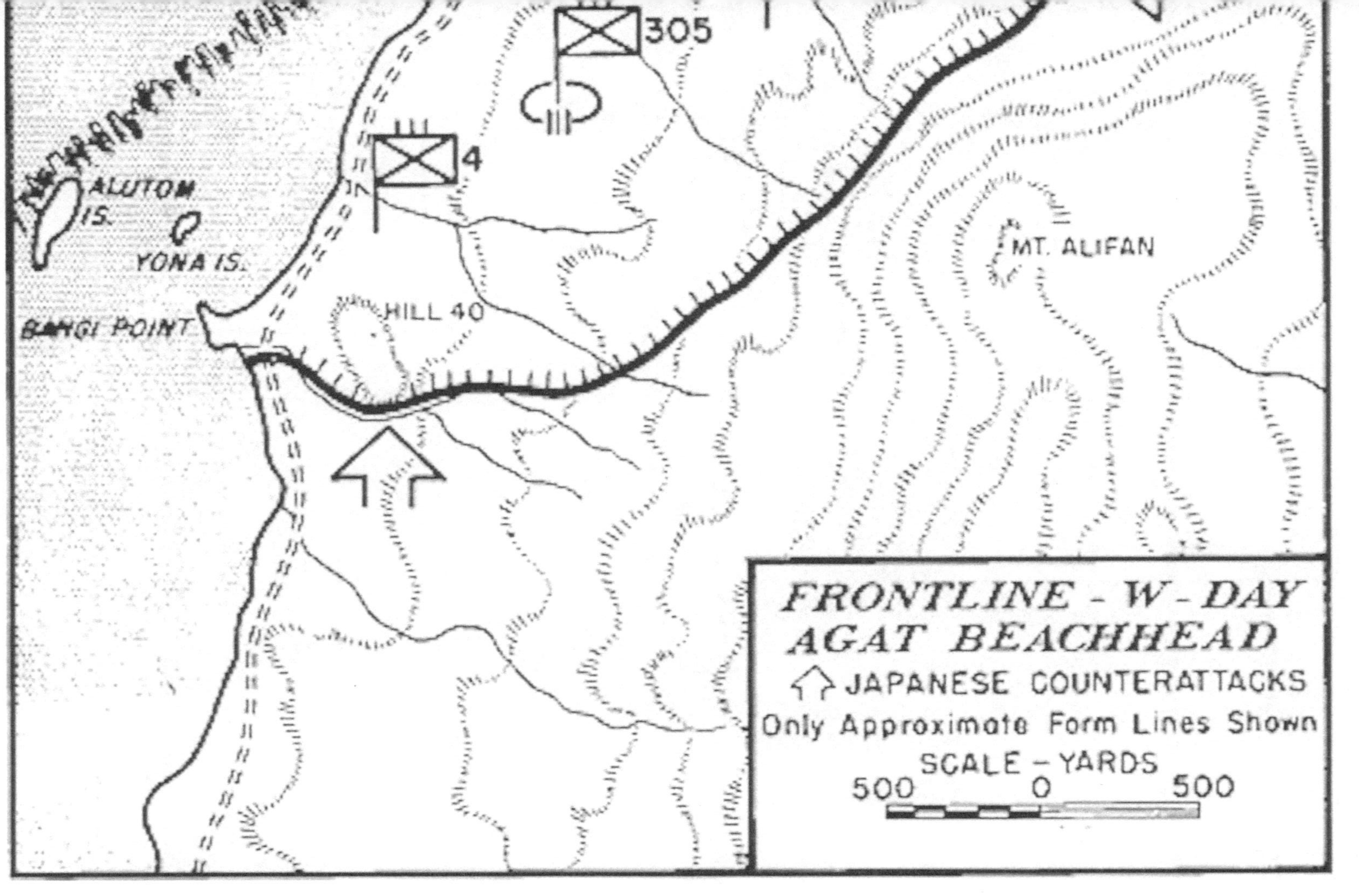

ALUTOM IS.
YONA IS.
BANGI POINT
HILL 40
MT. ALIFAN
305
4
FRONTLINE - W - DAY
AGAT BEACHHEAD
JAPANESE COUNTERATTACKS
Only Approximate Form Lines Shown
SCALE - YARDS
500   0   500

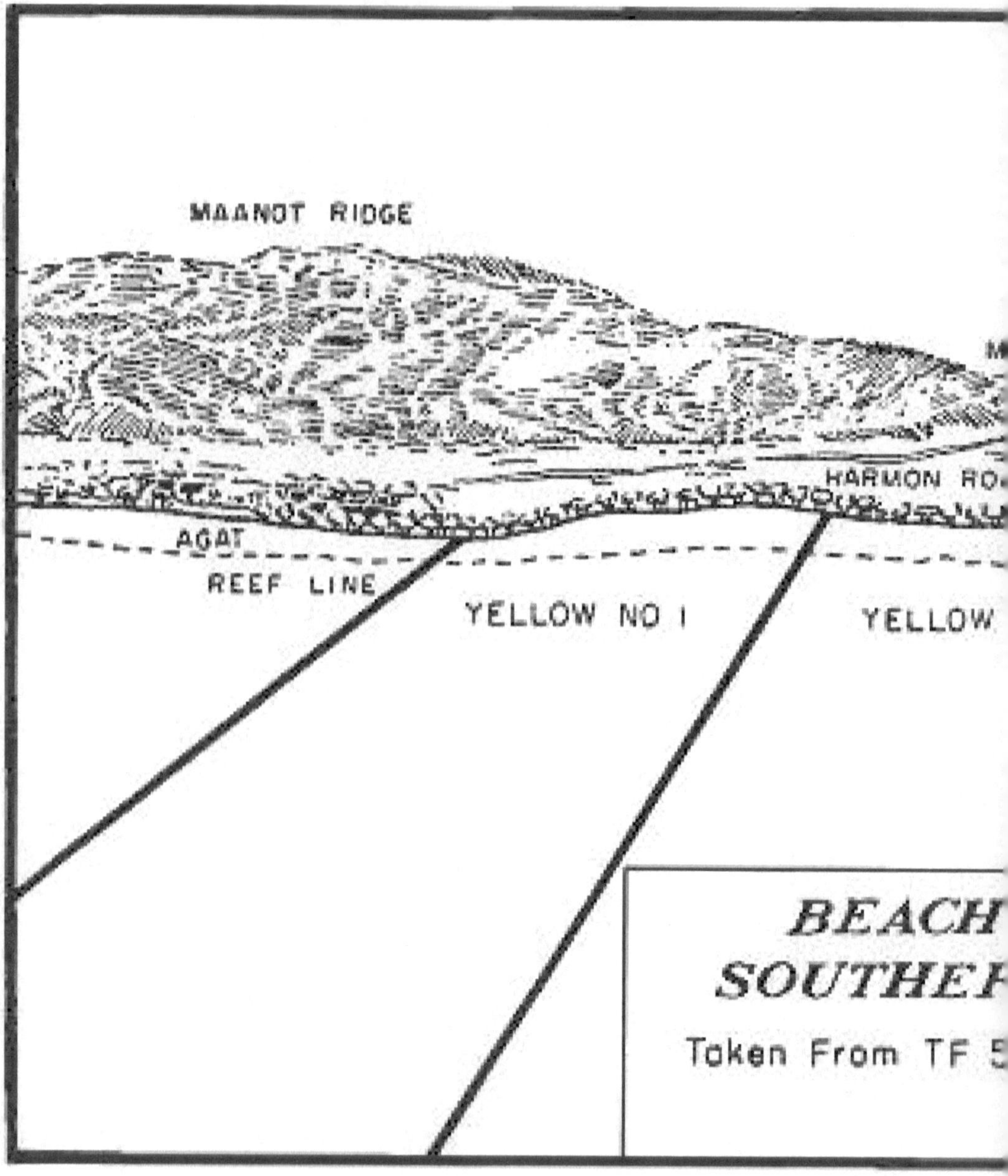

MAANOT RIDGE
HARMON RO
AGAT
REEF LINE
YELLOW NO I
YELLOW
BEACH
SOUTHE
Taken From TF 5

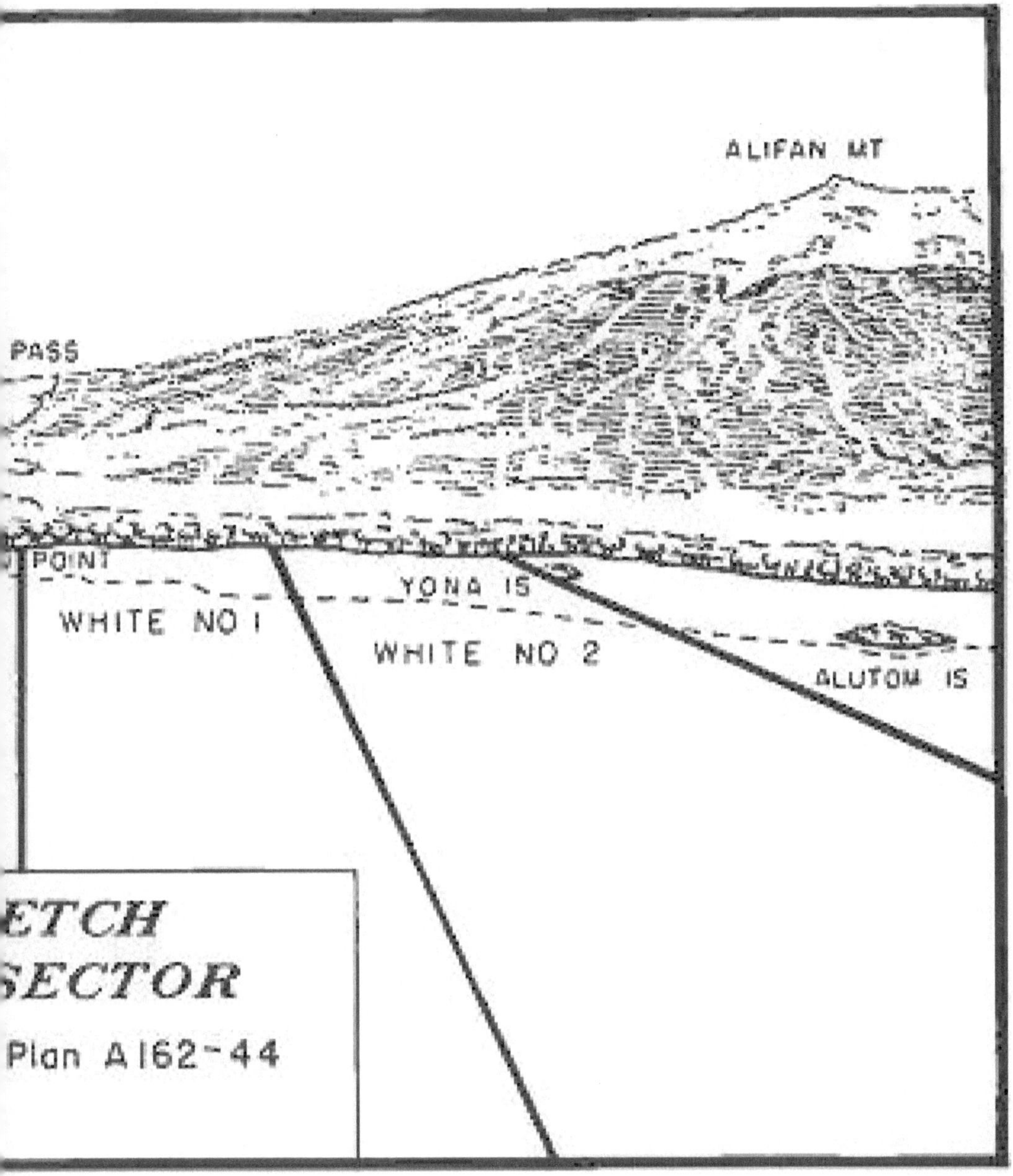

ALIFAN MT
PASS
POINT
YONA IS
WHITE NO 1
WHITE NO 2
ALUTOM IS
ETCH
SECTOR
Plan A 162-44

THE JAPANESE COUNTERATTACK

Colonel Suenaga commanded the *38th Regiment* from his command post on Mount Alifan. He watched the Americans overwhelm his forces below. Desperate to strike back, he called General Takashina and asked for permission for an all-out assault to drive the Marines back into the sea. He'd already ordered his remaining units to assemble for a counterattack. Takashina was not receptive at first. He said the losses would be too high and the *38th Regiment* would serve better defending the high ground and harassing the American advance.

Takashina did eventually give his permission and ordered any survivors to fall back on Mount Alifan if the attack failed—which he was certain it would. Colonel Suenaga must have shared the general's pessimism because he burned his regimental colors to prevent their capture before the counterattack.

The focal point of the Japanese attack came from the south on Hill 40. The brunt of the fighting would fall to the 3/4 Marines. A battalion of still mostly intact Japanese from the *38th Regiment* came north from reserve positions.

Lieutenant "Stormy" Sexton's Company K faced the brunt of the Japanese assault. Company K held, but barely. Sexton later wrote on that night's fighting: "if the Japs could've captured Hill 40, they would have kicked our asses off the Agat beaches."

The Japanese had 750 troops hit Company K at 2115 with their main thrust coming from the left or east of Hill 40.

According to Lieutenant Sexton: "They found a gap in our lines and overran the machine gun which covered the gap. The Japs broke through and advanced toward the beaches. Some elements turned left on Hill 40 and assaulted Company K from the rear. We fought them all night long with our 200 men from Hill 40 and a small hill to the rear and northeast. At daylight, Marines counterattacked with two squads and two tanks closing the gap. Many of our men from Company K died that night. All 750 Jap soldiers were destroyed. That hill symbolized the whole hard-fought American victory on Guam.

"All along the rest of the Marine front, and the reserve areas, the fighting was hot and heavy as the rest of the *38th* attacked. Colonel Suenaga pushed his troops to attack again and again. In the light of our flares, I watched them get mowed down from machine gun fire. General Shepherd was no novice to Jap tactics. He'd expected this attack and was ready for them.

"Jap reconnaissance patrols were numerous and around 2130 they tried to draw our fire and determine our positions. Suenaga was out in front of the center thrust, which began at 2315 after a brisk mortar flurry on the right flank of the 4th Marines. The enemy advanced in full force, charging with rifles carried at high port, yelling, and throwing grenades. Marines lurked in the dark shadows and moved across the skyline under the light of stars from the ships. Marines lined up hand grenades, waited, watched, and then reacted.

"Japs were everywhere trying to bayonet Marines in their foxholes. They even got down to the pack howitzer positions in the rear of the front lines. It was the same for the 22nd Marines. A whole company of Japs got close to the regimental command post. The defense was held largely by a reconnaissance platoon led by Lieutenant Dennis Chavez, who killed five Japs at point-blank range with a Thompson submachine gun.

"Six enemy tanks lumbered down Harmon Road. They were met by bazooka men. Private First Class Bruno Oribiletti knocked out the first two enemy tanks before Marine Shermans from the 4th Tank Company finished off the rest. Oribiletti was killed but was posthumously awarded the Navy Cross for his bravery.

"Enemy troops from the *38th* also stumbled into the perimeter of the newly arrived 305th Infantry and paid for it with their lives."

After a night and a day of furious battle, the *38th* ceased to exist. Colonel Suenaga, wounded in the first night's counterattack, continued to flail at the Marines until he also was cut down. Takashina ordered the shattered remnants of the regiment north to join the reserves he'd need to defend the high ground around Fonte Ridge above the beachhead. Here, the general would leave his troops to fend for themselves.

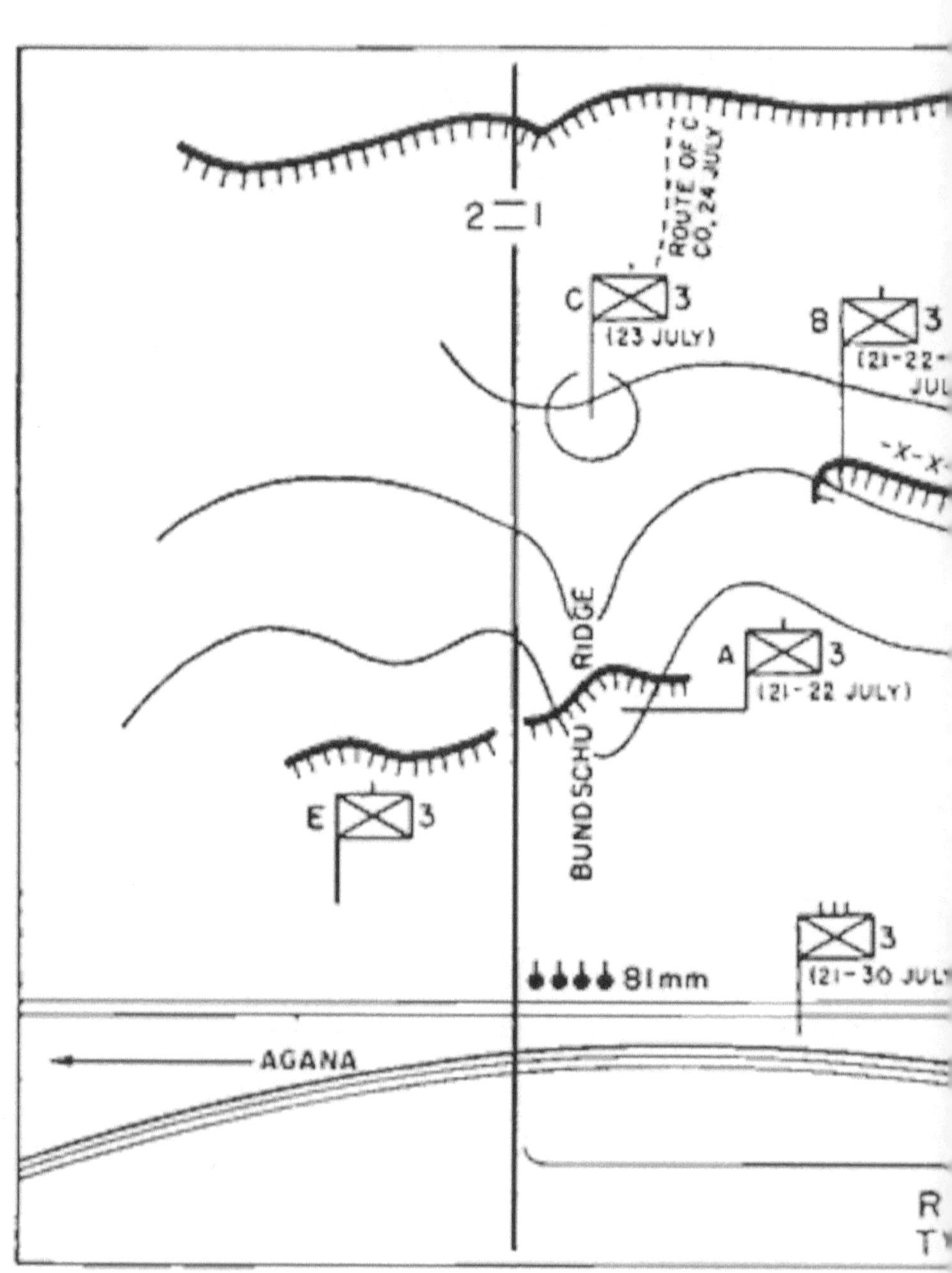
2 = 1
ROUTE OF C
CO. 24 JULY
C 3
(23 JULY)
8 3
(21-22-
JUL
-X-X-
A 3
(21-22 JULY)
BUNDSCHU RIDGE
E 3
3
(21-30 JUL
81mm
AGANA
R
T

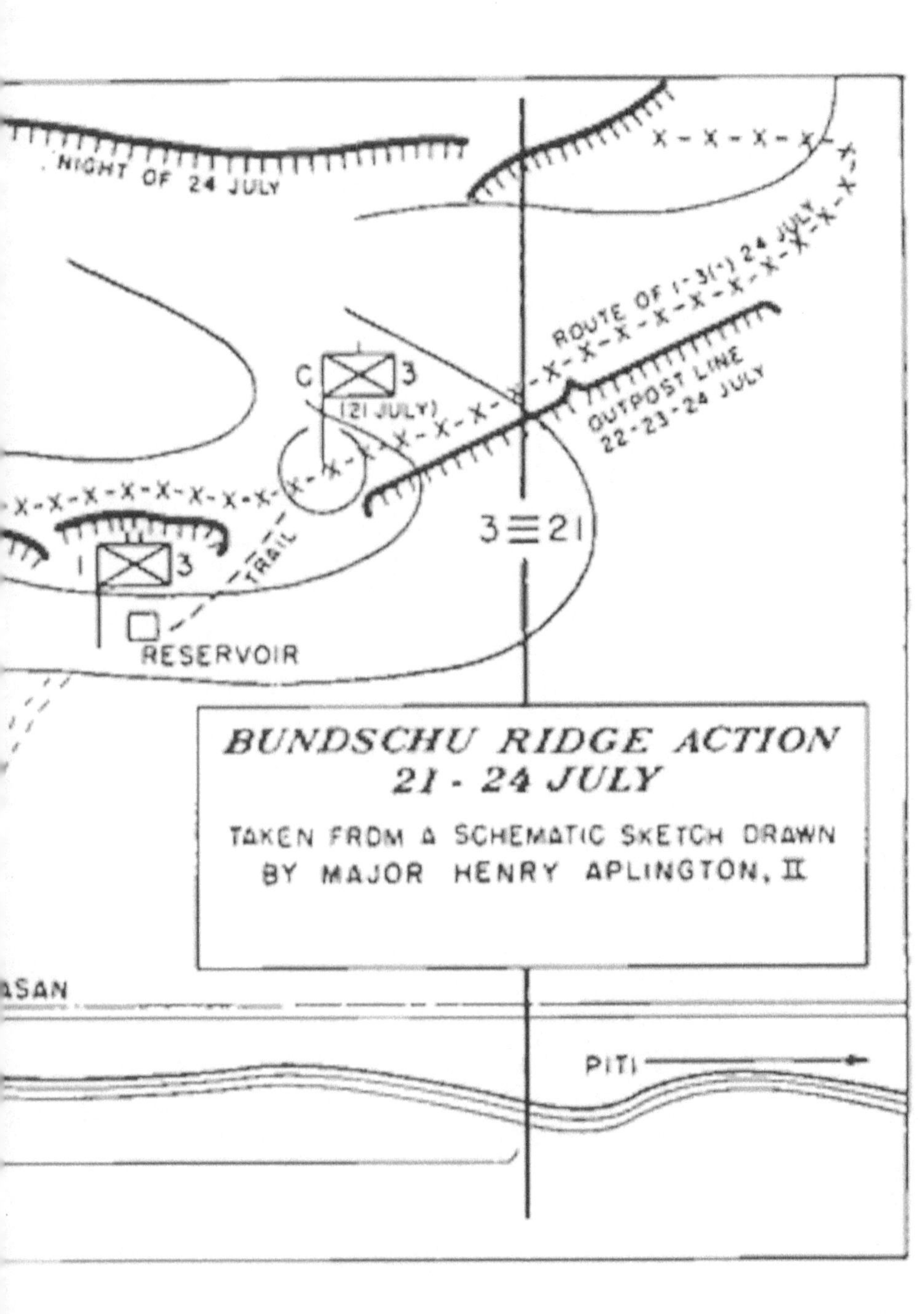

BUNDSCHU RIDGE ACTION
21 - 24 JULY

TAKEN FROM A SCHEMATIC SKETCH DRAWN
BY MAJOR HENRY APLINGTON, II

BATTLE OF FONTE RIDGE

After two days of fierce fighting on the left flank of the 3rd Division Marines' beachhead, in an area now known as Bundschu Ridge, the Marines suffered 613 casualties.

The 21st Marines, in the center, delayed their advance on July 22 until the 3rd could catch up. Marines in exposed ridge positions were getting hammered by Japanese mortar fire. The barrage was so intense that Colonel Arthur H. Butler, in charge of the regiment, called up the division reserve to replace the 1st Battalion with the 2nd.

The 9th Marines encountered little resistance while overrunning several abandoned Japanese positions in its drive to the shores of Apra Harbor. The 3rd Battalion, with the support of naval gunfire and bombs, assaulted Cabras Island. Marines landing in LVTs found hundreds of mines hidden in dense brambles.

General Turnage assessed the situation on July 22 and wrote: "Japanese resistance increased considerably today on the division's left and center. All of 3rd Battalion's combat team were committed to a continuous attack since landing. The 21st CT [combat team] has been relieved by division reserve. Former is forty percent depleted. Any further advance will continue to thin our lines. It is now apparent that an additional combat team is needed. The 9th is fully committed to the capture of Cabras and Piti. Urgently recommend an additional combat team be attached to this division at the earliest possible time."

Turnage was refused the additional combat team he sought. The night of W +1 was fairly quiet in the 3rd Division's sector. Except for the 1/21 Marines, who repulsed a Japanese counterattack complete with a mortar barrage and followed by a bayonet charge.

The III Amphibious Corps commander, General Geiger, was aware that most Japanese troops had not yet been encountered. He told the 3rd Division: "close contact between adjacent units needed to become established by late afternoon and maintained throughout the night."

Despite orders to close gaps and keep contact, the 3rd Division was spread too thin to hold. When they halted for the night, they realized the distance between the units had widened. As night fell, front-line troops held strong points with gaps between them covered by interlocking bands of fire.

The 3rd Marines reached the high ground of Bundschu Ridge on the 23rd. They hunted the remaining enemy stragglers. The enemy had withdrawn from the immediate area but hadn't gone far. When the 21st Marines' patrols tried to link up with the 3rd Marines, they were pushed back by fire from cleverly hidden machine guns. Nearly impossible to spot in the underground and rock-strewn ravines. All along the ridges that the Marines held were stretches of deadly open ground that completely blanketed enemy fire from higher positions.

On the night of the 23rd, the 9th Marines advanced through open territory dotted by hills, each of which a potential enemy bastion. Patrols sent south along the shoreline to contact the 1st Brigade took fire from the hills on its left flank. They also ran into a concentration of American artillery and naval gunfire directed at the enemy defenders on Orote. The patrol was permitted to turn back.

On the 24th, the 3rd and 21st Marine Regiments finally made contact on the heights. But the linkup was an illusion. There were no solid front lines, only strong points. No one could be certain that the Japanese had all been accounted for. But the areas that had been probed and attacked now seemed secure.

Every rifleman knew that much of the same lay ahead. They saw their next objective on the horizon to the front on the Mount Tenjo Road that crossed the high ground, framing the beachhead.

The division had already suffered over 2,000 casualties—the majority in the infantry units. The Japanese, who'd lost just as many if not more men in the north alone, showed no signs of abandoning their ferocious defense. General Takashina gathered his forces to prepare an all-out counterattack as Marines were advancing to their first objective on the FBHL (Force Beachhead Line), securing the high ground and linking up the two beachheads.

Takashina had been bringing his reserve troops into the rugged hills along Mount Tenjo Road since the American landings. He called in his reserves from scattered positions all over the island. By July 25, W-DayCaptain4, he had over 5,000 men, mostly made up of the *10th Independent Mixed Regiment,* in position and ready to attack.

The fighting on the 25th was as intense as any since the Marines invaded. The 2/9 Marines were attached to the 3rd Marines to bring a relatively intact unit into the fight and give the battered 1/3 Marines a chance to recover. By nightfall, the 2/9 Marines had driven a wedge into the Japanese lines and took Mount Tenjo Road. They were only four hundred yards short of reaching their objective at Fonte.

Throughout the relentless firefights, the 3rd Marines blasted and burned their way through barriers of enemy cave defenses. They finally linked up with the 9th Marines on the left. At 1900, Company G of 9th Marines pulled back one hundred yards to position themselves forward of the road, giving them a better observation and field of fire. Company F reached an occupied rocky prominence some one hundred fifty yards ahead of Company G in the center while they also pulled back for a better defense. The scene was set for a pitched battle on Fonte Ridge. Captain Louis Wilson (who became the 26th Commandant of the Marine Corps in 1976) led Company F in the intense fight for Fonte Ridge in which casualties were caused on both sides from small arms fire at point-blank range.

Captain Wilson was awarded the Medal of Honor for his leadership, doggedness, and organizational skill under fire. Wilson was wounded three times while he led attacks into the core of the Fonte action. Part of his citation reads: "In fierce fighting and hand-to-hand encounters, he led his men in a furiously waged battle for ten hours and tenaciously held his line and repelled fanatic counterattacks from the Japanese until he crushed the last efforts of the hard-pressed enemy."

Captain Wilson led and organized the seventeen-man patrol that climbed the slope in the face of the continuous enemy fire, seizing Fonte's critical high ground.

Colonel Frazier West recalled the battle for Fonte Ridge as brisk, bitter, and close. A young officer, West commanded Company G and reinforced Wilson's unit. He joined Company F's flank and then reconnoitered to spot enemy positions and shared the night in a joint command post with Captain Wilson.

In late afternoon on the 25th, a platoon of four tanks from Company C made their way up Mount Tenjo Road and got into position facing the Japanese strongpoints. At the climax of the battle, Wilson and West's companies were still holding their positions. First Lieutenant Wilcie O'Bannon, the XO of Company F, got downslope from his exposed position and brought up two tanks. By using telephones mounted in the rear of these tanks to communicate with the Marines inside, O'Bannon described targets for the tanks as he positioned them to support West's and Wilson's Marines.

The tanks came up with the precious cargo of ammunition. Volunteers stuffed grenades in their pockets and hung bandoleers over shoulders, pocketed clips, and carried grenade boxes on their shoulders to deliver like birthday presents all along the line to Companies F and G—and what was left of Company E.

Colonel West used a tank radio circuit to call in naval gunfire. This guaranteed that all the terrain before him would be lit all night by star shells and high explosive naval gunfire.

At dawn on July 26, over 600 dead Japanese laid in front of the 2/9 Marine positions. But the battle was not over. General Turnage ordered the crest of the reverse slope taken. More Japanese counterattacks would come, and again fighting would be hand-to-hand. But by July 28, the capture of Fonte Ridge was no longer in question. Companies E, F, and G took their objectives on the crest, costing the battalion 242 casualties in four murderous days.

The 21st Marines did not have it any easier on the 25th. After a hard morning of fighting, they were able to clear the front in the center of the line. The 2/21 Marines dealt with similar pockets of diehard enemy soldiers like those that held up the 2/9 Marines on Fonte. Hidden in cave positions on the eastern draw of the Asan River, inland from the beachhead.

The Japanese were destroyed only after repeated Marine assaults and close-in fighting. According to the official Marine Corps history of the campaign: "every foot of ground that fell to the Marines were paid in heavy casualties, and every man available was needed in the assault."

The 9th Marines made good progress on the 25th and reached their objective of the Sasa River by 0915. The 9th Marines had even taken more ground than was planned. From there, General Turnage repositioned the 9th Marines to support the fighting on the struggling left flank. The 2nd Battalion pulled out of position to reinforce the 3rd Marines, and the remaining two battalions spread out a little further in their position.

A determined enemy counterattack hit the 3rd Division Marines on the night of July 25. The intensity of the Japanese counterattack was matched across the 3rd Division's front. It wasn't long before Japanese troops roaming the rear slipped into Marine perimeters and snuck downstream into valleys and ravines leading to the beaches.

Major Henry Aplington II commanded the 1/3 Marines, the only infantry reserve. His Marines held positions on the hills of what had been a quiet sector. He wrote: "Heavy rain came when it got dark. On the line, Marines huddled under ponchos in their wet foxholes, trying to figure out the meaning of the obvious activity by the Japanese.

"Near midnight the Japs were probing the 21st Marines' lines and slopping over into those of the 9th Marines. All was quiet in our circle of hills, and we received no notifications when the probing increased its intensity or at 0400 when the enemy opened their attack. My first inkling came at about 0430 when my three companies on the hills erupted into fire and called for mortar support. I talked to the company commanders and asked them what was going on, only to be told that the Japs were all around them. The enemy was close. Three of my dead had been killed by bayonet attacks."

Private Dale Fetzer was a dog handler assigned to the 1/9 Marines with his black Labrador Retriever. His dog Skipper was asleep in front of his handler's foxhole. Suddenly Skipper bolted upright. His nose pointed up and toward Mount Tenjo. Private Fetzer shouted, "get the lieutenant. The Japs are coming."

Japanese troops poured down the slopes at 0400 in a furious banzai attack. The enemy had been sighted drinking during the afternoon in the higher hills and now some appeared drunk.

The 21st Marines were along a low ridge close to Mount Tenjo Road. The banzai charge smashed against the 3rd Battalion, and the enemy seized a machine gun position—quickly recaptured by Marines. The 3rd Division held a thin front on the right flank of the 21st Marines and to the left of the 9th Marines.

Some of the Japanese raiders got through the sparsely manned gap between the battalions. The Japanese charged fearlessly at the artillery, tanks, and ammunition supply dumps. Their attack was scattered and unorganized. But fighting was brutal and shattered the hastily erected Marine roadblock between the battalions.

Some attackers got through the lines along the front. Fifty enemy troops reached the division hospital. Doctors evacuated the gravely wounded, but the walking wounded joined stretcher-bearers, cooks, bakers, and corpsmen to form a line fighting off the attackers. One of the walking wounded, Private Michael Ryan, ran with a wounded foot through crossfire to join the line and help fight off the enemy assault.

Colonel George Van Orden assembled two companies of the 3rd Pioneer Battalion to eliminate this threat. Marine pioneers killed thirty-three enemy troops in less than three hours and only lost three of their men. The 3rd Medical Battalion took twenty casualties, but only one patient was killed in the fighting.

For many men in this furious and confused melee breaking out over Marine positions, Corporal Charles Moore's experiences weren't unique. His outfit held a position along a quarter mile from Fonte plateau. He later wrote: "We set up on the road that made a sharp turn overlooking a draw. It was Second Platoon's last stand. Three attacks that night, and by the third, no one was left to fight— so they broke through. They came in droves, throwing hand grenades and hacked up some of our platoon. In the morning, I only had ten rounds of ammo left and half the clip for my BAR. I was holding those rounds back in case I needed them to make a break for it. Everyone was quiet, either wounded or dead. The Japs came in to take out their dead and wounded steps from the edge of my foxhole. I held my breath. I watched them as they milled around until dawn, and then they left."

With the seizure of Fonte Ridge, the capture of the beachhead was now complete. The 3rd Division fought bravely throughout the bloody night until they finished off the determined Japanese enemy on Guam. What made the fighting for Fonte important was the fact that the advance to the north end of the island could not take place until Fonte Ridge was seized and held.

The enemy attack also failed in the south, although it was touch and go at times. However, Japanese sailors on Orote were just as committed as the soldiers on Fonte to drive the Allies from Guam.

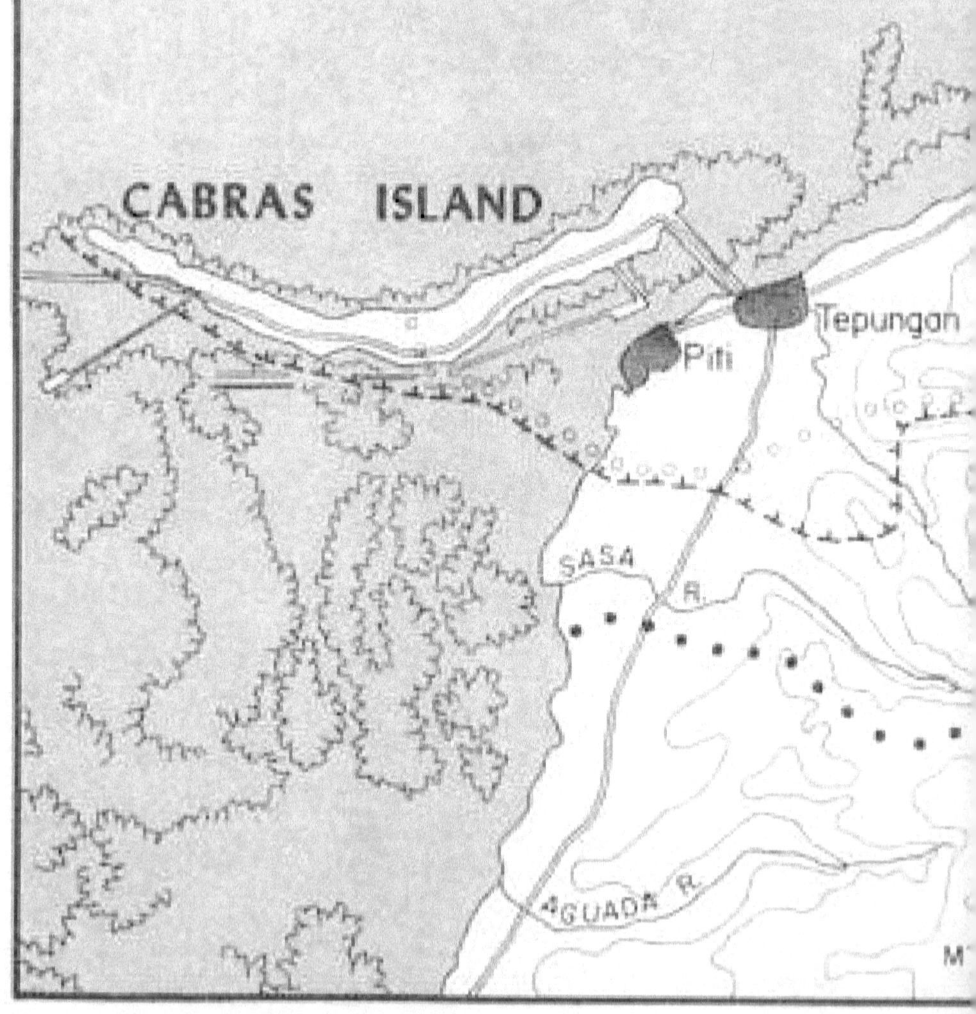

3D MARINE DIVISION PROGRESS
22-26 JULY 1944
POSITIONS AT 1800
22 JULY
24 JULY
26 JULY
1000
0
1000
2000
3000
YARDS
CONTOUR INTERVAL 100 FEET
CABRAS ISLAND
Pili
Tepungan
SASA
R.
AGUADA R.
M

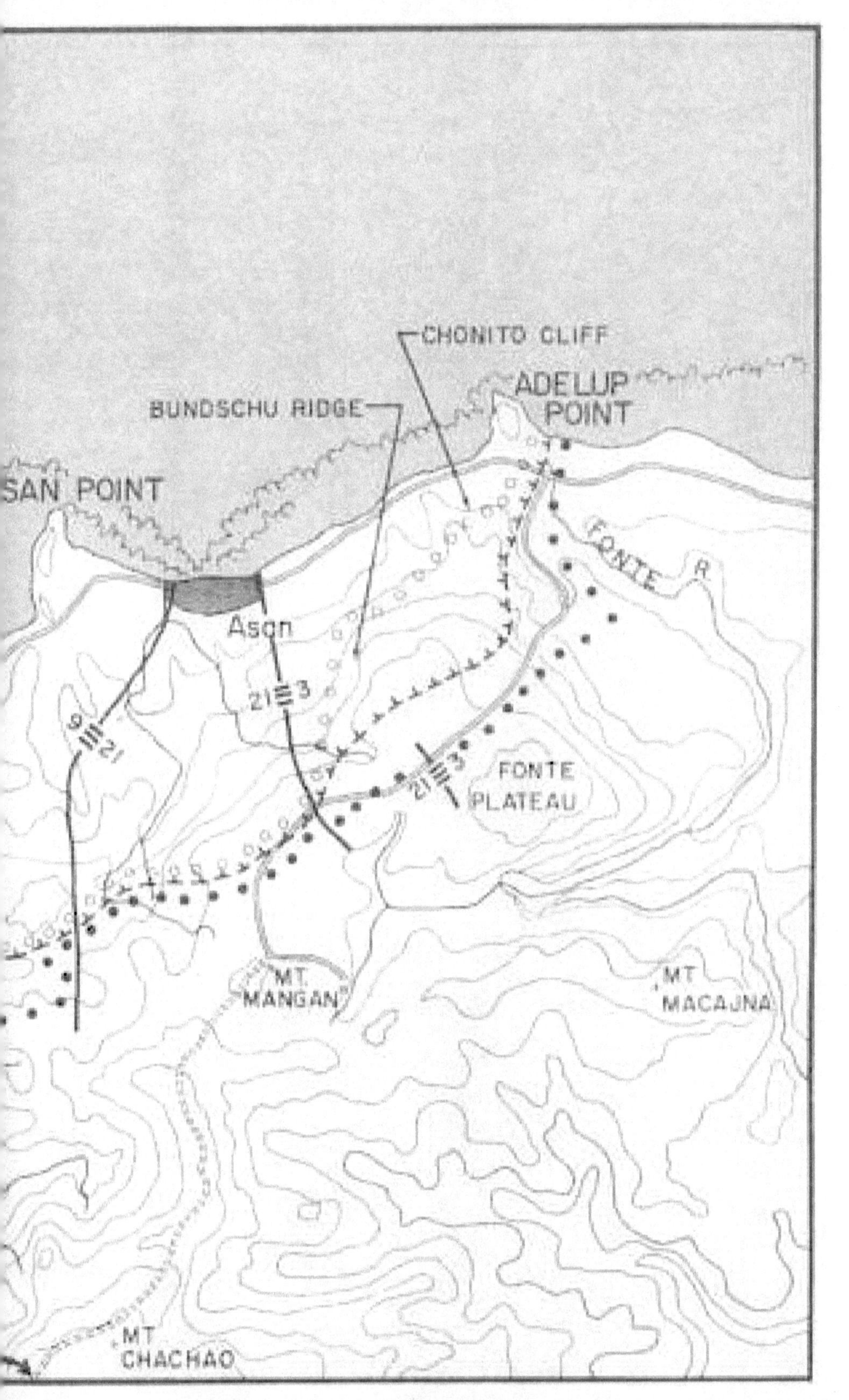

CHONITO CLIFF
BUNDSCHU RIDGE
ADELUP POINT
SAN POINT
FONTE R.
Ason
FONTE PLATEAU
MT. MANGAN
MT. MACAJNA
MT. CHACHAO

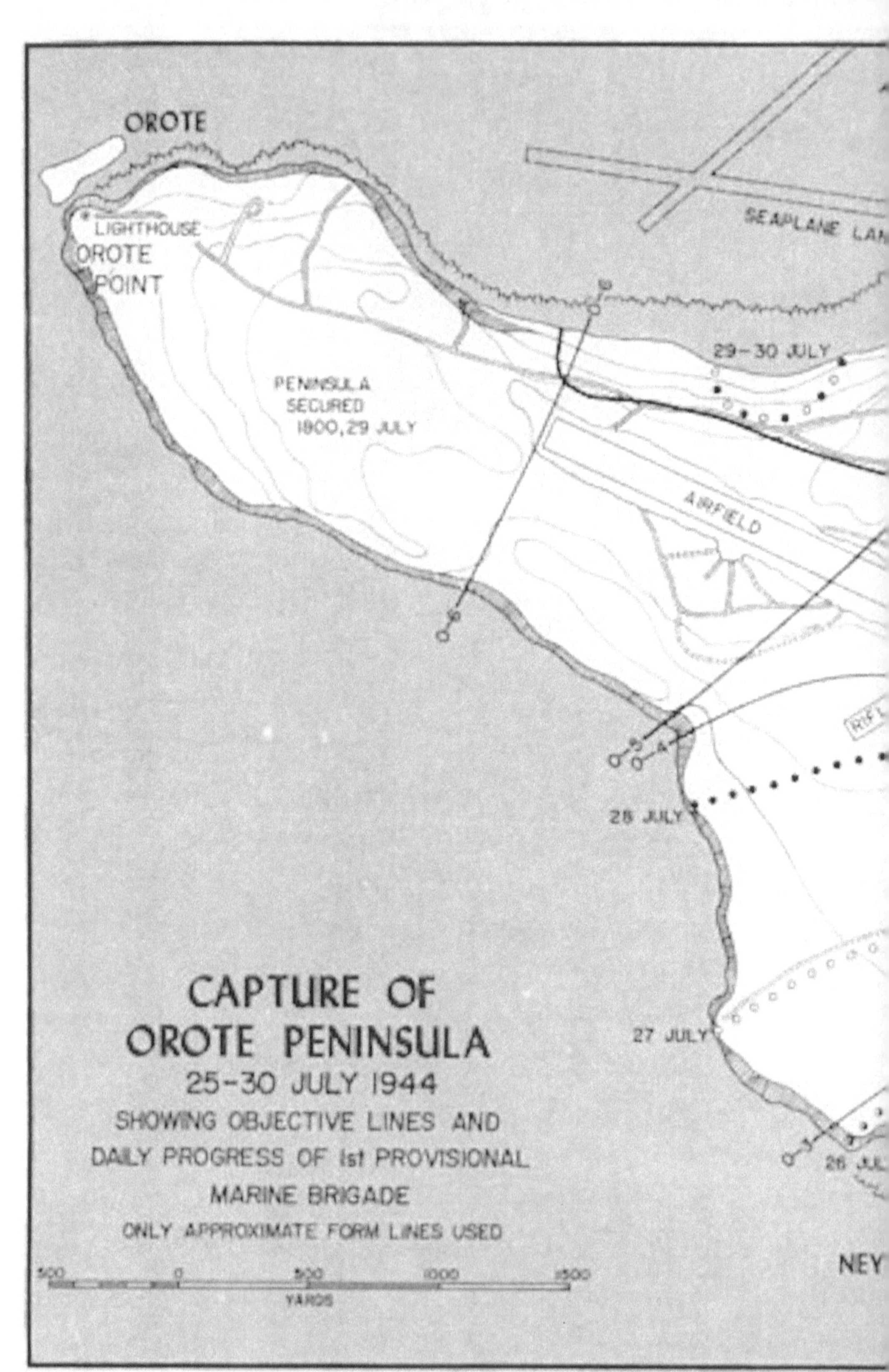

OROTE
LIGHTHOUSE
OROTE
POINT
PENINSULA
SECURED
1800, 29 JULY
SEAPLANE LA
29-30 JULY
AIRFIELD
RIFL
28 JULY
27 JULY
26 JUL
CAPTURE OF
OROTE PENINSULA
25-30 JULY 1944
SHOWING OBJECTIVE LINES AND
DAILY PROGRESS OF 1st PROVISIONAL
MARINE BRIGADE
ONLY APPROXIMATE FORM LINES USED
500   0   500   1000   1500
YARDS
NEY

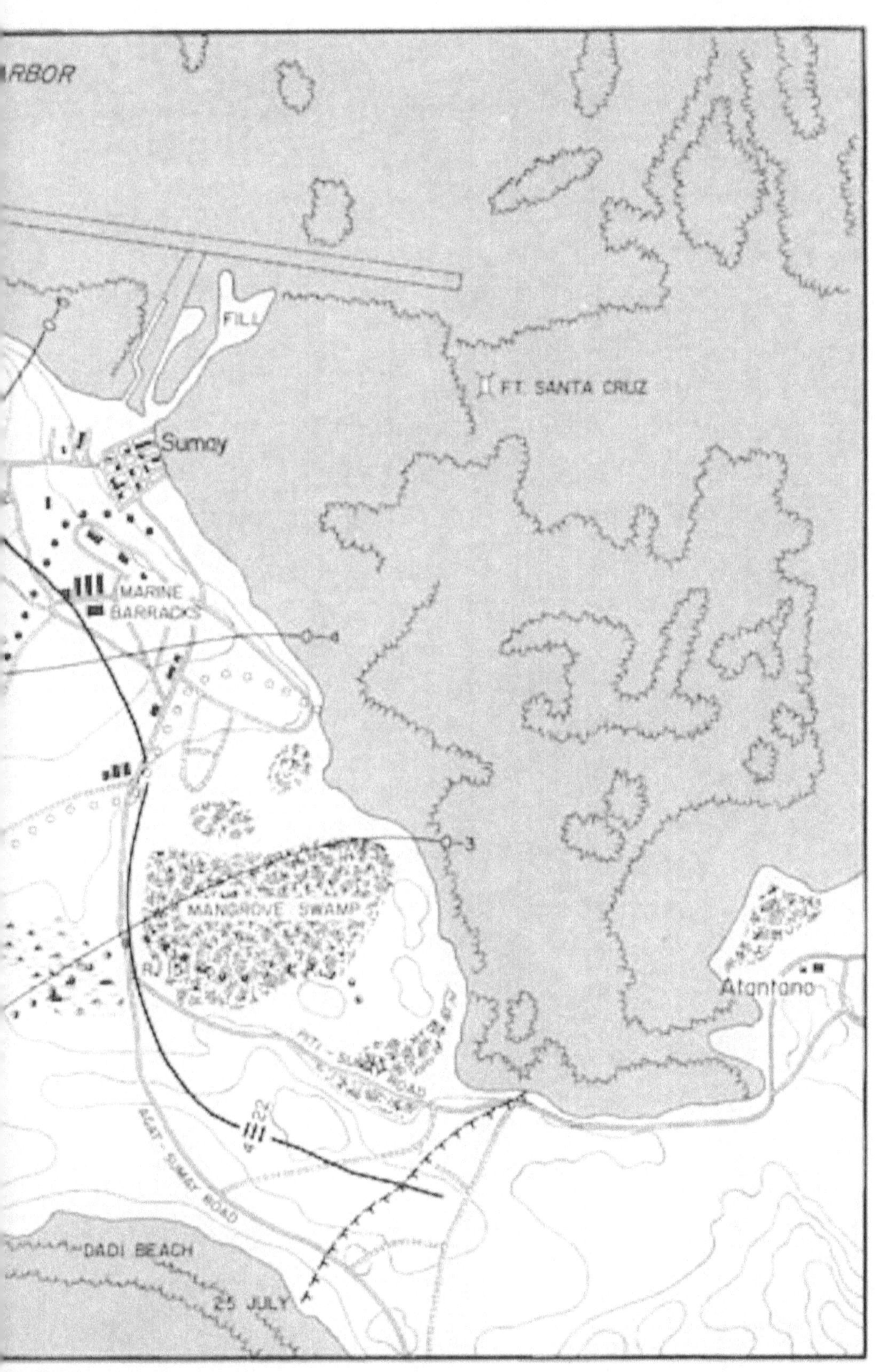

RBOR
FILL
FT. SANTA CRUZ
Sumay
MARINE
BARRACKS
MANGROVE SWAMP
Atantano
FT. SUMAY ROAD
AGAT - SUMAY ROAD
DADI BEACH
25 JULY

CAPTURE OF OROTE PENINSULA

The 22nd Marines advanced up the coast from Agat and fought a series of brutal battles against stubborn enemy defenders. The 4th Marines swept up the slopes of Mount Alifan and secured the high ground overlooking the beachhead. By the 25th, the brigade lined up across from the mouth of the Orote Peninsula. They faced formidable Japanese defenses. Enemy defenders were anchored in swamps and low hillocks concealed by heavy undergrowth—bristling with automatic weapons.

The 77th Infantry Division took over the rest of the southern beachhead, relieving the 4th Marines of their patrolling duties in the hills to the west. Artillery and naval guns pounded the Japanese on Orote without letup. In case of an enemy air attack, beach defenses from Bangi Point to Agat were manned by the 9th Defense Battalion. Few Japanese planes were still in the sky, so antiaircraft gunners concentrated their firing across the water into the southern flank of enemy positions on Orote.

The 14th Defense Battalion on Cabras Island moved into position to provide direct flanking fire on the Peninsula's northern coast. They stood ready to elevate their guns and fire at enemy planes in the skies.

At dawn on July 26, over 5,000 Japanese troops on Orote took part in General Takashina's desperate counterattack. Enemy soldiers stormed out of the mangrove swamp and charged with swords, grenades, and small arms fire. Like in the north, many of the Japanese attackers had fortified themselves with *sake*. Japanese officers led senseless soldiers who attacked Marine tanks armed only with samurai swords. There were also skilled and deadly attacks. Marines were stabbed and sliced in their foxholes.

In charge of Company L of the 22nd Marines, Captain Robert Frank was on the front relaying enemy positions to brigade artillery. He later wrote: "The artillery response was effective and intense. The fire was drawn in closer to our front lines. We threw over 25,000 shells into the pockets of the Japanese between midnight and 3 AM. Screaming banzai attacks came at 1230 and then again at 0145 and 0315. At daylight, muddy ground in front of Marine positions was slick with blood. Over 400 Japanese bodies were sprawled out in the driving rain."

General Shepherd knew his front-line troops, the 4th Marines on the left and 22nd Marines on the right, could withstand the night's banzai attacks. He ordered a counterattack launched at 0730. But first, there would be another artillery barrage. At dawn, the bombardment opened with the 77th Infantry Division's 105s and 155s, and whatever other guns the 12th Marines could spare. This became one of the most intense barrages of the campaign.

Major Charles Davis of the 77th Division Artillery later wrote about General Shepherd's request to turn the heavy guns to face Orote in order to soften Japanese positions. The 105s and 155s hammered the enemy defenders' well-prepared positions and shredded the protection, covering, and camouflage from bunkers and trenches. Pieces of Japanese troops hung in trees. Marines saw that this fire was effective and made it a point to return and congratulate the section leaders from the 77th Artillery.

When the advance came, it only moved one hundred yards before it was attacked by a blistering front of machine gun and small arms fire. Enemy artillery fell furiously, leaving Marines wondering if the fire was from their own guns—a favorite Japanese tactic. The Japanese return fire stalled the 22nd Marine's advance. It wasn't until 0830 before the attack was in full force again, spearheaded by Army tanks.

In front of the 22nd Marines was that mangrove swamp where the banzai attack was mounted the night before. Still heavily occupied by the Japanese, the only way to penetrate it was through a 200-yard-long corridor along the regimental boundary covered by Japanese fire. It could only be navigated under cover of tanks. Armor gunners and commanders directed their fire just over the head of prone Marines into the gun ports of enemy pillboxes.

By 1250, Marines had worked their way through the bottlenecks and passed the mangrove swamps—destroying bunkers with flamethrowers and demolitions. The 4th Marines' assault battalions kept pace with this advance and found it somewhat easier terrain, but the defenders were just as determined. By evening, the brigade advanced 1,100 yards from its jump-off line. Both regiments were weary and dug in with an all-around defense.

After a massive pre-attack barrage on the 27th, Marines were stalled again before they'd gone a hundred yards. The 3/4 Marines were up against a well-defended ridge, a sinister clearing, and a coconut grove. This ridge was close to the tactically essential goals of the old Marine barracks, its rifle range, and the Orote Airfield runways. With heavy tank support, the 22nd Marines surged past their initial obstacles, and by midafternoon, they reached positions well beyond the morning's battles.

On the left flank, the 4th Marines faced a lighter resistance. They were led by tanks that knocked down the brush. Colonel Samuel Puller, brother of the famous Colonel "Chesty" Puller, was killed by a sniper.

By early afternoon, assault elements of the 4th Marines broke out of the grove short of the rifle range. They were stalled by enemy dug-in defenses and minefields. A Japanese officer emerged and brandished his sword at a tank. Not an unusual sight in the climax of this losing engagement. This was easier than a ritual suicide.

The horror of the American guns must've been too much for the enemy defenders on the immediate front. They cut and ran from their strong and well-defended positions. Marines didn't care why the enemy ran—just that they ran—and dug in less than 300 yards from the prized target. This squeezed the enemy into the last quadrant of the peninsula. All their entrenched defenses failed to hold. The Orote Airfield, old Marine barracks, and old parade ground, which hadn't seen American boots since December 10, 1941, were recaptured.

On July 28, General Shepherd ordered an all-out barrage of the Japanese naval defenders: a thirty-minute naval gunfire bombardment, a forty-five-minute airstrike, joined by whatever guns the brigade, 77th Division, and any antiaircraft battalions could muster. At 0830, the brigade launched an attack to retake Orote Airfield.

The 22nd Marines would assault the barracks, while the 4th Marines would advance on the airfield and rifle range. Japanese mortar fire and artillery had lessened, but small arms and machine guns were still intense when the Marines attacked. To the bitter end, Japanese defenders evoked a last-ditch stubbornness. American tanks were called up, but most had problems with control and visibility. Wherever there was a thick scrub brush, the enemy was concealed.

General Shepherd wanted this battle over. He ordered a massive infantry and tank advance jumping off at 1530 on the 28th. The Japanese refused to quit: it was do or die. By nightfall, the objectives were in sight, but there were still a few hundred yards to gain. Marines dug in for the night and hoped the Japanese would sacrifice themselves in another counterattack—no such luck.

The next day, the attack resumed. After the usual artillery barrage and heavy airstrikes, Marine and Army tanks led the way onto the airfield. Resistance was meager. By early afternoon, the airfield was secured. The 22nd Marines occupied what was left of the old Marine barracks. A bronze plaque, once mounted mounted on the barracks entrance, but now removed, was recovered and put up for reinstallation at a future date.

The Japanese found this latest advance too hard to accept. Suicides were random and many enemy soldiers jumped off cliffs, cut their own throats, and hugged exploding grenades.

Private First Class George Eftang watched several enemy suicides and later wrote: "I watched the Japanese jump to their deaths. I actually felt sorry for them. I knew they had families and sweethearts just like anyone else."

While the peninsula still swarmed with patrols, Generals Geiger, Larson, Shepherd, Admiral Spruance, and others who could be spared, took part in a ceremonial flag-raising and heartfelt tribute to an old barracks and those Marines who'd made it home. General Geiger called it hallowed ground and told those assembled, a hastily cleaned up honor guard of brigade troops: "you've avenged the loss of our comrades who were overcome by a numerically superior force three days after Pearl Harbor. Under our flag, this island again stands ready to fulfill its destiny as an American fortress in the Pacific."

Many of the Marines taking part in the ceremony could only thank God that they were still alive. At the end of the ceremony, engineers moved on to the airfield and filled many of the bomb and shell holes. Just six hours after the first bulldozer had clanked out onto the runway, a navy torpedo bomber made an emergency landing. Soon after, light artillery spotting planes flew in regularly. The capture of the Orote Peninsula cost the brigade 874 casualties, with 115 men killed. Japanese dead was a staggering 1,633. On Orote, like Fonte, many enemy troops were still unaccounted for and likely ready to fight to prevent the capture of the island.

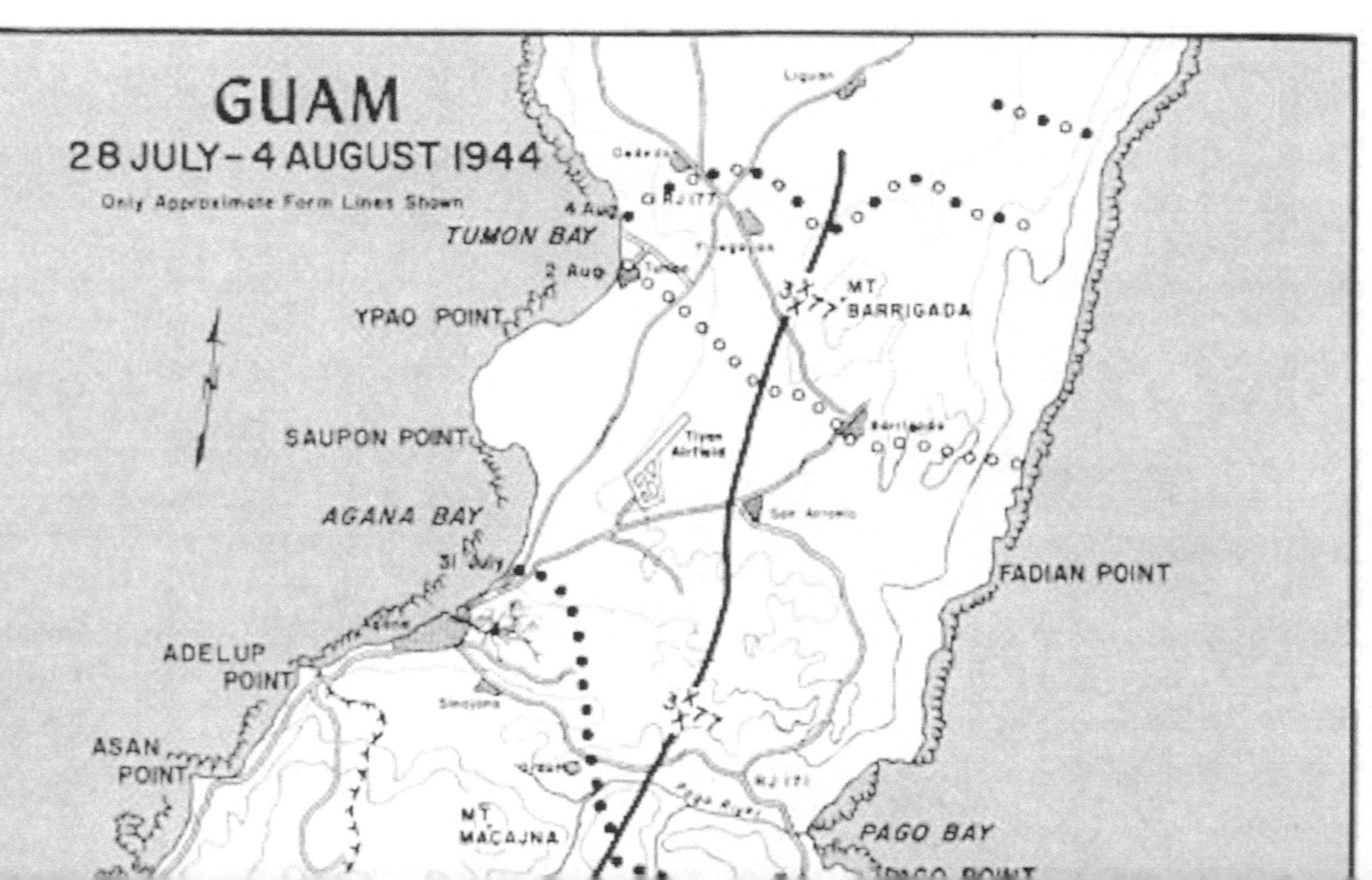

GUAM
28 JULY – 4 AUGUST 1944
Only Approximate Form Lines Shown
TUMON BAY
YPAO POINT
SAUPON POINT
AGANA BAY
ADELUP POINT
ASAN POINT
MT MACAJNA
PAGO BAY
FADIAN POINT
MT BARRIGADA
Tiyan Airfield
N
4 Aug
2 Aug
31 July
3 X 77
3 X 77

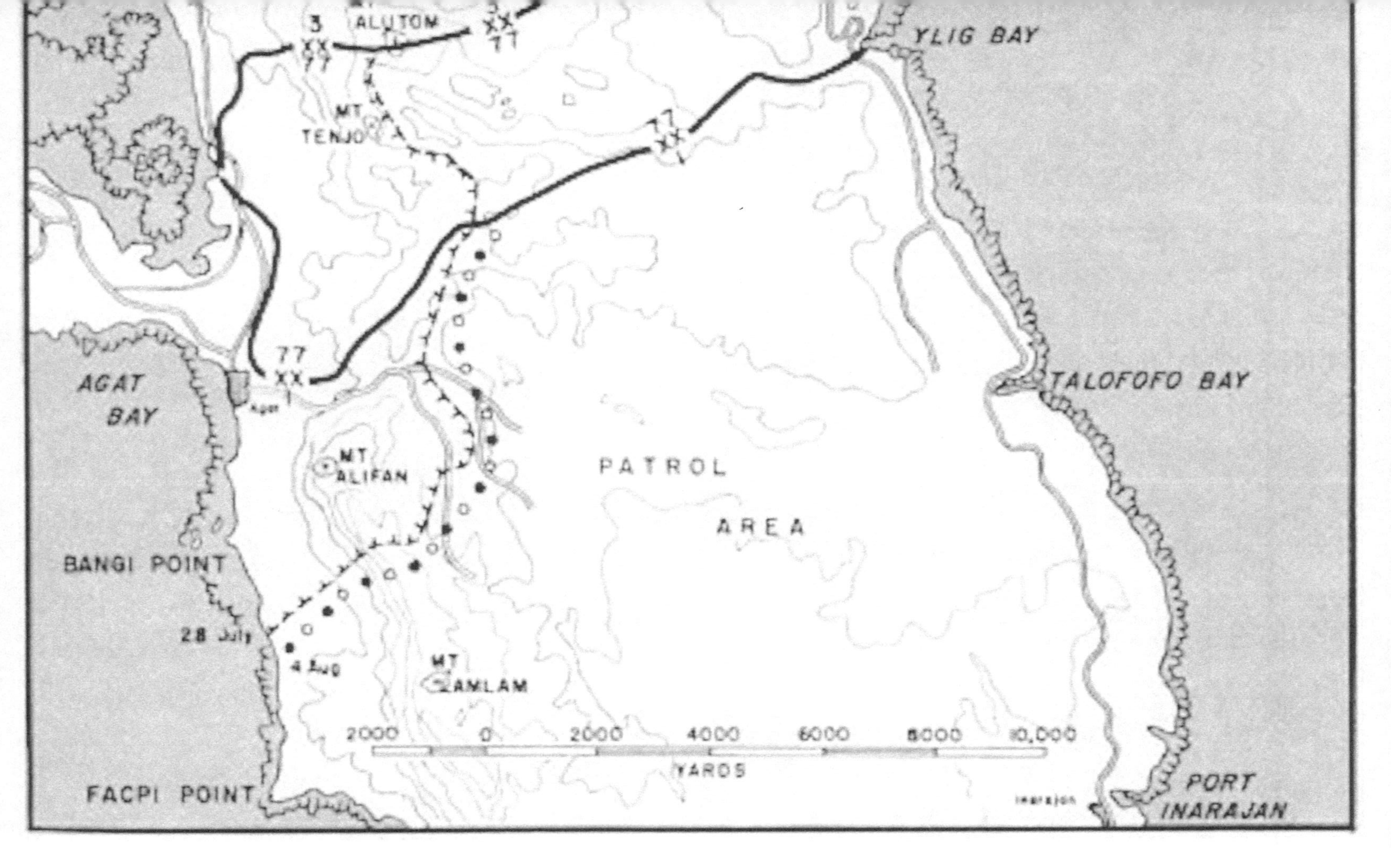
3 ALUTOM
XX 77
XX 77
MT TENJO
77 XX
YLIG BAY
77 XX
AGAT BAY
TALOFOFO BAY
MT ALIFAN
PATROL AREA
BANGI POINT
28 July
4 Aug
MT LAMLAM
FACPI POINT
2000 0 2000 4000 6000 8000 10,000
YARDS
PORT INARAJAN

TURNING POINT ON GUAM

After the breakthrough at Fonte and the failure of General Takashina's counterattack, American positions could now be consolidated. The 3rd and 21st Marines tightened their grasp on the heights, while the 9th Marines advanced up to Mount Chachao and Mount Alutom.

Across the hills at the base of Mount Chachao was the fiercest resistance. Major Donald Hubbard, in charge of the 3/9 Marines, called down artillery, and after the barrages, Marines attacked with bayonets and grenades. They destroyed everything that stood in their way. When the fight was over, Major Hubbard's Battalion counted over 130 dead Japanese. As their assault force pushed up the slopes, Marines spotted men from Company A of the 305th Infantry on top of Mount Tenjo to the west. Mount Tenjo had initially been in the 3rd Division's zone, but command wanted to get men on high ground so they could push ahead along the heights and not get trapped in ravines.

Japanese dead from the counterattack was 3,200. The destruction of General Takashina's infantry officers was estimated at 96%. Takashina himself was killed from a machine gun on an American tank as he urged survivors out of the Fonte position and on to the north to fight again. After Takashina's death, the tactical command of all Japanese forces on Guam was assumed by General Obata. He only had a handful of senior officers remaining to rally the Japanese defenders and organize a cohesive unit from the battalions' destroyed remnants.

On the night of July 28, Obata's defenders trudged along the path that led from Ordot to Fonte. They found their way by the light of the American flares. Two traffic control points guided men toward Barrigada, where three infantry companies were forming. General Obata fully expected the Americans to engage in an aggressive pursuit on the 29th. Obata organized a delaying force to hold back Marines until the Japanese withdrawal could be made.

General Geiger instead decided to rest his battle-weary troops before launching another full-scale attack to the north. His orders to the 3rd and 77th Divisions on July 29 were to eliminate any Japanese resistance and organize a line of defense and patrol in strength to the front. By capturing the beachhead line and its critical high ground, they were able to annihilate great numbers of Japanese—the turning point on Guam had finally been reached.

Still, the few enemy who'd surrendered, and those captured were wounded, dazed or unable to resist. Nearly all the enemy died fighting. Even when their lives were lost without purpose or sense. Yet, a substantial number of troops from the *29th Division* were not accounted for. General Geiger's intelligence sections estimated only one-quarter of the island's enemy troop strength had been on the island. He needed to make sure his rear was secure from attack before chasing north after the enemy. Captured Japanese prisoners, documents, and sightings from aircraft indicated to Geiger that the Japanese had withdrawn north to better roads. The north was denser and had a more concealing jungle—a better terrain for strong points.

General Geiger had the 77th Division scour Guam's southern half to ensure his rear was not threatened. He intensified and repeated the searches the brigade had made. Soldiers like the

Marines before them found native Guamanians everywhere—some on farms and ranches and others in Japanese camps.

The natives were surprised to see Americans so soon after the landings and reported only small Japanese bands, usually only single soldiers. It became clear to Geiger that the combat units remaining were in the north and not the south. Best estimates of enemy strength were around 6,000 men.

General Obata expected a swift pursuit and set up a strong rearguard to give his retreating forces time to organize. While victory was no longer even a dream, the Japanese could still extract a painful cost. Geiger moved his troops back into attack positions across the width of the island. Frequent strong patrols were sent out to find cross-country routes and clues of enemy strength and dispositions.

General Obata organized a delaying defensive on the south slopes of Mount Barrigada and into the little town of Barrigada itself—only twenty houses. On all the approaches to the final defensive positions in the northwest corner of the island, Obata organized roadblocks at trail and road junctions. He concealed troops in the jungle to interdict the roads that were the only practical approach route to the northern end of the island.

General Obata felt overwhelmed as he later revealed in his notes: "the enemy air force seeks out our units during daylight hours in the forest and will bomb and strafe even a single soldier."

Even more damaging than the air attacks were the continuous naval gunfire and artillery bombardments brought down on men, guns, and trenches, by Army spotter planes—constantly patrolling overhead.

THE NORTHERN ASSAULT

General Geiger knew the probable route of the Japanese retreat. He drew up a list of objectives across the island to seize all the enemy's strong points.

The jump-off for this drive north was 0630 on July 31. The 3rd Marine Division would be on the left, the 77th Infantry Division on the right—splitting the island down the middle. Marine zones would include the island capital of Agana, enemy airfields at Finegayan, Tiyan, and Tumon Bay's beachhead.

The 77th took Mount Santa Rosa, Mount Barrigada, and Yigo. The 1st Marine Brigade would relieve the 77th in the south and continue to patrol the southern half of Guam. As the attack gained momentum northward and the island widened, the 1st would join in the drive to the island's extreme north coast.

When the 3rd Division reached Ordot, in the center of their zone, the 3/21 Marines smashed into enemy troops and one of their pillboxes. Marines destroyed fifteen Japanese troops and two light tanks with M1s and bazookas.

The 3/3 Marines had the honor of liberating Agana. Riflemen entered the town ruins and tread carefully, sizing up dusty, stark building walls for snipers. A few enemy snipers emerged from behind concrete outcroppings before falling back into eternity. The Japanese in Agana were stragglers, wounded or foolish enough to stay. In one of the houses, a Marine opened the closet to reveal a Japanese officer with sword in hand. The Marine slammed the door, fired at it with his automatic rifle, and didn't even bother to look again. The majestic and beautiful Plaza de Espana was back in American hands less than twenty minutes after Marines entered the town. By noon, it was secured.

The 3rd Marines advanced along the Agana-Pago Road. At 1340 they caught up with the 21st Marines after several engagements with snipers, pillboxes, and tanks. By 1500, the 9th Marines on the division's right were across the road and had seized the remaining portion of the highway. It was a hard-surfaced road with two lanes crossing the island's midriff. The Agana-Pago Road was vital to liberating Guam.

After the historic rescue of the island's capital at Agana, the 3/3 Marines advanced with relative ease. Before nightfall, the battalion had seized over 1,500 yards of roads and trails needed to defend the strategic strong points of Barrigada and Finegayan.

General Turnage got close to the Tiyan Airfield and the village of San Antonio on August 1, but his advance was seriously slowed by mines. It took the steady hands and cool skill of the bomb disposal specialists of the 25th Naval Construction Battalion and the 19th Marine Engineers to reduce and remove those obstacles.

Many historians and those who were there consider taking the cross-island Agana-Paco Road a major factor in guaranteeing the northern advance's success. Its capture solved several logistical problems for the 77th. The Army division had no roads heading north and desperately needed a road to resupply their troops as they came down from the hills and cut their way through the jungle. Army front-line troops were running low on supplies—especially water. General Bruce promised his soldiers a hot breakfast as soon as the Marines would give him the road. Not long after, trucks were thick on the road, even while the Seabees and engineers enlarged and repaired it.

The 77th moved out at daylight on July 31. Enemy resistance to the Army advance was insignificant. In under two hours, the Army division had secured the cross-island road in their zones. They also rescued over 3,000 Guamanians at the Japanese detention camp in Asinan. Now unopposed, the 77th were across the Pago River. Residents of the area said the Japanese fled to Barrigada, where intelligence had expected the enemy to hide. The mountain was covered by a jungle, 650 feet high, and it dominated the area.

General Bruce ordered the 77th to capture Barrigada. They would keep contact with the 3rd Marine Division on the left and push through the village and then the one mile to seize Mount Barrigada. The village was a clearing fully swept with defensive machine-gun fire. In the same clearing was a much desired well. Capturing it meant everything to the thirsty troops.

On August 2 at 0630, General Bruce dispatched a dozen tanks of the 706th Tank Battalion to reconnoiter the area. As the tanks turned toward the village, the Japanese opened up with a surge of fire. The stubborn enemy defenders resisted and were determined to stop the assault companies from outflanking them. Heavy artillery support and repeated tank attacks netted only a few yards at a time, but the soldiers kept advancing. By August 4, the 77th Division finally held the village, or what was left of it, along with the precious well.

Captured documents and interviews with prisoners left little doubt that the 77th Division's major obstacle would be the heavily creviced, rugged jungle of Mount Santa Rosa. Seven miles northeast of Barrigada and close to the ocean on the east coast.

But first, well-armed enemy outposts blocking the way had to be destroyed. Yigo and Finegayan would be assaulted first. While each outpost promised a bloody battle and several casualties, General Geiger used the 77th to annihilate Yigo and then take Santa Rosa. The 3rd Marine Division would capture Finegayan and take the rest of northern Guam. He brought up General Shepherd's brigade to assist in the final drive. The 1/22 Marines would protect the force beachhead line and care for the Guamanians while still hunting down enemy stragglers in the south.

The 1/22 Marines aggressively sought out enemy holdouts. They also brought terrified Guamanians into friendly compounds and provide security for those who decided to remain in their homes and work their ranches. By August 2, Marine patrols approached Talofofo Bay on the southern coast. They found another 2,000 natives, still terrified of the Japanese, and directed them to a compound that promised safety and a small amount of comfort. In their own residential and farm areas, many Guamanians could still call upon this civil affairs section for protection, medicine, food, and shelter. This civil care was vital to the American occupation now that the island was once again under the American flag.

During the night of August 2, the 12th Marines delivered 750 rounds of harassing and interdictory fire onto the roads and trails that the division would encounter around Finegayan. At dawn, Marines moved in and passed Tinian Airfield. At 0700, they encountered a block at the crossroads approaching the Finegayan village. This terrain favored the Japanese with the excellent fields of fire. After the enemy position was finally overrun with tanks, Lieutenant Colonel Carey Randall said that these defenses were: "the toughest he had faced on Guam."

The battle for Finegayan was the last major battle for the 3rd Division on Guam. The Japanese made it a fight to remember. A 3rd Division armored reconnaissance patrol headed for Ritidian Point, on the northern tip of the island, ran into Japanese defenses. The enemy had dug in on the Finegayan trails and bristled with antitank weapons and artillery pointed at the patrol. Americans were bruised and surprised and did the Japanese some harm—but canceled their mission and withdrew.

The enemy was feisty at Finegayan. In a brave thrust, they dispatched two medium tanks skirting the crossroads of the 9th Marines at Junction 177. Nearly invulnerable to Marine fire, they shot up the area and got away. Another tank force rumbled down over a mortar barrage that seemed like the beginning of a counterattack. Marine artillery stalled the enemy effort, and Japanese tanks were driven off but survived to reappear another day.

LIBERATION OF GUAM

On August 4, new front lines and maneuvers were established to keep the pressure on General Obata and his remaining holdouts. During the afternoon, the brigade reached its northern assembly area, and General Shepherd set up his command post near the small town of San Antonio. In this final advance north, the brigade would be on the left with its inland flank less than a mile from the western beaches. The 3rd Division would advance in the center and deploy its units into a three-regiment front that would swerve to the east, taking in the whole northern end of the island and supporting the 77th Infantry Division.

The enemy defenders faced overwhelming odds. General Bruce's soldiers attacked Mount Santa Rosa and destroyed any remaining Japanese. The Army had priority of fire from air support, corps artillery, and naval gunfire.

The Marines also made strides to end the campaign. The 21st Marines progressed, while the 9th Marines kept running into a denser jungle. It was a tangled mess where tanks passed each other within fifteen feet without knowing where the other was. The division sped up its advance in battalion columns. By August 6, they'd advanced over 5,000 yards along the road to Ritidian Point. The end of the island and the end of the battle for Guam. That night, the 3rd Division made visual contact with the 77th—wherever the jungle would allow.

The Army Air Force bombing, Marine artillery, and naval shelling had been going on in enemy areas for days. Night fighters also supported the advance. Even in darkness, the enemy defenders had no protection or reprieve. By August 6, General Obata's defensive line across Guam was shattered and overrun. Only isolated pockets of enemy troops were left on the island.

American commanders still could not say when the fight for Guam would be over. The assault on Mount Santa Rosa began at noon on August 7. In the rumble of artillery and rattle of tanks, the 77th took Yigo, the gateway to Santa Rosa, and continued its wheeling maneuver. Tanks and infantry overran machine gun positions while bulldozers blazed trails. By the night of August 7, the 77th was dug into positions and ready for the final attack on the mountain. The Japanese counterattacks still did not come. The rapid American advance accompanied by heavy artillery likely stalled any enemy counterattack.

On August 8, the northern half of Mount Santa Rosa was in American hands, and troops moved to secure the rest of the mountain. By early afternoon, the Army reached the cliffs of the sea and looked right down into the ocean. The infantry had also completed an enveloping move by taking the northern slopes of Mount Santa Rosa.

Over 650 enemy bodies were found after the two-day battle. Estimates of enemy troops at Santa Rosa had been as high as 5,000. This meant enemy troops in significant numbers still infested the jungle terrain everywhere on Guam. Worse, several enemy tanks were unaccounted for. Japanese survivors from the battle drifted into the 9th Marines' lines on the Army flank and slowed the regiment's advance. Sharp-eyed Marines noted significant enemy movement at a hill in the Army's zone—General Obata's command post.

The 3rd Marines on the left advanced through light enemy opposition. A twenty-man roadblock held up the Marines but was quickly destroyed. After searching through a corridor, Marines found the bodies of thirty dead Guamanians. They were beheaded.

The brigade had it easier on the far west flank. They encountered light resistance and advanced along a fairly good trail. On August 8, the 22nd Marines finally reached Ritidian Point at the islands' northernmost tip. Moving along a twisted cliff trail to the beach, Marines encountered less than aggressive Japanese defenses, which they quickly overran. The 1st Marine Brigade had the honor of being first to reach both the southernmost point of the island and Guam's northernmost tip at Ritidian Point.

Marines patrolled the area they occupied but found few Japanese. General Geiger ordered the naval gunfire to be reduced, while the Saipan-based P-47s made their last bombing and strafing runs at Ritidian Point. The 22nd Marines scoured the cliffs below and along the beaches searching for enemy caves. On August 9, at 1800, General Shepherd declared all organized resistance had ceased in his zone.

But it wasn't that easy for the 3rd Marines. On August 9, near Tarague, the regiment was hit by an enemy tank and mortar attack. Marine antitank grenades and bazooka rockets were wet and ineffective against the enemy assault. The Japanese soldiers blazed away with impunity before ducking back into the woods. When Major Bill Culpepper, commanding the 2nd Battalion, counted heads, he noted his Marines hadn't suffered one-single-casualty.

The 9th Marines had advanced to Pati Point on the northeastern tip of the island. Intelligence reported that 2,000 Japanese troops were held up at Savana Grand in a wild tract of jungle and coconut trees and high grass near the coast. Command did not want to risk any casualties so close to the campaign's end and called in artillery—2,275 rounds. Japanese survivors were routed, and either killed or taken prisoner.

The final American positions were formed along the coast, and by nightfall on August 8, the 9th Marines waved to the soldiers of the 77th patrolling to their south.

General Geiger wanted the pocket of enemy tanks destroyed before he would declare Guam secure. This had to be completed by the 10th, because Admiral Nimitz was scheduled to arrive on a visit. Major Culpepper's 2/3 Marines were tasked with finding and eliminating the remaining enemy tanks. At 0730, Culpepper's battalion and a platoon of American Sherman tanks found two enemy medium tanks firing 400 yards up the trail from the Marines. The Shermans left their counterparts hunks of burning metal when they were finished. Seven more enemy medium tanks were abandoned. The remaining Japanese troops withdrew to the cliffs and were destroyed.

On August 10 at 1130, after hearing the remaining Japanese tanks were destroyed, General Geiger declared all organized resistance on Guam over. A great day for the Guamanians—their island was theirs again.

This was also the end for General Obata. On the morning of August 11, when the general knew his headquarters had been discovered, and the enemy was coming for him, he signaled a message to the Emperor: "We continue this desperate battle. We now have only our bare hands to fight with. The holding of Guam is now hopeless. Our souls will defend the island to the very end. I am overwhelmed with sorrow for the families of the many slain officers and men. I pray for the prosperity of the Empire."

The 77th made its assault on Obata's headquarters, supported by demolition squads and tanks. Enemy defenders killed seven Americans and wounded fifteen others before they were destroyed and buried in the rubble of blown caves and emplacements. It is still unclear if General Obata committed suicide or was killed in those last hours of the battle for Guam.

General Henry Larsen assumed command of Guam on August 15. Under him were the forces of the 3rd Marine Division to continue the mopping up.

A terrible cost for the Japanese on Guam was the already counted 10,970 bodies. And there were still supposedly 10,000 more Japanese on the island. At first, some of the enemy defenders fought in staged ambushes, and some sniped at Americans, but soon the remaining Japanese sought only one thing—food. Most others fled when encountered. The Japanese had no central command. They died of dysentery, starved, became too weak to run, and finally blew themselves up with the one precious grenade they saved to take their own lives. American patrols were aggressive in killing and capturing near eighty Japanese sailors and soldiers a day. A few daring Japanese snuck into Marine food storage areas at night.

In addition to the battlefield casualties, over 8,800 Japanese were captured or killed on Guam between August 1944 and the end of the war on August 1945.

The twenty-one-day Guam campaign ended on August 10. Marine units of the III Amphibious Corps reported 5,308 wounded and 1,567 men killed in action. The 77th Division's casualties were 843, with 177 soldiers killed.

The Marines and Army ran a closely-knit team in the liberation of Guam. General Holland Smith referred to General Bruce's troops as "the 77th Marines."

According to Major Aplington, a battalion commander in the 3rd Marines: "The fatigues are so different from our herringbone utilities and their olive drab ponchos so different from us. But there is no doubt the 77th were good men to have alongside us in a fight, and as a result, we refer to them as the 77th Marine Division."

On August 10, on the same busy day, only hours after Major Culpepper's battalion knocked out the last of the Japanese tanks. The *Indianapolis* steamed into Apra Harbor with Marine Commandant Alexander Vandergrift on board accompanying Admiral Nimitz. On August 15, Nimitz directed his forward headquarters be established on Guam, and from there he directed the rest of the Pacific War.

Soon after, from airfields on Guam and Tinian, B-29s blasted the Japanese home islands. While there was still more hard fighting to come, Peleliu, Iwo Jima, and Okinawa, the end of the war was less than one year away.

OPERATION STALEMATE

1944 BATTLE FOR PELELIU

SEIZING "THE POINT"

On September 15, 1944, five infantry battalions of the 1st Marine Division embarked in amphibian tractors. They clambered across 700 yards of coral reef to smash into the island of Peleliu.

Marines in the amphibian tractors (LVTs) were told the operation would be tough but quick. A devastating amount of naval gunfire had been unleashed before their landing.

The 1st Division Marines still had grim images of their sister division, the 2nd's bloody attack across the reefs at Tarawa—two months earlier. But the 1st Division Marines peered over the gunwales of their landing craft and saw an incredible scene of blasted and churned earth along the shore.

Geysers of smoke and dust caused by exploding bombs and large-caliber naval shells gave the Marine's hope. Maybe the enemy would become quick casualties from the pre-landing bombardment. Or at least, they'd be too stunned to react and defend against the hundreds of Marines storming the beach.

Ahead of the Marines were waves of armored amphibian tractors mounted with 75mm howitzers. They were tasked to assault any surviving enemy strongpoints or weapons on the beach before the Marines landed. Ahead of these armored tractors, naval gunfire was lifted toward deeper, more dug-in targets. Navy fighter aircraft strafed north and south along the length of the beach defenses—parallel to the assault waves. Their mission was to keep the enemy defenders subdued and intimidated on the beach as the Marines closed in.

Naval gunfire was shifted to target the ridge northeast of the landing beaches and used to blind enemy observation and limit Japanese fire on the landing waves. This ridge would later be known as the Umurbrogol Pocket (or just the Pocket) and was one of two deadly unknowns to command planners.

The other unknown was the natural traits of the Pocket. Aerial images showed it as a gently rounded north-south hill that commanded the landing beaches 3,000 yards distant. From these early images, this elevated terrain was camouflaged in jungle scrub, almost entirely unaffected from the preparatory bombardment and artillery fire directed at it.

But instead of a gently rounded hill, the Pocket was a complex system of sharply uplifted coral knobs, ridges, valleys, and sinkholes. It rose 300 feet above the island and offered superb positions for tunnels and cave defenses. The enemy had made most of what this terrain provided during their extensive occupation and defensive preparations before the Allied assault.

Another problematic issue for the Marines was the plan developed by Colonel Nakagawa, the Japanese commander of the force on Peleliu and his superior, General Inoue on Koror Island. The Japanese defense tactics had changed considerably from their defeats on Guadalcanal and Cape Gloucester.

Instead of depending on spiritual superiority, Japanese defenders would use their *bushido* spirit and *banzai* tactics to throw Allied troops back into the sea. Japanese forces would delay and try to bleed attacking Marines as long as possible. The enemy planned to combine the devilish terrain with a resolute discipline. Japanese soldiers would only relinquish Peleliu at a horrible price in blood to the Marine invasion. This wicked surprise marked a new and vital change to Japanese defensive tactics compared to what they employed earlier in the war.

Nothing during the trip to the beach revealed any elements of the revised Japanese tactical plan. They bounced across a mile of coral fronting the landing beaches. Amphibian tractors passed several hundred mines intended to destroy any craft approaching or running over them. These mines were aerial bombs detonated by wire control from observation points on shore. But the preliminary bombardment had disrupted the wire controls and the mines did little to slow or destroy any assaulting tractors.

As the LVTs neared the beaches, they came under fire from mortars and artillery. This fire against moving targets generated more anxiety than damage, as only a few vehicles were lost. But this fire did show that the preliminary bombardment had not eliminated the enemy's fire capability. Even more disturbing was when the leading waves of LVTs nearing the beaches were hit by heavy artillery and anti-boat gunfire from concealed bunkers on the north and south flanking points.

Enemy defenses on White Beach 1 were especially deadly and effective. The 3/1 Marines under Colonel Steve Sabol were in a savage beach fight with no means of communication to understand the situation. Japanese guns knocked out several amphibian tractors carrying essential control personnel and equipment.

The mission of seizing "The Point" had been given to Captain George Hunt (a decorated veteran of the New Britain and Guadalcanal campaigns). Hunt developed his plans, which entailed specific assignments for each element of his company. These plans were rehearsed until every Marine knew his role and how it fit into the company's strategy.

H-hour on D-Day brought heavier than expected casualties. One platoon was pinned down all day in beach fighting. Survivors wheeled left as planned, onto the flanking point. While they advanced, they pressed their assault on several enemy defensive emplacements. Pillboxes and casements were carpeted with small arms fire, and smoke from demolitions and grenades.

The climax came when a rifle grenade hit the gun muzzle and ricocheted into a casement, setting off explosions and flames. Enemy defenders ran out of the rear of the block house with their clothes on fire and ammunition exploding in their belts. Marines waited in anticipation of the enemy's flight and cut them down with small arms fire as they burned alive.

Captain Hunt's Marines held the Point, but his company was reduced to platoon strength with no other nearby units. Sketchy radio communications got through to bring in supporting fire and a desperately needed resupply. One LVT made it to the beach before dark with mortar shells, grenades, and water—evacuating casualties as it departed. This ammunition made all the difference in that night's brutal struggle against a determined enemy's attempt to recapture the Point.

* * *

The next afternoon, Colonel Raymond Davis of the 1/1 Marines moved his Company B to establish contact with Captain Hunt to help hold the desperately contested positions. Hunt's company regained the platoon survivors that were pinned down on the beach fight during the day.

The newly reinforced company recovered their artillery and naval gunfire communications, which proved critical during the second night. That evening the enemy counterattacked the Marines at the Point. The Japanese were narrowly defeated. By midmorning, survivors of the two Marine companies had secured the Point and looked out on 500 dead Japanese soldiers.

On the right of Colonel "Chesty" Puller's struggling 3rd Battalion, Colonel Russell Honsowetz, commanding the 2nd Battalion, took artillery, mortar, and machine-gun fire from still effective enemy beach defenders during their landing.

The 5th Marines' two assault battalions also took heavy enemy fire as they fought through the beach defenses toward the clearing's edge, looking out eastward over the airfield.

On the right flank, the 3/7 Marines crossed in front of an imposing defensive fortification flanking the beach. Luckily, it wasn't as close as the Point position and did not suffer heavy damage. But its enfilading fire, along with natural obstructions on the beach, caused Company K to veer off their planned landing and end up out of position and out of contact. After the confused and delayed battalion regrouped, they used a line of large anti-tank ditches to guide their eastward advance.

Any further delay would be a disaster to the division. Momentum was the key to success. The divisional plan on the right called for the 7th Marines to land two battalions in a column on Orange Beach 3. As the 3/7 advanced, it would be followed by the 1/7. These units would tie into the right flank and attack southeast on the beach.

After a bloody hour of fighting, all five battalions were ashore. The closer each battalion got to the Pocket, the more tenuous its hold was on the shallow beachhead. For another two hours, three more of the division's four remaining battalions joined the attack and pressed the momentum that General Rupertus had ordered.

Colonel Puller landed his forward command group close behind the 3/1 Marines. He was ready to fight, even if his location would deny him the best position for supporting fire. With reduced communications and inadequate numbers of LVTs to follow in waves, he struggled to improve his regiment's situation.

His left flank had two platoons desperately struggling to gain control of the Point. Puller landed the 1st Battalion behind the 3/1 to reinforce the fight for the left flank but was hindered by multiple losses in the LVTs. The 1st Battalion companies had to be landed singly and committed piecemeal into the action.

On the regiment's right flank, the 2/1 Marines recaptured the west edges of the scrub, looking out to the airfield.

In the beachhead's southern sector, the 1/7 Marines were delayed by the heavy LVT losses. This successful early opposition was felt throughout the rest of the day. Most of the 1/7 eventually landed on the correct beach, but many Marines were driven leftward from heavy enemy fire and landed in the 5th Marines' zone.

This caused the 1/7 to join in with the 3/7 and advance east to assault prepared enemy positions.

The battle raged with heavy opposition from both east and south. In the midafternoon, Marines ran into a blockhouse (supposedly destroyed by pre-landing naval gunfire) but had not been touched and put up a strong resistance.

The cost in Marine lives and lost momentum by having to assault these heavily defended blockhouses was harsh and unnecessary.

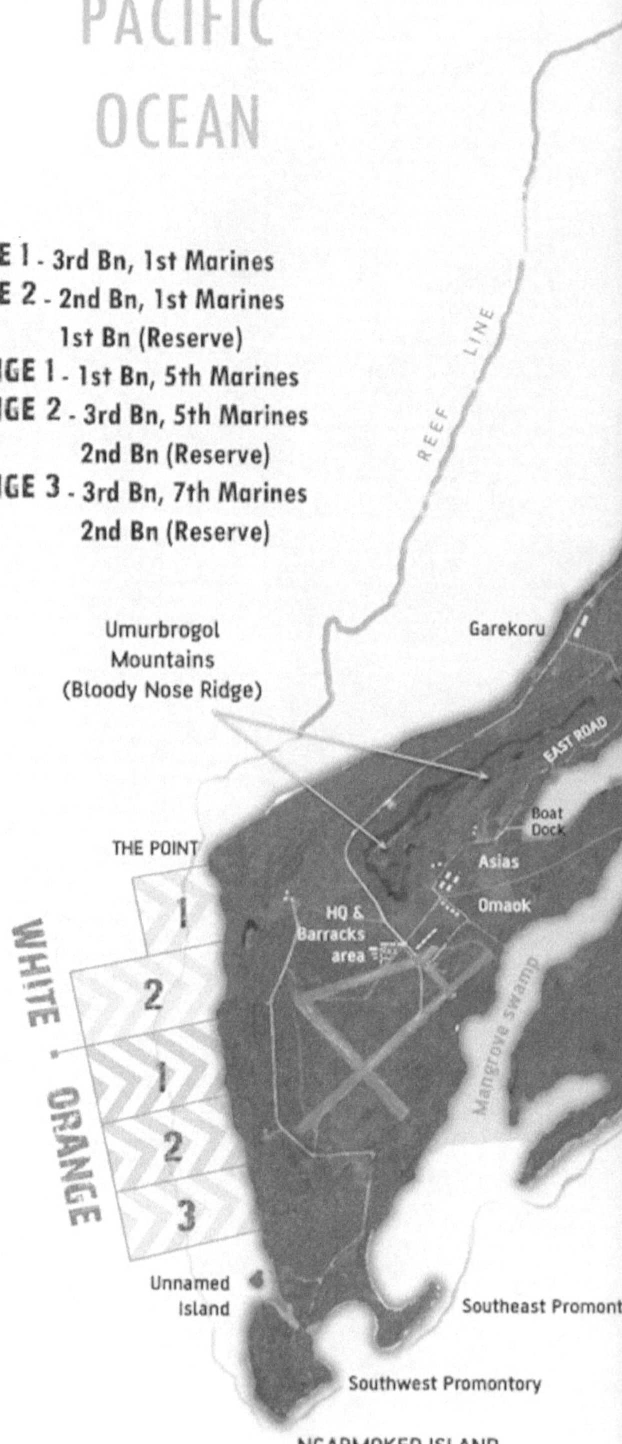

PACIFIC OCEAN
WHITE 1 - 3rd Bn, 1st Marines
WHITE 2 - 2nd Bn, 1st Marines
1st Bn (Reserve)
ORANGE 1 - 1st Bn, 5th Marines
ORANGE 2 - 3rd Bn, 5th Marines
2nd Bn (Reserve)
ORANGE 3 - 3rd Bn, 7th Marines
2nd Bn (Reserve)
REEF LINE
Umurbrogol Mountains (Bloody Nose Ridge)
Garekoru
EAST ROAD
Boat Dock
Asias
Omaok
THE POINT
HQ & Barracks area
1
2
WHITE
ORANGE
1
2
3
Mangrove Swamp
Unnamed Island
Southeast Promontory
Southwest Promontory
NGARMOKED ISLAND

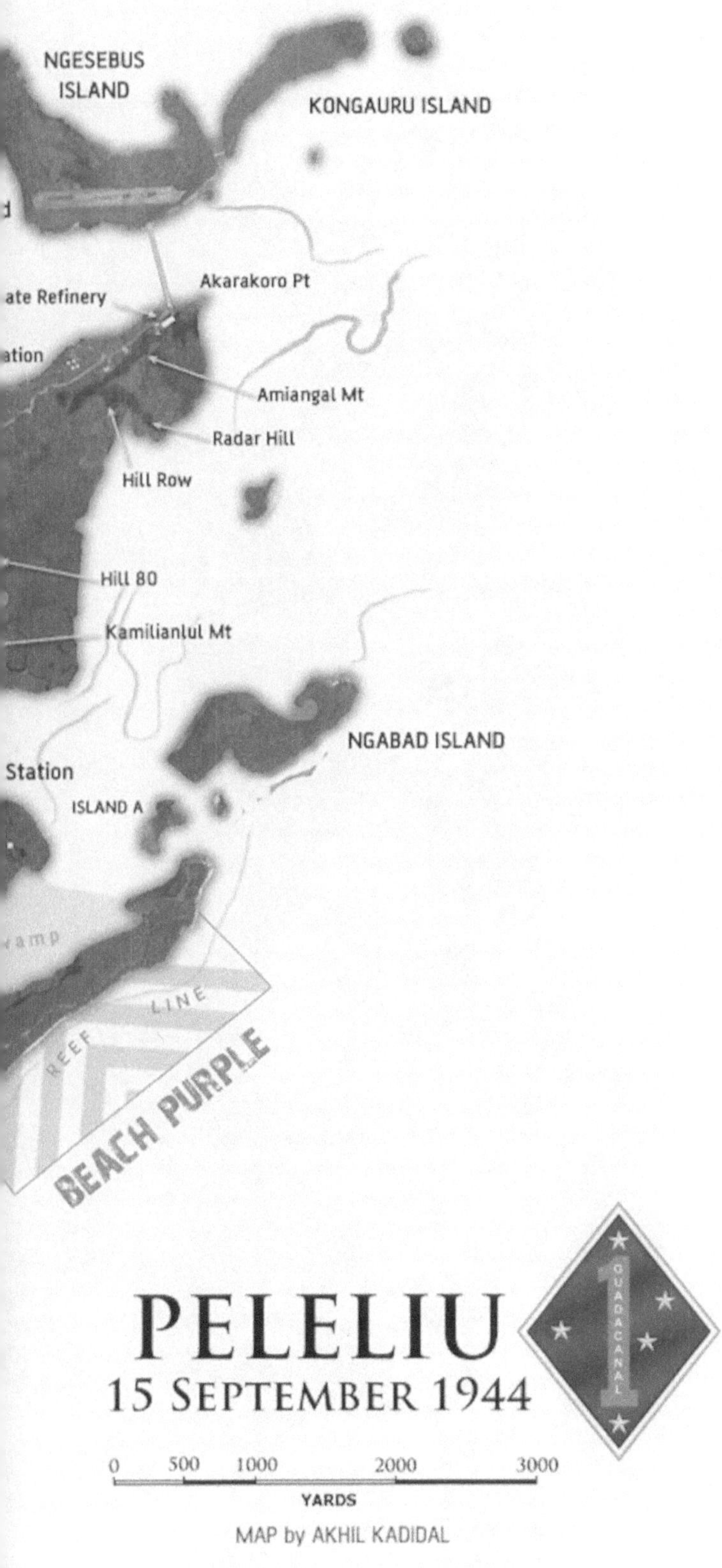

NGESEBUS
ISLAND
KONGAURU ISLAND
ate Refinery
Akarakoro Pt
ation
Amiangal Mt
Radar Hill
Hill Row
Hill 80
Kamilianlul Mt
NGABAD ISLAND
Station
ISLAND A
REEF LINE
BEACH PURPLE
PELELIU
15 SEPTEMBER 1944
GUADACANAL
1
0   500   1000   2000   3000
YARDS
MAP by AKHIL KADIDAL

THE JAPANESE DEFENDERS

General Sadae Inoue, a fifth-generation warrior with a robust military reputation, commanded the *14th Infantry Division.* He'd just arrived from the *Kwangtung Army* in China. In March 1944, Inoue met Japanese Premier Tojo in Tokyo to discuss the war.

Tojo decided Japan could no longer hold the Palaus against the Allied naval dominance in the Western Pacific. Tojo gave General Inoue command of all Japanese forces in the Palaus. His orders: take the *14th Infantry* and kill Americans while denying its use to the Allies for as long as possible. He ordered Inoue to sell the Palaus at the highest possible cost in blood and time.

As the enemy sailed for the Palaus, Inoue flew ahead and surveyed his new locale for two days before deciding Peleliu was the key to his defense. The earlier Task Force 58 strikes confirmed his decision. Peleliu had been under the administrative command of a rear admiral. The admiral used his forces to build blockhouses and reinforced concrete structures above ground while improving the existing caves and tunnels under Peleliu's rich natural camouflage of jungle, scrub, and vines.

In these underground installations, the admiral and his troops survived the March attacks from Task Force 58. The above-ground structures and planes were demolished. when the Japanese emerged, they repaired what they could with a focus on the underground installations. Together with Korean labor troops, their numbers swelled to 7,000 (most lacking training and leadership for any infantry action).

Colonel Nakagawa arrived on Peleliu with his *2nd Infantry Regiment*—a 6,500-man reinforced regiment. They were veterans from the war in China and had two dozen 75mm artillery pieces, a dozen tanks, fifteen 81mm heavy mortars, over a hundred .50-caliber machine guns, and thirty dual-purpose anti-aircraft guns. There were many heavy 141mm mortars and naval anti-aircraft guns already on the island.

Colonel Nakagawa had been awarded nine medals for his leadership against the Chinese. His regiment was regarded as elite veterans within the Japanese Army.

Immediately upon arriving, Nakagawa reconnoitered his battle position from the ground and air. He identified the western beaches (the White and Orange Beaches) as the most likely landing sites. Nakagawa ordered his troops to dig in and construct beach defenses. But a conflict arose when the senior naval officer, Admiral Itou, resented taking orders from a junior army officer.

From Koror, General Inoue sent General Murai to Peleliu. Murai assumed command and maintained a liaison with Nakagawa. Murai was a highly regarded, personal representative of General Inoue and considered senior to the admiral.

Murai left the mission firmly in Nakagawa's hands. Throughout the campaign, Nakagawa exercised operational control and was assisted and counseled but not commanded by General Murai.

Nakagawa fully understood his objective and the situation and firepower the Allies possessed. He turned his attention to making the fullest use of his primary advantage—the terrain. Nakagawa deployed and installed his forces to inflict all possible damage and casualties at the landing. Then his troops would defend in-depth to the last man. Peleliu offered a vertical and a horizontal dimension to its defense.

Nakagawa registered artillery and mortars over the width and depth of the reef on both eastern and western beaches. With a planned heavy concentration along the fringe of the western reef, he expected the Allies need to transfer follow-on waves from landing craft to the reef crossing amphibian vehicles. He registered weapons from the water's edge to subject landing troops to a hellish hail of fire. Offshore, he laid over 500 wire-controlled mines.

Nakagawa ordered the construction of beach obstacles using logs and rails and ordered multiple anti-tank ditches dug. He put troops in machine-gun and mortar pits along the inland from the beaches supported by all available barbed wire. He constructed concrete emplacements to shelter and conceal anti-tank and anti-boat artillery on the north and south beaches.

Inland, he used the already built blockhouses with adjacent rein-forced buildings. He made them into mutually supporting defensive complexes and added communication lines in the trenches.

Nakagawa believed the western beaches were the most probable route of attack. But he did not leave the southern and eastern beaches undefended. He committed one battalion on each beach to organize defenses. The eastern beaches were thoroughly prepared with contingents of defenders to move into central Peleliu if the battle expanded from the west as he expected.

Colonel Nakagawa assigned 600 infantry and artillery to defend Ngesebus and 1,100 Naval personnel to defend northern Peleliu. The only troops not under his command were the 1,500 defenders on Angaur.

The central part of his force and effort was committed to the 500 tunnels, caves, and firing embrasures in the coral ridges of central Peleliu. The naval units' prior extensive tunneling into lime-stone ridges rendered the occupants mainly immune to any Allied bombardments. Only an occasional lucky hit in the cave's mouth or a point-blank direct fire could damage the hidden defenses and the enemy troops.

Tunnels were designed for several purposes: command centers, hospitals, barracks, storage, ammunition dumps, and cooking areas with freshwater springs and basins—and of course, firing embrasures. He added elaborate concealment and protective devices including a few sliding steel doors.

Nakagawa expected an intense pre-landing bombardment. He believed his troops would endure it and carry out their mission of delaying and bleeding the Allies for as long as possible before Peleliu fell.

General Inoue was busy with his troops on Koror. He prepared for expected Allied attacks against Babelthuap. The Allied plan, Operation Stalemate, also called for the invasion of Babelthuap. As the expected invasion drew closer, Inoue made a statement to his troops, reflecting Tojo's instructions to bleed and delay the American forces. He pointed out the necessity to expect and endure the naval bombardment and how to use terrain to inflict casualties on the attacking force.

General Inoue said: "Dying and losing the territory to the enemy would contribute to opening a new phase of the war. We are ready to die honorably."

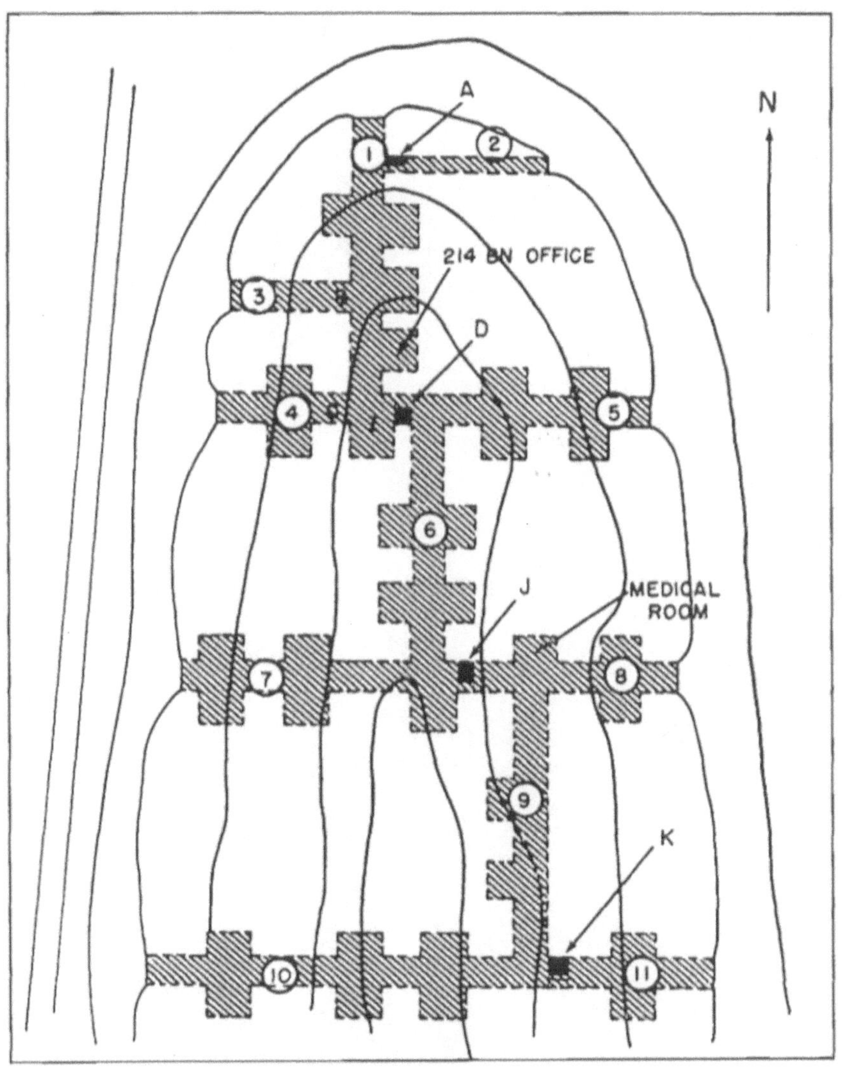

Map of most elaborate tunnel system on Peleliu

D-DAY CENTER ASSAULT

The 1st Marines fought to secure the left flank. The 7th Marines battled to isolate and reduce enemy defenses on the southern end of Peleliu. The 5th Marines were tasked with driving across the airfield to cut the island in half, reorient north, and secure the island's eastern half.

The 2/5 Marines under Major Gordon Gayle landed on Orange Beach 2 and advanced east through scrub jungle and dunes.

They moved in and out of the anti-tank barrier to the west edge of the clearing surrounding the airfield.

Gayle's battalion passed through the lines of the 3/5 Marines and attacked scattered resistance through the scrub in dugouts and bomb shelters near the southern end of the airfield. The 3rd Battalion's mission was to clear that scrub and maintain contact with the 3/7 Marines on the right flank, while the 2/5 Marines advanced across the open area to reach the far side of the island.

The 2/5 Marines advanced in the center and right, fighting entirely across the island by midafternoon. They kept contact with the 1/5 Marines and moved to reorient their attack northward.

* * *

The Japanese anti-tank ditch along the center and right of the Orange Beaches was notable because of the several command posts along its length.

The 1st Tank Battalion's M-48A1 Shermans—a third of which were left behind at the last moment—finally crossed the reef. These tanks had developed special reef-crossing maneuvers in anticipation of terrain obstacles.

Moving the fire and logistical support onto the beach was challenging and under direct observation from Japanese observers. This was an inescapable risk because of Peleliu's terrain. As long as the enemy had observation posts atop the Umurbrogol Point over the airfield and beach—there was no alternative but to advance rapidly and coordinate fire support.

The rapid beach advance caused heavy casualties. General Rupertus' concern for early momentum seemed to be correct. Marines on the left flank assaulted the foot of the Pocket's ridges and swiftly got to the crest. In the center, the 5th Marines advanced and secured all likely routes to outflank the Pocket. In the south, the 7th Marines destroyed the now cut-off forces before they could regroup and join the fight in central Peleliu.

The 5th Marines moved across the airfield to the western edge of the lagoon. They separated the airfield area from the eastern peninsula. They created a line of attacking Marines across the eastern and northern part of the island, believed to be the center of the enemy's strength.

Colonel Hanneken's 7th Marines pushed south and divided the Japanese forces. Hanneken's troops were fully engaged and mostly concealed against enemy observation.

It was becoming clear that the D-Day line objectives would not be met in either the north or south. General Rupertus was alarmed by the loss of his momentum, and he ordered the 2/7 (his last uncommitted infantry battalion), under Colonel Spencer Berger, into the fight. No commander onshore felt a need for the 2/7 Marines. Colonel Hanneken cleared an assembly area for them where they wouldn't be in the way.

General Rupertus was now fully committed. He told his staff that he'd "shot his bolt." On the crowded beachhead, more troops were not needed—they needed more room to maneuver them and more artillery.

Rupertus decided to land himself and the key elements of his command group onshore. His chief of staff, Colonel John Selden, convinced the general to stay on the flagship because it was too dangerous. So Rupertus ordered Colonel Selden ashore.

The shortage of LVTs stalled the timely landing of the following waves. Neither Selden's small command post group nor Berger's 2/7 Marines could get past the transfer line. The landing craft had to return to the ships, despite their orders to land.

At 1700, Colonel Nakagawa launched his counterattack. Marine commanders had been alerted to the Japanese capability to make an armored attack on D-Day and were well prepared. The enemy assault came from north of the airfield and headed south across the 1st Marines' line on the eastern edge of the airfield clearing.

This attack went directly into the 5th Marines' sector, where the 1/5 was dug in across the southern area of the airfield. Marines opened up on the enemy attackers' infantry and tanks. A bazooka gunner in front hit two tanks. The CO of the 1/5 Marines had his tanks in defilade behind the front lines. They fired on the enemy armor, running through the front lines as they advanced. The Marines' lines held, and they fired on the enemy infantry and tanks with all available weapons.

Major John Gustafson of the 2/5 was in the forward command post halfway across the airfield and had his tank platoon close at hand. While the enemy had not yet come into his zone, he launched a platoon of tanks into the fight. In minutes it was over. The enemy tanks were destroyed, and the Japanese infantry was ripped apart.

While Colonel Nakagawa's attack was bold, it was a failure. Even where the Japanese tanks broke through Allied lines, the Marines did not retreat. Instead, all anti-tank fire of every caliber concentrated on the enemy armor. Japanese light tanks were blown apart into pieces on the battlefield. Over one hundred were destroyed, although that figure may be exaggerated because of the amount of fire directed their way. Each Marine anti-tank gunner and grenadier thought they destroyed each tank they fired at and reported it that way.

* * *

With the Japanese counterattack repulsed and the enemy in shambles, Marines resumed their attack. They moved north along the eastern half of the airfield and advanced halfway up the length of the clearing before stopping to re-organize for the night. This was the farthest advance of the day over favorable terrain on the division's front. This advance provided the needed space for logistics and artillery deployment to support the next day's attack.

But this quick advance left a hole in the right flank. The 3/5 Marines were supposed to keep contact with the north-facing 2/5. But 3/5 command and control had been destroyed. The battalion's XO, Major Robert Ash, was killed earlier in the day from a direct hit into his LVT.

When the Japanese attack started, a mortar barrage hit the 3/5 command post in the anti-tank ditch and killed several staff officers and caused the evacuation of the battalion commander. At 1700, the 3/5 Marine companies weren't in contact with each other—nor their battalions.

The 5th Marines CO ordered his XO, Colonel Lewis Walt, to take command of the 3/5 and redeploy them in between the gap of the 5th and 7th Marines. Walt moved the 2nd Battalion's reserve company to his right flank in a tie-in position to form a more continuous regimental line. By 2200, he came under several sharp counterattacks from central and southern defenders throughout the night.

Enemy attacks came from the north and south. None had any significant success but were persistent enough to require an ammunition resupply. At dawn, dozens of Japanese bodies laid ripped to pieces north of the Marine lines.

Elsewhere across the front, there were more menacing night counterattacks. None drove the Marines back or penetrated Allied lines in significant strength.

In the south, the 7th Marines expected substantial night attacks from the enemy battalion opposing them. Marines were dug in and in strength. They had communications to call in fire support, including naval gunfire and star shell illumination—they easily turned back the sporadic enemy attacks.

At the end of the first twelve hours ashore, the 1st Marine Division held its beachhead across their projected front. Marine positions were strong everywhere except on the extreme left flank. General Smith, from his forward command post had communication with all three regimental commanders. The report he received from Colonel Puller was not a realistic assessment of the 1st Marines' weak hold on the Point. This was because of Colonel Puller's own limited information.

Besides all three infantry regiments, the 1st Division had three battalions of light artillery emplaced onshore. All thirty tanks were also now onshore. The shore party was operating on the beach under sporadic enemy fire and full daylight observation. The division was preparing to press their advance on D +1. Their objective was to capture the commanding crests on the left, advance farther into the center, and destroy isolated enemy defenders in the south.

By the end of the day, at least two colonels on Peleliu had misleading information about their situations and gave inaccurate reports to their superiors. When General Smith finally got a telephone wire into the 1st Marines' command post, he was told the regiment had secured the beachhead and was on the objective line. He was not told about the gaps in his lines nor of the gravity of the

1st Division's struggle on the Point—where thirty-eight Marines battled to keep the position.

Colonel Nakagawa reported that the Marines' landings attempt had been routed. He also reported that his brave counterattack had thrown the Marines into the sea.

THE UMURBROGOL POCKET

General Rupertus was irritated that after his failed efforts to land, his division reserve into the southern sector of the beachhead. Now he was informed that his northern sector—on the extreme left flank —needed reinforcements. Rupertus ordered the 2/7 into Colonel Puller's sector to assist.

Division headquarters afloat had reported the Marine D-Day casualties had exceeded 1,100, of which 210 Marines were killed in action. While not a substantial percentage of the total divisional strength, this number threatened the overall cutting-edge strength. Most of those 1,100 casualties were from each of the division's nine infantry battalions (with the exception of the center). General Rupertus was still not on the O-1 objective line—the first of his eight planned phase lines.

Rupertus had inaccurate information about the 1st Marines' situation. The general was determined to get ashore and see what he could do to reignite the lost momentum. He had a broken ankle from a pre-assault training exercise. His foot was in a cast, but his gimpy leg dragging in a sandy trench would not hold him back from seeing the situation on Peleliu for himself.

* * *

On Colonel Nakagawa's side, he saw a different situation from his high ground because of the incredible reports being sent out from his headquarters. The Marine landing force had *not* been routed. He watched while a division of Marines deployed across two miles of beach. While the Marines had been punished on D-Day, they were still in the fight.

Nakagawa predicted the next assault would be preceded by a hailstorm of naval artillery, gunfire, and aerial bombardments. Also, that they'd be supported by the US tanks that annihilated the Japanese armor on D-Day.

In Nakagawa's D-Day counterattack, he lost one of his five infantry battalions.

Across Peleliu, he lost hundreds of beach defenders in fighting across the front, and in futile night attacks. Still, he had several thousand courageous, well-armed and well-trained soldiers ready to fight and die for the empire. They were deployed through strong defensive complexes and fortifications, with abundant underground support facilities. Nakagawa's troops were determined to kill as many Marines as they could before they fell.

Colonel Nakagawa had the terrain advantage. He focused his defensive strategy around the occupation and organization of that terrain. Until he was driven from the commanding crests of the Point, he still had a dominant position. He could observe and direct hidden fire on the attackers while his forces were largely invisible to the Marines and their fire superiority. Continuing to hold this terrain was a key component of his overall defensive strategy.

The Marines were assaulting fortified positions, and precise fire preparations were needed. Marines on the left flank were under extreme pressure to advance rapidly, sacrificing speed for careful preparation. General Rupertus understood that enemy weapons and observation dominated the Marine position and troops were getting picked off at the enemy's leisure. Rupertus' concern for momentum was a priority and would save Marine lives.

The rapid advance burden was on the 1st Marines—on the left flank—and on the 5th in the airfield area. In the south, the 7th Marines already held the edge of the airfield's terrain. The scrub jungle screened the regiment from enemy observation.

Colonel "Chesty" Puller's 1st Marines had suffered the most

casualties on D-Day. They fought through the most formidable terrain and assaulted the toughest positions. They had to attack and relieve Company K of the 3/1 on the Point and then assault the Pocket ridges north to south.

Puller's Marines (aided by the 2/1) swung leftward and secured the built-up area between the airfield in the ridges. When Puller was at the foot of the cliffs, his Marines fought in a savage, scratch and scramble attack against the enemy troops in the ridges.

Puller closed the gaps on his left flank and swung his entire regiment north. With the help of the 3/1, he reinforced Company K on the Point. Then he moved north, keeping his left on the beach and his right close to the West Road, along the foot of the Pocket. While the terrain allowed for tank support, maneuverability was tight, and hard fighting was involved.

The rapid rate of movement along the boundary and the more open zone created a pressing need for reserves. Tactically, it was necessary to press east into and over the rough terrain and destroy enemy defenses. That job was given to the 1st and 2nd Battalions of the 1st Marines and the 2nd Battalion of the 7th Marines. But more troops were still needed to move north and encircle the rugged landscape of the Umurbrogol Pocket area. By September 17, reserves were needed along the 1st Division's western (left) advance, but neither division nor III Amphibious Corps had reserves.

The 3/1 Marines battled up easier terrain on the left flank. In the center, the 1/1 Marines advanced between the coral ridge and an open flat zone. One of their early surprises, as they approached the foot of the ridge area, was another enemy blockhouse. Admiral Oldendorf had reported that blockhouse destroyed from pre-landing naval gunfire, but the Marines who first encountered it reported the enemy placement as "not even having a mark on it."

This blockhouse was part of an impressive defensive complex. It was connected and supported by a web of adjacent emplacements and pillboxes. It had four-foot-thick walls of reinforced concrete. The naval gunfire support team from the USS *Mississippi* was called on to help. They annihilated the entire complex. The 1/1 Marines advanced again until running into the far more challenging

Japanese ridge defense systems. Major Davis, in command of the 1/1 Marines (later to earn a Medal of Honor in Korea) said the attack into and along the ridges: "was the most difficult assignment I'd ever been tasked with."

All three of the 1st Marines' Battalions battled beside each other onto the Pocket and its wicked, cave-filled coral ridges. The initial reserve, the 2/7 Marines, was assigned to the 1st Marines and immediately thrown into the fight. Colonel Puller fed companies into the battle piecemeal. Shortly afterward, the 2/7 took the central zone of action between the 1st and 2nd Marine Battalions.

The 1st Marines continued to assault the stubborn enemy defenders in their underground caves and fortifications. Every new advance opened the Marines to new fire from the incredible number of cliffs and ridges and concealed positions in the caves above and below the newly won ground.

Nothing exemplified this tactical dilemma better than the September 19 seizure and withdrawal from Hill 100. This ridge bordered the Horseshoe Valley on the eastern limit of the Pocket. The 2/1 Marines landed with 240 Marines. Now they had only 90 Marines left when they were ordered to take Hill 100. The Japanese called it East Mountain (Higashiyama).

Marines were at first supported by tanks but lost that support when the leading two tanks slipped off the approach causeway. The Marines continued with only mortar support into the face of heavy machine gun and mortar fire. When the Marines reached the summit at twilight, they discovered the ridge's northeast extension continued to even higher ground, where Japanese troops poured fire on the hill.

Just as threatening was fire from enemy caves on the parallel ridge to the west—known as Five Brothers. Into the setting darkness, Marines supported by heavy mortars hung on. Throughout the night, a series of enemy counterattacks on the ridge top were turned back. Marines repulsed them with mortars and hand-to-hand brawls, knives, and rifles. Marines even threw rocks when their grenade supplies ran low.

Marines were still clinging to the ridge-top when dawn broke. Only eight Marines were left. The remaining Marines, under the command of Captain Everett Pope, withdrew and successfully evacuated their wounded. The dead were left behind on the ridge until October 3, when the ridge was finally captured for good. Another example of the enemy's expert use of mutually supporting positions on the Umurbrogol Pocket.

By D +4, the 1st Marines was a regiment in name only. They'd taken over 1,500 casualties. General Rupertus had continued to urge Puller's under-strength Marines forward. General Geiger (commander of III Amphibious Corps and Rupertus' superior) was an experienced ground operations commander from Guam to Bougainville. He understood the lower combat efficiency that these types of losses imposed on a committed combat unit.

On October 2, General Geiger, after visiting Puller in his forward command post and observing the exhausted condition of his Marines, met with General Rupertus and his staff. Rupertus wasn't willing to admit that his division needed to be reinforced, but Geiger overruled him. He ordered the Army's 321st Regiment Combat Team and 81st Infantry Division (on Angaur) to be attached to the 1st Marine Division.

Geiger ordered Rupertus to stand down and send the 1st Marines to the division's rear area base on Pavuvu, in the Russell Islands.

On September 21, the 1st Marines had 1,749 casualties. They reported killing over 4,000 Japanese soldiers and capturing ten heavily defended coral ridges. They reported the destruction of three blockhouses, twenty-five pillboxes, fourteen anti-tank guns, and over 140 defended caves.

The 1st Marines' assault battalions had captured much of the crest required to deny the enemy observation and effective fire on the airfield and logistical areas. Light aircraft flew on September 25 from the scarred and still under repair airfield.

With the Pocket now in Allied control, the division's logistical lifeline was assured. While the Japanese still had some observation capability on the airfield, they could only harass rather than threaten.

The Marine front lines were now close to the final Japanese defensive positions. While intelligence couldn't verify it—the terrain and situation suggested that all assault requirements had been met, and it was time for siege tactics.

Enemy defenders learned that when aerial observers were overhead, they could no longer run their weapons out of caves and fire on the beach or the airfield. After one or two rounds, they were answered with a quick counter-battery fire or a dreaded aerial attack from carrier-based planes.

On September 24, Marines used attack planes operating from the airfield on Peleliu.

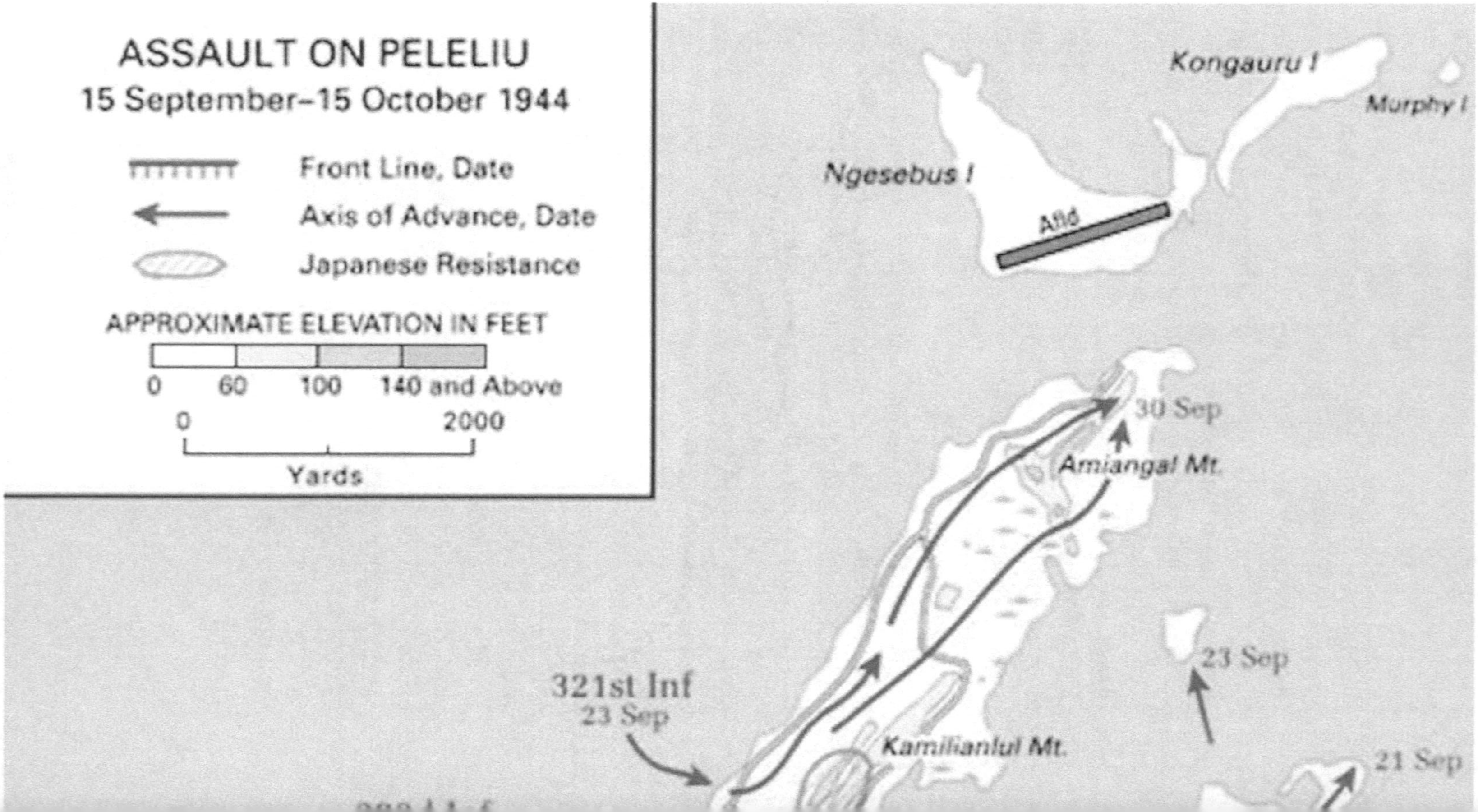

ASSAULT ON PELELIU
15 September–15 October 1944
Front Line, Date
Axis of Advance, Date
Japanese Resistance
APPROXIMATE ELEVATION IN FEET
0   60   100   140 and Above
0   2000
Yards
Kongauru I
Murphy I
Ngesebus I
Afld
30 Sep
Amiangal Mt.
23 Sep
21 Sep
321st Inf
23 Sep
Kamilianlul Mt.

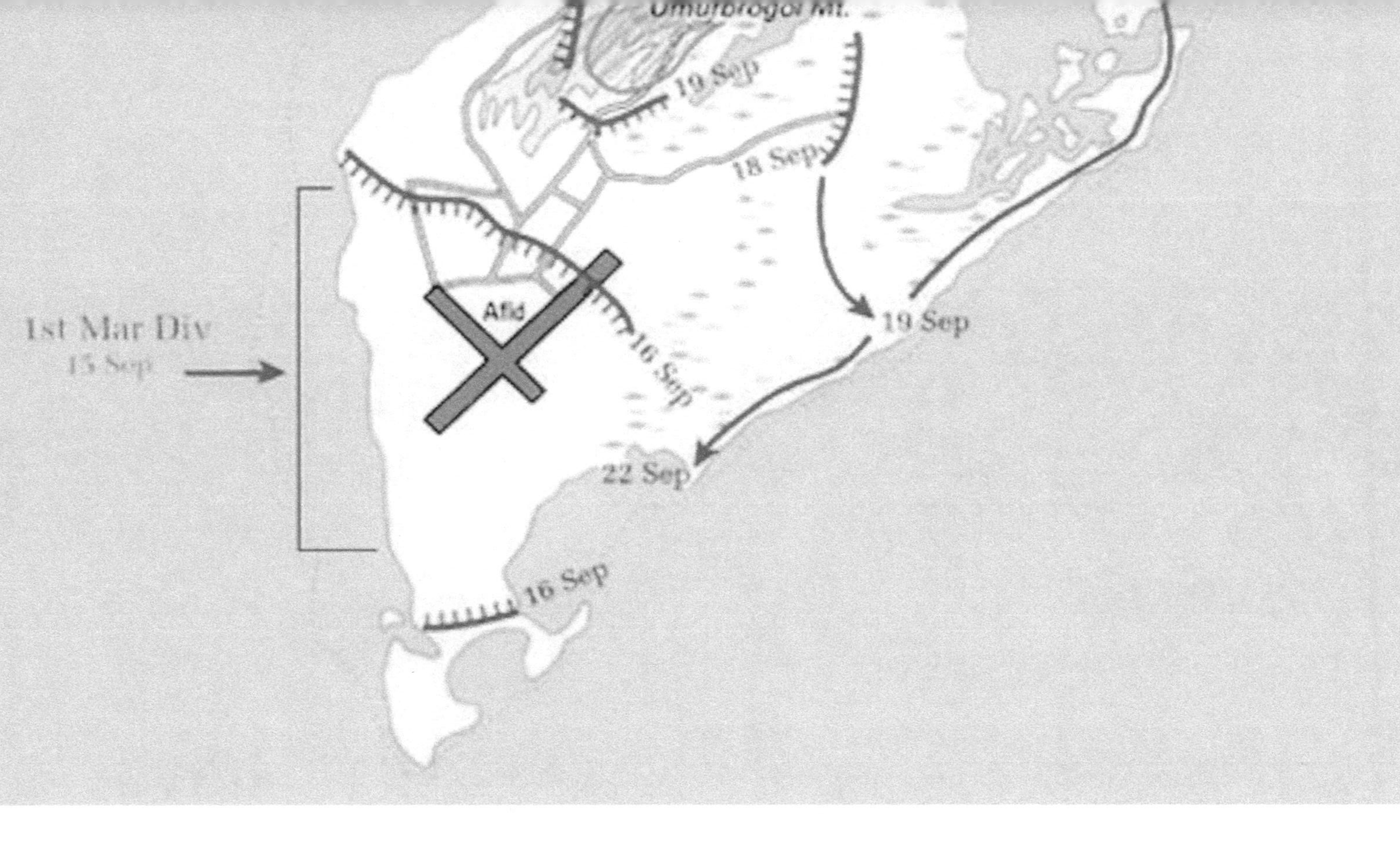

Umurbrogol Mt.
19 Sep
18 Sep
1st Mar Div
15 Sep
Afld
16 Sep
19 Sep
22 Sep
16 Sep

PELELIU'S EASTERN PENINSULA

On D +1, when the 1st Marines launched their bloody assault on the Pocket, the 5th Marines (on the right flank) found less opposition and easier terrain to navigate.

The 1/5 fought southwest to northeast across the airfield through a built-up area similar to what the 2/1 Marines faced. The battalion took fire from the Pocket and assorted small arms from hidden defenders in the rubble-filled built-up area.

The 1/5's tank-infantry attack carried the day. Marines had control of the east to west cross-island road—the next step in securing Peleliu's eastern peninsula.

The 2/5 Marines had a more difficult time. Their progress was opposed by infantry from the woods, and artillery directly from the Pocket, which targeted their tanks supporting the attack along the wood's edge.

Whether the Japanese troops in those woods were posted to defend that position or just trying to survive was never established. The battle took all day, and Marine battalions suffered heavy casualties. By nightfall, the 2/5 Marines had fought past the north end of the airfield and halted to spend the night in the woods, concealing the approaches to the eastern peninsula.

The two-battalion Marine assault was deeply engaged on its front and right. Regimental headquarters near the beach was hit by an artillery barrage that, coupled with the 3/5 Marines' CO and XO losses, prompted a considerable rearrangement of command assignments. The barrage at the regimental command post took out most of the staff and buried the regimental commander in the crumbling Japanese anti-tank trench.

Luckily, it was a temporary burial, and the regimental commander, Colonel Harris, crawled out with a twisted and battered leg but could still hobble. Two of his staff officers were casualties, and the sergeant major was killed. Harris didn't evacuate but needed help in his CP. Harris ordered Colonel Walt back from the 3rd Battalion and had the XO of the 2/5, Major John Gustafson, take command of the 3/5.

Fortunately, the 3/5 Marines were having a quiet day, unlike their hair-raising regrouping on the night of D-Day. After daylight, the 2/5 attacked to the north, and the 3/5 stretched along the east edge of a mangrove lagoon, separating Peleliu from the eastern peninsula. From that position, the 3rd Battalion 5th Marines tied into the 3/7 Marines as they attacked south.

This maneuver protected each regiment's flank against enemy

movement across the lagoon and into the rear of the attacking Marines. While no such threat developed, a more pressing concern emerged for the 3/5 Marines. Major Gustafson was tasked with getting the 3/5 into position to bolster and relieve the 1/5 Marines as they closed in on their objective.

The next day, the 5th Marines tied in with the 1st on their left and secured the foot of the East Road. To the right, the 2/5 Marines hacked their way through the jungle north of the airfield and alongside a road leading to the eastern peninsula. A thick and almost impenetrable scrub reduced progress to a crawl. The scrub concealed most of the advancing Marines from enemy observation on the high ground to the northwest.

The 5th Marines' position overlapped with the northeast sector. Securing that visual boundary meant frontline Marines were spared hostile, directed fire from Pocket. Like the 7th Marines, hidden mainly in the jungle to the South, this would lessen the need for a frontal assault.

Now Marines had the freedom to maneuver purposefully and coordinate supporting fire more carefully into enemy positions.

7TH MARINES IN THE SOUTH

In the south, starting on D +1, the 7th Marines' spirited assault against enemy fortifications smashed into the elite *2nd Battalion, 15th Regiment.*

Even though the enemy was isolated and surrounded by Marines, this Japanese battalion showed skill and an understanding of Colonel Nakagawa's orders and mission: to sell Peleliu at the highest price possible.

The 7th Marines attacked. The 3/7 were on the left and the 1/7 on the right. Marines had the advantage of assaulting the extensive and well-prepared defenses from the rear—with heavy fire support. Both sides fought bitterly, but by 1530 on September 8, the battle was over. Marines destroyed the fortified elite Japanese infantry battalion in their stronghold.

General Rupertus was informed that the 7th Marines' objectives had been met, through the courage, bravery, skill, and many casualties of the 7th Marines infantry companies. Now the 7th advanced out of their successful battle area and into another bloody assault— better known as a siege.

The 5th Marines were still battling bitterly for the eastern "lobster claw" peninsula. By the end of D +2, the 5th Marines stood at the approach to the eastern peninsula off the East Road—near the 1st Marines' vicious fight at the Pocket.

They'd planned an assault on the eastern peninsula across a narrow causeway the Japanese were sure to defend. But a recent reconnaissance revealed that the causeway was not defended. The 2nd Battalion advanced swiftly to seize the opportunity. They moved across in strength but were turned back by friendly fire. The battalion was strafed by Navy planes and then hit by an artillery airburst that killed eighteen Marines.

Still, a bridgehead across the causeway was established and on D +3 the 5th Marines moved in. By the afternoon, Marines advanced to capture and clear the eastern peninsula. Marines expected an attack against a strong defending force that never materialized, this provided an opportunity to secure Purple Beach quickly—a massive logistical prize.

Just before dark, two companies of the 3/5 Marines moved across the causeway to plan the next day's advance. They hoped for little resistance but armed their point units with war dogs to guard against a nighttime ambush. Their lead companies moved out just after dawn, while nearly ambushed, the war dogs warned the Marines and thwarted the enemy's attempted surprise attack.

By the end of D +4, the two battalions had secured the main body of the eastern peninsula and reached Purple Beach from the rear. While the Japanese defenses were extraordinary, many were unmanned. The enemy troops encountered were more interested in hiding than fighting. This added to the speculation that Colonel Nakagawa's trained infantry had been moved west. By D +5, Purple Beach was secured along with the southwest and northeast of the long peninsula of Purple Beach.

From that position and others near the island of Ngardololok, Marines could direct fire against the cave-infested ridges of central and northern Peleliu.

* * *

Now that eastern and southern Peleliu was captured, the Allies planned to encircle the Japanese defenders in central Peleliu and assault nearby Ngesebus and Kongauru in the north. While this was the obvious next tactical phase for the fighting, securing it was unnecessary for strategic and tactical goals.

General Oliver Smith, the 1st Marine Division's assistant commander, believed that the island's mop-up operations should take priority. He wrote: "by the end of the first week, the division controlled everything on the island that was needed, or later even used."

The airfield was secured and under improvement and repair— and in use. There was now no threat to MacArthur's long-heralded return to the Philippines. Purple Beach, Peleliu's best strategic axis, was secured and provided a protected logistic access to the major battle areas. While enemy defenders in their caves on northern Peleliu could still somewhat harass Allied rear installations, Marine counterattacks would quickly silence them.

Only two significant Japanese capabilities remained: they could reinforce Peleliu from Babelthuap and bitterly resist from their cave positions.

The Allied encirclement of the Pocket suffered from a lack of reinforcements.

The III Amphibious Corps reserves were fully committed to the seizure of Angaur. The Angaur operation's planning and timing were heavily affected by the Peleliu operation. Division planners proposed landing on Angaur before Peleliu, but General Julian Smith said that would cause the Japanese in northern Palau to reinforce Peleliu.

Division agreed that Angaur should only be assaulted after the landing on Peleliu was sure to succeed. But in the end, the assault on Angaur began before the Peleliu landing was resolved. The 81st

Division's commanding general wanted to land as soon as possible and was supported by Admiral Bill Valenti. General Julian Smith argued that committing the III Corps' Reserve before the operations on Peleliu were more fully developed was premature and costly. Admiral Wilkinson ignored his advice.

On September 17, the III Corps' final reserve was assigned to the Western Attack Force and ordered to use "all available forces." Against General Smith's advice, Wilkinson committed the entire 323rd RCT and the 81st Division's other maneuver element. The 321st successfully occupied an undefended Ulithi, while reserves were desperately needed on Peleliu.

By September 20, the 81st Division had destroyed or cornered Angaur's 1,400 enemy troops, and Anguar was declared secure. The 322nd RCT would complete mop-up operations, and the 321st RCT was now available for further operations.

General Rupertus believed his Marines could do it without help from the Army. The III Corps' plan had the 81st Division reinforcing Marines on Peleliu and then relieving the 1st Marine Division for the mop-up. But General Rupertus refused to accept the help and continued to tell his commanders to "hurry up."

Rupertus also shrugged off suggestions from 5th Marines "Bucky" Harris that he should take a look at the Pocket from the newly available light planes of the Marine Observation Squadron 3. Harris' newest aerial reconnaissance on September 19 changed his view of the Pocket from sober to serious. He believed attacking the Pocket from the north would be less costly than the original plan, and Rupertus told Harris that he had his own map.

The Marines' plan was built on the tactical concept that the 1st Marine Division would push in a northern line across the island's width after capturing the airfield. Once close to the southern edge of the Pocket, Marines would advance in four west-to-east phase lines. It was expected that the advance along with flatter zones east and west of the Pocket would be roughly the same pace as along the high central ground of Peleliu. Maybe this thinking was consistent with Rupertus' prediction of a three-day assault, but developments in Marine sectors to the west and east didn't change division-level thinking. Until additional forces were available, this linear advance may have seemed the only possible advance.

There was no re-examining the planned south-to-north advance, and for days, the Pocket was sealed off at its northernmost extremity. Still, the division commander kept ordering attacks from south to north following the initial landing plan. As "Bucky" Harris reported from his aerial reconnaissance of the overall Pocket, these attacks would only bring severe casualties. Heavily supported Marines could advance into "the Horseshoe" and "Death Valley," but their positions would soon prove untenable, and they'd need to withdraw by day's end.

The failure in this thinking may have come from the mapping use. The 5th Marines in early October created a newer sketch map to locate and identify the details within the Umurbrogol Pocket.

Even after General Geiger had ordered General Rupertus to stand down Puller's shattered 1st Marines on September 21, Rupertus made it known that *his Marines alone* would clear the entire island. After taking a closer look at the situation on the ground, General Geiger ordered the 321st RCT from Angaur and attached them to the 1st Marine Division—the encirclement of the Umurbrogol Pocket was possible.

Capturing Ngesebus and northern Peleliu became a priority. Allied forces discovered on September 23 that considerable enemy troop strength in the northern Palaus was being ferried by barge from Koror and Babelthuap. Even though the Navy patrol set up to protect against those reinforcements had discovered and destroyed some of the Japanese barges, many enemy troops had waded ashore on the early morning of September 23.

Colonel Nakagawa now had reinforcements on northern Peleliu.

NORTHERN PELELIU SEIZURE

General Rupertus held a meeting with III Corps staff and General Geiger. They formed a plan to encircle the Pocket and deny reinforcements to the enemy on northern Peleliu. The Army's 321st Infantry would advance up the West Road with the 5th Marines. After they reached the Pocket, Marines would pass through Army lines and continue north to assault Ngesebus and northern Peleliu.

The 321st Army Regimental Combat Team was now a battle-tested and hardened outfit. They would advance up the West Road along the edge of the elevated coral plateau. The plateau was 300 yards west to east and formed the western shoulder of the Pocket. It rose seventy feet, and its western cliff was a jumble of small ridges that dominated the road. This cliff would have to be cleared and secured to allow for an un-harassed use of the road.

After the 321st passed this cliff, they could probe east in search of any routes to the eastern edge of Peleliu. Any openings in that direction would be a chance to encircle the Pocket on the north. Following the 321st, the 5th Marines would press their attack into northern Peleliu. The 7th Marines (relieving the 1st) were stood down on the eastern peninsula and relieved the 5th Marines of their passive security role. This allowed the 5th to focus on the capture of northern Peleliu and Ngesebus.

The West Road would be used as a tactical route north and then as a communication line for continuing operations. The road was paralleled by the jagged cliff, which made up the western shoulder of the plateau. This was *not* a level plateau and had a moonscape of sinkholes, coral knobs, and karst.

With no defined ridges or patterns, the sinkholes varied from room size to house size, and some were over twenty feet deep and covered by jungle and vines. This plateau was ninety feet above the road. And another 300 yards to the east, it dropped off into a sheer cliff (known as the China wall). Marines who looked up at it from the eastern approaches to the Pocket claimed the western edge of the plateau was "virtually impassable."

The plateau was also impenetrable to vehicles. Coral sinkholes forced all infantry to crawl, climb, and clamber into small compartments of jagged and rough terrain. Having to evacuate any casualties would involve rough handling of stretchers and the wounded men.

The enemy defended this area with scattered small units who bitterly resisted movement into their moonscape. Japanese troops ignored individuals and only fired on groups or what they considered rich targets.

The tactical decision along the West Road was to seize and hold the cliffs and coral spires. From here, they could command the road and defend these positions against any attacks. Once these heights were secured, troops and trucks could move along the West Road. But until secured, this cliff gave cover and concealment to the enemy. Until these cliff positions were taken and held, the Japanese could only be temporarily silenced from heavy firepower.

On September 23, this was the situation the 321st launched their assault into. Following an hour-long naval bombardment against the high ground of the West Road. Army patrols moved in and were screened from the Japanese still on the cliff. These small-unit tactics worked well until larger units of the 321st moved out alongside the West Road. From here, the enemy unleashed hell from above.

Two battalions of the 321st advanced along an east-west line across the road and up to the heights. Soldiers secured the west edge of the cliff and advanced northward, but some elements of the cliff were outpaced to the west. Instead of fighting to seize the ridge, some units responsible for securing the cliff abandoned it and side-stepped down to the road.

Colonel Hanneken ordered the 3/7 to capture the high ground that the 321st had abandoned. After that, the 3/7 Marines were committed along the ridge within the 321st zone of action. This stretched the Marines, who still needed to maintain contact to their right. Farther north, the 321st pressed on and regained some of the heights above their advance and held onto them.

On the northern end of the Pocket, the sinkhole terrain blended into regular ridgelines. The 321st assaulted Hill 100, along with a nearby hill east of East Road, and designated it Hill B. This position was the northern cap of the Pocket. The 321st would fight for Hill B and the northern cap of the Pocket for the next three days.

The 321st probed the eastern path across the north end of the Pocket. They sent patrols north up to the West Road. In an area of buildings designated "radio station," they found the junction of East and West Roads. Colonel Bob Dark, commanding the 321st, sent a mobile task force (Task Force Neal), heavy with flamethrowers and armor, to circle southeast and join with the 321st at Hill 100. Below that battle, the 7th Marines continued to put pressure on the south and east fronts of the Pocket.

As this was underway, the 5th Marines were ordered to help in the battle for northern Peleliu. The 5th motored, marched, and waded to the West Road and sidestepped the 321st to join in the fight. The Marines found flat ground, some open, and some covered with palm trees. The familiar limestone ridges broke the ground. But the critical difference here was that most of the ridges stood alone.

Marines were not exposed to flanking fire from parallel ridges like they were in the Pocket. The Japanese fortified the northern ridges with extensive tunnels and concealed gun positions. But these positions could be attacked individually with flamethrowers, demolitions, and tank tactics. Many of the enemy defenders were from Naval construction units and not trained infantrymen.

On the US side of the fighting, Colonel "Bucky" Harris was determined to direct all available firepower before sending his infantry into the fight. His newer aerial reconnaissance gave him a better understanding of the terrain.

On September 25, the 1/5 Marines secured the radio station complex. When the 3/5 arrived, they were ordered to seize the next high ground to the east of the 1/5's position. From there, they would extend the regimental line back to the beach. This broke contact with the 321st's operations in the south but fulfilled Colonel Harris's plan to advance north as rapidly as possible without overextending their lines.

By suddenly establishing this regimental beachhead, the 5th Marines had surprised the enemy with powerful forces in position to engage them fully in their cave defenses the next day.

5TH MARINES NORTHERN ATTACK

On September 26, the 321st launched a three-pronged attack
against Hill B. The 5th Marines attacked the four hills running east

to west across Peleliu (Hills 1,2,3, and Radar Hill). This row of hills was perpendicular to the south of the last northern ridge —Amiangal.

These hills were defended by 1,500 enemy infantry, artillery, naval engineers, and the shot-up reinforcing infantry battalion, which landed on the night of September 23. The enemy were well protected in the caves and interconnected tunnels within the hills and ridges.

As the fighting started, Colonel Harris side-stepped his 2nd Battalion west of the hills and attacked Amiangal Ridge to the north. By dark, the 2nd Battalion had secured the southern end of the ridge but took heavy fire from positions in the central and north-western slopes.

The Marines now confronted the most wide-ranging set of tunnels and caves on Peleliu. They were trying to invade the homes and defensive positions of a long-established naval construction unit. Most of whose members were better miners than infantrymen. As night settled, the 2nd Battalion cut itself loose from its southern units and formed a small battalion beachhead for the night.

The next morning, the 2/5 Marines tried to advance along the route leading to the northern nose of Amiangal Ridge. They ran into a wide and deep anti-tank ditch that denied them the close tank support they'd successfully used earlier. Again, the 5th Marines asked for point-blank artillery.

This time division responded. Major George Hanna's 155mm Gun Battalion moved one of its pieces into position. This gun was 175 yards from the face of the ridge. The sight of that gun prompted enemy machine-gun and small arms fire, inflicting casualties upon the artilleryman.

Enemy fire was quickly suppressed by Marine rifle fire and then by the 155mm gun. Throughout the morning, the heavy 155mm fire pounded across the face of the ridge and destroyed or closed all identified caves on the west face—except one. That cave was a tunnel mouth that led down to the ground level in the northwest base of the hill. It was too close to Marine lines to permit the 155mm to fire on it.

After a bulldozer filled in a portion of the anti-tank ditch, tank-infantry teams moved into blast and bulldoze the tunnel mouth closed. Marines swept over the slopes above the tunnel and secured the crest of the northern nose of Amiangal. While Marines held the outside of the hill, stubborn Japanese defenders still occupied the interior.

A maze of interconnected tunnels extended throughout the length of the small Amiangal mountain. Enemy defenders would blast open the previously closed cave or tunnel mouth and surge out in a banzai attack. Apart from the surprise, these counterattacks were a rare and welcome opportunity for Marines to see and kill their enemy in daylight. These tactics were inconsistent with the overall enemy strategy on Peleliu and shortened the fight for the island's northern end.

As the fighting raged on, the 5th Marines assembled its 3rd Battalion with supporting tanks, amphibian tractors, naval gunfire, and air support to assault and secure Ngesebus 700 yards to the north of Peleliu on September 28.

This operation involved a single, reinforced battalion against 500 prepared and entrenched enemy infantry. In just over forty hours, the 3/5 Marines fought the most cost-effective single battalion battle in the Peleliu campaign.

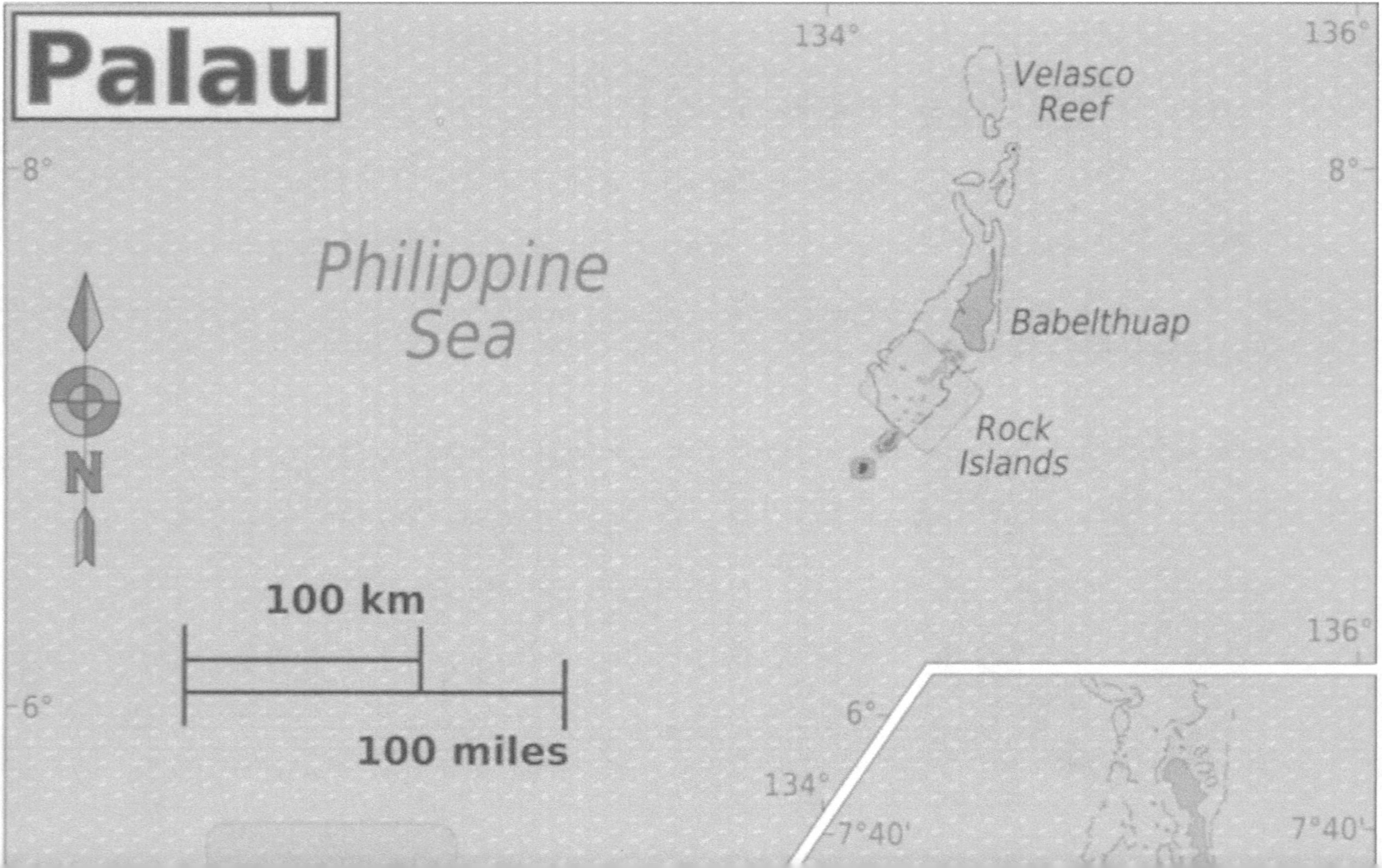

Palau

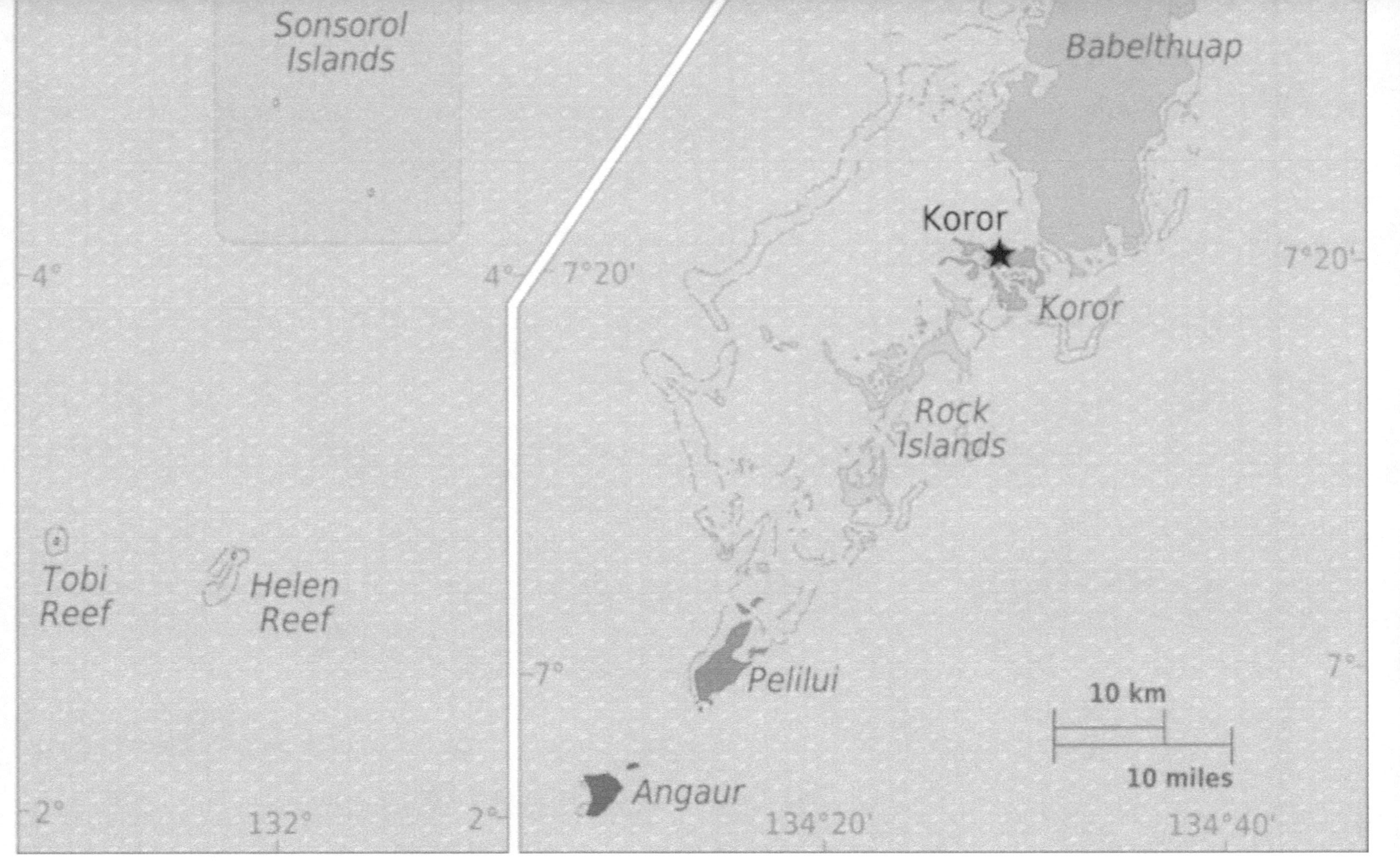

Sonsorol
Islands
Babelthuap
Koror
Koror
Rock
Islands
Tobi
Reef
Helen
Reef
Pelilui
Angaur
10 km
10 miles
4°
4°
2°
132°
2°
7°20'
7°20'
7°
7°
134°20'
134°40'

SEIZURE OF NGESEBUS

The 3rd Battalion got ashore with no casualties. They immediately knocked out all the enemy's beach defenses. Then they turned their attention to the cave positions in the ridges and blockhouses. The ridges here were like those in northern Peleliu in that they stood individually and not part of a complex ridge system.

This denied enemy troops the opportunity to have a mutual defense between cave positions. The attacking Marines could use supporting tanks and concentrate all their fire on each defensive system—without taking fire from their flanks.

By dusk on September 28, the 3/5 Marines had overrun most of the enemy opposition. The next day at 1500, Ngesebus was declared secure. The island was turned over to the 321st, and the 3/5 Marines were put into the division reserve.

The seizure of Ngesebus by one depleted infantry battalion illustrates an enduring principle of war: effective concentration of means. General Rupertus concentrated all his available firepower: divisional and corps artillery, two cruisers, a battleship, nearly all the division's remaining armor, armored and troop-carrying amphibian tractors, and all Marine aviation on Peleliu.

This concentrated support allowed the heavily depleted 3/5 Marines to secure Ngesebus and destroy 477 of Colonel Nakagawa's battle-hardened, entrenched soldiers in forty-one hours at the cost of forty-eight Marine casualties.

As the 3/5 Marines were securing Ngesebus, the rest of the 5th Marines fought the Japanese still hunkered down in northeast Peleliu. After seizing Akarakoro Point past Amiangal Mountain, the 2/5 Marines turned south and swept through enemy defenses east of the mountain with flamethrowers and demolitions. Then they moved southward to Radar Hill, the stronghold of Hill Row.

Radar Hill was under attack from the south and west by the 1/5 Marines. After two days, two battalions were on the top side of the hills. But inside, there were still stubborn enemy defenders continuing to resist.

Marines solved this problem by blasting the cave and tunnel mouths closed—silencing the enemy forever.

FIGHT FOR THE POCKET

The Umurbrogol Pocket was the scene of the bloodiest and most costly fighting along with the campaign's best and worst tactical decisions.

Its terrain was the most challenging on the island. Pre-landing planners didn't realize the Pocket for what it was: a complex cave fortress perfect for a suicidal defense. The southern slopes (known as Bloody Nose) dominated the landing beaches and airfield through where the Pocket had to be assaulted.

After Colonel Puller's 1st Marines conquered those heights through a costly and brave assault, command sent in artillery controlled by aerial observers. This radically changed the situation. The Pocket's defenders could only delay and harass Allied forces with sporadic fire attacks and nighttime raids. After D +4, enemy defenders in the Pocket could no longer seriously threaten the division's mission.

After more enemy observation sites were secured, General Rupertus continued to urge his Marines forward. He pressed his commanders to keep up momentum. As though the seizure of the Pocket was as crucial as securing the commanding heights guarding it from the south. But the challenging terrain and fanatical defenders became entangled with Rupertus' determined character.

This was only sorted out by time and the intervention of General Geiger. Most of the offensive into the Pocket between September 21-29 was directed into the cave mouths, ridges, and twin box canyons. Infantry, tanks, air support, and flame-throwing LVTs penetrated the low ground but were then surrounded on three sides. Enemy positions inside canyons and ridges were hidden from observation. Japanese troops were protected in their caves and were skilled at making the captured low ground untenable.

Other attacks to seize the heights of the eastern ridges were initially successful. Small infantry units scrambled up onto the bare ridge tops but came under fire from facing parallel ridges and caves. They were also harassed by strong enemy counterattacks who left their caves under cover of darkness in suicide attacks.

On September 20, the 7th Marines relieved the 1st Marines along the southwest front of the Pocket and resumed the attack the next day. These assaults achieved limited success behind heavy fire support and smoke. But these positions became impossible to maintain after the fire support and smoke lifted. Assault troops were withdrawn under renewed fire support to their original jump-off positions. There was little to show for the day's bloody fighting.

On September 22, against the west shoulder of the Pocket (Wildcat Bowl), Allied troops gained ground on their early advances —most of which were surrendered at day's end. Marines came under heavy fire from concealed defenders in their mutually supporting cave positions. The 7th Marines had advanced to within a hundred yards of Colonel Nakagawa's cave position. But several supporting hilltops and ridges would have to be reduced before a direct attack on the cave would have any hope of success.

The fight for the Pocket was turning into a siege, but the 1st Marine Division believed they could break through enemy opposition. Rupertus ordered continued battalion and regimental assaults believing they would soon bring victory.

When the 321st's eastward probes brought them within grasp of sealing off the Pocket from the north, they deployed two battalions to complete the encirclement. This assault would absorb the 321st Infantry's full attention until September 26, while the 5th Marines were fighting in northern Peleliu. The 7th Marines continued to pressure the Pocket from the south. When the 321st broke through on the 26th, their mission was expanded to assault the Pocket from the north.

The 321st broke through in the north and cleared the sporadically defended Kamilianlul Ridge. Their attack along adjacent ridges allowed for the Allied forces' consolidation on the north side of the Pocket—now 400 yards wide. On September 29, the 7th Marines were ordered to relieve the Army units in the northern sector.

Now that the 2/7 and 3/7 Marines were on static guard duty, hundreds of non-infantry were stripped from combat positions and put into support units. These "infantillery" units were assigned to hold the earlier held sectors. They faced the karst plateau between the Pocket and West Road.

On the 30th, with the 7th Marines' flexibility restored, they moved south and secured Boyd and Walt's Ridge. They controlled the East Road, but enemy defenders still harassed them from caves on the west side.

On October 3, the 7th Marines organized a four-battalion attack. This plan called for the 1/7 and 3/7 to attack Boyd's Ridge from the north, while the 2/7 would attack Walt's Ridge from the south. The 3/5 would make a diversionary southern attack into Horseshoe Canyon and Five Sisters to its west.

This regimental attack committed four battalions (closer to company strength) against the heights in the southern edge of the Pocket. The assault succeeded, but with heavy casualties. Four of the Five Sisters were scaled but were untenable and had to be abandoned. The next day, the 7th Marines made another attack to seize —then give up positions on Five Sisters.

During this fight, the 3/7 Marines' push led to a rapid advance that gained them Hill 120. They hoped this would provide a jump-off point for the next day's operation against the ridge to the west. But Hill 120, as with so many others in the Pocket, came under enemy crossfire, making it completely untenable.

The 3/7 withdrew and suffered heavy casualties. Among these was Captain "Jamo" Shanley, who commanded Company L. When several of his men fell wounded, Captain Shanley dashed forward under heavy fire to rescue two men, bringing them behind a tank. When he returned to help another wounded Marine, a mortar round exploded behind him—killing him instantly. His XO was shot by a Japanese sniper when he ran up to help, but collapsed on top of Shanley with a bullet in his brain.

Captain Shanley was awarded a gold star for the Navy Cross he earned in Operation Backhander at Cape Gloucester on New Britain, where he led his company in the seizure of Hill 660 in the Borgen Bay area.

The 7th Marines had been in the savage Umurbrogol Pocket

struggle for two weeks. Under the *advice* of General Geiger, Rupertus relieved them but was still determined to have his Marines secure the Pocket and turned to his only remaining regiment. Colonel Harris moved in with his 5th Marines. He planned to attack from the north and chip off one ridge at a time.

SUBDUING THE POCKET

On September 30, Peleliu aerial reconnaissance convinced Allied planners that siege tactics were required to clear positions in the Pocket. Colonel Harris believed in being lavish with ammunition and stingy with Marine lives. Harris would use all available fire support before ordering advances.

The 2/5 Marines were in position on October 5, but only reconnoitered positions where heavier firepower could come into play. Bulldozers prepared paths on the north end of the box canyons for tanks and LVT flamethrowers to operate. Light artillery batteries were placed along the West Road to fire point-blank into cliffs at the north end of the Pocket.

Cliffs considered "troublesome" were obliterated by direct fire. The rubble created a ramp for tanks to climb into better firing positions. Light mortars were used to strip vegetation from areas with suspected enemy caves. Planes loaded with napalm-filled belly tanks were also used to bomb enemy targets selected by the 5th Marines as their key objective.

While the 2/5 Marines picked off enemy firing positions in the north, on October 7, the 3/5 assaulted Horseshoe Ridge with tanks. This time the mission wasn't to seize and hold but to destroy all targets on the faces of Five Sisters and the lower western face of Hill 100.

When all the ammunition was used, tanks withdrew to rearm and then returned accompanied by flame-throwing LVTs and small infantry fire teams. This tactic killed many cave-dwelling Japanese, along with finally silencing their heavy weapons. Before this, single enemy artillery pieces firing from Horseshoe Ridge had harassed the airfield. After the October 7 assaults, no further enemy attacks occurred.

For six more days, the 5th Marines provided all available support to small incremental advances from the north. Light mortars were used to clear vegetation and routes of advance. Both tanks and artillery were used at point-blank range, firing into suspected caves or rough coral areas.

Napalm aerial bombardments cleared vegetation and drove the Japanese defenders farther back into their caves. All advances were limited and aimed at seizing new firing positions. Small platoons and squads made these advances. After Hill 140 was taken, they had a firing site for a 75mm howitzer. The howitzer was wrestled in, disassembled, reassembled, sandbagged, and then fired from position. The 75mm fired into the mouth of a huge cave at the base of the next ridge from where enemy fire had come from for days.

Sandbagging the 75mm howitzer posed several problems. The only available loose sand or dirt had to be carried in from the beach or came from occasional debris slides. The use of sandbags in forward infantry positions increased, and this technique was later widely used when the 81st Infantry Division took over Pocket operations.

SECURING THE EASTERN RIDGES

The 2/5 carefully advanced through several small ridges and knobs and finally seized two murderous box canyons. Direct fire could now be poured into the west face of Boyd and Walt Ridges. But these cave-filled western slopes were protected by other caves on the parallel ridge known as Five Brothers.

After a week of siege-like activity pushed the northern boundary of the Pocket another 600 yards south, the 3/5 Marines were called in to relieve the 2/5. The forward positions being relieved were so close to the enemy that snipers picked off several incoming Marines (even the company commander).

During this exchange, a small enemy group reoccupied a position earlier secured by frequent interdiction fires. Even through these losses and interruptions, the relief was completed on schedule, and on October 13, the 3/5 Marines continued their slow and deliberate advance.

Terrain prohibited any advance south of Hill 140, so the 3/5 shifted southwest, paralleling the West road and into the coral badlands. This terrain was earlier judged unsuitable, but with the aid of fire-scouring napalm bombs, it was traversed. Major "Cowboy" Stout's VMF-114 bombs fell incredibly close to the advancing 3/5 Marines front and the stationary units east of the West Road.

The 1/7 Marines launched a similar effort. Together, these two battalions advanced and secured one-half of the depth of the coral badlands. Between the West Road and the China Wall this clearing allowed the "infantillery" unit to advance their lines eastward and then hold as far as the infantry had cleared.

In early October, the 5th and 7th Marines' actions had reduced the Pocket to an oval shape 700 yards north to south and 350 yards east to west. According to Colonel Nakagawa's radio report, he still had over 700 troops within the Pocket, and eighty percent were still effective.

Division command suggested enclosing the Pocket with barbed wire and designating it as a prisoner of war closure. The Pocket no longer counted in the strategic balance nor in completing the effective seizure of Peleliu. General Rupertus wanted to subdue the Pocket before turning it over to General Mueller's 81st Army Division for mop-up operations. Rupertus' successful seizure of northern Peleliu and Ngesebus had ended the enemy's capability to reinforce the isolated Japanese troops on Peleliu.

Without pressing for a declaration that Peleliu had been secured (which would formalize the completion of the 1st Marine Division's mission), General Geiger ordered Rupertus to relieve the 5th and 7th Marines with his freshest and largest infantry regiment, the 321st RCT (still attached to the 1st Marine Division). General Rupertus replied that "very shortly," his Marines would subdue and secure the Pocket.

Admiral Nimitz sent a message to General Geiger. He directed him to turn command over to General Mueller's 81st Division, relieve the 1st Marine Division, and begin mop-up operations and garrison duty on Peleliu.

MOPPING UP PELELIU

On October 20, General Mueller took responsibility for mop up operations on Peleliu. He described the tactical situation as a siege —and ordered his troops to proceed accordingly.

For six weeks, his two infantry regiments, the 322nd and 323rd, plus the 2nd Battalion of the 321st Regiment, did just that. They used sandbags as an assault device, carrying sand up from the beaches and inching them forward. They pressed closer to enemy caves and dug-in strong points. They used tanks and flamethrowers and even improved on the vehicle-mounted flamethrower. They made a gasoline pipeline from a road-bound gas truck, enabling them (with booster pumps) to launch napalm hundreds of feet into the enemy's defensive area. They took advantage of the 75mm howitzer on Hill 140 and found other sites to put howitzers and fire point-blank into enemy caves.

To support the growing need for sandbags on ridge-top foxholes, army engineers strung high lines to transport them (along with ammo and rations) up to the peaks and ridge tops. Army troops still took casualties, even with these siege tactics, as they ground down the stubborn Japanese defenses. The Umurbrogol Pocket siege consumed the 81st Division's full attention and both regimental combat teams until November 27, 1944.

This prolonged siege operation was carried out within twenty miles of a much larger enemy force of 25,000 soldiers in the northern Palaus. The US Navy had the enemy isolated with patrols and bombing from Marine Aircraft Group 11 operating from Peleliu.

As costly and challenging as the Allied advances were, Japanese defenders had similar demanding, and even more discouraging, situations in their underground positions. Sanitation was crude. They had little to no water, rations were nearly nonexistent, and ammunition was even more scarce. As time wore on, some Japanese were given the opportunity to leave the defenses and make suicidal banzai night attacks. Very few were ever captured.

In late November, General Murai suggested in a radio message to General Inoue on Koror to make one final banzai attack for the honor of the empire. Inoue turned him down. By this time, Nakagawa's only external communications were by radio to Koror. As he'd expected, all local wire communications were destroyed.

Tanks and infantry carefully pressed on in their relentless advance. The 81st Divisions' engineers improved the roads and ramps leading into the heart of the final Japanese position. Flamethrower and tank attacks steadily reduced each cave position as the infantry pushed its foxhole sandbags forward.

On November 24, Colonel Nakagawa sent his final message to Koror. He'd burned the colors of the *2nd Infantry Regiment* and split the remaining fifty-six men into seventeen infiltration parties. They would slip through Allied lines and "attack the enemy everywhere."

On the night of November 24, twenty-five Japanese soldiers (including two officers) were killed. One soldier was captured the following day. His interrogation, along with post-war records, revealed that General Murai and Colonel Nakagawa committed *Seppuku* (Japanese ritual suicide by disembowelment) in their command post.

The final two-day advance of the 81st Division was indeed now a mop-up operation. Carefully conducted to eliminate any holdout opposition. By noon on November 27, north-moving units, guarded by other infantry units, met face-to-face with the battalion moving south near the Japanese command post. Colonel Arthur Watson, commanding the 323rd, reported to General Mueller that the operation was over.

* * *

The tenacious determination of the enemy was symbolized by the last thirty-three prisoners captured on Peleliu. In March 1947, a small Marine guard attached to a navy garrison on the island found unmistakable signs of a Japanese military presence in a cave.

Patrols captured a straggler, a Japanese sailor who said there were thirty-three Japanese soldiers under the command of Lieutenant Yamaguchi. While the straggler reported some dissension in the ranks, a final banzai attack was still under consideration.

The Navy garrison commander moved his personnel and their dependents to a secure area and radioed Guam for reinforcements and a Japanese war crimes witness. Admiral Michio Sumikawa flew in and traveled by Jeep along the roads near the suspected enemy positions. Through a loudspeaker, he recited the existing situation.

No response. The Japanese sailor who'd been captured earlier went back to the cave armed with letters from Japanese families and former officers on the Palaus, informing the holdouts that the war was indeed over.

On April 21, 1947, the holdouts surrendered. Lieutenant Yamaguchi led a haggard twenty-six soldiers to a position of eighty battle-dressed Marines. Yamaguchi bowed and handed over his sword to the on-scene US Navy commander.

CONDITIONS ON PELELIU

Robert "Pepper" Martin from *Time* magazine was one of the few civilian correspondents who chose to share the fate of the Marines on Peleliu. He wrote the following account: "Peleliu was a horrible place. Suffocating heat and sporadic rain—a muggy rain that brings no relief—only more misery. Coral rocks soak up heat during the day, and it's only slightly cooler at night.

"The Marines were in the finest possible physical condition, but they wilted on Peleliu. By the fourth day, there were as many casualties from heat as from wounds. Peleliu was worse than Guam in its bloodiness, climate, terror, and tenacity of the Japs. The sheer brutality and fatigue has surpassed anything yet seen in the Pacific, indeed from the standpoint of troops involved in the time taken to make the island secure.

"On the second day, the temperature had reached 105 degrees in the shade. There was little to no shade in most places where the fighting was going on, and arguably there was no breeze anywhere. It lingered at that level of heat as days dragged by (temperatures were recorded as high as 115 degrees).

"The water supply was a serious problem from the start. While this had been anticipated, the solution proved less complicated than expected. Engineers discovered productive wells could be drilled almost anywhere on low ground. Personnel semi-permanently stationed at the beach found that even shallow holes dug in the sand would yield a mildly repulsive liquid that could be purified for drinking with halazone tablets.

"It continued to be necessary to supply the assault troops from scoured out oil drums and 5-gallon fuel cans. But steaming out the oil drums didn't remove the oil, which resulted in many troops drinking water and getting sick. When the captains of the ships in the transport area learned of this and the shortage of water, they rushed cases of fruit and fruit drinks to the beaches to ease the problem.

"The water situation was a problem for troops operating on the relatively open and level ground. Once the fighting entered the ridges, just traversing the difficult terrain without having to fight caused the debility rate to shoot up quickly. An emergency call was sent to all the ships offshore—requisitioning every available salt tablet for the 1st Marines."

The statement that heat casualties equaled wound casualties was misleading. Most evacuated troops were returned to duty after a day or two of rest. Their absence from the front lines did not permanently impair the combat efficiency of their units. But these several cases strained the already overburdened medical core.

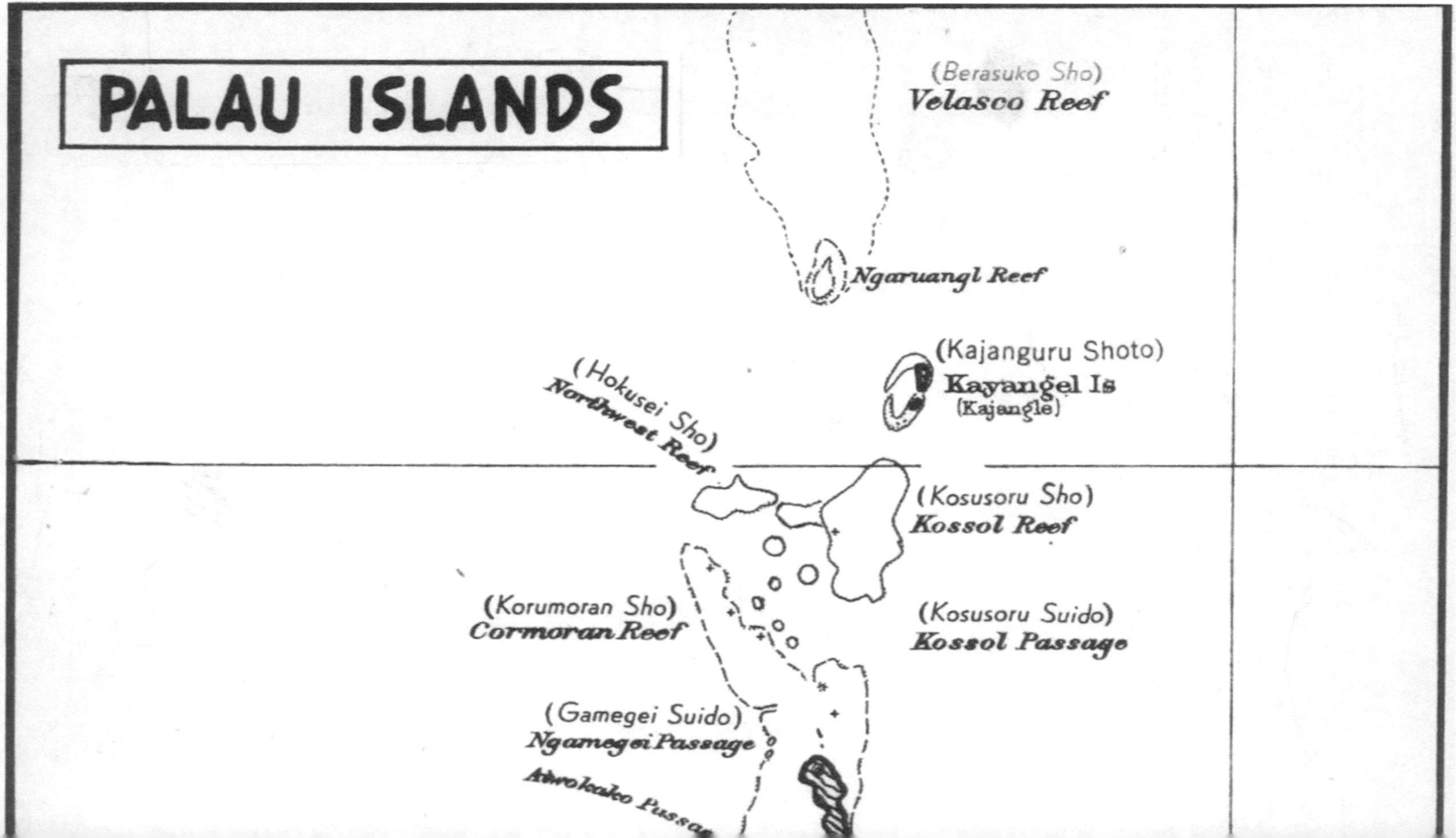
PALAU ISLANDS
(Berasuko Sho)
Velasco Reef
Ngaruangl Reef
(Kajanguru Shoto)
Kayangel Is
(Kajangle)
(Hokusei Sho)
Northwest Reef
(Kosusoru Sho)
Kossol Reef
(Korumoran Sho)
Cormoran Reef
(Kosusoru Suido)
Kossol Passage
(Gamegei Suido)
Ngamegei Passage

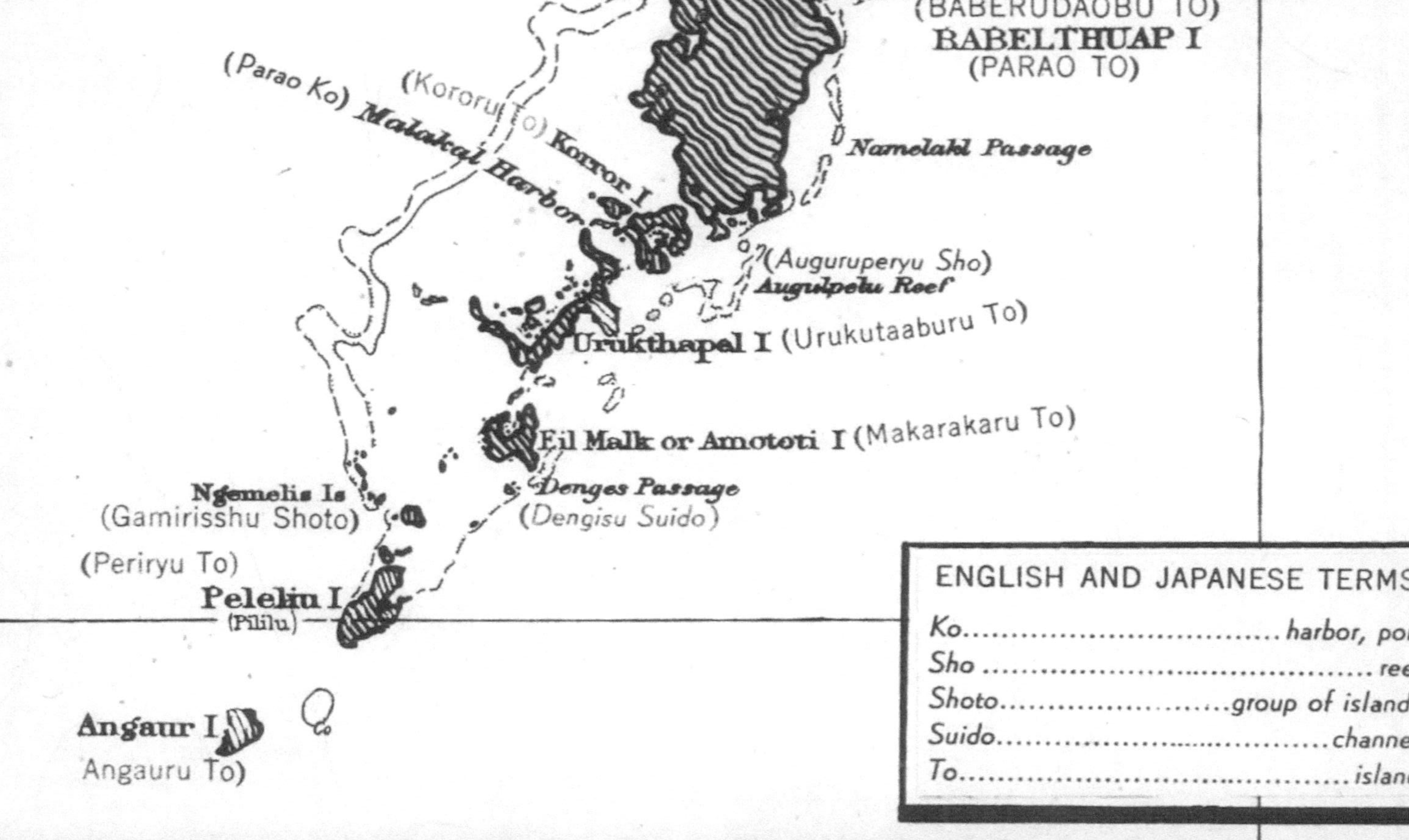

(BABERUDAOBU TO)
BABELTHUAP I
(PARAO TO)
Namelaki Passage
(Parao Ko)
(Kororu To)
Malakal Harbor
Koror I
(Auguruperyu Sho)
Augulpelu Reef
Urukthapel I (Urukutaaburu To)
Eil Malk or Amototi I (Makarakaru To)
Denges Passage
(Dengisu Suido)
Ngemelis Is
(Gamirisshu Shoto)
(Periryu To)
Peleliu I
(Pililu)
Angaur I
Angauru To)
ENGLISH AND JAPANESE TERMS
Ko.........................harbor, port
Sho.........................reef
Shoto.........................group of islands
Suido.........................channel
To.........................island

CONQUEST OF PELELIU

Was the seizure of Peleliu necessary?

What were the advantages to the US war effort from securing Peleliu?

It assured the absolute domination of all the Palau Islands. It also added to the security of General MacArthur's right flank as he continued westward with his Philippines campaign. Within the Palaus group, the conquest destroyed enemy facilities that survived Admiral Mitscher's destructive strike in March 1944.

Securing Peleliu also ensured a total denial of support to Japanese forces from the submarine base at Koror. Reducing the already waning enemy submarine capability east of the Philippines.

The Allied position on Peleliu contributed to neutralizing 25,000 enemy troops in northern Palau. The Peleliu landing *did not* contribute to the RLT 323's (regimental landing team) unopposed seizure of Ulithi. Admiral Halsey had earlier believed his forces could seize Ulithi without first taking Peleliu.

The most significant visible benefit of a subdued Peleliu was its use as a link in the flight path and communication lines from Hawaii to the Philippines. It was convenient but not a necessity.

Survivors of the *Indianapolis* during the July 29, 1945 sinking were saved indirectly by the seizure of Peleliu. After delivering atomic bomb parts to Tinian, the ship was heading for the Philippines when it was torpedoed. The *Indianapolis* sunk in twelve minutes. There was no received report of the contact or the sinking. Four days after it sunk, the 316 survivors (from a crew of 1,197) were spotted by a Navy patrol bomber flying out of Peleliu. This sighting directly led to the rescue and most likely would not have happened but for the Allied occupation of Peleliu.

PRICE OF PELELIU

Marine Casualties were 6,526. This included Navy doctors and corpsmen with 1,252 killed. The Army's 81st Division had 3,088 casualties, 404 were killed in action. Total US troop casualties were 9,616 (1,657 killed) on Peleliu, Angaur, and Ngesebus

The Japanese were successful in implementing their bleed and delay strategy. Their actions cost them an estimated 11,000 casualties (all but a small portion killed). Only 202 prisoners of war were captured, and of them, only nineteen were Japanese military (twelve Navy and seven Army). The rest were Korean laborers. Statistically, less than two out of every thousand Japanese military defenders were captured.

The bloody battle at Peleliu was a warning for the remaining Allied operations being conducted across the Pacific. Even with total naval and air superiority and a four to one troop advantage—the conquest of Peleliu cost one Allied casualty and 1,590 rounds of ammunition per Japanese soldier killed or driven from his position. A couple of months later, the attacks on Iwo Jima and Okinawa would confirm this grim calculation.

On September 13, 1944, two days before D-Day, Admiral Halsey recommended to Admiral Nimitz that the Peleliu landing should be canceled. But by that time, it was too late: Peleliu would be added to the long list of brutal battles in which Allied forces fought, suffered, and ultimately prevailed.

Seventy-seven years later, the question of whether Operation Stalemate was necessary remains debatable. The heroism and commendable conduct of the 1st Marine Division, its Navy corpsmen, and soldiers of the 81st Infantry on that miserable island will forever be written in blood.

OPERATION DETACHMENT

1945 BATTLE OF IWO JIMA

JAPAN
Tokyo

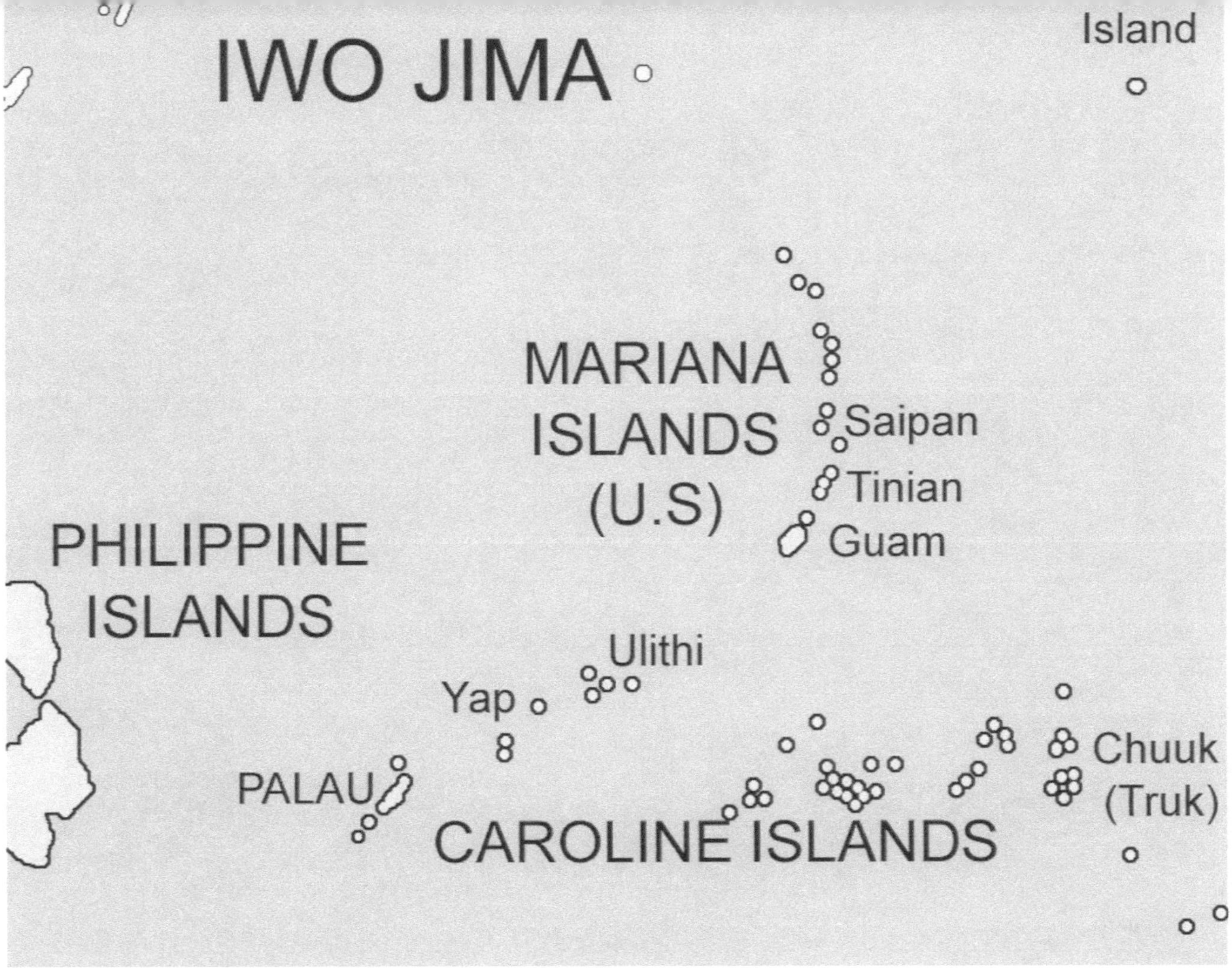

IWO JIMA
Island
MARIANA
ISLANDS
(U.S)
Saipan
Tinian
Guam
PHILIPPINE
ISLANDS
Ulithi
Yap
PALAU
CAROLINE ISLANDS
Chuuk
(Truk)

THE PACIFIC OFFENSIVE

March 4, 1945 was the second week of the Allied invasion of Iwo Jima. By now, the assault elements of the 3rd, 4th, and 5th Marine Divisions were drained, and their combat efficiency was seriously reduced.

The thrilling sight of the American flag being raised by the 28th Marines on Mount Suribachi had happened ten days earlier—a lifetime ago on Sulfur Island. The Amphibious Corps landing forces had already suffered 13,000 casualties, including 3,000 dead. The front was a jagged serration across Iwo Jima's fat northern half. Smack in the middle of the primary Japanese defenses. The Allied landing force had to advance uphill against a well-disciplined, entrenched, and rarely visible enemy.

In the center of the island, the 3rd Marine Division spent the night turning back a small, but determined, enemy counterattack, which found a gap between the 21st and 9th Marines. Savage hand-to-hand combat had cost both sides heavy casualties. The counterattack ruined the division's preparation for a morning advance, but both regiments made gains against stubborn enemy opposition.

In the east, the 4th Marine Division secured Hill 382 at the cost of their combat efficiency plummeting below fifty percent. By nightfall, it would fall another five percent. The 24th Marines, supported by flame-throwing tanks, only advanced one hundred yards before stopping to detonate two tons of explosives against enemy cave positions. The 23rd and 25th Marines entered the most challenging terrain yet—a broken ground with visibility less than a few feet.

On the western flank, the 5th Marine Division took Hill 362-B (Nishi Ridge) at the cost of over 500 casualties. They'd engaged a sizeable enemy force throughout the night. While the enemy attacks lacked coordination, exhausted Marines were barely able to hold them off. Most rifle companies were now at less than half strength. The division reported the net gain for the day as "practically nothing."

* * *

The battle took its toll on the enemy garrison as well. Japanese General Tadamichi Kuribayashi knew his *109th Division* had inflicted heavy casualties on the assaulting Marines, but his losses were comparable. The Allied capture of the critical hills the day before denied him his prized artillery observation sites.

Kuribayashi's brilliant chief of artillery, Colonel Chosaku Kaido, had been killed. Kuribayashi moved his command post from the central highlands to a large cave on the northwestern coast. Imperial Headquarters in Tokyo had reached him by radio that afternoon, but the general was in no mood for heroic rhetoric. He replied: "Send air and naval support, and I will hold the island. Without them, I cannot hold."

That afternoon, the combatants witnessed a glimpse of Iwo Jima's fate. Through the overcast skies, a giant silver bomber (the largest aircraft yet seen), the B-29 "Dinah Might," came in for an emergency landing on the scruffy island airstrip. Allied troops held their breath as the bomber swooped in and landed with a thud. Clipping a field telephone pole with its wing and rumbling to a stop three feet from the end of the strip.

Pilot Fred Malo and his ten-man crew didn't stay long. Every enemy gunner within range wanted to bag this prize. Mechanics made hurried field repairs, and the sixty-five-ton Super Fortress scrambled through a hail of enemy fire, returning to its base on Tinian.

The battle of Iwo Jima raged for another twenty-two days and claimed 11,000 more Allied casualties and the lives of nearly the entire Japanese garrison. A historic and colossal fight between two well-armed veteran forces. This was the bloodiest and biggest battle in the history of the Marine Corps. But after March 4, leaders on both sides had no doubts as to the ultimate outcome.

OPERATION DETACHMENT

Iwo Jima was an amphibious landing where assault troops saw the value of the objective. They were finally within a thousand miles of the Japanese homeland—and contributing clearly in support of the Allied bombing campaign.

This bombing campaign was a new wrinkle on an old theme. For forty years, Marines had been developing the skills to seize advanced naval bases in support of the fleet. In the Pacific war—especially at Tinian, Saipan, and now Iwo Jima—they secured advanced airbases to further the bombing of the Japanese home islands.

Allied forces had waited for the arrival of the B-29s for years. These long-range bombers became operational too late for the European Theater—but they'd been hitting Japan since November 1944 with disappointing results. The problem wasn't the planes or the pilots, but a little spit of volcanic rock halfway across the path from Saipan to Tokyo—Iwo Jima.

Radar on Iwo gave the enemy two hours' advance notice of every B-29 strike. Japanese fighters on Iwo's airfields would swarm and harass the unescorted Super Fortresses going in and especially returning to base. Enemy fighters picked off the B-29s crippled from antiaircraft fire. This caused the B-29s to fly higher and with a reduced payload.

The Joint Chiefs decided Iwo Jima must be secured with an Allied airfield built there. This would stop Japanese bombing raids and early warning interceptions. The airfield would offer fighter escorts through the treacherous portions of the B-29's missions and greater payloads at longer ranges. Iwo Jima in Allied hands would also provide emergency airfield support and landing for crippled B-29s returning from Tokyo and protect the Allied flank for the Okinawa invasion. Admiral Chester Nimitz was given three months to seize and develop Iwo Jima: codename Operation Detachment

Iwo Jima translates to "Sulfur Island" in Japanese. An ugly, foul-smelling, barren chunk of volcanic rock and sand—not even ten square miles in size. According to a Japanese Army officer: "an island of sulfur, no sparrow, no swallow, no water."

Less poetic Marines described Iwo's resemblance to a pork chop with a 556-foot volcano. Mount Suribachi dominated the southern end of the island and overlooked all potential landing beaches. Iwo rose unevenly over onto the Motoyama Plateau in the north before falling sharply off into the coast and steep cliffs and canyons. The northern terrain was a defender's dream: an intricate, broken, cave-dotted jungle of stone. Ringed by volcanic steam and a twisted land-scape that seemed like a barren moon wilderness. More than one surviving Marine compared the eerie silence to something out of Dante's *Inferno*.

Iwo Jima in 1945 had two redeeming characteristics: the military value of its airfields and the psychological status of the island as a historical Japanese possession. The Allies were now within Japan's Inner Defense Zone. According to a Japanese officer: "Iwo Jima is the doorkeeper to the Imperial capital."

Even with the slowest aircraft, Tokyo could be reached in three flight hours from the island. In the Iwo Jima battle, 20,000 Allied and Japanese troops would be killed during brutal fighting in the last winter months of 1945.

No one suggested taking Iwo Jima would be easy. Admiral Nimitz assigned this mission to the same team who'd done so well in the earliest amphibious assaults in the Gilberts, Marshalls, and Marianas. Admiral Raymond Spruance would commend the 5th Fleet, Admiral Richmond Kelly Turner would commend the expeditionary forces, and Admiral Harry Hill would command the attack force.

Operation Detachment required unrelenting military pressure on the enemy and an accelerated planning schedule. The Amphibious task force preparing to assault Iwo Jima was getting squeezed on both ends. Admiral Hill desperately needed amphibious ships, shore bombardment vessels, and landing craft that were currently in use by General Douglas MacArthur and his reconquest of the Philippines. Poor weather and stiff enemy resistance combined to delay the completion of that operation.

The Joint Chiefs reluctantly postponed D-Day on Iwo from January 20 to February 19. The new schedule provided no relief for Allied planners. D-Day on Okinawa could be no later than April 1 because of the monsoon season. This tight timeframe held grim implications for Marine landing forces.

General Harry Schmidt would command the V Amphibious Corps in the assault. Schmidt's landing force consisted of three Marine divisions (3rd, 4th, and 5th). Schmidt would have the honor of commanding the largest US Marine force ever committed into a single battle—a force totaling over 80,000 troops.

Over half of these troops were Marine veterans from earlier fighting in the Pacific. Realistic training had prepared new Marines for the hard fight to come. The Iwo Jima assault force was arguably the most proficient amphibious force the world had yet to see.

Two senior Marines shared the limelight on Iwo Jima, and history has done them both an injustice. General Holland M. Smith, who then commanded the FMF (Fleet Marine Force), was tasked to participate in Operation Detachment as the Expeditionary Troops' Commanding General. This was an unnecessary billet. Schmidt had the rank, experience, staff, and resources to execute core level responsibility without being second-guessed.

General Smith was an amphibious pioneer and veteran of landings in the Gilberts, Marshalls, and the Marianas. According to him:

"My sun had nearly set by then. I think they asked me along in case something happened to Harry Schmidt." Smith would try to keep out of Schmidt's way, but his decision to withhold the 3rd Marines (Expeditionary Troops Reserve) remains as controversial as it was in 1945.

General Smith proved himself an asset to the Iwo Jima campaign. He was always a voice in the wilderness in the top-level planning stage. Smith predicted severe casualties unless more effective preliminary naval bombardment was provided. He diverted visiting dignitaries and the press away from Schmidt and always offered a realistic counterpoint to some of the rosier staff estimates. According to Smith: "It's a tough proposition, that's why we're here."

General Schmidt's few public statements left him saddled with predicting Iwo Jima would be conquered in ten days. According to post-war accounts, Schmidt resented Smith's perceived role: "I was the commander of all troops on Iwo Jima at all times. Holland Smith never had an onshore command post, never issued a single order, and never spent a single night ashore. Isn't it important from a historical standpoint that I commanded the greatest number of Marines ever to be engaged in a single action in the entire history of the Marine Corps?"

General Smith did not disagree with those points. While Smith proved to be useful, Schmidt and his staff should be credited for planning and executing the difficult and bloody Iwo Jima campaign.

The V Amphibious Corps' conquest of Iwo Jima was even more remarkable due to tough enemy opposition on the island. General Kuribayashi was one of the most fearsome opponents of the war. Kuribayashi was a fifth-generation samurai handpicked by the emperor. The Japanese general combined combat experience with an innovative mind and an iron will.

Although this would be his only struggle against US forces, he learned much about his opponents from earlier service in the US. Kuribayashi appraised with an unblinking eye the results of previous Japanese attempts to repel Allied invasions of Japanese-held garrisons.

Aside from the heroic rhetoric, Kuribayashi saw little value in the defend-at-the-water's-edge tactics and suicidal *banzai* attacks that branded Japan's failures from Tarawa to Tinian. Kuribayashi was a realist. He did not expect much help from Japan's depleted fleet and air forces. His best chance was to fortify Iwo's forbidding terrain with an in-depth defense, similar to the defense on Peleliu. Kuribayashi would shun coastal defenses, anti-landing, and banzai tactics. Instead, he'd wage a battle of attrition: a war of patience, nerves, and time. A delay and bleed strategy. Would the Allied forces lose heart and abandon the campaign?

A passive policy this late in the war was radical to senior Japanese Navy and Army leaders. It was counter to the deeply ingrained *Bushido* samurai code: a warrior code that viewed the defensive as only an unpleasant delay before the glorious offensive could resume—where the enemy would be destroyed by fire and sword. Imperial Headquarters was nervous. There was evidence of a top-level request for guidance in defending against Allied storm landings from Nazi Germany, whose experience trying to defend Normandy at the water's edge had proven disastrous.

Japanese command was unconvinced. Kuribayashi used his connection to the Emperor to avoid being relieved. But it was not a complete victory—the Navy insisted on building blockhouses and gun casements along the obvious landing beaches. Kuribayashi demanded assistance from the finest mining engineers and fortification specialists in the Empire.

The island favored the defender. Iwo's volcanic sand mixed with cement produced an exceptional concrete for installations. The soft rock was easy to dig. Over half of the Japanese garrison put their weapons aside and picked up picks and spades. When Allied bombers from the Seventh Air Force began a daily pummeling of the island in early December 1944, Kuribayashi just moved everything underground: weapons, command post, barracks, and aid stations. The engineering achievements he accomplished were extraordinary. Kuribayashi masked gun positions, created interlocking fields of fire, and miles of tunnels linking key defensive positions. Every cave had multiple outlets and ventilation tubes. One installation inside Mount Suribachi ran seven stories deep. Allied troops rarely encountered a live Japanese on the island until the bitter end.

Allied intelligence, aided by documents captured in Saipan and by an almost daily flow of aerial surveillance, was puzzled by the Japanese garrison's disappearing act. The photo interpreters, using stereoscopic lenses, listed 775 potential targets, but all were covered, hardened, and masked. Allied planners knew there was no fresh water available on the island. They saw the rainwater cisterns and knew what the average monthly rainfall would deliver. They determined the enemy garrison couldn't survive under those conditions in numbers greater than 12,000 for long. But Kuribayashi's force was twice that size. His troops had existed on half rations of water for months before the battle even began.

Unlike the earlier amphibious assaults on Guadalcanal and Tarawa, Allies would not have a strategic surprise on Iwo. Japanese headquarters believed Iwo would be invaded after the loss of the Marianas. Six months before the battle, Kuribayashi wrote to his wife: "the Americans will most definitely invade Iwo Jima—do not look for my return."

Kuribayashi ruthlessly worked his men to complete the defensive and training preparations by February 11, 1945. The general met his objective. Kuribayashi had a mixed force of recruits and veterans, soldiers and sailors. His artillerymen and mortar crews were the best in the Empire. Still, he trained and disciplined them all. Each fighting position had the commander's "Courageous Battle Vows" prominently posted above the firing apertures. Troops were cautioned to maintain their position and to take ten Marine lives for each Japanese death.

General Schmidt issued the operational plan on December 23, 1944. This plan wasn't fancy. Mount Suribachi towered over the potential landing beaches, but the 3,000 yards of black sand along the southeastern coast were more sheltered from the prevailing winds. It was here the V Amphibious Corps would land on D-Day. The 4th Marine Division on the right, the 5th on the left and the 3rd in reserve. The primary objectives were the lower airfield and

Suribachi. Then, the assault force would swing into line and attack north shoulder to shoulder.

Anticipating a significant enemy counterattack on the first night, General Holland Smith said: "We welcome their counterattack. That's generally when we break their back."

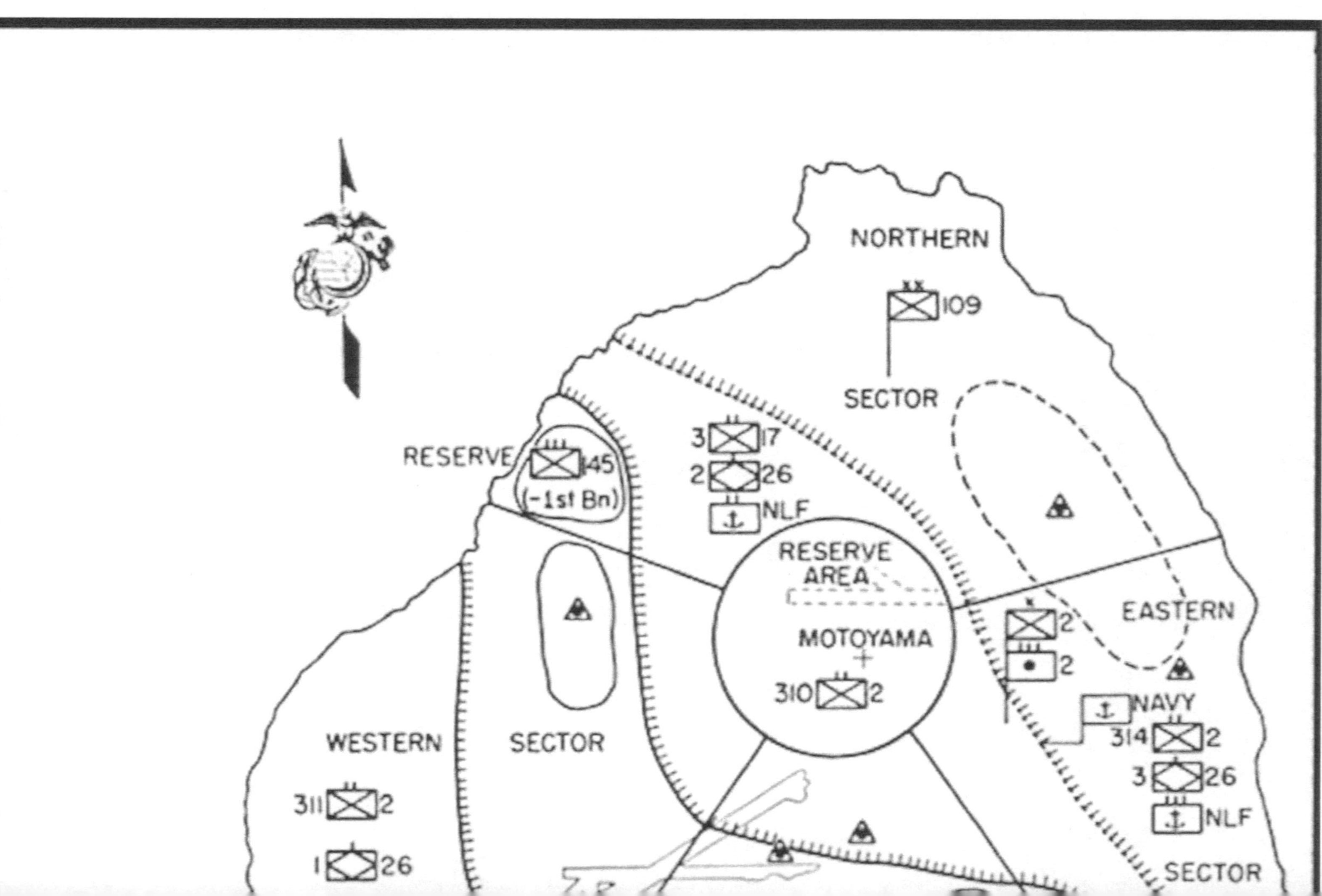

NORTHERN
SECTOR
109
RESERVE
45
(-1st Bn)
3 17
2 26
NLF
RESERVE
AREA
MOTOYAMA
310 2
EASTERN
2
2
NAVY
314 2
3 26
NLF
WESTERN
SECTOR
311 2
1 26
SECTOR

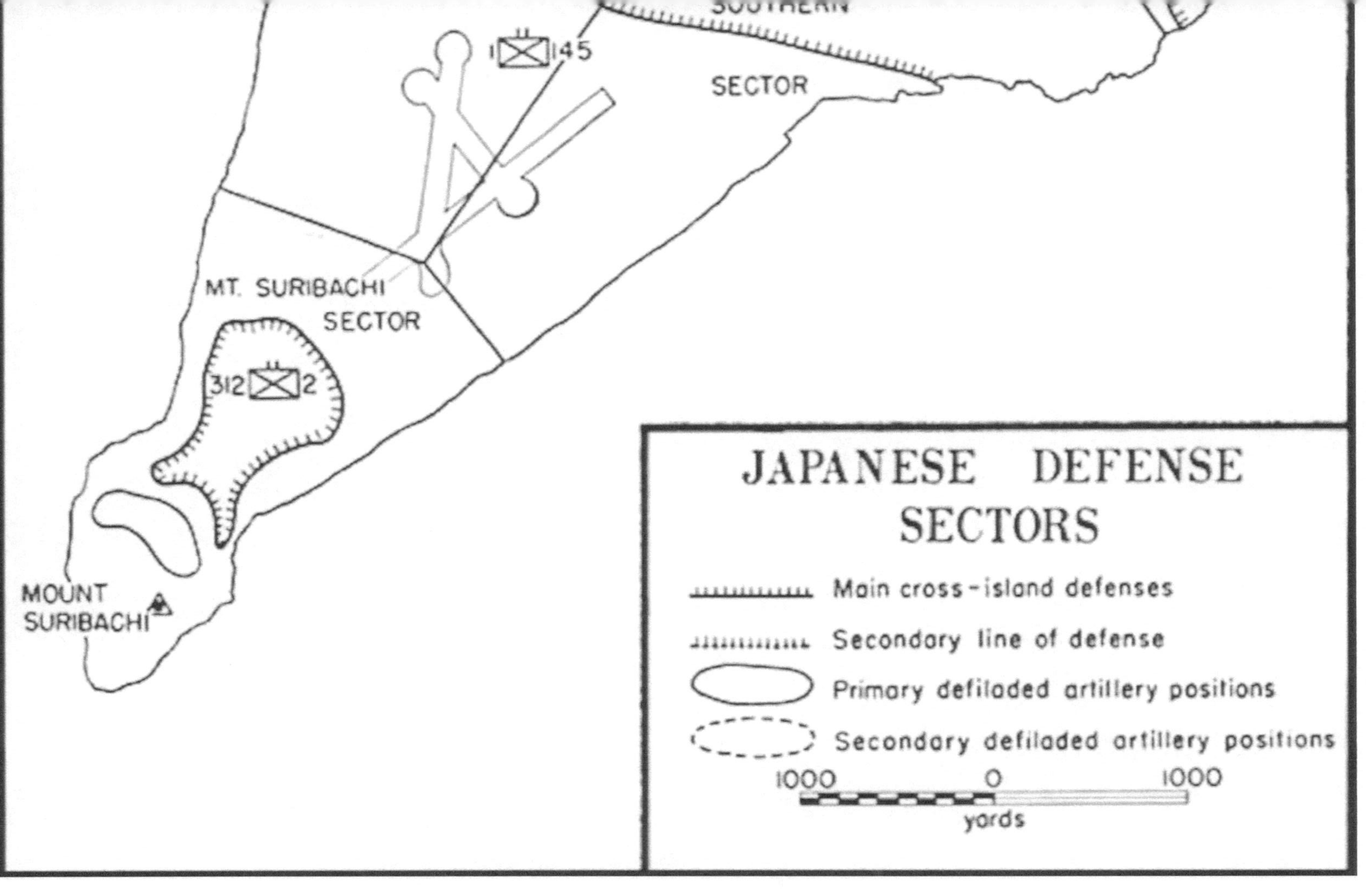

JAPANESE DEFENSE SECTORS
Main cross-island defenses
Secondary line of defense
Primary defiladed artillery positions
Secondary defiladed artillery positions
1000
0
1000
yards
SOUTHERN
SECTOR
MT. SURIBACHI SECTOR
MOUNT SURIBACHI
145
312
2

KURIBAYASHI'S BIG MISTAKE

The physical separation of the three Marine divisions from Hawaii to Guam had no apparent adverse effect on their training. The proficiency of small units in combined arms assaults on fortified positions and amphibious landing were where it counted most. Each division was well prepared for the invasion.

The 3rd Marine Division had just completed their part in the liberation of Guam. Their field training often included active combat patrols to root out and destroy stubborn enemy survivors.

On Maui, the 4th Marine Division prepared for their fourth assault landing in thirteen months with quiet confidence. According to Major Fred Karch: "We had a continuity of veterans that was unbeatable."

The 5th Marine Division prepared for their first combat experience on the big island of Hawaii. The unit's newness would prove misleading. Over half of the officers and men were veterans, including several former Marine Raiders and Parachutists who'd fought in the Solomons. Colonel Don Robertson took command of the 3rd Battalion, 27th Marine Regiment with less than two weeks before embarkation and immediately ordered them into the field for sustained live-fire exercises. Their confidence and competence impressed and convinced Robertson that these Marines were professionals.

Among the veterans preparing to deploy on Iwo Jima were two Medal of Honor recipients from Guadalcanal. Gunnery Sargent John Basilone and Colonel Robert Galer. The Marine Corps preferred to keep these distinguished veterans in the US for morale (bond raising) purposes, but both men wrangled their way back into the fight. Basilone led a machine gun platoon and Galer led a new radar unit for the Landing Force Air Support. The Guadalcanal veterans were amazed at the abundance of amphibious shipping available for Operation Detachment. Admiral Turner commanded 497 ships (140 of these were configured for amphib operations). This armada was ten times the size of the Guadalcanal task force.

But there were still problems. Many of the ships and crews were so new that each rehearsal featured an embarrassing collision or other accident. New bulldozers (TD-18s) were an inch too wide for the LCMs. Newly modified M4A3 Sherman tanks were so heavy that the LCMs rode with a dangerously low freeboard. The 105mm howitzers overloaded the DUKWs (amphibious trucks) to the point of unseaworthiness. These factors would soon prove treacherous in Iwo Jima's unpredictable surf.

Still, the massive Allied armada embarked and began the familiar move westward in good shape, well-trained, well-equipped, and thoroughly supported.

* * *

General Kuribayashi had benefited from the Allied delays of Operation Detachment due to the Philippines campaign. He felt as ready and prepared as possible. When the Allied armada sailed from the Marianas on February 13, he was warned. He deployed one infantry battalion into the lower airfield and ordered the bulk of his garrison into their assigned fighting holes—to await the inevitable storm.

Two issues divided the Navy/Marine team as D-Day on Iwo approached. The first was Admiral Spruance's decision to detach

Task Force 58 (the fast attack carriers under Admiral Marc Mitscher) to attack strategic targets on Honshu (Main island of Japan) with the simultaneous bombardment of Iwo. Marine officers suspected a Navy/Air Force rivalry at work: Mitscher's targets were aircraft factories that the B-29s had missed a few days earlier. Mitscher took all eight Marine Corps fighter squadrons assigned to the fast carriers, plus the new fast battleships with their 16-inch guns. While Task Force 58 returned in time to offer fire support on D-Day, they were off again for good, two days later.

There was a continuing argument between senior Navy and Marine officers over the extent of the preliminary naval gunfire. Marines looked at their intelligence reports on Iwo Jima and requested ten days of preparatory fire. The Navy said it did not have the time nor the ammunition to spare; three days would have to suffice. Generals Smith and Schmidt pleaded their case to Admiral Spruance. Their request was denied. Admiral Spruance ruled that three days of preparatory fire along with the daily hammering administered by the Seventh Air Force would be good enough to get the job done.

Lieutenant Colonel Don Weller was the Task Force 51 naval gunfire officer, and no man knew the business more thoroughly than him. Weller had absorbed the Pacific War's lessons well. Especially the terrible failures at Tarawa. He argued the issue was not the weight of shells and other caliber but rather the time. The destruction of heavily fortified enemy targets took deliberate and pinpoint firing from close range. They had to be assessed and adjusted by aerial observers. His seven hundred plus hard targets would need time to knock out—a lot of time.

Admiral Spruance did not have time to give for strategic, tactical, and logistical reasons. Three days of firing would deliver four times the shells than Tarawa and would be one and a half time as much delivered against the larger Saipan. It would have to do.

Iwo's notoriously foul weather and strong enemy fortifications dissipated the three-day bombardment. According to General William Rogers: "We got about 13 hours with the fire support during the 34 hours of available daylight."

General Kuribayashi committed his only known tactical error during this battle. On D minus 2, a force of one-hundred Navy and Marine frogmen approached the eastern beaches. They were escorted by a dozen rocket-firing LCI (Landing Craft Infantry). Kuribayashi believed this was the main assault and authorized the coastal batteries to open fire. This exchange was hot and heavy with the LCIs getting the worst of it, but the US battleships and cruisers hurried to blast the casement guns that were suddenly revealed on Suribachi's right flank.

That night, seriously concerned about the hundreds of Japanese targets untouched by two days of firing, Admiral Turner authorized a "war council" on his flagship and junked the original plan. He ordered the gunships to concentrate exclusively on beach areas. This was done with considerable effect on D minus 1 and D-Day morning.

Kuribayashi noted most of the positions the Imperial Navy insisted on building along the beach were destroyed—just as he predicted. But his central defensive force that crisscrossed the Motoyama Plateau remained intact. "I pray for a heroic fight," Kuribayashi told his staff.

The press briefing held the night before D-Day on Admiral Turner's flagship was uncommonly somber. General Holland Smith predicted heavy casualties: upwards of 15,000, which shocked everyone. A man clad in khakis without a rank insignia then stood and addressed the room. It was the Secretary of the Navy, James Forrestal: "Iwo Jima, like Tarawa, leaves very little choice. Except to take it by force of arms, by character, and by courage."

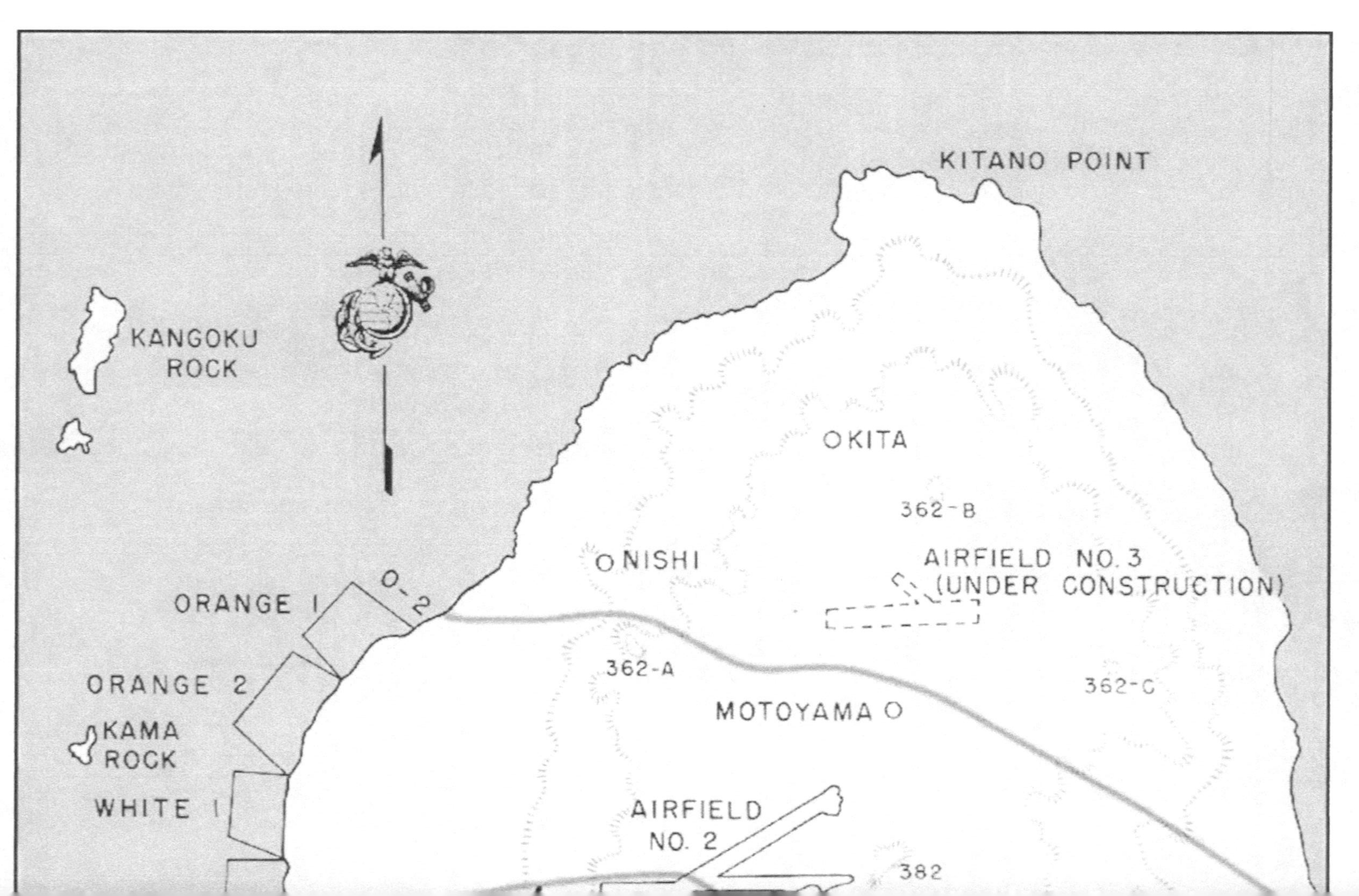

KITANO POINT
KANGOKU ROCK
OKITA
362-B
O NISHI
AIRFIELD NO. 3
(UNDER CONSTRUCTION)
362-A
362-C
MOTOYAMA O
O-2
ORANGE 1
ORANGE 2
KAMA ROCK
WHITE 1
AIRFIELD NO. 2
382

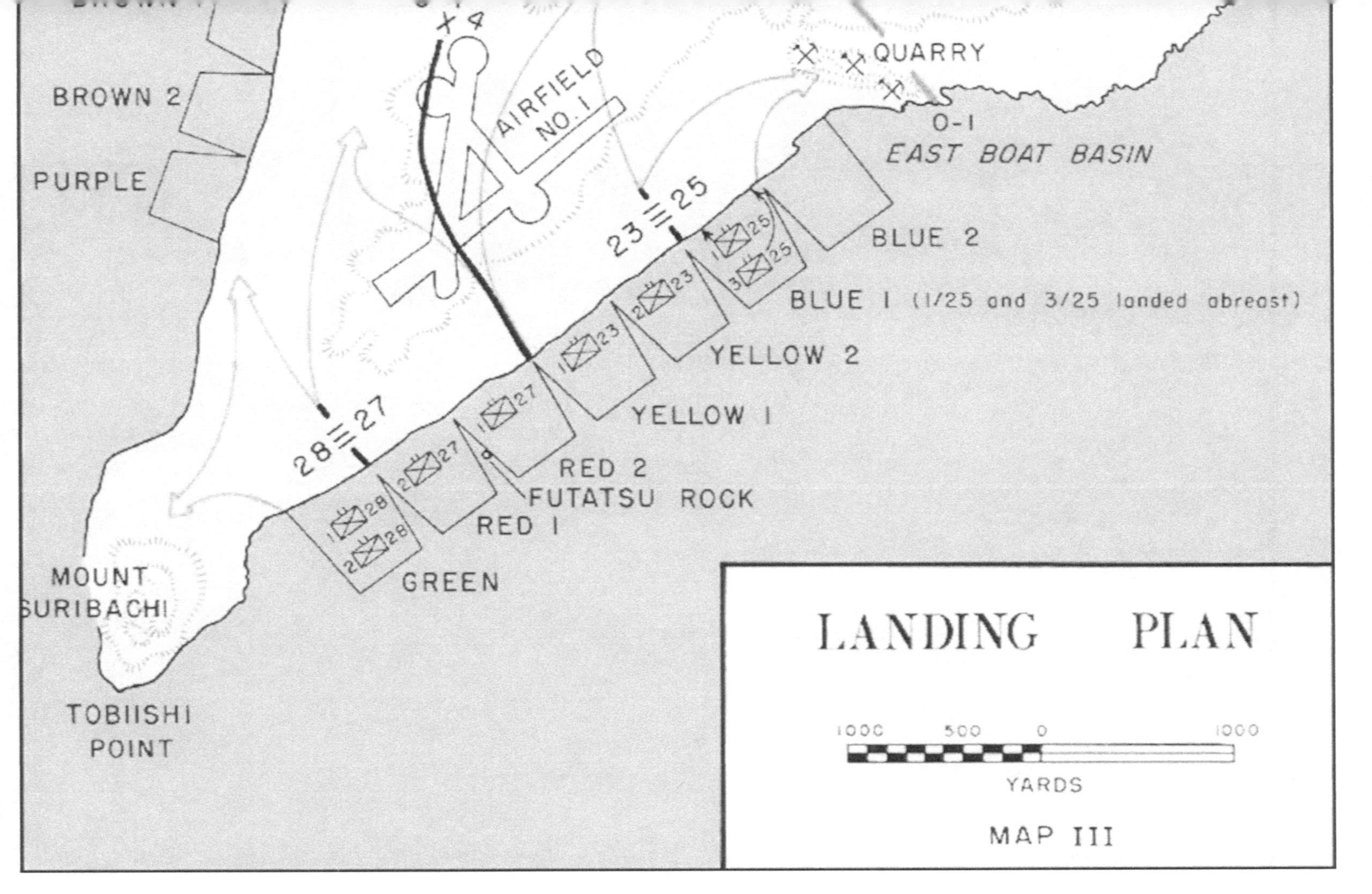

BROWN 2
PURPLE
QUARRY
AIRFIELD NO. 1
O-1
EAST BOAT BASIN
23 ≡ 25
BLUE 2
BLUE 1 (1/25 and 3/25 landed abreast)
YELLOW 2
YELLOW 1
28 ≡ 27
RED 2
FUTATSU ROCK
RED 1
GREEN
MOUNT SURIBACHI
TOBIISHI POINT
LANDING PLAN
1000 500 0 1000
YARDS
MAP III

D-DAY ON IWO JIMA

On D-Day morning, February 19, Iwo's weather conditions were ideal. At 0645, Admiral Turner signaled: "Land the landing force."

Shore bombardments had engaged the enemy island at near point-blank range. Battleships and cruisers steamed in as close as 1,500 yards to level their guns against their island targets. Many of these older battleships had performed this dangerous mission in other theaters of the war. The *Nevada*, raised from the muck and ruin of Pearl Harbor, led the bombardment force. The battleship *Arkansas*, built in 1912, had joined the armada from the Atlantic where she'd battered German positions at Normandy during the Allied landing on June 6, 1944.

Colonel "Bucky" Buchanan devised a modified form of the "rolling barrage" used by the bombarding gunships against beachfront targets. This concentration of naval gunfire advanced gradually as troops landed. Always 400 yards to the front. Air spotters would regulate the pace. This innovation was appealing to the division commanders who'd served in World War I France. In those days, a rolling barrage was often the only way to break a stalemate.

The amount of shelling was shocking. Admiral Hill later wrote: "there were no proper targets for shore bombardment remaining on

D-Day morning." This was an overstatement. No one denied the fury of firepower delivered against the landing beaches and surrounding areas. General Kuribayashi admitted in an assessment report to Imperial headquarters: "we need to reconsider the power of bombardment from ships. The violence of enemy bombardments is far beyond description."

When the task force appeared over the horizon, troop ships crowded with combat-equipped Marines gazed at the stunning fireworks. The Guadalcanal veterans among them watched with grim satisfaction as battleships hammered the island. The world had come full circle from the dark days of October 1942: when the 1st Marines and the Cactus Air Force suffered a similar shelling from Japanese battleships.

Sailors and Marines were eager to get their first glimpse of the objective. War correspondent John Marquand wrote of his first impressions on Iwo: "a silhouette like a sea monster, with a little dead volcano for a head and the beach area for the neck and a scrubby brown cliff for the body."

Navy Lieutenant David Susskind wrote his thoughts from the bridge of the troopship *Mellette*: "Iwo Jima was an ugly and rude sight. Only a geologist could look at it and not be disgusted."

A surgeon in the 25th Marines, Lieutenant Mike Keleher wrote: "the naval bombardment had already begun. I saw the orange-yellow flashes as the cruisers, battleships, and destroyers blasted away at the island with broadsides. We were close to Iwo, just like the pictures and models we'd been studying for weeks. A volcano was on our left and long flat beaches in a rough, rocky plateau was on our right."

General Clifton Cates studied the island through binoculars from his ship. Each division would land two reinforced regiments abreast. From left to right, the beaches were designated Green, Red, Yellow, and Blue. The 5th Division would land the 27th and 28th Marines on the left flank on Green and Red Beaches, While the 4th would land the 23rd and 25th Marines on the right flank at Blue Beach.

General Schmidt reviewed the latest intelligence reports with growing anxiety and requested that General Holland Smith reassign the reserve forces. Schmidt wanted the 3/21 Marines to replace the 26th Marines as the core reserve and release them to the 5th Division. Schmidt envisioned the 28th Marines cutting the island in half before turning to capture Suribachi. The 25th would scale the rock quarry, serving as the hinge for the entire corps to swing north. The 23rd and 27th Marines would then capture the first airfield, before pivoting north into their assigned zones.

General Cates was concerned about Blue Beach on the right flank. Blue Beach was directly under the observation and fire of suspected enemy positions in the rock quarry. Steep cliffs overshadowed their right flank, while Suribachi dominated the left. The 4th Division figured that the 25th Marines would have the most challenging objective to take on D-Day. General Cates said: "if I knew the name of the man on the extreme right of that squad, I'd recommend him for a medal before we even get there."

Iwo Jima was the pinnacle of a forced amphibious landing against a heavily fortified shore. A complex art mastered by the Fifth Fleet through many painstaking campaigns. B-24 bombers from the Seventh Air Force flew in to strike the smoking island. Rocket ships moved in to saturate shore targets. Fighter and attack squadrons from Mitscher's Task Force 58 joined in. While Navy pilots showed their skills at bombing and strafing, the troops started cheering at the sight of F4U Corsairs flown in from Marine fighter squadron 213.

Colonel Vernon McGee was the air officer for the Expeditionary Troops. He urged this special show for the men in the assault waves. "Drag your bellies on the beach," McGee said to the Marine fighters. The F4U Corsairs made an aggressive approach parallel to the island. They streaked low over the beaches and savagely strafed enemy targets. The Pacific War geography since Bougainville kept ground Marines separated from their air support. According to McGee: "it was the first-time many troops had ever seen a Marine fighter plane, and they were not disappointed."

Not long after the planes left, naval gunfire resumed. Gunfire carpeted the beach with a crescendo of high explosive shells. Ship-to-shore movement was underway, an easy thirty-minute run for the LVTs.

For Operation Detachment, there were enough LVTs to get the job done. Sixty-eight LVT (A)4 armored amtracs, with snub-nosed 75mm cannons, blasted the way forward with 385 troop laden LVTs following close behind. The assault waves crossed the line of departure on time and confidently chugged toward the smoking beaches.

On Iwo, there was no coral reef or killer neap tides to worry about. Navy frogmen cleared the approaches of tetrahedrons and mines. There was no premature secession of fire. The modified rolling barrage was in effect, and no vehicles were lost from enemy fire. Assault waves hit the beaches within two minutes of H-hour. Enemy observers watching the drama unfold from a cave on the slopes of Suribachi reported: "At 9 am, several hundred landing craft with amphibious tanks rushed toward shore like an enormous tidal wave."

Colonel Robert Williams, XO of the 28th Marines, later wrote: "The landing was a magnificent sight to see—two divisions landing abreast—you could see the whole show from the deck of a ship. At this point, so far so good."

The first obstacle didn't come from the Japanese, but from the beach and its parallel terraces. Iwo was a volcano with steep beaches that sharply dropped off into a narrow and violent surf zone. Soft black sand immobilized all wheeled vehicles and caused many tracked amphibious vehicles to belly down and get stuck.

The following boat waves had even more trouble. When ramps dropped and a Jeep or truck would drive out, they got stuck too. Then, plunging waves would smash into the stalled craft before they could unload, filling their sterns with water and sand and broaching them broadside. The beach quickly became a salvage yard.

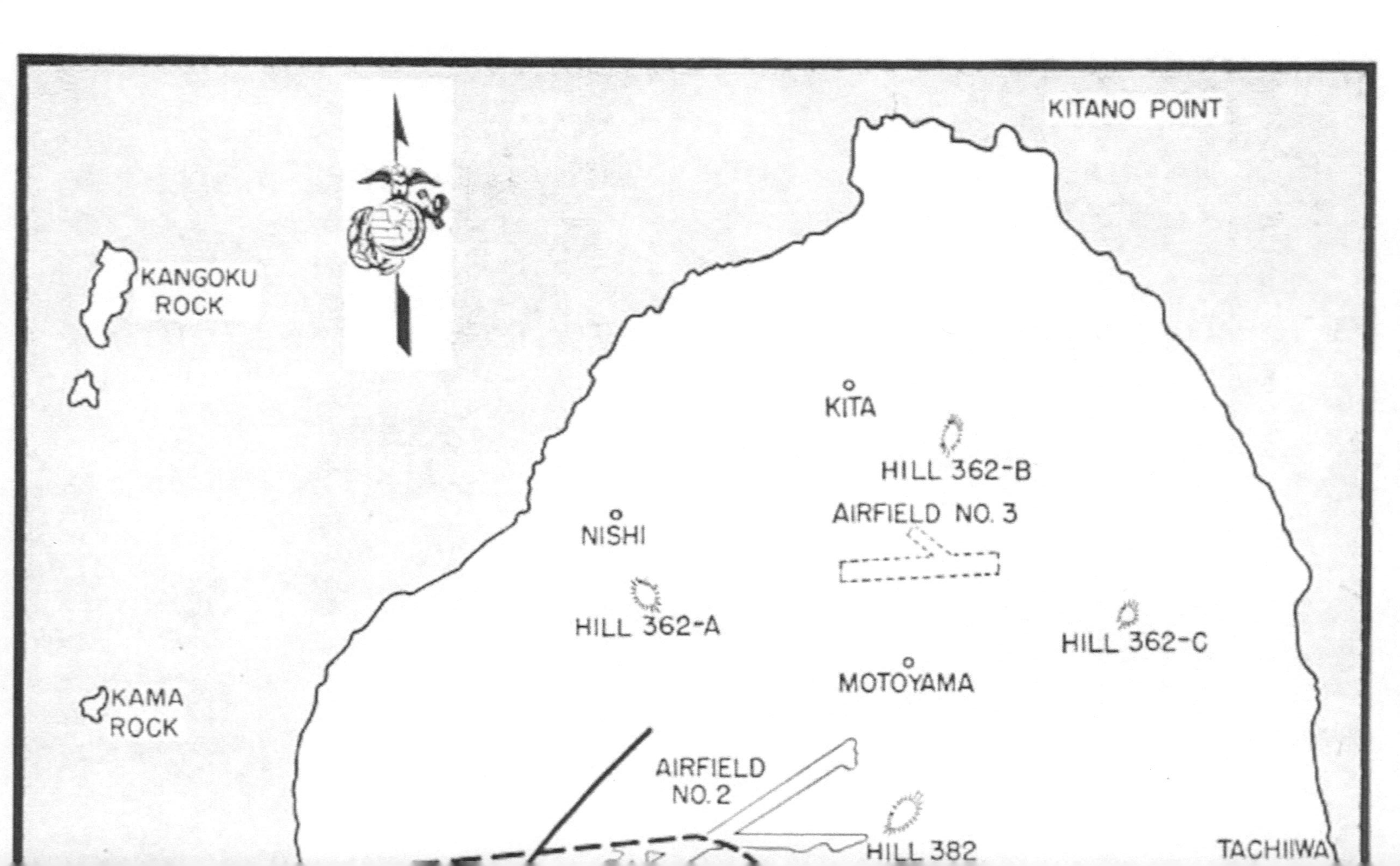

KITANO POINT
KANGOKU ROCK
KITA
HILL 362-B
AIRFIELD NO. 3
NISHI
HILL 362-A
HILL 362-C
MOTOYAMA
KAMA ROCK
AIRFIELD NO. 2
HILL 382
TACHIIWA

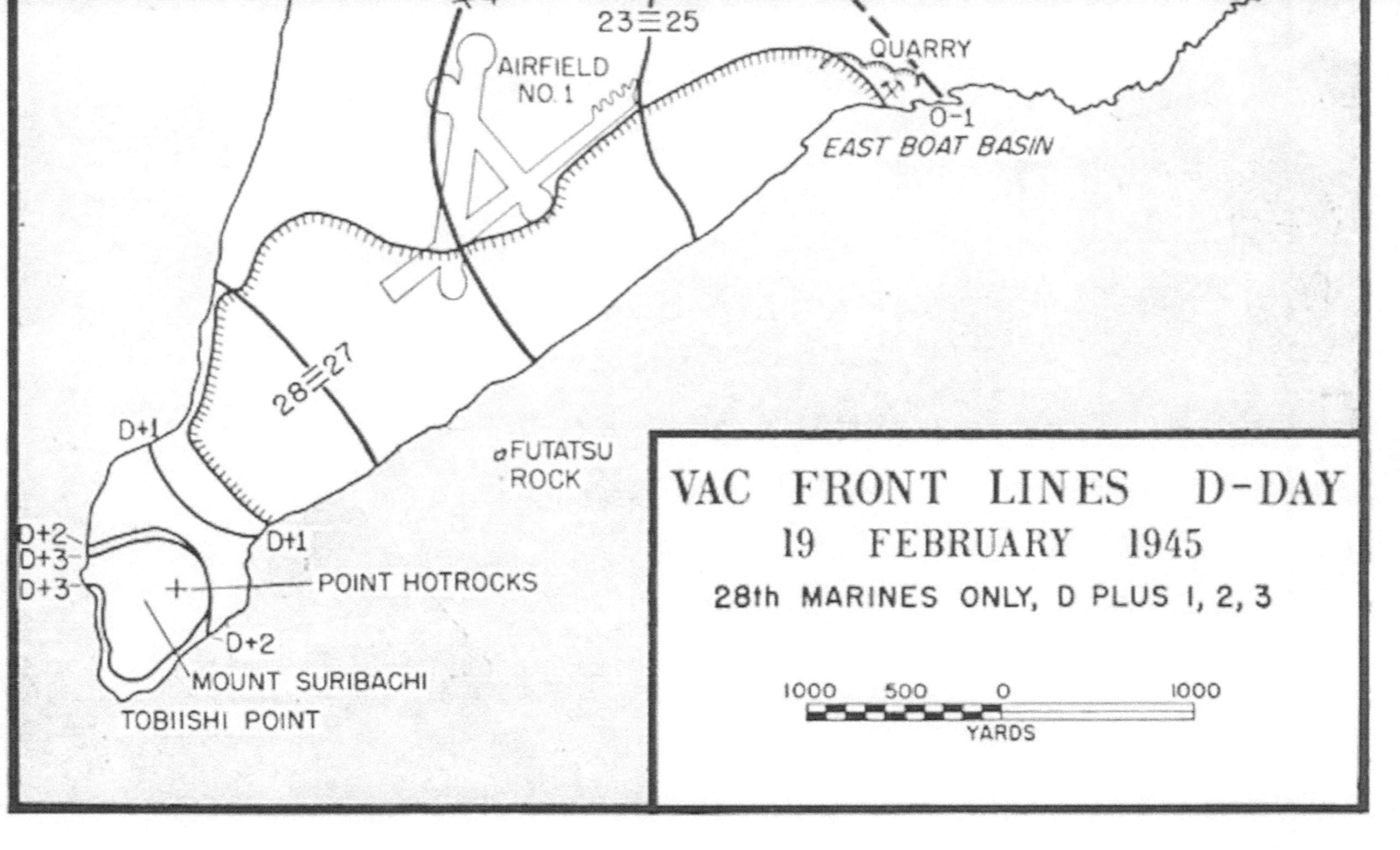

VAC FRONT LINES D-DAY
19 FEBRUARY 1945
28th MARINES ONLY, D PLUS 1, 2, 3
1000 500 0 1000
YARDS
QUARRY
23≡25
AIRFIELD NO. 1
O-1
EAST BOAT BASIN
28≡27
FUTATSU ROCK
D+1
D+1
D+2
D+3
D+3
POINT HOTROCKS
D+2
MOUNT SURIBACHI
TOBIISHI POINT

GETTING THE GUNS ASHORE

The heavily laden infantry was bogged down. According to Corporal Ed Hartman, a rifleman in the 4th Marine Division: "the sand was so soft, it was like trying to run in loose coffee grounds." The 28th Marines' first report after getting ashore: "resistance moderate, terrain awful."

The rolling barrage and carefully executed landing produced the desired effect: suppressing enemy fire while providing enough shock and awe to allow the first assault waves to clear the beach and advance inward. In less than fifteen minutes, 6,000 Marines were ashore. Many were hampered by increasing fire over the terraces and down from the highlands, but hundreds leaped forward and maintained their assault momentum.

The 28th Marines on the left flank had rehearsed this landing on the volcanic terrain of Hawaii's Big Island. Now, despite increasing casualties among company commanders and the usual landing disorganization, elements of the regiment used their initiative to advance across the narrow neck of the peninsula. This became much bloodier as enemy strong points along Suribachi's base sprung to life.

Ninety minutes after landing, elements of the 1/28 Marines

reached the western shore—700 yards from Green Beach—Iwo had been severed. According to one Marine: "it was like we cut off the snake's head." This was the deepest penetration of what would become a costly and bloody day.

The regiments had difficulty getting across the black-sand terraces toward the airfield. The terrain was like an open bowl in a shooting gallery. In full view of Suribachi on the left and a rising table to the right. Any thoughts of this operation being a cakewalk quickly vanished as registered machine gun fire whistled across the open ground and mortar rounds dropped along the terraces. Through this hardship, the 27th Marines made good initial gains and reached the southern and western edges of the first airfield by noon.

The 23rd Marines on Yellow Beach took the brunt of the first round of enemy combined arms fire. Troops crossing the terrace were confronted by two massive concrete pillboxes—still lethal after the bombardment. Overcoming these positions proved costly in men and time and. More fortified positions rose from the broken ground beyond. Requests for tank support could not be fulfilled because of the congestion problems on the beach. Still, the regiment clawed its way several hundred yards toward the eastern edge of the airstrip.

The 25th Marines immediately ran into a "Buzz-Saw" trying to move across Blue Beach. General Cates was correct in his appraisal: "The right flank was a bitch, if there ever was one." The 1/25 Marines scratched, scrambled, and clawed their way 300 yards forward under heavy enemy fire in the first half-hour. The 3/25 Marines took the heaviest beating of the day on the extreme right flank while trying to scale the cliffs leading to the rock quarry.

According to Lieutenant Colonel Justice Chambers leading the 3/25 Marines: "Crossing that second terrace, there was fire from automatic weapons coming from all over. I could've held up a cigarette and lit it on the stuff going by. I knew immediately we were in for one hell of a fight."

But this was only the beginning. When the landing forces tried to overcome the enemy's infantry weapons, they were blind to an imperceptible stirring taking place among the rocks and crevices in the interior highlands. General Kuribayashi's gunners unmasked their big guns—giant mortars, heavy artillery, rockets, and antitank weapons held under the tightest discipline for just this precise moment. Kuribayashi had waited patiently until the beaches were clogged with troops and material. Gun crews knew the range and deflection at each landing beach by heart: all weapons had been pre-registered on these targets long ago. At Kuribayashi's signal, hundreds of weapons opened fire. It was shortly after 1030.

This bombardment was as horrifying and deadly as any Marines had ever experienced. There was no cover. Enemy mortar and artillery rounds blanketed every corner of the 3,000-yard-wide beach. Large caliber coastal defense guns and dual-purpose antiaircraft guns fired horizontally. This created a deadly scissor of direct fire from high ground on both flanks. Marines stumbled over the terraces to escape the rain of lethal projectiles only to encounter machine-gun fire and minefields. Landing force casualties mounted at a shocking rate.

Major Karch of the 14th Marines expressed a begrudging admiration for the Japanese gunners: "it was one of the worst bloodlettings of the war. They rolled artillery barrages up and down the beach—I don't see how anybody could've lived through such a heavy fire barrage. The Japanese were superb artillerymen—someone was going to get hit every time they fired."

At sea, naval gunfire support desperately tried to deliver fire against enemy gun positions shooting down from the rock quarry. It took longer to coordinate this fire: the first enemy barrages wiped out the entire 3/25 Marines Shore Fire Control Party.

When the Japanese fire reached a crescendo, assault regiments issued grim reports to the flagship. Within fifteen minutes, these messages buzzed over the command net:

From 25th Marines 1036: Catching hell from the quarry. Heavy mortar and machine-gun fire.

From the 23rd Marines 1039: Taking heavy casualties and cannot move forward. Mortars are killing us.

From the 27th Marines 1042: All units pinned down by mortars and artillery. Heavy casualties. Need tank support fast to move.

From the 28th Marines 1046: Taking heavy fire and forward movement stopped. Artillery and machine-gun fire heaviest yet seen.

The landing force was getting bled but did not panic. The abundance of combat veterans throughout the rank-and-file beach regiments helped the rookies focus on the objective. Communications were still effective. Aerial observers spotted some of the now exposed gun positions and directed effective naval gunfire. Carrier planes screeched in low and dropped napalm from their belly tanks. But heavy enemy fire continued to take an awful toll throughout the first day and night—but would never again be as murderous as that first hour.

Sherman tanks played hell getting into the action on D-Day. Later in the battle, these combat vehicles were the most valuable weapons on the battlefield. This day was a nightmare. The assault divisions had embarked many tanks on board LSMs (Landing Ship Medium), sturdy craft that could deliver five Shermans at a time. But it was a challenge to disembark them on Iwo's steep beaches. The LSMs' stern anchors couldn't hold in the loose sand and the bow cables parted under the strain.

One lead tank stalled on top of the ramp and blocked the others, leaving the LSM at the mercy of the violent surf. Other tanks threw tracks or got bogged down in loose sand. Several tanks that made it over the terraces were destroyed by huge horn mines or were disabled by accurate 47mm antitank fire from Suribachi. Still, the tanks kept coming. Their mobility, armor protection, and 75mm guns were a welcome addition to the scattered infantry along Iwo's lunar-looking, shell-pocked landscape.

The division commanders committed their reserves. The 26th Marines were ordered in just after noon, General Cates ordered two battalions of the 24th Marines to land at 1400. The 3/24 Marines followed several hours later. The reserve suffered heavier casualties than the initial assault units crossing the beach, because of the punishing enemy bombardment from all island points.

Aware of a probable Japanese counterattack in the night to come, and despite the fire and confusion along the beaches, both divisions ordered their artillery regiments ashore. This frustrating and costly process took most of the afternoon. The surf and wind picked up as the day wore on and caused more than one low-riding amphibious truck to swamp with its precious 105mm howitzer cargo. Getting the guns ashore was one thing; getting them up off the sand was another.

The 75mm howitzers did better than the heavier 105s. Marines could quickly move them up over the terraces—at significant risk. But the 105s had a mind of their own in the black sand. The effort to get each weapon off the beach was a saga. Despite unforgiving terrain and enemy fire, Marines managed to get the batteries in place and registered them to render close-fire support before dark.

Plunging surf and enemy fire turned the battlefield into utter chaos. Later that afternoon, Lieutenant Mike Keleher, the battalion surgeon, went ashore to take over the aid station. (A sniper had killed the previous surgeon.) Lieutenant Keleher was a veteran of three assault landings. He was shocked by the carnage on Blue Beach: "such a sight on the beach. Wrecked boats, bogged down jeeps and tractors and tanks. Burning vehicles and casualties. Limbs of dead Marines were scattered all over the beach."

PROWLING WOLVES

An enemy mortar shell took the life of the legendary John Basilone. He'd led his machine gun platoon in a brave attack against the southern portion of the airfield. All Marines on the island felt this loss. Farther east, Colonel Rob Galer (one of the Pacific War's first fighter aces) survived the afternoon's battle along the beaches and reassembled his scattered radar unit in a deep shell-hole near the base of Suribachi.

Later that afternoon, Colonel Donn Robertson led his Marines onshore to Blue Beach. He was shocked at the intensity of fire still directed at the troops so late on D-Day: "they were ready for us. I watched with pride and wonderment as young Marines landed under fire, took casualties, and stumbled forward to clear the beach. I asked myself, what impels a young man landing on the beach in the face of fire?"

Then it was Robertson's turn. His boat slammed into the beach too hard. The ramp wouldn't drop. His Marines had to roll over the gunwales into the churning surf and crawl ashore.

The savage battle to capture the rock quarry cliffs on the right flank raged. The beachhead was exposed to direct enemy fire all day. Marines had to storm them before any more supplies or troops could be landed. In the end, it was the fighting spirit of Captain James Headley and Colonel "Jumping Joe" Chambers who led the survivors of the Marines to the top of the cliffs.

The battalion paid a high price for this feat. They'd lost twenty-two officers and five hundred troops by nightfall. Assistant division commanders Generals Hart and Hermle of the 4th and 5th Marine Division spent most of D-Day on board the control vessels marking both ends of the line a departure—4,000 yards offshore. This was another lesson in amphibious techniques learned from Tarawa. Having senior officers close to the ship-to-shore movement provided landing force decision-making from the forward most vantage point. By dust, General Hermle chose to come ashore. On Tarawa, he'd spent the night of D-Day out of contact on a fire-swept pierhead. This time he would be in the fight.

Hermle had the bigger operational picture in mind. He understood that the corps' commanders insistence on forcing the reserves and artillery units onshore despite the carnage to build combat power. Hermle knew that whatever the night brought, the Allies had more troops on the island than the Japanese could muster. His presence would help his division forget about the earlier days' disaster and focus on preparing for the inevitable enemy counterattacks.

Enemy mortar and artillery fire raked the beachhead. An enormous spigot of mortar shells (Marines called them "flying ashcans") and rocket-boosted aerial bombs were loud, whistling projectiles that tumbled end over end. Many of them sailed over the island, but those that landed along the beaches of the southern runways caused dozens of casualties. Few Marines could dig a proper foxhole in the sand. It was like trying to dig a hole in a barrel of wheat. With urgent calls to the control ship for plasma and stretchers and mortar shells came repeated sandbag requests.

War combat correspondent Lieutenant Cyril Zurlinden (soon to become a casualty himself) described his first night ashore: "On Tarawa, Saipan, and Tinian, I saw Marines killed and wounded in a shocking manner. But I never saw anything like the ghastliness that hung over the Iwo Jima beachhead. It was utter frustration, anguish, and a constant inner battle to maintain at least some semblance of sanity.

Accounting for personnel was a nightmare under those conditions. But assault divisions eventually reported a combined loss of 2,375 men to General Schmidt—503 killed and 1,755 wounded, 18 missing, and 99 combat fatigues. While these statistics were sobering, Schmidt had gotten 30,000 Marines ashore. A casualty rate of eight percent left the landing force in better condition than Saipan or Tarawa's first day. It was a miracle the casualties hadn't been twice as high. Did Kuribayashi wait too long to use his big guns?

The first night in Iwo Jima was an eerie affair. Mists of sulfur spiraled from the earth. Marines who were used to the tropics now shivered in the cold, waiting for Kuribayashi's samurai warriors to come screaming down the hills. Marines learned this Japanese commander was different. There would be no wasteful banzai attack tonight. Instead, small teams of infiltrators, "Prowling Wolves," would probe the Marine lines and gather intelligence. A barge full of the elite Japanese *Special Landing Forces* tried a counter landing on the western beaches—they died to a man under the alert guns of the 28th Marines and supporting LVT crews.

That night was one of continuous indirect fire from the Highlands. A high velocity round landed directly in a fighting hole occupied by the 1/23 Marines commander Colonel Ralph Hass and instantly killed him. Marines took other light casualties throughout the night, but at dawn, the veteran landing force stirred.

Five infantry regiments moved to the north, while the sixth turned to the business at hand in the south: Mount Suribachi

SURIBACHI-YAMA

Marines knew this dormant volcano as "Hotrocks."

The Japanese called it Suribachi-yama. Allied planners knew their drive north would never succeed without first securing that hulking rock dominating the southern plain. According to one Marine: "Suribachi took on a life of its own. It watched over us. It loomed over us. That mountain represented more evil to us than the Japanese."

Colonel Atsuchi commanded 2,000 enemy soldiers and sailors in the Suribachi garrison. The Japanese had honeycombed the mountain with machine-gun nests, tunnels, and observation sites. But Atsuchi had lost many of his large-caliber guns from the three-day naval bombardment. Atsuchi's command at Suribachi was semiautonomous. General Kuribayashi realized the invaders would soon cut communication lines across the island's narrow tip. Kuribayashi hoped Atsuchi could hold out for at least ten days and maybe even two weeks.

Some of the strongest defenses on Suribachi were down along the rubble-strewn base. Here, over seventy camouflaged concrete blockhouses protected the mountain's approaches. Another fifty blockhouses bulged from the slopes within the first hundred feet of elevation. Then came the caves, and the first of hundreds the Marines would face on Iwo Jima.

The 20th Marines took 407 casualties cutting across the neck of the island on D-Day. The following day in a cold rain, they prepared their assault. Colonel Chandler Johnson, commanding the 2/28 Marines, set the morning's tone as he deployed his tired troops forward: "it's going to be a hell of a day in one hell of a place to fight this damn war."

Several 105mm batteries opened up overhead. Gun crews fired from positions dug in the black sand next to the 28th Marine's command post. Troops learned that even their 155mm howitzers would hardly shiver the enemy's concrete pillboxes. As the preparatory fire lifted, infantry advanced into heavy mortar and machine-gun fire. Colonel "Harry the Horse" Liversedge requested tanks.

But the 5th Tank Battalion was having a frustrating morning. Tanks desperately searched for a defilade spot to rearm and refuel for the assault. But in those first few days on Iwo, there was no such spot. Every time the tanks gathered to service their vehicles, they were walloped by enemy artillery and mortar fire from the entire island. Getting the tanks serviced to join in on the assault took most of the morning. After getting battered all day, the tankers would now only refit, rearm, and re-equip at night.

The day's slow start led to more setbacks for the 5th Tank Battalion. Enemy antitank gunners hid in the hodgepodge of boulders and knocked out the first approaching Shermans, crippling the assault's momentum. While the 20th Marines overran forty enemy strongpoints and gained 200 yards a day, they lost a Marine for every yard gained. The tankers redeemed themselves when a 75mm round caught Colonel Atsuchi poking his head out of a cave entrance—blowing him apart.

Elsewhere on the morning of D +1 were discouraging sites of chaos along the beaches from Kuribayashi's unrelenting artillery barrages and the violent surf. According to one Marine: "The wreckage was indescribable. I saw two miles of debris that was so thick there were only a few places our landing craft could still get in. The wrecked hulls of dozens of landing boats testified to the price we had to pay to put our troops ashore. Tanks and half-tracks laid there crippled from getting bogged down in the coarse sand. LVTs and amphibian tractors were victims of mines and well-aimed shells and were now flopped on their backs. Cranes were brought in to unload cargo and were tilted at insane angles. Our bulldozers were smashed in their own roadways."

Then bad weather set in and complicated the unloading. Strong winds whipped sea swells into a nasty chop. The surf got uglier. These were the conditions Colonel Carl Youngdale faced while trying to land the 105mm howitzer batteries of his 4/14 Marines. All twelve of these guns were preloaded in amphibious trucks (DUKWs) one to a vehicle. Adding to that was the problem of marginal seaworthiness and contaminated fuel. Youngdale watched in shock as eight amphibious trucks suffered engine failures, swamped, and sank with a terrible loss of life. Two more amphibious trucks broached in the surf zone and spilled their guns into deep water. Youngdale managed to get the two remaining guns ashore and into firing position.

General Schmidt committed one battery of the 105mm howitzers to the narrow beachhead on D +1. These guns reached the beach intact, but it took hours to get the amphibious tractors to drag the heavy guns up over the terraces. The 105's were in place and firing before dark. The deep bark of the guns was a welcome sound to the Marines. Concerned about heavy casualties in the first twenty-four hours, General Schmidt committed the 21st Marines from the core reserve. But the seas were too rough. Troops had a harrowing experience trying to climb down the cargo nets and into the small boats—violently bobbing alongside the transports. Many Marines tumbled into the sea. The boating process took hours to complete. Once afloat, troops circled endlessly in the small Higgins boats waiting for the call to land. But after six hours of bobbing in the water and awful seasickness, the 21st Marines returned to the ships for the night.

Even the larger landing craft, the LSMs and LCTs, had a hard time breaching. Sea anchors were needed to keep the craft perpendicular to the breakers, and they rarely held fast in that soft bottom. Admiral Hill later wrote: "dropping that stern anchor was like dropping a spoon in a bowl of mush."

Hill contributed to the development of amphibious operations in the Pacific War. He and his staff developed armored bulldozers to land in the assault waves. They experimented with hinged *Marston* matting, used as a temporary road on airfields to get vehicles over soft sand. On the beach at Iwo, bulldozers were worth their weight in gold. The Marston matting was only partially successful: the LVTs chewed it up, but all hands could see the true potential.

Admiral Hill worked with the Naval Construction Battalion (Seabees) to bring the supply-laden pontoon barges ashore. But again, the surf prevailed and broached the craft, spilling the cargo. Now desperate, Hill's beachmasters turned to a round-the-clock use of amphibious trucks and LVTs to keep the combat cargo flowing.

Once amphibious trucks got free of their crippling loads, they were fine.

Amphibian tractors could cross the soft beach without help. They resupplied and conducted medevac missions directly along the front lines. These vehicles suffered from inexperienced crews in the LSTs who wouldn't lower their bow ramps enough to accommodate the amphibious trucks and tractors approaching after dark. Many times, vehicles loaded with wounded Marines got lost in the dark or ran out of gas and sank. The amphibian tractor battalions lost over 147 LVTs at Iwo Jima. Unlike Tarawa, where enemy gunfire and mines accounted for less than twenty percent of this total. Thirty-four LVTs perished from Iwo's crushing surf, and eighty-eight sank in the deep water.

Once ashore and clear of the loose sand along the beaches, half-tracks, tanks, and armored bulldozers collided with the strongest minefield defenses yet encountered in the Pacific. Under Kurib-ayashi's direction, enemy engineers had planted irregular rows of antitank and horned anti-boat mines along the exits from both beaches.

The enemy accompanied these weapons by rigging massive makeshift explosives from 500-pound aerial bombs, torpedo heads, and depth charges triggered by a pressure mine. The loose soil on Iwo had enough metallic characteristics to render standard mine detectors inaccurate. Marines and engineers were on their hands and knees in front of tanks, probing for mines with bayonets and wooden sticks.

While the 28th Marines battled to encircle Suribachi, the shore party and beachmasters struggled to clear the wreckage from the beaches. In the 5th Marine Division zone, the relatively fresh troops of the 1/26 and 3/27 Marines got bloodied. They forced their way across the western runways and took heavy casualties from time-fused airbursts and enemy dual-purpose antiaircraft guns. In the 4th Division zone, the 23rd Marines captured and secured the airstrip—advancing 800 yards with massive casualties.

Some of the most savage fighting was along the high ground above the Rock Quarry on the right flank. Here, the 25th Marines were engaged in the fight of their lives. Rifleman Richard Wheeler found the landscape, and the embedded enemy surreal: "there was no cover from enemy fire. Japs were in reinforced concrete pillboxes and laid down interlocking bands of fire that cut entire companies to pieces. Camouflage hid all their positions. The high ground on either side was honeycombed with layer after layer of Jap emplacements. They had a perfect observation of us. Whenever a Marine made a move, those damn Japs smothered the area with a murderous blanket of fire."

The second day of battle proved unacceptable on every front for the Marines. When the 1/24 Marines finally broke through along the cliffs late in the day, they were rewarded with back-to-back cases of friendly fire. A naval airstrike caused eleven casualties. Misguided salvos from an unidentified gunfire support ship took down another ninety troops. Nothing was going right.

The morning of D +2 promised more frustration. Marines shuddered in the chilly rain and wind. Admiral Hill twice closed the beach because of dangerous undertows and wicked surf. But during one of the grace periods, the 3/21 Marines came ashore, glad to be free of the heaving small boats.

The 20th Marines continued their attack on Suribachi's base. It was a slow, grinding, and bloody fight—boulder by boulder. On the western coast, the 1/28 Marines made the most of naval and field artillery gunfire support and reached the mountain's shoulder. Everywhere else, murderous enemy fire restricted any progress to a matter of yards. Enemy mortar fire from all over the volcano rained down on the 2/28 Marines, clawing their way along the eastern shore. Rifleman Richard Wheeler recalled: "it was terrible. Worst I can remember us ever taking. Jap mortar men played checkers with us as the squares."

The Marines used *Weasels*, handy tracked vehicles that made their first field appearance in this battle to hustle forward flamethrower canisters and evacuate the wounded. That night the amphibious task force experienced the only significant air attack of the battle. Forty-nine *kamikaze* pilots from the *22d Mitate Special Attack Unit* smashed into ships on the outer ring of Iwo Jima. In a desperate action, serving as a prelude to Okinawa's fiery hell, kamikaze pilots sank the escort carrier *Bismarck Sea* with heavy loss of life. They damaged several ships and knocked the veteran *Saratoga* out of the war. All forty-nine Japanese planes were destroyed.

On D +3, it rained even harder. Marines darted forward under fire, hitting the deck to return fire. They discovered that the loose volcanic sand, combined with rain, jammed their weapons. The 21st Marines at the vanguard ran headfirst into a series of enemy emplacements at the southeastern end of the Japanese defenses. Marines battled all day to scratch and claw and advance 200 yards. Casualties were disproportionate and horrific.

On the right flank, Colonel Chambers rallied the 3/25 Marines through the rough and rugged terrain above the Rock Quarry. While Chambers directed the advance of his decimated companies, an enemy sniper shot him in the chest. Chambers went down hard, thinking it was all over: "I faded in and out. I don't remember too much about it except a frothy blood gushing from my mouth. Then someone started kicking the hell out of my feet. It was Captain Headley yelling, 'get up, you were hurt worse on Tulagi.'"

Captain Headley knew Chamber's sucking chest wound was life-threatening. He tried to reduce his commander's shock until he could get him out of the line of fire. Lieutenant Mike Keller, the battalion surgeon, crawled forward with one of his corpsmen. They lifted Chambers onto a stretcher and through enemy fire, carried him down the cliffs to the aid station, and eventually onboard an amphibious truck to make the evening's last run out to the hospital ship. All three battalion commanders on the 25th Marines were now casualties. Chambers survived and received the Medal of Honor. Captain Headley took command of the shot-up 3/25 Marines for the rest of the fight.

The 20th Marines on D +3 made progress against Suribachi. They reached the shoulder on all points late in the day. Combat patrols from the 28th Marines linked up at Tobiishi Point: the southern tip of the island. Reconnaissance patrols reported they found few signs of life along the mountain's upper slopes and on the north side.

Admiral Spruance authorized Task Force 58 to strike Okinawa and Honshu at sundown. After that, they would go to Ulithi and prepare for the Ryukyuan campaign. All eight Marine Corps fighter squadrons left Iwo Jima for good. Navy pilots flying from the ten remaining escort carriers picked up the slack. While there was no question of the courage and skill of these pilots, the quality of close air support for the troops fighting ashore plummeted after the Marine fighter squadrons departed.

The escort carriers had too many other missions: combat air patrols, anti-submarine sweeps, downed pilot searches, and harassing strikes against neighboring Chichi Jima. Marines reported a slow response time for air support requests, light payloads, and high delivery altitudes. The navy pilots delivered several napalm bombs, but many failed to detonate. This wasn't the pilots' fault. The early napalm bombs were old wing-tanks filled with the mixture and activated by unreliable detonators. Marines on the ground were concerned about these notoriously inaccurate weapons being dropped from high altitudes.

On February 23, D +4, the 28th Marines were poised to capture Suribachi. This honor was given to Lieutenant Harry Schrier and Company E, 3rd Platoon. They were ordered to summit, secure the crater, and raise a 54" x 28" American flag for everyone to see. At 0800, Schrier led his forty-man patrol forward. The regiment had already blasted dozens of pillboxes with demolitions and flame. They'd rooted out snipers and knocked out the mass batteries. The combined arms hammering by planes, naval guns, and field pieces had finally taken their toll on the enemy. Any Japanese soldier who popped out of a cave to resist was cut to shreds. Marines carefully walked up the steep northern slope, sometimes resorting to crawling on hands and knees.

The Suribachi flag-raising drama has endured for so long because so many people observed it. All over the island, Marines tracked the progress of the tiny column of troops during their ascent. Hundreds of binoculars from offshore ships watched Schrier's Marines climb. When they finally reached the top, they disappeared. Those closest to the volcano heard gunfire. Then at 1020, there was movement on the summit—the Stars & Stripes fluttered bravely in the breeze.

Cheers roared from the southern end of the island. Ships sounded sirens and whistles. Wounded men propped up on their litters to get a glimpse. Marines wept. Navy Secretary Forrestal was thrilled. He turned to General Holland Smith: "raising that flag means a Marine Corps for another five hundred years."

Three hours later, an even larger flag went up. Few knew that Associated Press photographer Joe Rosenthal had just captured the American war-fighting spirit on film. *Leatherneck* magazine Staff Sergeant Lou Lowery had taken a picture of the first flag raising and immediately got into a firefight with a handful of enraged enemy defenders. His photograph would become a valuable collector's item—but it was Rosenthal's that would enchant the free world.

Captain Tom Fields of Company D's 1/26 Marines heard his men yell: "Look up there!" and he turned in time to watch the first flag go up. His first thoughts were on the battle still at hand, and he remembered in the moment saying: "Thank God the Japs won't be shooting us down from behind anymore."

The 28th Marines captured and secured Mount Suribachi in three days at the cost of 900 casualties. Colonel Liversedge reoriented his regiment for operations to the north. Unknown to all, the battle of Iwo Jima still had another bloody thirty days before it would be over.

THE MEATGRINDER

It wasn't until the ninth day of battle that intelligence officers realized General Kuribayashi led the Japanese forces on Iwo Jima.

The unexpected early loss of the Suribachi garrison was a setback for Kuribayashi, but he still held a strong position. He had eight infantry battalions, two artillery and three heavy mortar battalions, and a tank regiment. Admiral Ichimaru had 5,000 naval infantry and gunners under his command, but unlike other besieged garrisons in the Central Pacific—these two Japanese leaders worked well together.

Kuribayashi was pleased with the quality of his artillery and engineering troops. His chief of artillery, Colonel Kaido, commanded from an impregnable concrete blockhouse in the east-central sector of the Motoyama Plateau. A lethal landmark the Marines called "Turkey Knob."

General Senda was an artillery officer with combat experience in Manchuria. He commanded the *2d Independent Mixed Brigade*, whose central units would be locked into a 25-day death struggle against the 4th Marine Division. The *204th Naval Construction Battalion* had built some of the most formidable defense systems on the island in his sector. One cave had an 800-foot-long tunnel with fourteen separate exits. It was only one of the hundreds defended to the bitter end.

Well-armed and confident enemy troops waited for the advance of the V Amphibious Corps. Kuribayashi ordered occasional company-sized attacks to recapture lost terrain or disrupt enemy assault preparations—but these were not sacrificial or suicidal. These mainly were preceded by stinging mortar and artillery fires and aimed at gaining limited objectives. General Kuribayashi's iron will kept his troops from large-scale, futile banzai attacks until the last few days.

An exception was on the evening of March 8. General Senda, frustrated at the noose the 4th Division were applying, ordered 800 of his surviving troops into a ferocious counterattack. Finally, the Marines had targets out in the open. The suicidal Japanese attackers were cut to pieces with machine-gun and small arms fire.

For the first week of the drive north, the Japanese on Iwo had the assaulting Marines outgunned. The enemy's 120mm mortars and 150mm howitzers were superior to most of the weapons of the landing force. Marines found the enemy's direct fire weapons deadly. Especially the dual-purpose antiaircraft guns and the 47mm tank guns, buried up to their turrets. Retired General Donn Robertson said: "the Japs could snipe with those big guns. They also had the advantage of knowing the ground."

Most of the casualties in the first three weeks of battle were from high explosives: rocket bombs, grenades, mines, artillery, and hellacious mortars. Robert Sherrod (*Time* correspondent) wrote that the dead on Iwo Jima, both Japanese and Marine, had one thing in common: "they all died with the greatest possible violence. Nowhere in the Pacific War had I seen such badly mangled bodies. Many men were cut squarely in half."

The close combat was savage. Another constant stress for Marines was no secure rear area to put wounded troops. Kuribayashi's gunners hammered the beaches and airfields. Massive spigot mortar shells and rocket bombs tumbled from the sky. Japanese defenders were drawn to softer targets in the rear. Antipersonnel mines and booby-traps were everywhere and on a large scale for the first time in the Pacific.

Exhausted Marines stumbled out of the front line, seeking nothing more than a helmet full of water to bathe in and a deep hole to sleep in. Instead, Marines spent their rare rest repairing weapons, dodging incoming rounds, humping ammo, or having to repel another nighttime enemy probe.

General Schmidt planned to assault the northern Japanese positions with three divisions abreast. The 5th on the left, the 3rd in the center, and the 4th on the right. This northern drive would jump off on D +5: the day after securing Mount Suribachi. Preparatory fires along the high ground north of the second airfield would last for an hour. Then three regimental combat teams would advance abreast: 26th Marines on the left, 24th on the right, and the 21st in the center. For this assault, Schmidt merged all three divisions' Sherman tanks into one armor task force—commanded by Colonel "Rip" Collins. This would be the largest concentration of Marine tanks in the Pacific War: an armored regiment.

Marines recognized they were trying to force a passage through Kuribayashi's primary defensive belt. The assault deteriorated into multiple desperate small unit actions along the front. While the 26th Marines (with the help of tanks) gained the most yards, it was still relative. Airfield runways were lethal killing zones. Mines and high-velocity direct fire destroyed Sherman tanks all along the front. On the right flank, Colonel Alexander Vandegrift (son of Marine Commandant Alexander Vandegrift) was wounded.

During the fighting on D +5, General Schmidt moved his command post onshore from the amphibious force flagship *Auburn*. Schmidt now had eight entire infantry regiments committed to the battle. General Holland Smith still had the 3rd Marines and expeditionary troops in reserve. Schmidt made his first of multiple requests to Smith to release that seasoned outfit. The V Amphibious Corps had already taken 6,845 casualties.

On February 25, D +6, enemy resistance intensified. Small

Marine units escorted by tanks made progress along the runway. Each Marine was under the impression he was alone in the middle of a giant bowling alley. Often, holding newly gained positions across the runway proved more deadly than capturing them. Resupplying the troops became virtually impossible. Precious Sherman tanks were getting destroyed at an alarming rate.

General Schmidt got two battalions of 105mm howitzers ashore under the command of Colonel John Letcher. Well-directed fire from these heavy field pieces eased some of the pressure on the assaulting Marines. While fire from destroyers and cruisers was marginally effective, air support was a total disappointment. The 3rd Marine Division later complained that the Navy's assignment of eight fighters and eight bombers on station was utterly inadequate.

At noon, General Cates sent a message to Schmidt requesting the strategic Air Force in the Marianas immediately replace Navy air support. Colonel McGee, air commander on Iwo, took heat from the frustrated division commanders. He later wrote: "those little spit kit Navy fighters up there were trying to help but were never enough and were never where they needed to be."

In fairness, it's debatable if any service could have provided adequate air support within the opening days of the northern drive. The air liaison parties within each regiment played hell trying to identify and mark targets. The enemy kept a masterful camouflage. Japanese frontline units were often eyeball to eyeball with Marines, and the air support request net was often overloaded.

Navy squadrons flying from the decks of escort carriers eventually improved by adding heavier bombs and improving their response times. A week later, General Cates rated his air support as satisfactory. But the battle of Iwo Jima would continue to frustrate Allied forces; the Japanese never assembled legitimate targets in the open. Captain Fields of the 26th Marines wrote after the war: "the Japs weren't *on* Iwo Jima. They were *in* Iwo Jima."

Richard Wheeler, who survived Iwo Jima with the 28th Marines, wrote two books about the battle. "This was one of the strangest battlefields in history. One side fought wholly above ground, and the other operated within it. During the battle, American aerial observers marveled that one side of the field had thousands of figures milling around or in foxholes while the other side was deserted. But the strangest of all was that the two contestants sometimes made troop movements simultaneously in the same territory with one maneuvering on the surface and the other using tunnels below."

As the Marines fought like hell to capture the second airfield from the Japanese, the terrain features rising to the north caught their attention. While there were three hills named 362 on the island, Marines had different nicknames for them: "Amphitheater" and "Turkey Knob." But the bristling complex of hills and terrain would be forever known as "The Meatgrinder."

The 5th Marine Division earned their spurs and lost many of their precious veteran leaders fighting on "The Gorge" and attacking Nishi Ridge (Hills 362-A and B).

The 3rd Marine Division focused their assault north of the second airfield and then onto the heavily fortified Hill 362-C beyond the airstrip. Finally, they attacked the moonscape jungle of stone, soon to be known as "Cushman's pocket."

Colonel Robert Cushman commanded the 2/9 Marines on Iwo. Cushman and his Marines were veterans of heavy fighting on Guam but were stunned by their first sight of the battlefield. Burned out and smoldering Sherman tanks dotted airstrips. Casualties streamed to the rear. The terrific and horrific echo of machine-gun fire was everywhere. Cushman mounted his troops on the surviving tanks and rumbled across the field. They met the same reverse-slope defenses that dogged the 21st Marines. But after three days of savage fighting, Cushman's Marines secured the two Hills north of the second airfield, Peter and 199-Oboe.

General Schmidt made the 3rd Division attack in the center of his main effort. He gave the 3rd priority fire support from the corps artillery. He directed the other two divisions to allocate half of their regimental fire support to the center. The other commanders were not pleased. Neither the 4th Marine Division, who took heavy casualties in the Amphitheater, nor the 5th Division, who struggled to seize Nishi Ridge, wanted to dilute their organic fire support.

General Graves Erskine argued the main effort should receive the primary fire. Schmidt never solved this problem. His corps artillery was too late, and he needed twice as many battalions and bigger guns: the 8-inch howitzers, which the Marines had not yet fielded. Schmidt had plenty of naval gunfire support available and used it abundantly. But unless targets were in ravines facing the sea —he lost the advantage of observed direct fire.

General Schmidt's fire support problems were eased on February 26. Two Marine observation planes flew in from the carrier *Wake Island* and were the first planes to land on Iwo's recently recaptured, fire swept main airstrip. These were single-engine observation planes (Grasshoppers). They were followed the next day by similar planes from VMO-5. The pilots of these fragile planes had already had an exciting time in the waters off Iwo. Many were launched from the experimental catapult on *LST-776*: "like a peanut from a slingshot."

All fourteen of these observation planes took heavy enemy fire airborne and while serviced on the airstrips. But these two squadrons flew 612 missions supporting all three divisions. Few units contributed as much to the eventual suppression of Kuribayashi's murderous artillery fire. The mere presence of the small planes overhead caused Japanese gunners to cease fire and button-up against the inevitable counter-battery fire soon to follow. Grasshopper pilots would fly predawn or dust missions to extend a protective umbrella over the troops. This was risky flying because of Iwo's unlit fields and snipers hidden in the hills.

When the 4th Marine Division finally secured Hill 382 at the highest point north of Suribachi, they still suffered heavy casualties moving through the Amphitheater against Turkey knob. The 5th Marine Division seized Nishi Ridge and bloodied themselves on Hill 362-A's elaborate defenses. Colonel Tom Wornham, CO, 27th Marines: "they had interlocking fields of fire the likes of which I'd never seen before."

General Cates redeployed the 28th Marines into the fight. On March 2, an enemy gunner fired a high-velocity shell that killed Colonel Chandler Johnson one week after his glorious seizure of the

Suribachi Summit. The 28th Marines captured Hill 362-A—at the cost of 200 casualties.

The same day, Colonel Lowell English, CO 2/21 Marines, took a bullet in his knee. Colonel English was upset that his battalion was not rotating to the rear: "We took heavy casualties and were disorganized. I had less than 300 Marines left of the 1,200 I came ashore with." Colonel English received orders to turn his Marines around and plug a gap in the front lines. "It was an impossible order. I couldn't move that disorganized battalion a mile back to the north in thirty minutes."

But General Erskine did not want excuses: "tell that *God-damned* English he'd better be there."

Colonel English replied: "you tell that son of a bitch I will be there, and I was, but my men were still half a mile behind me, and I got a hole in my knee!"

The 26th Marines fought their bloodiest and most successful attack of the battle on the left flank—finally securing Hill 362-B. This all-day battle cost 500 Marine casualties and produced five Medals of Honor. For Captain Frank Caldwell of Company F, 1/26 Marines, it was the worst day of his life. His company took forty-nine casualties on that hill—as well as the first sergeant and all the original platoon commanders.

The first nine days of the V Amphibious Corps' northern drive produced a net gain of only 4,000 yards at a horrific cost of 7,000 Marine casualties. Several of these pitched battles in The Meat-grinder would've been worthy of a separate book. The fighting was one of the most brutal and bloody in the Marine Corps' history.

On D +13, March 4, came the turning point. After alarming and frightful losses, Marines had torn through a substantial chunk of General Kuribayashi's primary defenses. Forcing the enemy commander to shift his command post to a northern cave. On this afternoon, the first crippled B-29 landed. In terms of Allied morale, it couldn't have come at a better time. General Schmidt ordered a standdown on March 5 to enable the exhausted assault forces a brief rest and the opportunity to absorb replacements.

The issue of replacement troops throughout this battle is controversial—even seventy-seven years later. General Schmidt had suffered losses approaching the equivalent of an entire division (6,561 Marines). Schmidt urged Holland Smith to release the 3rd Marines. While each division had been assigned several thousand Marine replacements, Schmidt wanted the cohesion and combat experience of Colonel Jim Stewart's regimental combat team. Holland Smith argued the replacements would suffice and believed that each replacement Marine in these hybrid units had received sufficient infantry training to fulfill immediate assignment to the frontline outfits.

The next challenge was distributing the replacements in small arbitrary numbers—not teamed units—to plug the gaping holes in the assault battalions. These new men were expected to replace the vital veterans of the Pacific War. These replacement Marines were not only new to combat but also to each other—an assortment of strangers that lacked the lifesaving bonds of unit integrity.

One frustrated Marine officer said: "they get killed the day they go into battle." Losses among the replacement Marines within the first forty-eight hours of combat were shocking. Those who survived and learned the ropes established a bond with the veterans and contributed significantly to the battle's victory. Division commanders criticized the wastefulness of this policy and urged for replacements from the veteran battalions of the 3rd Marines.

General Erskine later wrote: "I asked Kelly Turner and Holland Smith to give us the 3rd. They said, 'you got enough Marines on the island now. There are too damn many here already.' I said, 'this is an easy solution. Some of these Marines are tired and too worn out, so take them out and bring in the goddamn 3rd Marines.' They said, 'keep your mouth shut. We made our decision.' And that was that."

Most surviving officers agreed that the decision not to use the veteran 3rd Marines at Iwo was wasteful and ill-advised. But Holland Smith never wavered: "sufficient troops were on Iwo Jima for the capture of the island. Two regiments were sufficient to cover the frontal assault assigned to General Erskine."

On D +14, March 5, General Holland Smith ordered the 3rd Marines to sail back to Guam.

* * *

While Holland Smith may have known the overall statistics of the battle losses sustained by the landing force at that point—he did not fully appreciate the tremendous attrition of experienced junior officers and senior noncoms taking their place every day. For example, the day after the 3rd Marines sailed for Guam, the 2/23 Marines' E Company suffered the loss of their seventh company commander since the start of the battle.

Colonel Cushman's experiences with the 2/9 Marines were typical: "casualties were brutal. By the time Iwo was over, we'd gone through two complete sets of lieutenants and platoon leaders. After that, we had forward artillery observers commanding companies and sergeants leading half strength platoons. It was that bad."

Colonel English wrote: "After twelve days, we'd lost every company commander. I had one company exec left. I'd lost all three of my rifle company commanders killed by the same damn shell."

Many infantry units and platoons ceased to exist. Depleted companies were merged to form half-strength outfits.

NORTHERN ALLIED DRIVE

The Allied drive continued north after the March 5 standdown. It did not get any easier. The Japanese had changed tactics: fewer big guns and rockets and less observed fire from the highlands. But now, the terrain had deteriorated into narrow gorges, enveloped in sulfur mists—killing zones.

Allied casualties mounted. Gunshot wounds now outnumbered the high explosive shrapnel hits. A myth among Marine units was that the Japanese were nearsighted and poor marksmen. In close quarters fighting in northern Iwo, Japanese riflemen shot down hundreds of advancing Marines in the head or chest with well-aimed fire. Captain Caldwell of the 1/26 Marines said: "Poor marksmen? All the Japs we faced were expert shooters."

Supporting arms coordination became more effective during the battle. Colonel "Buzz" Letcher established the first SACC (Supporting Arms Coordination Center), where senior artillery, naval gunfire, and air support representatives pooled their talents and resources. While Letcher lacked the manpower and communications equipment to run a full-time SACC, his efforts significantly advanced this challenging art.

Colonel McGee's Landing Force Air Support Control Unit worked in harmony with the fledgling SACC. Still, friendly fire incidents happened. Perhaps friendly fire was inevitable on that crowded island, but positive control at the highest level did much to reduce the frequency of these accidents.

The lack of preliminary naval bombardment on Iwo angered Marines. While all hands valued the responsive support received from D-Day onward, the lack of initial fire was blamed for the horrific Marine casualties. The gunfire ships stood in close—less than a mile offshore—and hammered the flanks and front lines. Many ships took hits from the hidden enemy coastal defense batteries. There were no safe zones in or around Iwo Jima.

Two characteristics of naval gunfire on Iwo were notable: The extent ships provided illuminating rounds over the battlefield, especially during the early days before the landing force artillery could assume the bulk of these missions. Second was the degree of assistance provided by the smaller gunships, frequently modified with 4.2-inch mortars, 20mm guns, or rockets. These "small boys" were vital along the northwestern coast as they worked in lockstep with the 5th Marine Division advancing toward The Gorge.

While the Marines comprised most of the landing force on Iwo, they still received support from the army. Two of the four amphibious truck companies on D-Day were army units. The 138th Antiaircraft Artillery Group placed their 90mm batteries around the newly captured airfields. General Jim Chaney (later to become Iwo's island commander) landed on D +8 with elements of the Army's 145th Infantry.

Army units flew into Iwo on March 6 (D +15). The 15th Fighter Group arrived to escort B-29s over Tokyo. This group was a seasoned outfit that included the famous 47th Fighter Squadron and their P-51 Mustangs. While the army pilots had little to no experience in direct air support of ground troops, Colonel McGee was impressed with their "eager beaver attitude" and willingness to learn.

McGee appreciated the fact the Mustangs could deliver thousand-pound bombs. He had the Army pilots trained on how to strike designated targets on nearby islands. In three days, they were ready for duty on Iwo. McGee instructed the Mustang pilots to arm their bombs with twelve-second delay fuses and attack parallel to the front lines approaching from a 45° angle.

These tactics often produced stunning results—especially along the west coast—where the thousand-pound bombs blew sides of entire cliffs off into the ocean. This exposed enemy caves and tunnels to direct naval gunfire from the sea. According to McGee: "those Air Force boys did a lot of good."

The field medical support given to the assaulting Marines was a major contributor to victory on Iwo. Integrating chaplains, surgeons, and corpsmen within the FMF (Fleet Marine Force) paid valuable dividends. Most times, corpsmen were as tough and combat savvy as the Marines in that company. Wounded Marines knew their corpsman would move heaven and earth to reach them, bind their wounds, and start the long evacuation process.

Marines on Iwo Jima echoed the views of Staff Sergeant Al Thomas: "we had outstanding corpsmen. They were our family." The luxury of having first-rate medical help so close to the front took a terrible toll. Eight hundred twenty-seven corpsmen and twenty-three doctors were wounded or killed on Iwo Jima—a casualty rate twice as high as Saipan.

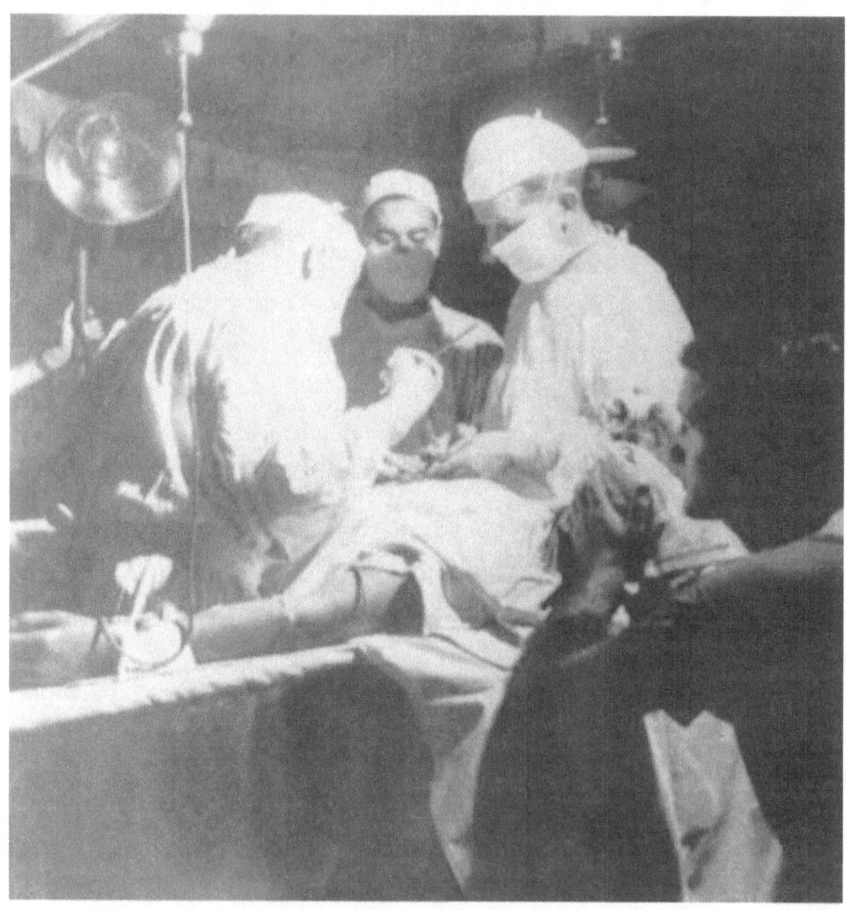

Combat medical support was thoughtfully prepared and provided on Iwo. Past the crude aid stations and toward the rear, the Army and Navy field hospitals arose. Wounded Marines would receive treatment in a field hospital, then recuperate in a bunker before returning to the lines to often receive their second or third wound. The more seriously wounded were evacuated by air to Guam or to one of the several fully-staffed hospital ships operating around the clock. Within the first month of fighting on Iwo, 13,747

Marines and corpsmen casualties were evacuated by hospital ship and another 2,489 by airlift.

When a Marine was wounded, the first few minutes were the most dangerous after going down. Enemy snipers had no hesitations about picking off corpsmen, litter crews, or even the wounded man himself as his buddies tried to slide him out of the fire.

Corporal Ed Canter was a rocket truck crew chief in the 4th Marine Division. Rocket trucks always drew an angry barrage of counter-battery fire from the enemy. A Japanese sniper shot Canter through the stomach. Corporal Canter's comrades knew they had to get him away from that launch site fast. As a nearby motion picture crew recorded the drama, four Marines carried Canter down a mud-covered hillside. They heard the scream of an incoming shell and dumped Canter while they took cover.

The explosion killed the film crew and wounded each of the Marines, including Canter again. The film footage survived and appeared in US newsreels—before becoming a part of the movie *Sands of Iwo Jima*. Corporal Canter survived and was evacuated to a hospital ship and then to different hospitals in Guam and Hawaii before returning to the US. His war was over.

* * *

The shore party personnel and beachmasters performed remarkable feats of logistics to keep the advancing divisions equipped and armed. The logistical management and sheer backbreaking work needed to maintain such a high volume of supplies and equipment moving over these dangerous beaches was hard to imagine. A single beach on the west coast became functional on D +11, but by that time, most of the landing force supplies were already ashore.

The next day after the general unloading was completed, the vulnerable amphibious ships were released from their tether to the beachhead. Shortly after, well-aimed enemy fire detonated the 5th Marine Division's entire ammo dump. Ammunition resupply became vital. Then, the ammunition ship *Columbia Victory* came under direct enemy fire as she approached the western beaches to unload. Waiting Marines held their breath as the *Columbia Victory* was nearly destroyed. She narrowly escaped, but the potential for disaster still loomed.

An entire brigade of the 62nd Naval Construction Battalion (Seabees) extended and repaired the captured runways. Marines returning to the beaches from the northern highlands could scarcely recognize the place they'd first seen on D-Day. There were now over 80,000 Allied troops on the small island, and the Seabees had bull-dozed a two-lane road to the top of Mount Suribachi.

Communications had improved dramatically on Iwo compared to previous amphibious campaigns. Handsets and radios were now waterproof and had more frequencies. Forward observer teams used the backpack SCR-610, while companies and platoons preferred the walkie-talkie style SCR-300 or even lighter portables, the "Spam Can" SCR-536.

Colonel Jim Berkeley, XO of the 27th Marines said: "On Iwo, we had near-perfect communications. It was all any commander could ask for." Marines strung telephone lines between support units and four command posts as the battle raged, elevating the wire along upright posts to avoid damage by tracked vehicles.

Enemy counterintelligence expected to have an easy day splicing into allied phone lines, but Marines baffled them with Navajo code talkers. Each division employed twenty-four trained Navajos. The 5th Marine Division's command post had six established Navajo networks on the island. No one throughout the war could ever crack the Navajo code.

Black American troops played a major role in the capture of Iwo. Black troops drove army amphibious trucks and were active throughout the landing. Black Marines of the 8th Ammunition Company and the 36th Depot Company landed on D-Day and served as longshoremen on those chaotic, bloody beaches. The on-island Black Marines worked with the Shore Party and helped to sustain the momentum of the Allied northern drive. When the Japanese counterattacked penetrated these beach areas, Black Marines dropped their cargo, unslung their carbines, and engaged the enemy with well-disciplined fire.

Colonel Leland Swindler commanded the V Amphibious Corps Shore Party: "the entire body of Black Marines under my command conducted themselves with marked coolness and courage and inflicted more casualties on the enemy than they sustained."

News coverage of the Iwo Jima battle was extensive. Dozens of combat correspondents were embedded with the landing force throughout the battle. Marine Sergeant "Dick" Dashiell was a writer for the Associated Press and assigned to the 3rd Marine Division. Although sometimes terrified and filled with horror, Dashiell endured and wrote eighty-one frontline stories and pounded out news releases on his portable typewriter at the edge of his foxhole. Dashiell's eye for detail always caught the attention of the reader: "All is bitter. Frontal assault always uphill. A ceaseless wind filled the air with a fine volcanic grit." He described how Marines had to stop and clean the grit from their weapons—and how naked that made most Marines feel.

Occasionally, hot food was delivered to the exhausted Marines on the front lines. The deliveries of milk and fruit from nearby ships boosted morale. So did watching the crippled B-29s zoom in for an emergency landing. Sergeant "Doc" Lindsey was a squad leader in Company G, 2/25 Marines. He stated: "It was good to see them land. You knew they'd just come from hitting Tokyo."

DEFIANT TO THE END

General Erskine caught pneumonia but refused to evacuate. His Chief of Staff, Colonel Robert Hogaboom, kept the war moving behind the scenes. The division continued its advance, and when Erskine recovered—Hogaboom adjusted accordingly. The two were an effective team.

Erskine had long wanted to conduct a battalion-size night operation. It bothered him that throughout the war, the Allies had yielded the night to the Japanese. When Hill 362-C continued to thwart his advance, Erskine ordered a predawn assault without the trappings of preparatory fire, which always identified the time and place of attack.

The honor of leading this unusual attack was put to Colonel "Bing" Boehm, CO, 3/9 Marines. But this battalion was new to the sector and received their attack order too late to reconnoiter effectively. Absent of advance orientation, the battalion crossed the line of departure silently at 0500 and advanced toward Hill 362-C. The unit achieved total surprise. Before the sleepy Japanese knew it, the Marines swept across 500 yards of broken ground and roasted enemy outposts and strong points with flamethrowers.

When daylight revealed that Boehm's battalion had captured the wrong hill (Hill 362-C was still 250 yards distant), his battalion was surrounded by a sea of furious and wide-awake and counterattacking enemy infantry. Boehm redeployed his battalion and attacked toward the original hill. This was rough going and took most of the day, but before dark, the 3/9 Marines secured Hill 362-C—a main Japanese defensive anchor.

The Allied positions grew stronger after General Senda's counterattack against the 4th Marine Division. On D +18, a patrol from the 3rd Marine Division reached the northeast coast. The squad leader filled his canteen with saltwater and sent it to General Schmidt marked: "For Inspection, Not Consumption."

Schmidt welcomed the symbolism. The next day, the 4th Marine Division finally secured Turkey Knob and advanced toward The Amphitheater on the east coast. While the end was in sight, the intensity of the Japanese resistance did not fade. In the 5th Division's western zone, the 2/26 reported a casualty rate of seventy percent. General Keller Rockey reported his Marines were: "in a state of extreme fatigue and exhaustion."

Division commanders looked to relieve their shot-up men. General Cates formed a provisional battalion in the 4th Marine Division under Colonel Melvin Krulewitch. He was ordered to attack bypassed enemy positions. While the term "mopping up" was used, it was considered inaccurate by many Allied troops. Countless pockets of Japanese held out—defiant and well-armed to the end. Rooting them out was never easy. Marines used pioneers, motor transport units, and amtracs, as light infantry units to strengthen frontline battalions and conduct combat patrols.

In the extreme rear on Iwo Jima, the men had become overconfident. Movies were shown every night and ice cream could be found on the beach. Men swam in the surf and slept in tents in a deadly and false sense of security.

To the north, Colonel Cushman's 2/9 Marines were engaged in broken terrain east of the airfield. Marines ultimately encircled the enemy's position, but the battle of "Cushman's Pocket," raged on. Cushman's battalion commander reported the action: "The Jap position is a maze of pillboxes, caves, emplaced tanks, stonewalls, and trenches. We beat against them for eight continuous days using every support weapon. Our core objective in the sector still remains. Our battalion is exhausted, and most of our leaders are gone. Our battalion now numbers 387 with 350 replacements."

Cushman's 2/9 was ultimately relieved by elements of the 9th and 21st Marines (equally exhausted) and had just as difficult of a time. General Erskine had no reserves. He ordered Cushman back into the pocket, and by March 16, (D +25) enemy resistance in the thicket of jumbled rocks ended.

* * *

The 4th Marine Division poured over the hills in the east and secured the coastal road by blasting the last Japanese strong points from the rear. Ninety percent of Iwo Jima was in Allied hands.

Radio Tokyo announced the fall of Iwo Jima as: "the most unfortunate thing in the whole war situation."

General Holland Smith took the opportunity to declare victory and conduct a flag-raising ceremony. Following that, the old warhorse departed along with Admiral Kelly Turner. Now, General Schmidt and Admiral Hill finally had the campaign to themselves. Survivors of the 4th Marine Division began backloading on board ship—their battle finally over.

The killing continued in the north. The 5th Marine Division entered The Gorge, an 800-yard pocket of broken country the troops called "Death Valley." General Kuribayashi would make his last stand here in a command center in a deep cave. Fighting through this horrid moonscape was a fitting end to the battle—nine days of cave-by-cave assaults with demolitions and flamethrowers. Marine combat engineers used 9,000 tons of explosives to detonate one massive fortification. Progress was bloody and slow. General Rockey's depleted and drained regiments lost one man for every two yards gained. General Schmidt deployed the 3rd Division against Kitano Point in the 5th Division zone to ease the pressure.

Colonel Hartnoll Withers led the final assault with the 21st Marines against the extreme northern tip of the island. General Erskine's pneumonia be damned. He came along to look over Withers' shoulder. The 21st Marines felt the end was near. Their momentum was irresistible. In a few hours of sharp fighting, they cleared out the last of the resistance. Erskine signaled Schmidt: "Kitano Point Taken."

Allied forces tried to persuade Kuribayashi to surrender during these last days. They broadcasted appeals in Japanese and sent him personal messages, praising his bravery, and urging his cooperation. General Kuribayashi was a samurai to the end. In his last message to Tokyo: "We have not eaten or drank for five days, but our fighting spirit is still running high. We will fight to the end for our Emperor."

Imperial Headquarters tried to convey the good news that the emperor had approved his promotion to full general. There was no response from Iwo Jima. It would be a posthumous promotion.

Controversial Japanese evidence revealed that he committed *Seppuku* on the night of March 25.

The 5th Marine Division clawed their way forward in The Gorge. The average battalion that landed with thirty-six officers and 885 men on D-Day now only had sixteen officers and 300 men. This included the hundreds of replacements funneled in through the battle. Remnants of the 1/26 and 1/28 Marines squeezed the enemy into a final pocket and destroyed them.

On the evening of March 25 (D +34), the battle for Iwo Jima was over. The island became eerily quiet. Far fewer illumination shells flickered a false light on the shadowy figures moving south toward the airfield. General Schmidt got the good news that the 5th Marine Division had snuffed out the last enemy cave. As the corps commander prepared to declare the end of organized resistance on Iwo Jima—a well-organized enemy force emerged from the northern caves and snuck down the length of the island.

This last spasm of Japanese resistance reflected the enemy's tactical discipline. A 300-man Japanese force took all night to move into position around the island's vulnerable rear area. Newly arrived army pilots from the VII Fighter Command were surprised in their tents. The enemy force attacked the sleeping pilots with grenades, swords, and automatic rifles. The fighting was as savage and bloody as any on Iwo Jima.

Men from the 5th Pioneer Battalion and surviving pilots formed a skirmish line and launched a counterattack. Seabees and redeploying 28th Marines joined the fight. There were few suicides among the Japanese. Most died in battle. Grateful to strike one final blow for their emperor. Sunrise uncovered the carnage—300 dead enemy and over a hundred slaughtered pilots, Seabees, and pioneers along with another 200 wounded. It was a grotesque closing chapter to five savage weeks of killing and carnage.

LEGACY OF IWO JIMA

In thirty-six days of combat, the V Amphibious Corps killed nearly
22,000 Japanese sailors and soldiers. This was achieved at a stag-

gering cost. Marine assault units (along with organic Navy personnel) suffered 24,053 casualties—6,140 killed—the highest single action losses in Marine Corps history. Statistically, for every three Marines who landed on Iwo Jima, one became a casualty.

According to military historian Norman Cooper: "Seven hundred Americans gave their lives for every square mile. For every plot of ground the size of a football field, an average of one American and five Japanese were killed, and five Americans wounded."

Assault units bore the brunt of these casualties. Captain Bill Ketcham's Company I, 3/24 Marines, landed on D-Day with 133 Marines and three rifle platoons. Only nine of these men remained when his company re-embarked on D +35.

Captain Frank Caldwell reported a loss of 220 men from Company F, 1/26 Marines. By the end, a private first class commanded a platoon in Captain Caldwell's merged 1st and 2nd Platoons.

Captain Tom Fields relinquished command of Company D on the eighth day to replace his battalion's executive officer. When he rejoined his company at the end of the battle, Fields was sickened to find only seventeen of the original 250 Marines still alive.

Company B of the 1/28 Marines went through nine company commanders in the fight. Twelve different Marines served as platoon leaders of the 2nd Platoon—including two buck privates. Other divisions reported similar conditions.

The American public reacted with shock and sadness as they had fourteen months earlier on Tarawa. The debate about the high cost of forcibly seizing an enemy island raged in the press while the battle was being fought. The Marine Corps released only one statement on February 22 about detailed battle losses during the fighting. They reported casualties of nearly 5,000.

William Randolph Hearst was an early supporter of the MacArthur for President campaign. Hearst ran a front-page editorial in the *San Francisco Examiner* blaming the horrific Marine losses on poor tactics: "it's the same thing that happened on Saipan and Tarawa." The editorial urged for the elevation of General

MacArthur to supreme commander of the Pacific: "HE SAVES THE LIVES OF HIS OWN MEN."

One hundred off-duty Marines disagreed and stormed the offices of the examiner and demanded an apology. But the Hearst editorial had already received wide play. Many families of men fighting in the Pacific were forwarded the clippings. Marines received these in the mail while the fighting still raged on Iwo—an unwelcome blow for morale.

FDR, an expert in manipulating public opinion, kept a lid on the outcry by emphasizing the troops' sacrifice as symbolized by Joe Rosenthal's Suribachi flag-raising. While this photograph was already famous, Roosevelt made it the official logo of the Seventh War Bond Drive. He ordered the six flag raisers be reassigned home to boost morale, but three out of those six men had already been killed in the fighting on Iwo Jima.

The Joint Chiefs studied Iwo's losses. No one questioned the objective: Iwo Jima was an island that had to be secured to launch an effective strategic bombing campaign. The island could not have been bypassed or leapfrogged. There was evidence the Joint Chiefs considered using poison gas during the planning phase. Neither the US nor Japan had signed the international cessation on poison gas, and there were no civilians on the island. The US had stockpiled mustard gas shells in the Pacific Theater. When FDR read the report, he shot down the idea. He publicly stated that the United States would never make *first use* of poison gas. This left the landing force with no other option but a frontal amphibious assault against the most heavily fortified island the United States had ever faced.

The capture of Iwo Jima provided other strategic and symbolic benefits. Marines raised the flag over Suribachi the same day MacArthur entered Manila. The parallel captures of the Philippines and Suribachi were followed immediately by the invasion of Okinawa—accelerating the pace of the war and bringing it at long last to Japan's doorstep. These three campaigns proved to the Japanese command that the Allies had the capability and will to overwhelm even the most resolutely defended islands. Honshu and Kyushu would be next.

The capture of Iwo Jima delivered immediate benefits to the strategic bombing campaign. Marines fighting on the island were reminded of this mission repeatedly as crippled B-29s flew in from Honshu. Securing and rebuilding Iwo's airfields increased the operating range payload and survival rate of the big bombers. The monthly tonnage of high explosives dropped on Japan by the B-29s based in the Marianas increased eleven-fold in March alone. On April 7, eighty P-51 Mustangs took off from Iwo, escorting the B-29s bombing the Nakajima aircraft engine plant in Tokyo.

The great value of Iwo's airfields was that they could be used as emergency landing fields. By war's end, 2,252 B-29s made forced landings on Iwo. These forced landings included 24,765 flight crewmen. Many of these men would have perished at sea without Iwo's safe haven. According to one B-29 pilot: "whenever I landed on that island, I thanked God for the men who fought and died for it."

General Kuribayashi proved to be one of the most competent field commanders the Marines had ever faced. His expert understanding of simplicity and economy of force made maximum use of Iwo's formidable terrain. He deployed his mortars and artillery with great skill and commanded his troops with an iron will—to the end. He was a realist. With no hope of naval or air superiority, he knew he was doomed from the start. Allied forces took five weeks to breach every strong point and exterminate his forces on the island.

Iwo Jima was the pinnacle of Allied amphibious capabilities in the Pacific. The sheer magnitude of planning the assault and sustaining the landing forces made Operation Detachment an enduring model of detailed planning and violent execution. The element of surprise was not available. But the speed of the landing force and the toughness with which assault units withstood the withering barrages amazed the enemy defenders.

Colonel Wornham of the 27th Marines said: "The Iwo landing was the epitome of everything we'd learned over the years about amphibious assaults. Bad as the enemy fire was on D-Day, there were no reports of 'Issue in doubt.'"

Colonel Galer compared his Guadalcanal experience to the

battle on Iwo: "then, it was can we hold? On Iwo, the question was simply, when can we get this over?"

While the ship-to-shore assaults were impressive, the actual degree of amphibious effectiveness was seen in the massive, sustained logistical support which flowed over the treacherous beaches. Marines had all the ammunition and flamethrower refills they needed around the clock. They also had many less obvious necessities that marked this battle differently than its predecessors. Marines on Iwo had enough quantities of whole blood, most donated two weeks in advance, flown in, refrigerated, and always available.

Marines had mail call, clean water, radio batteries, fresh-baked bread, and prefabricated burial markers. The Iwo Jima operation was a model of interservice cooperation. Marine and Navy teams functioned efficiently together. The Navy earned the respect of the Marines on D -2 when a flotilla of tiny LCI gunboats fearlessly attacked the coastal defense guns to protect the Navy and Marine frogmen. Marines appreciated the contributions of the Coast Guard, Army, Red Cross, and embedded combat correspondents; all shared in the misery and glory of this battle.

The US Military occupied Iwo Jima until 1968, when jurisdiction was transferred back to Japan. Seventy-seven years later, the island remains a military-only island. It is no longer a baren moonscape, but covered in rich greenery, yet two aspects of this battle are still controversial: inadequate preliminary bombardment and the decision to use piecemeal replacements instead of organized units to strengthen the assault forces. Both decisions were made in the context of several competing factors and were made by experienced commanders in good faith. Iwo Jima's highest cost was the loss of so many combat veterans while taking the island. While this battle created a new generation of veteran heroes among the survivors, many proud regiments suffered devastating losses.

Those veteran regiments had already been designated as crucial landing force components in the Japanese home islands assault—these losses had severe potential implications. It may have been these factors that influenced Holland Smith's unpopular decision to withhold the 3rd Marines from the battle.

To many exhausted Marines and commanders fighting on Iwo Jima, Holland Smith's decision to withhold the 3rd Marines was unforgivable—then and now. But whatever his flaws, General Holland Smith almost certainly knew amphibious warfare better than anyone at the time.

According to Holland Smith: "We had no hope of surprise, either tactical or strategic. There was little possibility for tactical initiative. The entire operation was fought on virtually the enemy's terms. The strength, conduct, and disposition of the enemy's defense required a major penetration of his prepared positions in the center of the Motoyama Plateau and a subsequent reduction of his positions in rugged terrain sloping to the shore on the flanks.

"The terrain and size of the island precluded any Force Beachhead Line. It was a one-phase and one-tactic operation. From the time the engagement was joined until the mission was completed, it was a frontal assault maintained with relentless pressure by a superior force in supporting arms against a position fortified to the maximum practical intent.

"We Americans of a subsequent generation in the profession of arms find it difficult to imagine a sustained amphibious assault under these conditions. In some respects, the fighting on Iwo Jima took the features of the Marines fighting in France in 1918. We sensed the drama repeated every morning on Iwo Jima after the prep fires lifted, when the rifleman, engineers, corpsman, flame tank crews, and armored bulldozers somehow found the fortitude to move out again into The Meatgrinder or Death Valley. Few of us today can study the defenses, analyze the after-action reports, or walk that broken ground without experiencing a sense of reverence for the men who fought and won that epic battle."

While the fighting was raging on Iwo, Admiral Nimitz said: "Among the Americans serving on Iwo Jima, uncommon valor was a common virtue." This line was chiseled into the base of Felix de Weldon's giant bronze sculpture of the Suribachi flag-raising.

On Iwo, Twenty-two Marines, four Navy corpsmen, and one

LCI skipper were awarded the Medal of Honor for bravery during the battle—half were awarded posthumously.

General Erskine put the Allied sacrifices into perspective during his remarks at the dedication of the 3rd Marine Division's Cemetery on Iwo Jima: "Our victory was never in doubt. Its cost was. What was in doubt, in all of our minds, was whether there would be any of us left to dedicate this cemetery at the end. Or if the last Marine would die knocking out the last Japanese gunner."

OPERATION ICEBERG

1945 VICTORY ON OKINAWA

SEIZING SHURI CASTLE

At dawn on May 29, 1945, the 1st Marine Division began their fifth consecutive week of frontal assaults. This was part of the Tenth

Army's relentless offensive against Japanese defenses in southern Okinawa.

Operation Iceberg's mission to secure Okinawa was now two months old and badly bogged down. The fast-paced opening had been replaced by weeks of exhausting and bloody attrition warfare against the Shuri Castle.

The 1st Division were hemmed in between two other divisions. They had precious little room to maneuver and had advanced less than a thousand yards in eighteen days. An average of fifty-five murderous yards per day. Their sector was one bristling, honeycombed ridgeline after another—Kakazu, Dakeshi, and Wana.

But just beyond was the long shoulder of Shuri Ridge. Nerve center of the Imperial Japanese *Thirty-second Army*. The outpost of dozens of forward artillery observers, who'd made life miserable for the Allied landing force. On this wet, rainy, and cold morning, things were different. It was quieter. After days of savage and bitter fighting, Allied forces overran Conical Hill to the east and Sugar Loaf to the west. Shuri Castle no longer seemed invincible.

The 1/5 Marines moved out cautiously and expected the usual firestorm of enemy artillery at any moment. But there was none. Marines reached the crest of Shuri Ridge without a fight. Amazed, the company commander looked west along the road toward the ruins of Shuri Castle: a medieval fortress of ancient Ryukyuan kings.

Soldiers in the Tenth Army expected the Japanese to defend Shuri to the death, but the place seemed lightly held. Spiteful small arms fire came from nothing more than a rearguard. Field radios buzzed with this surprising news. Shuri Castle laid in the distance, ready for the taking. Marines asked for permission to seize their long-awaited prize.

General Pedro del Valle, CO of the 1st Marine Division, didn't hesitate. According to corps division boundaries, Shuri Castle belonged to soldiers of the 77th Infantry Division. General del Valle knew his counterpart, Army General Andrew Bruce, would be furious if the Marines snatched their long-sought trophy before his soldiers could arrive. This was a unique opportunity to grab the

Tenth Army's primary objective. General del Valle gave the go-ahead, and with that, the 1/5 Marines raced along the west ridge against light opposition and secured Shuri Castle.

After General del Valle's staff did some fancy footwork to keep peace with their army neighbors, they learned the 77th had scheduled a massive castle bombardment that morning. Frantic radio calls averted the near-catastrophe just in time. General Bruce was infuriated by the Marines' unauthorized initiative. Del Valle later wrote: "I don't think a single Army commander would talk to me after that."

Through the inter-service aggravation, Allied forces had achieved much this morning. For two months, Shuri Castle had provided the Japanese with a superb field of observed fire—covering southern Okinawa's entire five-mile neck. But as the 1/5 Marines deployed into a defensive line within the castle's rubble, they were unaware that a Japanese rearguard still occupied a massive subterranean headquarters underneath them. Marines soon discovered that directly under their muddy boondockers was the underground headquarters of the Japanese *Thirty-second Army*. This mammoth complex was over 1,200 feet long and 160 feet deep: all dug by pick and shovel.

The enemy had stolen a march on the approaching Tenth Army. Japanese forces retreated south during the rains and occupied the third (final) ring of their prepared underground defenses: a series of fortified escarpments on the Kiyamu Peninsula.

Seizing Shuri Castle was an indisputable milestone in the Okinawa campaign. Still, it was a hollow victory. Like the flag-raising on Iwo Jima's Suribachi signified the end of the beginning of that prolonged battle. The capture of Shuri Castle did not end the fighting. The savage slugfest on Okinawa continued for another twenty-four days—while the plum rains fell and the horrors and dying on both sides continued.

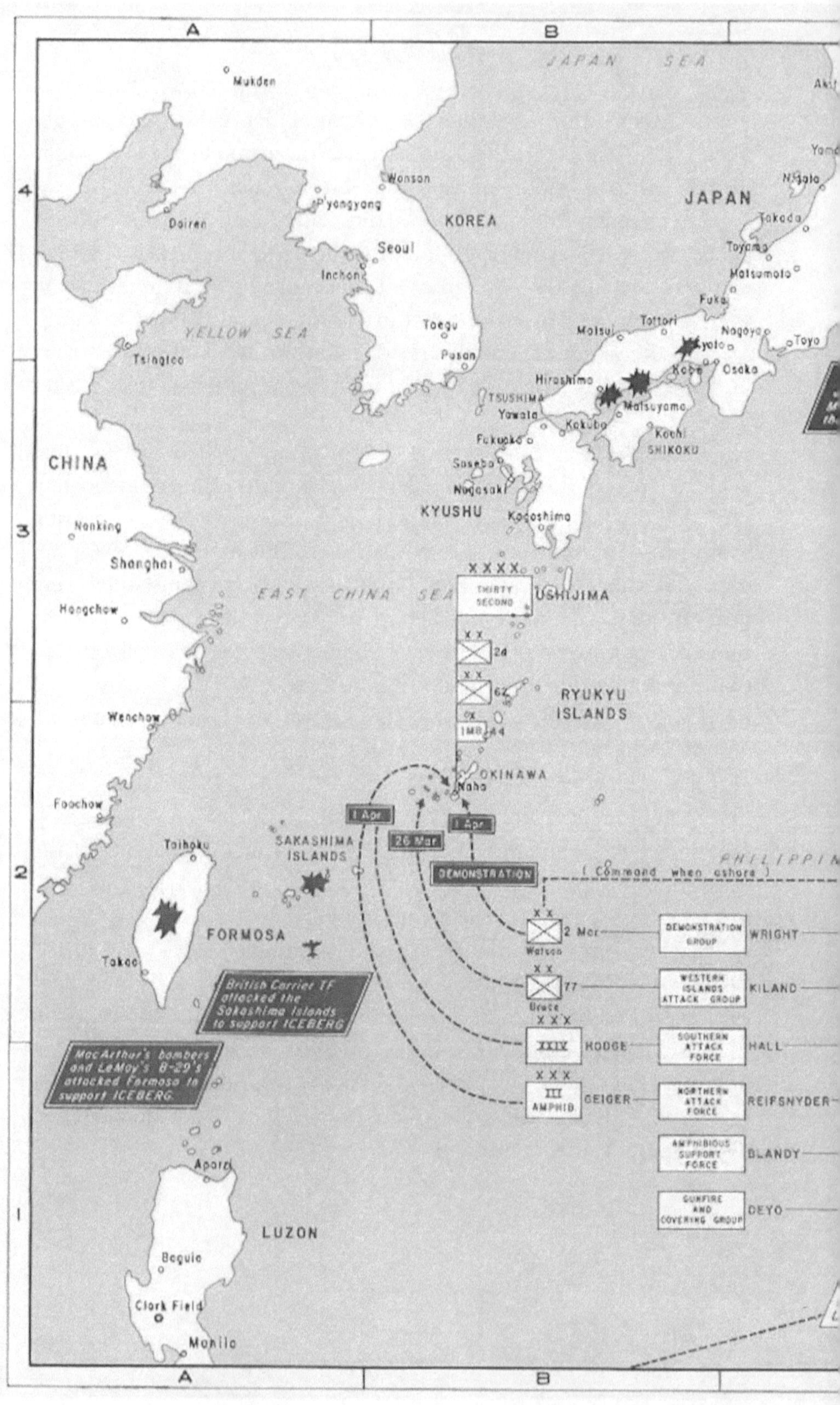

JAPAN SEA
Akit
Mukden
Yama
Wonson
N'gata
JAPAN
P'yongyang
Takada
Dairen
Toyama
Seoul
Matsumoto
Inchon
Fuka
KOREA
Tottori
YELLOW SEA
Toegu
Matsui
Nagoya
Kyoto
Toyo
Pusan
Kobe
Osaka
Tsingtao
Hiroshima
Matsuyama
TSUSHIMA
Yawata
Kochi
Nanking
Yawata
Kokubo
SHIKOKU
Fukuoka
Shanghai
Sasebo
CHINA
Nagasaki
Hangchow
KYUSHU
Kagoshima
EAST CHINA SEA
XXXX
THIRTY
USHIJIMA
SECOND
Wenchow
XX
24
XX
62
RYUKYU
ISLANDS
Foochow
IMB 44
OKINAWA
Naha
1 Apr
1 Apr
26 Mar
PHILIPPIN
Taihoku
SAKASHIMA
DEMONSTRATION
(Command when ashore)
ISLANDS
XX
2 Mar
DEMONSTRATION
WRIGHT
FORMOSA
Watson
GROUP
Takao
XX
WESTERN
77
ISLANDS
KILAND
British Carrier TF
Bruce
ATTACK GROUP
attacked the
XXX
Sakashima Islands
XXIV
SOUTHERN
to support ICEBERG
HODGE
ATTACK
HALL
FORCE
XXX
MacArthur's bombers
III
NORTHERN
and LeMay's B-29's
AMPHIB.
GEIGER
ATTACK
REIFSNYDER
attacked Formosa in
FORCE
support ICEBERG.
AMPHIBIOUS
Aparri
SUPPORT
BLANDY
FORCE
LUZON
GUNFIRE
AND
DEYO
Baguio
COVERING GROUP
Clark Field
Manila

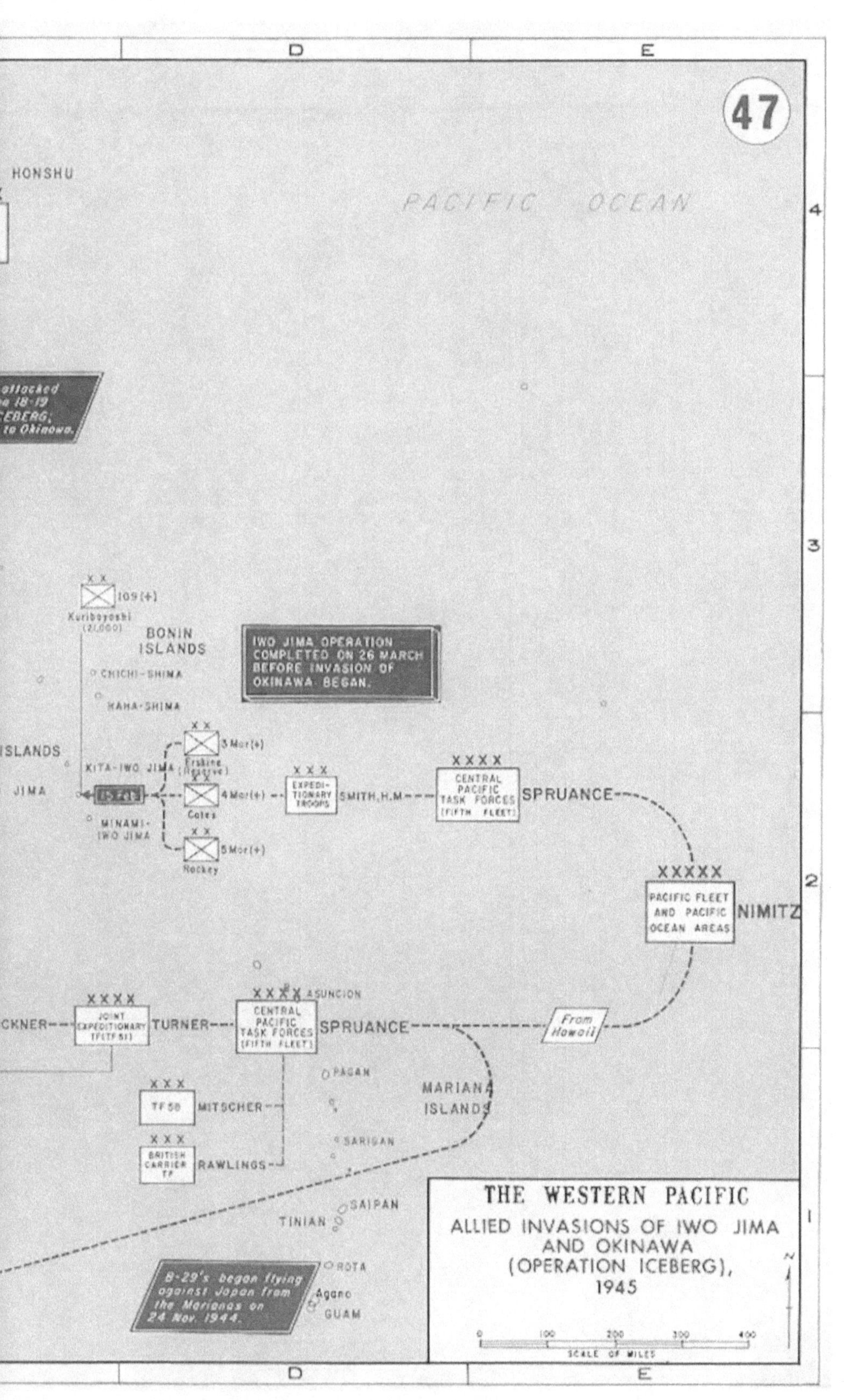
47
HONSHU
PACIFIC OCEAN
attacked
18-19
CEBERG,
to Okinawa.
XX
109(+)
Kuriboyoshi
(21,000)
BONIN
ISLANDS
CHICHI-SHIMA
HAHA-SHIMA
IWO JIMA OPERATION
COMPLETED ON 26 MARCH
BEFORE INVASION OF
OKINAWA BEGAN.
ISLANDS
KITA-IWO JIMA
XX
3 Mar(+)
Erskine
(Reserve)
O JIMA
XX
4 Mar(+)
Cates
XXX
EXPEDI-
TIONARY
TROOPS
SMITH, H.M
XXXX
CENTRAL
PACIFIC
TASK FORCES
(FIFTH FLEET)
SPRUANCE
MINAMI-
IWO JIMA
XX
5 Mar(+)
Rockey
XXXXX
PACIFIC FLEET
AND PACIFIC
OCEAN AREAS
NIMITZ
XXXX
JOINT
EXPEDITIONARY
TF(TF 51)
UCKNER
TURNER
XXXX
CENTRAL
PACIFIC
TASK FORCES
(FIFTH FLEET)
ASUNCION
SPRUANCE
From
Hawaii
PAGAN
MARIANA
ISLANDS
XXX
TF 58
MITSCHER
XXX
BRITISH
CARRIER
TF
RAWLINGS
SARIGAN
SAIPAN
TINIAN
THE WESTERN PACIFIC
ALLIED INVASIONS OF IWO JIMA
AND OKINAWA
(OPERATION ICEBERG),
1945
ROTA
Agano
GUAM
B-29's began flying
against Japan from
the Marianas on
24 Nov. 1944.
0   100   200   300   400
SCALE OF MILES

OPERATION ICEBERG

The battle of Okinawa covered a seven-hundred-mile arc from Kyushu to Formosa. It involved a million combatants—Japanese, Americans, British, and Okinawan natives. This battle rivaled the Normandy invasion because it was the biggest and bloodiest operation of the Pacific War. In eighty-two days of combat, Allied forces and unfortunate noncombatants suffered an average of 3,000 lives lost a day.

By the spring of 1945, the Empire of Japan was a wounded wild animal: desperate, cornered, and furious. Japanese leaders knew Okinawa under Allied control would be transformed into "the England of the Pacific." It would serve as a staging point for the invasion of the sacred homeland. The Japanese would sacrifice everything to avoid the unspeakable disgrace of unconditional surrender and foreign occupation.

The US Navy was presented with its greatest operational challenge to date: how to protect a gigantic and exposed amphibious task force tethered to the beachhead against Japanese *kamikaze* attacks. Okinawa would be the ultimate test of US amphibious power and projection. Could Allied forces in the Pacific Theater plan and execute such a massive assault against a heavily defended landmass? Could the Allies integrate the tactical capabilities of all the services and fend off every imaginable form of counterattack while maintaining operational momentum?

Operation Iceberg was not executed in a vacuum. Preparatory action to the invasion kicked off at the same time campaigns on Iwo Jima and the Philippines were still being wrapped up—another strain on Allied resources. But as dramatic and sprawling as the battle of Okinawa proved to be, both sides saw this contest as an example of the even more desperate fighting soon to come with the invasion of the Japanese home islands. The closeness of Okinawa to Japan was well within medium bomber and fighter escort range. Its valuable military ports, anchorages, airfields, and training areas made this skinny island imperative for Allied forces—eclipsing their earlier plans for the seizure of Formosa.

Okinawa is the largest of the Ryukyuan Islands. The island sits at the apex of a triangle nearly equidistant to strategic areas. Formosa is 330 miles to the southwest, Kyushu is 350 miles to the north, while Shanghai is 450 miles to the west. As on so many Pacific battlefields, Okinawa had a peaceful heritage. Officially an administrative prefecture of Japan (forcibly seized in 1879), Okinawans were proud of their long Chinese legacy and unique sense of community.

Imperial headquarters in Tokyo did little to garrison or fortify Okinawa at the beginning of the Pacific War. After the Allies conquered Saipan, Japanese headquarters sent reinforcements and fortification materials to critical areas within the "Inner Strategic Zone," Peleliu, the Philippines, Iwo Jima, and Okinawa.

Imperial Japanese headquarters on Okinawa formed a new field army: the *Thirty-second Army*. They funneled different trained components from Japan's armed perimeter in China, Manchuria, and the home islands. American submarines took a deadly toll on these Japanese troop movements. On June 29, 1944, the USS *Sturgeon* torpedoed the transport *Toyama Maru*. She sank with a loss of 5,600 troops of the *44th Independent Mixed Brigade* en route for

Okinawa. It would take the Japanese the rest of the year to replace that loss.

In October 1944, US Joint Chiefs decided to act on the strategic value of the Ryukyus. They tasked Admiral Nimitz with seizing Okinawa after the Iwo Jima campaign. The Joint Chiefs ordered Nimitz to seize, occupy, and defend Okinawa before transforming the captured island into an advanced staging base for the invasion of Japan.

Nimitz turned to his most veteran commanders to execute this mission. Admiral Spruance, the victor of Midway and the Battle of the Philippine Sea, would command the US Fifth Fleet (debatably the most powerful armada of warships ever assembled). Admiral Kelly Turner, veteran of the Solomons and Central Pacific landings, would command all amphibious forces under Spruance. But Kelly Turner's military counterpart would no longer be the old warhorse General Holland Smith. Iwo Jima was Smith's last fight. Now the expeditionary forces had grown to the size of a field army with 182,000 assault troops. Army General Simon Buckner (son of the Confederate general who fought against Grant at Fort Donaldson in the American Civil War) would command the newly formed US Tenth Army.

General Buckner made sure the Tenth Army reflected his multi-service composition. Thirty-four Marine officers served on Buckner's staff, including General Oliver P. Smith as his deputy Chief of Staff. Smith later wrote: "the Tenth Army became, in effect, a joint task force."

Six veteran divisions, two Marine and four Army, composed Buckner's landing force. A division from each service was marked for reserve duty—another sign of the growth of Allied amphibious power in the Pacific. Earlier in the war, Americans had landed one infantry division on Guadalcanal, two in the Palaus, and three each on Iwo Jima and Saipan. But by spring 1945, Buckner and Spruance could count on eight experienced divisions besides those still on Luzon and Iwo Jima.

The Tenth Army had three major operational components.

Army General John Hodge commanded the XXIV Corps, composed of the 77th and 96th Infantry Divisions (with the 27th Infantry Division in floating reserve and the 81st Infantry Division in area reserve). Marine General Roy Geiger commanded the III Amphibious Corps, composed of the 1st and 6th Marine Divisions (with the 2nd Marine Division held in floating reserve). Marine General Francis Mulcahy commanded the Tenth Army's Tactical Air Force and the 2nd Marine Aircraft Wing.

The Marine components for Operation Iceberg were scattered. The 1st Marines had returned from Peleliu to "Pitiful Pavuvu" in the Russell Islands to prepare for the next fight. The 1st Marine Division had been the first to deploy into the Pacific. They executed brutal amphibious campaigns on Guadalcanal, Cape Gloucester, and Peleliu. Over one-third of the 1st Marines were veterans of two of those battles.

Pavuvu's tiny island limited work-up training, but a large-scale exercise on neighboring Guadalcanal enabled the division to integrate its replacements and returning veterans. General del Valle drilled his Marines in tank-infantry training under the protective umbrella of supporting howitzer fire.

The 6th Marine Division was the only division formed overseas in the war. General Lemuel Shepherd activated the colors and assumed command on September 12, 1944. While this unit was newly formed, it was not green—several former Marine Raiders with combat experience comprised the heart of this Marine division. General Shepherd used his time and the more extensive facilities on Guadalcanal to conduct work-up training from the platoon to the regimental level. He looked ahead to Okinawa and emphasized rapid troop deployments and large-scale operations in built-up combat areas.

General LeRoy Hunt commanded the 2nd Marine Division. Hunt's Marines had returned to Saipan after the conquest of Tinian. The division had absorbed 8,000 replacements and trained for a wide-ranging series of mission assignments as a strategic reserve. The 2nd Division possessed a vital lineage in the Pacific

War at Guadalcanal, Tarawa, Saipan, and Tinian. Its presence in the Ryukyus' waters would establish a fearsome "amphibious force-in-being" to distract the Japanese on Okinawa. This division would pay an unequal price for its bridesmaid role in the coming campaign.

The Marine assault force preparing for Okinawa was dealt another organizational change—the fourth of the war. Marine headquarters constantly reviewed "lessons learned" in the war and had just completed a series of revisions to the table of organization for its divisions and components. While it would not become official until a month after the landing, the divisions had already made most changes.

The overall size of each division increased to 19,176 (from 17,465). This was done by adding an assault signal company, a rocket platoon (Buck Rogers Men), a fifty-five man assault platoon in each regimental headquarters, and a war dog platoon. Motor transport, artillery, and service units also received slight increases, as did machine-gun platoons in each rifle company. But the most timely weapons change happened by replacing the 75mm half-tracks with the new M-7s (105mm self-propelled howitzer). Artillery regiment purists did not approve of these weapons being deployed by the infantry. These M-7s would not be used as massed howitzers but as direct fire "siege guns" against the thousands of fortified caves on Okinawa.

Marine Corps Headquarters backed up these last-minute changes by providing the required replacements to land the assault divisions at full strength. Sometimes the skills required did not match. Some artillery regiments absorbed a flood of radar technicians and anti-aircraft artillery gunners from old defense battalions. But the manpower and equipment shortfalls that had plagued earlier operations were overcome by the time the assault force embarked on Operation Iceberg.

Even this late in the war, operational intelligence was unsatisfactory before the landing. At Tarawa and Tinian, the pre-assault combat intelligence had been brilliant. But at Okinawa, the landing force did not have accurate figures of the enemy's weapons or abilities.

The cloud cover over the island prevented accurate and complete photo-reconnaissance. Also, the ingenuity of the Japanese commander and the extraordinary digging skills of the enemy garrison helped disguise the island's true defenses.

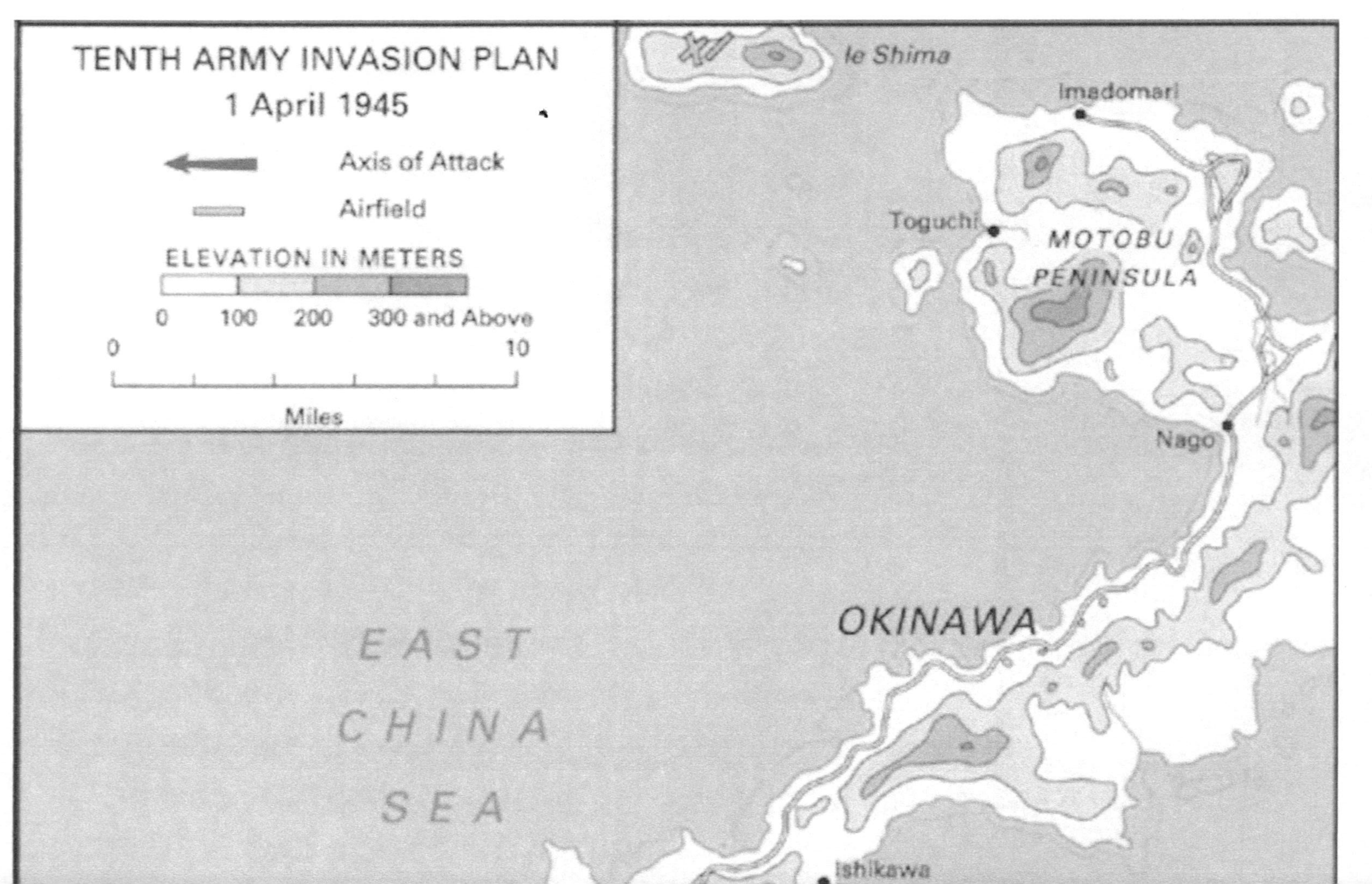

TENTH ARMY INVASION PLAN
1 April 1945
Axis of Attack
Airfield
ELEVATION IN METERS
0   100   200   300 and Above
0   10
Miles
Ie Shima
Imadomari
Toguchi
MOTOBU PENINSULA
Nago
OKINAWA
EAST CHINA SEA
Ishikawa

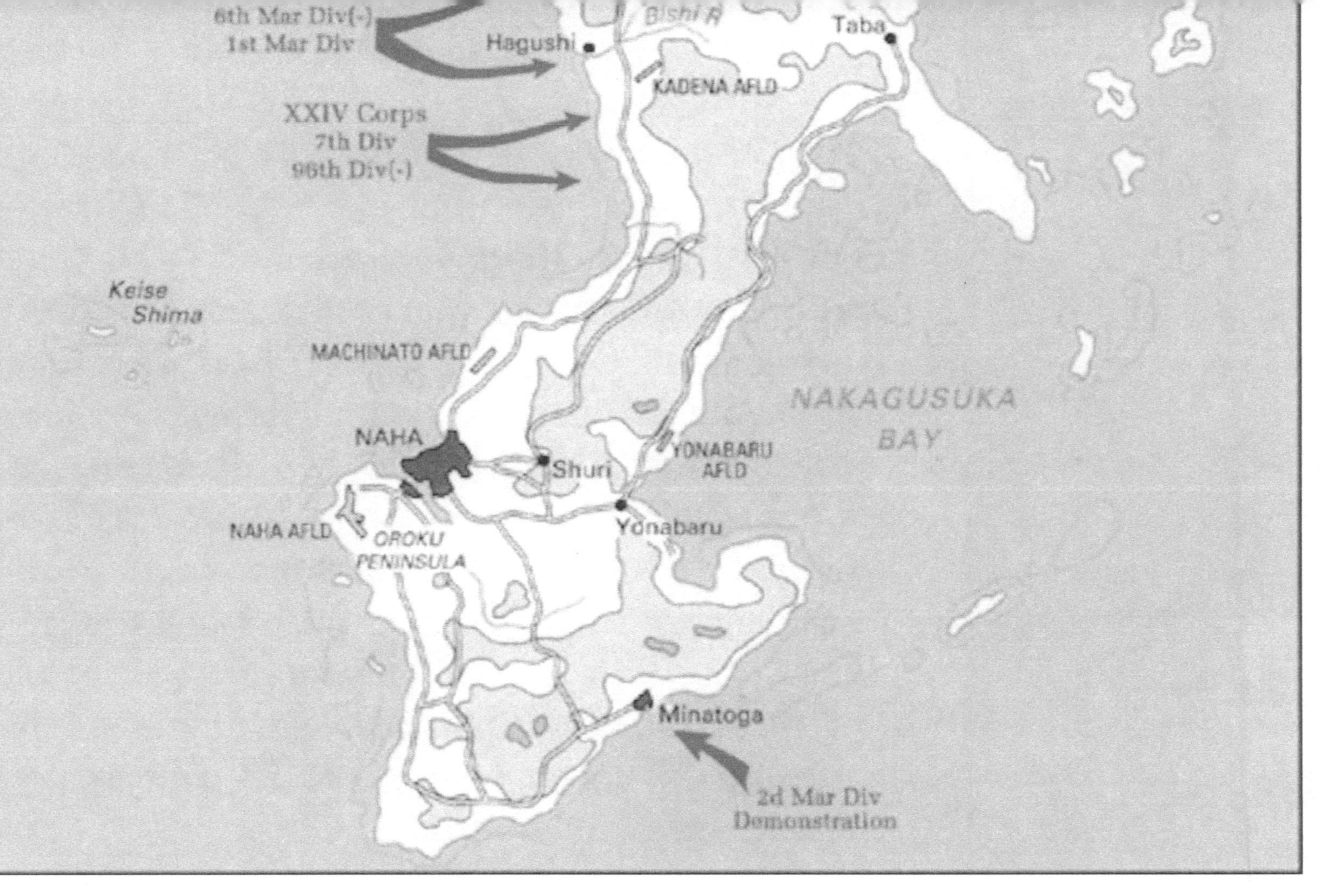
6th Mar Div(-)
1st Mar Div
Hagushi
Bishi R
Taba
KADENA AFLD
XXIV Corps
7th Div
96th Div(-)
Keise Shima
MACHINATO AFLD
NAKAGUSUKA BAY
NAHA
Shuri
YONABARU AFLD
NAHA AFLD
OROKU PENINSULA
Yonabaru
Minatoga
2d Mar Div Demonstration

JAPANESE DEFENSES

Okinawa is sixty miles long, but only the lower third of the island had the military objectives of anchorages, ports, and airfields. In August 1944. Japanese General Mitsuru Ushijima took command of the *Thirty-second Army*. He understood the fight would be fought in the south and concentrated his forces there.

He decided to not challenge the probable Allied landings in Hagushi along the broad beaches of the southwest coast. He believed that doing so would lose him the Kadena and Yontan Airfields. This decision allowed him to conserve his forces and fight the only battle that stood a chance: an in-depth defense, underground and protected from the overpowering Allied air and arms superiority.

This clash of cave warfare and attrition would be like the recent battles on Peleliu and Iwo Jima. Each had taken a terrifying cost to Allied invaders. General Ushijima sought to replicate this strategy. He would go underground and sting the Allies with high caliber gunfire from his freshly excavated fire-port caves. He believed by bleeding the landing force and bogging down their momentum, he could buy the Imperial Army and Navy's air arms enough time to destroy the fifth fleet with massed *kamikaze* attacks.

General Ushijima had 100,000 Imperial troops on the island, including thousands of Okinawan Home Guard (conscripts known as *Boeitai*). He had a disproportionate number of heavy weapons and artillery in his command. The Allies in the Pacific would not encounter a more formidable concentration of 47mm antitank guns, 320mm spigot mortars, 120mm mortars, and 150mm howitzers. The strategic decision to invade Peleliu, Iwo Jima, and the Philippines before Okinawa gave the enemy seven months to develop their defenses.

Allied forces had already seen what the Japanese could do to fortify a position in a short time. On Okinawa they achieved stunning success. They worked almost exclusively with hand tools: not one bulldozer on the entire island. The Japanese dug miles of underground fighting positions and honeycombed southern Okinawa's ridges and draws. They stocked each position with reserves of food, water, ammunition, and medical supplies. Allied forces anticipated a fierce defense of the southwestern beaches and the airfields, followed by a general counterattack. Then, the battle would be over except for some mop-up and light patrolling.

The Allies could not have been more mistaken.

The assault plan called for the advance seizure of the Kerama Retto Islands after several days of preparatory air and naval bombardment. Followed by a massive four-division assault on the Hagushi Beaches. During the primary assault, the 2nd Marine Division, with a separate naval task force, would duplicate the assault on Okinawa's southeast coast (Minatoga Beaches).

Love-Day (chosen to avoid planning confusion with D-Day being planned for Iwo Jima) would happen on April 1, 1945. Hardly anyone failed to remark about the irony of April Fool's Day and Easter Sunday.

The US Fifth Fleet was a breathtaking sight as it steamed toward the Ryukyus. Marines who'd returned to the Pacific from the original amphibious offensive on Guadalcanal thirty-one months earlier gaped at the quantity of landing craft in the assault ships. The armada stretched to the horizon—a genuinely incredible, mind-boggling vista.

* * *

On March 26, the 77th Infantry Division skillfully secured Kerama Retto. A move that surprised the Japanese and generated enormous operational dividends. Admiral Turner now had a series of sheltered anchorages to repair ships likely to be damaged by *kamikaze* attacks. Soldiers discovered stockpiled Japanese suicide boats—over 300 powerboats equipped with high explosive rams to sink the thin-skinned troop transports.

Major James Jones commanded the Force Reconnaissance Battalion. His battalion paved the way before each landing with stealthy scouting missions the night before. Jones' recon Marines scouted and found the barren sand spits of Keise Shima unde-fended. After reporting that welcome news, the Army landed a battery of 155mm "Long Toms" on the small inlets, adding to their significant firepower and the naval bombardment of Okinawa's southwest coast.

Admiral Turner's minesweepers cleared approaches to the southwestern beaches. Navy frogmen and Marines detonated hundreds of man-made obstacles. After seven days of preliminary bombardment, Allied ships fired over 25,000 rounds of 5-inch shells. This shelling produced more of a spectacle than a destructive effect. The Allied forces believed General Ushijima's troops would be arrayed around the beaches and airfields. While that scale and duration of bombardment would've saved many lives on Iwo Jima: on Okinawa, this precious ordinance was largely wasted and produced few results.

Tensions were high in landing force transports. The 60mm mortar section of Company K, 3/5 Marines learned that the casu-alty rates on Love-Day were estimated to reach 85%. According to Private First Class Eugene Sledge: "this is not conducive to a good night's sleep."

A Japanese soldier observing the massive armada bearing down on Okinawa wrote in his diary: "it's like a frog meeting a snake and waiting for the snake to eat him."

LAND THE LANDING FORCE

The Allied invasion got off to a roaring start. The few enemy defenders still in the area at dawn on April 1 immediately agreed with the wisdom of conceding the beaches to the landing force.

The massive armada gathered from ports all over the Pacific

now bore down on Okinawa's southwest coast: ready to deploy a 182,000-man landing force onto the beach. The ultimate forcible entry—the embodiment of all painfully learned amphibious lessons from the crude beginnings at Guadalcanal and North Africa.

Admiral Turner made his final review of the weather conditions in the objective area. As at Iwo Jima, the amphibious assault was fortunate to have good weather for the critical initial landing. Skies were clear, winds and surf were moderate. The temperature was 75 degrees.

At 0406, Turner ordered: "Land the landing force." That phrase set off a sequential countdown to the first assault waves smashing into the beaches at H-hour. Combat troops crowded the rails of the transports to witness an extraordinary display of Allied naval power. A sustained bombardment by rockets and shells from hundreds of ships. Formations of Allied attack aircraft streaked low over the beaches: strafing and bombing at will. Japanese fire was ineffective and scattered, even against this massive armada assembled offshore.

The diversionary force carrying the 2nd Marine Division set out to bait the Japanese with a feint landing on the opposite coast. This amphibious force steamed into position and launched amphibian tractors and Higgins boats loaded with combat Marines in seven waves toward Minatoga Beach. The fourth wave commander paid careful attention to the clock and crossed the line of departure at exactly 0830—the time of the actual H-hour assault on the western coast. Then, the Higgins boats and LVTs turned away and returned to the transports: mission accomplished.

The diversionary landing achieved its purpose. General Ushijima had placed several front-line infantry and artillery units in the Minatoga Beach area for several weeks as a contingency against an expected secondary landing. His officers reported to Imperial headquarters on Love-Day morning: "enemy landing attempt on east coast blocked with heavy enemy losses."

This deception came at a high cost. *Kamikaze* pilots were convinced this was the main assault. They came in waves and struck the small force that morning, damaging the troopships *LST 844* and *Hinsdale*. The 3/2 Marines and the 2nd Amphibian

Tractor Battalion suffered fifty casualties. The troopships lost an equal number of sailors. Ironically, the division that was expected to have the most minor damage or casualties in the battle lost more men than any other division in the Tenth Army that day. According to Operation Officer Colonel Sam Taxis: "we'd requested air cover for the feint but were told the threat was 'incidental.'"

In the southwest, the main assault force faced little resistance. A massive coral reef provided an offshore barrier to the beaches on Hagushi. But by early evening, the reef no longer presented a threat to the landing force. Unlike on Tarawa, where the reef dominated the tactical progress of the battle. General Buckner had over 1,400 LVTs to transport the assault waves from ship to shore without delay.

Eight miles of LVTs churned across the line of departure just behind 360 armored LVT-As that blasted away at the beach with their snub-nosed 75mm howitzers as they advanced the final four thousand yards. Behind the LVTs were 750 amphibious trucks with the first of the direct support artillery battalions. The horizon behind the amphibious trucks was filled with lines of landing boats. They paused at the reef to marry with the outbound LVTs. Marines and soldiers had exhaustively rehearsed transfer line operations—there was no pause in the assault momentum.

The Bisha Gawa river mouth marked the boundary between IIIAC and XXIV Corps along the Hagushi beaches. The tactical plan called for the two divisions to land abreast—the 6th on the left and the 1st on the right. The endless rehearsal of thousands of hours paid off. The initial assault touched down at 0830: the designated H-hour. Marines stormed out of their LVTs, swarming over the sea walls and berms into the great unknown. The Okinawa invasion had begun. Within the first hour, the Tenth Army had over 16,000 combat troops ashore.

Despite the dire intelligent predictions and their own combat experience, the troops' landing was a cakewalk—almost unopposed. Private First Class Eugene Sledge's mortar section began singing "Little Brown Jug" at the top of their lungs. He later wrote how he couldn't believe his good luck: "I didn't hear a single shot all morning. It was unbelievable."

Many Marine veterans expected enemy fire at any second. Later that day, General del Valle's LVT got stuck in a pothole en route to the beach. "It was the worst twenty minutes I'd ever spent in my life," the general later wrote.

That morning continued to deliver pleasant surprises to the assault force. No mines along the beaches, the main bridge over the Bishi River was still intact, and both airfields were lightly defended. Marines took Yontan Airfield at 1300 while soldiers from the 7th Infantry Division had no problem securing nearby Kadena.

After securing the assault beaches, the landing force left plenty of room for the follow-on forces. Division commanders accelerated the landing of artillery battalions, tanks, and reserves. This massive buildup was hampered by a few glitches. Four artillery pieces went down when their amphibious trucks foundered along the reef. Several other Sherman tanks grounded on the reef. The 3/1 Marines arrived at the transfer line by 1800 but spent an uncomfortable night in their boats because enough LVTs were not available for the last leg at that hour. While only minor inconveniences, by the day's end, the Tenth Army had 60,000 troops ashore and occupied an expanded beach eight miles long and two miles deep.

The landing was not bloodless. Snipers wounded Major John Gustafson, CO of the 3/5 Marines, later that afternoon. Other men went down to enemy mortars and machine-gun fire. But the Tenth Army's entire losses (including the hard-luck 2nd Division) were 159 casualties with twenty-eight killed.

This was less than ten percent of casualties suffered by V Amphibious Corps on the first bloody day of Iwo Jima.

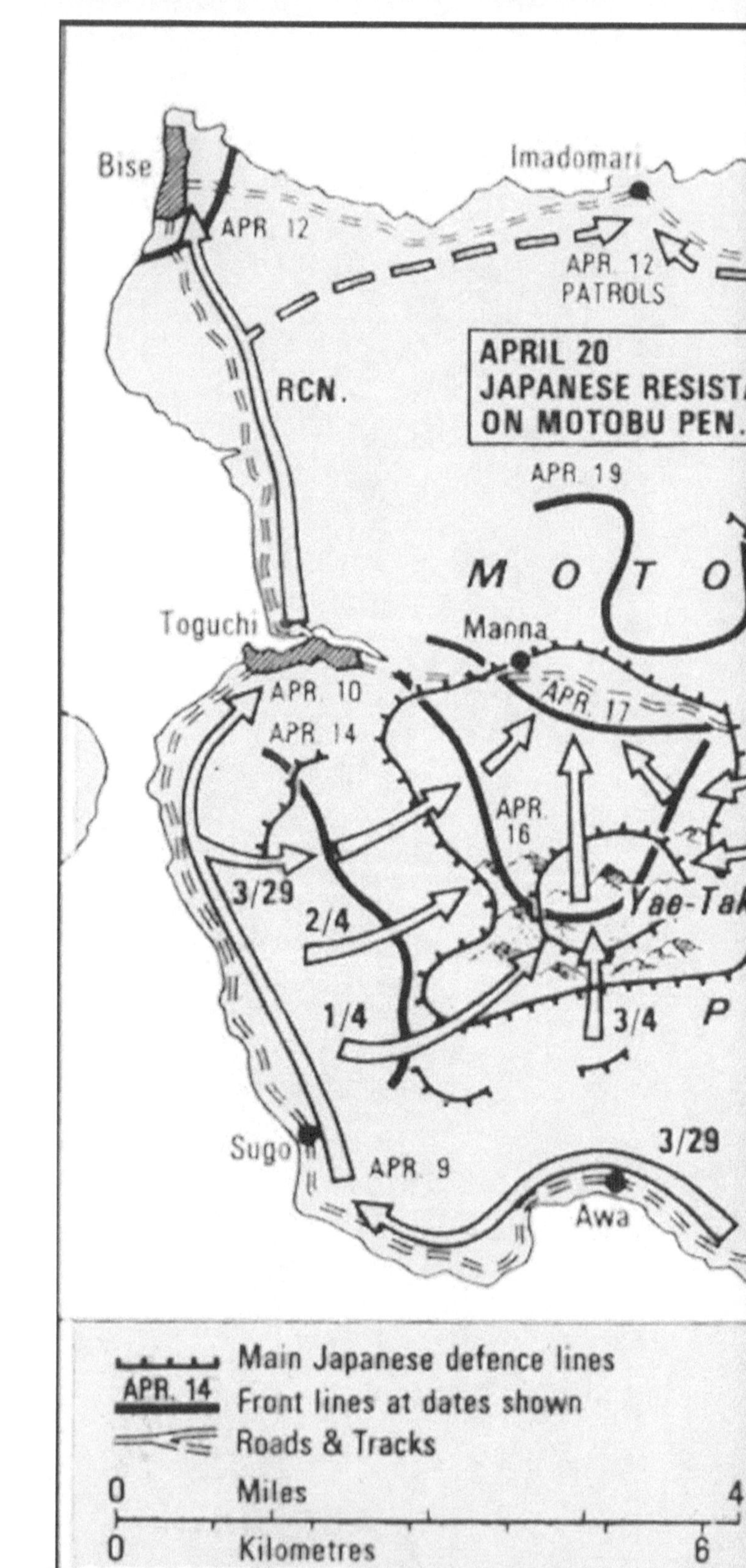

Bise
Imadomari
APR. 12
APR. 12
PATROLS
RCN.
APRIL 20
JAPANESE RESISTA
ON MOTOBU PEN.
APR. 19
M O T O
Toguchi
Manna
APR. 10
APR. 14
APR. 17
APR. 16
3/29
2/4
Yae-Tak
1/4
3/4
P
Sugo
3/29
APR. 9
Awa
Main Japanese defence lines
APR. 14   Front lines at dates shown
Roads & Tracks
0   Miles   4
0   Kilometres   6

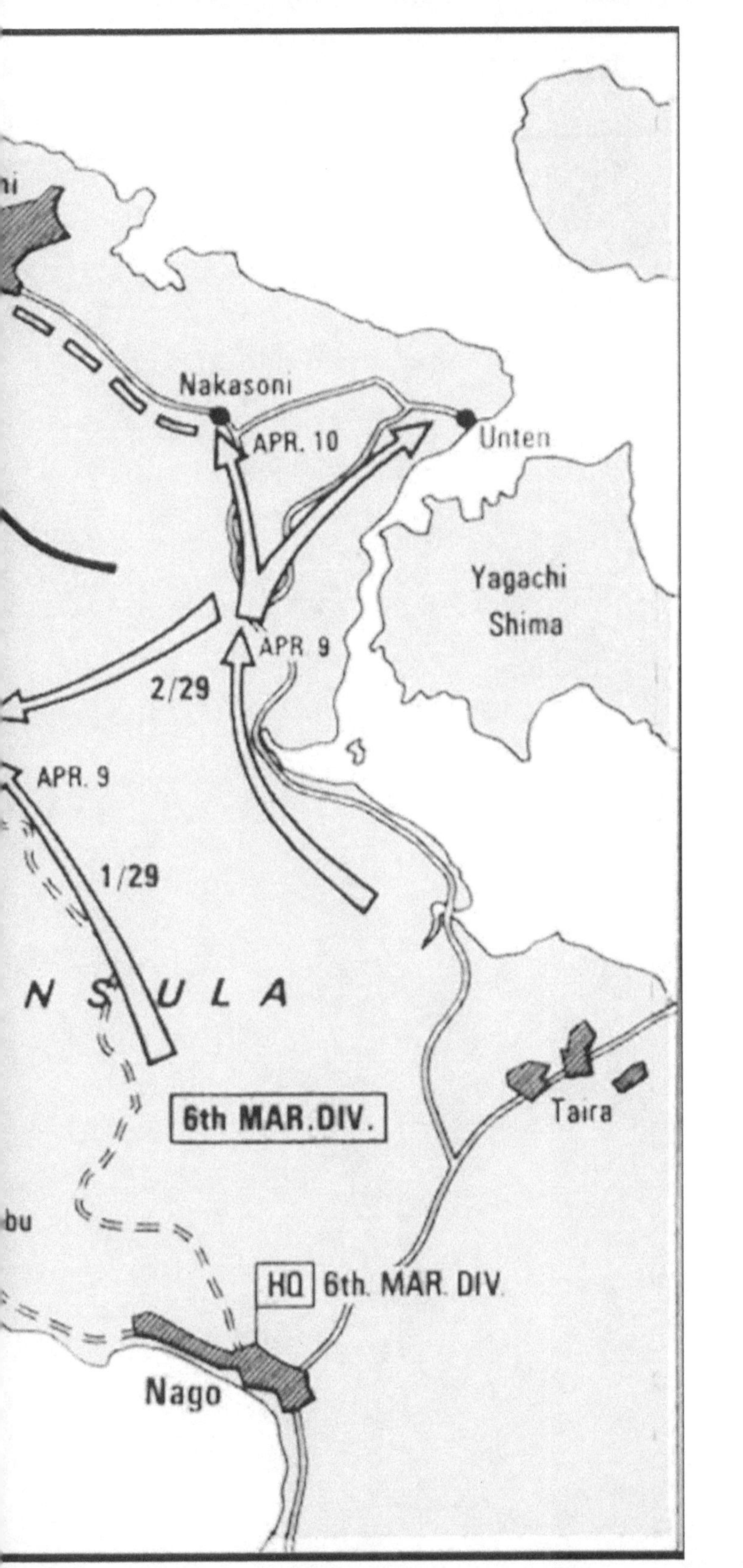

Nakasoni
APR. 10
Unten
Yagachi
Shima
APR. 9
2/29
APR. 9
1/29
N S U L A
6th MAR. DIV.
Taira
HQ 6th. MAR. DIV.
bu
Nago

BATTLE OF YAE TAKE

The assault force's momentum did not slow down after the Tenth Army broke out of the beachhead. The 7th Infantry reached the east coast on the second day. On the third day, the 1st Marine Division secured the Katchin Peninsula and cut the island in two. By now, elements of the III Amphibious Corps had reached their objective initially thought to require eleven days. Colonel Victor Krulak, 6th Marine Division operations officer, recalled General Shepherd's orders: "Plow ahead as fast as you can. The Japs are on the run."

Krulak thought: *Well hell, we didn't have them on the run. They weren't there.*

The 6th Division swung north, while the 1st Marine Division moved to the northwest—their immediate problems stemming not from the enemy but a slow supply system still processing on the beach. The reef-side transfer line worked well for troops but not for cargo.

Navy Seabees worked to build a causeway for the reef. At the same time, the 1st Division demonstrated their amphibious know-how learned on Peleliu. They mounted swinging cranes on powered causeways and secured craft to the seaward side of the reef. When boats pulled alongside, cranes lifted nets filled with combat cargo into open hatches of waiting LVTs and amphibious trucks. This worked so well that the division divided its assets within the Tenth Army.

Beach congestion slowed the logistical process. Both Marine divisions used their replacements as shore party teams. Inexperience combined with a constant call for new replacements caused traffic control problems in establishing functional supply dumps and pilferage. This was not new. Other divisions in earlier operations had had the same problems. The quickly advancing divisions desperately needed bulk fuel and motor transport—but these were slow to land and distribute.

The undeveloped road network on Okinawa made this problem worse. Colonel Ed Snedeker, CO of the 7th Regiment in the 1st Marine Division, wrote: "The movement from the west coast landing beaches on Okinawa across the island was difficult because of the rugged terrain. It was physically exhausting for personnel to be on the transports for such a long time. This also presented an initial impossible supply problem in the Seventh's zone of action because of the lack of roads."

General Mulcahy brought the Tactical Air Force command post ashore on L +1. Operating out of crude quarters between Kadena and Yontan Airfields, Mulcahy closely watched the Seabees and Army-Marine engineers progress repairing the captured airfields. A Marine observation plane was the first Allied aircraft to land on April 2. Two days later, the airfields were ready to accept fighters. By the eighth day, General Mulcahy could accommodate medium bombers and assumed control of all ashore fleet aircraft.

Mulcahy's fighter arm, the Air Defense Command, was established on shore under the command of Marine General William Wallace. Graceful F4U Corsairs of Marine Aircraft Group (MAG 31) flew in from escort carriers. Wallace tasked them with flying combat air patrols over the fleet to tackle the vicious mass of *kamikaze* attacks plaguing the fleet. Most Marine fighter pilots' initial missions were combat air patrols, while (ironically) Navy squadrons on board escort carriers handled the close air support jobs.

At dawn, Marine Corsairs took off from the airfields and flew combat air patrols over the far-flung fifth fleet. They passed Navy Hellcats coming in from the fleet to support the Marines fighting on the ground. Other air units poured into the two Army airfields: night fighters, torpedo bombers, and an Army Air Forces fighter wing. The Okinawan airfields were not safe-havens. They received nightly artillery fire from long-range bombing the entire first month ashore. But the two airfields remained in operation around the clock. They were an invaluable asset in support of Operation Iceberg.

* * *

General Roy Geiger unleashed the 6th Marine Division to sweep north while the 1st Division hunted down and destroyed small bands of enemy guerrillas in the center of the island. Riflemen rode topside on tanks and self-propelled guns streaming northward against the fleeing enemy. Not since Tinian did Marines enjoy such invigorating mobility. On April 7, Marines seized Nagano, the largest town in northern Okinawa. The Navy swept for mines and deployed Underwater Demolition Teams to breach obstacles and open the port for direct seaborne delivery of crucial supplies.

Corporal James Day with the 22nd Marines was impressed at the momentum of the operation. He wrote: "Hell, here we are in Nago. It wasn't tough at all. Up until that time, our squad hadn't lost a man." The 22nd Marines continued north through a rugged and broken country. They reached Hedo Misaki at the far end of the island on L +12 after advancing fifty-five miles from the landing beaches at Hagushi.

The honeymoon was coming to a swift end for the rest of the 6th Division. Northwest of Nago, on its bulby nose, the Motobu Peninsula jutted out into the East China Sea. In a six mile area around the 1,200 foot Mount Yae Take, Colonel Takesiko Udo and his *Kunigami Detachment* were in prepared defensive positions. The delaying tactics were over. Udo's force comprised two thousand seasoned troops from the *44th Independent Mixed Brigade*. He had two rifle battalions, a regimental gun company, and an anti-tank company at his disposal.

Mount Yae Take was a defender's dream. Steep vines tangled with dense vegetation. Japanese troops booby-trapped the approaches with mines and mounted 20mm machine cannons and heavier weapons deep inside their caves. According to Colonel Krulak: "They were just there. They weren't going anywhere. They were going to fight to the death. They had a lot of Navy guns that came off disabled ships. They dug them way back in holes where their arc of fire was not more than ten degrees." An artillery battalion of fifteen Marines had the misfortune to lay their guns directly within the narrow arc of a hidden 150mm cannon. "They lost two howitzers before you could spell cat."

The battle of Yae Take was the first real fight for the 6th Marine Division. Five days of difficult and deadly combat against a determined enemy. The 4th and the 29th Marines earned their spurs here. They developed teamwork and tactics, putting them in a good position for the long, bloody campaign ahead.

One aspect of General Shepherd's success in this battle stemmed from his desire to place proven leaders in command of his troops. On the 15th, Shepherd relieved Colonel Victor Bleasdale (a decorated World War I Marine) and installed Guadalcanal veteran Colonel William Whaling as the commanding officer of the 29th Marines. After an enemy sniper killed Major Bernard Greene, commanding the 1/4 Marines, Colonel Alan Shapley assigned his own XO, Colonel Fred Beans (former Marine Raider), as his replacement.

The ferocious fighting continued with three Allied battalions attacking from the west and two from the east. They were protected against friendly fire by the steep pinnacle separating them. Logistics were essential in this fight. Every Marine (from private to general) who climbed that mountain to the front lines carried either a 5-gallon water can or a case of ammo. All hands coming down the mountain helped carry the stretchers of wounded Marines. On April 15, a company of the 2/4 Marines took sixty-five casualties—including three consecutive company commanders.

The next day Marines secured the ridge with the help of the battleship *Tennessee's* 14-inch guns and Marine Corsairs low-level pocket bombing.

Colonel Udo and his troops from the *Kunigami Detachment* died to the last man. On April 20, General Shepherd announced the Motobu Peninsula was secured. His Marines had earned a precious victory, but the cost did not come cheap. The 6th Marine Division suffered 757 wounded and 207 killed in the battle.

In his journal, an impressed General Oliver Smith wrote: "This northern campaign should dispel the belief held by some that Marines are beach-bound and not capable of rapid movement. Our Marines raced over rugged terrain and repaired roads and blown bridges while successfully opening new unloading points. They reached the island's northern tip—over fifty miles away from the landing beaches—in fourteen days. Followed by a seven-day campaign to secure the Motobu Peninsula."

The 77th Infantry Division landed on the island Ie Shima and seized its airfields during the battle for Motobu Peninsula. On April 16, Major Jones' recon Marines paved the way by taking a small islet 6,200 yards offshore called Minna Shima. Here, soldiers positioned a 105mm battery to support onshore operations. The 77th needed plenty of fire support to fight the 5,000 enemy defending the island. The Army soldiers overwhelmed them in six days of hard fighting at the cost of 1,100 casualties.

A popular war correspondent named Ernie Pyle, who'd landed with the Marines on L-Day, was shot in the head by a Japanese sniper. Marines and soldiers alike grieved over Pyle's death just as they'd done six days earlier with the news of FDR's passing.

TYPHOON OF STEEL

The 1st Marine Division fought a different campaign in April than
their sister division to the north. They spent their days processing

refugees and their nights on ambushes and patrols. Snipers and guerrillas exacted a steady but small toll.

The "Old Breed" Marines welcomed this style of low intensity. After many months in the tropics, they found Okinawa refreshing and rustic. Marines were concerned about the welfare of the thousands of Okinawan refugees streaming in from the heavy fighting.

According to Private First Class Eugene Sledge: "The most pitiful things about the Okinawan civilians were that they were totally bewildered by the shock of our invasion, and they were scared to death of us. Countless times they passed us on the way to the rear with sadness, fear, and confusion on their faces."

Sledge and his companions in the 5th Marines could tell by the sound of the intense artillery fire to the south that the XXIV Corps had smashed into General Ushijima's ring of outer defenses. Inside that first week, soldiers from the 7th and 96th Divisions figured out the riddle: Where the hell are the Japs? By the second week, General Buckner and General Hodge were aware of Ushijima's intentions and the depth and range of his defensive positions.

Along with minefields, caves, and reverse slope emplacements, the Shuri defensive complex contained the most large-caliber weapons the Allies had ever faced in the Pacific. These positions had mutually supporting fires from the adjacent hills and ridgelines— honeycombed with fighting holes and caves. Keeping a strict adherence to these intricate networks of mutually supporting positions required an iron discipline from enemy troops. The enemy's discipline prevailed. Allied forces found themselves entering into savage killing zones.

Japanese tactics along the front were to isolate and contain Allied penetration by grazing fire from supporting positions. Then, they'd overwhelm exposed troops with a storm of preregistered heavy mortar shells while enemy troops swarmed out of their tunnels and counterattacked. Japanese troops often shot down more Allied troops during their extraction from a fire swept hilltop than they did in the initial advance.

General Buckner committed the 27th Infantry Division to the southern front. He had General Geiger loan him his corps artillery and 11th Marines to help beef up fire support. The XXIV Corps now had an additional four 155mm battalions, three 105mm battalions, and one 75mm pack howitzer battalion to add to the underway bombardment of Ushijima's outer defenses. Colonel Fred Henderson took command of a field artillery group composed of a 155mm gun battalion and an eight-inch howitzer battalion (the Henderson Group), which provided massive fire support for the Tenth Army.

It took time to build the adequate units of fire for field artillery battalions to support the mammoth, three-divisional offensive that General Buckner wanted. After a week of inactivity passed along the front, the Japanese made their own adjustments and prepared for the coming offensive.

On L +7 (April 18) General Buckner moved the command post of the Tenth Army onshore, and the new offensive began the following day. It was preceded by a wicked preliminary bombardment (typhoon of steel) of twenty-seven artillery batteries, six hundred aircraft, and eighteen ships. But the enemy just burrowed deeper into their subterranean fortress and waited. They waited for the hellish pounding to stop. They waited for the Allied infantry to advance into their well-designed killing traps.

On April 19, XXIV Corps executed the assault. They made *some* gains before getting thrown back with heavy casualties. The enemy extracted a heavy toll from Allied tanks—particularly those supporting the 27th Infantry Division. The fighting around Kakazu Ridge had separated tanks from supporting infantry by fire, and the Japanese knocked off twenty-two of them with everything from hand-delivered satchel charges to 47mm guns.

This disastrous battle on April 19 gave the Tenth Army a dose of reality. The walk in the sun was over. Overcoming enemy defenses around Shuri would require several divisions, massive firepower, and much more time. General Buckner requested General Geiger give him the 1st Tank Battalion to help the 27th Division along the Machinato-Kakazu lines.

General del Valle was livid and complained to Geiger: "They can have my division, but not piecemeal." Marine tank crews and infantry trained together as a team. The 1st Marine Division had perfected tank-infantry offensive attacks in the crucible on Peleliu. Committing tanks to the Army without trained infantry squads would be catastrophic.

Fortunately, Generals Oliver Smith and Roy Geiger made del Valle's points crystal clear to General Buckner. The Tenth Army commander agreed to refrain from any piecemeal commitments of the Marines. On April 24, he ordered Geiger to designate one division as a Tenth Army reserve and make one regiment in that division ready to move south in less than twelve hours. Geiger gave the mission to the 1st Marine Division, and General del Valle advanced the 1st Marines south.

General Buckner and his senior advisers seriously debated opening a second front with an amphibious landing on the Minatoga Beaches. The bloody fighting on the Shuri front helped him decide. As casualties piled up at a shocking rate, Buckner concentrated all of his resources on one front. On April 27, he assigned the 1st Marine Division to the XXIV Corps. Over the next three days, the division advanced south and relieved the shot-up 27th Infantry Division on the right flank. The 6th Division was ordered to prepare for a similar displacement to the south.

The long battle for the southern highlands of Okinawa was now shifting into gear.

Throughout April and with unparalleled ferociousness, Japanese *kamikazes* punished Fifth Fleet ships supporting the operation. The aerial battles became so intense that the western beaches received a deadly, steady rain of shell fragments from thousands of antiaircraft guns in the fleet. There were no safe havens in this battle.

SITUATION AT SEA

The Japanese strategy to defend Okinawa was to make the most of the nation's shrinking resources and zealous patriotism.

General Ushijima planned to bloody the Allied forces in a lengthy battle of attrition, while the Japanese air forces would savage the Fifth Fleet—tethered to the island to support ground forces. Ushijima's strategy would combine passive ground defense with a violent air offensive. Suicidal *kamikaze* tactics were planned on an unprecedented scale.

By spring of 1945, the Allies understood the enemy's decision to sacrifice planes and pilots in reckless *kamikaze* attacks from their time in the Philippines. Individual suicide attacks by anti-shipping swimmers near Iwo Jima and the "human bullet" anti-tank demolitions on Peleliu were common. Japanese headquarters had escalated these tactics to an overwhelming level at Okinawa. They unleashed their newest weapon: *Operation Kikusui* (floating chrysanthemums) devastating mass suicide airstrikes against the fleet.

While small groups of *kamikazes* struck the fleet nightly and achieved some damage, the worst destruction came from concentrated *Kikusui* raids. The Japanese launched ten separate *Kikusui* attacks during the battle on Okinawa—each with over 350 aircraft. Japanese headquarters coordinated these raids and other tactical surprises, like the sacrificial sortie of the *Yamato* and other formidable counter-attacks. These tactics resulted in a shocking loss of life on both sides.

Kamikaze swarms harassed the Fifth Fleet from the time they entered Ryukyuan waters and throughout the battle. Some senior Navy commanders dismissed the threat—inexperienced pilots and rundown planes launched with insufficient fuel to reach Okinawa. While it was true that many of the 2,377 *kamikaze* pilots did not fulfill their mission, Special Attack Unit pilots who got through the air and surface screens inflicted a wicked toll on the Fifth Fleet.

At the end of the campaign, the Fifth Fleet had endured thirty-four ships sunk, 360 damaged, and over 9,000 casualties: the worst losses ever sustained in a single battle in the history of the US Navy.

The situation at sea became so devastating that smoke from burning ships and offshore escorts blinded Kadena Airfield and caused four returning combat air patrol planes to crash. As the onslaught continued, Admiral Spruance said: "The suicide plane is an effective weapon which we must not underestimate." Spruance spoke from first-hand experience. *Kamikaze* attacks knocked out his first flagship, the heavy cruiser *Indianapolis*, early in the campaign. Then they damaged his replacement flagship—the battleship *New Mexico* two weeks later.

Enemy pilots attacking the fleet off Okinawa had a new weapon: the *Ohka* (Cherry Blossom) bomb. The Allies called this bomb "Baka" (the Japanese word for foolish). A manned rocket packed with 4,400 pounds of explosives launched at ships from the belly of a twin-engine bomber.

The Ohka bombs were the first antiship guided missiles. They shrieked toward their target at an unheard of speed of 500 knots. This new weapon blew the destroyer *Manert L. Abele* out of the water. But luckily for the Allies, most Ohka's missed their targets— the missiles were too fast for the inexperienced pilots to control in their last seconds of glory.

The ultimate suicide attack was the final sortie of the super battleship *Yamato*. One of the world's last great dreadnoughts. She had 18.1-inch guns that could outrange any US battleship. Imperial headquarters dispatched the *Yamato* on her last mission. A bizarre maneuver with no air cover and only a handful of surface escorts— with enough fuel for a one-way trip.

Her mission was to distract American carriers while the Japanese launched a massive *Kikusui* attack against the rest of the fleet. Afterward, the *Yamato* would beach on the west coast of Okinawa and use her massive guns to shoot up the onshore landing force and the thin-skinned amphibious shipping. This daring plan proved to be a complete failure.

This colossal warship would've terrified the fleet protecting an amphibious beachhead in the early years of the war. But not now. US submarines gave Admiral Spruance early warning of the *Yama-to's* departure from Japanese waters. Admiral Mark Mitscher asked Spruance: "Shall I take them or will you?" Mitscher commanded the fast carriers of Task Force 58. While Spruance knew his battle-ship force was eager to avenge their losses at Pearl Harbor—this was no time for nostalgia.

Spruance signaled: "You take them." And with that, Mitscher's Avengers and Hellcats roared into action. They intercepted the *Yamato* a hundred miles from the beach. They sunk her quickly with torpedoes and bombs. It cost the Allied forces eight planes and twelve pilots.

Another bizarre Japanese suicide mission was more effective. On the evening of May 25, seven enemy transport planes loaded with *Giretsu* (Japanese commandos) approached the Yontan Airfield. Vigilant antiaircraft guns flamed five planes, but the surviving plane made a wheels-up belly landing on the airstrip—discharging troops as she slid in sparks and flames along the long surface. Giretsu commandos destroyed eight planes and damaged twice as many more. They ignited 70,000 gallons of aviation fuel, creating chaos and confusion through the night. Jumpy security troops fired into the shadows and injured more of their own men than the Japanese. It took twelve hours to hunt down and destroy the enemy commandos.

Admiral Spruance desperately tried to reduce the effectiveness of the *kamikaze* strikes. His fast-attack carriers hit enemy airfields in Formosa and Kyushu repeatedly, but the Japanese were experts at camouflage. Marine landing parties were sent to seize the outlying islands to establish fire direction and early warning outposts. Fighter aircraft from all three services took to the skies to intercept the massed waves of suicidal enemy planes.

Not all of these enemy airstrikes were *kamikazes*. Equal numbers of fighters and bombers attacked Allied targets while guiding in the suicide planes. The Japanese used several of their later model fighters like the Nakajima in death-defying air-to-air duels over hundreds of miles of blue ocean.

The far-reaching fast carriers usually made the first interceptions. While many pilots were from the Navy, the task force included two Marine fighter squadrons on the carriers *Bennington* and *Bunker Hill*. Marine pilot Lieutenant Ken Huntington flew the only Marine Corsair in the attack on the *Yamato*. Huntington swept through heavy antiaircraft fire to deliver a bomb on the battle ship's forward turret. Described by war correspondent Robert Sherrod: "one Marine, one bomb, and one Navy Cross."

Marine pilots from MAGs 31 and 33 flying out of Yontan Airfield provided most combat air patrol missions over the fleet. Under General Mulcahy's command, the combat air patrol missions surged from an initial twelve planes to as many as thirty-two, with another dozen on alert. These missions involved countless hours of patrolling in rough weather spiked by sudden violent encounters from enemy raiders. Marine planes ran a double risk. Battling with Japanese fighters often brought both planes within range of jittery shipboard antiaircraft gunners—who sometimes shot down both planes.

On April 16, Marine Corsairs raced to help the picket ship *Laffey* under attack from five *kamikaze* planes. Allied aircraft shot down seventeen enemy planes. Only one Corsair was lost in the fight while chasing an enemy *kamikaze* so low that they both clipped the ship's superstructure and crashed.

Major George Axtell and his "Death Rattlers" (VMF-323) intercepted a large flight of enemy raiders approaching the fleet at dusk. Three Marine pilots shot down sixteen enemy planes in twenty minutes. Major Axtell, the squadron commander, shot down five and became an instant ace. He later described these dog fights: "You'd be flying in and out of clouds and heavy rain. Friendly and enemy aircraft would wind up in a big melee. You'd just keep turning into any enemy aircraft that appeared. It was fast and furious, and the engagement would be over within thirty minutes."

Despite the brave efforts of pilots and ground crews, a few *kamikazes* always got through. Kerama Retto's protected anchorage resembled a floating graveyard of severely damaged ships. The small groups of suicide pilots who appeared every night in the fleet were especially vulnerable during the full moon. A naval officer described the nighttime raids as "witches on broomsticks." The main victims of these nocturnal attacks were the "small boys," amphibs and picket ships.

Nick Floros was a 19-year-old signalman who manned a 20mm gun on the tiny *LSM-120*. One moonless night a *kamikaze* appeared out of nowhere. She glided in, cut her engine off, looking like a giant bat. The Japanese plane smashed into the LCM with a horrific explosion before anyone could fire a shot. While the small LSM loaded with landing force supplies somehow survived the fiery blast, she was immediately towed to Kerama Retto's "demolition yard."

* * *

Japanese headquarters believed the exaggerated claims that the *Kikusui* attacks had crippled the US fleet. Wishful thinking. While the Fifth Fleet may have been battered and bruised by the *kamikaze* onslaught, they were too massive of a force to deter. The fleet endured the worst of these endless air attacks. They never wavered from their primary mission of supporting Okinawa's amphibious assault.

Naval gunfire support had never been so effective. Over 4,000 tons of munitions were delivered on L-Day. Frontline regiments received direct support from a "call-fire" ship and one illumination ship throughout the campaign. The quantity and quality of naval gunfire was summed up in this message from General Shepherd: "The effectiveness of our naval gunfire support was measured by the large number of Japanese encountered. Dead ones."

Even through the most intense *Kikusui* attacks in early April, the fleet still unloaded over half a million tons of supplies onto Hagushi's beaches to support the Tenth Army. They opened the port of Nago by clearing mines and obstacles under fire. The only direct consequence from the massed *kamikaze* attacks was the April 6 sinking of ammunition ships *Hobbs Victory* and *Logan Victory*. This caused a shortage of 155mm artillery and delayed General Buckner's first offensive against Shuri by three days. But the Fifth Fleet deserved its nickname "The fleet that came to stay."

But as April dragged into May, the Tenth Army was bogged down because of lackluster frontal assaults along the Shuri line. Admiral Spruance pressured General Buckner to speed up his attack to reduce the fleet's vulnerability. Nimitz was concerned and flew to Okinawa to "counsel" Buckner. Nimitz said: "we're losing a ship and a half each day we're out here. You gotta get this thing moving."

Senior Marine commanders urged Buckner to play the "amphib card" and execute a massive landing on the southeast coast to turn the enemy's right flank. Several Army generals agreed with this recommendation and mentioned that continuing to assault Shuri with frontal assaults was like putting forces through a meatgrinder.

General Vandegrift, Commandant of the Marine Corps, visited the island and seconded the recommendations given to Buckner. Vandegrift pointed out that Buckner still controlled the 2nd Marines. This veteran amphibious outfit had already demonstrated its capability against the Minatoga Beaches on L-Day. Buckner had sent the 2nd Marine Division to Saipan to reduce their vulnerability from *kamikaze* attacks. But the 2nd Division still had combat-loaded ships at hand and could have opened a second front in Okinawa within days.

General Buckner was a capable and popular commander, but his experience with amphibious warfare was limited. His staff warned of a potential logistical nightmare in opening a second front. His intelligence predicted stiff resistance around the Minatoga beachhead. Buckner knew the high cost of the bloody Anzio operation and the consequences of an amphibious landing far from the main effort. Buckner believed the defenses on Shuri would soon crack under a coordinated application of his massive infantry firepower. Buckner rejected the amphibious option. Admirals' Nimitz and Sherman agreed. But not Admirals Turner and Spruance or the Marines.

Spruance wrote in a private letter: "There are times when I was impatient for some of Holland Smith's drive." And General Shepherd stated: "General Buckner did not cotton to amphibious operations."

Even Colonel Yahara of the *Thirty-second Army*, conceded later under interrogation that he'd been puzzled by the adherence to a wholly frontal assault from north to south: "The absence of a landing in the south puzzled the *Thirty-second Army*. Especially after the beginning of May, when it was impossible to put up anything more than a token resistance in the south."

But by then, the 2nd Marine Division was feeling like a yo-yo preparing for their assigned missions. Colonel Samuel Taxis had sharp words after the war about Buckner's decision. "I will always feel that the Tenth Army should've been prepared the instant they were found bogged down. They should've thrown a left hook down there in the southern beaches. They had one hell of a powerful reinforced division down there—trained to a gnat's whisker."

General Buckner stood by his decision. There was to be no "left hook." Instead, both the 1st and 6th Divisions joined in the Shuri offensive as infantry divisions under the Tenth Army, and the 2nd Division would remain in Saipan.

BLOWTORCH AND CORKSCREW

According to the Tenth Army's after-action report: "Japanese defensive efforts and continued development and improvement of cave warfare was the most outstanding feature of enemy tactics on Okinawa."

General Ushijima selected the best terrain to defend the Shuri highlands across the southern neck of the island. His troops dominated two of Okinawa's strategic features: the sheltered anchorage of Nakagusuku bay (later called Buckner Bay) to the east, and the port of Naha to the west. Because of this, Allied troops would have to force their way into the enemy's preregistered killing zones to secure their objectives.

Everything about the terrain favored the defenders. The elaborate topography of ridges, draws, and escarpments grouped the battlefield into sections of small unit firefights. The lack of dense vegetation gave the Japanese troops full, interlocking fire and observation from immediate strong points.

Like Iwo Jima, the enemy fought primarily from underground positions to counteract the Allied supremacy in supporting arms. The enemy modified thousands of concrete Okinawa tombs to use as combat outposts. While there were blind spots in the defenses, finding and exploiting them was costly in time and blood.

The most savage fighting of the campaign took place on a compressed battlefield. The distance from Yonabaru on the east coast to the Asa River bridge on the other side of the island was only 9,000 yards. General Buckner advanced abreast with two Army divisions. By May 8, he'd doubled his force by adding two Marine divisions from IIIAC and sent them west. His two XXIV Corps Army Divisions were sent east. Each of these divisions fought brutal, bloody battles against disciplined enemy soldiers defending entrenched and fortified terrain.

By rejecting the amphibious flanking plan in late April, Buckner had fresh divisions ready to deploy and join the general offensive against Shuri. The 77th relieved the 96th in the center, and the 1st Marine Division relieved the 27th Infantry in the west. Colonel Ken Chappell's 1st Marines entered the lines on April 30 and took heavy fire the moment they approached. When the 5th Marines arrived to supplement the relief, enemy gunners were pounding anything that moved.

PFC Eugene Sledge later wrote: "It was hell in there. We raced across an open field with Jap shells screaming and roaring around us with increasing frequency. The thunder and crash of explosions was a nightmare. I was terribly afraid."

General del Valle took command of the western zone on May 1 at 1400. He issued orders for a major assault the following morning. That evening, a staff officer brought a captured Japanese map annotated with all the American positions. Del Valle realized that the enemy already knew where the 1st Marine Division had entered the fight.

At dawn, Marines attacked into a jagged country (known as the Awacha Pocket). With all their combat expertise, Marines were no more immune to the relentless storm of shells and bullets than the soldiers they relieved. This frustrating day was a forewarning of future conditions. It rained hard as Marines secured the closest high ground. They came under such intense fire from nearby strongholds and other higher ground that they had to retreat. Dozens of Japanese infiltrators snuck up on the withdrawing Marines and engaged them in savage hand-to-hand combat. According to a Marine survivor: "That, was a bitch."

The 1st Division's veterans from Peleliu weren't strangers to cave warfare. No other division had as much practical experience. While nothing on Okinawa could match the Umurbrogol Pocket's steep cliffs, heavy vegetation, and array of fortified ridges, the "Old Breed" of the 1st Division faced a more numerous and smarter enemy. The 1st Division fought through four straight weeks of hell. The funnel created by the cliffs and draws reduced most of the Allied attacks to savage frontal assaults by fully exposed infantry/tank/engineer teams. General Buckner described this small unit fighting as: "a slugging match with temporary and limited opportunity to maneuver."

General Buckner captured the media's imagination with his "blowtorch and corkscrew" tactics needed for successful cave warfare. But to the Marine and Army veterans of Peleliu, Iwo Jima, and Biak, he was just stating the obvious—flamethrowers were the blowtorch and demolitions the corkscrew. But both weapons had to be delivered from close range by tanks and exposed infantry covering them.

On May 3, the rains finally let up, and the Marines resumed their assault. This time they took and held the first tier of vital terrain in the Awacha Pocket. But even after a methodical reduction of enemy strong points, it would take another full week of fierce fighting. Fire support proved to be an excellent asset. Now it was the Army's time to return the favor of inter-service artillery support. The 27th Division's Field Artillery Regiment stayed on the line with its forward observers and linemen familiar with the terrain.

Here, Japanese defensive discipline began to crack. General Ushijima encouraged discussion and debate from his staff regarding tactical courses of action. These heated discussions were generally between chief of staff, Lieutenant General Cho and conservative operations officer, Colonel Yahara. So far, Yahara's strategy of a "delay and bleed" holding action had prevailed. The *Thirty-second Army* had resisted the massive Allied invasion for over a month. With their Army still intact, they could continue to inflict heavy casualties on their enemies for months while massed *kamikaze* attacks wreaked havoc on the fleet.

But maintaining a sustained defense was not *Bushido* and against General Cho's code of honor and morals. He argued for a massive counterattack. Against Yahara's protests, Ushijima sided with General Cho. The great Japanese counterattack of May 4 was ill-advised and foolhardy. Manning the assault forces would forfeit Japanese coverage of the Minatoga sector and bring Ushijima's troops forward into unfamiliar territory. To deliver the mass of the fire necessary to cover the assault, Ushijima brought most of his mortars and artillery pieces into the open. He planned to use the *26th Shipping Engineer Regiment* and other elite forces in a frontal attack. At the same time, a waterborne double envelopment would alert the Allied forces to a massive counteroffensive. Yahara winced in despair.

General Cho's recklessness was now clear. Navy "Flycatcher" patrols on both coasts interdicted the first flanking attempts by Japanese raiders in slow-moving barges and canoes. On the west coast, near Kusan, the 1/1 Marines and the 3rd Armored Amphibian Battalion greeted the enemy trying to come ashore with deadly fire—killing 727. Farther down the coast, the 2/1 Marines intercepted and killed another 175, while the 1st Reconnaissance Company and the war dog platoon hunted down and destroyed the last sixty-four men hiding in the brush. The XXIV Corps took the brunt of the overland assault. They scattered the Japanese troops into small groups before ruthlessly shooting them down.

Instead of the 1st Marine Division being surrounded and annihilated per the Japanese plan—they launched their own counterattack and advanced several hundred yards. The *Thirty-second Army* took 6,000 front-line troop casualties and lost sixty pieces of artillery in this disastrous counterattack. A tearful Ushijima promised Yahara he would never again disregard his advice. Yahara was the only senior officer to survive the counterattack and described this debacle as: "the decisive action of the campaign."

General Buckner took the initiative and organized a four-division front. He tasked General Geiger to redeploy the 6th Division south from the Motobu Peninsula. General Shepherd asked Geiger to assign his Marines to the seaward flank, to continue receiving the benefit of direct naval gunfire support. Shepherd noted his division's favorable experience with fleet support throughout the northern campaign. There was also another benefit: General Shepherd would have only one nearby unit to coordinate maneuvers and fire with— the veteran 1st Marine Division.

At dawn on May 7, General Geiger reclaimed control of the 1st Marine Division and his Corps Artillery and set up his forward command post. The next day, the 22nd Marines came in to relieve the 7th Marines on the lines north of the Asa River. The 1st Division had suffered over 1,400 casualties in the last six days while trying to cover a vast front. The two Marine divisions advanced shoulder to shoulder in the west. They were greeted by heavy rains and ferocious fire as they entered the Shuri lines. The situation was dire along the front. On May 9, the 1/1 Marines assaulted Hill 60 in a spirited attack but lost their commander, Colonel James Murray, to a sniper. Later that night, the 1/5 Marines joined in savage hand-to-hand fighting against a force of sixty Japanese troops—appearing like phantoms out of the rocks.

The heavy rains delayed the 22nd Regiment's attempt to cross the Asa River. Engineers built a narrow footbridge under intermittent fire one night. Hundreds of infantry troops raced across before two enemy soldiers wearing satchel charges strapped to their chests darted into the stream and blew themselves and the bridge to pieces. Engineers spent the next night building a more stable "Baily Bridge." Allied troop reinforcements and vehicles poured across it, but the tanks had a hell of a time traversing the soft mud along the banks. Each attempt was a new adventure. But the Marines were now south of the river in force: encouraging progress on an otherwise stalemated front.

On May 10, the 5th Marines finally fought clear of the hellish Awacha Pocket, ending a week of frustration and point-blank casualties. Now it was the 7th Marines' turn to engage their own nightmarish terrain. South of their position was Dakeshi Ridge. Buckner urged his commanders to keep up the momentum and declared a general offensive along the entire front. This announcement was probably in response to the growing criticism Buckner had been receiving from the Navy and in the media for his attrition strategy.

But the rifleman's war had progressed past high-level persuasion. The assault troops knew full well what to expect—and had a good idea of what the price in blood would be.

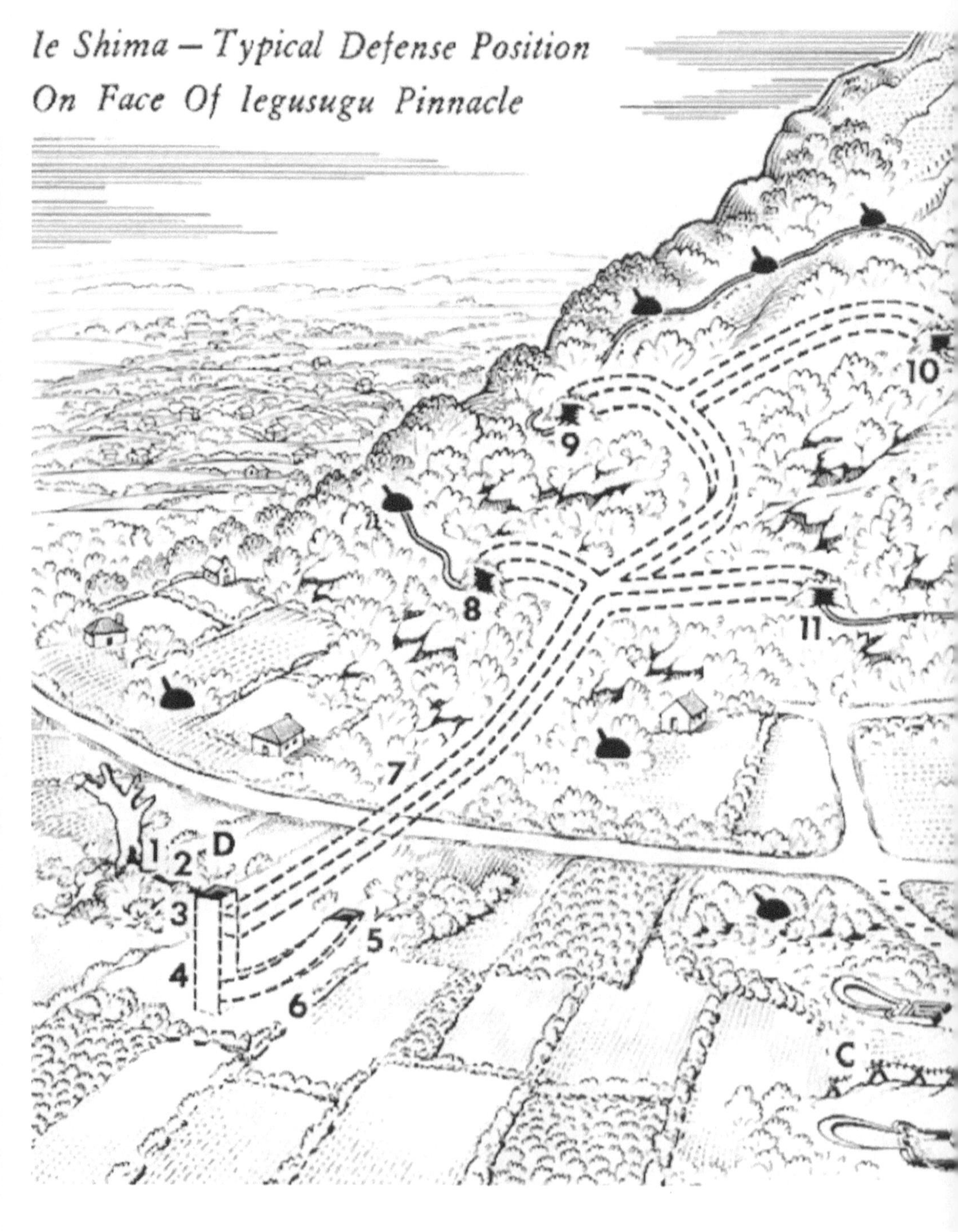

le Shima — Typical Defense Position
On Face Of Iegusugu Pinnacle
1
2
D
3
4
5
6
7
8
9
10
11
C

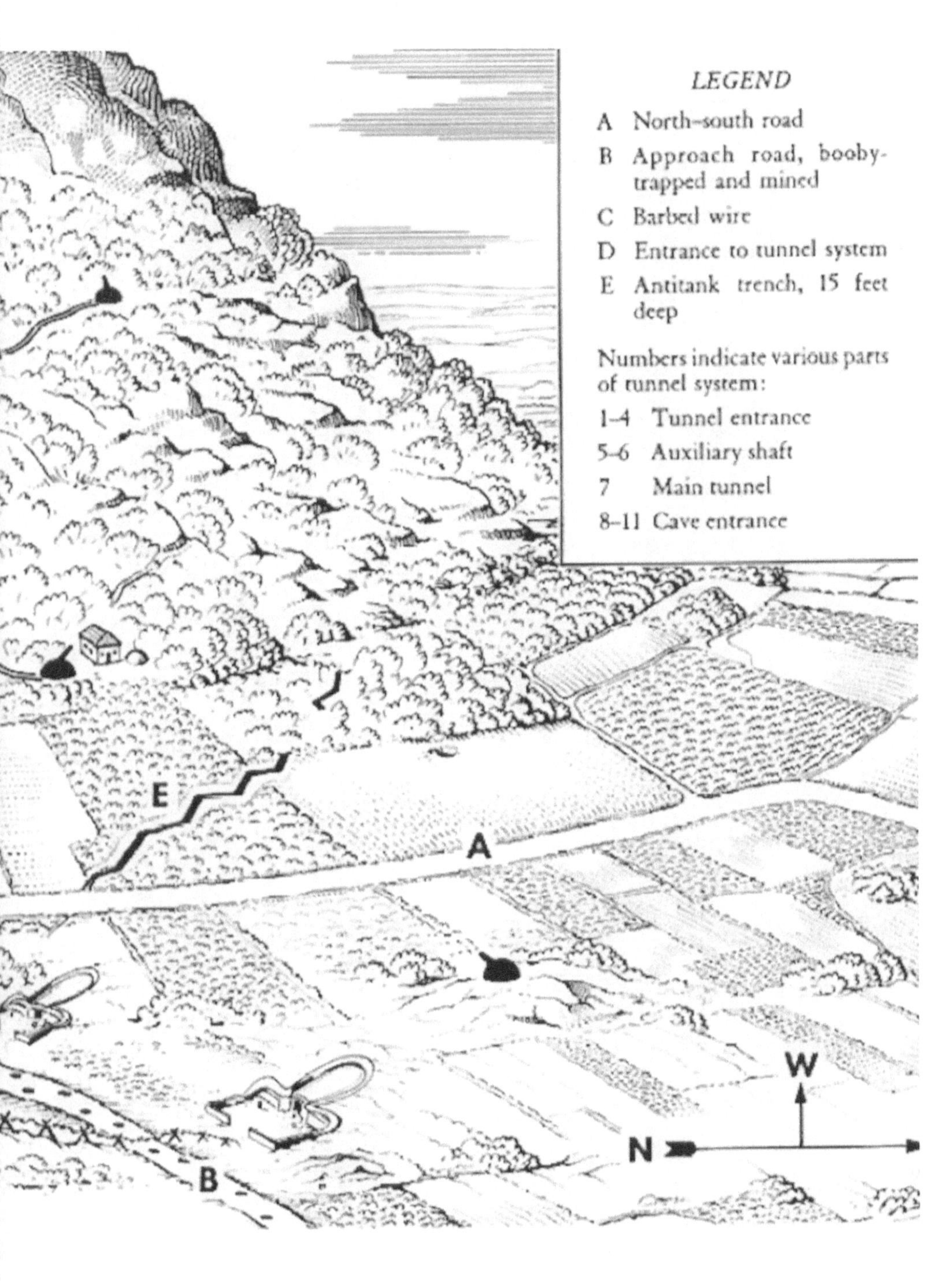

LEGEND
A   North–south road
B   Approach road, booby-trapped and mined
C   Barbed wire
D   Entrance to tunnel system
E   Antitank trench, 15 feet deep
Numbers indicate various parts of tunnel system:
1-4   Tunnel entrance
5-6   Auxiliary shaft
7   Main tunnel
8-11   Cave entrance
A
E
B
N
W

SUGAR LOAF HILL

Colonel Edward Snedeker was a veteran commander with experience fighting on Bougainville and Guadalcanal. "I was fortunate on Okinawa," Snedeker said, "in that each of my battalion commanders had fought at Peleliu. Still, our regiment had its hands full on Dakeshi Ridge. It was our most difficult mission."

After a full day of ferocious fighting, Colonel John Gormley's 1/7 Marines fought their way to Dakeshi's crest but withdrew after enemy counterattacks swarmed them like a hive of angry hornets. The next day, the 2/7 Marines retook the crest and cut down the Japanese counterattacks pouring out from the reverse slope bunkers. Now the 7th Marines were on Dakeshi to stay—another major Allied breakthrough.

The Old Breed Marines briefly celebrated this achievement before the difficulties to come dawned on them. Advancing the next 1,200 yards would take eighteen days of brutal fighting. Their most formidable obstacle would be the steep and twisted Wana Draw rambling off to the south—a lethal killing ground surrounded by towering cliffs, pockmarked with caves and mines, and covered by interlocking fire at every approach. According to General Oliver Smith: "Wana Draw was the toughest assignment the 1st Division ever encountered on Okinawa." The remains of the Japanese *62nd Infantry Division* was prepared to defend Wana to the death.

Historians have paid little attention to the 1st Division's fight against the Wana Draw defenses. Mainly because the celebrated 6th Division's assault on Sugar Loaf Hill happened at the same time. But the Wana Draw battle was just as deadly of a man-killer as the Sugar Loaf Hill battle. Colonel Arthur Mason (now leading the 1st Marine Regiment) began the assault on the Wana complex on May 12. All three infantry regiments took turns assaulting this narrow gorge to the south. The division made full use of their medium Sherman tanks and attached Army flame tanks. Both were instrumental in their assault and fire support roles. On May 16, the 1st Tank Battalion fired over 5,000 rounds of 75mm and 175,000 rounds of 30-caliber along with 650 gallons of napalm.

Crossing the gorge was a heart-stopping race through a gauntlet of enemy fire—and progress came slowly. Typical of the fighting was the division's summary for its progress on the 18th: "Gains were measured by yards won, lost, and then won again." On May 20, Colonel Stephen Sabol's 3/1 Marines improvised a new method to dislodge enemy defenders from their reverse slope positions.

In five hours of grueling, muddy work, troops manhandled several drums of napalm up to the north side of the ridge. There, Marines split the barrels open and tumbled them into the gorge, setting them on fire by dropping white phosphorus grenades in their wake. These small successes were undercut by the Japanese ability to reinforce and resupply their positions during darkness—usually screened by small-unit counterattacks.

The close-quarters fighting was a vicious affair. General del Valle watched his casualties mount daily at an alarming rate. The 7th Marines lost 700 men taking Dakeshi and another 500 in the first five days of fighting for the Wana Draw. On May 16, Colonel E. Hunter Hurst's 3/7 Marines lost twelve officers among his rifle companies. The other regiments suffered just as terribly. From May 11-30, the division lost 200 Marines for every one hundred yards gained.

Heavy rains started again on May 22 and continued in a torrential downpour for ten days. The 1st Marine Division's sector had no roads. General del Valle committed his LVTs to deliver ammo and extract the wounded. Valle resorted to using replacements to hand-carry food and water to the front. This was not acceptable for General del Valle. He brought in torpedo bombers from Yontan Airfield and airdropped supplies by parachute. The low ceilings, heavy rain, and intense enemy fire made for hazardous duty. General del Valle did everything in his power to keep his troops supported, reinforced, supplied, and motivated—even through these grim and treacherous conditions.

To the west, the 6th Marine Division advanced south below the Asa River and collided into a trio of low hills in the open country leading to Shuri Ridge. The first of these hills was steep and unassuming (soon to be known as Sugar Loaf Hill). In the southeast was Half Moon Hill, and in the southwest was the village of Takamotoji and Horseshoe Hill. These three hills represented a singular defensive complex: the western anchor of the Shuri line.

An attack on any one of the mutually supporting defenses of these three hills would prove ineffective unless the others were simultaneously assaulted. Colonel Mita and his *15th Independent Mixed Regiment* would defend this sector to the last man. Its anti-tank guns and mortars were expertly placed to cause maximum damage to the enemy. The western slopes of Half Moon Hill had some of the most sophisticated machine-gun nests the Marines had encountered in the Pacific War. Sugar Loaf Hill had intricate, concrete-reinforced, reverse-slope positions. All approaches to this complex lay within a no-man's-land of heavy artillery from Shuri Ridge, dominating the battlefield.

Sugar Loaf Hill had an elevation of 245 feet, Half Moon at 220, and Horseshoe at 190. In comparative terms, Sugar Loaf though steep, only rose fifty feet above the northern approaches—it was no Mount Suribachi. The significance of Sugar Loaf was in the genius of the defensive fortifications and the unbridled ferocity with which the Japanese would counter-attack every US assault.

The Sugar Loaf complex was like a smaller version of Iwo Jima's Turkey Knob. As a tactical objective, Sugar Loaf lacked the physical dimensions to accommodate anything larger than a rifle company. But after eight days of fighting, that small ridge managed to chew up a handful of companies from two regiments.

Corporal James Day was a squad leader from Weapons Company 2/22. He "debatably" had the best seat in the house to watch the battle. Corporal Day's squad spent four days and three nights isolated in a shell hole in Sugar Loaf's western shoulder. On May 12, Day got orders to cross the Asa River and support Company G's attack against the small ridge. Corporal Day's squad arrived too late to do anything more than cover the fighting withdrawal of G Company. His company lost half their number in the all-day assault, including their gutsy commander, Captain Owen Stebbins (shot in both legs by a Japanese machine gunner). Corporal Day later wrote that Stebbins was: "a brave man whose tactical plan for assaulting Sugar Loaf became the pattern for all successive units to follow."

Concerned about unrestricted fire from the Half Moon Hill area, Major Henry Courtney, battalion XO, took Corporal Day and his squad with him. They moved out on the morning of May 13 on a dangerous trek to reach the 29th Marines and coordinate the upcoming assault. The 29th Marines were then committed to protecting the 2/22 Marines' left flank. Courtney tasked Corporal Day and his squad to support Company F in the following day's assault.

Day's rifle company comprised seven Marines. On the 14th, they joined Company F's assault on Sugar Loaf Hill and scampered up the left shoulder. Day got orders to backtrack his squad around the hill and take up defensive positions on the right western shoulder—this was not easy. By late afternoon Company F had been driven off their exposed left shoulder, leaving Corporal Day with just two of his squad mates in a large shell hole on the opposite shoulder.

That evening, Major Courtney led forty-five volunteers from George and Fox Companies up the left shoulder of Sugar Loaf. In a frantic battle of close-quarters fighting, the Japanese killed Major Courtney and half of his force. According to Corporal Day: "We didn't know who they were. Even though they were only fifty yards away, they were on the opposite side of the crest, we were out of visual contact. But we knew they were Marines, and we knew they were in trouble. We did our part by shooting and grenading every Jap we saw moving in their direction."

Then, Corporal Day heard the sounds of Courtney's force getting evacuated from the hill and knew they were alone on Sugar Loaf. Nineteen-year-old Corporal Day's biggest concern was letting the other Marines know where they were and replenishing their ammo and grenades. "Before dawn, I went back down the hill and there were a couple of LVTs trying to deliver critical supplies to the folks who made it through the earlier penetration. But both had been knocked out just north of the hill. I was able to raid those disabled vehicles several times for ammo, rations, and grenades. We were fine."

On May 15, Corporal Day and his men watched another Marine attack come from the northeast. This time Marines on the eastern crest of the hill were fully exposed to raking fire from the mortars on Half Moon and Horseshoe Hills. Corporal Day's Marines directed their rifle fire into a column of enemy troops running toward Sugar Loaf from Horseshoe: "we really needed a machine gun."

But good fortune provided them with a 30-caliber air-cooled M1919A4 left behind in the wake of the withdrawing Marines. Day's gunner put the weapon into action on the forward parapet of their hole. But an enemy 47mm crew opened up from Horseshoe Hill, killing the Marine gunner and destroying the gun. Now there were only two riflemen left on the ridgetop.

DAY AND BERTOLI

On May 15, tragedy struck the 1/22 Marines. A crushing Japanese bombardment caught the command group assembled at their observation post while they planned their next attack. Shellfire killed the CO, Major Tom Myers. Every other company commander was wounded, including the CO and XO of the supporting tank company. General Shepherd wrote: "it was the greatest single loss the division had sustained. Major Myers was an outstanding leader."

Major Earl Cook, the battalion XO, took command and continued to make assault preparations. Division staff released a warning: "The enemy is able to accurately locate our OPs and CPs because of the commanding ground he occupies. The dangerous practice of permitting unnecessary crowding exposure in these areas will have serious consequences."

That warning was worthless. Commanders had to observe the action to command. Exposure to interdictive fire was a risk you had to take as an infantry battalion commander. The following day, Colonel Jean Moreau, CO of the 1/29 Marines, suffered a serious wound when an enemy shell hit his observation post. His XO, Major Robert Neuffer, took over, and the battle raged on.

According to Corporal Day's last surviving squad mate, Private First Class Dale Bertoli: "The Japs were the only ones up there, and they gave us their full attention. While we had plenty of grenades and ammo, it was still pretty hairy."

Sugar Loaf Hill's south slope was the steepest. Japanese troops swarmed from their caves on the reverse slopes but had a tough climb to get at the Marines on the ridge. Day and Bertoli greeted enemy troops scrambling up the rocks with grenades. The Japanese troops who survived this mini-barrage were backlit by flares as they struggled over and back down the ridge. Day and Bertoli were back to back in the dark side of the crater—an excellent position to shoot down fleeing Japanese troops.

According to Corporal Day: "I believed that Sugar Loaf would fall on the 16th. We looked back and down and saw the battle shaping up. A great panorama." The two squad mates hunkered down while artillery, mortars, and tanks hammered the ridge. Day saw the fire coming from the enemy had not slackened: "Sugar Loaf's real danger wasn't the hill where we were, it was a 300-yard kill zone the Marines had to cross to approach the hill from the north. It was a grim sight. Men falling, tanks getting knocked out . . . division must've suffered over 600 casualties in that one day." Looking back, the 6th Marine Division considered May 16 to be the bloodiest day of the entire campaign.

The battered 22nd Marines were down to forty percent effectiveness. General Shepherd relieved them with the 29th and installed fresh regimental leadership, replacing the CO and XO with Colonels Harold Roberts and August Larson. When the weather cleared during the late afternoon on the 16th, Day and Bertoli could see well past Horseshoe Hill and all the way to the Asato River. Steady columns of Japanese reinforcements surged northward through Takamotoji village and toward the battlefield. Day and Bertoli kept firing at them from 600 yards away, keeping a small but persistent thorn in the enemy's defenses. Their rifle fire drew substantial attention from crawling squads of nighttime enemy raiders.

Corporal Day recalled: "They came at us from 2045 and on all night. All we could do was to keep tossing grenades and firing at them with our M-1s. Marines north of Sugar Loaf tried to help us with mortar fire, but it came a little too close, and both me and Bertoli were wounded by shrapnel and burned by white phosphorus."

At dawn on the 17th, a runner from the 29th Marines scrambled up to their shell-pocked crater with orders to "get the hell out of there." A massive naval, air, and artillery bombardment was underway. Day and Bertoli did not hesitate. They were exhausted and partially deaf, but still had the energy to stumble back down the hill to safety. Day and Bertoli endured a series of debriefings from staff officers, while a roaring bombardment crashed down on the three hills.

May 17 was the fifth day of battle for Sugar Loaf Hill. It was 2/29 Easy Company's turn to attack the complex's defenses. While brave and persistent, Easy Company's several assaults fared little better than their predecessors. During one of these ferocious attacks, the 29th Marines reported to division: "E Company moved to the top of the ridge and had thirty men south of Sugar Loaf. [E Co.] sustained two close-in charges and killed a hell of a lot of Nips. Moving back to base to reform and at dusk, we are going again, We will take it."

But Sugar Loaf did not fall. At dusk, after overcoming another savage onslaught of bayonets, flashing knives, and hand-to-hand combat against a brutal counterattack, Easy Company withdrew—taking 160 casualties.

May 18 marked the beginning of incessant rain. In this soupy mess, Dog Company, 2/29 Marines, attacked Sugar Loaf Hill. They were supported by tanks that braved the minefields on both shoulders of Sugar Loaf to penetrate the no-man's-land just to the south. When the enemy swarmed out of their reverse-slope caves for another counterattack—tanks destroyed them. Dog Company earned the honor of becoming the first rifle company to hold Sugar Loaf overnight. Marines would not give up that bloody and costly ground.

The shot-up and exhausted 29th Marines still needed to take Half Moon and Horseshoe Hills. General Geiger adjusted the tactical boundaries westward and brought the 1st Marine Division into the fight for Horseshoe Hill. Geiger also released the 4th Marines from Corps reserve.

General Shepherd deployed the fresh Marines into the battle on the 19th. The battle raged, and the 4th Marines took seventy casualties just relieving the 29th Marines. But with Sugar Loaf now in Allied hands, the battle's momentum shifted. On May 20, Colonel Reynolds Hayden's 1/4 Marines (with help from the 2/4 and 3/4) made notable gains on both flanks. By the end of the day, Marines had secured Half Moon Hill and a good portion of Horseshoe.

Enemy reinforcements funneled into the fight from the southwest. The Marines prepared for nighttime visitors at Horseshoe Hill. Japanese troops came in massive numbers: 700 sailors and soldiers smashing into Marine defenders throughout much of the night. Colonel Bruno Hochmuth's 3/4 Marines had six artillery battalions in direct support of the attack and fifteen battalions at the height of the fighting. Throughout the crisis on Horseshoe, Hochmuth kept in radio contact with Colonel Bruce Hemphill, who commanded the support artillery battalions.

This exchange between commanders reduced the number of short rounds and allowed Marines to provide accurate fire on the Japanese. This hellish rain of shells blew massive holes into the ranks of every Japanese advance: Marine riflemen met those who survived with their bayonets. The enemy counter attackers died to the man.

The victory at Sugar Loaf lacked a climactic finish. There was no celebration ceremony here. The sniper-infested ruins of Naha loomed ahead, with Shuri Ridge in the distance. The 1st Marine Division sidestepped the last of the Wana defenses to the east. The 6th Marine Division crept west while the 4th Marines crossed the chest-high Asa River on May 23. The III Amphibious Corps stood primed on the outskirts of Okinawa's capital city.

* * *

The Army's XXIV Corps matched the Marines' breakthroughs and success. On the east coast, the 96th Division secured Conical Hill (opposite Sugar Loaf on the Shuri anchor line) after weeks of fierce fighting. On May 22, the 7th secured Yonabaru.

Now, the Japanese Thirty-*second Army* faced a real risk of being cut off from both flanks. General Ushijima (this time) took Colonel Yahara's advice. Instead of fighting to the death at Shuri Castle, the remaining Japanese troops took advantage of the awful weather. They streamed southward to their last line of prepared defenses in the Kiyamu Peninsula. General Ushijima masterfully executed this maneuver. While Allied pilots spotted and interdicted the south-bound columns, they reported other columns moving north. General Buckner believed the Japanese were rotating units in defense of Shuri. But these northbound troops were ragtag units tasked with a suicide rearguard action. At this, they succeeded.

On May 29, a South Carolina company commander raised the "Stars and Bars" Confederate flag over the abandoned Shuri Castle. According to General del Valle: "every damn OP that could see that flag started telephoning me and raising Cain. I had one hell of a hullabaloo on the telephone. I agreed to replace that rebel flag with the Stars and Stripes, but it took two days to get it through the Japs rear guards."

On May 31, Colonel Richard Ross, CO of the 3/1 Marines, raised the Stars and Stripes over Shuri Castle and then took cover. Unlike Sugar Loaf Hill, Shuri Castle could be seen from all over southern Okinawa. Every Japanese gunner within range opened up on the hated American colors. Even though the Stars & Stripes fluttered over Shuri Castle, and the formidable enemy defenses had been breached, the Japanese *Thirty-second Army* still remained as deadly a fighting force as ever. The enemy would sell their lives dearly for the final eight shell-pocked, rain-soaked miles of southern Okinawa.

SCREAMING MIMI

Withdrawing Japanese troops did not easily escape from their Shuri defenses. US Navy spotter planes found the southbound column and called in a devastating fire from every available attack craft and half a dozen ships.

Soon after, many miles of that muddy road were littered with wrecked field guns, trucks, and corpses. General del Valle congratulated the Tactical Air Force: "Thanks for the prompt response this afternoon when the Nips were caught on the road with their kimonos down."

Still, most of General Ushijima's *Thirty-second Army* survived and made it to their "Alamo" on the Kiyamu Peninsula. The Tenth Army missed an opportunity to end the battle a month early—stalled by heavy rains and deep mud—simply too encumbered to swiftly respond.

Allied infantry trudged south, cursing the weather but glad to be past the Shuri line. Every advance exacted a price in blood. A Japanese sniper killed Colonel Horatio Woodhouse, CO of the 2/22 Marines (and General Shepherd's cousin) as he led his battalion toward the Kokuba Estuary. Shepherd grieved privately at the loss of his young cousin and put the battalion XO, Colonel John G. Johnson, in command.

As troops of the III Amphibious Corps continued south, Marines came upon a series of east-west ridges that dominated open farmlands. Colonel Snedeker wrote: "The southern part of Okinawa consisted primarily of cross ridges that stuck out like the bones of a fish." In the meantime, divisions from the Army's XXIV Corps carefully approached the towering escarpments in their zone. The remaining Japanese troops had gone to ground again along the ridges and peaks—lying in wait to ambush the Allied advance.

Rain and mud plagued the advancing Allied forces. In Eugene Sledge's book, he described this battlefield as a "five-mile sea of mud." PFC Sledge wrote: "The mud in camp on Pavuvu was a nuisance. But the mud on that Okinawan battlefield was misery beyond description."

The 96th Division reported the results of a full day's efforts under these conditions: "those on the reverse slope slid back and those on the forward slope down—otherwise no change."

Marines chafed at the heavy-handed controls of the Tenth Army, which seemed to stall at each encounter with a Japanese outpost. General Buckner preferred a massive application of fire-power and destroying every obstacle before committing troops into the open. Colonel Shapley, CO of the 4th Marines, disagreed: "I'm not too sure that sometimes when they whittle you away, ten to twelve men a day, that maybe it would be better to take a hundred losses a day to get out sooner."

Colonel Wilburt "Bigfoot," Brown, CO of the 11th Marines (legendary veteran artilleryman) believed the Tenth Army relied too heavily on firepower. "We dumped a tremendous amount of metal into those Jap positions. Nothing could have lived through that churning mass of roaring and falling shells—but when we advanced, the Nips were still there—and mad as hell." Colonel Brown also had strong feelings about the overuse of star shells for night illumination: "It was like we were the children of Israel in the wilderness: living under a pillar of fire by night and a cloud of smoke by day."

This heavy reliance on artillery support stressed the amphibious supply system. The Tenth Army's demand for heavy ordinance grew to over 3,000 tons of ammunition per day. Each round had to be delivered to the beach and distributed along the front. This reduced the availability of other supplies, including rations. Front-line troops began to go hungry. Partial support came from the friendly skies when Marine torpedo-bombers air-dropped rations during the first three days of June.

Offshore, the fleet endured waves of *kamikaze* attacks. On May 17, Admiral Turner announced an end to the amphibious assault phase and departed. General Buckner now reported to Admiral Spruance. Admiral Harry Hill assumed command of the enormous amphibious force still supporting the Tenth Army. On May 27, Admiral "Bull" Halsey relieved Spruance. And the Fifth Fleet officially became the Third Fleet: same crew, same ships, different designation. Turner and Spruance began plotting their next amphibious assault—Operation Downfall—the invasion of the Japanese home islands.

General Shepherd appreciated the vast amphibious resources available and decided to inject some tactical mobility into this sluggish campaign. For the 6th Division to secure the Naha Airfield, Shepherd had to first overcome the Oroku Peninsula. The hard way of achieving this would be to attack from the peninsula's base and scratch seaward. Or Shepherd could launch a shore-to-shore amphibious assault and surprise the enemy on their flank. "The Japanese expected us to cross the Kokuba," Shepherd said. "I wanted to surprise them."

Shepherd convinced General Geiger of the wisdom of this approach, but getting General Buckner's approval took much longer. Eventually, Buckner agreed but only gave the 6th Marine Division thirty-six hours to plan and execute this division-level amphibious assault.

Colonel Krulak relished this challenge. Scouts from Major "Cold Steel" Walker's 6th Recon Company crept across the statuary at night to gather intelligence on the enemy defenders and Nishikoku Beaches. Scouts confirmed a cobbled force of Japanese Navy units under an old adversary. The final opposed amphibious landing of the Pacific War would be launched against one of the last surviving SNLF (Special Naval Landing Force) commanders—Admiral Minoru Ota.

Admiral Ota was fifty-four years old and a graduate of the Japanese Naval Academy. A veteran of the elite SNLF service from as early as 1932 in Shanghai. Ten years later, he commanded the *2nd Combined Special Landing Force* meant to assault Midway but was prevented by the catastrophic naval defeat suffered by the Japanese.

In November 1942, he commanded the *8th Combined Special Landing Force* in the Solomons, defending Bairoko against the 1st Marine Raiders. By 1945, the SNLF had mostly disappeared. Ota was in command of a motley outfit of several thousand coastal defense and antiaircraft gunners, aviation mechanics, and construction specialists. Ota still breathed fire into his forces. He equipped his ragtag troops with hundreds of machine cannons from wrecked aircraft and made them sow thousands of mines.

Shepherd knew he was in for a fight and that he faced a skilled opponent; he also realized that he had the advantage of surprise if his forces could act quickly. The final planning details centered on problems with the division's previously dependable LVTs. The hard-fighting onshore had taken a hefty toll on the tracks and suspension systems of these amphibious assault vehicles—and there were no repair parts available. Worse, the first typhoon of the season was approaching, and the Navy was getting jumpy. General Shepherd remained resolute in executing the assault on June 4, and Admiral Halsey backed him up.

Shepherd chose Colonel Shapley to lead the 4th Marines in the assault. Shapley divided the 650-yard Nishikoku Beach between the 1/4 Marines on the right and the 2/4 on the left. Despite the heavy rains, the assault jumped off on schedule. The Oroku Peninsula exploded in smoke and flame under the hammering of hundreds of naval guns, aerial bombs, and artillery batteries. Scouts secured Ono Yama island while the 4th Marines swept across the statuary. LCIs and LCMs loaded with tanks appeared from Loomis Harbor in the north.

The amphibious force achieved total surprise. Many of the busted-up LVTs broke down en route, causing delays, but enemy fire was negligible. Empty LVTs from the first waves quickly returned to rescue the stranded troops. The 4th Marines rapidly advanced with Colonel Whaling's 29th Marines close behind. By dusk, Marines occupied 1,200 yards on Oroku Peninsula. A furious Admiral Ota redeployed his sailors to the threat from the rear.

This amphibious assault had been near-perfect and a model for future study in amphib ops. The typhoon blew through while the Marines occupied the peninsula and captured the airfield in two days. On June 7, when the 1st Division reached the southwest coast north of Itoman, Admiral Ota's force had no chance of escape. General Shepherd ordered a threefold enveloping movement with his regiments—leading to the inevitable outcome.

The battle for the Oroku Peninsula was savage. Admiral Ota

was no ordinary enemy commander. His 5,000 troops fought with a warrior's spirit and were heavily armed. No similar size Okinawan force had so many automatic weapons or so effectively placed mines. Marines encountered devastating enemy weapons at short range—rail-mounted 8-inch rockets, "the Screaming Mimi," and massive 320mm spigot mortars firing "Flying Ashcans."

On June 9, the 4th Marines reported: "Stubborn defense of high ground by MG and 20mm fire. Character of opposition unchanged. L Hill under attack from two sides. Another tank shot on right flank, thinking 8-inch gun."

Admiral Ota saw the end coming. On June 6, he reported to Tokyo: "The troops have fought valiantly in the finest tradition of the Japanese Navy. While fierce bombardments may have deformed the mountains of Okinawa, they cannot alter the loyal spirit of our men." Three days later, Ota sent his final message to General Ushijima: "Enemy tank groups now attack our cave headquarters. The naval force will have a glorious death." Ota committed ritual suicide —his duty now done.

General Shepherd had defeated a competent and worthy foe. In his Oroku operation after-action report he said: "In ten days of fighting we killed 5,000 Japanese and took 200 prisoners. Mines disabled thirty of our tanks. One tank was destroyed by two direct hits from an 8-inch naval gun at point-blank range. 1,608 Marines were wounded or killed."

WRAPPING UP THE FIGHT

When the 1st Marine Division reached the coast near Itoman, it was the first time the division had access to the sea in over a month. This relieved the veteran division's extended supply lines. Colonel Snedeker, CO of the 7th Marines, wrote: "As we reached the shore we were helped a great deal by amphibian tractors that had come down the coast with supplies. Otherwise, there was no way in hell we could get supplies overland."

The wide-open southern country allowed General del Valle to further refine the deployment of his infantry-tank teams. No unit in the Tenth Army surpassed the 1st Marine Division's synchronization of these two supporting arms. Using those painfully learned tactical lessons from Peleliu, the 1st Division never allowed their tanks to range beyond the support of accompanying artillery and infantry. This resulted in the 1st Tank Battalion being the only armored unit in the battle not to lose a tank to Japanese suicide squads—even during the swirling close-quarter combat at Wana Draw.

General del Valle appreciated his attached Army 4.2 mortar battery: "My tanks had such good luck because the 4.2s were vital in

Okinawa. We developed the tank infantry training to a fare-thee-well in those swales—backed up by the 4.2-inch mortars."

According to Colonel "Bigfoot" Brown of the 11th Marines: "Working with Lieutenant Colonel 'Jeb' Stuart and the 1st Tank Battalion, we developed a new method of protecting tanks and reducing infantry vulnerability during the assault. We'd put an artillery observer in one of those tanks with a radio to one of the 155mm howitzer battalions. We used both packs of the 75mm, and LVT-As with the airburst capabilities. If any Jap [suicider] showed his face anywhere, we opened fire with an airburst and kept a pattern of pattering shell fragments around the tanks."

On June 10, Colonel Jim Magee's 2/1 Marines used similar tactics in a bloody all-day assault on Hill 69—west of Ozato. Magee's Marines lost three tanks to enemy artillery in the approach. But they still took the hill and held it through a savage enemy counterattack that night.

Kunishi Ridge loomed beyond Hill 69. A steep coral escarpment dominated the surrounding grasslands and rice patties. Kunishi was longer and higher than Sugar Loaf, but equally honeycombed with enemy caves and tunnels. While it lacked cover with Half-Moon and Horseshoe on its rear flanks, it was still protected from behind by Masato Ridge—500 yards south. Fragments of the veteran *32nd Infantry Regiment* defended the many hidden bunkers. This was the last of General Ushijima's organized frontline troops. Kunishi Ridge would be as deadly a killing ground as the Marines would ever face in the Pacific War.

On June 11, enemy gunners repelled the first tank-infantry assaults by the 7th Marines. Colonel Snedeker had a different plan: "I realized, due to the losses of experienced leadership, we'd never be able to take Kunishi Ridge in the daytime. I thought a night attack could be successful."

Snedeker flew over his objective and devised his plan. Tenth Army night assaults were rare in this campaign—especially Snedeker's ambitious plan of deploying two battalions. But General del Valle approved his plan, and at 0330 the next morning, the 1/7 and

2/7 departed the combat outpost for the dark ridge. By 0500, lead companies of both battalions swarmed over the crest and surprised several enemy groups calmly cooking breakfast. Then, a brutal battle to expand the toehold on the ridge exploded into action.

As dawn broke, enemy gunners targeted relief infantry columns as Marines clung to the crest and endured showers of shrapnel from grenades and mortar rounds. According to General del Valle: "This situation was one of the tactical oddities in this type of peculiar warfare. We were *on* the ridge, and the Japs were *in* the ridge, on both the forward and reverse slopes."

Marines on Kunishi desperately needed supplies and reinforcements. The growing number of wounded needed evacuation. Only the medium Shermans had the bulk and the ability to provide relief. Over the next several days, the 1st Tank Battalion (even losing twenty-two Shermans to enemy fire) made remarkable achievements. They removed two crewmen to make room for six replacement riflemen inside each tank. Once on top of the hill they exchanged replacements for wounded, but no one could stand without getting shot. So, all the exchanges had to take place through the escape hatch in the bottom of the tanks.

This became a familiar sight on Kunishi Ridge: a buttoned-up tank lurching up to besieged Marine positions while replacements slithered out via the escape hatch carrying ammo, rations, water, and plasma. Then, other Marines crawled under the Shermans, dragging their wounded on ponchos—manhandling them through the small escape hatch. For those severely wounded, they had the unsavory privilege of riding down to safety lashed topside behind the turret. Tank drivers provided maximum protection to their exposed stretcher cases by backing down the entire 850-yard gauntlet. In this meticulous way, tankers delivered fifty fresh troops and evacuated thirty-five wounded men the day after the 7th Marines' night assault.

General del Valle was pleased with these results and ordered Colonel Mason to execute a similar night assault in the 1st Marine sector of Kunishi Ridge. This mission went to the 2/1 Marines, who accomplished it on the night of June 13 despite careless lapses of illumination fire by forgetful supporting arms.

Furious Japanese swarmed out of their bunkers in a massive counterattack. Losses mounted quickly in Colonel Magee's ranks. One company lost six of seven officers that morning, before the 1st Tank Battalion came to the rescue delivering reinforcements and evacuating 110 wounded Marines by nightfall.

General del Valle wrote: "The Japs were so damn surprised. They used to counterattack us at night all the time. I bet they never felt we'd have the audacity to go out and do it to them."

During Colonel Yahara's interrogation, he admitted the Marine night attacks effectively caught his troops off-guard—psychologically and physically.

By June 15, the 1st Marines had been fighting for twelve straight days: sustaining 500 casualties. The 5th Marines replaced them with an elaborate nighttime relief on June 15. The 1st Marines, back in the safety of division reserve, received their newest orders: *If not otherwise occupied, you will bury Japs in your area.*

The battle for Kunishi Ridge raged. PFC Sledge approached the embattled escarpment with dread. He later wrote: "That crest looked so much like Bloody Nose that my knees nearly buckled. I felt like I was back on Peleliu and had to go through that hell all over again." The fighting along that crest and its slopes took place at point-blank range—even for Sledge's 60mm mortars. His crew then became stretcher-bearers in this highly hazardous duty. Half of his company was wounded within the next twenty-two hours.

Getting wounded Marines off Kunishi Ridge was no easy task. The seriously wounded needed to endure another half day of evacuation by field ambulance over bad roads and enemy fire. Then, pilots stepped in with a great idea. Engineers cleared a rough landing strip suitable for "Grasshopper" observation aircraft. Corpsmen hustled to deliver casualties from Kunishi and Hill 69 to the crude airfield. They were gently loaded into waiting "Piper Cubs" and flown back to the field hospitals in the rear—an eight-minute flight. This was the dawn of tactical medevacs, which saved so many lives in the subsequent Asian wars. Marine pilots flew out 640 casualties in eleven days: saving countless lives.

The 6th Marine Division joined the southern battlefield after securing the Oroku Peninsula. The *32nd Infantry Regiment* died a hard death after the combined forces of III Amphibious Corps swept north and overlapped Mezado Ridge and could smell the sea along the south coast. In Ira Saki, Marines from Company G (2/22) raised the 6th Division's colors on the island's southernmost point.

The long-neglected 2nd Marine Division finally got into the fight in the closing week of the campaign. Colonel Clarence Wallace and his 8th Marines arrived from Saipan to capture the two outlying islands—Aguni Shima and Iheya Shima—this would give the fleet more early warning radar sites against *kamikaze* raids. Colonel Wallace commanded a considerable force (essentially a brigade), including the 2/10 Marines and the 2nd Amphibian Tractor Battalion. General Geiger assigned the 8th Marines to the 1st Division, and on June 18, they relieved the 7th Marines and swept southeast with ferocity.

PFC Sledge recalled the arrival of the 8th Marines: "We scrutinized these Marines with the hard professional stare of old salts sizing up another outfit. Everything we saw brought forth remarks of approval."

General Buckner was interested in observing the 8th Marines' first combat deployment. Earlier, he'd been impressed with Colonel Wallace's outfit during an inspection visit to Saipan. Buckner went to a forward observation post on June 18 to watch the 8th Marines advance along the valley floor. Enemy gunners on the opposite ridge saw the official party and opened up. A shell struck a close coral outcrop and drove a lethal splinter into the general's chest. Buckner died in ten minutes. One of the few senior American officers killed in action in World War II.

General Geiger assumed command. His third star became effective immediately. The Tenth Army was in capable hands. Geiger became the only Marine—and the only pilot of any service—to command a field army. The Okinawan soldiers had no qualms about this. Senior Army echelons elsewhere did. Army General Joseph Stillwell received urgent orders to Okinawa. Five days later, he relieved Geiger. But by then, the battle was over.

When news of General Buckner's death reached the *Thirty-second Army* headquarters in its cliff-side cave near Mabuni—the enemy officers cheered—but General Ushijima remained silent. He respected Buckner's military ancestry and appreciated that they'd both once commanded their respective service academies: Buckner at West Point and Ushijima at Zama.

Ushijima knew his end was approaching fast. The 7th and 96th Divisions were nearly on top of Japanese command. On June 21, General Ushijima ordered his men to "save themselves so they could tell the story to Army headquarters." Then he committed *Seppuku*. Ushijima plunged his *Tantō* (short knife) into his belly, drawing the blade from left to right before Colonel Yahara shot him in the back of the head—Ushijima collapsed into a pool of his own blood.

General Geiger declared the end of organized resistance on Okinawa the same day. True to form, a final *kamikaze* attack struck the fleet that night, and sharp fighting broke out on the 22nd. Undeterred, General Geiger ordered the 2nd Marine Aircraft Wing in action and ran up the American flag at Tenth Army headquarters.

The long battle was finally over.

LEGACY OF OKINAWA

The exhausted Marines on Okinawa showed little joy at the official proclamation of victory. The death throes of the *Thirty-second Army*

kept the battlefield deadly. The last of General Ushijima's infantry may have died defending Yuza Dake and Kunishi Ridge, but the remaining mishmash of support troops sold their lives dearly to the last man.

On June 18, diehard enemy survivors wounded Major Earl Cook, CO of the 1/22 Marines, and Colonel Hunter Hurst, CO of the 3/7. Even Day and Bertoli, who'd survived so long in that crater on Sugar Loaf, watched their luck run out in the final days. Private First Class Bertoli died in action. Corporal Day was seriously wounded by a satchel charge and required urgent evacuation to the hospital ship *Solace*.

The butcher's bill on Okinawa was costly to both sides. Over 120,000 Japanese died defending the island, while 7,000 surrendered at the end. The native Okinawans suffered the worst. Recent studies show that over 150,000 civilians died in the fighting—one-third of the island's population. The Tenth Army suffered over 45,000 combat casualties, including 7,264 dead Americans. An additional 26,000 nonviolent casualties were incurred: primarily cases of combat fatigue.

The Marine Corps' overall casualties: air, ship detachments, and ground were 19,821. In addition, 562 members of the Navy Medical Corps were wounded or killed. General Shepherd described the corpsmen on Okinawa as: "the finest and most courageous men that I'd ever known. They did a magnificent job."

Losses within the infantry (as usual) were disproportionate with other Allied outfits. Colonel Shapley reported his losses as 110 percent in the 4th Marines. This number represents the replacements and their high attrition in the battle. Corporal Day of the 2/22 Marines experienced the death of his battalion and regimental commanders, plus the killing and wounding of his two company commanders, seven platoon commanders, and every other member of his rifle squad.

The legacy of this epic battle can be defined through the following points:

Foreshadow to the Invasion of Japan

Admiral Spruance described the Okinawan battle as: "the bloody and hellish prelude to the invasion of Japan." As wicked a nightmare as Okinawa was, every survivor knew the subsequent battles on Honshu and Kyushu would be worse. The operational plans for invading Japan specified the use of surviving veterans from Iwo Jima and Luzon. The reward for the Okinawan survivors would be to land on the main island of Honshu. Most of the men were fatalistic—no man's luck could last through those hellish infernos.

Mastery of amphibious tactics

The massive and nearly flawless amphibious assault on Okinawa happened thirty years (to the month) after the disaster at Gallipoli in World War I. By 1945, the Allied forces had refined this difficult naval mission into an art form. Admiral Nimitz had every advantage in place for Okinawa: specialized ships and landing craft, a proven doctrine, mission-oriented weapons systems, flexible logistics, trained shock troops, and unity of command. Everything clicked and everything worked. The projection (and execution) of 60,000 combat troops landed ashore on L-Day validated an amphibious doctrine earlier considered suicidal.

Attrition style warfare

Ignoring the great opportunities for maneuver and surprise available in the amphibious task force, the Tenth Army executed most assaults on Okinawa using an unimaginative attrition style of warfare, which played to the Japanese defenders' strength. This unrealistic reliance on firepower and siege tactics only prolonged the fighting. The Oroku Peninsula and Ie Shima Landings (despite being successful) comprise the only division-level amphibious assaults after L-Day. Also, the few night attacks made in unison by the Army and Marine forces (which were successful) were not encouraged. The Tenth Army squandered several opportunities for tactical innovations that could have hastened a breakthrough into enemy defenses.

Unity of service

Excluding squabbles between the 77th Infantry Division and 1st Marine Division after the Marines' seizure of Shuri Castle (in the Army's zone), the battle for Okinawa represented joint service cooperation at its finest. This was General Buckner's finest achievement, and General Geiger continued with this level of teamwork after Buckner was impaled through the chest and killed in action. The battle of Okinawa today is still a model of study in inter-service cooperation for succeeding generations of military professionals.

The best training

Marines deployed in Okinawa received the most practical and thoroughly advanced training of the war. Well-seasoned and battle-hardened division and regimental commanders anticipated Okinawa's requirements for cave warfare. They built-up areas to conduct realistic rehearsals and training. This battle produced few surprises.

Many Marines who survived Okinawa went on to top positions of leadership that influenced the Marine Corps for the next two decades. Two Marine Corps commandants emerged from this hellish ordeal: General Lemuel Shepherd of the 6th Marine Division and Colonel Leonard Chapman, CO of the 4/11 Marines. Oliver Smith and Vernon McGee were promoted to the rank of four-star general. At least seventeen others achieved the rank of lieutenant general—including George Axtell, Alan Shapley, Ed Snedeker, and Victor Krulak.

Corporal James Day recovered from his wounds and returned to Okinawa forty years later as a Major General in command of all Marine Corps bases on the island.

During the taping of the battle's fiftieth anniversary, General Victor Krulak gave a fitting epitaph to the brave men who gave their lives on Okinawa. Speaking on camera, he said: "The cheerfulness with which they went to their death has stayed with me forever. What is it that makes them all the same? I watched them in Korea, I watched them in Vietnam, and it's the same. American youth is one hell of a lot better than he is usually credited."

grueling struggle for the island of Guadalcanal and its vital strategic position.

Operation Galvanic, an incredible account of the battle for the Tarawa Atoll and base that would give them a steppingstone into the heart of Japanese-controlled waters.

Operation Backhander, a gripping retelling of the war for Cape Gloucester, New Guinea, and the Bismarck Sea.

Battle for Saipan, Marines stormed the beaches with a goal of gaining a crucial air base from which the US could launch its new long-range B-29 bombers directly at Japan's home islands.

Invasion of Tinian, is the incredible account of the assault on Tinian. Located just under six miles southwest of Saipan. This was the first use of napalm and the "shore to shore" concept.

Recapture of Guam, a gripping narrative about the liberation of the Japanese-held island of Guam, captured by the Japanese in 1941 during one of the first Pacific campaigns of the War.

Operation Stalemate, Marines landed on the island of Peleliu, one of the Palau Islands in the Pacific, as part of a larger operation to provide support for General MacArthur, who was preparing to invade the Philippines.

Operation Detachment, the battle of Iwo Jima was a major offensive in World War II. The Marine invasion was tasked with the mission of capturing airfields on the island for use by P-51 fighters.

Operation Iceberg, the invasion and ultimate victory on Okinawa was the largest amphibious assault in the Pacific Theater. It was also one of the bloodiest battles in the Pacific, lasting ninety-eight days.

This gripping narrative sheds light on these often-overlooked facets of WWII, providing students, history fans, and World War II buffs alike with a captivating breakdown of the history and combat that defined the ultimate victory of US forces in the Pacific.

Wings of Victory: World War II adventures in a war-torn Europe

"Historical fiction with a realistic twist." – Reviewer

Thrilling World War II adventures like you've never seen them before.

As the Nazis invade Europe on a campaign for total domination, a brutal war begins to unfold which will change the course of the world forever—and John Archer finds himself caught in the middle of it. When this amateur pilot joins the Allied war effort and is tasked with a series of death-defying missions which place him deep into German-occupied territory, his hair-raising adventures will help decide the fate of Europe.

In **War Heroes**, John is caught up in the devastating Nazi invasion of France while on vacation. Teaming up with ambulance driver Barney, John will need his amateur pilot skills and more than a stroke of luck to pull off the escape of the century.

In **Bombs Over Britain**, the Nazis have a plan which could change the course of the entire war . . . unless Archer can stop them. Air-dropped into Belgium on a top-secret mission, Archer must retrieve vital intelligence and make it out alive. But that's easier said than done when the Gestapo are closing in.

And in **Desert Scout**, Archer finds himself stranded beneath the scorching Libyan sun and in a race against time to turn the tide of the war in North Africa. But with the Luftwaffe and the desert vying to finish him off, can he make it out alive?

Packed with action and filled to the brim with suspense, these thrilling stories combine classic adventures with a riveting and historical World War II setting, making it ideal for history buffs and casual readers. If you're a fan of riveting war fiction novels, WW2 aircraft, and the war for the skies, Archer's next adventure will keep you on the edge of your seat.

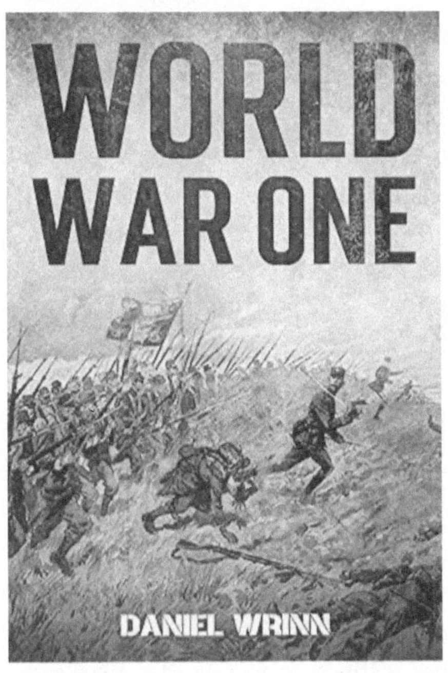

Dive into the incredible history of WWI with these gripping stories.

With a unique and fascinating glimpse into the lesser-known stories of the War to End All Wars, this riveting book unveils four thrilling stories from the trenches, seas, skies, and desert of a war-torn world. From one captain's death-defying mission to smuggle weapons for an Irish rebellion to heroic pilots and soldiers from all corners of the globe, these stories shed light on real people and events from one of the greatest conflicts in human history.

• **WWI: Tales from the Trenches**, a sweeping and eerily realistic narrative which explores the struggles and endless dangers faced by soldiers in the trenches during the heart of WWI

- **Broken Wings**, a powerful and heroic story about one pilot after he was shot down and spent 72 harrowing days on the run deep behind enemy lines
- **Mission to Ireland**, which explores the devious and cunning plan to smuggle a ship loaded with weapons to incite an Irish rebellion against the British
- And **Journey into Eden**, a fascinating glimpse into the lesser-known battles on the harsh and unforgiving Mesopotamian Front

World War I reduced Europe's mightiest empires to rubble, killed twenty million people, and cracked the foundations of our modern world. In its wake, empires toppled, monarchies fell, and whole populations lost their national identities.

Each of these stories brings together unbelievable real-life WWI history, making them perfect for casual readers and history buffs alike. If you want to peer into the past and unearth the incredible stories of the brave soldiers who risked everything, then this book is for you.

REFERENCES

Information regarding the WWII Pacific Theater is vast. The information I gathered for this book came from several sources. The USMC archives maintained by the Washington National Records Group in Suitland, Maryland, were a source of reference information as well as websites, newspaper articles, and even History Channel documentaries.

First-hand accounts, as recorded by the surviving participants, also contributed to my research.

Allen, Robert E. *The First Battalion of the 28th Marines on Iwo Jima: a Day-by-Day History from Personal Accounts and Official Reports, with Complete Muster Rolls*. McFarland, 1999.

Alexander, Colonel Joseph H. *Across the Reef: the Marine Assault of Tarawa*. Quantico, VA: Marine Corps History Division, 1993.
Alexander, Colonel Joseph H. "'In for One Hell of a Time': Bloody Sacrifice at the Battle of Iwo Jima." HistoryNet.com and

World War II magazine. HistoryNet.com and World War II magazine, February 2000.

Alexander, Colonel Joseph H. *The Final Campaign: Marines in the Victory on Okinawa*. Washington, D.C.: Marine Corps Historical Center, 1996.

"Amphibious Operations: Capture of Iwo Jima." Naval History and Heritage Command, October 23, 2019.

Anderson, Charles R. *Western Pacific*. The U.S. Army Campaigns of World War II. U.S. Army Center of Military History, 1994. CMH Pub 72-29.

Antill, Peter D. "The Battle for Iwo Jima." History of War, April 6, 2001.

Appleman, Roy Edgar, James Burns, Russel Gugeler, and Stevens John. *Okinawa: The Last Battle*. Washington: United States Army Center of Military History, 1948.

Bradley, James, and Ron Powers. *Flags of Our Fathers*. New York: Bantam Books, 2006.

Bradley, James. *Flyboys: a True Story of American Courage*. Boston: Little, Brown, 2003.

"Breaking the Cycle of Iwo Jima Mythology: A Strategic Study of Operation Detachment." *The Journal of Military History* 68, no. 4 (October 2004)

Buell, Hal. *Uncommon Valor, Common Virtue: Iwo Jima and the Photograph That Captured America*. New York, NY: Berkley, 406AD.

Burbeck, James. "Invasion of Peleliu". *Animated Combat Map*. The War Times Journal, 2008

References

Burke, Davis. *Marine: The Life of Chesty Puller*. Boston: Little, Brown, 1962.

Burrell, Robert S. *The Ghosts of Iwo Jima*. College Station: Texas A&M University Press, 2006.

Chapin, Captain John C. "Breaching the Marianas - United States Marine Corps." U.S. Marine Corps Reserve (RET), 1994.

Chen, C. Peter. "Mariana Islands Campaign and the Great Turkey Shoot." World War II Database. Lava Development, LLC, 2004.

Chen, C. Peter. "Palau Islands and Ulithi Islands Campaign," World War II Database. Lava Development, LLC, 2007.

Cheser, S. Matthew, and Nicholas Keefauver Roland. *Galvanic: Beyond the Reef: Tarawa and the Gilberts, November 1943*. Washington, DC: Naval History and Heritage Command, Department of the Navy, 2020.

Cressman, Robert J. *The Official Chronology of the U.S. Navy in World War II*. Annapolis, MD: Naval Institute Press, 1999.

Denfeld, D. Colt, and Eugene L. Rasor. "Hold the Marianas: The Japanese Defense of the Islands." *The Journal of Military History*, 1997.

Drea, Edward J. "An Allied Interpretation of the Pacific War." 1998.

Drea, Edward J. Essay. In *In the Service of the Emperor: Essays on the Imperial Japanese Army*. Lincoln, Neb.: University of Nebraska Press, 2003.

Dull, Paul s. *A Battle History of the Imperial Japanese Navy, 1941-1945*. Annapolis: Naval Institute Press, 1978.

Dyer, George Carroll. *The Amphibians Came to Conquer: the Story of Admiral Richmond Kelly Turner*. Washington, D.C, Dept. of the Navy,: United States Government Printing Office – via Hyperwar Foundation, 1973.

Fisch, Arnold G. *Ryukyus*. Washington, D.C.: U.S. Army Center of Military History, 2004.

Gailey, Harry A. *The Liberation of Guam, 21 July-10 August 1944*. Novato, CA: Presidio, 1988.

Gailey, Harry A. *Peleliu, 1944*. Annapolis, MD: Nautical & Aviation Pub. Co. of America, 1983.

Gayle, Gordon D., BGen USMC. *Bloody Beaches: the Marines at Peleliu*. Washington, D.C.: Marine Corp Historical Center, 1996.

Gnam, Carl. "Marine Fight for Tinian: A squabble between a general and an admiral led to 'the most perfect amphibious operation of the Pacific War.'" Warfare History Network, June 16, 2020.

Goldberg, Harold J. *D-Day in the Pacific The Battle of Saipan*. Bloomington: Indiana University Press, 2007.

Guillaume, Marine. "Napalm in US Bombing Doctrine and Practice, 1942-1975." Sciences Po portal, December 10, 2016.

Gypton, Jeremy. "Bloody Peleliu". MilitaryHistoryOnline, 2008.

Hallas, James H. *The Devil's Anvil: The Assault on Peleliu*. Westport, CT: Praeger, 1994.

Hammel, Eric M. *Iwo Jima: Portrait of a Battle: United States Marines at War in the Pacific*. St. Paul, MN: Zenith Press, 2006.

Hammel, Eric. *Coral and Blood: The U.S. Marine Corps' Pacific Campaign*. Pacifica, CA: Pacifica Military History, 2010.

Harwood, Richard. "A Close Encounter: The Marine Landing on Tinian." 1994.

Hastings, Max. *Retribution: the Battle for Japan, 1944-45*. New York: Alfred A. Knopf, 2009.

Hearn, Chester G. *Sorties into Hell: The Hidden War on Chichi Jima*. Guilford, CT: Lyons Press, 2005.

HistoricalResources. "Ivo Jima Maps - February 19, 1945–March 26, 1945." Historical Resources About The Second World War RSS, September 15, 2008.

Hobbs, David. *The British Pacific Fleet: the Royal Navy's Most Powerful Strike Force*. Barnsley, South Yorkshire: Seaforth Publishing, 2012.

Hoffman, Major Carl W., USMC. *Saipan: the Beginning of the End*. Washington, D.C.: Historical Division, U.S. Marine Corps, 1950.

Hoffman, Major Carl W., USMC. *The Seizure of Tinian:* Washington, DC: Historical Division, Headquarters, U.S. Marine Corps, 1951.

Horie, Yoshitaka, Robert D. Eldridge, and Charles W. Tatum. *Fighting Spirit: The Memoirs of Major Yoshitaka Horie and the Battle of Iwo Jima*. Annapolis, MD: Naval Institute Press, 2011.

Hough, Frank O. *The Assault on Peleliu*. Washington, D.C.: Historical Division, Headquarters, U.S. Marine Corps, 1950.

Hough, Frank O., and John A. Crown. *The Campaign on New Britain*. Washington: Historical Division, Headquarters, U.S. Marine Corps, 1952.

Kier, Mike. "PELELIU". Archived from the original on December 19, 2006.

Kindersley, Dorling. *World War II: The Definitive Visual History*. New York: DK Publishing, 2009.

Lacey, Laura Homan. *Stay Off the Skyline: The Sixth Marine Division on Okinawa: an Oral History*. Potomac Books, 2005.

Manchester, William. *Goodbye Darkness*. Boston, Mass: Little, Brown and Co., 1980.

McMillan, George. *The Old Breed: a History of the First Marine Division in World War II*. Washington: Infantry Journal Press, 1949.

Miller Jr., John. *Cartwheel: the Reduction of Rabaul*. Washington: Office of the Chief of Military HistoryDeptarment of the Army, 1959.

Moran, Jim, and Gordon L. Rottman. *Peleliu 1944: the Forgotten Corner of Hell*. Oxford: Osprey, 2002.

Morison, Samuel Eliot. *History of United States Naval Operations in World War II, Vol. 5: The Struggle for Guadalcanal, August 1942-February 1943*. Boston, MA: Little, Brown, 1950.

Morison, Samuel Eliot. *Victory in the Pacific, 1945 Vol. 14 of History of United States Naval Operations in World War II*. Urbana: University of Illinois Press, 2002.

Morison, Samuel Eliot. *Leyte: June 1944-January 1945, Vol. 12*. Boston: Little, Brown and Company, 1958.

Nash, Douglas. *Battle of Okinawa III MEF Staff Ride Battle Book*. U.S. Marine Corps History Division, 2015.

Nichols, Chas S., and Henry I. Shaw. *Okinawa: Victory in the Pacific (PDF)*. Washington, D.C.: Government Printing Office, 1955.

O'Brien, Cyril J. "Liberation: Marines in the Recapture of Guam", Marine Corps Historical Center, United States Marine Corps, 1994.

O'Brien, Francis. *Battling for Saipan*. New York: Ballantine Books, 2003.

"'Rare Photos of the Battle of Iwo Jima from the U.S. National Archives and the Department of Defense, USMC.'" Awesome Stories. Accessed June 2021.

Ross, Bill D. *Peleliu: Tragic Triumph: the Untold Story of the Pacific War's Forgotten Battle*. New York: Random House, 1991.

Rottman, Gordon L. *Okinawa, 1945: the Last Battle*. Oxford: Osprey Pub., 2002.

Rottman, Gordon L. *Saipan & Tinian 1944: Piercing the Japanese Empire*. Oxford: Osprey, 2004.

Salomon, Henry. *Victory at Sea Volume 23: Target Suribachi*. United States of America: The National Broadcasting Company, 1954.

Shively, John C. *The Last Lieutenant: A Foxhole View of the Epic Battle for Iwo Jima*. Bloomington: Indiana University Press, 2006.

Shread, Paul. "The Battle of Peleliu and the scars of war". *The Concord Monitor*. Archived from the original on September 19, 2014.

Sledge, E. B. *With the Old Breed: At Peleliu and Okinawa*. New York: Oxford University Press, 1991.

Sledge, E. B., and Paul Fussell. *With the Old Breed At Peleliu and Okinawa*. New York: Oxford University Press, 1991.

Sloan, Bill. *Brotherhood of Heroes: the Marines at Peleliu, 1944: the Bloodiest Battle of the Pacific War*. New York: Simon & Schuster, 2005.

Sperling, Milton. *To the Shores of Iwo Jima*. United States of America: United States Navy and United States Marine Corps, 1945.

The Battle for Iwo Jima 1945. Stroud: Sutton, 2006.

Toland, John. *The Rising Sun: The Decline and Fall of the Japanese Empire, 1936-1945*. New York: Random House, 1970.

Toll, Ian W. *TWILIGHT OF THE GODS: War in the Western Pacific, 1944-1945*. S.l.: W W NORTON, 2020.

Vandegrift, A. A., and Robert B. Asprey. *Once a Marine: The Memoirs of General A.A. Vandegrift*. W. W. Norton & Company, 1964.

Veronee, Marvin D. *A Portfolio of Photographs: Selected to Illustrate the Setting for My Experience in the Battle of Iwo Jima, World War II, Pacific Theater, as a Naval Gunfire Liaison Officer with the First Battalion, 28th Marines, 19 February-26 March 1945*. Quantico: Visionary Pub., 2001.

Wells, Keith. *Give Me Fifty Marines Not Afraid to Die: Iwo Jima*. Abilene, TX: Produced by Quality Publications, 1995.

Wheeler, Richard. *Iwo*. Annapolis, MD: Naval Institute Press, 1994.

World War 2 Pictures. "Iwo Jima Pictures." WW2-Pictures.com, April 16, 2010.

World War 2 Pictures. "Okinawa Pictures." WW2-Pictures.com, April 16, 2010.

Wright, Derrick. *Iwo Jima 1945: The Marines Raise the Flag On Mount Suribachi*. Oxford: Osprey Publishing Ltd, 2004.

Wright, Derrick. *To the Far Side of Hell: the Battle for Peleliu, 1944.* Tuscaloosa: University of Alabama Press, 2005.

ABOUT THE AUTHOR

Daniel Wrinn writes Military History & War Stories. A US Navy veteran and avid history buff, Daniel lives in the Utah Wasatch Mountains. He writes every day with a view of the snow capped peaks of Park City to keep him company. You can join his readers group and get notified of new releases, special offers, and free books here: